THE INTERNATIONAL LIBRARY OF ESSAYS ON AVIATION POLICY
AND MANAGEMENT

THE INTERNATIONAL LIBRARY OF ESSAYS ON AVIATION POLICY AND MANAGEMENT

Edited by

LUCY BUDD AND STEPHEN ISON
De Montfort University, Leicester

Volume II
Aviation Planning and Operations

LONDON AND NEW YORK

First published 2020
by Routledge
2 Park Square, Milton Park, Abingdon, Oxon OX14 4RN

and by Routledge
52 Vanderbilt Avenue, New York, NY 10017

Routledge is an imprint of the Taylor & Francis Group, an informa business

© 2020 selection and editorial matter, Lucy Budd and Stephen Ison; individual owners retain copyright in their own material.

The right of Lucy Budd and Stephen Ison to be identified as the authors of the editorial material, and of the authors for their individual chapters, has been asserted in accordance with sections 77 and 78 of the Copyright, Designs and Patents Act 1988.

All rights reserved. No part of this book may be reprinted or reproduced or utilised in any form or by any electronic, mechanical, or other means, now known or hereafter invented, including photocopying and recording, or in any information storage or retrieval system, without permission in writing from the publishers.

Trademark notice: Product or corporate names may be trademarks or registered trademarks, and are used only for identification and explanation without intent to infringe.

British Library Cataloguing-in-Publication Data
A catalogue record for this book is available from the British Library

Library of Congress Cataloging-in-Publication Data
A catalog record has been requested for this book

ISBN: 978-0-367-28136-6 (set)
ISBN: 978-1-4724-5156-9 (volume II)

Typeset in Times New Roman
by codeMantra

Publisher's Note
References within each chapter are as they appear in the original complete work

Contents

Acknowledgments   ix

Introduction   1

Part I Forecasting

1. Arthur S. De Vany and Eleanor H. Garges, 'A Forecast of Air Travel and Airport and Airway Use in 1980', *Transportation Research*, 6, 1972, 1–18.   9

2. Tobias Grosche, Franz Rothlauf and Armin Heinzl, 'Gravity Models for Airline Passenger Volume Estimation', *Journal of Air Transport Management*, 13, 2007, 175–183.   27

3. Erma Suryani, Shuo-Yan Chou and Chin-Hsien Chen, 'Air Passenger Demand Forecasting and Passenger Terminal Capacity Expansion: A System Dynamics Framework', *Expert Systems with Applications*, 37, 2010, 2324–2339.   37

Part II Infrastructure Planning and Provision

4. Roland A. A. Wijnen, Warren E. Walker and Jan H. Kwakkel, 'Decision Support for Airport Strategic Planning, *Transportation Planning and Technology*, 31, 1, 2008, 11–34.   55

5. Ron Vreeker, Peter Nijkamp and Chris Ter Welle, 'A Multicriteria Decision Support Methodology for Evaluating Airport Expansion Plans', *Transportation Research Part D*, 7, 2002, 27–47.   79

6. Peter Forsyth, 'Airport Infrastructure for the Airbus A380: Cost Recovery and Pricing', *Journal of Transport Economics and Policy*, 39, 3, 2005, 341–362.   101

Part III Capacity

7. Miltiadis A. Stamatopoulos, Konstantinos G. Zografos and Amedeo R. Odoni, 'A Decision Support System for Airport Strategic Planning', *Transportation Research Part C*, 12, 2004, 91–117.   125

8. Alan Carlin and R. E. Park, 'Marginal Cost Pricing of Airport Runway Capacity', *American Economic Review*, 60, 3, 1970, 310–319. 151

9. Eric Pels and Erik T. Verhoef, 'The Economics of Airport Congestion Pricing', *Journal of Urban Economics*, 55, 2004, 257–277. 161

10. Gernot Sieg, 'Grandfather Rights in the Market for Airport Slots', *Transportation Research Part B*, 44, 2010, 29–37. 183

11. David Starkie, 'Allocating Airport Slots: A Role for the Market?', *Journal of Air Transport Management*, 4, 1998, 111–116. 193

12. Senay Solak, John-Paul B. Clarke and Ellis L. Johnson, 'Airport Terminal Capacity Planning', *Transportation Research Part B*, 43, 2009, 659–676. 199

Part IV Scheduling

13. Cynthia Barnhart and Amy Cohn, 'Airline Schedule Planning: Accomplishments and Opportunities', *Manufacturing & Service Operations Management*, 6, 1, 2004, 3–22. 219

14. Guy Desaulniers, Jacques Desrosiers, Yvan Dumas, Marius M. Solomon and François Soumis, 'Daily Aircraft Routing and Scheduling', *Management Science*, 43, 6, 1997, 841–855. 239

15. Christopher A. Hane, Cynthia Barnhart, Ellis L. Johnson, Roy E. Marsten, George L. Nemhauser and Gabriele Sigismondi, 'The Fleet Assignment Problem: Solving a Large-scale Integer Program', *Mathematical Programming*, 70, 1995, 211–232. 255

16. Amy Mainville Cohn and Cynthia Barnhart, 'Improving Crew Scheduling by Incorporating Key Maintenance Routing Decisions', *Operations Research*, 51, 3, 2003, 387–396. 277

Part V Safety and Security

17. Milan Janic, 'An Assessment of Risk and Safety in Civil Aviation', *Journal of Air Transport Management*, 6, 2000, 43–50. 289

18. Robert L. Helmreich, Ashleigh C. Merritt and John A. Wilhelm, 'The Evolution of Crew Resource Management Training in Commercial Aviation', *The International Journal of Aviation Psychology*, 9, 1, 1999, 19–32. 297

19. Bradley F. Blackwell, Travis L. DeVault, Esteban Fernández-Juricic and Richard A. Dolbeer, 'Wildlife Collisions with Aircraft: A Missing Component of Land-use Planning for Airports', *Landscape and Urban Planning*, 93, 2009, 1–9.   311

20. Thomas A. Birkland, 'Learning and Policy Improvement After Disaster: The Case of Aviation Security, *American Behavioral Scientist*, 48, 3, 2004, 341–364.   321

21. Peter Adey, 'Surveillance at the Airport: Surveilling Mobility/Mobilising Surveillance', *Environment and Planning A*, 36, 2004, 1365–1380.   345

Part VI Disruption Management and Resilience

22. Niklas Kohl, Allan Larsen, Jesper Larsen, Alex Ross and Sergey Tiourine, 'Airline Disruption Management—Perspectives, Experiences and Outlook', *Journal of Air Transport Management*, 13, 2007, 149–162.   363

23. Jens Clausen, Allan Larsen, Jesper Larsen and Natalia J. Rezanova, 'Disruption Management in the Airline Industry—Concepts, Models and Methods', *Computers & Operations Research*, 37, 2010, 809–821.   377

24. Shan Lan, John-Paul Clarke and Cynthia Barnhart, 'Planning for Robust Airline Operations: Optimizing Aircraft Routings and Flight Departure Times to Minimize Passenger Disruptions', *Transportation Science*, 40, 1, 2006, 15–28.   391

25. Lucy Budd, Morag Bell and Tim Brown, 'Of Plagues, Planes and Politics: Controlling the Global Spread of Infectious Diseases by Air', *Political Geography*, 28, 2009, 426–435.   405

Index   415

Acknowledgments

The Publishers would like to thank the following for permission to reprint their material:

Elsevier for permission to reprint Arthur S. De Vany and Eleanor H. Garges, 'A Forecast of Air Travel and Airport and Airway Use in 1980', *Transportation Research*, 6, 1972, 1–18.

Elsevier for permission to reprint Tobias Grosche, Franz Rothlauf and Armin Heinzl, 'Gravity Models for Airline Passenger Volume Estimation', *Journal of Air Transport Management*, 13, 2007, 175–183.

Elsevier for permission to reprint Erma Suryani, Shuo-Yan Chou and Chih-Hsien Chen, 'Air Passenger Demand Forecasting and Passenger Terminal Capacity Expansion: A System Dynamics Framework', *Expert Systems with Applications*, 37, 2010, 2324–2339.

Taylor & Francis for permission to reprint Roland A. A. Wijnen, Warren. E. Walker and Jan H. Kwakkel, 'Decision Support for Airport Strategic Planning, *Transportation Planning and Technology*, 31, 1, 2008, 11–34.

Elsevier for permission to reprint Ron Vreeker, Peter Nijkamp and Chris Ter Welle, 'A Multicriteria Decision Support Methodology for Evaluating Airport Expansion Plans', *Transportation Research Part D*, 7, 2002, 27–47.

Bath University Press for permission to reprint Peter Forsyth, 'Airport Infrastructure for the Airbus A380: Cost Recovery and Pricing', *Journal of Transport Economics and Policy*, 39, 3, 2005, 341–362.

Elsevier for permission to reprint Miltiadis A. Stamatopoulos, Konstantinos G. Zografos and Amedeo R. Odoni, 'A Decision Support System for Airport Strategic Planning', *Transportation Research Part C*, 12, 2004, 91–117.

Alan Carlin and R. E. Park, 'Marginal Cost Pricing of Airport Runway Capacity', *American Economic Review*, 60, 3, 1970, 310–319.

Elsevier for permission to reprint Eric Pels and Erik T. Verhoef, 'The Economics of Airport Congestion Pricing', *Journal of Urban Economics*, 55, 2004, 257–277.

Elsevier for permission to reprint Gernot Sieg, 'Grandfather Rights in the Market for Airport Slots', *Transportation Research Part B*, 44, 2010, 29–37.

Elsevier for permission to reprint David Starkie, 'Allocating Airport Slots: A Role for the Market?', *Journal of Air Transport Management*, 4, 1998, 111–116.

Elsevier for permission to reprint Senay Solak, John-Paul Clarke and Ellis L. Johnson, 'Airport Terminal Capacity Planning', *Transportation Research Part B*, 43, 2009, 659–676.

INFORMS for permission to reprint Cynthia Barnhart and Amy Cohn, 'Airline Schedule Planning: Accomplishments and Opportunities', *Manufacturing & Service Operations Management*, 6, 1, 2004, 3–22.

INFORMS for permission to reprint Guy Desaulniers, Jacques Desrosiers, Yvan Dumas, Marius M. Solomon and Francois Soumis, 'Daily Aircraft Routing and Scheduling', *Management Science*, 43, 6, 1997, 841–855.

Springer for permission to reprint Christopher A. Hane, Cynthia Barnhart, Ellis L. Johnson, Roy E. Marsten, George L. Nemhauser and Gabriele Sigismondi, 'The Fleet Assignment Problem: Solving a Large-scale Integer Program', *Mathematical Programming*, 70, 1995, 211–232.

INFORMS for permission to reprint Amy Mainville Cohn and Cynthia Barnhart, 'Improving Crew Scheduling by Incorporating Key Maintenance Routing Decisions', *Operations Research*, 51, 3, 2003, 387–396.

Elsevier for permission to reprint Milan Janic, 'An Assessment of Risk and Safety in Civil Aviation', *Journal of Air Transport Management*, 6, 2000, 43–50.

Taylor & Francis for permission to reprint Robert L. Helmreich, Ashleigh C. Merritt and John A. Wilhelm, 'The Evolution of Crew Resource Management Training in Commercial Aviation', *The International Journal of Aviation Psychology*, 9, 1, 1999, 19–32.

Elsevier for permission to reprint Bradley F. Blackwell, Travis L. DeVault, Esteban Fernández-Juricic and Richard A. Dolbeer, 'Wildlife Collisions with Aircraft: A Missing Component of Land-use Planning for Airports', *Landscape and Urban Planning*, 93, 2009, 1–9.

Sage Publications for permission to reprint Thomas A. Birkland, 'Learning and Policy Improvement After Disaster: The Case of Aviation Security', *American Behavioral Scientist*, 48, 3, 2004, 341–364.

Sage Publications for permission to reprint Peter Adey, 'Surveillance at the Airport: Surveilling Mobility/Mobilising Surveillance', *Environment and Planning A*, 36, 2004, 1365–1380.

Elsevier for permission to reprint Niklas Kohl, Allan Larsen, Jesper Larsen, Alex Ross and Sergey Tiourine, 'Airline Disruption Management—Perspectives, Experiences and Outlook', *Journal of Air Transport Management*, 13, 2007, 149–162.

Elsevier for permission to reprint Jens Clausen, Allan Larsen, Jesper Larsen and Natalia J. Rezanova, 'Disruption Management in the Airline Industry—Concepts, Models and Methods', *Computers & Operations Research*, 37, 2010, 809–821.

INFORMS for permission to reprint Shan Lan, John-Paul Clarke and Cynthia Barnhart, 'Planning for Robust Airline Operations: Optimizing Aircraft Routings and Flight Departure Times to Minimize Passenger Disruptions', *Transportation Science*, 40, 1, 2006, 15–28.

Elsevier for permission to reprint Lucy Budd, Morag Bell and Tim Brown, 'Of Plagues, Planes and Politics: Controlling the Global Spread of Infectious Diseases by Air', *Political Geography*, 28, 2009, 426–435.

Disclaimer

The publishers have made every effort to contact authors/copyright holders of works reprinted in the *International Library of Essays on Aviation Policy and Management*. This has not been possible in every case, however, and we would welcome correspondence from those individuals/companies whom we have been unable to trace.

Introduction

Lucy Budd and Stephen Ison

Introduction to *the International Library of Essays on Aviation Policy and Management*

This collection comprises 6 distinct but interrelated volumes that contain previously published academic essays that collectively address important issues in international civil aviation policy and management. Despite air transport's relatively short presence in world history, it has evolved into one of the world's most significant modes of international and long-distance mobility that facilitates the routine transnational movement of billions of passengers and millions of tonnes of highly valuable freight annually. Understanding the policy and management implications of this rapidly developing transport mode has been considered by disciplines as diverse as civil engineering and the social sciences, and tens of thousands of essays, both empirical and theoretical, have been published in the field. In this collection, we limit ourselves to essays published in the English language; while we do not (and cannot) claim to be comprehensive, the aim of this collection is to present essays which showcase significant and thought-provoking essays that have sought to stimulate debate in this diverse and dynamic field of academic inquiry.

The collection comprises 6 volumes, each covering a different aspect of aviation policy and management. The collection seeks to provide useful insight into key areas of aviation that are of interest both to academics and practitioners worldwide. The choice of essays is necessarily subjective; however, every effort has been made to be as inclusive and informative as possible by drawing on a wide range of disciplinary perspectives and journal titles. Given the diversity of the empirical, theoretical and disciplinary approaches that have been applied to the study of aviation, this is no straightforward task and is inherently problematic and subjective. We appreciate that not every reader will agree with our selection and may have his or her own opinion concerning which essays should have been included or excluded. Nevertheless, it is our intention that this collection will act as a foundation from which readers can make their own further forays into the academic research base surrounding aviation.

The 6 volumes have been configured and presented as follows:

Volume 1 addresses aspects of *Aviation Law and Regulation*. This volume sets the scene for the legal and regulatory operation of international civil aviation from the earliest days to the present. It contains 4 Parts and 18 essays that cover aviation law, regulation and deregulation, competition and contestability and open skies.

Volume 2 *Aviation Planning and Operations* comprises 25 essays with Parts covering forecasting, infrastructure planning and provision, capacity, scheduling, safety and security, disruption management and resilience.

Volume 3 *Aviation Business Strategy* comprises 26 essays that cover market structure, revenue cost and pricing, mergers and acquisitions, global airline alliances and marketing and customer loyalty.

Volume 4, which focuses on *Aviation Performance and Productivity*, includes Parts relating to privatization and commercialization, efficiency, service delivery and service quality, human resources and industrial relations. This volume comprises 26 essays.

Volume 5 *Aviation Social and Economic Impacts* contains 26 essays divided into 5 Parts, namely airports and economic development, airports, logistics and supply chains, air transport and tourism, air transport in remote regions and environmental externalities.

Volume 6 *Aviation Design and Innovation* comprises 20 essays presented in 4 Parts – airport design and sustainability, aircraft design and manufacturing, alternative fuels and business model innovation.

Introduction to Volume 2 *Aviation Planning and Operations*

The 25 essays in this volume are presented in 6 Parts as follows:

Part I Forecasting

Accurately forecasting consumer demand for air travel is a vitally important aspect of aviation policy formation and management, not least in terms of infrastructure planning and provision. However, forecasting demand is notoriously challenging owing to the fact that air travel is a derived demand and global economic activity is uncertain. Forecasts of airline and airport activity may differ, often substantially, from original predictions, and there have been many examples of routes, airlines and airports failing owing to inaccurate forecasts and traffic levels failing to materialise whereas, at the other extreme, underestimating demand can lead to congestion, delays, inefficiency and lost productivity (de Neufville, 2017).

In recognition of the importance of forecasting, the first paper in this part, by De Vany and Garges (1972), provides a forecast of air traffic and airway use in the United States during the period of economic regulation. Their methodology, which seeks to capture the complex interdependencies in the domestic aviation network in the United States, is used to forecast anticipated loads on airports, air traffic control and airlines across the country in 1980.

Grosche, Rothlauf and Heinzl (2007) present two gravity models for estimating air travel demand between city-pairs using data on flights between Germany and other European countries on routes where air services may or may not already be present.

The final paper in this part, by Suryani, Chou and Chen (2010), found that the price of airline tickets, level of service, GDP, population, flights per day and dwelltime all combined to determine air passenger volumes, runway utilisation and the additional space required for passenger terminal expansion and makes explicit the link between forecasts and infrastructure utilisation and future provision. This essay leads into the second Part of the volume relating to infrastructure planning and provision.

Part II Infrastructure Planning and Provision

This section contains three essays that discuss the importance of airport infrastructure planning and provision worldwide. The first, by Wijnen, Walker and Kwakkel (2008), examines the role of airport Master Plans in airport strategic planning and the uncertainties that must be accommodated in order to create flexible and adaptable development proposals. The second, by Vreeker, Nijkamp and Welle (2002), provides a multi-criteria decision support methodology for evaluating airport expansion plans and helps deal with conflicts in the decision-making process.

The paper by Forsyth (2005) concerns the airport infrastructure that is required to accommodate the Airbus A380 'super jumbo'. It shows the importance of accurate forecasting as the infrastructure investment required is a sunk cost that has implications for cost recovery, pricing and evaluation of investment decisions.

Part III Capacity

Capacity refers to the ability of a component of the aviation network to accommodate demand. The first paper, by Stamatopoulos, Zografos and Odoni (2004), provides a set of models to estimate airfield capacity and associated delays. The models they document account for the dynamic characteristics of airfield geometry, capacity and demand. Very often, delays and congestion result from insufficient runway capacity. The paper, by Carlin and Park (1970), examines the marginal cost pricing of airport runway capacity as a means to optimise the use of this scarce resource. Congestion pricing as a policy response to growing delays at airports is also discussed by Pels and Verhoef (2004) who develop a model of airport pricing.

One contentious aspect of airport operations concerns the use of airport slots as a demand management measure. Sieg (2010) discusses the role of Grandfather Rights at airports in the European Union and the implications of their preference for a 'use it or lose it' rule to unconditional property rights. The issue of slot allocation at capacity-constrained airports is also addressed by Starkie (1998) who considers the role of the market in allocating access to this scarce resource.

Congestion and delays can also occur in the terminal building. In addition to runway infrastructure planning, airport operators also need to be conversant with planning future airport terminal capacity. The final paper in this part, by Solak, Clarke and Johnson (2009), develops a model to provide an efficient solution for capacity requirements for each section of the airport terminal.

Part IV Scheduling

Scheduling forms a vital part of airline operations as it is concerned with making the optimum use of scarce resources, both material and human, and meeting consumer demand. The 4 essays in this section concern various aspects of airline scheduling planning and management. The first, by Barnhart and Cohn (2004), examines the accomplishments and opportunities of airline scheduling and demonstrates how optimisation approaches can help improve decision-making and, by definition, profitability in the airline sector. Optimising the use of a heterogeneous fleet of aircraft is a challenge that many airlines face and the paper, by Desaulniers, Desrosiers, Dumas, Solomon and Soumis (1997), addresses this issue by focusing on the daily routing and scheduling of aircraft. The fleet assignment problem is an issue also addressed in the paper by Hane, Barnhart, Johnson, Marsten, Nemhauser and Sigismondi (1995). In it, they present and then efficiently solve a domestic fleet assignment problem. The final paper in this section, by Cohn and Barnhart (2003), seeks to improve the efficiency of crew scheduling by including aircraft maintenance routing in scheduling decisions.

Part V Safety and Security

The importance of safety and security in the aviation industry cannot be overstated. The 5 essays in this section examine different aspects of these two inextricably interrelated aspects of aviation planning and operations. The first essay in this section, by Janic (2000), introduces the concept of risk and safety in civil aviation, describes the main causes of aircraft accidents and proposes a methodology for quantifying risk and safety. Investigations of aircraft accidents have revealed the importance of communication on the flightdeck; the paper, by Helmreich, Merritt and Wilhelm (1999), examines the evolution of Crew Resource Management (CRM) in commercial aviation and its importance in helping to identify, manage and mitigate safety incidents. As well as human factors, a further element of risk relates to wildlife collisions on and around the airfield which is an issue that is often overlooked when considering issues of aviation planning and operations. The paper, by Blackwell, DeVault, Fernández-Juricic and Dolbeer (2009), reviews legislation, identifies information gaps and future research requirements and seeks to demonstrate how data on wildlife-strike risk hazards can be utilised by airport operators and planners to assess and manage the risk of wildlife collisions.

The final two essays in this section focus on aviation security. The paper, by Birkland (2004), examines the extent to which actual or apparent security breaches that resulted in fatal aircraft crashes have led to changes in global aviation security policy. One of the most significant yet, on occasion, controversial interventions has been the increased surveillance of airline passengers and employees, with technologies including profiling, biometrics and CCTV being used to monitor flows of people and goods within and between airports. This aspect of security is explored by Adey (2004).

Part VI Disruption Management and Resilience

Planned flight schedules and routine airports operations can be disrupted by a number of internal and external factors including industrial action, equipment failures and adverse weather. Any disruption has the potential to cause delays, inconvenience and lost productivity. Responding and managing disruptive events by ensuring a quick and orderly return to normal routine operations is of paramount importance. The 4 essays in this section address various aspects of disruption. The first, by Kohl, Larsen, Larsen, Ross and Tiourine (2007), introduces the field of airline disruption management and provides a description of the planning processes that are required to address various sources of disruption. This theme also forms the basis of the paper by Clausen, Larsen, Larsen and Rezanova (2010). In it, they review the state of the art in aircraft, crew and passenger recovery. The third paper in this section, by Lan, Clarke and Barnhart (2006), investigates approaches to minimising passenger disruption and designing schedules that are more robust and less vulnerable to disruption.

An example of an external factor that has the potential to cause significant disruption is the emergence of human infectious diseases that have the potential to be spread around the world by air travel. The final paper in this section, by Budd, Bell and Brown (2009), explores the mechanisms through which individual nation-states have sought to control the spread of infectious disease by air travel by introducing legislation and screening technologies that seek to protect national borders and safeguard human health.

Reference

De Neufville R. (2017) *Airport Systems Planning and Design* in Budd L. and Ison S. (Eds) *Air Transport Management An International Perspective* Abingdon, Routledge, 61–78.

Part I:
Forecasting

1

A FORECAST OF AIR TRAVEL AND AIRPORT AND AIRWAY USE IN 1980†

Arthur S. De Vany

and

Eleanor H. Garges

I. INTRODUCTION

Projections of air travel demand and airline flights form an important input to government decision-making and policy formation. For example, the Civil Aeronautics Board uses travel projections in making route awards to airlines and in evaluating proposed mergers. The Federal Aviation Administration employs projections of air travel demand and airline flights to forecast future loads on airports, and elements of the Air Traffic Control System. The airlines use them in planning routes and making equipment acquisitions, and airport authorities use forecasts to plan facility expansions.

Air transportation is a system with many interrelated parts; each airport is tied to the system through the airways and the other airports with which it exchanges flights. Thus, the traffic at any one airport depends upon traffic at all others. For example, an increase in international flights leaving Dulles Airport would tend to decrease international flights at Kennedy Airport as well as reduce the number of flights from Washington and Chicago to New York. To allocate resources to airports in the system the full incremental benefits of expanding capacity at any one location must be calculated, including the effect on other airports. This can only be done if forecasts indicate the volume of flights exchanged between airports in the entire system.

Existing forecasts do not adequately capture these interdependencies because they are either too aggregative or too narrow. Broad national forecasts of total passenger miles or airline flights, such as have been prepared by the Civil Aeronautics Board (1967) and the Federal Aviation Administration (1970), are the easiest to make but are of little real use. They must be broken down to the level of individual airports and air traffic control regions to serve any planning purpose. Yet the process for breaking these aggregate projections down into sub-totals is ad hoc and lacks a solid basis.

On the other hand, forecasting of flights is carried out by each individual airport authority (see, for example, Port of New York Authority, 1970; Port of San Diego Authority, 1969). Since every commercial airline flight involves at least two airports, it is doubtful that forecasts that do not reflect this interdependence can be accurate or consistent with

---

† This work is part of a study of the competition for airspace entitled Project Blue Air conducted for the Navy at Center for Naval Analyses under contract N00014–68–A–0091. The conclusions do not necessarily represent the opinion of the Department of the Navy.

each other. (That so many airport authority forecasts forsee a rising share of the national market for their airport is an indication of a possibility very serious lack of consistency.)

The forecasts presented in this paper represent our attempt at removing some of these deficiencies. Specifically, our objective is to forecast air traffic in such a fashion that traffic forecast for any one airport is consistent with that forecast for each other airport. To do this, it is necessary to simultaneously forecast traffic between all cities in the system.

There are advantages of proceeding in this manner over and beyond merely being consistent. This procedure indicates the jet routes used, the mix of aircraft, trip length and number of passengers per flight. Route structures consistent with the growth of travel and its origin and destination distribution can be determined to assist airline planning and shed light on merger or route proposals that may come before the Civil Aeronautics Board. Any national totals can be obtained by simply aggregating over individual routes and airports.

We shall treat United States domestic passenger travel and commercial trunk airline traffic in this paper. In Section II, a function giving passenger demand for travel between cities is estimated with cross-sectional data. In Section III, a simple model of an airline is developed and its ability to predict flights in domestic city-pair markets is tested. In Section IV, these models are brought together to project passenger demand and airline service patterns. In the last section some rather surprising conclusions are presented.

II. THE DEMAND FOR AIR TRAVEL

Economic theory predicts that the determinants of passenger demand for air travel between two cities are the cost of an air trip in time and money relative to the cost by other modes, the incomes of consumers and the populations of the cities (see, for example, Gronau, 1970; Becker, 1965; De Vany, 1971). Our problem is to estimate a function relating these variables to the volume of air passenger trips between cities.

The model to be estimated is

$$\ln Q_{ij} = a + b_1 \ln p_{ij} + b_2 \ln t_{ij} + b_3 \ln M_{ij} + b_4 \ln I_{ij} + b_5 \ln P_{ij} + u$$

The dependent variable, $\ln Q_{ij}$, is the natural log of domestic passenger trips between (both directions) city i and city j, net of international passengers on a domestic leg of an international flight.

The fare variable, $\ln p_{ij}$ is the log of the fare for a one-way flight in coach service between i and j, divided by the distance between i and j. The constant b_1 is, therefore, the fare elasticity of demand, expressing the percentage change in the quantity of passengers traveling between i and j that will be induced by a change in the fare per mile of travel. The parameter b_1 should be negative according to theory.

The time variable, $\ln t_{ij}$, is the log of the scheduled trip time per mile for the best direct flight published in the Official Airline Guide. The constant b_2 is therefore the elasticity of demand with respect to time cost and should be negative.

The next term, $\ln M_{ij}$, is the log of the one-way distance between the cities. Since we are using cross-sectional data with varying trip distances between cities, we have normalized fare and time by expressing them in units per mile. Adding distance into the equation translates these averages into total cost per trip. Thus the coefficient b_3 expresses the change in trips as total cost of the trip increases with distance, holding fare and time per mile constant. This should be negative.

The income term, $\ln I_{ij}$, is the product of income in cities i and j. This is a convenient way to express income when two cities are involved. Using the product reduces the two income figures to one, which characterizes the travel *arc* rather than the individual cities. The coefficient of the log of the income product, b_4, is expected to be positive.

The term for population, $\ln P_{ij}$, combines the population of the two cities forming the pair into a single number. Since Q_{ij} is total number of trips rather than trips *per capita*, there is some presumption—and some evidence (see Elle, 1968)—that increasing the population of one or both cities will increase passenger trips. The coefficient of the log of the population term should be positive, although we have no theory on which to base this expectation.

The last term of the equation u, is an error term; u is assumed to be normally distributed with mean 0, and variance σ_u^2.

Sources of data

Passenger trips are measured as annual origin and destination passengers net of those passengers who are on the domestic leg of an international flight. The data are for the year 1968 and come from the Origin and Destination Survey, 1968. They include only those city pairs in the top 1000 that received at least one non-stop flight per week. Distances are measured on great circles, in miles, from city center to city center and come from the same survey.

Fare and travel time are taken from the Official Airline Guide, 1 May 1968. Coach fare was used in all cases and divided by distance to obtain fare per mile, expressed in cents per mile. Travel time is measured by the difference between scheduled arrival and departure time for the fastest equipment serving the route. Travel time is divided by distance to obtain time in minutes per mile.

Current and projected income and population statistics are not available for all cities in our sample. It was therefore necessary to combine some cities into regions that corresponded with the regions for which income and population projections are available. The area surrounding a city, of course, forms a part of the economic base that generates trips through the city, and should be included in the analysis.

As a consequence of grouping cities in our sample into the regions defined in this report, five city pairs were lost, leaving a total sample of 576. Under the circumstances, the grouping can be considered quite accurate for our purposes. Current population figures were taken from Rand McNally (1968) and grouped into regions corresponding to Standard Metropolitan Statistical Areas. Incomes figures were obtained from Department of Commerce (1970) and grouped according to the above procedure.

Empirical results

The demand equation was estimated by ordinary least-squares regression. The regression results are given in Table 1. The results are in agreement with expectations given by economic theory.

Fare. The overall fare elasticity of demand of -1.10 is significant, of the correct sign and in agreement with other work (Brown and Watkins, 1968).

Time. The elasticity with respect to time per mile is of the correct sign (negative) and is significant at the 70 per cent confidence limit.

Distance. The coefficient for distance is negative as expected and is significant.

Income. The elasticity with respect to income products is positive and/or roughly the same magnitude as found by Brown and Watkins (1968).

Population. The population variable is significant. The coefficient is positive as intuition would suggest.

III. THE SUPPLY OF AIRLINE FLIGHTS

The number of flights that airlines will supply is not wholly determined by passenger demand. Airlines will schedule the number of flights between cities that maximize profits. In this section we seek to develop a model that predicts airline flights in each market on the basis of passenger demand, fare and operating cost of the airline.

TABLE 1. REGRESSION RESULTS: CROSS-SECTIONAL ANALYSIS OF AIR TRAVEL IN 576 DOMESTIC CITY PAIRS

Degrees of freedom	571
R^2	0·49
s_Q	0·65
Coefficients and t-values:	
Constant	−5·81
Fare per mile	−1·10
	(3·89)
Trip time per mile	−0·21
	(1·14)
Distance	−0·39
	(5·10)
Income product	0·20
	(13·92)
Population product	(15·36)

Theory of the airline

Air travel is a good having money price (fare) and an earnings cost (time). Total trip time is made up of several elements that depend upon aircraft speed, check-in and check-out time, travel to and from airports and, perhaps most important, waiting time for a flight. The more frequent that airline flights are, the shorter the period is between a passenger's desired departure or arrival time and the time he actually departs or arrives. In addition, the total amount of time it takes to make a trip depends upon schedule frequency.

An airline would seek to offer travelers a combination of fare and travel time (including schedule frequency) that would maximize its profits. However, airlines are not free to choose the fares they wish to charge. Airline fares are regulated by the Civil Aeronautics Board (CAB), and regulated airlines competing on a given route usually charge identical fares. Therefore an airline can affect the demand for its product only by varying its quality (decreasing time cost or increasing utility to the traveler). The CAB discourages most forms of non-price competition, e.g. seating density, in-flight meals, drinks and entertainment. However, the CAB has not attempted to regulate flight frequency. Thus an airline could maximize its profits by choice of its schedule frequency subject to the regulated fare.

A simple model of the airline is given by the maximization problem

$$\max \pi = pQ_{ij}(p,f) - (c+m)f - vQ_{ij}(p,f) - k$$

by choice of number of flights f, where π is profits p, the regulated fare, $Q_{ij}(p,f)$ a demand function relating the number of passengers to p and f, c the marginal cost of flight frequency, m the landing charge, v the variable cost per passenger, and k fixed cost.

The necessary condition for a relative maximum is

$$\frac{\partial \pi}{\partial f} = p\frac{\partial Q}{\partial f} - c - m - v\frac{\partial Q}{\partial f} = 0$$

If we let e be the elasticity of demand with respect to flight frequency, then profit-maximizing flights are

$$f^* = \frac{(p-v)Qe}{c+m}$$

Equilibrium load factor, when s is number of seats per plane, is

$$L^* = \frac{c+m}{(p-v)es}$$

It can be shown (De Vany, 1970) that at a profit maximum e must be less than one, which implies

$$\frac{\partial L^*}{\partial f} = \frac{s(e-1)}{f} < 0$$

In other words, load factor falls with further increases in flights, and a profit-maximizing airline would schedule flights in that region where load factor declines with increases in flights.

The equation expressing profit-maximizing flights can be used to predict flights given information on passenger demand, fare and cost, only if we know the elasticity of demand with respect to flights, e. Based upon analysis of time series, estimates of e range between 0·45 and 0·59 (De Vany, 1970). Using the value of 0·59 and neglecting v and m, both of which are trivial, we have predicted 1968 flights for 15 city pairs for comparison with flights actually scheduled between these cities in 1968 as a check of the validity of the equation. The predicted and actual flights are shown in Table 2.

TABLE 2. COMPARISON OF ACTUAL WITH PREDICTED FLIGHTS

City pairs	Actual 1968 one-way flights	Predicted one-way flights
New York–Miami	47	72
–Los Angeles	27	33
–Chicago	73	47
–Boston	110	93
–Philadelphia	27	4
–Atlanta	20	10
Los Angeles–San Diego	28	7
–San Francisco	51	47
–Chicago	34	20
–Houston	7	5
Chicago–Minneapolis	38	18
–Detroit	29	20
–Atlanta	6	2
–Cleveland	27	11
Atlanta–Houston	6	2

The agreement is good, particularly in view of the fact that we used a simple and arbitrary procedure to assign aircraft to the routes and made no attempt to consider flights which stop in the city that carry passengers bound for other cities. We assigned aircraft by mileage as follows:

Length	Equipment
0–300 miles	2 engine
300–600 miles	3 engine
More than 600 miles	4 engine

Flights on highly competitive routes, such as New York–Chicago, are underpredicted, as one would expect, since on a highly competitive route, the elasticity with respect to flights approaches unity for the individual airline even though the market elasticity may be closer to 0·5 or 0·6. However, each route earns a positive profit with our assignment of flights. The predictions tend to underestimate flights for city pairs that receive a high percentage of their service as a continuation of flight between more dominant city pairs. For example, many flights between Los Angeles and San Diego are continuations, or first legs, of flights between Los Angeles and cities in the Middle West and South West. Our prediction is of the number of flights that would be scheduled to carry people originating or departing at San Diego and therefore omits flights that may go from Los Angeles to Houston with a stop in San Diego. We resolve this problem in our projections by allowing for this type of service through the hub and spoke pattern explained below.

IV. PROJECTIONS

In this section we forecast passenger demand and airline flights with the models of the preceding sections. The projections of passenger demand are made by introducing forecasted changes in levels of population and income for each city pair into the demand function along with assumed changes in levels of fare and trip time. The projections of passenger demand and the various assumptions are then fed into the expression for profit-maximizing flights to obtain flights between each pair of cities.

Projections of population and income

The projected population and income of each city is given in the Department of Commerce (1968). These projections are incorporated into the demand function, along with assumptions of fare and travel time, to individually forecast the demand for travel between each city pair.

The assumed structure of fare and travel time

In order to estimate travel time between each city pair, we need an equation that relates time to the distance between each city. Using the 1968 schedules, trip per mile is given by

$$t = \frac{25 \cdot 6 + 0 \cdot 115 M}{M}, \quad R^2 = 0 \cdot 94, \quad s = 16 \cdot 7$$

This equation is plotted as t_c in Fig. 1. As can be seen, time per mile is a declining function of trip length. This is due to the presence of a fixed time component of about 25 mins flight. Once aloft, average travel time is 0·115 min/mile, giving an average airborne speed of about 520 miles/hr.

We have made forecasts under several assumed trip times. These assumptions are shown in Fig. 1 by curves t_1 and t_2. The rationale for the shape of these curves is that airborne speed is unlikely to increase much, while there is a high probability that time in the terminal area (the intercept of the equation) will rise. The sensitivity of the forecasts to these assumptions is discussed below.

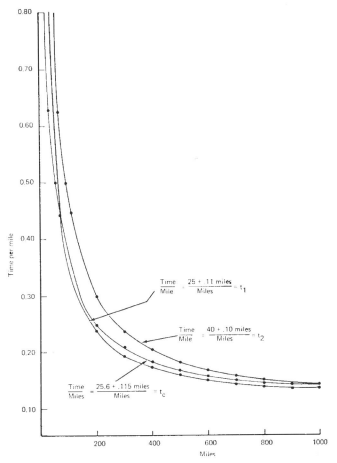

Fig. 1. Current and assumed future structure of travel time.

The structure of airline fares by distance is shown in Fig. 2. The equation for real fare per mile in 1968 is

$$p = \frac{6 \cdot 62 + 0 \cdot 0448M}{M}, \quad R^2 = 0 \cdot 97, \quad s = 5 \cdot 6$$

and is plotted as p_c in Fig. 2. Our alternative assumptions of the fare structure are shown in the two curves, p_1 and p_2, in Fig. 2.

We have hypothesized a "twisting" of the fare structure, with the fixed element rising somewhat and the contribution of distance declining somewhat. This reflects the operating economies of the aircraft likely to be in service during the 1970's. The wide-body aircraft are most economical for trips of 600 miles and more, which is reflected in the fact that the assumed fare curves cross beneath the curve of current fares at about this distance. The prospects for reduction of fares in the shorter haul markets are not particularly good. STOL aircraft may require a premium fare, which would be offset by somewhat lower travel times; and airport and airway congestion will raise the cost of short trips relatively more than long trips. Thus, a continuation of congestion, or the onset of congestion at new airports, would raise fares for shorter trips relative to fares for longer trips.

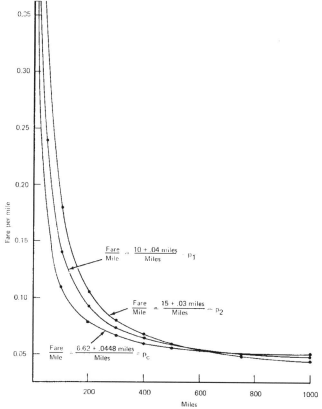

FIG. 2. Current and assumed future structure of fare.

Sensitivity. In Table 3 we have listed projections of passenger demand under various combinations of assumed fare and trip time for 15 selected pairs of cities. Variation of the assumptions affects short-haul markets most strongly. As the estimated elasticities would imply, the greatest variation is caused by changing fare, and our assumptions of a twist in the fare structure exerts a damping effect on travel over short routes.

The longer haul markets are next most affected by the assumptions. The longest haul markets (New York–Los Angeles, Los Angeles–Chicago) are at their highest levels under assumption (p_2, t_2) and their lowest under (p_c, t_c). This is the reverse of the pattern for the short-haul markets as is implied by the twist in fare structure.

In no case is the projected traffic under (p_1, t_1) either highest or lowest for a city pair; in most cases this projection lies between extremes. Because of this, assumption (p_1, t_1) is used to project passenger demand for all city pairs.

Sensitivity of Flights. The question now is: how sensitive are forecasts of flights to these same alternative assumptions: To check this, we have forecast flights under the same five assumptions on which demand forecasts were made. These are listed in Table 4.

TABLE 3. SENSITIVITY OF FORECASTS OF DAILY ONE-WAY PASSENGERS

City pairs	Assumptions				
	p_c and t_c	p_1 and t_1	p_1 and t_2	p_2 and t_1	p_2 and t_2
New York–Miami	2,922,866	3,045,729	3,022,182	3,392,261	3,366,035
–Los Angeles	1,374,276	1,491,635	1,504,269	1,802,176	1,817,441
–Chicago	2,232,915	2,260,138	2,218,735	2,389,392	2,345,621
–Boston	3,550,910	3,050,795	2,847,400	2,564,475	2,393,503
–Philadelphia	159,295	126,343	115,602	97,677	89,373
–Atlanta	585,695	595,102	585,003	633,300	622,553
Los Angeles–San Diego†	237,166	192,171	176,726	151,724	139,529
–San Francisco	2,463,772	2,301,104	2,199,479	2,148,507	2,053,621
–Chicago	872,899	934,618	937,298	1,097,613	1,100,760
–Houston	216,706	229,344	228,939	263,145	262,680
Chicago–Minneapolis	691,400	649,788	622,288	612,012	586,111
–Detroit	639,831	575,046	543,414	510,244	482,177
–Atlanta	256,595	255,385	249,223	262,459	256,126
–Cleveland	624,626	585,842	560,695	550,210	526,592
Atlanta–Houston	84,061	84,832	83,189	89,225	87,497

† Does not include traffic of Pacific Southwestern Airlines.

TABLE 4. SENSITIVITY OF FORECASTS OF DAILY ONE-WAY FLIGHTS

City pairs	Assumptions				
	p_c and t_c	p_1 and t_1	p_1 and t_2	p_2 and t_1	p_2 and t_2
New York–Miami	41·6	43·7	42·0	43·4	41·8
–Los Angeles	16·8	17·6	18·4	17·5	18·2
–Chicago	31·1	32·6	29·8	32·5	29·7
–Boston	54·2	53·5	40·9	49·8	38·0
–Philadelphia	2·1	2·2	1·4	2·3	1·4
–Atlanta	8·1	8·5	7·8	8·5	7·8
Los Angeles–San Diego†	3·2	3·4	2·2	3·4	2·3
–San Francisco	38·2	40·2	32·2	40·3	32·3
–Chicago	10·5	11·1	11·2	11·0	11·1
–Houston	2·6	2·7	2·7	2·7	2·6
Chicago–Minneapolis	10·7	11·3	9·1	11·3	9·2
–Detroit	9·6	10·1	7·6	10·1	7·7
–Atlanta	4·1	4·4	3·9	4·4	3·9
–Cleveland	9·7	10·2	8·2	10·2	8·2
Atlanta–Houston	1·1	1·2	1·1	1·2	1·1

† Does not include traffic of Pacific Southwestern Airlines.

Evidently flights are less sensitive to the variety of assumptions than passenger demand. This is a natural consequence of the relationship between passenger demand, fare and flights. As fare increases, the demand for trips decreases, but profit-maximizing load factor decreases as well, which tends to offset the reduction in flights that would be caused by the fall in passenger trips.

Equipment assignments and service patterns

As a final step in our procedure we must determine the class of aircraft to be used in individual city-pair markets. Two steps were necessary to accomplish this. First, it had to be determined what service patterns were likely to emerge between city pairs. Would all flights be direct or would some city pairs be likely to receive primarily indirect service? Second, aircraft had to be assigned to markets in light of the nature of the service they were to receive. We adopted two service hypotheses: direct service, and hub and spoke.

Direct service. Under this hypothesis, direct flights were scheduled between all city pairs according to the following distribution.

TABLE 5. ASSIGNMENT—DIRECT SERVICE

Market characteristics	Class of aircraft	Operating cost†
0–300 miles	B-737/DC-9	$450/hr
300–600 miles		
Less that 100 passengers/day	B-727	$550/hr
More than 100 passengers/day	DC-10/L-1011	$1050/hr
600–1200 miles	B-747 DC/10/L-1011	$1250/hr
1200–more miles	B-747	$1500/hr

Source: CAB (1969a), b), numbers are rounded for convenience.
† Composite.

Hub and spoke service. Under this hypothesis, the economies of the wide-body jets are fully exploited. City pairs are regrouped into wheels, with the spoke cities becoming feeders to the hub cities (the actual groupings are shown in Fig. 3–7). The wide-body jets are then assigned to the hub-to-hub routes and to some larger spoke-to-hub routes; the remaining feeder cities are then served by smaller aircraft. The assignment procedure is shown in Table 6.

TABLE 6. ASSIGNMENT—HUB AND SPOKE

Market characteristics	Class of aircraft	Operating cost
0–300 miles; less than 100 passengers/day	B-737/DC-9	$450/hr
0–300 miles; more than 100 passengers/day	DC-10/L-1011	$1050/hr
300–600 miles; less than 100 passengers/day	B-727	$550/hr
300–600 miles; more than 100 passengers/day	DC-10/L-1011	$1050/hr
600–1200 miles	B-747 DC-10/L-1011	$1250/hr†
1200–or more miles	B-747	$1500/hr

† Composite.

A forecast of air travel and airport and airway use in 1980

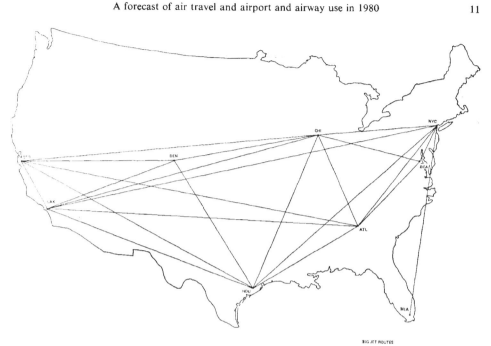

Fig. 3

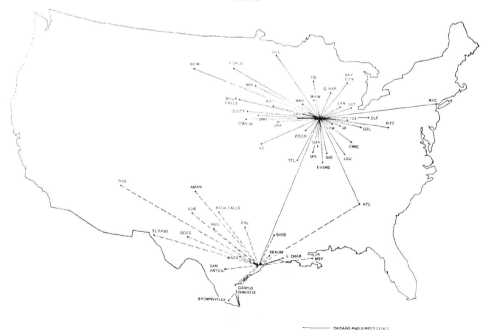

Fig. 4

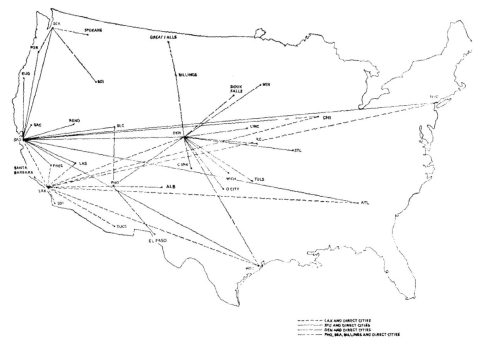

Fig. 5

Fig. 6

A forecast of air travel and airport and airway use in 1980

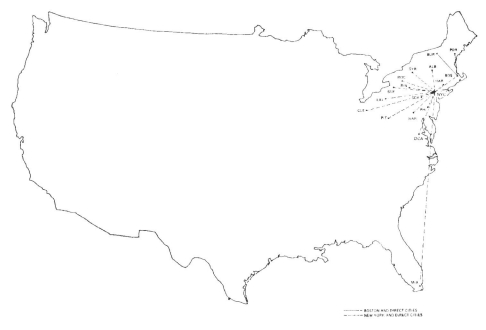

Fig. 7

Our grouping of the hubs represents an early try and could be improved upon through use of a simultaneous equations model that permits solution for fare, flights and travel time which would permit optimization of the route structure (see De Vany, 1971). For example, to travel from Memphis to Nashville with hub-and-spoke service, a distance of 200 miles, one must go through Atlanta for a total trip distance of 546 miles. However, there would be only 4 direct one-way flights per day from Memphis to Nashville, whereas with indirect service there would be 25 flights between Memphis and Atlanta and 15 between Nashville and Atlanta. Thus the longer trip time may be made up for by higher frequencies.

There are other city pairs, however, where not only frequency but class of aircraft are improved, with some penalty in travel time. For example, the direct flight distance from St. Louis to Pittsburg is 553 miles, whereas our indirect routing through Chicago requires the passenger to travel 810 miles. The benefits of the indirect routing are an increase of flight frequency from 2 direct flights between St. Louis and Pittsburg to a situation having 20 flights from Chicago to Pittsburg and 35 flights from St. Louis to Chicago. In addition, the indirect routing employs air bus equipment and the direct routing receives 727-class equipment, permitting a fare reduction because of the higher productivity of the wide-body aircraft. The higher schedule frequency is sufficient to offset the increased trip time alone, however.

Perhaps the major question is what the direction of traffic around the hubs will be. Two possibilities exist for the same route structure shown in the figures. Flights could move along the spokes from the feeders to the hubs. Alternatively, flights between hubs might touch down at feeder cities along the way. The basic pattern of feeders and hubs would remain the same under either arrangement, but the pattern of flights would differ.

V. CONCLUSIONS

The demand function estimated here sheds light on the historical sources of growth of air travel and indicates that these forces are largely played out and will not contribute as strongly to growth in the future.

Passenger miles carried by the domestic trunk airlines have grown an average of 14·1 per cent a year over the past 20 yr. Some of this growth has been due to the steady increase of the average trip length from 450 to 650 miles. Passenger originations have grown more slowly, averaging 11·7 per cent a year. The high-income elasticity of demand of our demand function (2·00) accounts for a 7 per cent rate of growth of passenger originations based on an average annual rate of growth of real GNP of about 3·5 per cent. The remaining 5 per cent annual growth is explained by a combination of factors. Real average fare per mile declined 37 per cent over the period, or about 1·8 per cent a year. This would account for about 2 per cent annual growth of passenger originations and for a lengthening of the average trip as explained in De Vany (1971). Travel time per mile declined an average of 6·5 per cent a year which, based on our time elasticities, would result in 1·36 per cent annual growth of travel. The remaining annual growth of about 1·6 per cent would be accounted for by the increase in frequency of flights. Overall aircraft departures performed rose from 1·66 million in 1949 to 3·00 million, or about 8 per cent a year, but not all routes experienced so substantial a rise in scheduled flights because many flights were added through creation of new routes. If half the increase in frequency of flights went to new routes and half to existing routes, this remaining 1·6 per cent annual growth would be accounted for by increased schedules.

Just how these forces will work in the future is somewhat speculative, but our forecasts indicate the following. Consumer income will continue to be the strongest source of growth in air travel. Not only does income provide the purchasing power necessary for air travel, it also affects the cost of time (see Becker, 1965; Gronau, 1970; De Vany, 1971) which will induce further substitution toward air travel on longer trips, but may also induce substitution away from it on shorter trips as alternative travel modes begin to rival the speed of air travel.

Further fare reductions are heavily dependent upon use of wide-body jets. Since wide-body jets are more economical on medium- and long-haul routes their further use will contribute to the twisting of the fare structure. The twist in fare structure will contribute further to a lengthening of average trip length.

Our forecasts indicated that the effect of these wide-body jets on schedules will eliminate schedule frequency as a source of growth of air travel in the future. Further introduction of wide-body jets into service will result in a substantial decrease in schedule frequencies in many city-pair markets and very modest growth in most others, if the present pattern of direct flights is adhered to. The data in Table 7 allow us to examine the underlying reasons for this. These data indicate daily one-way passengers and flights in 1968 and in 1980 for both direct and hub-and-spoke service patterns.

The entries in this table require some explanation before they can be interpreted. One-way passenger travel from the origin city (on the left) to the destination city (on the right) is shown for 1968 and 1980 under the basically direct-service pattern in use today. The next column indicates 1980 passengers under the hub-and-spoke pattern. A blank in this column indicates all passengers going between the cities of the pair go via an indirect route, therefore they show up as traffic between the cities along the route. For example, the blank for Boston–Syracuse indicates that the 121 daily passengers going from Boston to Syracuse go via on indirect route—from Boston to New York and then to Syracuse in this case—therefore, these passengers are added to totals for Boston–New York and New York–Syracuse. The flight columns are easily interpreted except for the hub-and-spoke column.

TABLE 7. ONE-WAY DAILY PASSENGERS AND FLIGHTS FOR SELECTED CITY PAIRS

City pair	One-way daily passengers			One-way daily flights		
	1968	1980 direct	1980 hub and spoke	1968	1980 direct	1980 hub and spoke
Boston–Syracuse	103	121	†	4	4	156, 16
Boston–Chicago	459	587	†	14	7	156, 116
Albany–Buffalo	82	117	†	4	4	11, 28
New York–Boston	3499	3662	11,974	110	111	156
New York–Syracuse	573	660	1234	25	20	16
New York–Philadelphia	97	96	5200	27	3	69
New York–Miami	2433	3663	6128	47	39	65
New York–Chicago	2226	2842	10,981	74	30	116
New York–San Francisco	863	1237	2395	25	11	21
New York–San Diego	107	145	†	1	2	28, 14
Washington D.C.–Cleveland	255	322	†	13	5	106, 36
Washington D.C.–New York	2785	3205	8182	84	97	106
Washington D.C.–Milwaukee	61	88	†	2	1	50, 17
Atlanta–Washington D.C.	238	367	2865	15	5	37
Atlanta–Cleveland	72	112	†	4	2	59, 29
Chicago–Houston	151	199	†	4	3	23, 46
Chicago–Portland	67	100	†	7	1	21,
Denver–Milwaukee	36	58	†	2	1	14, 17
San Francisco–Chicago	518	728	2347	27	7	21
San Francisco–Phoenix	152	228	†	4	3	74, 27
Los Angeles–Atlanta	107	183	565	3	2	5

† Receives indirect service under the hub-and-spoke arrangement.

A double entry here indicates the number of one-way daily flights on each leg of the hub-and-spoke patterns as depicted in Figs. 3–7. Thus, for example, there would be four direct flights from Boston to Syracuse under the direct service pattern in 1968 and in 1980; whereas, under the hub-and-spoke pattern there would be 156 flights from Boston to New York and 16 from Boston to Syracuse.

Perhaps the clearest pattern to emerge from our forecasts is the tendency for flights to decline in 1980 under the direct-service pattern. It was largely an attempt to keep frequencies from declining too much with use of wide-body jets that led us to adopt the hub-and-spoke pattern with its high frequencies but indirect routes. There is little question that the passenger would prefer direct flights; however, two factors tend to militate against this preference if our forecasts are correct. First, for some city pairs the number of flights consistent with fares, operating costs and number of passengers will be so low as to reduce the likelihood that the direct flight will depart near a desired time. The hub-and-spoke pattern offers higher frequencies in most cases which can offset the lengthened time of flight. Second, this pattern establishes a feeder structure which permits more filling of the wide-body jets and more efficient route assignments. One of the key issues facing the airlines concerns the willingness of passengers to bear a longer flight time in order to have the fare reductions and higher flight frequencies permitted by use of the wide-body jets in some version of a hub-and-spoke pattern. Unless some form of hub-and-spoke pattern is used—with some direct flights as well—flights will fall too much under the route assignment of wide-body jets as hypothesized in Table 8. The lack of a feeder structure to adequately fill these jets will result in low load factors, high cost per passenger and a failure of the wide-body jets to produce the fare reductions they now promise and upon which a good deal of the growth in the air travel depends.

In this regard, the introduction of the big jets in the 1970's is similar to the situation in the early 1960's as the first generation jets came into service. Frequency of flight declined, passengers per flight increased and a hub-and-spoke type service pattern emerged. Aircraft departures declined from 2·4 million in 1959 to 1·99 million in 1962, climbing to 3·0 million in 1968. Passengers per flight over the same years were 18·3, 23·5 and 36·3. These changes are roughly comparable to what we forecast for the coming decade (see below). The difference is that the big jets are not as revolutionary a change from conventional jets as conventional jets were from piston aircraft. This, in conjunction with a lack of the other strong growth factors experienced in the 1960's, indicates that the wide-body jet will not penetrate air travel markets as deeply as might be supposed unless existing patterns of service are modified toward an indirect pattern containing more flight segments per passenger trip.

TABLE 8. DAILY DOMESTIC FLIGHT OPERATIONS (LANDINGS AND TAKE-OFFS) OF THE REGULATED TRUNK AIRLINES FOR SELECTED CITIES

City	1968 scheduled		1980 hub and spoke		1980 direct	
	Operations	% of total	Operations	% of total	Operations	% of total
Boston	476	3·2	284	2·6	468	4·2
New York City	1520	10·2	1668	15·4	1456	13·0
Philadelphia	416	2·8	174	1·6	288	2·6
Washington, D.C.	852	5·7	598	5·5	628	5·6
Miami	350	2·3	286	2·6	318	2·8
Atlanta	662	4·4	856	7·9	336	3·0
Memphis	166	1·1	52	0·5	112	1·0
Pittsburgh	322	2·2	130	1·2	242	2·2
Detroit	360	2·4	180	1·7	288	2·6
Chicago	1430	9·6	1694	15·7	832	7·4
St. Louis	352	2·4	140	1·3	268	2·4
Dallas	498	3·3	181	1·7	304	2·7
New Orleans	218	1·5	80	0·7	144	1·3
Houston	252	1·7	504	4·7	186	1·7
Denver	288	1·9	394	3·6	176	1·6
Seattle	216	1·5	154	1·4	158	1·4
San Francisco	520	3·5	456	4·2	400	3·6
Los Angeles	740	5·0	560	5·2	584	5·2
San Diego	86	0·6	32	0·3	54	0·5
Total operations for all cities in sample	14,972		10,812		11,192	

The implications of these considerations for airport operations can be seen by examining the data in Table 8. Here total daily operations that result from flights to and from all other cities in our forecasts are listed for 1968 and both 1980 patterns. The city's percentage of the national operations total is also shown. As can be seen, the totals at the bottom indicate that domestic trunk airline flights would decline by 1980 under either service pattern, but the decline would be greatest under the hub-and-spoke. The individual pattern at each airport, however, may not be inferred from the national totals. There is substantial growth at some airports, New York, Chicago and Las Vegas, for example. At other airports, notably Philadelphia, Washington, D.C., and Los Angeles, there are substantial declines. Almost every airport's share of 1980 national traffic differs from its 1968 share which emphasizes the danger of forecasting under an assumption of constant shares.

In terms of daily passengers, the differences between the hub-and-spoke and direct-service patterns are more dramatic than flights. These are shown in Table 9. Airports such as New York, Atlanta, Chicago and San Francisco would handle many more passengers under the hub-and-spoke arrangement than under the direct arrangement because they function as hubs. Passengers at other cities, such as St. Louis or Detroit, would be independent of the service pattern adopted since they do not serve as hubs under either.

TABLE 9. DAILY PASSENGERS (IN AND OUT) FOR SELECTED CITIES

City	1980 hub and spoke		1980 direct	
	Passengers	% of total	Passengers	% of total
Boston	21,366	2·5	20,198	3·8
New York City	139,700	16·6	77,927	14·7
Philadelphia	12,973	1·5	12,973	2·4
Washington, D.C.	45,080	5·3	28,114	5·3
Miami	23,953	2·8	23,664	4·5
Atlanta	63,607	7·5	14,490	2·7
Memphis	3,967	0·5	3,967	0·7
Pittsburgh	9,858	1·2	9,858	1·9
Cleveland	10,896	1·3	10,986	2·1
Detroit	13,813	1·6	13,813	2·6
Chicago	138,544	16·4	45,496	8·6
St. Louis	11,116	1·3	11,116	2·1
Dallas	14,045	1·7	14,045	2·6
New Orleans	5,937	0·7	5,937	1·1
Houston	39,068	4·6	7,708	1·5
Denver	32,327	3·8	9,794	1·8
Seattle	11,011	1·3	9,098	1·7
San Francisco	47,569	5·6	27,594	5·2
Los Angeles	48,345	5·7	40,328	7·6
San Diego	2,232	0·3	2,232	
Total passengers for all cities in sample	842,832		531,050	

It is clear that the role an airport serves in the national system is fundamentally important to the flights and passengers it must service. The more likely is a hub-and-spoke type of pattern, the more interdependent are airports and the less likely is it that the pattern at any one airport will resemble the national pattern of flights and passengers. It is especially clear that the old methods of forecasting either national totals or individual airport traffic independent of service patterns will produce many mistakes in airport planning over the next decade if service patterns change even roughly along the lines we have forecast. It is our fear that, using these methods of forecasting, excess capacity will be created in many smaller airports and too little capacity will be added at existing major hub cities and at cities that will be hubs tomorrow. In addition, the airport problem will become more a problem of handling passengers and less a problem of handling aircraft, so that greater emphasis must be given to terminals and less to runways.

REFERENCES

BECKER G. S. (1965). A theory of the allocation of time. *Econ. J.* **LXXV**, 494–514.
BROWN S. S. and WATKINS W. S. (1968). *The demand of air travel: a regression study of time-series and cross sectional data in the U.S. domestic market.* Civil Aeronautics Board Research Study, Washington D.C.

CIVIL AERONAUTICS BOARD (1967). *Forecast of Scheduled Domestic Air Passenger Traffic for the Eleven Trunkline Carriers.* CAB Research Study, Washington, D.C.
CIVIL AERONAUTICS BOARD (1968). *A Study of the Domestic Passenger Air Fare Structure.* CAB Research Study, Washington, D.C.
CIVIL AERONAUTICS BOARD (1969a). *Impact of New Large Jets on the Air Transportation System, 1970–1973.* CAB Research Study, Washington, D.C.
CIVIL AERONAUTICS BOARD (1969b). *Aircraft Operating Cost and Performance Report.* Washington, D.C.
CIVIL AERONAUTICS BOARD (1969c). *Domestic Origin-Destination Survey of Airline Passenger Traffic.* Washington, D.C.
CIVIL AERONAUTICS BOARD (1970). *Wide-bodied Jet Aircraft Operating Cost and Performance Report, U.S. Certificated Route Air-Carriers,* Vol. 2. Washington, D.C.
DEPARTMENT OF COMMERCE (1970). *Survey of Current Business.* V5QNN5.
DEPARTMENT OF COMMERCE (1968). *Preliminary Report on Economic Projections for Selected Geographic Areas, 1929 to 2020.* Washington, D.C.
DE VANY, A. S. (1970a). *Time in the Budget of the Consumer: The Theory of Consumer Demand and Labor Supply under a Time Constraint.* Ph.D. Dissertation, University of California, Los Angeles, California.
DE VANY, A. S. (1970b). The value of time in air travel: theory and evidence. *Center for naval analyses. Research Contribution No. 162.* Arlington, Virginia.
DE VANY A. S. (1971). *The Economics of Quality Competition: Theory and Evidence on Airline Flight Scheduling.* (Mimeo.)
ELLE B. J. (1968). *Issues and Prospects in Interurban Air Transport.* Almqvist & Wiksell, Sweden.
FEDERAL AVIATION ADMINISTRATION (1969). *Air Traffic Activity, Fiscal Year* 1968. FAA, Washington, D.C.
FEDERAL AVIATION ADMINISTRATION (1970). *Aviation Forecasts, Fiscal Years* 1970–1981. FAA, Washington, D.C.
GRONAU R. J. (1970). The effect of traveling time on the demand for passenger transportation. *J. Polit. Econ.* **8**, 377–394.
OFFICIAL AIRLINE GUIDE (1968). Donelley, New York.

2

Gravity models for airline passenger volume estimation

Tobias Grosche, Franz Rothlauf, Armin Heinzl

Abstract

This paper presents two gravity models for the estimation of air passenger volume between city-pairs. The models include variables describing the general economic activity and geographical characteristics of city-pairs instead of variables describing air service characteristics. Thus, both models can be applied to city-pairs where currently no air service is established, historical data is not available, or for which factors describing the current service level of air transportation are not accessible or accurately predictable. One model is limited to city-pairs with airports not subject to competition from airports in the vicinity, while the other model includes all city-pairs. Booking data of flights between Germany and 28 European countries is used for calibration. Both models show a good fit to the observed data and are statistically tested and validated.
© 2007 Elsevier Ltd. All rights reserved.

Keywords: Passenger volume estimation; Gravity model; Forecasting

1. Introduction

Demand forecasts are used by airlines to predict the travel behavior of potential passengers. Accurate forecasts are of major importance for an airline's overall success. An important element in forecasting is passenger volume estimation. The objective is to predict the number of expected passengers between two cities for a given time interval. Based on such forecasts, airlines can make decisions regarding new routes or additional flights on existing routes.

A variety of different techniques exist for passenger volume estimation. Since no single technique guarantees accuracy, airlines in fact compare forecasts from several different models. Within this set of forecasting methods, the most widely used is the gravity model.

Two gravity models for the estimation of passenger volume between city-pairs are examined here. By excluding service-related or market-specific input variables, and using cross-sectional calibration data, the models are particularly applicable to city-pairs where no air service exists, historical data is unavailable, or factors describing the current service level of air transportation are not available.

2. Air travel demand forecasting

2.1. Driving forces

In Gravity models it is assumed that air travel supports other targeted activities such as business or vacation trips (O'Connor, 1982), and that it can be derived from other selected economic or social supply variables. In general, these variables can be categorized into two groups: geo-economic and service-related factors (Rengaraju and Thamizh Arasan, 1992; Kanafani, 1983). Geo-economic factors describe the economic activities and geographical characteristics of the areas around the airports and the routes involved (Jorge-Calderón, 1997). Service-related factors are characteristics of the air transport system and are, in contrast to geo-economic factors, under the control of the airlines.

Geo-economic factors involve the economic activities and geographical characteristics of cities served by an airline. The most commonly used activity-related factors are income and the population of the metropolitan area served. A more aggregate measure can be the historical passenger volumes at each airport (Doganis, 1966). Other activity-related variables that have been used are income distribution, percentage of university degree holders, number of full-time employees, type of city, employment composition, structure of the local production sector, and economic, political and cultural relationships between two countries (Russon and Riley, 1993). An important geographical factor affecting inter-city air travel demand is the distance between cities. It has two conflicting effects: increasing distance leads to lower social and commercial interactions but longer distances increase the competitiveness of air transport compared to other transportation modes (Jorge-Calderón, 1997). Competition between airports in close proximity also influences demand. For example, an airport offering better schedules may attract more passengers than airports in closer proximity (Ubøe, 2004; Fotheringham, 1983b; Fotheringham and Webber, 1980).

The main service-related factors focus on the quality and the price of airline service (Jorge-Calderón, 1997). Various studies have looked at factors influencing airline service quality (Gardner Jr., 2004; Ghobrial and Kanafani, 1995; Gursoy et al., 2003; Park et al., 2004). Travel time between cities, often represented as the difference between the desired departure time of a passenger and the actual arrival time, is generally found important. Travel time partly depends on the frequency of flights offered because with increasing frequency, passengers are able to select a flight that departs closer to their preferred time. The average load factor also influences travel time as it indicates the probability of free seats at the preferred departure time. An airline's overall on-time performance is another factor as flight delays increase the travel times. Also relevant for service quality are an airline's reputation, market presence, frequent flyer membership programs, and aircraft equipment. In general, the demand for air travel decreases with increasing fares. On short-haul routes, airlines face competition of other modes that gain a relative advantage with increasing airfares (Jorge-Calderón, 1997). A survey of German passengers showed that 52% would not have traveled at all if no low-priced low-cost airline flights had been available (Tacke and Schleusener, 2003). However, some reject consideration of air fares when forecasting demand. Often, the airfare is highly correlated with the distance or travel time and is omitted to avoid issues of multicollinearity (Rengaraju and Thamizh Arasan, 1992). It may also be assumed an exogenous factor; an airline has only limited control over price in competitive markets (O'Connor, 1982). In addition, it is difficult for airlines to forecast fares reliably because determinants such as oil prices are highly volatile and hard to predict (Doganis, 2004). Finally, the use of average fares is problematic because fares often depend on route density and competition as well as on the fare classes (Lee, 2003). Jorge-Calderón (1997), for example, showed that air travel demand is price inelastic with respect to the unrestricted economy fare, and that moderately discounted restricted fares do not generate significant additional traffic.

3. Gravity model development

Gravity models were the earliest causal models developed for traffic forecasting. The gravitational law states that the gravity between two objects is directly proportional to their masses and inversely proportional to their squared distances. A simple formulation of a gravity model for human spatial interaction used for the prediction travel demand between two cities i and j is

$$V_{ij} = k \cdot \frac{(A_i A_j)^\alpha}{d_{ij}^\gamma}, \qquad (1)$$

where V_{ij} is the passenger volume between i and j ($V_{ij} = V_{ji}$ and $i \neq j$), A_i and A_j are attraction factors of i and j, $d_{ij} = d_{ji}$ is the distance between the cities, and k is a constant. γ is a parameter that controls the influence of the distance on travel demand and α controls the influence of the attraction factors. Usually, the attraction and deterrence is expressed not only by a single variable but by a combination of various factors. This undirected gravity model can be extended to a directed model if V_{ij} measures directed passenger flows from i to j. Then, separate variables represent travel production (push) factors P_i^β the originating city and travel attraction (pull) factors A_j^α of the destination city. This distinction is sometimes only made by allowing the variables to have different parameter values for the origin and destination city while using the same variables for both.

Parameters are calibrated to lead to the most accurate prediction of the expected travel demand (the difference between predicted and observed travel demand should be low). Thus, data including historical passenger demand as well as characteristics of the influencing factors is used. Because accurate values for unconstrained demand can only be obtained by extensive and detailed market research, most models are calibrated using traffic figures as a substitute for the unconstrained demand. These figures, however, are influenced by the available aircraft capacity of the airlines on the routes involved, and thus only approximate unconstrained demand. In most cases, the calibration involves ordinary-least-squares methods. Table 1 offers some results from previous work.

4. Gravity models

Two new gravity models are developed for passenger volume estimation. The first (BM) minimizes the effects of competing destinations by excluding city-pairs involving multi-airport cities such as London or Berlin. The second (EM) is an extension of the BM that includes multi-airport locations using the independent variables of the BM and additional variables that describe effects of competing airports. Because both models primarily deploy geo-economic variables as inputs, and cross-sectional data for calibration, they can be used for the estimation of air passenger volume in new markets. A second motivation for using only geo-economic variables is that the airline industry is facing a more flexible business environment with volatility in competition, changes in alliances, different business models, volatile fuel prices, etc.

Table 1
Properties of selected previously estimated gravity models

Study	Factors	Obs.	R^2
Doganis (1966)	Observed passenger number at airports, distance	22	0.740[a]
Brown and Watkins (1968)	Income, sales competition, average fare per mile, journey time per mile, number of stops, distance, phone calls, international passengers on domestic flight, competition index	300	0.870
Verleger (1972)	Income, price, phone calls, distance, flying time	441	0.720[b]
Moore and Soliman (1981)	population on city-level, income, economy fare	69	0.370
	Population of airport catchment regions, income, airport catchment, economy fare	58	0.810
Fotheringham (1983b)	attractiveness/population, traffic outflow of origin, distance	9900	0.730; 0.760[c]
Rengaraju and Thamizh Arasan (1992)	Population, percentage of employees, university degree holders, big-city proximity factor, travel time ratio (travel time by rail divided by travel time by air), distance, frequency of service	40	0.952
Russon and Riley (1993)	Income, population, highway miles distance, number of jet/propeller nonstop/connection flights, driving time minus connection flight time, distance to competing airports, political state boundary	391	0.992
O'Kelly et al. (1995)	Nodal attraction, distance	294	0.850[d]
Jorge-Calderón (1997)	Population, income, proximity of hub airport, hub airport, distance, existence of body of water between cities	339	0.371
	Additional variables: tourism destination, frequency, aircraft size, economy fare (not/moderately/highly discounted restricted)	339	0.722
Shen (2004)	Nodal attraction, impedance	600	0.568[e]
Doganis (2004)	Scheduled passenger traffic at airports, economy fare, frequency	47	0.941

[a]This value is the "rank coefficient". The city-pairs are ranked according to the actual and estimated passenger volumes and the correlation between the ranks yields the rank coefficient.
[b]The study is based on the model from Brown and Watkins (1968).
[c]The model with the higher R^2 includes the "accessibility" of a destination to all other destinations of an origin" as an additional variable to consider the effects of spatial structure.
[d]Different methods for a reverse calibration of the gravity model were used.
[e]The focus is on an algebraic approach for reverse-fitting of the gravity model. Therefore, the nodal attraction is estimated endogenously from exogenous spatial interaction and impedance.

Therefore, the selection of service-related factors that are subject to continual change often play a minor role in long-term forecasting. In addition, airline-specific variables such as available aircraft, overall capacities and airport facilities are excluded because the output of the models is the number of passengers which is the basis for developing airline-specific schedules.

Market Information Data Tapes (MIDT) bookings are used as a substitute for the unconstrained demand for calibration. The data sets describe travel itineraries between airports in Germany and 28 European countries between January and August 2004. City-pairs for which data is unavailable are excluded. To reduce the effects of competing modes, only medium and long-haul routes are considered (distances greater than 500 km) as are only traffic routes with at least 500 passengers over the time period. Typical tourist routes or destinations with low-cost airlines traffic are not considered because traffic on these routes is expected to depend on different factors to routes with significant amounts of business traffic (Jorge-Calderón, 1997). The sample contains 1228 city-pairs with 137 embracing cities, and 9,091,082 passengers.

4.1. Basic gravity model

The basic gravity model is

$$V_{ij} = e^{\varepsilon} P_{ij}^{\pi} C_{ij}^{\chi} B_{ij}^{\beta} G_{ij}^{\eta} D_{ij}^{\delta} T_{ij}^{\tau}, \qquad (2)$$

where V_{ij} is total passenger volume between cities i and j. Table 2 lists the functional forms of the independent variables.

- *Population*: City populations are based on data from the statistical offices of the countries where they are located. The latest figures were always considered. Population

Table 2
Independent variables used in the basic model

Notation	Functional form	Factor
P_{ij}	$P_i P_j$	Population
C_{ij}	$C_i C_j$	Catchment
B_{ij}	$B_i + B_j$	Buying power index
G_{ij}	$G_i G_j$	Gross domestic product
D_{ij}		Geographical distance
T_{ij}		Average travel time

refers only to the city where each airport is located with potential passengers from an airport's vicinity included its catchment data.

- *Catchment*: A catchment area covers the vicinity of an airport. Usually it includes only those areas that are within a certain driving time of an airport (60 minutes). The data is derived from population data of the regions at the NUTS3-level for 2003.[1]
- *Buying power index*: The average buying power index is based on an airport's catchment area and is given at the NUTS3-level with 100 as the European average. The index is an indicator for the size of the travel budget of the population within an airport's catchment in 2003.
- *Gross domestic product*: The gross domestic product of the country of the airport is given at market prices in € millions for 2003. Because data on income distribution is not available, the GDP is considered as a representative variable for the level of economic activity.
- *Geographical distance*: The distance between two airports is the great circle distance in kilometers between their coordinates.
- *Average travel time*: The travel time is calculated from the MIDT-bookings and averages non-stop and connecting flights for each city-pair.

Distance and the travel time are expected to be deterrent factors for air travel; airfare is omitted because appropriate data is unavailable. Excluding tourist routes and destinations of low-cost airlines reduces the effect of not including fares because the remaining routes are expected to have a high proportion of business travelers who are largely time-sensitive and price-insensitive. The model's parameters are calibrated using ordinary least squares (Table 3).

The results indicate that the model is statistically valid. The null hypothesis that the independent variables have no effect can be rejected for each variable at the 1%-level and the significance of the combination of all coefficients is high, exceeding the critical F-statistics value at the 1%-level. Tests for multicollinearity produce contradictory results. The maximum variance inflation factor indicates collinearity but the maximum correlation coefficient between any two independent variables is 0.700 for distance and travel time. However, omitting one of these variables would substantially reduce the model fit. As the goal is to obtain a reliable estimation of the passenger volume, both variables were included.

The results of the statistical tests use the information available within the sample to test specific hypothesized values of individual regression coefficients (Huang, 1970). However, it is important to study model validity by testing its structural stability after calibration and a test requiring additional observations not already considered is used. Because additional observations are not available, we split the total sample into sub-samples. For the sub-samples, the stability of the input coefficients and the coefficient of determination are analyzed. The separation into subsets is conducted through two experimental setups.

For the first experimental setup (setup 1), the sample is split into two subsets of equal size (Rengaraju and Thamizh Arasan, 1992). Five experiments are conducted each with two different subsets. In the first, observations are assigned randomly to one of the subsets and in the other the observations are split into two subsets with one subset having 50% of the observations with the highest value of the selection criteria: distance, aggregate population, aggregate catchment, and observed passenger volume. For each of the experiments, one subset is used to calibrate the coefficients of the gravity model using regression analysis—the calibration sample (CS). Then coefficients obtained from the CS are used to estimate the passenger volume for the observations of the other subset (estimation sample ES), and vice versa. The results of this validation setup are presented in Table 4.

In the second experimental setup (setup 2), subsets are constructed by building successive intervals with respect to the different selection criteria used in the first experimental setup leading to subsets with different numbers of observations (Table 5).

A formal procedure to test the stability of the set of coefficients in a regression equation for different subsets is presented by Huang (1970). s is defined as the number of subsamples, β_i as the coefficients of the ith subsample ($i \in \{1,...,s\}$), and β^* as the coefficients of the complete sample. The following hypotheses are tested:

$$H_0: \beta_1 = \beta_2 = \cdots = \beta_s (= \beta^*), \quad (3)$$

$$H_1: \beta_1 \neq \beta_2 \neq \cdots = \beta_s. \quad (4)$$

SSR* is the sum of the squared residuals for the complete sample and SSR_s is the sum of the squared residuals of subsample s. The following variables are constructed:

$$Q_1 = SSR^*, \quad (5)$$

$$Q_2 = \sum_s SSR_s, \quad (6)$$

$$Q_3 = Q_1 - Q_2, \quad (7)$$

where n is the number of observations and v is the number of independent variables including the constant term.

---
[1] Nomenclature des unités territoriales statistiques (NUTS) are levels of territory of about the same population size that provide the basis for regional statistics of the European Union.

Table 3
Calibration results of the basic model

Model	Obs.	Coefficients						R^2	F
		P_{ij}	C_{ij}	B_{ij}	G_{ij}	D_{ij}	T_{ij}		
BM	956	0.156	0.164	1.452	−0.065	2.085	−3.297	0.761	503.4
		−7.254	−9.340	−9.023	(−3.276)	−28.592	(−41.103)		
		[0.132]	[0.201]	[0.161]	[−0.075]	[0.692]	[−1.018]		

Table 4
Validation results for the BM, setup 1

Selection criteria	Coefficients						F	R^2 (CS)	R^2 (ES)
	P_{ij}	C_{ij}	B_{ij}	G_{ij}	D_{ij}	T_{ij}			
BM	0.156	0.164	1.452	−0.065	2.085	−3.297	503.4	0.761	
Random	0.158	0.120	1.284	−0.053	2.047	−3.299	258.3	0.767	0.752
	0.153	0.205	1.633	−0.079	2.130	−3.301	247.4	0.759	0.761
Distance	0.190	0.058	1.053	0.017	1.941	−3.283	348.4	0.816	0.668
	0.104	0.239	1.783	−0.120	2.192	−3.537	186.4	0.704	0.799
Population	0.148	0.169	1.103	−0.036	1.877	−2.960	188.9	0.706	0.762
	0.138	0.118	1.719	−0.095	2.271	−3.606	263.3	0.770	0.679
Catch-ment	0.199	0.129	1.144	−0.083	1.707	−3.065	191.3	0.709	0.735
	0.077	0.129	1.497	−0.002	2.634	−3.623	256.3	0.766	0.614
Passenger volume	0.059	0.036	0.425	−0.038	0.345	−0.478	7.8	0.090	0.697
	0.155	0.172	1.255	−0.037	1.850	−2.680	227.3	0.743	0.078

Table 5
Validation results for the BM, setup 2

Selection criteria	Interval	Coefficients						F	R^2	Obs.
		P_{ij}	C_{ij}	B_{ij}	G_{ij}	D_{ij}	T_{ij}			
BM		0.156	0.164	1.452	−0.065	2.085	−3.297	503.4	0.761	956
Distance	500–1000 km	0.199	0.046	1.126	0.017	1.968	−3.310	347.9	0.822	460
	1000–1500 km	0.092	0.217	1.464	−0.092	2.259	−3.420	102.0	0.682	292
	>1500 km	0.114	0.271	2.127	−0.143	2.829	−3.610	89.3	0.731	204
Population	0–200 Bill.	0.178	0.180	1.136	−0.059	1.861	−2.889	102.6	0.661	322
	200–400 Bill	0.167	0.205	0.845	−0.063	2.115	−3.231	121.8	0.751	250
	400–600 Bill	−0.196	0.109	1.716	−0.086	1.930	−3.401	64.8	0.728	152
	600–800 Bill	1.909	0.066	2.356	−0.065	2.710	−3.823	42.3	0.791	74
	>800 Bill.	0.158	0.007	1.971	−0.074	2.401	−3.894	70.1	0.736	158
Catchment	0–4 Mrd.	0.192	0.116	1.078	−0.071	1.643	−2.947	148.8	0.711	370
	4–8 Mrd.	0.151	0.084	1.014	−0.040	1.799	−3.366	92.5	0.726	216
	8–12 Mrd.	0.156	0.877	2.728	−0.133	2.341	−2.785	86.8	0.824	118
	12–16 Mrd.	0.091	−0.935	1.353	−0.016	2.930	−3.593	54.5	0.813	82
	>16 Mrd	−0.010	−0.050	1.719	0.063	3.197	−4.300	89.6	0.767	170
	500–1000	0.020	0.006	0.048	−0.008	−0.025	−0.014	0.9	0.020	284
	1000–1500	−0.006	0.013	0.052	0.010	0.045	−0.014	1.2	0.050	150
Passenger volume	1500–2000	0.017	0.014	0.183	0.007	0.065	0.021	5.1	0.254	96
	2000–2500	−0.025	−0.010	0.061	0.003	0.032	−0.038	2.5	0.223	60
	2500–3000	−0.013	−0.024	−0.094	0.013	−0.100	0.069	3.6	0.316	54
	>3000	0.180	0.235	0.957	−0.006	2.182	−2.819	123.1	0.708	312

Then, Q_1/σ^2 has a χ^2 distribution with n degrees of freedom, Q_2/σ^2 has a χ^2 distribution with $n-sv$ degrees of freedom, and Q_3/σ^2 has a χ^2 distribution with $(s-1)v$ degrees of freedom. The test statistic for the null hypothesis is

$$F = \frac{Q_3/((s-1).v)}{Q_2/(n-s \cdot v)}, \qquad (8)$$

which follows an F-distribution with $((s-1)v, n-sv)$ degrees of freedom. For example, splitting the sample according to the city-pair distances into two subsamples of equal size results in $F = 5.31$. The critical value of $F(8, 940)$ at the 1%-level is 2.51 (2.5%-level: 2.19). Therefore, the null hypothesis is not rejected. Table 6 presents all F-values for the two experimental validation setups.

To summarize, the basic gravity model was derived by testing all possible combinations of input variables and the model offering the best fit selected using as independent variables the factors population, catchment, GDP, buying power, travel time, and distance. For this model, the overall fit is comparable to results found in other studies. To eliminate the effects of competing airports, multi-airport cities were excluded from the data set reducing the number of observations to 956.

The model is statistically valid and all variables significant at the 1%-level. Tests for multicollinearity produced inconsistent results. If it exists, an interpretation of the individual coefficients and their order of magnitude would not be possible. Here, for example, the positive value for the distance runs counter to the common assumption for gravity models that distance has a negative impact on travel demand. However, because distance is correlated with travel time, the negative coefficient of travel time may be overcompensating the positive effect of distance. For forecasting, however, multicollinearity is not relevant as long as the model offers a good fit between the observations and the estimates and the collinearity is not expected to change significantly in the future.

The model is validated by testing its structural stability. With the exception of passenger volume as a selection criteria, the validation results (Table 4) show good fits for the subsamples, and for the estimation samples (ES) compared to the CS. The high correlation between the estimated and observed values for the ES indicates good explanatory power. Additional tests of structural stability (Table 5) show that the coefficients are only subject to minor variations across the different subsets. Changes of sign for some variables occur when using distance as a selection criterion in setup 1 (Table 4), and for all different selection criteria in setup 2 (Table 5). The results emphasize that the gravity models should, if possible, be applied to homogeneous data sets. However, the high coefficient of determination for all subsets and the results in Table 6 indicate broad applicability of the model.

A poor fit is found when separating the data by passenger volume that may be a result of the highly diverse observation data. However, the results are obtained ex post. When using the model for forecasting purposes (ex ante), it is not possible to use different models or coefficients for passenger volume groups because passenger volume is the subject of forecasting. Because the validation using the other selection criteria yielded good results, the presented model is meaningful.

4.2. Extended gravity model

In the basic model, multi-airport cities were not considered but are now brought into consideration. Rengaraju and Thamizh Arasan (1992), for example, include a "big-city proximity factor" as a dummy variable in their model to identify small cities in proximity of larger ones. Jorge-Calderón (1997) also uses dummies for airports that have a hub within a 200 km radius, and another to indicate if the airport is itself a hub; hubs being defined as the top two cities in an airline's host country where the airline carries out international services and that are among the top 20 destinations in terms

Table 6
F-test on structural stability of the BM

Model	F-value (setup 1)	F-value (setup 2)
Distance	5.31	3.53
Population	4.44	2.37
Catchment	6.98	3.98
Passenger volume	127.50	94.60

Table 7
Results of the BM including multi-airport cities

Model	Obs.	Coefficients						R^2	F
		P_{ij}	C_{ij}	B_{ij}	G_{ij}	D_{ij}	T_{ij}		
BM	956	0.156	0.164	1.452	−0.065	2.085	−3.297	0.761	503.4
		−7.254	−9.340	−9.023	(−3.276)	−28.592	(−41.103)		
BM (all cities)	1228	0.136	0.193	1.558	−0.085	1.893	−3.082	0.713	506.8
		−7.383	−10.858	−9.411	(−4.137)	−25.526	(−38.400)		
BM (agg. cities)	1178	0.281	0.189	2.071	−0.102	1.846	−2.974	0.708	476.4
		−14.664	−10.279	−12.242	(−4.815)	−24.223	(−35.130)		

of passenger throughput. Fotheringham (1983a) introduced a variable describing the accessibility of a destination airport as perceived by the passengers of the origin airport.

Table 7 shows results when applying the basic model to all city-pairs including multi-airport cities. The first line replicates the results of Table 3 and shows results when omitting all multi-airport cities. The second line offers results when applying the basic model to all observations without any modification. In the third line, airports of multi-airport cities are aggregated to represent only one generic airport for each city (input values are averaged among those airports).

For the extended model, additional variables that describe the competition faced by each airport are included in the basic model. Multi-airport destinations are characterized by the number of competing airports and their individual characteristics. It is assumed that the number of competing airports depends on distances between airports with airports defined as competing airports if the distance is less than a given maximum distance. The set of possible variables describing a competing airport are the independent variables of BM and these variables divided by the distance to the airport.

For the BM, the final set of additional variables, their functional form and the relevant distance $d_{comp-max}$ is determined by testing all possible combinations of variables. The overall structure of the EM is

$$V_{ij} = e^{\varepsilon} P_{ij}^{\pi} C_{ij}^{\chi} B_{ij}^{\beta} G_{ij}^{\gamma} D_{ij}^{\delta} T_{ij}^{\tau} N_{ij}^{\nu} A_{ij}^{\alpha} W_{ij}^{\omega}, \qquad (9)$$

where N_{ij}, A_{ij}, and W_{ij} are variables that describe the spatial characteristics.

The additional variables offering the best fits are seen in Table 8. The best results are found when considering airports within a distance of 200 km as competing airports. In contrast to other models the EM does not use variables for service levels or that are obtained by personal judgment (for example the identification of an airport as a hub or large city). The results of the EM model are presented in Table 9.

The EM is statistically valid with all variables significant at the 1%-level. As in the BM, no clear results are obtained when testing for multicollinearity. The maximum variance inflation factor indicates no effects of collinearity. On the other hand, as in the BM, the maximum correlation between any two independent variables is 0.696 for distance and travel time.

We validate the structural stability of the model in the same way as for the BM. First, the structural stability is tested in two experimental setups. We study the coefficients and fit for different subsets of the total observation data. Table 10 presents results for EM using setup 1 while Table 11 presents results for setup 2. The results of the test on structural stability are presented in Table 12.

To summarize, like the BM, the EM is statistically valid and all variables are statistically significant. Tests on multicollinearity lead to inconsistent results. Thus, the interpretation of the individual coefficients and their order of magnitude is not possible, but the joint impact of correlating variables is not affected.

The results on structural stability of the EM follow the results of the BM. With the exception of passenger volume as a selection criteria, Table 10 indicates good fits for the subsamples, and for the estimation and calibration samples. The coefficients are subject to minor variations across the different subsets (Table 11). The formal test on structural stability produced the same results as for the BM (Table 12) and indicate a broad applicability of the model at the 2.5%-level for all subsets, and at the 1%-level for all subsets excluding population.

5. Conclusions

This paper presents two gravity models that can be used for air passenger volume forecasting between city-pairs. Both models use mainly geo-economic variables as independent factors. Traditionally, service-related factors or additional variables such as passenger income, are used

Table 8
Additional independent variables of the EM

Notation	Functional form	Factor
N_{ij}	$N_i N_j$	Number of competing airports
A_{ij}	$A_i A_j$	Average distance to competing airports
W_{ij}	$W_i W_j$	Number of competing airports weighted by their distance

Table 9
Calibration results of the EM

Model	Obs.	Coefficients									R^2	F
		P_{ij}	C_{ij}	B_{ij}	G_{ij}	D_{ij}	T_{ij}	N_{ij}	A_{ij}	W_{ij}		
EM	1228	0.154	0.224	1.856	−0.089	1.804	−3.032	−0.704	−1.141	0.181	0.730	366.2
		−7.562	−12.170	−11.099	(−4.457)	−24.158	(−38.503)	(−7.825)	(−4.575)	−7.250		
		[0.146]	[0.265]	[0.231]	[−0.100]	[0.562]	[−0.912]	[−0.180]	[−0.088]	[0.155]		

Table 10
Validation results of the EM, setup 1

Selection criteria	Coefficients									F	R^2 (CS)	R^2 (ES)
	P_{ij}	C_{ij}	B_{ij}	G_{ij}	D_{ij}	T_{ij}	N_{ij}	A_{ij}	W_{ij}			
EM	0.154	0.224	1.856	−0.089	1.804	−3.032	−0.704	−1.141	0.181	366.2	0.730	
	0.164	0.198	1.560	−0.077	1.790	−3.167	−0.504	−1.004	0.148	180.4	0.729	0.677
Random	0.142	0.251	2.162	−0.103	1.837	−2.912	−0.926	−1.349	0.212	185.9	0.735	0.658
	0.191	0.120	1.488	0.006	2.068	−3.160	−0.501	−1.105	0.057	250.6	0.789	0.521
Distance	0.108	0.285	2.098	−0.154	1.674	−2.890	−0.671	−0.761	0.254	129.1	0.658	0.750
	0.090	0.245	1.538	−0.061	1.749	−2.792	−0.716	−0.716	0.169	156.3	0.700	0.630
Population	0.144	0.160	2.311	−0.135	1.842	−3.229	−0.590	−1.056	0.168	157.2	0.701	0.618
	0.234	0.136	1.384	−0.088	1.394	−2.638	−0.497	−0.758	0.221	129.8	0.659	0.644
Catchment	0.073	0.327	1.833	−0.038	2.236	−3.349	−1.137	−2.367	0.220	185.5	0.734	0.618
	0.040	0.071	0.629	−0.048	0.293	−0.405	−0.395	−0.367	0.103	10.2	0.131	0.410
Passenger volume	0.167	0.207	1.661	−0.054	1.679	−2.535	−0.298	−0.687	0.106	178.9	0.727	0.057

Table 11
Validation results of the EM, setup 2

Selection criteria	Interval	Coefficients									F	R^2	Obs.
		P_{ij}	C_{ij}	B_{ij}	G_{ij}	D_{ij}	T_{ij}	N_{ij}	A_{ij}	W_{ij}			
EM		0.154	0.224	1.856	−0.089	1.804	−3.032	−0.704	−1.141	0.181	366.2	0.730	1228
Distance	500–00	0.197	0.117	1.851	0.001	2.031	−3.160	−0.466	−1.150	0.058	251.8	0.788	618
	1000–1500	0.083	0.251	2.225	−0.138	1.757	−2.918	−0.472	−0.434	0.191	72.6	0.641	376
	1500	0.123	0.316	1.796	−0.168	1.995	−3.007	−0.930	−1.061	0.324	56.5	0.694	234
Population	0–200 Bill.	0.141	0.238	1.320	−0.074	1.873	−2.813	−0.560	−0.252	0.120	72.4	0.668	334
	200–400 Bill.	0.071	0.283	1.951	−0.043	1.698	−2.837	−0.882	−0.810	0.166	75.8	0.714	284
	400–600 Bill.	−0.494	0.084	2.154	−0.090	2.255	−3.419	0.212	−0.339	0.043	55.1	0.749	176
	600–800 Bill.	−0.049	0.247	1.294	−0.059	2.467	−3.812	−1.279	−1.078	0.161	52.9	0.832	106
	>800 Bill.	0.148	0.171	1.467	−0.165	1.388	−2.889	−0.808	−1.276	0.175	62.3	0.638	328
Catchment	0–4 Mrd.	0.234	0.161	1.406	−0.107	1.380	−2.580	−0.537	−0.910	0.207	101.8	0.677	446
	4–8 Mrd.	0.184	0.270	4.755	−0.057	1.635	−2.967	−0.566	−0.843	0.207	68.1	0.694	280
	8–12 Mrd.	0.125	1.188	2.797	−0.075	1.926	−2.790	−1.240	−3.163	0.225	64.2	0.796	158
	12–16 Mrd.	0.054	−0.130	5.613	−0.112	2.408	−2.911	−0.582	−0.394	0.414	21.4	0.702	92
	>16 Mrd.	−0.016	0.404	2.020	0.047	3.094	−4.124	−1.437	−3.887	0.259	72.6	0.730	252
	500–1000	0.022	0.012	−0.003	−0.005	−0.043	0.020	−0.093	0.049	0.036	1.9	0.048	340
	1000–1500	−0.007	0.023	0.114	0.002	0.091	−0.102	−0.013	−0.099	0.017	2.6	0.121	182
Passenger volume	1500–2000	0.006	0.027	−0.018	−0.005	0.031	0.070	−0.050	0.050	0.003	2.9	0.202	112
	2000–2500	−0.002	−0.017	0.258	0.014	0.109	−0.201	−0.033	−0.206	−0.009	3.2	0.284	82
	2500–3000	−0.005	−0.028	0.148	0.016	−0.147	0.113	−0.021	0.034	0.016	4.1	0.414	62
	>3000	0.201	0.273	5.824	−0.038	1.732	−2.325	−0.369	−0.821	0.158	96.9	0.665	450

Table 12
F-test on structural stability of the EM

Model	F-value (setup 1)	F-value (setup 2)
Distance	7.37	4.07
Population	3.55	2.06
Catchment	6.49	3.66
Passenger volume	143.13	73.17

in explanatory modeling but in new markets usually no service-related factors are available and an alternative is needed. This has been done here.

References

Brown, S., Watkins, W.S., 1968. The demand for air travel. A regression study of time series and cross-sectional data in the US domestic market. Highway Research Record, 21–34.

Doganis, R., 1966. Traffic forecasting and the gravity model. Flight International, 547–549.

Doganis, R., 2004. Flying Off Course—The Economics of International Airlines, Third ed. Routledge, London, New York.

Fotheringham, A.S., 1983a. A new set of spatial-interaction models the theory of competing destinations. Environment and Planning A15, 15–36.

Fotheringham, A.S., 1983b. Some theoretical aspects of destination choice and their relevance to production-constrained gravity models. Environment and Planning A15, 1121–1132.

Fotheringham, A.S., Webber, M.J., 1980. Spatial structure and the parameters of spatial interaction models. Geographical Analysis 12, 33–46.

Gardner Jr., E.S., 2004. Dimensional analysis of airline quality. Interfaces 34, 272–279.

Ghobrial, A.A., Kanafani, A., 1995. Quality-of-service model of intercity air-travel demand. Journal of Transportation Engineering 121 (2), 135–140.

Gursoy, D., Chen, M.-H., Kim, H.J., 2003. The US airlines relative positioning based on attributes of service quality. Tourism Management 26, 57–67.

Huang, D.S., 1970. Regression and Econometric Methods. Wiley, New York.

Jorge-Calderón, J.D., 1997. A demand model for scheduled airline services on international European routes. Journal of Air Transport Management 3, 23–35.

Kanafani, A., 1983. Transportation Demand Analysis. McGraw-Hill, New York.

Lee, D., 2003. Concentration and price trends in the US domestic airline industry, 1990–2000. Journal of Air Transport Management 9, 91–101.

Moore, O.E., Soliman, A.H., 1981. Airport catchment areas and air passenger demand. Transportation Engineering Journal of ASCE 107, 569–579.

O'Connor, W.E., 1982. An Introduction to Airline Economics, Third ed. Praeger, New York.

O'Kelly, M.E., Song, W., Shen, G., 1995. New estimates of gravitational attraction by linear programming. Geographical Analysis 27, 271–285.

Park, J.-W., Robertson, R., Wu, C.-L., 2004. The effect of airline service quality on passengers' behavioural intentions: a Korean case study. Journal of Air Transport Management 10, 435–439.

Rengaraju, V.R., Thamizh Arasan, V., 1992. Modeling for air travel demand. Journal of Transportation Engineering 118, 371–380.

Russon, M.G., Riley, N.F., 1993. Airport substitution in a short haul model of air transportation. International Journal of Transportation Economics 20, 157–173.

Shen, G., 2004. Reverse-fitting the gravity model to inter-city airline passenger flows by an algebraic simplification. Journal of Transport Geography 12, 219–234.

Tacke, G., Schleusener, M., 2003. Bargain airline pricing—how should the majors respond? Travel and Tourism White Paper Series, Simon, Kucher and Partners, Bonn.

Ubøe, J., 2004. Aggregation of gravity models for journeys to work. Environment and Planning 36, 715–729.

Verleger Jr., P.K., 1972. Model for the demand for air transportation. Bell Journals of Economics and Management Science 3.

3

Air passenger demand forecasting and passenger terminal capacity expansion: A system dynamics framework

Erma Suryani, Shuo-Yan Chou, Chih-Hsien Chen

ARTICLE INFO

Keywords:
Demand forecasting
System dynamics
Simulation
Capacity expansion
Scenario

ABSTRACT

This paper deals with how to develop a model to forecast air passenger demand and to evaluate some policy scenarios related with runway and passenger terminal capacity expansion to meet the future demand. System dynamics frameworks can be used to model, to analyze and to generate scenario to increase the system performance because of its capability of representing physical and information flows, based on information feedback control that are continuously converted into decisions and actions. We found that airfare impact, level of service impact, GDP, population, number of flights per day and dwell time play an important roles in determining the air passenger volume, runway utilization and total additional area needed for passenger terminal capacity expansion.

© 2009 Elsevier Ltd. All rights reserved.

1. Introduction

Analyzing air travel demand is an integral part of an airport's plan that reflects the capacity utilization, which will be considered to make decisions. Regarding to the development of infrastructure facilities and to reduce the airport risk, it is important to evaluate and to forecast the volume of air passenger demand in the future. Peak demand in passenger flows at the airports, typically determined by seasonal and cyclical patterns. Therefore, it is essential to manage the facilities such as runway and passenger terminal capacity planning and design, to cover demand during the planning horizon. Runway utilization, terminal capacity and the availability of facilities to handle arrival and departure of passengers flow, are the main entities that will affect the required landside capacity.

According to Lyneis (2000), the air travel demand can be affected by two factors, e.g. external and internal factors. Assumption about future demand and performance are essential for business decisions. He considered airfare as the internal factor, and Gross Domestic Product (GDP) and population as the external factors. People play in a dominating role in the city life, the scale of population will determine the air travel demand (Jifeng, Huapu, & Hu, 2008).

Miller and Clarke (2007) have developed a model to evaluate the strategic value of air transportation infrastructure. They considered airfare impact and level of service impact as the internals variables that affect the air travel demand. These two variables were determining using the concepts of price and time elasticity, respectively.

According to Transportation Research Board (1987), landside elements in the passenger terminal can be classified into three classes, those are processing facilities that will process passengers and their luggage; holding facilities that passengers wait for some events such as check in and flight boarding; and flow facilities that passengers use them to move among the landside elements.

Brunetta, Righi, and Andreatta (2000) note that there are essentially three ways that have been used to analyze the flows and determine the amount of space and the number of servers required for the airports, those are queuing theory, graphical analyses using cumulative diagrams and computer simulations. According to their research, formal applications of pure queuing theory (Lee, 1966) have not proven efficient for design because the processes in airports are essentially never in a steady-state condition, they are almost always in transient condition. Graphical analyses of the cumulative arrivals and service (Newell, 1971) does not tie in well to the process of designing a complete terminal, since each major alternative is likely to change the pattern of flows into a particular activity area. Simulations provide the way of investigating the flows throughout an entire building. The airport landside capability is influenced by the terminal capacity that can be evaluated for each individual functional component of the airport landside.

In this paper, we developed model to analyze and to forecast air passenger demand in the future related with runway and passenger terminal capacity to support long-term growth. For this study, we analyzed air passenger demand in Taiwan Taoyuan International Airport (TTIA) by utilizing system dynamics model. System dynamics framework is a method that can be used to analyze and to develop a model to forecast the air passenger demand and to evaluate some scenarios of runway and passenger terminal capacity expansion related with the air passenger demand in the future. While the demand for air travel is difficult to forecast, it is important to utilize system dynamics for several reasons (Lyneis, 2000):

1. Forecasts come from calibrated system dynamics models, that are likely to be better and more informative than those from other approaches.
2. System dynamics model can provide more reliable forecasts of short- to mid-term trends than statistical models, and therefore lead to better decisions.
3. System dynamics model provide a means of determining key sensitivities, and therefore of developing more robust sensitivities and scenarios.

In general, there are two kinds of scenarios: the first one is parameter scenario, which means that the scenario is made by changing the value of the parameter. The second one is structure scenario, which means that the scenario is made by adding some feedback loops, adding new parameters, or by changing the structure of the feedback loops.

The simulation tool (Vensim) that we use allows us to conceptualize, document, simulate, and analyze the system dynamics model. The tool also provides a simple and flexible way to build simulation models from causal loops and flow diagrams. Under uncertain demand, industry players are forced to take a cautious approach towards capacity expansion, therefore the right information becomes critical in ensuring high level of service (LOS) availability. The focus of system dynamics framework is identifying the feedback loops that dominate the dynamics behavior of the system.

In the process we identify information flow(s) that provide the alternative policy for determining runway and terminal capacity expansion to meet the future demand. The information gathered from the system was used to analyze the structure and the behavior of systems to provide a scientific basis for decision making. Although such analysis may differ from one airport to another, we keep the proposed of the model as generic as possible to facilitate its implementation on a wide spectrum of real-world cases.

This paper is organized as follows. Section 2 provides the literature review and Section 3 presents the system dynamics model as a method for model development. Section 4 describes the base model development. Base model run results is provided in Section 5. Model validation is explained in Section 6. Section 7 demonstrates scenario development in terms of modifying the information structure and parameter values to design policy. Finally in Section 8, conclusion, the important aspect of system dynamics framework, and the successfulness of model, assumption we use in developing some scenarios are presented.

2. Literature review

The rapid growth of air transportation in Asia Pacific region has attracted considerable attention of researchers and academics. Increasing numbers of flights and volumes of traffic, make the demand analysis plays an important role in determining the adequacy of runway and passenger terminal capacity. Various studies have emerged to explain some factors that influence the air travel demand and airport capacity.

Poore (1993) has developed a study to test the hypothesis that forecasts of the future demand for air transportation offered by aircraft manufacturers and aviation regulators are reasonable and representative of the trends implicit in actual experience. He compared forecasts issued by Boeing, Airbus Industry and the International Civil Aviation Organization (ICAO) which have actual experience and the results of a baseline model for revenue passenger kilometers (RPKs) demand.

Inzerilli and Sergioc (1994) have developed an analytical model to analyze optimal price capacity adjustments in air transportation. From this study, they used numerical examples to analyze the behavior of the policy variables (and the resulting load factor) under different degrees of uncertainty.

Matthews (1995) has done measurement and forecasting of peak passenger flow at several airports in the United Kingdom. According to his research, annual passenger traffic demand can be seen as the fundamental starting point, driven by economic factors and forecasting. While forecasts of hourly flows are needed for long-term planning related with infrastructure requirements. Hourly forecasts are almost always based on forecasts of annual flows.

Bafail, Abed, and Jasimuddin (2000) have developed a model for forecasting the long-term demand for domestic air travel in Saudi Arabia. They utilized several explanatory variables such as total expenditures and population to generate model formulation. Another study for air travel demand forecasting has done by Grosche, Rothlauf, and Heinzl (2007). According to their research, there are some variables that can affect the air travel demand, including population, GDP and buying power index. He considered GDP as a representative variable for the level of economic activity.

Swan (2002) has analyzed airline demand distributions model. The model explains when the Gamma shape will dominate and when the Normal will determine the shape. From his study, he found that Gamma shapes are probably better for revenue management and Normal for spill modeling. Fernandes and Pacheco (2002) have analyzed the efficient use of airport capacity. According to their research, on the basis of passenger demand forecast, it was possible to determine the period when capacity expansion would become necessary to maintain services at standards currently perceived by passengers.

Hsu and Chao (2005) have examined the relationships among commercial revenue, passenger service level and space allocation in international passenger terminals. They developed a model for maximizing concession revenues while maintaining service level, to optimize the space allocation for various types of stores.

Svrcek (1994) has analyzed three fundamental measures of capacity, including static capacity that is used to describe the storage capability of a holding facility or area, dynamic capacity which refers to the maximum processing rate or flow rate of pedestrians and sustained capacity that is used to describe the overall capacity of a subsystem to accommodate traffic demand over a sustained period.

Yamaguchi et al. (2001) have analyzed the economic impact analysis of deregulation for airport capacity expansion in Japanese domestic aviation market. According to their research, deregulation and airport capacity expansion play significant roles in realizing full benefit of aviation market growth. In line of deregulation policy, airport capacity expansion was accelerated to meet the growth demand.

3. System dynamics model

System dynamics was developed by Forrester (1961) in Massachusetts Institute of Technology (MIT). This framework is focused on systems thinking, but takes the additional some steps of constructing and testing a computer simulation model. The main characteristics of this method is the existence of complex system, the change of system behavior from time to time and also the existence of the closed loop feedback. This feedback describes the new information about the system condition, that will yield the next decision. Sterman (2000) has developed some steps to create system dynamics model such as depicted in Fig. 1. Modeling is a feedback process that go through constant iteration and an iterative cycle. It is embedded in the larger cycle of learning and action constantly taking place in organizations:

Step 1: Problem articulation: in this step, we need to find the real problem, identify the key variables and concepts, determine the time horizon and characterize the problem dynamically for understanding and designing policy to solve it.

Step 2: Dynamic hypothesis: modeler should develop a theory of how the problem arose. It guides modeling efforts by focusing on certain structures. In this step, we need to develop causal loop diagram that explain causal links among variables and convert the causal loop diagram into flow diagram. This flow diagram consists of some variables such as depicted in Table 1.

Step 3: Formulation: to define system dynamics model, after we convert the causal loop diagram into flow diagram, we should translate the system description into level, rate and auxiliary equations. We need to estimate some parameters, behavioral relationships and initial conditions. Writing equations will reveal gaps and inconsistencies that must be remedied in the prior description.

Step 4: Testing: the purpose testing is comparing the simulated behavior of the model to the actual behavior of the system.

Step 5: Policy formulation and evaluation. Once modelers have developed confidence in the structure and model behavior, we can utilize it to design and evaluate policies for improvement. The interactions of different policies must also be considered, because the real systems are highly nonlinear, the impact of combination policies is usually not the sum of their impacts alone.

System dynamics can be applied to a wide range of problem domains such as strategy and corporate planning, public management and policy, business process development, biological and medical modeling, energy and the environment, theory development in the natural and social sciences, dynamic decision making, complex nonlinear dynamics, software engineering, and supply chain management.

Lyneis (2000) has analyzed the use of system dynamics models to "forecast" the behavior of markets. He claims that the structural orientation of system dynamics models provides more accurate depictions of short and mid-term behavior than statistical models, which often become skewed by "noise" in the system. According to Sterman (2000), the dynamic behavior of a system is said to arise from the interaction among the various system components over time. Lyneis (1998) has developed system dynamics model to forecast demand of commercial jet aircraft industry. James and Galvin (2002) have utilized system dynamics to determine the future behavior of the principle components of the air traffic control (ATC) system over time.

System dynamics has three important roles in developing the model. The first and the most important one is the system structure that will characterize its behavior. The second one is the nature of the structure where the mental models play an important role in dynamic behavior of the system. The third one is that significant change can be used to alter the structure (structure scenario). This structure can be represented by feedback loops.

4. Base model development

In general, the demand for air passenger can be affected by two factors, those are external and internal factors. Some internal factors that affect the air passenger demand are airfare impact and level of service impact. While the external factors we consider *economic conditions* such as Gross Domestic Product (GDP) and *demographic factor*, e.g. population. Air transportation demand tends to evolve as a function of price changes and economic conditions (Department of Finance Canada, 2008). According to Seraj, Abdullah, and Sajjad (2001), there are several factors that affect the air travel demand, those are basically macroeconomic and demographic factor (population).

Fig. 2 represents the causal loop diagram of air passenger demand and passenger terminal capacity expansion. Causal loop diagrams have been used to describe basic causal mechanisms hypothesized to underlie the reference mode of behavior over time (Richardson, 1995; Sterman, 2000), to create a connection between structure and decisions that generate system behavior.

This causal loop diagram represents the relationship among *Population*, *GDP Growth*, *Level of Service Impact*, *Airfare Impact*, *Runway Utilization* and *Passenger Required Space*. This diagram shows the cause and effect of the system structure. Each arrow represents a cause and effect relationship between two variables. The '+' and '−' signs represent the direction of causality. A '+' sign indicates can increase the result to destination variable. While the '−' sign indicates can decrease the result to the destination variable. For example, increase *Population* can increase *Births*, but increase *Deaths* can decrease *Population*.

Each feedback loop has a polarity that will indicate the causality direction that implies how a change in any variables within the feedback loop. There are two kinds of feedback loop. The first one is reinforcing feedback loop, which means that feedback flows will generate exponential growth. The second one is balancing feedback loop, which means that feedback loop will maintain the system stability. The main causal loops in this model are depicted below:

Average number of flights per day $\rightarrow$ Congestion $\rightarrow$ Airline congestion cost $\rightarrow$ Airfare impact $\rightarrow$ Air passenger demand $\rightarrow$ Average number of flights per day

Average number of flights per day results in more congestion and airline congestion cost. As price elasticity has negative impact to airfare, the more airline congestion cost will cause airfare impact become more negative and decrease the demand of air passenger. Air passenger demand will increase in line with GDP growth and Population growth:

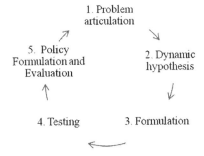

Fig. 1. System dynamics modeling process.

Table 1
Some variables in system dynamics.

Variable	Symbol	Description
Level	□	A quantity that accumulates over time, change its value by accumulating or integrating rates
Rate	⌧	Change the values of levels
Auxiliary	○	Arise when the formulation of a level's influence on a rate involves one or more intermediate calculations, often useful in formulating complex rate equations, used for ease of communication and clarity

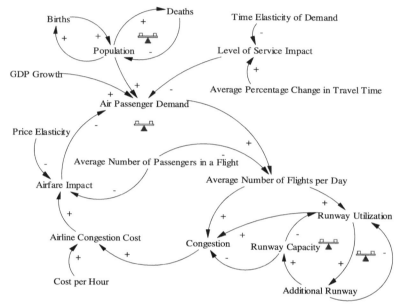

Fig. 2. Causal loop diagram of air passenger demand and passenger terminal capacity expansion.

Average number of flights per day $\xrightarrow{+}$ Runway utilization $\xrightarrow{+}$ Additional runway $\xrightarrow{+}$ Runway capacity $\xrightarrow{-}$ Congestion $\xrightarrow{+}$ Airline congestion cost $\xrightarrow{+}$ Airfare impact $\rightarrow$ Air passenger demand $\xrightarrow{+}$ Average number of flights per day.

Average number of flights per day attracts more runways utilization and additional runway. The more additional runway, the larger the runways capacity will be and will decrease the runways utilization. Runways capacity has negative impact to congestion, airline congestion cost and will decrease the effect of negative airfare impact to air passenger demand. The more air passenger demand, the more average number of flights per day will be.

Passenger required space $\rightarrow$ Dynamic capacity $\xrightarrow{-}$ Terminal space area $\rightarrow$ Terminal utilization $\xrightarrow{+}$ Passenger required space.

As the demand of air passenger increases, it generates more passenger required space. The growth of passenger required space will decrease the dynamic capacity and will need more terminal space area. However, increase the terminal space area will decrease the terminal utilization.

Causal loop diagrams emphasize the feedback structure of the system, it can never be comprehensive. We have to convert the causal loop diagram into flow diagram that emphasize the physical structure of the model. It has a tendency to be more detailed than causal loop diagram, to force us to think more specifically about the system structure. Fig. 3 shows the flow diagram of air passenger demand and runway utilization (base model).

This model consists of five sub-models: airfare impact, level of service impact, GDP, population and runway utilization.

4.1. Airfare impact sub-model

Airfare represents the fare for transportation on a commercial airplane. The airfare impact on air passenger demand is determined by utilizing the concept of price elasticity of demand. Price elasticity of demand is defined as the percentage change in demand as the impact of 1% change in average airfare. While time elasticity of demand is the percentage change in total travel demand that occurs with a 1% change in travel time. In this study, airfare impact is the change in demand from a percentage change in average travel cost times price elasticity (see Eqs. (1)–(5)):

$$\text{Airfare Impact} = \varepsilon_{price} * \Delta \text{Travel cost} \qquad (1)$$

$$\Delta \text{Travel cost} = \frac{\text{Congestion Cost/Passenger}}{\text{Average Airfare}} * \text{Transfer Cost} \qquad (2)$$

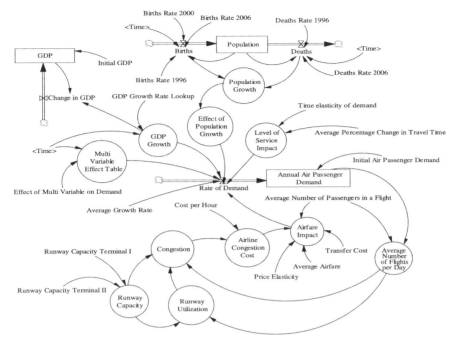

Fig. 3. Flow diagram of air passenger demand and runway utilization.

ε_{price} is the price elasticity of demand which represents the percentage change in air passenger demand as a result of a 1% change in travel cost due to the congestion costs. The price elasticity of demand has been estimated at approximately −1.6 for leisure passengers and −0.8 for business passengers (Belobaba, 2001).

In this study, congestion is defined as the waiting time (per peak hour of traffic) for each aircraft that's wants to land on the runway. According to Larson and Odoni (1981), the waiting time is obtained by utilizing M/G/1 queuing system such as depicted in Eq. (3):

$$\text{Congestion} = \frac{\lambda * \left(\left(\frac{1}{\tau}\right)^2 + \sigma_t^2\right)}{2 * (1 - \rho)} \quad (3)$$

$$\rho = \frac{\lambda}{\mu} \quad (4)$$

Congestion Cost = Congestion ∗ Cost per Hour (5)

where λ is the average number of flights for a specified of time determined by the Poisson distribution, σ_t is the standard deviation of service time and μ is runway capacity. While ρ can be defined as runway utilization.

4.2. Level of service impact sub-model

Level of service impact is the change in demand as the impact of the percentage change in average travel time times time elasticity (see Eqs. (6) and (7)):

Level of service impact = ε_{times} ∗ ΔTravel Time (6)
Travel Time = 0.4 + ABS(0.01 ∗ RANDOM NORMAL( )) (7)

where ε_{times} is the time elasticity of demand and ΔTravel Time is the percentage change in travel time. RANDOM NORMAL( ) is a function that provides a normal distribution of mean 0 and variance 1. Time elasticity of demand is the percentage change in total demand that occurs with a 1% change in travel time. We utilized ABS function to return to absolute value of RANDOM NORMAL( ). In this study, we assumed that the average percentage change in travel time was around 40% by considering that travel air kept a portion of its fleet in reserve (initially 40%, later much less) to resolve scheduling conflicts (Ingram, 2004).

4.3. Population sub-model

The growth of population can generate more travel demand. We classified the total population as the level variable, while birth rate and death rate as the auxiliary variables (see Eqs. (8)–(10)). Parameter dt represents the time interval of simulation. In this study, the time interval is 1 year. During 1996–1999, the births rate in Taiwan was ±13.2/1000 population, ±13/1000 population in 2000–2005 and ±11.14/1000 population in 2006. While for the deaths rate was ±6/1000 population during 1996–2005 and ±6.53 starting from 2006.

Based on these conditions, we utilize IF THEN ELSE function for the births and deaths formulation. This function has general format *IF THEN ELSE (condition, true value, false value)* which means that returns first value if condition is true, second value if condition is false. Condition must be a Boolean expression or an expression or variable that can be interpreted as Boolean. If condition is true, than the function evaluates and returns *true value*, otherwise *false value* is evaluated and returned:

Population(t) = Population$(t - dt)$ + (Births − Deaths) ∗ dt (8)

Deaths = IF THEN ELSE(Time < 2000, Deaths Rate 1996/1000
∗ Population, IF THEN ELSE(Time < 2006,
Deaths Rate 2000/1000 ∗ Population,
Deaths Rate 2006/1000 ∗ Population)) (9)

Births = IF THEN ELSE(Time < 2000, Births Rate 1996/1000
∗ Population, IF THEN ELSE(Time < 2006,
Births Rate 2000/1000 ∗ Population,
Births Rate 2006/1000 ∗ Population)) (10)

4.4. GDP sub-model

GDP is chosen as a level variable, and change in GDP as a rate variable. Change in GDP depends on GDP growth (see Eqs. (11) and (12)). In this study, we utilize lookup or table function for GDP growth based on consideration that GDP growth is a nonlinear function. Lookup table represents the dynamic behavior of a physical system by mapping multiple inputs to a single output in a multidimensional data array. In the simpler two-dimensional case, lookup tables can be represented by matrices. Each element of a matrix is a numerical quantity, which can be precisely located in terms of two indexing variables (see Eqs. (13) and (14)):

GDP(t) = GDP$(t - dt)$ + (Change in GDP) ∗ dt (11)
Change in GDP = GDP Growth/100 ∗ GDP (12)
GDP Growth = GDP Growth Rate Lookup(Time) (13)

GDP Growth Rate Lookup([(1996, −8)
− (2007, 10)], (1996, 8.4), (1997, 6), (1998, 5.7), (1999, 5.8),
(2000, −2.2), (2001, 3.2), (2002, 2.2), (2003, 5.2), (2004, 3.1),
(2005, 4.7), (2006, 4.5), (2007, 4.5)) (14)

4.5. Runway utilization sub-model

Runway capacity is the limiting factor that leads to congestion (Kessides, 1996). As demand for air travel increases, average number of flights requiring service on this runway also increases (see Eqs. (15)–(17)). If runway capacity is held constant, the increase in demand will lead to congestion, which raises the airline congestion cost. The higher airline congestion cost, the greater the airfare impact will be:

Runway Utilization = Average Number of Flights
× per Day/Runway Capacity (15)

Average Number of Flights per Day = Annual Air Passenger
× Demand/(365 ∗ Average Number of Passengers in a Flight)
(16)

Runway Capacity = Runway Capacity Terminal I
+ Runway Capacity Terminal II (17)

4.6. Main relationships of the model

Air passenger demand is very volatile and cyclical (Skinner, Dichter, Langley, & Sabert, 1999). In order to capture this nonlinear relationships, we utilized lookup or table functions. In this study, we consider multivariable effect table to accommodate the nonlinear relationships among demand, airfare impact, effect of population growth, GDP growth, level of service impact and multivariable effect (see Eqs. (18)–(21)). The general format can be described as follows:

Table for effect of X on $Y = (X1, Y1), (X2, Y2), \ldots, (Xn, Yn)$

where (Xi, Yi) represents each pair of points defining the relationship. We set the time as Xi and the effect of interaction among variables as Yi. The other function that we used in this model is MAX function. The MAX function format is given as follows:

MAX(A, B)

This function means that returns the larger of A and B. In this study, we set A as the level of service impact and B as the airfare impact:

Annual Air Passenger Demand(t)
= Annual Air Passenger Demand$(t - dt)$
+ (Rate of Demand) ∗ dt (18)

Rate of Demand = (Effect of Population Growth
+ MAX(Level of Service Impact/100, Airfare Impact/100))
∗ GDP Growth ∗ Average Growth Rate/MultiVariable Effect Table
(19)

MultiVariable Effect Table
= Effect of MultiVariable on Demand(Time) (20)

Effect of MultiVariable on Demand([(1996, −100)
− (2007, 100)], (1996, 12.83), (1997, −17), (1998, 3.2),
(1999, 2.45), (2000, 10.5), (2001, 2.32), (2002, −0.34),
(2003, 0.81), (2004, 1.7), (2005, 1.8), (2006, 3.3), (2007, 1))
(21)

4.7. Parameter estimation

Parameter estimation is the process of utilizing data or observation from a system to develop mathematical models. The assumed model consists of a finite set of parameters, the values of which are calculated using estimation techniques. Parameter values can be drawn from all available sources, not merely from statistical analysis of time series. All information is admissible in the modeling process. The estimation of parameters can be obtained is some ways, e.g. statistics data, published reports and statistical methods. The coefficient estimation results for effect of population growth and population growth are given in Eqs. (22) and (23). Other values of coefficients of the base model are listed in Table 2:

Effect of Population Growth = Population Growth/100,000
(22)
Population Growth = Births − Deaths (23)

5. Base model run results

As mentioned above, this study has focused on air passenger demand, runway and passenger terminal capacity expansion. In the base model, we set the simulation timing for 12 years starting from 1996 to 2007 based on consideration of learning the system behavior of air travel demand before and after terrorist attack in 2001 and the availability of the data. The simulation time step is 1 year.

Fig. 4 demonstrates Taiwan GDP during 1996–2007. As we can see from Fig. 4, average Taiwan GDP growth during 1996–2007

Table 2
Values of parameters of base model.

Parameter	Value	Unit
Average growth rate of demand	745,633	Passengers/year
Initial passenger demand	15,613,600	Passengers
Initial GDP	7,944,600	NT Million Dollar
Average airfare	140	$/one way
Average number of passenger in a flight	250	Passengers
Price elasticity	−0.8	–
Time elasticity of demand	−1.6	–
Cost per hour	6761	$/h
Runway capacity	420	Flights/day

was around 4.23% annually. The global slowdown in 2001 caused by terrorist attacks on the United States, made Taiwan GDP − 2.2% decline. Recovery began in 2002, real growth of 3.16% was recorded. Taiwan's economy had been growing rapidly, starting from 2004. GDP bounced back and rose by 5.1% in 2004, 3.16% in 2005, 4.6% in 2006 and 4.5% in 2007.

Fig. 5 represents Taiwan population during 1996–2007. Population grew around 0.47–0.75%. In 2007, population was around 23.14 million people with average births rate −0.76% and average deaths rate 1.49%. Fig. 6 shows the airfare and airline cost congestion. Airfare impact became more negative in line with increase in airline cost congestion.

Fig. 7 represents the impact of level of service to the demand growth. As we can see from Fig. 7, level of service had negative impact to the air travel demand. It has fluctuated around −64% to −67% as the results of time elasticity and the percentage change in travel time.

Fig. 8 shows the annual air passenger demand during 1996–2007 in TTIA. Average growth of air passenger demand was around 4.32% as the impact of airfare, effect of population growth, GDP growth, level of service impact, and multivariable effect. The causal relationship among rate of demand, airfare impact, effect of population growth, GDP growth, level of service impact and multivariable effect is given in Fig. 9. As we can see from Fig. 9, airfare impact had a very significant contribution to the demand growth (rate of demand). Multivariable effect is restricted by internal variables (airfare impact and level of service impact) and external variables (GDP growth and effect of population growth).

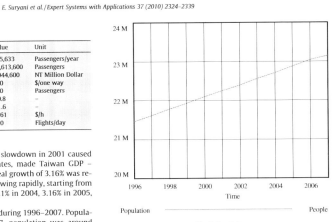

Fig. 5. Population.

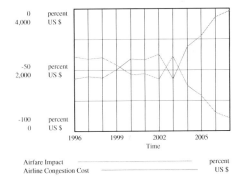

Fig. 6. Airfare impact and airline cost congestion.

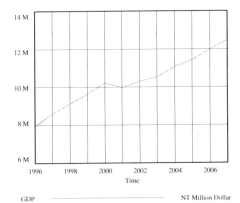

Fig. 4. GDP.

Fig. 10 represents the average number of flights per day in TTIA. During 1996–2007, the average number of Flights per day was around 171–257 flights. With this condition, the runways utilization was 0.404 in 2003 and 0.6101 in 2007. Runway utilization during 1996–2007 is given in Fig. 11.

6. Model validation

Validation process is required to help build confidence in the model. The objective is to achieve a deeper understanding of the model. To do this process, we need historical data during the time horizon of simulation of the base model (1996–2007). According to Barlas (1994), a model will be valid if the error rate, less than 5% (see Eqs. (24)–(26)). Valid implies being supported by objective truth. The comparison between model and data of air passenger demand, GDP and population are given in Figs. 12–14, respectively (see Table 3),

$$\text{Errorrate} = \frac{|\overline{S} - \overline{A}|}{\overline{A}} \quad (24)$$

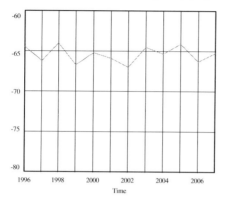

Fig. 7. Level of service impact.

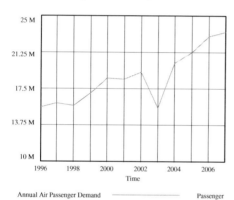

Fig. 8. Annual air passenger demand.

where

$$\bar{S} = \frac{1}{N} \sum_{i=1}^{N} S_i \quad (25)$$

$$\bar{A} = \frac{1}{N} \sum_{i=1}^{N} A_i \quad (26)$$

7. Scenario development

In this section, we show how the system structure of a valid model can be exchanged by adding some feedback loops, adding new parameters, and changing the structure of the feedback loops (structure scenario) and how the parameter model can be changed to see the impact to other variables (parameter scenario). Scenario development is a prognosis method where the present data is used to develop various possible, often alternative future scenarios (Reibnitz, 1988). In this study, we developed some scenarios that demonstrate how a future situation can be regarded as a logical consequence of possible events occurring in the future. A scenario

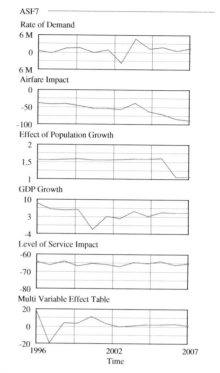

Fig. 9. Causal relationship among rate of demand, airfare impact, effect of population growth, GDP growth, level of service impact and multivariable effect.

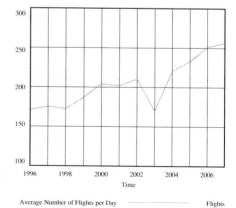

Fig. 10. Average number of flights per day.

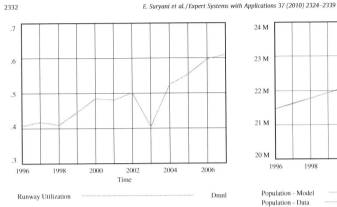

Fig. 11. Runway utilization.

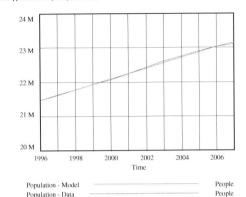

Fig. 14. Comparison between model and data of population.

Table 3
Comparison of model outputs with data.

Variable	Simulation ($\bar{S}$)	Data actual ($\bar{A}$)	Error rate
Demand	18,637,500	18,644,669	0.00038
GDP	10,272,916.7	10,239,629.3	0.003251
Population	22,317,500	22,325,320	0.000350253

can be seen as a movie, rather than as a photograph. We combined between structure scenario and parameter scenario to generate more robust sensitivity analysis. The scenario block diagram is given in Fig. 15.

7.1. Structure scenario

In this scenario, we modified the structure of airfare impact and add new structure to determine the flow of passenger in terminal building. In line with inflation rate, we assumed that airline congestion cost, average airfare and transfer cost will increase. We defined cost per hour, average airfare, and transfer cost as level variable, while average inflation rate will generate change in cost per hour, change in average airfare and change in transfer cost.

The flow of passenger depends on the air passenger demand, departure dwell time and arrival dwell time. We set the departure dwell time parameter = 1 h and arrival dwell time = 0.5 h based on our observation in TTIA. This passenger flow, will determine the excess of capacity of the terminal building. Additional daily capacity is required when excess of capacity is less than zero (see Eq. (34)). Total additional area for the terminal building is restricted by excess of capacity and the type of level of service of the standard area that will be utilized by the airport.

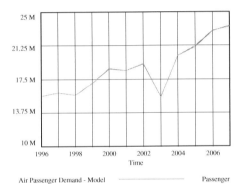

Fig. 12. Comparison between model and data of air passenger demand.

7.2. Parameter scenario

As parameter scenario, we developed optimistic and pessimistic scenarios to predict the future of air passenger demand related with runway and passenger terminal capacity expansion by utilizing 'A' level of service (LOS) area.

According to IATA (1981), the level of service can be divided into six levels (A, B, C, D, E and F). The best of LOS is 'A 'LOS which represents excellent service level and the worst is 'F' LOS which

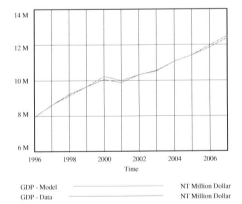

Fig. 13. Comparison between model and data of GDP.

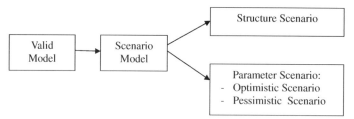

Fig. 15. Scenario block diagram.

represents unacceptable service level. Every LOS has different area requirement, such as depicted in Table 4.

7.2.1. Optimistic scenario

This scenario is made to check the runway and passenger terminal capacity to meet the future demand if *GDP* is predicted to grow with average growth rate 6% annually. This assumption is made by considering Taiwan government prediction. Based on this prediction, the average economic growth will achieve 6% annually (The China Post, 2008). We utilized RANDOM NORMAL to generate the GDP growth fluctuation. RANDOM NORMAL provides a normal distribution of mean 0 and variance 1. In this study, we set the *GDP Growth Scn* = 6 + RANDOM NORMAL( ) to provide *GDP Growth* with a normal distribution of mean 6% and variance 1% (see Eq. (27)). *Population* is expected to grow around 0.48% annually based on the births rate (11.14/1000 population) and deaths rate (6.53/1000 population) by considering the existing condition:

$$\text{GDP Growth Scn} = 6 + \text{RANDOM NORMAL}( ) \quad (27)$$

$$\text{Cost per Hour Scn}(t) = \text{Cost per Hour Scn}(t - dt)$$
$$+ (\text{Change in Cost Per Hour}) * dt \quad (28)$$

$$\text{Average Airfare Scn}(t) = \text{Average Airfare Scn}(t - dt)$$
$$+ (\text{Change in Average Airfare}) * dt \quad (29)$$

$$\text{Transfer Cost Scn}(t) = \text{Transfer Cost Scn}(t - dt)$$
$$+ (\text{Change in Transfer Cost}) * dt \quad (30)$$

$$\text{Average Inflation Rate Scn} = 1 + \text{RANDOM NORMAL}( ) \quad (31)$$

Percentage Change in Travel Time Scn
$$= 30 + \text{RANDOM NORMAL}( ) \quad (32)$$

All cost components such as *Cost per Hour Scn*, *Average Airfare Scn*, *Transfer Cost Scn* will increase as the impact of Inflation (*Inflation Rate Scn*) (see. Eqs. (28)–(30)). We assume that the inflation rate will grow with average 1% annually by considering the average inflation rate for the last 4 years (see Eq. (31)). Percentage change

Table 4
LOS parameters.

LOS area (sq. m.)	A	B	C	D	E
Baggage claim	2.00	1.80	1.60	1.40	1.20
Flow space	20.00	25.00	40.00	57.00	75.00
Check in	1.80	1.60	1.40	1.20	1.00
Holding area	2.70	2.30	1.90	1.50	1.00
Generic area	1.40	1.20	1.00	0.80	0.60

in travel time will be less than the existing condition in the base model, we assume that the percentage change in travel time will be around 30% (see Eq. (32)).

Fig. 16 shows the flow diagram of demand and passenger terminal capacity expansion optimistic scenario. As we can see from Fig. 16, annual demand forecast will determine passenger required space optimistic scenario. We can utilize this scenario model to check the runway utilization and passenger terminal capacity whether they can accommodate the forecast demand. In this study, arrival and departure dwell time have significant impact to passenger required space. If runway utilization is greater than one, means that the runway should be expanded in order not to make congestion longer (see Eq. (33)). If excess of capacity is strictly less than zero, means that they should expand the terminal capacity (see Eq. (34)):

Additional Runway Scn = IF THEN ELSE(Runways Utilization Scn
$$\geqslant 1,350,0) \quad (33)$$

Additional Daily Capacity Scn
$$= \text{IF THEN ELSE}(\text{Excess of Capacity Opt Scn} \leqslant 0 : \text{AND}$$
$$: \text{Excess of Capacity Opt Scn} > -1.7e + 007,$$
$$(1.7e + 007/365), \text{IF THEN ELSE (Excess of Capacity Opt Scn}$$
$$< -1.7e + 007, (3.4e + 007/365), 0)) \quad (34)$$

7.2.2. Pessimistic scenario

This scenario is made to check the runway and passenger terminal capacity to meet the future demand if *GDP* is predicted to grow with average growth rate 2.8% annually by considering that global GDP growth rate would be only 1% and 4.5% for developing countries (Zoellick, 2008). We utilized RANDOM NORMAL to generate the GDP growth fluctuation. In this study, we set the *GDP Growth Scn* = 2.8 + RANDOM NORMAL( ) to provide GDP growth with a normal distribution of mean 2.8% and variance 1% (see Eq. (35)).

By setting the average GDP growth around 2.8%, we expect that the scenario run result of GDP growth will be around 1–4.5%. For LOS impact and population, we adopt the variables from the base model, the percentage change of travel time will be around 40% and the population will grow with average growth rate around 0.48%. We assume that annual inflation rate will be around 2% based on Taiwan central bank prediction (Taipei times, 2008) (see Eq. (36)):

$$\text{GDP Growth Pessimistic Scn} = 2.8 + \text{RANDOM NORMAL}( ) \quad (35)$$

Average Inflation Rate Pessimistic Scn
$$= 2 + \text{RANDOM NORMAL}( ) \quad (36)$$

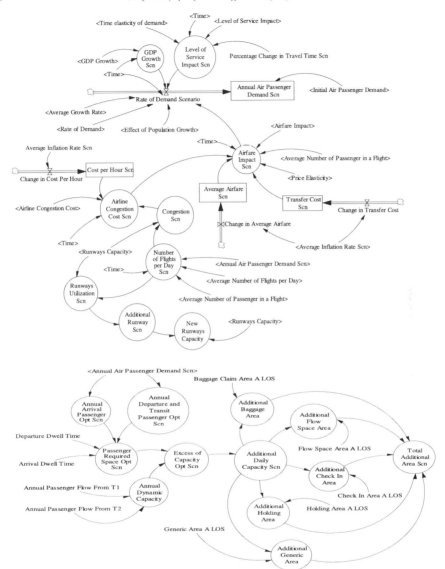

Fig. 16. Flow diagram of demand and passenger terminal capacity expansion optimistic scenario.

Fig. 17 shows the flow diagram of air passenger demand and passenger terminal capacity expansion pessimistic scenario. We can utilize this pessimistic scenario model to check the runway utilization and passenger terminal capacity whether they can accommodate the forecast demand in pessimistic condition. Average inflation rate will determine all components cost, e.g. average airfare, transfer cost and cost per hour (see Eqs. (37)–(39)):

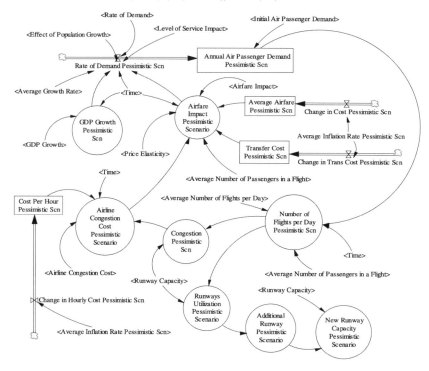

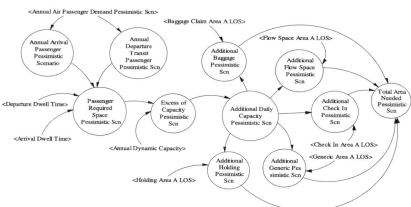

Fig. 17. Air passenger demand and passenger terminal capacity expansion pessimistic scenario.

Cost Per Hour Pessimistic Scn(*t*)
= Cost Per Hour Pessimistic Scn(*t* − d*t*)
  + (Change in Hourly Cost Pessimistic Scn) ∗ d*t*   (37)

Average Airfare Pessimistic Scn(*t*)
= Average Airfare Pessimistic Scn(*t* − d*t*)
  + (Change in Cost Pessimistic Scn) ∗ d*t*   (38)

Transfer Cost Pessimistic Scn(t)

= Transfer Cost Pessimistic Scn(t − dt)

+ (Change in Trans Cost Pessimistic Scn) ∗ dt   (39)

7.3. Scenarios run results

As we can see from Fig. 18, GDP will grow around 4.35–8% in optimistic condition and around 1.44–3.96% in pessimistic condition. *Level of Service Impact* that represents the change in demand from a percentage change in travel time has negative impact to the demand growth. Fig. 19 demonstrates level of service impact in optimistic and pessimistic condition. As we can see from Fig. 19, by reducing the percentage change in travel time, it will affect the level of service impact. Level of service impact become more positive and it will generate more air travel demand.

Fig. 20 demonstrates the airfare impact in optimistic and pessimistic condition. As we can see from Fig. 20, airfare impact also has negative impact to the demand growth in line with increase in all price components such as cost per hour, average airfare and transfer cost as the impact of inflation rate. Airfare impact in optimistic condition will be more negative than pessimistic condition as the impact of congestion. The greater the demand for air travel will increase the runway utilization and will lead to congestion. Population is predicted will grow ±0.48% annually. So, by the year 2028 the population will be around 25.48 million people.

Fig. 21 represents the annual passenger demand in optimistic and pessimistic condition. Demand will grow with average growth rate 6.6% annually in optimistic condition and 3.12% in pessimistic condition. So, by the year 2028, the air travel demand will achieve ±84.09 million passengers in optimistic condition and ±44.41 million passengers in pessimistic condition.

Fig. 22 shows the number of flights per day in optimistic and pessimistic condition. Average number of flights per day will be around 424 flights in 2013 and will achieve 922 flights in 2028 in optimistic condition. While for pessimistic condition, Average number of flights per day will be around 430 flights in 2024 and will achieve 487 flights in 2028.

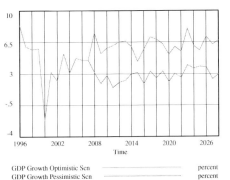

Fig. 18. GDP growth optimistic and pessimistic scenario.

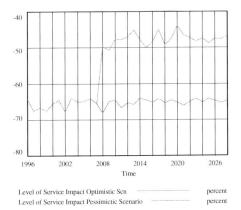

Fig. 19. Level of service impact optimistic and pessimistic scenario.

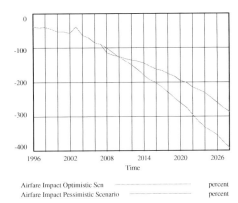

Fig. 20. Airfare impact optimistic and pessimistic scenario.

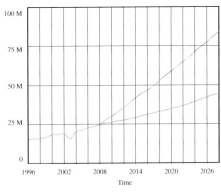

Fig. 21. Annual air passenger demand optimistic and pessimistic scenario.

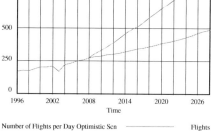

Fig. 22. Number of flights per day optimistic and pessimistic scenario.

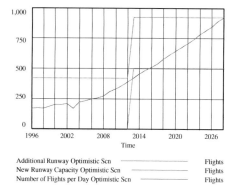

Fig. 23. Additional runway, new runway capacity, number of flights/day optimistic scenario.

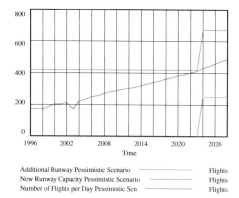

Fig. 24. Additional runway, new runway capacity, number of flights per day pessimistic scenario.

As we can see from Fig. 23, the airport needs additional runway that can provide ±500 flights starting from 2013 to cover demand

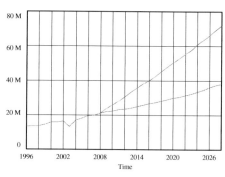

Fig. 25. Passenger required space optimistic and pessimistic scenario.

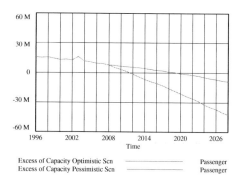

Fig. 26. Excess of capacity optimistic and pessimistic scenario.

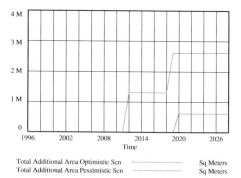

Fig. 27. Total additional area optimistic and pessimistic scenario.

Table 5
Scenario results summary.

Scenario	Average demand growth (%)	Runway expansion		Passenger terminal expansion	
		Year	Volume (F)	Year	Volume (sq. m)
Optimistic	6.6	2013	±500	2012	1.3 million sq. m → 17 million pax
Average GDP growth = 6%					
Average inflation rate = 1%				2019	1.3 million sq. m → 17 million pax
Average % change in travel time = 30%					
Pessimistic	3.12	2024	±250	2020	614,258 sq. m → 9 million pax
Average GDP growth = 2.8%					
Average inflation rate = 2%					
Average % change in travel time = 40%					

until 2028. Runway utilization will be greater than 1 starting from 2013 in optimistic condition. While Fig. 24 shows the additional runway, new runway capacity and number of flights per day in pessimistic scenario. Runway utilization will be greater than 1, starting from 2024, therefore it is better to expand/ build a new runway capacity that can accommodate ±250 flights to cover demand until 2028.

The other consideration, besides, runway capacity, is terminal building related with baggage claim, flow space, check in, holding and generic area. Fig. 25 represents the passenger required space in optimistic and pessimistic condition. The passenger required space is made to check the dynamic flow of the passengers in terminal area. As we can see from Fig. 25, passenger required space in optimistic condition will be greater than in pessimistic condition in line with increase in air travel demand for optimistic condition.

Fig. 26 shows the excess of capacity in optimistic and pessimistic condition. The lack of capacity of passenger terminal area in optimistic condition would be happened starting from 2012 and from 2020 for pessimistic condition. The lack of capacity would be around 1.4 million passengers in 2012 and will achieve 42.9 million passengers in 2028 for optimistic condition. While in pessimistic condition, the lack of capacity would be around 0.9 million passengers in 2020 and will achieve 9 million passengers in 2028. It would be better that the airport authority expand the terminal area starting from the year 2012 in optimistic condition and from the year 2020 in pessimistic condition.

Fig. 27 demonstrates the total additional area needed in optimistic and pessimistic condition. As we can see from Fig. 27, for optimistic condition model, by adding 17 million pax such as the dynamic capacity in Terminal II of TTIA, total requirement for the terminal area will be around 1.3 million square meters to cover demand until 2018.

Starting from 2019, again the airport authority needs to expand their terminal capacity to cover demand for the next future in optimistic condition. Because the demand for air travel in pessimistic condition are lower than in optimistic condition, they only need to expand the terminal area to cover 9 million of passengers in 2028, so the total area requirement in pessimistic condition will be around 614,258 square meters to cover the future demand. We summarized all these scenario results in Table 5.

8. Conclusion

This paper presents a method for developing model to forecast air passenger demand and some scenarios related with runway and passenger terminal capacity expansion to meet the future demand from system dynamics point of view. As demand for air travel is difficult to forecast, it is important to utilize system dynamics based on consideration that forecasts come from calibrated system dynamics models, that are likely to be better and more informative than other approaches to develop more robust sensitivities, in order to lead better decisions.

From the base model and scenario development, we summarized that airfare impact, level of service impact, GDP, population, number of flights per day and dwell time play an important roles in determining the air passenger volume, runway utilization and total additional area needed for passenger terminal capacity expansion. It is important to forecast air travel demand in order to support long-term planning to meet the future demand during the planning horizon. Specification of *Level of Service* standards has a significant impact in determining the terminal space, since every LOS standard has different area requirement. We assume that demand for air travel will grow as general economic trends were positive for the airline industry. Rapid growth in air travel demand will force the airport authority to expand the runway and the passenger terminal facilities, e.g. baggage claim, flow space, check in, holding and generic area.

The important aspect of system dynamics framework is that it focuses on information feedback control to organize the available information into computer simulation model. By using a feedback structure, the existing conditions of the system can lead to decisions that will change the surrounding conditions and will influence the next decisions. In creating system dynamics model, information is used as the basic building blocks of a model. The successfulness of model depends on a clear identification of important purpose and objective. The model should help us to organize information in a more understandable way, and should link the past into present condition and extent the present into alternative futures through several scenarios development.

This study could be considered as a pilot study to decide when the airport should expand the runway capacity, passenger terminal capacity and to determine the total area needed to meet the future demand. Furthermore, it is obvious that further research is required to analyze revenue and performance management if the airport expands the runway and passenger terminal facilities, e.g. aprons, gates and ground service facilities.

References

Bafail, A. O., Abed, S. Y., & Jasimuddin, S. M. (2000). The determinants of domestic air travel demand in the Kingdom of Saudi Arabia. *Journal of Air Transportation World Wide, 5*(2), 72–86.

Barlas, Y. (1994). Model validation in system dynamics. In *International system dynamic conference*.

Belobaba, P. (2001). *Characteristics of air transportation markets and demand for air travel*. Lecture notes from The Airline Industry course taught at the Massachusetts Institute of Technology.

Brunetta, L., Righi, L., & Andreatta, G. (2000). *An operations research model for the evaluation of an airport terminal*. European Union Research, DG VII R95 – B67161 – SIN000326.

Department of Finance Canada. (2008). *Air travel demand elasticity: Concepts, issues and measurement: 1*.

Fernandes, E., & Pacheco, R. R. (2002). Efficient use of airport capacity. *Transportation Research Part A, 36*, 225–238.

Forrester, J. W. (1961). *Industrial dynamics*. Cambridge: MIT Press.

Grosche, T., Rothlauf, F., & Heinzl, A. (2007). Gravity models for airline passenger volume estimation. *Journal of Air Transport Management, 13*, 175–183.

Hsu, C. I., & Chao, C. C. (2005). Space allocation for commercial activities at international passenger terminals. *Transportation Research Part E, 41*, 29–51.

IATA. (1981). *Guidelines for airport capacity/demand management*. Geneva, Switzerland: IATA.
Ingram, F. (2004). Flights options. *International Directory of Company Histories, 75*.
Inzerilli, F., & Sergioc, R. (1994). Uncertain demand, modal competition and optimal price-capacity adjustments in air transportation. *Transportation, 21*, 91–101 (Kluwer Academic Publishers, The Netherlands).
James, J., & Galvin, Jr. (2002). *Air traffic control resource management strategies and the small aircraft transportation system: A system dynamics perspective*. Dissertation submitted to the Faculty of the Virginia Polytechnic Institute and State University.
Jifeng, W., Huapu, L., & Hu, P. (2008). System dynamics model of urban transportation system and its application. *Journal of Transportation Systems Engineering and Information Technology*.
Kessides, C. (1996). *A review of infrastructure's impact on economic development, infrastructure and the complexity of economic development*. Berlin: Springer Verlag.
Larson, R., & Odoni, A. R. (1981). *Urban operation research*. New Jersey: Prentice Hall.
Lee, A. M. (1966). *Applied queuing theory*. London/New York: Macmillan/St. Martin's Press.
Miller, B., & Clarke, J. P. (2007). The hidden value of air transportation infrastructure. *Technological Forecasting and Social Science, 74*, 18–35.
Lyneis, J. (1998). *System dynamics in business forecasting: A case study of the commercial jet aircraft industry*.
Lyneis, J. (2000). System dynamics for market forecasting and structural analysis. *System Dynamics Review, 16*, 3–25.
Matthews, L. (1995). Forecasting peak passenger flows at airports. *Transportation, 22*, 55–72 (Kluwer Academic Publishers, The Netherlands).
Newell, G. F. (1971). *Applications of queuing theory*. Boston, MA/London, England: Barnes and Noble/Chapman and Hall.
Poore, J. W. (1993). Forecasting the demand for air transportation services. *Journal of Transportation Engineering, 19*(5), 22–34.

Reibnitz, U. V. (1988). Szenarien – Optionen fr die Zukunft. *Revista de Matem'atica: Teor'ıa y Aplicaciones, 1*, 39–47.
Richardson, G. P. (1995). Loop polarity, loop dominance and the concept of dominant polarity (System Dynamics Conference, Norway, 1984). *System Dynamics Review, 11*, 67–88.
Seraj, Y. A., Abdullah, O. B., & Sajjad, M. J. (2001). An econometric analysis of international air travel demand in Saudi Arabia. *Journal of Air Transport Management, 7*, 143–148.
Skinner, S., Dichter, A., Langley, P., & Sabert, H. (1999). *Managing growth and profitability across peaks and troughs of the airline industry cycle – An industry dynamics approach*.
Sterman, J. (2000). *Business dynamics: Systems thinking and modeling for a complex world*. Boston: McGraw-Hill.
Svrcek, T. (1994). *Planning level decision support for the selection of robust configurations of airport passenger buildings*. Ph.D. Thesis, Department of Aeronautics and Astronautics, Flight Transportation Laboratory Report R94-6, MIT, Cambridge, MA, USA.
Swan, W. M. (2002). Airline demand distributions: Passenger revenue management and spill. *Transportation Research Part E, 38*, 253–263.
The China Post. (2008). *Ma noticeable lacking sound political reason*.
Taipei times. (2008). *Central bank lowers key interest rates*.
Transportation Research Board (TRB). (1987). *Special report 215: Measuring airport landside capacity*. Washington, DC: TRB, National Research Council.
Yamaguchi, K., Ueda, T., Ohashi, T., Takuma, F., Tsuchiya, K., & Hikada, T. (2001). *Economic impact analysis of deregulation and airport capacity expansion in Japanese domestic aviation market*.
Zoellick, R. B. (2008). *Global slump hits developing countries as credit squeeze impedes growth and trade; tensions in commodity markets ease*. Retrieved 24 August, 2009. Available from: http://web.worldbank.org.

Part II:

Infrastructure Planning and Provision

4

Decision Support for Airport Strategic Planning

ROLAND A. A. WIJNEN, WARREN E. WALKER &
JAN H. KWAKKEL

ABSTRACT Master Planning is currently the dominant approach to airport strategic planning. However, history shows that this approach can often result in costly mistakes. Because there are many stakeholders with conflicting objectives, deep uncertainty about the future, and many *potential* strategies, planners often narrow their scope by using a single forecast for the future, leaving out alternative strategies, and excluding stakeholders, resulting in a Master Plan that quickly becomes obsolete and may be opposed by some stakeholders.

What is needed is a flexible, integrated approach that enables collaboration among stakeholders. Such an approach can be facilitated using a Decision Support System (DSS) that provides a way for decisionmakers and stakeholders to evaluate alternative strategies quickly and easily with respect to their outcomes of interest. We present the conceptual design for a DSS called HARMOS, showing how it meets the high-level requirements for airport strategic planning while addressing the problems associated with Master Planning.

KEY WORDS: Airport strategic planning; Master Planning; Decision Support System; policy analysis; HARMOS

Introduction

The history of powered flight over the past 100 years has been one of constant change: it took off after decades of empirical research, continued to be developed by trial and error, was accelerated by World War I, became more and more a means of mass transportation after World War II, and now has become a force that moves the planet. Airports are the elements of the aviation system that provide the ground infrastructure that is required for enabling organized flight across the globe. Today, the aviation industry is in the midst of rapid change, stimulated by both internal forces (e.g. airline mergers and low cost carriers) and external forces (e.g. terrorist threats and environmental regulations). Airports have been and are constantly affected by these changes, which force them to adapt accordingly. Looking at airport developments in retrospect shows that adapting is not always easy. Privatization and liberalization put pressure on airport decisionmaking: opportunities have to be seized and threats dealt with quicker than ever before. Merely trying to keep pace with growing travel demand is not enough; airport planners and decisionmakers also have to provide solutions for mitigating the adverse effects of growth that are satisfactory to their stakeholders (communities, air navigation service providers (ANSPs), airlines, governments, etc.). Doing this successfully is difficult, given the growing opposition to airport expansion plans around the world.

Currently, the airport Master Plan is the core artifact of airport strategic planning. Master Planning is a recommended practice by the International Civil Aviation Organization and required by the Federal Aviation Administration in the United States (ICAO, 2004; FAA, 2005). Most airports in the world, therefore, periodically create one. Although airport operators have increasingly involved a variety of stakeholders in their Master Planning and decisionmaking processes, this has generally not led to improved decisionmaking with respect to future development. In addition, most Master Planning studies take a very long time to complete and run the risk of becoming obsolete by the time they are completed because of new conditions that had not been taken into account. Just recently, construction began on the first project defined in the Master Plan for Los Angeles International Airport, after 10 years of analysis, public discussion, and negotiation (LAWA, 2006). During the planning study, the plan underwent major transformations and revisions in order to reflect the changing environment (LAWA, 2005). Other cases show that implementation of a plan is hampered by the fact that some stakeholders' perspectives have been misunderstood or their objectives or concerns had not been taken into account adequately. Two examples of plans that faced major opposition and implementation delay are the plans for the new runways at Boston Logan Airport (proposed in 1973 with the decision to build in 2006) and the so-called 'Polderbaan' at Amsterdam Airport Schiphol (proposed in the 1970s and opened in 2003).

A primary reason for the lack of success of current approaches to planning is the complexity and uncertainty that planners and decision-makers have to deal with. Not only are there many stakeholders with different objectives and concerns that need to be considered, but the airport system itself is also complex. It consists of many components that have to fit together so that both passengers and aircraft are processed efficiently and safely; at the same time, the adverse effects (e.g. noise, air pollution, road congestion) of these passenger and aircraft flows have to be considered as well. The context in which airports operate is subject to changes in terms of aviation demand, technological developments, demography, and regulations; the uncertainties associated with these changes need to be taken into account as well. Usually, there are large numbers of possible changes that can be made to an airport system, each having different effects on the airport's performance (e.g. delay, environmental impacts, profits). Because the effect of system changes on airport performance are interdependent and affect the objectives of the stakeholders differently, they need to be considered in an integrated way – as complete packages, not as separate, independent changes. It is also essential to consider the changes and their effects for different plausible futures.

The Master Planning effort itself involves the mobilization of an array of disparate resources (internal staff, consultants, stakeholder representatives) and the assembling of a great deal of data and information. Conducting the quantitative part of the analysis involves selecting the appropriate tools and processing their results. The inputs and the results need to be consistent and valid, which usually requires a significant effort. And all of these activities have to be repeated when a new problem has to be analyzed at some time in the future. Currently, there is not enough time or resources to perform the analysis in a quality way – to assemble the data, prepare the analytical tools, and explore future problems, issues, and bottlenecks in the airport system and their potential solutions to the satisfaction of all stakeholders.

Fortunately, the conditions outlined above provide an ideal setting for the application of a Decision Support System (DSS) that would support a multi-stakeholder approach for addressing the wide range of airport strategic planning problems and would efficiently integrate the analytical and human resources within the airport operator's organization. This paper provides the conceptual design for such a DSS as it emerged from the (iterative and incremental) software development process that is ongoing to actually build the software (Wijnen, 2006). Additionally, our experience with previous work on tools for airport strategic planning has been used as input (Walker *et al.*, 2003; Visser *et al.*, 2003). In what follows we use Turban's (1995) definition of a DSS as an interactive, flexible, and adaptable computer-based information system, developed for supporting the solution of a non-structured management problem for improved decision making.

The remainder of this paper is organized as follows. The current airport strategic planning process is examined in more detail with the purpose of identifying the people involved, the activities being employed, and the problems with this approach. Based on an understanding of the current strategic planning process, the role and functionality of a DSS to support the process is shown to be an approach that solves these problems. Finally, the key principles for designing such a DSS and the resulting conceptual design are presented.

Current Airport Strategic Planning

We provide a simplified, conceptual description of how current airport strategic planning is carried out in order to identify in more detail its problems and their causes. We define strategic planning to be the managerial activity that produces fundamental decisions and actions that shape and guide what the organization is, what it does, and why it does it (Bryson, 2004). This implies that strategic planning can be carried out through different approaches. In the case of airport strategic planning, Master Planning is currently the dominant approach, although there are alternatives (de Neufville, 1991; de Neufville & Odoni, 2003). Our description assumes that the airport operator is ultimately responsible for airport planning and coordinates the planning effort. In reality, airport planning consultants might be heavily involved and even responsible for creating the final plan; the relationship between the airport operator and the consultants depends on the local setting, size of the airport operator's organization, and regulatory framework. Figure 1 provides a conceptual map of current airport strategic planning. It is meant to provide a generic overview of airport strategic planning and is not meant to represent any specific airport's approach. The map has been determined empirically and shows that many resources are involved, both inside as well as outside the organization: a lot of *data* are involved, requiring a significant number of *people*, possibly using *tools*, to turn the data into *information* relevant for decisionmaking.

Decision Support for Airport Strategic Planning 15

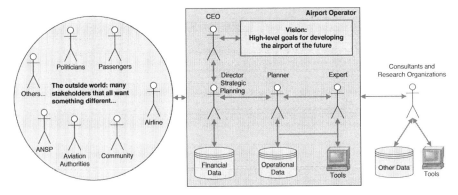

Figure 1. Current airport strategic planning: conflicts of interest and a huge coordination effort

People

The people involved in airport strategic planning can be divided into two groups – those inside the airport operator's organization and those outside the organization. People inside the airport operator's organization are the ones that are directly involved in the strategic planning process; they carry out different types of activities to support the creation of a strategic plan that supports the management's vision. People outside the airport operator's organization are typically associated with organizations or groups that have a stake in the airport's development, which we collectively call the airport's stakeholders. These stakeholders (e.g. airlines, ANSPs, aviation authorities, community groups) have conflicting goals and objectives with respect to the airport's development. The way the stakeholders are involved depends on the local setting, and their role may vary from merely making their views known to being official partners in making agreements about the actual airport development and operations. Stakeholders have significant power (e.g. public campaigns, lobbying, appealing to court) to influence an airport operator's planning process and will do so whenever they think that their objectives and goals are not being sufficiently taken into account.

Data and Information

Creating an effective strategic plan requires consistent data and information about a wide range of aspects. The types of data and information are: (i) the business goals, usually implicitly contained in an organization's vision and further specified (qualitatively or quantitatively) by the airport's management team; (ii) the future context for the airport's operation in terms of economic, technological, regulatory, and demographic developments; (iii) the airport system and its environment, modeled at the appropriate level of detail; (iv) system changes (structural, operational, and/or managerial) due to strategies; and (v) quantitative airport performance information for the given future context and strategies. With respect to airport performance, information at different levels of detail is required concerning capacity and delay, and environmental impacts (noise, emissions, and third-party risk). Nowadays, the financial implications of a plan are also important. Often, outside consultants are contracted to provide information about some or all of these airport performance aspects.

Tools

Much of the data and information are generated using analytical tools, typically related to capacity and delay, environmental impacts (noise, emissions, and third-party risk), and financial performance. In most cases, this data and information are not generated in a consistent, integrated way. Usually, only a single aspect of the airport's operation (e.g. its capacity and delay or noise or emissions) is evaluated at a single time. Only if there is a problem to be expected with another aspect, additional analyses are conducted. The reason for this is that different aspects are usually assessed by different experts, who are not all from the same organization. First, an expert needs to get appropriate data and information. Next, the data and information have to be processed in order to be used as input to the tools being used. Then the experts execute the appropriate runs with their tools, post-process the outcomes, and return the results to an advisor, who either uses it in a report or directly communicates it to the decisionmaker. If one of them is not satisfied with the results, or needs an assessment of another situation, the whole process is repeated. Airport staff may have automated some of the pre- and post-processing tasks, but there is still a risk of data redundancy and conflicting assumptions.

Problems with Current Airport Strategic Planning

Getting all the relevant stakeholders directly involved in the airport operator's strategic planning process is one of the general problems. The recent update of the FAA's advisory circular for Master Planning was specifically rewritten to address this issue (FAA, 2005). Other, more specific problems are:

- *Too few scenarios are considered.* Because of a lack of resources, planners analyze only a limited number of futures (usually only one). As stated by Ascher (1978) and repeated by many others (e.g. de Neufville & Odoni, 2003): *'the forecast is always wrong'*, which means that the traditional 'predict and act' approach is likely to produce a poorly performing plan.
- *Too few alternatives are analyzed.* The problems related to long-term airport development are not exhaustively explored with respect to all of the different aspects and stakeholder perspectives. Only a short list of alternatives is usually considered and combined in a single strategy, based on what is known to have more or less worked in the past. This eventually delays or halts implementation, because of the resulting lack of stakeholder and societal support for the proposed plan.
- *Resources are used inefficiently.* Often, people involved in estimating different outcomes of interest (e.g. noise, delays, finances) work on different parts of the analysis, each using different models/tools, assumptions, and data. This makes it difficult to produce a consistent, integrated set of results that can be used to support a specific plan. An integral view on the airport's performance can only be produced (if at all) by manually collecting, combining, and post-processing the individual results, which is usually not done.
- *Collaboration among stakeholders is problematic.* In addition to inconsistencies in data, assumptions, models, and results, the current approach does not facilitate easy and comprehensive collaboration among the stakeholders, resulting in excluding some of them altogether, or involving them too late. History shows that this causes serious problems when an airport operator tries to implement its Master Plan. Numerous examples, some of them very successful, are available of legal actions from the excluded stakeholders to prevent a plan from becoming reality (Caves & Gosling, 1999; Dempsey, 1999).
- *There are often conflicts among the various stakeholders.* Stakeholders are likely to argue about results, assumptions, and the methodologies that were used, either because they were not involved or do not understand each other (or both).

A major fundamental cause of these problems is a dispersion of data, tools, information, and knowledge within the organization of the airport operator and those of its stakeholders. Resources cannot be easily integrated, consolidated, and focused on producing an effective plan. The result is an inefficient strategic planning process that is not able to support the creation of a transparent plan, based on a thorough understanding of both the airport system and plausible future contexts, that is acceptable to all stakeholders.

In principle, such problems could be solved through the use of a DSS. However, the context in which decision support is to be realized, which has been described above for airport strategic planning, has often been forgotten in DSS development projects (Dodson, Arnott & Pervan, 2006; Brown, 2006). As a result, it is not clear what the DSS being designed is trying to support and what functionality it should provide, Hence, after the DSS is developed, it is not used in practical applications (Poon & Wagner, 2001; Briggs & Arnott, 2004; Arnott & Pervan, 2005).

Design Principles for a DSS for Airport Strategic Planning

The previous discussion makes it clear that there is much room for improvements in airport strategic planning. On the one hand, planners need to improve their understanding of the system and its problems, the airport's future performance given deep uncertainty about the future, and the strategies for addressing these problems. On the other hand, airport decisionmakers need to understand how their business decisions affect their goals and those of their stakeholders such that they are able to define a vision that satisfies both.

We propose that any approach to airport strategic planning should address both issues simultaneously, because we believe that only a holistic approach can meet the decision support needs of the airport of the future. This proposition is based on the observation that the success of an organization is determined by its ability to have people working together both within the organization as well as with its stakeholders. One of the prerequisites of working together is the ability to share information effectively. Just sharing information is, however, not enough; information should be shared in such a way that an organization and its stakeholders gain an understanding of each other's perspectives and objectives. Only when there is a mutual understanding is it possible to look for solutions that are satisfactory to all parties involved (see the left side of Figure 2).

As noted above, the current airport strategic planning and decision-making process includes many common, repetitive activities with data and tools dispersed throughout and outside the organization. It would be sensible to incorporate these into a DSS. By doing so, decisionmakers, decision advisors, and domain experts can work more efficiently and effectively in analyzing problems, thereby unlocking their creative powers, rather than spending large amounts of time on activities that a DSS can do faster and better. The DSS will also integrate and institutionalize the planning process, data and

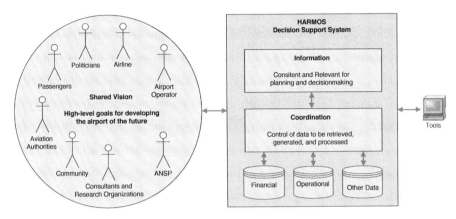

Figure 2. HARMOS: bringing people together

information, and tools within the organization so that a new strategic problem does not require starting from scratch every time it arises.

Our proposed solution, which we call the HARMOS DSS, enables an airport operator to deploy its resources – people (knowledge), data and information, and tools – more efficiently, resulting in an improved understanding of the airport system, its problems and potential solutions, while explicitly facilitating the involvement of stakeholders in the planning process. As a result, airport staff (e.g. management, planners, and experts) and airport stakeholders can work together on solving their problems and improving mutual understanding, so that a shared vision of the future airport can be created. The two key design principles underlying HARMOS are: (1) the adoption of the policy analysis approach; and (2) the integration of resources. We discuss these design principles below.

The Policy Analysis Approach

Policy analysis (Miser & Quade, 1985) is a systematic, well-defined, complete, and comprehensive approach for problem analysis and decisionmaking that evolved out of operations research and systems analysis (Davis et al., 2005). It is widely accepted for analyzing a diversity of problems, and generic enough for addressing the wide range of airport planning problems. Policy analysis explicitly recognizes that problems caused by systems affect many stakeholders, and hence finding solutions needs to be done by involving those stakeholders (van de Riet, 2003).

Figure 3 presents the approach for structuring a policy analysis study statically (framework) and dynamically (process), based on Walker (2000). The framework is an integral system description of a policy

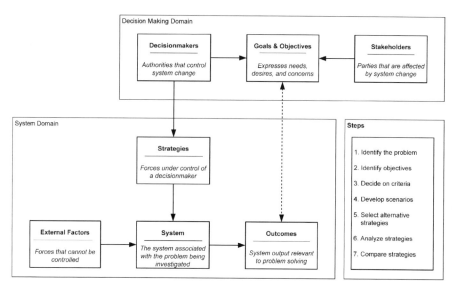

Figure 3. The policy analysis framework and process

field; at its heart is a description of the system domain in the form of a system model that clarifies the system by: (1) defining its boundaries; and (2) defining its structure – the elements, and the links, flows, and relationships among them. Two sets of forces act on the system: *external factors* outside the control, and *strategies* under the control of the actors in the decisionmaking domain. Both sets of forces affect the structure of the system and, hence, the outcomes of interest to the decisionmakers and stakeholders.

The process generally involves performing the same set of logical steps (Walker, 2000). These steps are not necessarily performed in the same order and there is usually feedback among the steps. More general information about the individual steps in the process is described in detail by Miser and Quade (1985) and by Quade (1989). The steps are:

- *Step 1: Identify the Problem.* Identify the planning problem, clarify constraints on possible strategies, identify the airport stakeholders, and discover the major operative factors.
- *Step 2: Identify Objectives.* Identify business objectives (i.e. from the airport operator) and the objectives of other stakeholders so that later it can be determined if: (1) a strategy solves the problem identified or seizes the opportunity; and (2) how a strategy affects the various stakeholders.
- *Step 3: Decide on Criteria.* Identify the consequences of a strategy that can be estimated (quantitatively or qualitatively) and that are directly related to the objectives. It is essential to have an integral

view of the airport's future performance so that bottlenecks and adverse effects of a specific strategy on the airport's overall performance can be correctly identified.
- *Step 4: Develop Scenarios.* Define the future contexts within which the problems are to be analyzed and the strategies will have to function. In this step, several plausible scenarios are developed. A scenario is a specification of the external factors influencing the system, including their effects on the structure or operations of the system over a specified planning period. Scenarios are not complete descriptions of the future; they include only those aspects that might strongly affect the outcomes of interest. It is important to include enough scenarios to cover a broad range of uncertainties. Omitting an uncertainty from the scenarios implies that the effects of that uncertainty are not important, since they will not be examined in the analysis.
- *Step 5: Select Alternative Strategies.* It is important to include as many strategies as stand any chance of being worthwhile ('think the unthinkable'). If a strategy is not included in this step, it will never be examined, so there is no way of knowing how good it may be. The current strategy (*business as usual*) should be included too (often referred to as the 'base case'), in order to determine how much of an improvement can be expected from the other strategies.
- *Step 6: Analyze Strategies.* Determine the consequences that are likely to follow if the strategy is actually implemented in each of the scenarios, where the consequences are measured in terms of the criteria chosen in Step 3.
- *Step 7: Compare Strategies.* Examine the strategies in terms of their estimated outcomes for each of the scenarios, making tradeoffs among them, and choosing a preferred strategy (or combination of strategies), which is robust across the future contexts. If none of the strategies examined so far are good enough to be implemented (or if new aspects of the problem have been found, or the analysis has led to new strategies), return to Step 5.

The policy analysis approach has been applied to many problems, both in the private and public domain. However, to our knowledge it has never been used as the basis for DSS design, since most policy analysis studies are designed to solve a single, unique problem once. Airport strategic planning should be a continual, repetitive process. The nature of airport strategic planning (a multi-stakeholder setting and a complex system under study) makes a way to structure the problem and a clear problem solving process an absolute must. An airport operator's organization and its stakeholders can be supported in their strategic planning by using a structured, comprehensive framework. Policy analysis provides such a framework.

The Integration of Resources

As already pointed out, one of the fundamental causes of problems in current airport strategic planning is a dispersion of data, tools, information, and knowledge within the organization of the airport operator and its stakeholders. An integrative approach toward the deployment of people, data/information, and tools is needed to address these problems. We discuss the integration of these three types of resources in the following three sections.

People. Many people are involved in airport strategic planning, both from inside and outside the organization (i.e. representatives from the stakeholders). Each of them plays a different role and conducts specific tasks, either throughout the entire duration of the planning study or at specific times. In order to achieve the integration of resources, it is necessary to identify the different roles of these actors. As pointed out, in order to be successful, airport strategic planning should be a collective effort of both the people within the airport operator's organization and its stakeholders. Therefore, both groups should be able to use the DSS.

A further division can be made with regard to the roles with respect to the strategic planning effort. Conceptually, those roles are shown in Figure 4, including the main sources of information that people with these roles use or have available. There are three major roles in the

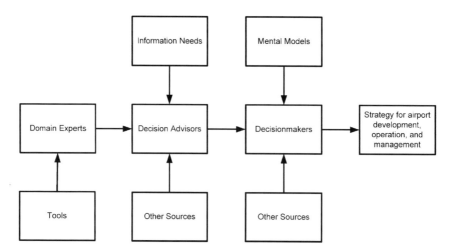

Figure 4. Roles of the people involved, their information needs and sources

planning process, which are performed by one or more persons, depending on the size of the airport operator's organization:

- *Decisionmakers*. The persons that have the decision power to develop and implement strategies for the airport's development, operation, and management. Strategies are developed such that they meet the business goals associated with the vision about the airport of the future. Decisionmakers usually do not make direct use of (analytical) computer tools. The sources these people use are very diverse (e.g. newspapers, meetings with airport staff and stakeholders, and their intuition) and include their own mental models and input from their advisors.
- *Decision Advisors*. The persons that advise the people that make the actual decisions. Decision advisors explore the strategies that could be implemented for meeting the goals set by the decisionmakers. In order to accomplish this task, they hire external consultants, use in-house computer tools, and consult domain experts.
- *Domain Experts*. The persons that have specific knowledge of the airport system (e.g. of the airside, landside, ground access infrastructure) and its operation. The domain expert uses various tools to provide quantitative information about the (future) airport performance (e.g. capacity and delay, environmental impacts, and financial results).

The realization of the DSS design that services the different needs of people with each of these roles is discussed in section 'Integrating People'.

Data and information. Integrating data and information helps reduce the coordination effort required for making sure that the decision advisors, domain experts, and external consultants use a consistent set of data and assumptions. It also makes data, such as current information about the airport infrastructure and operation, airlines and their flight schedules and networks, aircraft and their noise and emissions characteristics, and demographics (e.g. population densities, dwellings, housing projects) available for easy retrieval, analysis, and reuse. Moreover, it makes sure that the information is valid and consistent (and remains so) and that it can be easily shared. The aforementioned policy analysis framework can help in structuring the data in a clear manner (discussed in section 'Integrating Data and Information').

Tools. The dispersion of tools both within and across organizations leads to inconsistencies between assumptions and input data used for setting up the tools for airport performance analysis. A tool, such as the Integrated Noise Model (INM), is frequently used for land-use compatibility planning (Gulding et al., 1999; FAA, 1983) and for determining the effect of forecast airport operations within airport Master Planning studies. In order to use INM, an expert needs to first create and set up an INM study, which means selecting, checking, and setting up the INM default data for the specific airport under consideration. Next, an expert needs to provide input data about the airport infrastructure (runways and tracks) and the airport operation, prepare noise metrics and other computational settings, run the computations, and finally interpret the results. If another situation needs to be assessed, this process or parts of it need to be repeated. Because of this effort, detailed environmental analysis (i.e. the analysis of noise and emissions) is usually postponed until it is more or less clear which infrastructural developments are to be included in the plan. However if the use of all the tools for all the analyses were coordinated by a single DSS, an integral assessment of all relevant outcomes of a strategy could be carried out at the same time. These facts, and the need for consistent assumptions across all of the analyses, make it clear that it would be more efficient and effective if all of the tools were controlled centrally, as we will discuss in section 'Integrating Tools'.

Conceptual Design of the HARMOS DSS

The analysis of the current airport strategic planning approach shown in Figure 1 revealed that:

1. many people with different roles are involved, who conduct fundamentally different activities;
2. a huge amount of data and information is needed and generated; and
3. different tools need to be deployed and used.

Based on these observations, we defined three categories of resources: people, data and information, and tools. A concrete planning study involves specific resources from the airport operator and from its stakeholders. Currently, those resources are not embedded in a unified structure, which makes it difficult to use them efficiently. Adopting the principles described in section 'Design Principles for a DSS for Airport Strategic Planning' and using them consistently results in the conceptual design of the HARMOS DSS as presented in Figure 5.

HARMOS has a layered design, with each layer partitioned into packages, each of which has a clear responsibility. Within the packages there is a further partitioning so that the design is truly modular, making the DSS easy to maintain, extend, and/or customize for a potential customer. The layers are:

Decision Support for Airport Strategic Planning

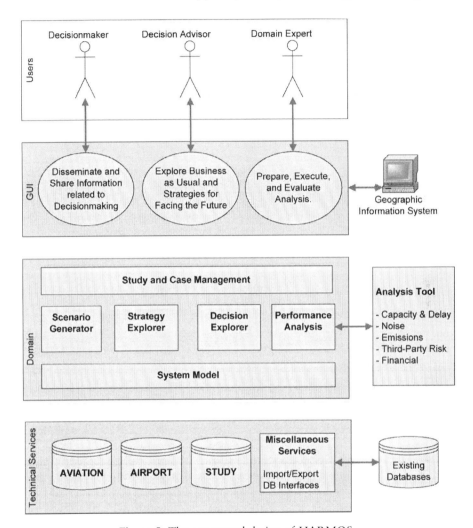

Figure 5. The conceptual design of HARMOS

- Graphical User Interface (GUI): the interface between the DSS' functionality and the users.
- Domain: incorporates the core functionality for supporting the strategic planning effort.
- Technical Services: incorporates lower-level, more generic services used by the higher-level layers.

The GUI is designed such that it meets the specific information and task requirements of the roles identified in Figure 4, but its components are not further discussed. The packages within the domain layer are:

- *Study and Case Management.* Provides functionality for organizing the strategic planning effort.
- *Scenario Generator.* Responsible for capturing data about the future developments of the external factors (one of the forces in the policy analysis framework, see also Figure 3), so that domain experts and decision advisors can create multiple scenarios representing a range of plausible futures. Those scenarios include future flight schedules in an Official Airline Guide (OAG) format, using current OAG data about scheduled airline operations as the starting point.
- *System Model Manager.* Incorporates a generic system description, being the heart of the policy analysis framework (see also Figure 3), as discussed in much more detail in section 'Integrating Data and Information'. The package provides functionality to create system models as a function of time within the planning period, including the effect of the forces (external factors and strategies) on the system. The package also provides functionality for retrieving, updating, and deleting specific system models.
- *Performance Analysis.* Provides an interface between the problem and the tools; it is responsible for transferring the information from the problem context to the tool context (pre-processing), so that quantitative results about the airport's performance can be generated (computations) and digested (post-processing) so that finally they can be evaluated by one of the DSS users. The tools are not incorporated into the DSS; instead the DSS calls upon some of the computational services of third-party tools through a so-called 'adapter'.
- *Strategy Explorer.* Provides the functionality for defining strategies, assessing their effect on the airport's future performance, and comparing them (business as usual strategy with new strategies and one new strategy versus another).
- *Decision Explorer.* Each of the strategies explored by the decision advisors will solve the future bottlenecks in a more or less satisfying manner, depending on the stakeholder that is considered. This package allows decision advisors to present the results of the strategy exploration to the decisionmakers from the perspectives of various stakeholders, so that they can discuss, negotiate, and decide upon a strategy (or combination of strategies) that is preferred for implementation. Obviously, the decisionmakers could also come up with new strategies that should be explored before coming to an agreement.

The technical services mainly provide functionality for disclosing data needed for setting up an airport planning study or permanently storing the user-generated information within an airport planning study. Three types of databases are incorporated:

- *Aviation.* Includes generic data, such as the world's airline fleets, and aircraft characteristics (e.g. flight performance, noise, and emissions data).
- *Airport.* Includes airport specific data, such as traffic demand data (based on the OAG format and data), historic wind data, and data related to economic forecasts.
- *Study.* Includes data and information related to a specific planning study (e.g. the decisionmaking context, scenarios, and strategies).

Another package that is incorporated in this layer provides miscellaneous services, such as data import and export functionality and functionality to interface with existing databases within the airport operator's organization.

Integrating People

The HARMOS GUI (the top layer in Figure 5) provides the interface between the DSS and its users, enabling them to interact with the DSS based on their role in the strategic planning effort. Their tasks are not independently executed anymore; they are interrelated, and connected within the workflow for problem solving that the HARMOS DSS provides. Through the GUI, the following functionality is provided for each role (note that these roles are adopted by people from the airport operator's organization as well as by representatives of the airport's stakeholders):

- *Decisionmakers* disseminate and share information related to decisionmaking. They compare the business as usual strategy with other strategies that have been explored so that they can discuss them with other stakeholders to find out which strategy is collectively preferred to be implemented.
- *Decision advisors* define and explore strategies for dealing with the future (either for solving problems or seizing opportunities). This task includes preparing scenarios resembling different futures, and analyzing the overall airport performance (airside and landside delays, environmental impacts, and profits or losses) for the business as usual strategy and any other proposed strategy (e.g. building a new runway, extension of the terminal, demand management).
- *Domain experts* prepare, execute, and evaluate quantitative analyses related to the airport's performance in terms of capacity and delay, noise, emissions, third-party risk, and financial aspects.

Integrating Data and Information

As pointed out, a huge amount of data need to be processed iteratively and interactively by different people before the relevant information for decisionmaking becomes available. Currently, this is done using a bottom-up approach in which the decision advisors analyze and digest large amounts of data to obtain the required information. The HARMOS DSS uses a top-down approach, which starts from what needs to be known from the problem point of view. Based on this view, the context for problem analysis is determined, which in turn reveals the data and information needs. Using a top-down or problem-oriented approach, there is much more focus on what is really needed in terms of information, which makes data gathering and processing much more efficient.

Categorizing data as well as turning data into useful information follows naturally from adopting the policy analysis framework. Based on the framework (see Figure 3), we defined four categories of data: system, external factors, strategies, and outcomes of interest. Each of those categories has been modeled in a similar fashion, but only the static structure of the system category is described in detail.

The system category captures data to describe and model the system, but we also need to capture the nature of the elements and the relationships among the elements. At the top level, the system model consists of three subsystems – the airport, its (physical) environment, and other systems. The last is a collection of systems that an airport depends on, such as the Air Traffic Management (ATM) system or the road network outside the airport property. The reason that those are not separately included in the system model is because we do not need to describe them in detail for the purposes of airport strategic planning. Only the characteristics that directly affect the airport operation have to be included. The system model hierarchy is depicted in Figure 6, which shows some of the details of the runway system (one of the components of the airside subsystem of an airport). In this way, the real world is reflected quite naturally in the DSS, while at the same time providing a single and consistent data model of the relevant airport subsystems, taking into account their interrelationships.

The most important advantage of structuring data and information according to the policy analysis framework is that there are clear distinctions among data that are related to the system, the external factors, the strategies, and the outcomes of interest for the problem at hand. Tables 1 and 2 provide concrete examples for each of the four categories of data (but they are not intended to provide an exhaustive overview of the data that need to be collected for each category).

Decision Support for Airport Strategic Planning 29

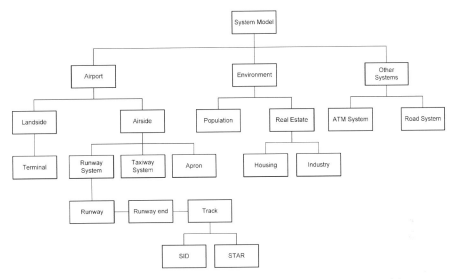

Figure 6. A hierarchical representation for defining the system model

Integrating Tools

Table 2 presented a number of outcome indicators for each of the outcomes of interest (i.e. capacity and delay, noise, emissions, third-party risk, and financial). During the strategic planning process, these outcome indicators need to be quantified for various different situations so that they can be assessed by a domain expert and/or decision advisor. The outcome indicators need to be quantified for a specific period of interest (either a day or a year). For each period, the performance analysis package is used (see Figure 5) for the actual quantitative analysis. The performance analysis package pre-processes data, executes tools, and post-processes the generated results to draw meaning from them. The tool adapter mentioned before is the interface between the DSS and the tool, which is responsible for converting information from the problem context to the tool context, control the execution of the tool, and convert the tool results back to the problem context. Returning to the activity of conducting noise analysis with the INM as described in section 'Tools', the sequence of events based on the need of a decision advisor to assess the noise impact of a strategy is the following:

1. Specific outcome indicators (e.g. noise contours and areas, population counts) are selected through the GUI.
2. HARMOS checks whether all the input required to quantify the selected outcome indicators is available:

Table 1. Organization of data according to the policy analysis framework: forces on the system

External factors	Strategies
Economy	*Strategies to improve airside capacity*
● Traffic demand and mix (regional jets, new large aircraft).	● Additional infrastructure: runways, taxiway system design.
● Growth rates.	● New operational concepts and technology.
● Type of demand: business, leisure, transfer.	● Change in aircraft mix.
● Market share low cost carriers and other airlines.	*Strategies to reduce environmental impact*
	● Noise abatement procedures (NAP).
● Aviation market conditions: deregulation, liberalization, globalization, competition, privatization.	● Reorganizing departure (SID) and arrival (STAR) routes.
	● Ban or curfews on noisy aircraft.
	● Single engine taxiing.
Technology	● Insulation of houses.
● New modes of transport.	● Runway allocation strategies.
● Air Traffic Management.	*Strategies to improve landside capacity*
● New aircraft designs.	● New check-in procedures.
● Noise reductions: engine & airframe.	● Additional landside infrastructure: new pier, new terminal.
● Emission reductions.	
Regulation	● Different security procedures.
● Effect of noise levels on disturbance.	*Strategies for increasing revenues*
● Effect of pollutant emissions on public health.	● Real estate developments.
	● Expanding shopping areas.
● New government regulations.	● Parking services.
● Slot allocation.	● Meeting facilities (golf course, conference centre).
Demographics	
● Population growth.	
● Effect of noise impact and third-party risk on population (distribution) and housing developments.	

a. if all input is available, the decision advisor proceeds with Step 3;

b. if input is missing (e.g. census data, departure/arrival tracks), HARMOS notifies the user so that the appropriate data can be retrieved and added to the system model (probably with the help of domain experts).

3. The domain expert starts the noise analysis from the GUI, which in turn calls upon the performance analysis package for doing the work. The performance analysis package:

   a. automatically creates an INM study, retrieves the appropriate data from the system model, and converts that into specific input for INM (pre-processing);

Table 2. Organization of data according to the policy analysis framework: system and outcomes of interest

System	Outcomes of interest
Airport	*Airport capacity and delay*
● Airside:	● Runway system, gate, and terminal capacity
○ Runway system: runways, configurations, tracks.	for a peak day.
○ Taxiway system: taxiways, holding bays and areas.	● Annual airport capacity.
	● Delay statistics for overall airport.
○ Apron.	● Delay statistics for different airport
● Landside:	components such as the runway and taxiway
○ Terminal system: terminals, people movers.	system, apron, gates, and terminal.
	Noise impact
	● Noise levels at specific locations.
○ Parking areas and garages.	● Noise contours.
○ Roads (circular drive).	● Population (annoyance) and houses affected.
Environment	*Third-Party Risk*
● Population and housing.	● Individual risk contours and group risk.
● Industry parks.	● Houses affected.
● Schools.	*Emissions*
● Wildlife.	● Inventory of pollutant emissions.
Other systems	● Concentration levels of pollutants.
● Air Traffic Management system.	*Financial*
● Train station.	● Costs and revenues (airport balance sheet).
● Access roads.	● Return on investments.

    b. starts INM, sends it a message to start the actual computations, and shuts it down when it is finished (tool execution and control);

    c. retrieves the results from INM, and converts those results into the appropriate format for presentation within the problem context. When noise contours and population counts have been requested, the contours are plotted on a background map, and calculations are made to determine the number of people inside those contours (post-processing).

Along the same lines, the HARMOS DSS provides functionality for obtaining information about any other performance aspect (i.e. capacity and delay, emissions, third-part risk, and financial) given any particular situation in the decisionmaking context.

Conclusions

Current airport strategic planning is primarily based on Master Planning, which is problematic because, in general, in Master Planning uncertainties about the future are not properly addressed, and involvement of stakeholders is inadequate. We have argued that, in today's rapidly changing world, there is a continuous need for airport operators to update their plans, which is why we propose that the practice of Master Planning should adopt a flexible and integrated approach to strategic planning. This approach should acknowledge the fact that the future is uncertain and is about exploring many different strategies that may contribute to realizing a vision about the airport of the future. It does not necessarily produce a single static plan. By adopting a flexible and integrated approach to strategic planning, airport management is able to change its strategy as the future unfolds. However, involvement of the entire organization and all airport stakeholders is essential for actually being able to implement new strategies. Current airport planning practice is already a cumbersome and resource intensive process, so transitioning to a planning process that allows continuous updating of plans will be difficult without appropriate support. We, therefore, proposed a DSS to support airport strategic planning. The high-level design principles for such a DSS were presented and we showed how those principles (the policy analysis approach and integration of resources) were adopted for the conceptual design of the HARMOS DSS. The resulting conceptual design shows great promise in enabling airport staff and stakeholders to be more efficient and effective in exploring strategies for achieving their visions of the airport of the future. The HARMOS DSS integrates and institutionalizes the planning process, data and information, and tools in a multi-stakeholder context, so that successive strategic planning studies can easily make use of the data and information, and tools, and results from previous studies, thereby reducing the time and resources needed to carry out a new planning study.

Our general conclusions are:

- Analyzing the current strategic planning approach is essential for identifying the problem that is to be solved by a DSS, and identifying the users, and their high-level needs.
- The conceptual design of HARMOS supports airport strategic planning through all levels – i.e. from the expert in the organization to the final decisionmaker.
- The policy analysis approach provides a well-defined and systematic framework for exploring airport planning problems within the context of an uncertain future. Adopting the policy analysis approach as the foundation for the design of the DSS is an effective way to deal with system complexity and uncertainty.
- The strategic planning process becomes institutionalized through the HARMOS DSS instead of remaining an ad hoc process. This enables

an organization to better respond to change with respect to the future that unfolds, the problems it brings, and solutions that can be provided. With the HARMOS DSS, solutions to new problems might even have been explored before, so that their results can be retrieved and the analyses do not have to be redone entirely from scratch.
- By using the HARMOS DSS, an organization can be provided with an effective learning capability and memory function, which initially helps to improve the strategic planning process and eventually enables strategic thinking across all levels of the organization.
- Using the HARMOS DSS, the focus of a planning effort shifts from rather technically oriented Master Planning to a stakeholder-oriented approach to strategic planning, in which the airport operator and stakeholders explore future problems and strategies for addressing them together, resulting in a flexible and adaptable strategic plan, instead of a fixed and rigid Master Plan.

The conceptual design outlined in this paper has already been implemented in prototype software. Our next step is to customize and test the DSS within the organizational context of an airport operator in Europe.

References

Arnott, D. & Pervan, G. (2005) A critical analysis of decision support systems research, *Journal of Information Technology*, 20(2), pp. 67–87.

Ascher, W. (1978) *Forecasting: An Appraisal for Policy-makers and Planners* (Baltimore, MD: Johns Hopkins University Press).

Briggs, D. & Arnott, D. (2004) Decision support systems failure, an evolutionary perspective, *Journal of Decision Systems*, 13(1), pp. 91–111.

Brown, R. V. (2006) Planning decision research with usefulness in mind: Toward quantitative evaluation, in: F. Adam, P. Brezillon, S. Carlsson & P. Humphreys (Eds) *Creativity and Innovation in Decision Making and Decision Support*, Vol. I (London: Decision Support Press).

Bryson, J. M. (2004) What to do when stakeholders matter: Stakeholder identification and analysis techniques, *Public Management Review*, 6(1), pp. 21–53.

Caves, R. E. & Gosling, G. D (1999) *Strategic Airport Planning* (Oxford: Pergamon).

Davis, P. K., Kulick, J. & Egner, M. (2005) *Implications of Modern Decision Science for Military Decision-support Systems*, Document Number: MG-360-AF, Santa Monica: The RAND Corporation.

Dempsey, S. (1999) *Airport Development and Planning Handbook: A Global Survey* (New York, NY: McGraw-Hill Professional).

Dodson, G., Arnott, D. & Pervan, G. (2006) The client and user in decision support systems: Review and research agenda, in: F. Adam, P. Brezillon, S. Carlsson & P. Humphreys (Eds) *Creativity and Innovation in Decision Making and Decision Support*, Vol. I (London, UK: Decision Support Press).

Federal Aviation Administration (FAA) (1983) *Advisory Circular 150/5020-1, Noise Control and Compatibility Planning for Airports* (Washington, DC: US Department of Transportation).

Federal Aviation Administration (FAA) (2005) *Advisory Circular 150/5070-6B, Airport Master Plans* (Washington, DC: US Department of Transportation).

Gulding, J. M., Olmstead, J. R., & Fleming, G. C. (1999) *Integrated Noise Model (INM) User's Guide, Version 6.0* (Washington, DC: US Department of Transportation, Federal Aviation Administration, Office of Environment and Energy).

International Civil Aviation Organization (ICAO) (2004) *Airport Planning Manual, Part 1 – Master Planning* (Doc 9184) (2nd edn, 1987). Reprinted July 2004.

LAWA (May 20, 2005) *News Release: FAA Publishes Record of Decision on Improvement Proposals at LAX* (Los Angeles: Los Angeles World Airports (LAWA)).

LAWA (January 18, 2006) *News Release: Los Angeles City Council Gives Final Approval to Settlement of LAX Master Plan Lawsuits* (Los Angeles: Los Angeles World Airports (LAWA)).

Miser, H. J. & Quade, E. S. Eds (1985) *Handbook of Systems Analysis: Overview of Uses, Procedures, Applications, and Practice* (New York, NY: Elsevier).

de Neufville, R. (1991) Strategic planning for airport capacity: An appreciation of Australia's process for Sydney, *Australian Planner*, 29(4), pp. 174–180.

de Neufville, R. & Odoni, A. (2003) *Airport Systems: Planning, Design, and Management* (New York, NY: McGraw-Hill Professional).

Poon, P. & Wagner, C. (2001) Critical success factors revisited: Success and failure cases of information systems for senior executives, *Decision Support Systems*, 30, pp. 394–418.

Quade, E. S. (1989) *Analysis for Public Decisions* (3rd edn) (New York, NY: Elsevier).

Turban, E. (1995) *Decision support and expert systems: management support systems* (Upper Saddle River, NJ: Prentice Hall).

van de Riet, O. W. A. T. (2003) *Policy Analysis in Multi-Actor Policy Settings: Navigating Between Negotiated Nonsense and Superfluous Knowledge* (Delft: Eburon Publishers).

Visser, H. G., Chin, R. T. H., Wijnen, R. A. A., Walker, W. E., Keur, J., Kohse, U., Veldhuis, J. & de Haan, A. R. C. (2003) The airport business suite: A decision support system for airport strategic exploration, in: *Proceedings of AIAA's 3rd Annual Aviation Technology, Integration, and Operations (ATIO) Technical Forum*, Denver.

Walker, W. E. (2000) Policy analysis: A systematic approach to supporting policymaking in the public sector, *Journal of Multicriteria Decision Analysis*, 9(1–3), pp. 11–27.

Walker, W. E., Lang, N. A., Keur, J., Visser, H. G., Wijnen, R. A. A., Kohse, U., Veldhuis, J. & De Haan, A. R. C. (2003) An organizational decision support system for airport strategic exploration, in: T. Bui, H. Sroka, S. Stanek & J. Goluchowski (Eds) *DSS in the Uncertainty of the Internet Age* (Katowice: Karol Adamiecki University of Economics in Katowice).

Wijnen, R. A. A. (2006) Adopting the Agile Unified Process for developing a DSS for airport strategic planning, in: *Proceedings of the 2nd International Conference on Research in Air Transportation (ICRAT)*, 24–28 June, 2006, Belgrade.

5

A multicriteria decision support methodology for evaluating airport expansion plans

Ron Vreeker, Peter Nijkamp, Chris Ter Welle

Abstract

Rational decision-making requires an assessment of advantages and disadvantages of choice possibilities, including non-market effects (such as externalities). This also applies to strategic decision-making in the transport sector (including aviation). In the past decades various decision support and evaluation methods have been developed in which a market evaluation played a prominent role. The intrinsic limitations of these approaches were also increasingly recognised. Gradually, a variety of adjusted multidimensional methods has been developed over the past years to complement conventional cost–benefit analysis (CBA). These methods aim to investigate and evaluate all relevant impacts of a choice possibility (e.g., project, plan, or programme) on the basis of a multitude of important policy criteria (so-called multicriteria methods). They have a particular relevance in case of non-priced or qualitative effects. There is a clear need for a systematic and polyvalent multicriteria approach to many actual planning issues, such as land use or transportation. This paper offers a new evaluation framework based on a blend of three types of approaches, viz. Regime Analysis, the Saaty method and the Flag Model. All these methods have been developed separately in the past; the paper makes an effort to offer a cohesive framework, which can be used for the e valuation of spatial-economic and environmental-economic policy issues. This new tool is tested by means of a case study on conflicting plans (and policy views) for airport expansion options in the Maastricht area in the southern part of The Netherlands. © 2001 Elsevier Science Ltd. All rights reserved.

1. Introduction

Economic developments are not solely the result of a proper combination of production factors such as labour, land and capital, but also a consequence of a balanced use of overhead capital in general and infrastructure (transport systems and related policies) in particular (Rietveld and

Bruinsma, 1999). There is quite some evidence that improving transport systems tends to lead to a higher productivity rate of private production factors.

Besides a static reallocation effect, a major dynamic driving force of economic adjustment is that investments in transport infrastructure and an implementation of efficiency-enhancing transport policies lead to changes in transportation costs (see Nijkamp and Blaas, 1996). These may affect trade relationships and hence also the location of production factors (see Fujita et al., 1999).

The complexity of transport-land use interactions prompts the need for sophisticated assessment methods and clear decision-making processes in order to assess all advantages and disadvantages of choice possibilities at the edge of infrastructure and sustainable land use.

In modern evaluation theory we witness an increasing emphasis on analytical decision support methods. After the popularity of cost–benefit analysis (CBA) and related financial-economic evaluation methods (such as cost-effectiveness analysis) we have seen an increasing popularity and widespread use of multicriteria methods. Such methods are capable of dealing with the multiple dimensions of evaluation problems (e.g., social, cultural, ecological, technological, institutional, etc.) and give due attention to interest conflicts among stakeholders involved. In general, the aim of these methods is to combine assessment methods with judgement methods and to offer a solid analytical basis for modern decision analysis (see for a general overview Nijkamp et al., 1990).

The focus of this paper concerns the foundation of these modern assessment methods. It aims to highlight their relevance for strategic transport decision-making from an operational perspective. From the large set of existing and recently developed evaluation methods, three frequently employed assessment techniques (viz. Regime Analysis, the Saaty method and the Flag Model) have been selected for a more thorough treatment. Each of these assessment techniques has a great potential for policy analysis in the transport sector and builds on the foundation of conventional CBA. The presentation of these methods follows a systematic framework set out by a newly developed coherent evaluation methodology. Besides, the functioning of the various methods is clarified by means of a case study on airport expansion in one of the southern provinces in The Netherlands.

The paper is organised as follows. Section 2 of the paper offers a description of the evaluation methodology. It provides a framework for evaluating transport policies and infrastructure investments in a multidimensional way. Section 3 is dedicated to the three methods included in our methodology. It takes a closer look at the principles of this methodology by means of a more detailed description of the various methods. Section 4 is concerned with the aviation case study; it clarifies the methodology and describes the results of the application of the evaluation techniques employed. In Section 5 we draw conclusions and offer some further reflections.

2. Evaluation methodology

The standard framework for evaluating transport policies and infrastructure investments from an economic perspective is CBA. CBA has already a long history in the evaluation of infrastructure projects.

The French engineer Dupuit has laid the theoretical basis for CBA many years back, in 1844. Dupuit introduced in his article the concept of a consumer's surplus, which has ever since played a crucial role in applied welfare theory (we refer here inter alia to Marshall, Pigou, Keynes, Hicks, Wicksell and Samuelson).

In the second part of the 20th century, CBA has become increasingly popular as a meaningful and practical evaluation technique for (public) projects. A CBA is originally a capital budgeting system primarily concerned with public projects. CBA is essentially not purely an accounting system, but an evaluation method based on applied welfare theory. It is a method to determine the net social surplus of public investments or of institutional decisions (Mishan, 1971).

If a choice has to be made by public authorities among alternative goods in order to achieve allocative efficiency, the criterion of a maximum willingness to pay has to be used. In this way, CBA can be employed as a monetary evaluation method for assessing the net (social) benefits of (public) projects (Layard, 1997). Clearly, right economic decisions can only be taken when the price system reflects the social revenues and sacrifices in an adequate manner. An essential problem in applying a CBA is indeed the determination of consistent and reliable values of project outcomes (particularly, if the market mechanism does not provide this price system).

A CBA represents thus a systematic enumeration and evaluation of all relevant (i.e., direct and indirect) (social) revenues and costs of a given set of choice possibilities. This analysis incorporates two important stages, viz. impact analysis and monetary assessment. After the execution of these steps the most favourable plan – at least from an economic perspective – can be identified in a straightforward way.

Unfortunately, in the history of application of CBA sometimes many intrinsic shortcomings and practical limitations of this evaluation approach have been overlooked. Therefore, it may be useful to examine in slightly more detail some important aspects of CBA.

Accuracy of information. In general, it will be very difficult to assess in an accurate manner all direct and indirect impacts of an infrastructure plan over a long-time horizon (for example, the long-term effect of infrastructure on biodiversity).

Distributional equity. In general, distributional effects are omitted in many evaluations, because the judgement of these effects is considered to be politically instigated. However, it has to be noted that distributional effects can in principle be taken into account by employing the notion of compensatory payments (e.g., Hicks–Kaldor compensation test) or attaining a Pareto-equilibrium.

Compensatory payments. A decline in utility of several individuals or groups can be assessed by means of a monetary amount that compensates this decline. The notion of compensation is a direct implication of welfare theory, but its precise amount is in general very hard to operationalise (due to lack of information on preference curves of individuals or a society at large). Furthermore, compensatory payments are frequently only introduced as fictitious payments to assess social costs; they are not meant to be out-of-pocket costs.

Discount rate. The time preference of plan impacts is reflected by the (social) rate of discount, but an operational determination of this parameter is very difficult. The value of a (social) discount rate is not an unambiguous parameter, but is essentially the result of a socio-political decision. This also explains the variety in values of the social rate of discount.

Lifetime of the project. The lifetime of a transportation project is sometimes hard to assess, as this is not only a technological issue, but also dependent on the emergence of alternative competing projects.

On the basis of the foregoing remarks, the conclusion can be drawn that CBA may, in principle, be a sound evaluation method for decisions in the public sector. It should be noted however, that several severe limitations do exist. As a consequence, also several complementary approaches have been deployed in the past decades, such as cost-effectiveness analysis, planning balance sheet methods and shadow project approaches; they all belong to the same family.

In the recent evaluation history a closer orientation towards actual decision-making processes can be observed, which means that – next to a monetary CBA-based approach – also complementary – in particular decision-making based and institutionally based – approaches have been deployed. In fact, nowadays one may distinguish at least four types of evaluation styles in the planning literature:

1. a *monetary* decision approach, based e.g., on cost–benefit or cost-effectiveness principles;
2. a *utility* theory approach, based on prior ranking of the decision-makers' preferences using multicriteria analysis;
3. a *learning* approach, based on a sequential (interactive or cyclical) articulation of the decision-maker's views;
4. a *collective* decision approach, based on multi-person bargaining, negotiation or voting procedures.

Information uncertainty and conflict management are thus critical issues. Many conflicting views may emerge in evaluating alternative plans. Especially modern approaches like multicriteria analysis may serve as a meaningful evaluation vehicle for taking explicitly account of such conflicts regarding the foreseeable impacts of a plan (Nijkamp et al., 1990). For example, everybody may agree on the fact that the expansion of an airport will destroy x hectares of the forest. Multicriteria analysis may then be helpful in taking into account such conflicting issues by considering priority schemes or weights as an ingredient in an evaluation analysis for investment projects. Of course, this will not always lead to a unique final solution, but the structure and consequences of conflicts among decision-makers can be made more explicit, so that also the range of politically feasible alternatives can be analysed in greater detail (see for an overview of evaluation procedures and methods related to infrastructure investments Rietveld, 2000; De Brucker, 2000; Rietveld and Rouwendal, 2000).

In general, one may argue that the efficiency test on an investment decision can most properly be carried out by means of CBA methods, while equity and sustainability checks need broader approaches based on MCA approaches. In addition, in case of 'soft' information (e.g., ordinal) the latter class of methods is also very suitable (see for example van Pelt, 1994). Thus, we are essentially seeking for the most appropriate decision support method in case of a complex evaluation problem.

To conclude, there is clearly no single assessment and evaluation method that can satisfactorily and unequivocally evaluate all complex aspects of choice possibilities. The choice of assessment methods in any given choice context therefore depends on the features of the problem at hand, on the aims of the analysis, and on the underlying information base. The proposed evaluation methodology gives insight into the above-mentioned aspects that determine the choice of the appropriate evaluation method or combination of evaluation methods. By means of systematically structuring the evaluation process, the methodology ensures the compatibility between the assessment method(s) used and the actual problem to be tackled.

The evaluation methodology proposed and deployed here is based on a blend of three multi-criteria evaluation methods. The core of the methodology is formed by Regime Analysis; this pairwise comparison method is extended with two complementary methods, notably the Flag Model and Saaty's analytic Hierarchical process (AHP) (see Fig. 1). Due to the assessment of impacts in qualitative terms CBA is inappropriate for the decision-making procedure in our case study. Therefore we have to rely on multicriteria analysis, in this case Regime Analysis. Since the plan impacts are all measured in qualitative terms we cannot use quantitative weights or preference statements in our analysis. Saaty's AHP is used in order to overcome this problem. By means of this method ordinal preference statements are transformed into metric (cardinal) data

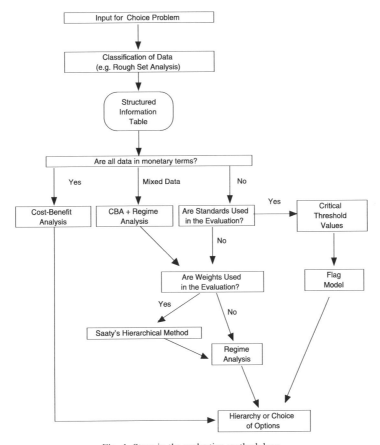

Fig. 1. Steps in the evaluation methodology.

and used in the multicriteria analysis. The existence of development constraints and so-called reference values makes it necessary to deploy an assessment technique that is capable to carry out such a kind of analysis. The Flag Model is capable of analysing policy alternatives in the light of *a priori* defined set of constraints. A concise description of the above-mentioned methods can be found in Section 3.

Step 1. Specification of choice problem

In this step of the evaluation methodology the generation and definition of alternatives takes place. Besides this, the selection of criteria, as well as the assessment of effects are considered. The assessment of relevant effects entails the changes in welfare positions of all stakeholders. Part of these effects can be measured in monetary terms, but part may have to be measured in other than monetary terms such as environmental effects, travel time, etc. Clearly, the identification of the effects of choice possibilities is not easy, but the valuation of these effects is quite a different issue, which also takes place in this step of the evaluation process. The result of this first step is the creation of a data set on the information architecture. This data set is still rudimentary and needs to be analysed more closely in the second step.

Step 2. Analysis of information

In this stage of the evaluation process a more in-depth analysis of the data gathered takes place. Questions on the type of data to be examined (ordinal, cardinal, etc.), the completeness of the data set, the mutual relationships among the data, reduction of the data set without losing information and so forth, are addressed. Data classification methods like Discriminant Analysis, Principal Component Methods or Rough Set Analysis may be meaningfully applied in this phase of the evaluation process (see for an overview of Rough Set Analysis Pawlak, 1991; Slowinski, 1995).

The result of this step is the assembly of a structured information table (impact table) which forms the input for an evaluation method (or combination of methods).

Step 3. Choice of appropriate evaluation method

The methods included in an evaluation methodology differ according to their aim and characteristics in practical decision support situations, in particular in terms of their level of measurement, their classification, and the use of reference values. Although the methods considered do differ in many respects they have one common feature, viz. the aim to evaluate the pros and cons of a planned transport policy initiative or infrastructure investment. The choice of the appropriate method (or combination of methods) in any given transport policy context depends therefore on the features of the policy problem at hand, on the aims of the policy analysis, and on the underlying information base. The ultimately proposed and deployed evaluation methodology has to ensure compatibility and consistency between the evaluation method used and the actual transport problem to be tackled.

Clearly, this approach towards the selection of the class of multicriteria methods becomes more relevant if traditional evaluation methods, such as CBA, cannot be applied due to information shortages or specific requirements in a decision-support environment.

The following steps seem to be indispensable in the rational selection of an appropriate evaluation method (see Fig. 1, Step 3):

1. If all effects are quantitative and in monetary terms, apply CBA.
2. If parts of the information are expressed in monetary terms and others in quantitative, non-monetary or qualitative terms, apply CBA to this part of the data set. This can only be done if all requirements are met for this type of evaluation. After the application of CBA, the results should be combined with the remaining part of the data set by introducing the cost–benefit ratio's in the database. Apply next to this newly created data set (quantitative or a mixed quantitative–qualitative data set) a proper multicriteria method, notably Regime Analysis.
3. If effects are quantitative and/or qualitative, but not monetary in nature, and if no standards (or critical levels) are used in the evaluation process, then the application of Regime Analysis is in order. In the Regime Analysis Software there is also an option available to include weights in the evaluation process. This can be done by means of Saaty's AHP method.
4. If standards or critical values are used in the evaluation process, one should resort to the Flag approach. The Flag Model evaluates the selected alternatives in relation to pre-defined standards.

Step 4. Evaluation of alternatives; hierarchy or choice of options

In this step the evaluation of alternatives takes place by means of the selected (combination of) evaluation method(s), weights or pre-defined standards. The final result will be a rank-order of alternatives, a classification of these alternatives or a final selection.

In conclusion, the methods included in our evaluation methodology are based on the foundations of CBA, and form a decision-support complement to this type of analysis in a modern evaluation process.

3. The evaluation methods used: a description

The designed methodology is based on a joint use of various multicriteria evaluation methods. The core of the methodology is formed by Regime Analysis, extended with complementary methods, viz. the Flag Model and Saaty's AHP method. We will now describe the methods in some more detail. We will start with a presentation of the so-called Flag Model.

3.1. The flag model

The main purpose of the Flag Model is to analyse whether one or more policy alternatives can be classified as acceptable or not in the light of an a priori set of constraints. The model does so by comparing impact values with a set of reference values called critical threshold values (CTV). The Flag Model has been designed to assess the degree to which competing alternatives fulfil pre-defined standards or normative statements in an evaluation process (see for applications of the Flag Model Nijkamp and Ouwersloot, 1998; Nijkamp and Vreeker, 2000). There are four important steps in applying the model:
- Identifying a set of measurable indicators.
- Assessing the impact of the alternatives on the above-mentioned indicators.
- Establishing a set of normative reference values (standards).
- Evaluation of the relevant alternatives.

The input of the Flag Model is formed by an impact matrix (structured information table) containing multi-dimensional information on a set of policy-relevant variables or criteria; this matrix contains the values that the indicators assume for each alternative considered. Therefore, the methodology requires the identification and definition of relevant indicators, which are suitable for further empirical treatment in the evaluation process.

The choice of indicators depends on the choice problem to be addressed; in general, the indicators should be in agreement with the nature of the choice issue under scrutiny and also consider the objectives to be taken into consideration. One significant threat always encountered when defining indicators is the likelihood that the number of indicators to be considered tends to grow limitless; and, to complicate matters, some indicators are encompassed within other indicators. In order to avoid the complication of a large number of indicators (which would be difficult to examine) and which often contain less relevant or unnecessary information, it may be a helpful approach to use a hierarchical approach based on a tree-like structure. Such an approach corresponds to the idea of aggregation and disaggregation of indicators that are deemed fundamental to the problem examined. For instance, a distinction can be made between macro, meso and micro indicators, or on the basis of relevant time or geographical scales. The indicators in the Flag Model have two formal attributes, class and type. There are normally three classes of indicators in the Flag Model, which correspond to the following dimensions: (1) environmental, (2) social, and (3) economical. The second attribute, type, relates to the fact that some indicators, e.g., accessibility to water, have high scores showing a preferable situation, whereas others, such as a pollution indicator, have low scores showing also a preferable situation. This difference, in terms of benefit or cost-criteria, is captured in the model under the attribute 'type of indicator'.

For each indicator in the Flag Model, preferably a CTV has to be defined. These values represent the reference system for judging alternatives. Since in many cases experts and decision-makers may have conflicting views on the precise level of the acceptable threshold values, a bandwidth of CTVs – by way of sensitivity analysis – can be used in the analysis. This bandwidth ranges from a maximum value (CTV_{max}) to a minimum value (CTV_{min}). This can be represented as follows:

Section A	Green	No reason for specific concern
Section B	Yellow	Be very alert
Section C	Red	Reverse trends
Section D	Black	Stop further growth

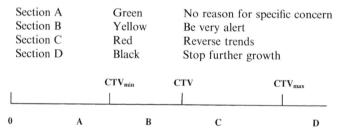

The assessment module of the Flag Model provides a number of instruments for the analysis of alternatives. This analysis can be carried out in two ways. The first option is the inspection of a single alternative. The second one is the comparison of choice options. In the first procedure we decide whether an alternative is acceptable or not. In the latter case of comparing two alternatives, we decide which alternative scores best. This last option may be interpreted as a basic form of multicriteria analysis.

The Flag Model can operate both as a classification procedure and as a visualisation method. In the former case – for example, in combination with Regime Analysis – the Flag Model can determine the acceptable alternatives; accordingly, the examined alternatives can then be ranked by means of Regime Analysis. In the latter case, we can utilise the Flag Model to visualise in an appealing way the results obtained, for example, from Regime Analysis or from another set of classification or evaluation methods.

One of the major merits of the Flag Model is its potential for representation. There are three approaches to such a representation: a qualitative, a quantitative and a hybrid approach. The idea of having three possible options for result representation is based upon the necessity for the Flag Model and the accompanying software to be flexible to the requirements of its users. Rather than to be used as substitutions, the three modes of analysis are complementary to each other.

The qualitative approach only takes into account the colours of the flags. This entails flag counts and cross-tabulation. This approach merely displays in various insightful ways the results obtained from the evaluation. The quantitative approach defines the values of the standards that may be acceptable or not. To achieve such results, we need to standardise the indicator (values), because they refer to different aspects, which are next expressed by different measurement scales. Finally, the hybrid form regards the existence of both qualitative and quantitative aspects.

3.2. Regime Analysis

Multi-criteria analysis comprises various classes of decision-making approaches. The multi-assessment method used in our methodology is Regime Analysis. Regime Analysis is a discrete multi-assessment method suitable to assess projects as well as policies. The strength of Regime Analysis is that it is able to cope with binary, ordinal, categorical and cardinal (ratio and interval scale) data, while the method is also able to use mixed data. This applies to both the effects and the weights in the evaluation of alternatives.

The fundamental framework of the method is based upon two kinds of input data: an impact matrix (structured information table) and a set of (politically determined) weights (Nijkamp et al., 1990; Hinloopen et al., 1983). The impact matrix is composed of elements that measure the effect of each considered alternative in relation to each policy relevant criterion. The set of weights incorporates information concerning the relative importance of the criteria in the evaluation. In case there is no prioritisation of criteria in the evaluation process, all criteria will be assigned the same numerical weight value.

Regime Analysis is a discrete multicriteria method, and in particular, it is a generalised form of concordance analysis, based in essence on a generalisation of pairwise comparison methods. In order to gain a better understanding of Regime Analysis; let us reiterate the basic principles of concordance analysis.

Concordance analysis is an evaluation method in which the basic idea is to rank a set of alternatives by means of their pairwise comparisons in relation to the chosen criteria. We consider a choice problem where we have a set of alternatives i and a set of criteria k. We begin our analysis by comparing alternative i with alternative k in relation to all criteria. After having done this, we select all criteria for which alternative i performs better than, or is equal to, alternative k. This class of criteria we call a "concordance set". Similarly, we define the class of criteria for which alternative i performs worse than, or is equal to, alternative k. This set of criteria is called a "discordance set".

We now need to rank the alternatives. In order to do so, we introduce the concordance index. The concordance index will be the sum of the weights that are related to the criteria for which i is better than k. We call this sum C_{ik}. Then we calculate the concordance index for the same alternatives, but by considering the criteria for which k is better than i, i.e., C_{ki}.

After having calculated these two sums, we subtract these two values in order to obtain the net concordance index $\mu_{ik} = C_{ik} - C_{ki}$.

Because in most cases we have only ordinal information about the weights (and no trade-offs), our interest is in the sign of the net concordance index μ_{ik}. If the sign is positive, this will indicate that alternative i is more attractive than alternative k; otherwise, the opposite holds.

We are now able to rank our alternatives. We note that due to the ordinal nature of the information in the indicator μ_{ik} no information exists on to the size of the difference between the alternatives; it is only the sign of the indicator that matters.

We may also solve the complicating situation that it may not be able to determine an unambiguous result, i.e., a complete ranking of alternatives, because of the problem of ambiguity in the sign of the index μ. In order to solve this problem we introduce a performance indicator – as a semi-probability measure – p_{ik} for the dominance of criteria i with respect to criteria k as follows:

$$p_{ij} = \text{prob}(\mu_{ij} > 0).$$

Next, we define an aggregate probability measure, which represents the success (performance) score as follows:

$$p_i = \frac{1}{I-1} \sum_{j \neq i} p_{ij},$$

where i is the number of chosen alternatives.

The problem here is to assess the value of p_{ij} and of p_i. The Regime Analysis then assumes a specific probability distribution of the set of feasible weights. This assumption is based upon the Laplace criterion in the case of decision-making under uncertainty.

In the case of a probability distribution of qualitative information, in principle, the use of stochastic analysis will suffice, which is consistent with an originally ordinal data set. This procedure helps to overcome the methodological problems we may encounter by applying a numerical operation on qualitative data.

From the viewpoint of numerical analysis, the Regime method identifies the feasible domain within which feasible values of the weights w_I must fall in order to be compatible with the condition imposed by their probability value. By means of a random generator, numerous values of the weights can be calculated. This allows us at the end to calculate the probability score (or success score) p_I for each alternative i. We can then determine an unambiguous solution and rank the alternatives.

Regime Analysis is able to examine both quantitative and cardinal data. In case of choice problems with qualitative data, we first need to transform the qualitative data into cardinal data and then apply the Regime method. The Regime Software method is able to do so consistently. [1] Due to this necessity, Regime Analysis is classified as an indirect method for qualitative data. This

---

[1] Regime analysis is included in the software package SAMIsoft, a deliverable of the EU project (SAMI, 1998).

is an important positive feature. When we apply the cardinalisation of qualitative data through indirect methods such as the Regime Analysis, we do not lose information like in direct methods. This is due to the fact that in the direct methods only the ordinal content of the available quantitative information is used.

3.3. Saaty's analytical hierarchical process method

The core of Saaty's method is an ordinal pairwise comparison of all criteria. In other words, it addresses in particular preference statements. Per pair of criteria the decision-maker is asked to which degree a criterion is of more importance than the other. By means of these comparisons the method defines the relative position of one criterion in relation to all other criteria. By using an eigenvalue matrix technique, quantitative weights can be assigned to the criteria.

The Saaty method (AHP method) has been developed by Thomas Lorie Saaty in the 1970s (Saaty, 1988). This method is based upon three important components:
1. The hierarchical articulation of the elements of the decision problem.
2. The identification of the priority scheme.
3. A check on the logic consistency of the priority expressed.

The procedure is conducted in different steps. The first steps consist of the definition of the problem and of the identification of the criteria in a hierarchy of five levels:
- Level 1: general objective(s),
- Level 2: criteria,
- Level 3: sub-criteria,
- Level 4: indicators,
- Level 5: index.

After defining the hierarchy articulation of the elements, the second step consists of assessing the value of the weights related to each criterion through a pairwise comparison between the elements.

The SAATY method employs a semantic 9-point scale (Table 1) for the assignment of priority values. This scale relates numbers to judgements, which express the possible results of the comparison in qualitative terms. In this way, different elements can be weighted with a homogeneous measurement scale.

Through this method, the weight assigned to each single criterion reflects the importance which every party/agent/group involved in the project attaches to the objectives. In addition, the method verifies the fit between the components of the weight vector and the original judgements. From the pairwise comparison a 'comparison matrix' is derived out of which, through the eigenvector

Table 1
Semantic scale of Saaty

Value	Definition
1	Equal importance
3	Moderate importance
5	Strong importance
7	Very strong importance
9	Extreme importance
2,4,6,8	Intermediate value

approach, it is possible to calculate the weight vector to be used for a subsequent evaluation and investigation. Finally, the method is able to check the consistency of the matrix through the calculation of the eigenvalues.

4. Application of the evaluation methodology and methods

Multicriteria methods have been applied to a great variety of environmental and land use problems. We will offer here an illustration from the aviation sector in The Netherlands.

In the past decades various stakeholders in The Netherlands discussed the problems concerning the development of the Dutch airports. These discussions were often focussed on environmental effects of airports (e.g., nuisance). The above-mentioned discussions and problems are not solely related to the national airport Schiphol Amsterdam, but also to the regional airports in The Netherlands.

While in the past discussions and decisions on the development of airports were often dominated by economic arguments favouring the extension of the airport concerned, nowadays an assessment of all related (direct and indirect) effects takes place.

In this part of the paper, we illustrate the application of the evaluation methodology developed above by means of a case study on conflicting plans (and policy views) for airport expansion in the Maastricht area in the southern part of The Netherlands.

First, we will describe the main characteristics of the problem at hand with the aim to illustrate its complexity and to identify the necessary information that plays a role in the evaluation and choice of alternatives. Next, we will apply Regime Analysis and the Flag Model in order to evaluate the choice alternatives.

4.1. Maastricht Aachen airport: a short description

In 1945, the US liberation army erected a military airport in the Maastricht area in the southern part of The Netherlands. In the subsequent decades this small military airport became a regional airport, which is nowadays named Maastricht Aachen airport (MAA).

At the moment most aircraft movements from MAA are related to passenger traffic. Each year, around 350.000 passengers use the airport as departure point or final destination. Airfreight handling at the airport is limited to 33.000 ton each year, since the landing strip is not long enough; it can only accommodate small freighter aircraft. Besides this, the strip is only opened for a limited period during the day (e.g., no flights during the night). This leads to a diminishing comparative advantage and a feeble position on the airfreight market with respect to other European (regional) airports.

To cope with these problems and to improve the profitability of the airport, four alternative development scenarios were designed as possible policy strategies. The four scenarios differ very much in nature and aims. The scenarios are heterogeneous and designed as extreme points of a so-called feasibility spectrum. The first scenario *Business as Usual* is designed as a reference scenario and refers to the situation where no changes in current trends and policies occur. The second scenario *MAA serving as passenger airport* is aimed at analysing the impacts of changes in the logistics of the airport. *MAA serving the Euregio* is constructed to evaluate the impacts of land use changes in the region. The last scenario *Tradable Permits* is dominated by changes in the institutional setting of the airport. In this scenario changes occur in the legislation regarding the emission of CO_2 in The Netherlands. This scenario differs in nature somewhat from the previous ones, but has been mentioned several times in recent discussions. It can also be applied in combination with the three preceding ones. These four options will now concisely be discussed.

4.1.1. Scenario 1: Business as Usual

This scenario serves as a reference scenario. Current trends are used to make predictions about the future. The main purpose of this scenario is to evaluate the situation where there are no changes in current trends and policies. This scenario can be summarised as follows:
1. A further decrease of aircargo handling at MAA; the decrease will be 5.000 tons a year.
2. A stabilisation of passengers traffic at a stable level of 350.000 passengers a year.
3. A substitution of slots and aircraft movements originally designated for airfreight services toward passenger transport.

4.1.2. Scenario 2: MAA serves as a Passenger Airport

In this choice option MAA will concentrate on the passengers market as a source of profit. Although freight handling will still be present at MAA, it is not recognised as the "core business". In this scenario a new runway (the east–west strip) is constructed in order to accommodate larger aircrafts at MAA. Besides this, the Dutch National Aviation School will leave the airport. This gives the opportunity to extend the number of passenger flights with 55.000 aircraft movements. This scenario can be summarised as follows:
1. Construction of a new runway.
2. Outplacement of the Dutch National Aviation School to another airport, thus leaving room for 55.000 additional aircraft movements.
3. No further expansion of freight handling at MAA.

4.1.3. Scenario 3: MAA as an Euregio airport

In this third scenario MAA will serve as the main regional airport in the Euregio (see Fig. 2). In this role MAA has to attract passengers from regions nearby in Belgium and Germany.

Besides this, MAA has to play a major role in the freight market for the Euregio. Therefore, the construction of a new (east–west) runway is necessary. This runway should be larger than the one in Scenario 2. To summarise:
1. Construction of a new large runway at MAA to accommodate larger passenger flows and freight aircraft.
2. Establishment of an open night regime, so that starts and landings are allowed for 24 h a day.

4.1.4. Scenario 4: Tradable Permits

In this scenario permits concerning the emission of CO_2 are traded among the regional airports in The Netherlands. The national number of permits is fixed. In such a case airports can only expand their activities, if they buy permits from other regional airports. In this scenario MAA is a buyer on the market of permits. This means in concise terms:
1. MAA is a buyer on the market of CO_2 permits.
2. MAA is not capable or allowed to expand its activities without buying additional permits.

Fig. 2. The Euregio.

3. Schiphol Amsterdam, the national airport of The Netherlands, is not a player on the market. In Section 5 of the paper we will pay attention to the criteria and indicators which are used to measure the effects exerted by the above-mentioned scenarios on the Maastricht region. The scores the scenarios assume on the indicators form an important input for our Flag Model and the Regime Analysis, and hence in the evaluation methodology.

4.2. Hierarchical definition of criteria and assembling the impact matrix

The choice process of a transport infrastructure project against the background of the concept of sustainability should be based upon a broad set of criteria which allow for the simultaneous consideration of a project impact from different viewpoints, notably economical, social and environmental. The corollary of adopting this view is that an optimisation of logistic functionality will not result in an excessive cost for the environment and for society (i.e., a burden higher than the system's carrying capacity). Such a carrying capacity is not solely related to the infrastructure's physical capacity, but also to the carrying capacity of the environment. The latter concept is defined through the inclusion of pollution (of water, air and soil, in visual and acoustic forms, etc.) of the territory's capability of accommodating new infrastructure and of the society's carrying capacity, expressed, e.g. in terms of safety levels.

Main attention in our case study is devoted to the attainment of the best possible solution, viz. one that is functionally effective and at the same time compatible with constraints imposed by relevant environmental and social circumstances. The evaluation criteria used in this assessment are defined in relation to the concept of sustainability, notably through the identification of three main classes of indicators: economy, accessibility and environment.

For each of these classes a list of indicators has been specified. The latter ones stem from a thorough analysis of site-specific problems and allow us to evaluate each alternative in respect to

Table 2
Criteria used in the airport evaluation process

Main criteria	Sub-criteria	Type	Scale	CTV_{min}	CTV	CTV_{max}
Economic	Economic benefits for the region	Benefit	Qualitative	3	5	7
	Employment in sector transport and logistics	Benefit	Qualitative	3	5	7
	Employment in sector finance and business to business	Benefit	Qualitative	3	5	7
	Employment in sector tourism and recreation	Benefit	Qualitative	3	5	7
	Development and supply of industrial sites	Benefit	Qualitative	3	5	7
	Infrastructure	Benefit	Qualitative	3	5	7
	Business traffic	Benefit	Qualitative	3	5	7
	Supply of skilled jobs	Benefit	Qualitative	3	5	7
Social	Nuisance	Benefit	Qualitative	3	5	7
	Safety	Benefit	Qualitative	3	5	7
	Health	Benefit	Qualitative	3	5	7
	Recreational traffic	Benefit	Qualitative	3	5	7
	Total income	Benefit	Qualitative	3	5	7
	Residential areas	Benefit	Qualitative	3	5	7
Environment	Natural conservation areas	Benefit	Qualitative	3	5	7
	Disturbance of Fauna's habitat	Benefit	Qualitative	3	5	7
	Air quality	Benefit	Qualitative	3	5	7
	Water quality	Benefit	Qualitative	3	5	7
	Soil quality	Benefit	Qualitative	3	5	7
	Biodiversity	Benefit	Qualitative	3	5	7

pre-defined objectives. In Table 2 the indicators are summarised according to their main types (economic, social, environment). At the right-hand side of Table 2, three columns are added that show the specified CTVs for each indicator; these CTVs are used as input for the Flag Model.

The various data referring to the sub-criteria are in our case study expressed and measured on an ordinal scale, through which numerical values on a 9-point scale (where the highest value represents the best score) were assigned to the various effects. We can now summarise the consequences each distinct alternative has by means of an impact matrix (see Table 3). In this matrix the pre-defined criteria are linked to the alternatives by means of the values each alternative scores on the pre-defined criteria.

4.3. Regime Analysis; obtaining a rank–order of alternatives

The Regime Method described in Section 3.2 allows us to analyse an impact matrix (Table 3) containing mixed data and a weight vector in order to calculate a rank–order of alternatives. The weights may be assumed to be equal, but also alternative weight compositions can be handled by means of a sensitivity analysis.

Table 3
The impact matrix for alternative airport expansion plans

Criterion	A	B	C	D
Economic				
Economic benefits for the region (+)	4	8	9	6
Employment in sector transport and logistics (+)	4	5	8	6
Employment in sector finance and business to business (+)	5	9	7	6
Employment in sector tourism and recreation (+)	6	5	1	3
Development and supply of industrial sites (+)	5	3	1	6
Infrastructure (+)	5	8	9	6
Business traffic (+)	6	9	8	6
Supply of skilled jobs (+)	4	7	9	6
Social				
Nuisance (+)	5	8	5	3
Safety (+)	5	7	2	3
Health (+)	5	6	5	3
Recreational traffic (+)	6	9	9	7
Total income (+)	4	6	7	6
Residential areas (+)	5	5	2	5
Environment				
Natural conservation areas (+)	5	4	1	3
Disturbance of Fauna's habitat (+)	5	8	1	3
Air quality (+)	4	6	1	4
Water quality (+)	4	5	2	4
Soil quality (+)	4	3	2	4
Biodiversity (+)	4	5	2	4

The software used to evaluate all alternatives in this case study (SAMIsoft) considers all the scores as benefit criteria; this means that the higher an alternative scores on a criteria the better. Therefore, our impact matrix (Table 3) is constructed of only benefit criteria and cost criteria were transformed into benefit criteria.

In our case study research, the Regime Analysis was conducted in two steps. First, a Regime Analysis was performed on each of the main classes (Economic, Social and Environment). By means of the values each alternative scores on the relevant sub-criteria, the scores for each main class were determined. These results are presented by the intermediate results in Table 4. In the second step the intermediate results formed the input, together with a uniform weight vector, for a final Regime Analysis. The results of this analysis are presented in Table 4 and Fig. 3.

The intermediate results show that alternatives B and C (Passenger Airport and Euregio) have the highest scores on the economic indicators. Besides this, alternative B scores also very well on the social and environmental indicators. It will be no surprise that this scenario is the most favoured one in the final Regime Analysis. Accordingly, the final rank–order is:

1. Scenario 2: Passenger Airport.
2. Scenario 3: MAA serving the Euregio.
3. Scenario 1: Business as Usual.
4. Scenario 4: Tradable Permits.

Table 4
Rank–order of alternatives (weights of criteria are equal)

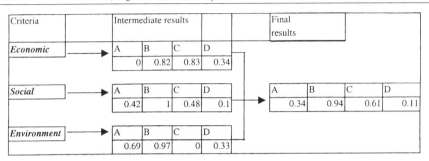

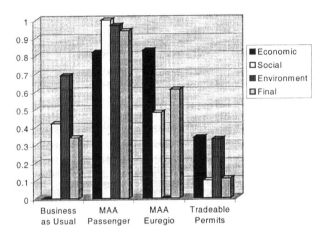

Fig. 3. Results of the regime analysis.

4.4. Acceptability of alternatives; application of the Flag Model

In this subsection we will illustrate the application of the Flag Model to check the acceptability of the four alternatives, in this case from the viewpoint of the sustainability concept, with regard to a set of reference values (CTVs). This analysis is carried out by means of the Flag Model that is included in the multicriteria evaluation software package SAMIsoft.

The Flag Model needs two types of input: an impact matrix (see Table 3) and a set of CTVs. The impact matrix is formed by the values that the indicators assume for each alternative considered. Besides the construction of the impact matrix, for each indicator a CTV has to be defined. These values represent the reference system for judging the alternatives.

The use of CTVs is related to a normative view on the concept of sustainability (see Nijkamp and Ouwersloot, 1998; Nijkamp and Vreeker, 2000, where more attention is paid to the question how sustainability can be identified as a normative orientation for policy). In other words, the question is: Is it possible to define a set of reference values or CTVs (limits, standards or norms) to trace and evaluate the impacts of policies and infrastructure projects on the environment and society?

In this context, the notion of carrying capacity is of importance, as it indicates the maximum use of environmental resources that is still compatible with an ecologically sustainable economic development. This means that a CTV cannot be exceeded without causing irreversible and unacceptable damage or costs to the environment or society.

Table 3 and the list of CTVs in Table 2 form the input for the Flag Model. Table 5 shows the results of the analysis by means of the frequency of flags per alternative in respect to each relevant main class of criteria. In Figs. 4–7 the frequencies of flags are presented by means of charts.

Our investigation of the results in Table 5 and Figs. 4–7 shows that Scenario 2 MAA Passenger Airport is generally most acceptable/sustainable; it has in fact 9 green and 8 yellow flags. Most of these flags are scored on the economic and social indicators. This scenario has however, some negative effects on some environmental indictors; three of them are even labelled red. Although the third scenario MAA serving the Euregio has 8 green and 2 yellow flags, it has a tremendous negative impact on the environment in the region, as is shown by the 6 black flags. The Tradable Permits scenario is not an option, since it is not economically viable, according to the 6 Red flags

Table 5
Frequencies of flags

	Business as Usual				MAA Passenger				MAA Euregio				Tradable Permits			
	B	R	Y	G	B	R	Y	G	B	R	Y	G	B	R	Y	G
Economic	0	3	5	0	0	1	2	5	2	0	0	6	0	6	0	0
Social	0	1	5	0	0	0	3	3	2	0	2	2	0	1	7	0
Environment	0	4	2	0	0	2	3	1	6	0	0	0	0	3	2	1

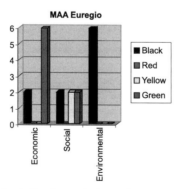

Fig. 4. Flag frequencies for Business as Usual.

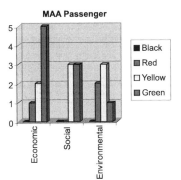

Fig. 5. Flag frequencies for MAA as Passenger Airport.

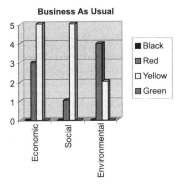

Fig. 6. Flag frequencies for MAA Euregio.

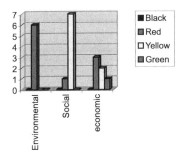

Fig. 7. Flag frequencies for Tradable Permits.

on the economic indicators. The impacts on the social indicators are positive. If we take a close look at the Business as Usual scenario, we see that this will not improve the development of MAA. In the long term it may be expected that the economic and environmental consequences of current trends and policies become more negative.

5. Some reflections

The aim of this paper is to offer decision-makers a methodology and a set of techniques in order to analyse the acceptability and priority of choice possibilities in the case of qualitative or mixed data on either effects of choices or policy priorities, or both. Three complementary evaluation methods have been proposed.

The application of the methods has led to the identification of the best possible ranking for each alternative as well as the degree of acceptability of each alternative with respect to a pre-defined set of CTVs. The results turned out to be plausible; they may perhaps not always coincide with prevailing political wisdom, but offer on the other hand a platform for a structured debate.

In conclusion, the application of the multicriteria methods points out that these are very useful tools to deal with conflicts in a decision-making process. Three critical points deserve thorough attention. First, the methodology and accompanying software allows the decision-maker to analyse conflicting choices and the degree of conflict among various policy objectives. Second, the methodology offers the decision-maker also the possibility to take into account the preferences of policy makers and stakeholders in a decision-making process, as well as to measure the impacts of these viewpoints. Finally, the use of CTVs provides the decision-maker with an operational framework for environmental sustainability analysis on a given site or in a given area.

References

De Brucker, K., Ontwikkeling Van Een Eclectisch Evaluatie-Instrument Voor De Sociaal-Economische Evaluatie Van Complexe Investeringsprojecten, Met Een Toepassing Op Het Project Seine-Scheldeverbinding. Ph.D. thesis, Universiteit Antwerpen, 2000.
Fujita, M., Krugman, P., Venables, A.J., 1999. The Spatial Economy. MIT Press, Cambridge, MA.
Hinloopen, E., Nijkamp, P., Rietveld, P., 1983. Qualitative discrete multiple criteria choice models. Regional Planning Regional Science and Urban Economics, pp. 77–102.
Layard, R. (Ed.), 1997. Cost–Benefit Analysis. Penguin Books, England.
Mishan, E.J., 1971. Cost–Benefit Analysis. Allen & Unwin, London.
Nijkamp, P., Rietveld, P., Voogd, H., 1990. Multicriteria Analysis for Physical Planning. Elsevier, Amsterdam.
Nijkamp, P., Blaas, E., 1996. Impact Assesment and Evaluation in Transport Planning. Kluwer Academic Publishers, Dordrecht.
Nijkamp, P., Ouwersloot, H., 1998. A decision support system for regional sustainable development. In: van den Bergh, J.C.J.M., Hofkes, M.W. (Eds.), The Flag Model Theory and Implementation of Sustainable Development. Kluwer Academic Publishers, Dordrecht.
Nijkamp, P., Vreeker, R., 2000. Sustainability assessment of development scenarios: methodology and application to Thailand. Ecological Economics 33, 7–27.
Pawlak, Z., 1991. Rough Sets. Kluwer Academic Publishers, Dordrecht.
Pelt, M.J.F. van, 1994. Ecological Sustainability and Project Appraisal. Aldershot, Avebury.

Rietveld, P., Bruinsma, F.R., 1999. Transport Systems Economic Change and Policy Analysis. Vrije Universiteit, Amsterdam.
Rietveld, P. Rouwendal, J., 2000. Welvaartsaspecten Bij de Evaluatie Van Infrastructuur-projecten. Ministerie van Verkeer en Waterstaat, Den Haag.
Rietveld, P., 2000. Afwegingskader voor Beleid in Verkeer en Vervoer. Vrije Universiteit Amsterdam, Amsterdam.
Saaty, T.L., 1988. Decision Making for Leaders. Rws Publication, Pittsburgh, PA.
SAMI, Strategic Assessment Methodology for the Interaction of CTP-Instruments, 1998. Deliverable 2: Review of Strategic Assessment Tool and Methods, DG7 Transport Research (Strategic), European Union, Fourth Framework Programme.
Slowinski, R., 1995. Intelligent Decision Support. Kluwer Academic Publishers, Dordrecht.

6

Airport Infrastructure for the Airbus A380

Cost Recovery and Pricing

Peter Forsyth

The author is grateful to Anthony Bell, Nathalie McCaughey, and Neelu Seetaram for helpful research assistance, and to Anming Zhang, Paul Hooper, David Starkie, and Cathal Guiomard for helpful comments, but claims any errors as his own.

Abstract

The introduction of the new large aircraft, the Airbus A380, will require investments by airports to enable them to handle it. These investments will be in the nature of sunk costs, such as in widening runways. As such they will pose problems for pricing, cost recovery, and investment evaluation. Short-run pricing efficiency involves not imposing any specific charge for the use of the aircraft, which will mean that users will not face the costs they impose. This, however, could create problems in terms of signals for investment. In addition, the ownership/regulatory environment within which most airports operate will further increase the incentives for excessive investment.

1.0 Introduction

The introduction of the new large aircraft, the Airbus A380, will pose cost recovery issues for airports. Some airports are able to handle the aircraft now, but only if they impose constraints on the use of the airport by other users. To handle the A380 without imposing these costs, they will need to invest, by widening runways, realigning taxiways, and by making modifications to terminals. Most of these investments will be in the nature of sunk costs. Once they have been made, the marginal costs of operating the A380 at an airport are likely to be negligible, and comparable to the marginal costs of operating other aircraft.

This then raises a question of how best to recover costs at airports that are investing to handle the A380. As with other cost recovery problems, a number of related problems arise:

- If the marginal cost of using the A380 at an airport is zero, should any additional specific charge on its use be levied?
- If not, and airports need to recover the costs of their investments to handle the A380, how should price structures be adjusted?
- What role might two-part tariffs play in efficient pricing, and can they ensure that 'users pay'?
- If prices for the use of the A380 are set at zero, how can investments by airports to accommodate them be assessed, and what signals will airlines face whether to purchase the aircraft?
- When efficient pricing and investment solutions can be devised, will the ownership/regulatory environment most airports operate within provide the incentives to set prices and assess investment correctly?

The nature of airport cost recovery, and the price structures that can be used to achieve it, are considered first. After this, the Airbus A380 and its airport requirements are considered. In Section 4, optimal pricing in the short run is considered, and in Section 5 investment for the long run is considered. In Section 6, the incentives for efficient pricing and investment are considered in a world where airports are either publicly owned or privately owned but subject to regulation; these incentives are weak, thus increasing the risk of excessive investment. Finally, the key points of the paper are synthesised and some broad conclusions are drawn.

2.0 Cost Recovery at Airports

Cost recovery is not normally a problem for all but small, lightly used, airports. Airports typically possess considerable market power, and have discretion over the level of their prices. Cost recovery is quite straightforward. The issue is not so much whether it can be achieved as how (for a discussion of several of these issues, see Oum and Zhang, 1990).

Airports are usefully thought of as consisting of two sets of facilities — the airside facilities, including runways, taxiways and aprons, and the landside facilities, including terminals. The airside facilities represent large sunk costs — ground preparation, land reclamation, and constructing runways and taxiways, are major costs that are sunk. They are very long lasting, and there are significant indivisibilities present, since one runway can handle a large amount of traffic, and very few airports have more than two or three runways. Many airports have ample airside capacity, and once it has been provided, it is generally taken that the marginal cost of using it is negligible (though for an alternative view, see Hogan and Starkie, 2004).

There are elements of sunk costs and indivisibilities with terminals, though these are less prominent than with airside facilities. Terminals can be expanded, though it is cost effective to build ahead of demand, and to avoid frequent matching increases in demand with increases in capacity. In addition, there are running costs of terminals, along with congestion costs as the throughput approaches the design capacity. Thus there will be positive costs associated with additional passengers, though these will be below average costs, except for busy terminals.

The indivisibility aspect of airport development creates problems for cost recovery. It often makes sense to construct very large and expensive new airports as a way of expanding capacity — this was the case with Osaka-Kansai and Hong Kong. These airports are built to a scale that results in considerable excess capacity for some time after they are built. Additions to airport capacity, such as new runways, come in discrete chunks. It is arguable that it is the indivisibility aspect of airports, rather than the presence of large sunk costs, which leads to a cost recovery problem.

Large sunk costs, *per se*, need not impose a cost recovery problem. If there are constant returns to scale, efficient pricing (at short-run marginal cost) is consistent with cost recovery. There is some evidence that most major airports fall within the range of approximately constant returns to scale (see Graham, 2003). There are some scale economies at low scale, but these peter out at the scale of moderately small airports. However, airports involve substantial indivisibilities, and cost recovery, with efficient pricing, may need to be accomplished over a period of several decades. A new airport is built, and for a long time capacity is ample, and efficient prices are minimal. Over time demand grows, and eventually it pushes against capacity. Marginal cost rises sharply, and efficient prices generate large revenues. Under constant returns to scale, efficient prices will cover costs, but it will be the revenues in a few busy years that cover most of the sunk costs.

Here there is not so much a problem of cost recovery *per se*, as one of the period over which it is to be achieved. Typically, owners wish to even out the revenue stream, and recover depreciation and the cost of capital on a year-by-year basis, even when the airport has ample capacity. The arbitrary insistence on year-by-year cost recovery results in a divergence from efficient pricing, with prices in ample capacity years being inefficiently high, and in excess demand years being inefficiently low. Cost recovery, over the long run, does not necessitate a divergence from efficient pricing; however, cost recovery on a year-by-year basis will.

Most major airports have a degree of market power, due to their locations. The typical city has one major centrally located airport, and most traffic will prefer to use the convenient central airport, even if there are other airports on or beyond the urban fringe. Some large cities have more than one airport, though mostly these are under single ownership (for example, BAA owns both Heathrow and Gatwick in London). Thus the typical airport will have considerable market power, and demand elasticities will be low or very low.

For an airport that does not face excess demand, prices set at marginal cost will fail to cover total cost. Marginal cost pricing of runways and taxiways would imply zero prices, and marginal cost pricing of terminals may yield non-zero prices, but ones that fail to cover all terminal costs. To cover costs, airports have traditionally set charges based on aircraft weight. Weight is a rough proxy for the inverse of the elasticity of demand. Large heavy aircraft carrying large loads of passengers on long haul flights have inelastic demand for the use of the airport. For smaller lighter aircraft on short haul flights airport charges make up a much higher proportion of total costs, and the elasticity with respect to airport charges will be correspondingly higher. Thus, weight based pricing schedules would amount to a rough approximation to Ramsey pricing, and would be a tolerably efficient means of covering costs. Recently many airports have been moving away from weight based charges to ones based on the number of passengers. Such charging schedules may explicitly recognise the marginal costs of terminal use, but they also have the property of being approximate Ramsey structures. The upshot of this is that while marginal costs at airports with ample capacity may be negligible, it is feasible to achieve cost recovery at very little cost in terms of efficiency. Few potential users of the airport are discouraged from using it by the charges (for more discussion, see Morrison, 1982).

While the majority of airports do have excess capacity, there are many that are subject to excess demand. Some, such as London Heathrow and

Frankfurt in Europe, and New York La Guardia and Chicago O'Hare in North America, are subject to substantial excess demand. Most of these airports still have weight or passenger based charges, even though the relevance of such charging structures has diminished or been eliminated. These airports have limited capacity, which for land availability or environmental reasons is difficult to increase. These airports have a cost recovery problem that is the reverse of that discussed above. Prices set at a level that would efficiently ration capacity would more than cover costs. In fact, prices tend to be kept to inefficiently low levels, either by regulation (in the case of London Heathrow) or by owners, perhaps as a result of pressure from users. Thus there is a problem of excess demand, and this needs to be resolved by other rationing devices: slots (London Heathrow and Frankfurt); congestion (Los Angeles); or by a combination of these two (New York La Guardia). Granted that congestion is costly, and even the best performing slot allocation methods actually used are imperfect, keeping prices below efficient rationing levels imposes an efficiency cost.

3.0 The Costs of Handling the Airbus A380

The Airbus A380 will be a substantially larger aircraft than the current largest, the Boeing 747. It will be around 50 per cent larger, at least, than the large aircraft currently selling well, such as the Airbus A340 and the Boeing 777. The larger size will enable it to achieve lower operating costs per seat kilometre. Several of the airlines that specialise in long haul routes, such as Singapore Airlines, Qantas, and Emirates, have ordered it, as have Lufthansa and Air France. It is expected to come into service in 2006 or 2007.

The A380 is wider and higher than the Boeing 747. It will be able to use most airports without the need for specific investments, but this will be at a cost in terms of restrictions being placed on other users. Other aircraft may not be able to use nearby runways while the A380 is landing or taking off. Because of the size of the A380, their movement around the airport is likely to be constrained while an A380 is taxiing. The A380 will take up more space when at a gate, and this may impact on aircraft at neighbouring gates. Thus the ability of the airport to handle traffic will be lessened, and its effective capacity reduced, while the A380 is being handled. Thus use by the A380 will impose costs on other users of the airport.

These costs can be avoided if the airport invests to upgrade facilities for the A380 (Barros and Wirasinghe, 2002; Holzschneider, 2004). For airports that expect to handle significant numbers of A380s, investment will be

Table 1
Cost of Investment to Handle Airbus A380

Airport	Cost
New York Kennedy	$US109m
Los Angeles	$US177–1215m
Atlanta	$US25–26m
London Heathrow	£450m ($US823m)
Frankfurt	€150m ($US194m)
Melbourne	$A50m ($US38m)

Sources: GAO (2002, Appendix V) — New York, Los Angeles, Atlanta; Rozario (2004) — London; Airport Media Announcements — Frankfurt, Melbourne.

worthwhile. The wider wingspan of the A380 will necessitate wider runways, and several airports are currently widening their runways. Greater separations between taxiways may need to be provided, and larger parking areas created. To make effective use of the aircraft, terminals will have to be adapted. It is a double-decker aircraft, and to move passengers on and off quickly double deck aerobridges will need to be installed. Larger passenger lounges at gates will need to be provided.

Some estimates of the likely cost of upgrading are given in Table 1 for selected airports. There is considerable variation in the cost. For some airports, such as Atlanta and Melbourne, the cost is not likely to be large, since they have ample land and modifications will not be difficult. Upgrading Los Angeles, by contrast, could be very costly, since this airport is very constrained by land availability, and modifications are not straightforward. In addition, there is considerable difference in the estimates for Los Angeles — Airbus considered that only $177m of proposed investment would be attributable to making the airport ready to handle the A380, whereas the airport estimated the cost at above $1billion. The estimate for London Heathrow is also high. This may be because the modifications to be made will add terminal capacity as well as tailor it for the A380 — if the terminal capacity was not augmented, the cost might be significantly less. Thus some of the quoted costs of adapting airports may be overestimates, in that they incorporate capacity increases or additional facilities that are not necessitated by the A380.

To put these into perspective, Frankfurt expects to handle about twenty landings and take offs per day by 2010 (a relatively high number). Annualising the investment at 10 per cent yields a cost of about $20m PA, which amounts to $2,740 per movement. This can be compared to the current charge for a Boeing 747 movement of about $8,000 (ATRS, 2005). If a specific charge for the A380 was levied, it would not add more than about 30 per cent to the charge based on the current schedule (and the operational cost savings from using the A380 are likely to exceed this substantially). This would be at the lower end of the scale of costs per movement of investing to handle the A380, because Frankfurt will handle a relatively large number of flights, and the costs of upgrading are about average. For those airports for which upgrading is costly, and which do not expect many A380 movements, a specific A380 per movement charge could be large relative to current movement charges.

Most of the costs of accommodating the A380 will be in the form of sunk costs of investment, such as the cost of widening the runway and realigning the taxiways. Once the investment has been made, the use of the A380 will impose no more costs on the airport than the use of other types of aircraft. There will be some additional costs that using the A380 will impose — for example, it will require parking space, and where this space is valuable, the opportunity cost of using an A380 will be greater than that of using smaller aircraft. However, the major costs are likely to be the sunk costs of upgrading the facilities.

This then poses a cost recovery and pricing problem. One aspect is who should pay for the costs of upgrading — the airlines that use the A380, or all users of the airport, or some subset of users, such as international movements? There are two potentially important efficiency aspects to the pricing problem.

The first concerns the short-run problem of ensuring the efficient use of the airport once investments have been made. This is best solved by facing users with charges that, as closely as possible, reflect the costs they impose on the airport, so they will choose a mix of aircraft that minimises costs overall. If the A380 does not impose any higher costs on using the airport than other aircraft, then there is a case for having no specific additional charge levied on the use of the A380. This, however, would be a departure from 'user pays', and airlines that do not schedule the A380 will be paying for the infrastructure to handle it. This may not be perceived as fair. Non-linear price schedules could be a way round this problem in some cases.

The second concerns the long-run problem of providing the right signals for investment. If the specific charge for using an A380 is set at zero, then airlines will not face any of the costs of investing to upgrade facilities so that the airport can handle the A380. Thus they may invest excessively in the aircraft. When the airport assesses whether it is worthwhile to invest to handle the A380, it will have little information about the airlines' willingness to pay for this, since the price it is likely to charge will be zero. If non-linear prices are feasible, they will help since they will facilitate cost recovery with short-run efficiency at the same time as giving airlines appropriate signals for investment in aircraft, since they will be faced with the long-run costs they are imposing on airports by their aircraft purchasing decisions. These issues are explored in the following two sections.

4.0 Efficient Pricing and the Short Run

4.1 Pricing without investment

One possibility is that the airport does not invest to accommodate the A380. In spite of this, it may be feasible for the airport to handle A380 flights, though at a cost. These costs will be primarily in the form of externalities imposed on other users.

Before examining the nature of these costs, it is relevant to note that there need be no necessary association between the type of airport and the extent of use of A380s. Clearly, airports such as London Heathrow, Frankfurt, and Singapore Changi are busy hub airports that will attract considerable use by A380s. A380s will tend to be in heavy use at hub airports. However, they may also be used at non-hub airports, such as Melbourne. Some of the airports they use will be very busy, such as London Heathrow, but other airports they use may have ample capacity. Some very busy airports may serve only a few A380 flights, and investment to upgrade may not be worthwhile.

The costs imposed by the use of an A380 at an airport that has not invested to accommodate A380s will come about because of restrictions on the use of flights by other aircraft. While the A380 is arriving or taking off, movements around the airport and on other runways will be restricted. This will impose a cost on other users, though there need not be much by way of additional cash costs. How high these externality costs are depends on the utilisation of the airport. For a non-busy airport, these costs could be low. When the A380 arrives or leaves, other users will be restricted. However, if the airport has ample capacity, output will not be reduced. Those users that are affected will face a cost as a result of delays or not being able to use the airport at their preferred time.

When an airport is busy, the cost will depend on whether it is slot controlled or demand is rationed by congestion. If restrictions are imposed on other users when an A380 arrives or leaves, there will be an effective reduction in capacity. If there are slot controls, fewer flights will be able to be accommodated. Since slots are valuable, there will be a cost. On the other hand, if congestion is the rationing device, as is usually the case at busy US airports, congestion costs will increase, though no reductions in output need take place (some users may be discouraged from using by higher congestion, however). For those airports for which slots are

348

expensive or congestion is high, the externality costs of handling a movement by an A380 could be considerable.

If prices are to be set to encourage efficient use of the airport, they should be set equal to short-run marginal cost. Since A380 flights impose higher marginal costs than other flights, a specific charge for such flights, in addition to the normal airport charges, would be efficient. Such pricing will result in the users of A380s facing the costs they impose. Efficient externality pricing will raise the airport's gross and net revenues, since the cash costs of handling the A380 need not be large. Airports that are setting prices to just cover costs will be able to reduce their overall price level (though only slightly). Possibly the main practical problem will be that of determining the marginal cost of A380 use. If there is an effective market for slots, and the impacts of the A380 on effective capacity are clear, it will be a simple matter to estimate the capacity reduction component of the externality cost. When the externality takes the form of additional delays imposed on other users, again it should be straightforward to make an estimate of marginal cost and the efficient price for A380 use. With less busy airports, marginal costs will be lower, but less easy to estimate, since the costs imposed on other users (for example requiring them to use different times) are less easy to estimate.

4.2 Pricing with investment

In this section, it will be assumed that for an airport to be able to handle the A380 without imposing costs on other users, it will be necessary for it to make some capital investments, such as in widening the runways. These investments will be sunk costs in nature, and there will be no significant changes in operating costs associated with them. The marginal costs of an A380 in using these facilities will be the same as for other aircraft. For example, once the runway has been widened, it will cost no more for an A380 than other aircraft to use it. In the main, the marginal costs of using the A380 will be taken as zero, though the case of positive marginal costs will also be considered briefly. Airports may have more than enough capacity, or they may be busy and congested or subject to excess demand. These possibilities are considered in turn.

4.2.1 Non-busy airports

Many airports around the world have more than adequate capacity, because investments such as runways are subject to substantial indivisibilities. Passenger related investments such as terminals can be more closely tailored to demand. Marginal costs of using the terminals are likely to be positive and closer to the average costs.

With this cost structure, there will be a cost recovery problem if prices are set efficiently at marginal rather than average costs. Efficient prices will fail to cover the costs of building and operating the airport. If cost recovery is imposed, as it is for most airports in this situation, then second-best pricing will be required. Ramsey pricing, which sets prices proportional to the inverse of the elasticity of demand for a particular user, will achieve cost recovery at minimum cost in terms of efficiency. Ramsey prices are often regarded as impractical and demanding of too much information. However, airports have long implemented an approximation to Ramsey prices. Charges for most non-busy airports are based on aircraft weight, or passenger numbers. Terminal costs depend on passenger numbers. Furthermore, aircraft size and passenger numbers are roughly correlated with the inverse of the elasticity of demand. Thus this pricing structure is tolerably close to a Ramsey price structure, and if so, cost recovery can be achieved at little cost in terms of efficiency (Morrison, 1982).

Suppose the case of a non-busy airport incurring a sunk cost to accommodate flights by A380s. How should these sunk costs be recovered in the way that is most consistent with efficiency? Should specific charges be levied on users of A380s, or should the extra sunk costs be included in the cost base to be recovered from all users?

Since the marginal costs associated with the A380 are the same as for other users, they should not be priced differently. There would be no specific charge for using the A380. The price structure would then be adjusted to recover the higher costs, including the sunk costs of the investment. This means that all users will pay more. The all-up price for using an A380 will be higher than for smaller aircraft, though the per kilogram or per passenger charge will be about the same. The choice of aircraft will be based on the operating and other costs of using different aircraft, and will be efficient. It is possible that the airport will recover the costs from a subset of users of the airport, such as international flights only. In general, this would be less efficient than spreading the cost recovery problem as widely as possible.

If there are positive marginal costs specifically associated with the A380, then it will be efficient to allow for these in the pricing schedule. Just as aircraft that stay longer in parking areas impose greater costs on the airport, the use of a very large aircraft may impose additional costs, such as provision of more land for parking, which it is efficient to recognise in the price structure.

This result, whereby sunk costs are recovered from all users, may not be seen as very 'fair', and it can be seen as a divergence from the principle of 'user pays'. A small number of airlines schedule A380s into an airport, which is then required to incur costs to accommodate them. The airlines that operate the A380s will enjoy reduced operating costs. Other airlines will shoulder most of the burden of the costs of providing for the A380s. However, once the facilities are upgraded, it is then efficient to make the best use of them, and this requires that airlines face no disincentive to schedule the A380 rather than other aircraft. While this may be an efficient solution, it could be regarded as not fair. Fairness is a concept that economists do not often use, but public decisions are often conditioned by perceptions of fairness (for a discussion, see Zajac, 1995).

4.2.2 Busy airports

The significance of the distinction between busy and non-busy airports is that while the pricing structures of the latter are mostly tolerably efficient, the pricing structures of busy airports are often quite inefficient. Three types of busy airports can be distinguished:

- Ones with slot limits and efficient price structures;
- Ones with slot limits and inefficient price structures; and
- Ones that use congestion to ration excess demand.

These are considered in turn.

4.2.2.1 Slot limited airports with efficient prices Pricing efficiency for slot constrained airports requires that both slots are efficiently allocated and prices for use of the airport reflect marginal costs and opportunity costs of capacity. Efficient allocation of slots will be present if there is a slot auction, or effective, unconstrained trading of slots. An efficient price structure for use of an airport subject to excess demand involves a flat charge for use of the runway and associated facilities, combined with a per passenger charge that reflects the marginal costs of terminal use. One efficient solution would be for the user charge for the airport to be sufficiently high to eliminate the slot premium. This rarely occurs — mostly, airport charges are held down by owners or regulators, and there is a premium for slots. The price to an airline for an aircraft to use the airport includes a flat amount equal to the slot premium and runway charge, plus a per passenger charge reflecting passenger related costs.

There are few airports that meet these conditions. The closest approximation is London Heathrow Airport. The pricing structure has a large fixed element in it, though there is also a per passenger charge, which, to an extent, reflects the costs of terminal use. Slots are tradeable, and there is a market for slots. However, there are few trades that take place and it is difficult to determine exactly how efficient this slot market is (see Humphreys, 2003).

Given a starting point of a tolerably efficient pricing structure, it would be efficient not to impose a separate charge on the use of the A380 to recover the sunk costs of accommodating it. If the sunk costs are to be recovered from airlines, the most efficient way of doing so would be to raise the flat per-flight charge for using the airport, while leaving the passenger charge unchanged. The price for using the airport would move closer to the market clearing level, and the slot premium would fall accordingly. There would be no efficiency cost in recovering the additional sunk costs in this way. Unless demand elasticities are very high, the substitution of smaller aircraft by the A380 will lead to a fall in the demand for slots, and the slot price will. As against this, the A380 will also encourage substitution of point-to-point services by services through the hub, and the demand for slots by feeder flights will increase. The ultimate impact on the slot price and premium is not clear.

With this pricing structure, airlines will face the right incentives when choosing whether to schedule the A380 or smaller aircraft. Each type will face the costs it imposes on the airport system. The price per flight will be the same, reflecting the fact that they impose the same cost of using scarce capacity. The A380 will pay more in total per passenger charges, reflecting its higher passenger load and greater passenger related costs. If slot prices are very high, as they are for London Heathrow, there will be an incentive for airlines to consider replacing smaller aircraft by the A380, thus economising on the scarce capacity.

If there are positive marginal costs of use, then it will be efficient for prices to reflect these. Thus if the A380 uses more parking space, and space is valuable, it will be efficient to charge it more than smaller aircraft.

As with the airports that are not busy, it will be the airlines in general that use the airport who will pay for the costs of accommodating the A380. Those who do not benefit from the use of the A380 will pay the costs associated with it. This will be essential if efficiency in the short run is to be achieved. Indirectly, some airlines may gain or lose, though changing slot prices or increased opportunities for feeder traffic, but there are not likely to be any systematic patterns of gain or loss.

4.2.2.2 Slot limited airports with inefficient pricing Inefficient pricing is the norm with slot limited airports. Except for the London airports, and a few US airports, slot trading is prohibited in many parts of the world, especially in Europe (NERA, 2004). In addition, most airports still operate with weight or passenger related charging systems, which, while efficient for non-busy airports, are quite inappropriate for busy airports. Even though capacity to handle flights is at a premium, it is cheaper for smaller aircraft with smaller passenger loads to use the airport than for large aircraft. The structure of pricing discourages the substitution of small by large aircraft, even though this would lead to better utilisation of the airport.

In this situation, the case for not imposing a specific charge on the A380 to recoup the sunk costs of accommodating is stronger than before. Such a charge would further discourage the use of the A380, and would compound the disincentives to use large aircraft noted above. Assuming that airport charges are levied to recover costs, airlines that use smaller aircraft will pay the costs of accommodating the A380. In this case, while the fairness issue also arises, most of the flights that pay increased charges are underpriced, and efficiency is enhanced, rather than reduced, by imposing the costs on them.

Even where there are some marginal costs specific to the A380, it may be efficient to absorb them in the general price structure, rather than to relate charges to them, as was the case when price structures were efficient. Because large aircraft are overpriced, an additional charge will lower, not raise, the efficiency with which the airport's scarce capacity is used.

4.2.2.3 Congested airports Most busy airports in the US that are subject to excess demand ration this demand by congestion. Service is predominantly on a first come first served basis, and queues form. In addition, airports recover costs with weight based or passenger based charges. Granted that each movement imposes the same external delay cost, this means that while prices are, in general, below marginal cost, large aircraft are relatively discouraged and small aircraft are encouraged. A specific charge for the A380, to recover the sunk costs of its infrastructure, would lower allocative efficiency, since the marginal cost of the A380 would be the same as that for other aircraft, but the higher charge would discourage its use. A zero specific charge for the A380 would enhance efficiency in the short run by encouraging some substitution of small by large aircraft, thus reducing congestion.

4.3 Non-linear pricing

So far, it has been assumed that simple unit pricing would be imposed. When there is a cost recovery problem, non-linear prices, such as two-part tariffs, are often more efficient (Brown and Sibley, 1986). This possibility needs to be considered in the context of recovering the sunk costs of accommodating the A380.

One possible solution would be to offer a contract that involved airlines that commit to using the A380 making a contribution to the sunk costs, in advance or by an annual subscription, and for those that do so zero specific charges for using the A380 would be levied. Other airlines, which do not contribute to the capital costs, would be charged a specific price when they use A380s at the airport. This solution would ensure efficient utilisation by airlines that contribute up front, since they face the marginal costs of use — namely zero. This would be attractive to the major users of the A380 at the airport. Other airlines would face a charge for use, and would not use the A380 to its full potential. Thus there would be some cost in terms of efficiency in the short run, though it would be small. This would have to be compared to the efficiency cost of recovering the cost from all users.

While, in principle, a two-part pricing schedule has desirable properties, it may be difficult to determine the up-front contributions. These might be on the basis of expected use of the aircraft, though this would result in some airlines making larger up front contributions than others. This could result in a *de facto* charge per use being levied. Alternatively, a fixed up-front contribution might be charged. As usual with two-part tariffs, this fixed charge would discourage some users, and would thus have some efficiency costs. Two-part tariffs work well if most users have similar demands. Where users have widely differing demands, it is difficult to determine the optimal fixed charge. This is a particular problem for airports where there might be considerable variation in the use by airlines of the A380. This said, however, the two-part tariff option might be suitable for some airports.

The two-part tariff approach thus has some efficiency costs — though these need to be compared to the efficiency costs of setting zero specific charges for the A380. While such a pricing policy optimises the use of the aircraft, it does have an efficiency cost in terms of raising prices to all users a little further above marginal cost. This cost is likely to be small if demand elasticities for use of the airport are low, as is likely to be the case. A possible efficiency advantage of the two-part tariff is that it creates the right signals for airlines to take into account the infrastructure costs of choosing the A380 (see Section 5). Other than this, the main practical advantage of the two-part tariff is that it results in users of the A380 paying for its infrastructure — it thus achieves a good mix of efficiency and fairness.

5.0 Efficient Investment and the Long Run

The long-run decision for an airport is whether to invest to accommodate the A380. Suppose that welfare maximisation is the objective. Whether an airport invests will depend on the likely use of the airport by airlines scheduling A380s. If there is only likely to be limited use by airlines of the aircraft, investment will not be worthwhile. For many airports it will

Airport Infrastructure for the Airbus A380   Forsyth

be still possible to handle flights by the A380, but this will be at a positive marginal (externality) cost. For some airports, such as London Heathrow and Singapore Changi, investment will be well worthwhile, since the A380 is likely to be used extensively. For many airports, there is a choice — for these, there is the risk of inefficient decisions if excessive investments are made, or provision is not made when warranted.

Given the welfare objective, the appropriate course of action is to undertake a cost benefit analysis of investment, balancing the costs of such investment against the benefits from it. In some situations, it may be that investment is essential for the airport to handle the A380. As noted earlier, for some land constrained airports (for example Los Angeles), the costs of such investment may be very large, while for other airports with ample land (for example Melbourne), the costs of upgrading for the A380 are modest. Airlines will gain from lower operating costs if they use the A380. For a slot limited airport, the use of the larger aircraft may make more slots available, which will be a benefit that will accrue to the airline. If the airport is capable of handling the A380 without investment, but at a cost, then investment will eliminate these costs. These costs are essentially the externality costs imposed on other users when restrictions are imposed on them to allow use by the A380. If the airport is congested, an increase in congestion arising from the use of the A380 will be avoided, and if the airport is slot controlled, a reduction in effective capacity of the airport is avoided. These costs could be substantial for busy airports. For airports that are not busy, the costs avoided will be smaller. If the additional infrastructure is provided, unless a two-part tariff is feasible, the optimal specific charge for the A380 will be zero. In this context, there will be only a limited role for prices to signal investment.

The choices facing an airport are summed up in Figure 1. Suppose that the marginal cost of handling the A380 without investment is constant (MC). A fixed sunk cost is required to enable the airport to handle the A380 at zero marginal cost — the average fixed cost is shown as AFC. If the number of A380 movements at the airport is less than N, it is efficient not to incur the sunk cost. If the use is greater than N, investment is worthwhile. If the airport is not upgraded, the efficient price P is equal to the marginal cost, MC. If upgrading takes place, the efficient price is zero.

If a substantial number of A380 movements is expected (demand curve D_1), investment is clearly worthwhile, the efficient price will be zero, and the number of movements X_1. If only a few flights are expected (demand curve D_2), upgrading is not worthwhile, the efficient price is P, and the number of movements will be X_2.

The airport's prices will not always give the airlines the right signals as to whether to schedule the A380. Suppose that airlines expect zero prices if use

Figure 1

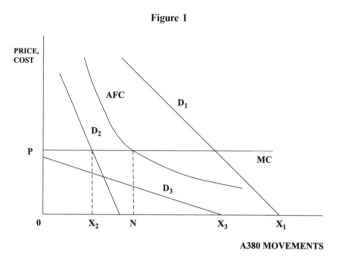

exceeds N, and the airport only knows that this number of movements will be scheduled (that is, it does not know the full demand curve D_3). The airport invests, sets a price of zero, and X_3 movements are scheduled. However, the benefits from upgrading (as indicated by the area under the demand curve) are less than the cost of the investment — upgrading is not worthwhile. The airport can inform the airlines of the price schedule, but this will not be sufficient information to ensure that the airlines make an efficient choice of aircraft to serve the airport. The airport can make the correct decision on upgrading if it accurately knows the size of the benefits to the airlines from using the A380, that is, it knows the full demand curve. In practice it may not have such accurate information, and there is the possibility that it will invest when not worthwhile.

In this situation, it is assumed that neither the airport nor the airlines are behaving opportunistically — both groups are making efficient choices based on the information available to them. There is a possibility that airlines may behave strategically, by purchasing the A380 and then facing the airport with a *fait accompli* — the airport may then find it worthwhile to upgrade even though it would not have if the airlines had not incurred the sunk cost of purchasing the A380. This is a dynamic inconsistency problem, in which optimal actions at all points of time can lead to less the optimal outcomes over time (it is explored in Forsyth, 2004).

Just as with the short-run problem, a two-part pricing structure can be a way around the investment signalling problem. Under such a structure, airlines will be faced with the costs they impose on the airport as a result of scheduling the A380. They will take this cost into account when determining whether to purchase and use the A380 on routes into this airport. Thus they will take all costs and benefits into account and will be given the incentive to make decisions that are efficient overall.

6.0 Airport Ownership, Regulation, and Incentives

In the discussion so far, it has been assumed that airports have the objective of maximising efficiency — pricing to maximise efficiency in the use of facilities, and investing where the net benefits are positive. This is the standard assumption of much public enterprise theory, and it has the merit of establishing a benchmark — if the enterprise is to seek to maximise efficiency, this is how it should do it. This said, however, most airports do not behave in this way.

Historically, many airports have been publicly owned, though there has been a significant move towards privatisation over the past two decades. In North America, airports are often owned by local communities or governments. While some airports are still operated by government departments, most publicly owned airports have been corporatised.

Even though airports may be publicly owned, they need not be welfare maximisers. The objectives of airport managements may be complex, but they could include size maximisation, quality maximisation, and maximisation of business for the local community. Typically, these airports will be subject to an overall cost recovery constraint. Such airports will not necessarily seek to implement price structures that make the most efficient use of their facilities (the widespread presence of inappropriate price structures for busy airports is clear evidence of this), or seek to invest only when benefits exceed costs.

Many airports are now privatised. These airports may be seeking to maximise profits, but all major private airports are subject to either explicit regulation or indirect regulation through price monitoring. Some are subject to either explicit or *de facto* rate-of-return regulation (Niemeier, 2004), while others are subject to price caps, which may or may not approximate rate-of-return regulation in fact (see Toms, 2004; Hendriks and Andrew, 2004).

The critical issue, for present purposes, is how they respond to investment proposals, such as proposals to invest to accommodate the A380. It is likely that public and private rate-of-return regulated airports will respond in a similar way. They will both seek to expand their capital base, to increase total profits in the case of the private airport, or to increase size, in the case of the publicly owned airport. In neither case do they have

357

any incentive to subject investment in accommodating the A380 to rigorous scrutiny, and to invest only if benefits exceed costs. If they make an investment, they will be permitted to pass on the costs to users. The size maximising airport will wish to invest because this is a way of increasing size. The quality maximising airport will see investment as being justified because it improves the range of services available to users. The profit maximising airport increases its regulated capital base and total profit. All have an incentive to invest in accommodating the A380 regardless of whether such investments are warranted or not.

The incentives facing the price capped airport are different, and depend on how the price cap is implemented. If a simple, unchanging, price cap is imposed over airport charges, the airport will have no incentive to invest to accommodate the A380, no matter how worthwhile doing so would be. Investment will increase the costs of the airport, but it will not lead to any price increases, and it will thus reduce profits. This disincentive to invest is frequently recognised (Hendriks and Andrew, 2004) and regulators devise methods to allow the regulated firm to recoup the costs of investment (Forsyth, 2002). If this is done, it will result in the regulator exercising discretion over the investment. The firm will come to the regulator with a proposal to allow pass-through of investment costs (that is, to allow a price increase on top of the cap) and the regulator then assesses the investment and chooses whether to allow pass-through. In effect, the regulator evaluates the investment, and could choose to use welfare maximising/ cost benefit criteria or alternative criteria. In this situation, there will be an explicit evaluation of whether the investments needed to accommodate the A380 are worthwhile or not. Just as in the case of welfare maximising airports, discussed in the previous section, there is the chance that the regulator will be pressured into allowing accommodation by airlines committing to purchase the larger aircraft.

Pure price caps are rare, though they have been implemented on occasions (for example in Australia from 1997 to 2002). A more common form of regulation is a hybrid of price caps and cost based regulation. With this arrangement, price caps are set so as to be able to recover forecast costs, including capital costs. Prior to setting the price cap for a period, the regulator makes a forecast of capital expenditure, and evaluates whether all the airport's forecast expenditure is efficient. Under these arrangements, the costs of accommodating the A380 will be forecast, and the regulator may set the price cap at a level that allows recovery of them. If the regulator simply accepts the airport's own capital expenditure programme, then this will be similar to rate-of-return regulation, and there is a chance that inefficient investments will be made. If the regulator assesses the proposed capital investment on cost benefit criteria, then the outcome will be similar to that under the pure price cap, where the regulator determines whether to allow pass-through or not.

Regulation and ownership also have implications for incentives to price efficiently. Public size maximising or quality maximising airports and private rate-of-return regulated airports do not have clear incentives to price efficiently. While pricing of non-busy airports is tolerably efficient, pricing of most busy airports is seriously inefficient. Pricing incentives under price caps are better and interestingly, the busy airports that have the best price structures are those in London, which are subject to a price cap regime, albeit not a pure price cap.

It has been suggested above that the best pricing structure for the A380 would involve either no specific charge for use of this aircraft, or a two-part tariff scheme as outlined. What incentives are there for airports to price in this way? It is likely that public and regulated airports will choose not to implement a specific charge, partly because it is simpler not to do so, and partly because they will seek not to discourage traffic. To an extent, they (and in particular, local communities) may see being able to accommodate the A380, and encouraging its use, as a matter of prestige. They may also wish to encourage the use of the airport by A380s in the hope that this may foster the development of the airport as a hub. To this end they will choose to avoid specific charges.

It is also possible that they may respond to the fairness argument. Their existing airlines will not like being charged more to provide facilities for a small number of airlines. If so, they will be under pressure to ensure that users of the A380 cover the costs of the infrastructure they require. They can do this at least cost in terms of efficiency by implementing a two-part tariff schedule if this is feasible, though whether they have a strong enough incentive to handle the issue in this way is not obvious.

7.0 Synthesis and Conclusions

There are several main propositions in the discussion above. These include the following points.

- The introduction of the Airbus A380 imposes pricing and investment problems for airports and airlines, especially since there are significant sunk costs associated with upgrading airports to accommodate the A380, along with possible sunk costs when airlines commit to purchasing the aircraft. Achieving cost recovery is not a problem, since most airports have market power. However, there is an issue of how cost recovery can be achieved at minimum cost in terms of efficiency.

- There are two aspects of choice that are important from an efficiency point of view. These are first, achieving efficient use of airports and aircraft in the short run, and second, ensuring that efficient investments are made, and especially ensuring that investments that are not warranted in terms of net benefits are not made.
- From a short-run perspective, to optimise the use of the A380 it is desirable that airports that have upgraded do not levy specific charges for the use of the A380 in addition to normal airport charges. This is so for most airports regardless of the price structures already in place. For most busy airports price structures are already inefficient in that they discourage the use of larger aircraft. In this environment the case for zero specific charges is stronger.
- If zero specific charges are levied, so airports can recover the additional costs of accommodating the A380, charges will have to be increased across the board. This will imply that other airline users of the airport will pay most of the costs so that users of the A380 enjoy the cost savings. This may be seen as unfair.
- A two-part tariff approach, which involves zero charges for users that make an initial capital contribution, and specific charges for others, could achieve the goal of fairness at little or no cost in terms of efficiency. In this situation, the primary reasons for the imposition of a two-part tariff would be to achieve fairness, and to provide signals for investment by airlines, rather than the more usual short-run efficiency goal.
- To the extent that the A380 imposes additional operating costs, and the marginal costs to the airport of it being used exceed zero, there is a case for specific charges based on these, but only if initial price structures are efficient. If they are not, there may be a case for absorbing them within the general pricing structure.
- When there are no specific charges for using the A380 at airports, prices cease to serve as signals for investment by airports and airlines. Granted this, the role of investment criteria in determining whether investments should go ahead becomes more critical.
- It is possible for airports to use cost benefit analyses to determine whether investment to accommodate the A380 should be made. However, granted that airlines will face only some of the costs they impose when purchasing and scheduling A380s, they may schedule too many. This in turn could lead to airports investing to handle the A380 when it would otherwise be more efficient not to make the investments.
- While airports may make efficient choices about investments, the ownership and regulatory environments in which most operate create

incentives for inefficient choices. Publicly owned and rate-of-return regulated airports have an incentive to invest excessively, and to pass on the costs to users. In this type of environment, many airports will invest to accommodate the A380 even when doing so is not worthwhile.
- Price capped airports have no incentive to overinvest in this way. Their incentive to invest to accommodate the A380 will depend critically on the cost pass-through arrangements that the regulator imposes. The regulator effectively decides whether an airport should accommodate the A380.

It may well be that the short-run aspects of the problem are easier to solve, in a practical way, than the long-run aspects. It is easy for airports to make investments to accommodate the A380 and recover the costs of doing so by raising charges across the board. This is a violation of 'user pays', and it may not be regarded as fair, though it will lead to efficient choices of aircraft. In cases where there is pressure for user pays, the two-part tariff option is an efficient one, though not always feasible.

Implementing an efficient solution of the long-run aspect of the problem is more difficult to achieve. There are at least two forces that will lead to pressure for airports to invest excessively, and upgrade facilities to accommodate the A380 in situations where this is not worthwhile. Excessive investment in accommodating new aircraft types has arguably happened more than once in the past. The fact that airlines will not face the full costs of using the A380 can lead to this result, and coupled with this, most airports operate in a regulatory environment that weakens incentives to scrutinise investment proposals. For them it is easy to make questionable investments and pass the costs on to users. It is likely that many airports that need not upgrade their facilities to accommodate the A380 will nonetheless make the investments, and pass the costs on to airlines, and ultimately, their passengers.

References

Air Transport Research Society (ATRS) (2005): *2005 Airport Benchmarking Report: Part II Full Results and Analysis*, Vancouver, Air Transport Research Society.

Barros, A. and S. Wirasinghe (2002): 'Designing the Airport Airside for the New Large Aircraft,' *Journal of Air Transport Management*, 8, 121–12.

Brown, S. and D. Sibley (1986): *The Theory of Public Utility Pricing*, Cambridge, Cambridge University Press.

Brueckner, J. (2002): 'Airport Congestion when Carriers have Market Power,' *American Economic Review*, 92, 1357–75.

Doganis, R. (1992): *The Airport Business*, London and New York, Routledge.

Forsyth, P. (2002): 'Privatisation and Regulation of Australian and New Zealand Airports,' *Journal of Air Transport Management*, 8, 19–28.

Forsyth, P. (2004): 'Pricing the Airport Infrastructure for the Airbus A380: Efficient Pricing and Dynamic Inconsistency,' Mimeo, Monash University, Dept of Economics.

General Accounting Office (GAO) (2002): *Airport Infrastructure: Unresolved Issues Make it Difficult to Determine the Cost to Serve New Large Aircraft. Report to Congressional Requesters*, GAO -02-251, US GAO, Washington.

Graham, A. (2003): *Managing Airports – An International Perspective*, Oxford, Elsevier Butterworth Heinemann.

Hendriks, N. and D. Andrew (2004): 'Airport Regulation in the UK,' in P. Forsyth, D. Gillen, A. Knorr, O. Mayer, H.-M. Niemeier, and D. Starkie (eds), *The Economic Regulation of Airports: Recent Developments in Australasia, North America and Europe*, Aldershot, Ashgate.

Hogan, O. and D. Starkie (2004): 'Calculating the Short-Run Marginal Infrastructure Costs of Runway Use: An Application to Dublin Airport,' in P. Forsyth, D. Gillen, A. Knorr, O. Mayer, H.-M. Niemeier, and D. Starkie (eds), *The Economic Regulation of Airports: Recent Developments in Australasia, North America and Europe*, Aldershot, Ashgate.

Holzschneider, M. (2004): 'Are Airports Fit for the Next Decade? Integrating the New Super Jumbo in the World's Airport System,' mimeo, Dornier Consulting.

Humphreys, B. (2003): 'Slot Allocation: A Radical Solution,' in K. Boyfield (ed), *A Market in Airport Slots*, London, Institute of Economic Affairs.

Morrison, S. (1982): 'Landing Fees at Uncongested Airports,' *Journal of Transport Economics and Policy*, 14, 151–60.

National Economic Research Associates (NERA) (2004): *Study to Assess the Effects of Different Slot Allocation Schemes – A Final Report for the European Commission*, London, D. G. Tren.

Niemeier, H.-M. (2004): 'Capacity Utilization, Investment and Regulatory Reform of German Airports,' in P. Forsyth, D. Gillen, A. Knorr, O. Mayer, H.-M. Niemeier, and D. Starkie (eds), *The Economic Regulation of Airports: Recent Developments in Australasia, North America and Europe*, Aldershot, Ashgate.

Oum, T. and Y. Zhang (1990): 'Airport Pricing: Congestion Tolls, Lumpy Investment and Cost Recovery,' *Journal of Public Economics*, 43, 353–74.

Rozario, K. (2004): 'Boarding the A380,' *Jane's Airport Review*, September, 27–9.

Toms, M. (2004): 'UK-Regulation from the Perspective of the BAA, plc,' in P. Forsyth, D. Gillen, A. Knorr, O. Mayer, H.-M. Niemeier, and D. Starkie (eds), *The Economic Regulation of Airports: Recent Developments in Australasia, North America and Europe*, Aldershot, Ashgate.

Zajac, E. (1995): *The Political Economy of Fairness*, Cambridge, MA, MIT Press.

Part III:

Capacity

7

A decision support system for airport strategic planning

Miltiadis A. Stamatopoulos, Konstantinos G. Zografos, Amedeo R. Odoni

Abstract

This paper describes an integrated set of models for the estimation of the capacity of an airfield and the associated delays. The aim is to develop a decision support tool suitable for airport planning at the strategic level. Thus, the emphasis is on obtaining reliable approximations to the quantities of interest quickly and with a limited set of inputs. The models account for the dynamic characteristics of airfield capacity and demand, as well as for some stochastic aspects of airfield operations. They are sensitive to airfield geometry, the operational characteristics of the airfield and of the local air traffic control system, and the characteristics of the local air traffic demand for airport access and services. Through its integrated structure, the decision support tool can account for interactions among operations at different parts of the airfield.
© 2003 Elsevier Ltd. All rights reserved.

Keywords: Aerodrome; Airport; Airside; Apron; Capacity; Decision support system; Delays; Runway; Sequencing

1. Motivation and objectives

The demand for air transport has been increasing rapidly over the years and all forecasts suggest that this trend will continue. In response, airports worldwide are making large investments aimed at increasing capacity and operating efficiency and controlling congestion. The busiest commercial airports in the United States spent $7.2 billion on capital investments in 2000 and had already committed another $24 billion between 2001 and 2006 (ACI-NA, 2001). The corresponding figures for the whole world are probably at least twice as large.

Expansion planning at airports must typically adopt a long-term perspective with time horizons of 15–50 years. In this paper, we present an integrated set of models that has been developed to assist airport operators and managers in planning strategically for expanding and optimizing the airfield (runways, taxiways, aprons) and for improving operating procedures or managing demand ("slot control and allocation"). Planning at the strategic level requires the ability to examine approximately the implications for the level of service at the airport of a wide range of different scenarios and hypotheses about future conditions. The goal of MACAD (MANTEA Airfield Capacity And Delays model), the decision support system described in this paper, is to provide such a tool for performing this type of analysis quickly, reliably and with limited effort.

A number of existing simulation models (e.g., SIMMOD, TAAM and the Airport Machine) aim at providing assistance in the detailed design of the airfield. However, such microscopic models are not well suited to serve as strategic decision-support tools because their use requires a great amount of time, effort and expense. They also have a steep learning curve, requiring well-trained, expert users. It may take several person-months of effort to set up the simulation of an airport using these tools. Significant modifications to some of the original assumptions or airport configuration may also take much additional time to implement. Moreover, these models suffer from the somewhat paradoxical disadvantage of often providing too much detail for the needs of a strategic planning exercise, instead of focusing on the aggregate characteristics of interest (Odoni, 1991). A detailed discussion of these issues, as well as descriptions of existing models, can be found in Odoni et al. (1997).

On the opposite side, numerous analytical, macroscopic (low level of detail) models also exist for computing approximate capacities and/or delays associated with each of the individual elements of the airfield, i.e., the runways, taxiways and apron areas (Odoni et al., 1997). However, these models have been used in a stand-alone mode to date, e.g., for runway capacity studies or for apron capacity studies. They have not been integrated in a fashion that would permit examination of the airfield as a whole, including possible interactions among the various elements of the airfield. The approach described here is an attempt to provide such a macroscopic, integrated tool.

In what follows we first provide a brief overview of the integrated system, and then describe some of the individual models that its main module, the Airside Module, is composed of. The reader is referred to Stamatopoulos (2000) for a far more detailed description.

2. Overview of the decision support system

MACAD integrates macroscopic airside models to provide approximate estimates of the capacity and delays associated with every element of the airfield. Its primary advantages are that it is fast, flexible and easy to use, and thus suitable to support strategic decision-making. In recognition of the fact that the availability of data and the statistics of interest differ widely from case to case, the user is offered several options in this respect. For example, MACAD will accept as an input a detailed daily schedule of arrivals and departures at the airport of interest or will assist the

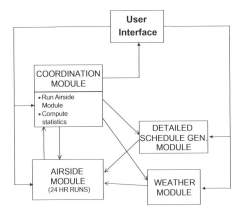

Fig. 1. Overview of the proposed integrated system of models.

user in constructing a hypothetical schedule that complies with some general specifications. MACAD consists of five modules, as shown in Fig. 1. A very brief description of each follows.

The "Co-ordination" module. As the name suggests, this module "co-ordinates" the sequence in which other modules are called up, depending on the options chosen by the user. It also manages the flow of data within MACAD and the output of statistics as specified by the user.

The "Airside" module. This module is the principal component of the system and the focus of this paper. The Airside module computes the capacity of the various elements of the airfield and the associated delays, given the runway configuration in use, the air traffic control (ATC) separation requirements, the airfield's operational characteristics, and a demand profile for a 24-hour period (see also the Weather module below).

The operation of the Airside module is outlined in Fig. 2. An airfield (or "airport airside") can be viewed as a service network that consists of a series of components, which are used sequentially

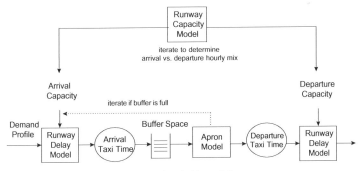

Fig. 2. The airside module.

by aircraft operators. These components are the arrival runways, the arrival taxiways, the gate/apron area, the departure taxiways and the departure runways. It is noteworthy that the capacity of the arrival and departure runway systems are often closely coupled. For example, in the case where a single runway is used both for arrivals and for departures, a direct trade-off exists between arrival capacity and departure capacity.

The Airside module consists of a set of models that examine all the stages of aircraft processing on airside from the final approach path for landings to the takeoff runway. Briefly, the following computations are performed to determine the capacity and level of service of the airside (see Fig. 2): A runway capacity model is used to determine the capacity envelopes (see Section 3) for all possible runway sets and configurations available. MACAD then uses a runway delay model to estimate delays to arriving aircraft at the runways, taking into consideration the schedule of arrivals, the runway configuration(s) used (provided on an hourly basis), the mix of arrivals versus departures computed on an hourly basis and the available arrival capacity as previously computed by the runway capacity model. Next, a revised schedule of arrivals at the apron area is computed, using the previously derived estimates of arrival delay and adding an estimated taxi time. Based on this revised schedule of arrivals, the apron model is then used to estimate the utilization of the apron area and any delays that may be incurred by an incoming aircraft waiting for a suitable stand. If the capacity of the apron buffer space is exceeded, the arrival process may be discontinued for some time. In this case, MACAD re-computes arrival delays using a reduced capacity for arrivals to account for the length of time during which the arrival process is blocked. Next, the departure time of each aircraft from its apron stand is computed, taking into consideration the scheduled departure time, the actual arrival time at the stand and the minimum required ground turn-around time for each type of aircraft. MACAD thus prepares a revised schedule for departures. Using this revised schedule and after taking into account the estimated taxi-out time, the system estimates departure delays using the departures capacity computed for the traffic and operations mix at hand. Finally, because the mix of arrivals versus departures in the original schedule may no longer be valid due to arrival and/or apron delays, the system repeats the process using a mix computed with the revised schedule for departures.

The "Weather" module. Weather affects airfield capacity and delays in a major way. This module gives MACAD users the option of investigating the performance of the airfield over periods of time longer than 24 h under a range of weather conditions. The user may elect to "re-play" historical weather data for the airport covering an extended period of time (e.g., one year). A look-up table identifies the runway configuration(s) and associated ATC separations and other operating rules to be used for each set of weather conditions. In the absence of such a detailed weather record, the user has the alternative of "simulating" in rough terms weather conditions through a Markov chain model. The states of the chain correspond to a small number of user-defined weather categories (e.g., "visual flight rules—VFR" conditions, "instrument flight rules—IFR" conditions, "low IFR—LIFR" conditions). Runway configurations are associated, in a deterministic or probabilistic way, with each state and a random number generator is used to determine the configuration in use for each hour. The transition probabilities between states and the occupancy time for each state are provided on the basis of statistical records from the airport site.

The "Detailed Schedule Generation" module. MACAD requires as an input a detailed daily schedule of arrivals and departures at the airport of interest, along with relevant information for each flight operation (e.g., the type or size of the aircraft involved). In recognition of the fact that such a detailed schedule may not always be available, especially if the analysis is concerned with hypothetical conditions several years into the future, the Detailed Schedule Generation module assists users of MACAD in generating a range of alternative demand scenarios with a minimum of effort. The function of the module is to generate detailed schedules based on aggregate descriptions of the demand. The number of scheduled arriving flights is provided on an hourly base for each aircraft category. Unless otherwise specified, the module then assumes that arrivals are randomly distributed within each hour and uses a random number generator to create a detailed flight schedule for arrivals throughout the duration of a single day. In parallel, for each arrival, it generates a scheduled departure time, again using a pseudo random number generator given the statistics provided on the amount of time between the scheduled arrival and the scheduled departure of aircraft, while always respecting the required minimum "turnaround" time for the handling of the aircraft. The required share of the different airlines and/or aircraft ground handlers in the composition of the traffic, as well as the proportion of domestic versus international flights, are also taken into account in generating schedules.

The user interface. A Windows-based user-friendly interface has been developed for MACAD. The user interface facilitates the data entry process by guiding users in a structured manner in providing the required information, depending on the mode of MACAD operation chosen. The interface also illustrates the results graphically and textually, so that users can readily obtain the information of interest.

3. The runway capacity model

A stochastic analytical model has been developed for the estimation of the capacity envelope of an airport's runway system. The capacity envelope identifies capacity limits for every possible mix of arrivals and departures during a period of airfield operations.

Runway complexes consist of one or more runways that can be used under different configurations. Each configuration consists of a distinct set of runways for landings and takeoffs. The scope of the model extends from a configuration with a single runway to configurations with two simultaneously active runways under different geometric and operational characteristics. Runway configurations consisting of more than two simultaneously active runways can be modelled in most cases by decomposing them into more easily analysable runway sets, each set consisting of one or two runways. In this section we describe: (1) the detailed logic of the single-runway capacity model; (2) the extension of the single-runway capacity model to a set of two-runway configurations that span the entire range of possible interactions between two simultaneously active runways; and (3) a simple model for the assessment of the potential capacity benefits obtainable from sequencing arriving aircraft.

3.1. The single runway capacity model

Runways are operated with various constraints and ATC separation standards designed to ensure the safety of operations. Although the constraints are of a similar nature, the values of the separation standards vary considerably from country to country—and even across airports within the same country—and depend on the geometry of the active runway system. The (maximum throughput) capacity of a runway system is typically defined as the expected number of movements (landings and takeoffs) that can be performed in one hour without violating ATC separation standards in the presence of continuous demand. Note that this definition recognizes that the actual number of movements in any given hour is a random variable.

3.1.1. The runway capacity envelope

The best-known early model for estimating the capacity of a single runway is due to Blumstein (1959, 1960). It introduced an approach, which was subsequently used by several other, increasingly sophisticated, single-runway models. The most advanced of these in many respects is the "LMI model" (Lee et al., 1997). The logic of the single-runway capacity model presented here is based on that of the LMI model, with some significant modifications (see also Section 3.5). The model computes the runway capacity envelope, i.e., the set of points that define the maximum throughput capacity that can be achieved at the runway for the entire range of arrival and departure "mixes" (Gilbo, 1993). Specifically, it identifies four points (Fig. 3) on the runway capacity envelope as defined below. The entire envelope can then be obtained approximately by simply interpolating between pairs of points with straight-line segments. The four points are the following:

Point 1. The "all arrivals" point, i.e., the capacity of the runway when it is used for arrivals only.
Point 2. The "freely inserted departures" point which has the same arrivals capacity as Point 1 and a departures capacity equal to the number of departures that can be inserted into the arrival stream by only exploiting large interarrival gaps and without increasing any separations between arriving aircraft.
Point 3. The "alternating arrivals and departures" point, i.e., the point at which equal numbers of departures and arrivals are performed under the assumption of a sequencing strategy under which each arrival is immediately followed by a departure and vice versa.
Point 4. The "all departures" point, i.e., the capacity of the runway when it is used for departures only.

3.1.2. Details of the model

3.1.2.1. Point 1. Arrivals only. First, we discuss the computation of Point 1, i.e. the situation in which the runway is used only for arrivals. Landing aircraft approach the runway in a single file

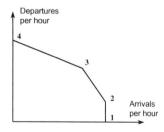

Fig. 3. The runway capacity envelope.

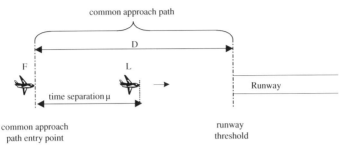

Fig. 4. Final approach for landing.

along a common approach path that typically begins between 5 and 8 nautical miles from the runway threshold. The capacity of the runway is then subject to two constraints. The first is that, during the final approach, consecutive aircraft are required to maintain a separation that exceeds an ATC-specified distance, which depends on the types of the leading and following aircraft (Fig. 4). The second constraint is that the runway cannot be occupied by more than one aircraft simultaneously—or a similar rule to essentially the same effect. Air traffic controllers impose a longitudinal separation between every pair of consecutive landings at the beginning of the common approach path such that these constraints are satisfied with high probability.

Aircraft are categorized for ATC purposes into several "types," with each type having its own characteristics in terms of separation requirements, approach speed and runway occupancy time. The speed at which each aircraft flies on the common approach path is assumed to remain constant. It is also assumed that this speed is sampled from a normal distribution, with a different mean and standard deviation applying to each type of aircraft. As is the case in practice, the standard deviation is assumed to be much smaller than the mean for all types of aircraft. Runway occupancy times and the actual position of aircraft (as compared to the position shown on the controller's radar screen) are also treated as normal random variables.

The parameters involved in computing Point 1 are now defined in Table 1.

The model computes the time μ by which controllers must separate successive arrivals at the entry point of the common approach path. This is done in two stages. First, the model computes the time by which controllers must separate successive arrivals, such that, with 95% confidence, the aircraft will not violate the minimum in-air separation requirement during the final approach (μ_1). Then, it calculates again the time by which controllers must separate successive arrivals, such that they can be 98.7% confident that the single-occupancy rule for the runway is met (μ_2). This is based on the perception that the single-occupancy rule on the runway is adhered to somewhat more strictly. The more restrictive of μ_1 and μ_2 is the separation sought, i.e. $\mu = \max(\mu_1, \mu_2)$.

Based on the separation imposed as aircraft enter the common approach path, the model computes the distribution of the interarrival times, i.e. of the times between two consecutive crossings of the runway threshold, for all possible pairs of aircraft types. The overall mean interarrival time is determined based on the weighted average of the means of the interarrival times of the different possible pairs. The analysis is performed separately for (1) the case where the

Table 1
Parameters involved in the computation of "Point 1" of the single runway model

V_i	Approach speed of aircraft of type i
δV_i	Uncertainty in the approach speed of aircraft of type i. It is assumed to be a normal random variable with mean zero and standard deviation σ_{V_i}
X_n	Distance of aircraft n from the starting point of the common approach path
p_i	Fraction of aircraft of type i
t_{L0}	Time when an aircraft L crosses the runway threshold
D	Length of common approach path
S_{ij}	Minimum separation requirement (distance) during the final approach when an aircraft of type i follows an aircraft of type j
μ	The time separation imposed by controllers between two consecutive entries to the common approach path
Ra_i	Arrival runway occupancy time of aircraft of type i
δRa_i	Uncertainty in the arrival runway occupancy time. It is assumed to be a normal random variable with mean zero and standard deviation σ_{Ra_i}
IAT_{ij}	Interarrival time between two consecutive arrivals, when an aircraft of type i follows an aircraft of type j

following aircraft is faster than or has the same speed as the leading one and (2) the case where the following aircraft is slower. In either case we denote the leading aircraft as L and the following aircraft as F. The detailed steps are as follows:

Case I: $V_F \geqslant V_L$

(a) Miles-in-trail minimum separation requirement

Let the time separation between the two aircraft when the following aircraft enters the common approach path be μ_1. In what follows, the distance is measured from the starting point of the common approach path, and time $t = 0$ is the time when the leading aircraft enters this path. The positions of the two aircraft at time t are given by

$$X_L = (V_L + \delta V_L)t \quad \text{and} \tag{1}$$
$$X_F = (V_F + \delta V_F)(t - \mu_1) \tag{2}$$

Note that, from (2), $X_F = 0$ when $t = \mu_1$. Since the following aircraft is faster, the distance between the two consecutive arrivals is decreasing during the final approach, and thus the critical time point in this case (i.e., the point where the in-air separation between L and F is minimal) is the instant when the leading aircraft flies over the runway threshold. This happens at time t_{L0}, given by

$$t_{L0} = \frac{D}{V_L + \delta V_L} \tag{3}$$

From (2) and (3), the position of aircraft F at that time can be derived:

$$X_F(t_{L0}) = (V_F + \delta V_F)\left(\frac{D}{V_L + \delta V_L} - \mu_1\right) \tag{4}$$

This can also be written as

$$X_F(t_{L0}) = \left(\frac{DV_F + D\delta V_F}{V_L + \delta V_L}\right) - \mu_1 V_F - \mu_1 \delta V_F \tag{5}$$

but,

$$\frac{DV_F + D\delta V_F}{V_L + \delta V_L} \approx \frac{DV_F + D\delta V_F}{V_L} - \frac{DV_F \delta V_L}{V_L^2} = \frac{DV_F}{V_L} + \frac{DV_F \delta V_F}{V_L V_F} - \frac{DV_F \delta V_L}{V_L^2}$$

because

$$\frac{a}{b} - \frac{ac}{b^2} = \frac{a}{b+c} - \frac{ac^2}{b^2(b+c)} \approx \frac{a}{b+c} \quad \text{when } \frac{c^2}{b^2} \ll 1$$

(let $a = DV_F + D\delta V_F$, $b = V_L$, $c = \delta V_L$ and ignore the $\delta V_L \cdot \delta V_F$ term). Then we can write:

$$X_F(t_{L0}) \approx \frac{DV_F}{V_L}\left(1 + \frac{\delta V_F}{V_F} - \frac{\delta V_L}{V_L}\right) - \mu_1 V_F\left(1 + \frac{\delta V_F}{V_F}\right) \tag{6}$$

From (6), and under the assumption that δV_F and δV_L are normal, zero mean, independent random variables, it follows that $X_F(t_{L0})$ is a normal random variable with mean

$$\overline{X}_F(t_{L0}) = \frac{DV_F}{V_L} - \mu_1 V_F \tag{7}$$

and variance

$$\sigma_1^2 = \frac{D^2 V_F^2}{V_L^2}\left(\frac{\sigma_{V_F}^2}{V_F^2} + \frac{\sigma_{V_L}^2}{V_L^2}\right) + \mu_1^2 V_F^2 \frac{\sigma_{V_F}^2}{V_F^2} \tag{8}$$

Then, the condition that F is at least a distance S_{FL} from L, when L crosses the runway $(D - X_F(t_{L0}) \geqslant S_{FL})$, with 95% confidence, can be written as

$$\mu_1 \geqslant \frac{D}{V_L} - \frac{D - S_{FL}}{V_F} + \frac{1.65\sigma_1}{V_F} \tag{9}$$

Based on (9) the smallest acceptable μ_1 can be computed iteratively. More specifically, in the implementation of the model, the starting point for μ_1 is

$$\frac{D}{V_L} - \frac{D - S_{FL}}{V_F}$$

Then σ_1 is computed from (8), the next μ_1 is computed from (9) by treating (9) as an equality, σ_1 is recomputed from (8), and so on until the difference between two consecutive values of μ_1 is less that 10^{-6}.

(b) Runway occupancy requirement

In order to meet the requirement that no more than one aircraft can be on the runway at any time, the leading aircraft must leave the runway before the following aircraft crosses the runway threshold. Runway occupancy times are assumed to be normal random variables that depend on the type of the aircraft. Let the time separation imposed for this reason as the aircraft enter the common approach path be μ_2. L will exit the runway at time t_{LX} given by

$$t_{LX} = t_{L0} + Ra_L + \delta Ra_L = \frac{D}{V_L + \delta V_L} + Ra_L + \delta Ra_L \tag{10a}$$

and F will cross the runway threshold at time t_{F0}, given by

$$t_{F0} = \frac{D}{V_F + \delta V_F} + \mu_2 \tag{10b}$$

Then, the difference between these times is given by

$$t_{F0} - t_{LX} = \frac{D}{V_F + \delta V_F} + \mu_2 - \frac{D}{V_L + \delta V_L} - Ra_L - \delta Ra_L \tag{11a}$$

After some algebra and ignoring second order terms, in a similar way as for Eq. (5), we can write (11a) as

$$t_{F0} - t_{LX} \approx \frac{D}{V_F} - \frac{D\delta V_F}{V_F^2} + \mu_2 - \frac{D}{V_L} + \frac{D\delta V_L}{V_L^2} - Ra_L - \delta Ra_L \tag{11b}$$

From (11b), the mean and variance of $t_{F0} - t_{LX}$ are computed:

$$\overline{t_{F0} - t_{LX}} = \frac{D}{V_F} + \mu_2 - \frac{D}{V_L} - Ra_L \tag{12a}$$

$$\sigma_2^2 = \sigma_{Ra_L}^2 + \frac{D^2}{V_F^2} \frac{\sigma_{V_F}^2}{V_F^2} + \frac{D^2}{V_L^2} \frac{\sigma_{V_L}^2}{V_L^2} \tag{12b}$$

Under the assumption that δV_F, δV_L, and δRa_L are independent, zero mean, normal random variables, $t_{F0} - t_{LX}$ is also a normal random variable. Then, the condition on μ_2 for a 98.7% confidence level is

$$\mu_2 \geq \frac{D}{V_L} - \frac{D}{V_F} + Ra_L + 2.215\sigma_2 \tag{13}$$

The smallest μ_2 that satisfies (13) is computed by treating (13) as an equality.

The single-runway occupancy requirement has, in recent years, been somewhat "relaxed" at airports with long runways. For instance, in the United States, in some cases, the follower aircraft can touch down on a runway as long as the leading aircraft is 8000 feet or more away from the runway threshold. For such cases, the runway occupancy time (Ra_i) in our model can be redefined appropriately to reflect the time it takes the leading aircraft to be at a safe distance from the runway threshold.

The time increment μ between two consecutive entries of aircraft in the common approach path actually applied by the controllers will be the most restrictive of the time increments:

$$\mu = \max(\mu_1, \mu_2) \tag{14}$$

Case II: $V_F < V_L$

(a) Miles-in-trail requirement

In this case the separation between the two aircraft will be increasing during the final approach. Thus, the critical point is now at the beginning of the common approach path. Specifically, the controllers must make certain that F will enter the common approach path after the leading aircraft has advanced a distance S_{FL} along it. The separation between the two aircraft when F enters the common approach path will be equal to the distance that L will have travelled during the time separation interval μ_1. This distance is given by

$$X_L(\mu_1) - X_F(\mu_1) = (V_L + \delta V_L)\mu_1 \tag{15a}$$

with mean and variance

$$\overline{X_L(\mu_1) - X_F(\mu_1)} = V_L\mu_1 \tag{15b}$$

$$\sigma_1^2 = \mu_1^2 \sigma_{V_L}^2 \tag{15c}$$

Under the assumption that the speed of the leading aircraft is a normal random variable, the distance it will have travelled is also a normal random variable. Then, the condition that the miles-in-trail requirement is not violated with 95% confidence is

$$\mu_1 \geqslant \frac{S_{FL}}{V_L} + 1.65 \frac{\sigma_1}{V_L} \tag{15d}$$

(b) Single runway occupancy requirement

The analysis and the results for the single-occupancy rule are identical with Case I. As in Case I, the most restrictive among μ_1 and μ_2 is applied, i.e., $\mu = \max(\mu_1, \mu_2)$.

Arrival capacity

Given μ, the time between threshold crossings of successive arrivals is given by the following equation:

$$IAT_{FL} = \frac{D}{V_F + \delta V_F} - \frac{D}{V_L + \delta V_L} + \mu \tag{16a}$$

After some algebra and ignoring second order terms, as was done for Eq. (11a), we can write (16a) as

$$IAT_{FL} \approx \frac{D}{V_F} + \frac{D\delta V_F}{V_F^2} - \frac{D}{V_L} - \frac{D\delta V_L}{V_L^2} + \mu \tag{16b}$$

Then, the mean interarrival time is

$$\overline{IAT}_{FL} = \frac{D}{V_F} - \frac{D}{V_L} + \mu \tag{17a}$$

and its variance can be approximated as

$$\sigma_{IAT_{FL}}^2 = \frac{D^2}{V_F^2} \frac{\sigma_{V_F}^2}{V_F^2} + \frac{D^2}{V_L^2} \frac{\sigma_{V_L}^2}{V_L^2} \tag{17b}$$

Under the assumption that δV_F and δV_L, are independent, zero mean, normal random variables, IAT_{FL} is also a normal random variable.

One important aspect of the spacing between arrivals is the additional separation that controllers typically allow to compensate for the uncertainty about the true position of aircraft that arises from resolution limitations of the radar screens they use, as well as tracking inaccuracies in older ATC systems. In the implementation of our model, this is taken into account by increasing the minimum separation standards during the final approach before carrying out the computations described above. The length to be added is computed such that, with 95% confidence, no violations will occur as a result of this uncertainty, under the assumption that the measurement error is a normal random variable with mean 0 and standard deviation σ_x. Thus, S_{ij} is replaced by $S_{ij} + 1.65\sigma_x$ for all i and j.

Once the interarrival times for all possible pairs have been computed, the "all arrivals" capacity (Point 1) is calculated based on the inverse of the weighted average of the interarrival times. Under a first-come, first-served policy of sequencing aircraft to the runway, the maximum throughput capacity is given by

$$C_{\text{arrivals}} = \frac{1}{\sum_i \sum_j p_i p_j \overline{\text{IAT}}_{ij}} \qquad (18)$$

3.1.2.2. Point 2. Arrivals plus "free departures". When a single runway is used for both arrivals and departures, one or more departures may be inserted between two consecutive arrivals (Fig. 5). The departing aircraft is cleared to enter the runway as soon as the leading arrival passes in front of it, prepares for takeoff while the leading arrival decelerates on the runway and begins its takeoff run immediately or soon after the leading arrival exits the runway. The takeoff run should begin before the following arrival comes within an ATC-specified distance from the runway's threshold. This ensures that the takeoff will have lifted off the far end of the runway by the time the following arrival touches down. For Point 2, the model calculates the number of departures that can be inserted into the arrival stream in one hour without affecting the interarrival times, i.e. without "stretching" the separation between any two consecutive arrivals to achieve the departure.

The ATC requirements that are involved in this process are that the departure (1) cannot start to roll before the first arrival exits from the runway, (2) cannot start to roll unless the second arrival is at least a minimum specified distance away from the runway threshold and (3) must lift off the runway before the second arrival crosses the runway threshold. The model assumes that a departure can start to roll immediately after the first aircraft exits the runway with a possible additional delay for communication between the pilot and the controller. It then computes the probability of inserting one or two departures between each possible pair of arrivals without violating ATC requirements (2) and (3) above.

The additional parameters involved in the computations for "Point 2" are defined in Table 2.

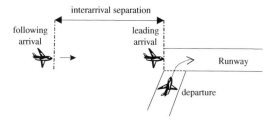

Fig. 5. Inserting a departure between two arrivals.

Table 2
Additional parameters involved in the computations for "Point 2" of the single runway model

G_{ij}	Minimum separation requirement (time) between two consecutive takeoffs (starts of roll) when an aircraft of type i follows an aircraft of type j
Rd_i	Departure runway occupancy time of aircraft of type i
δRd_i	Uncertainty on the departure runway occupancy time. It is assumed to be a normal random variable with mean and standard deviation σ_{Rd_i}
c	Communication time delay in departures; assumed to be a normal random variable with mean $\bar{c}$ and standard deviation σ_c
TFA_i	The time for a type i aircraft to reach the runway threshold when it is at the minimum allowable distance such that a departure can be released
SD	The minimum allowable distance of an approaching aircraft from the runway threshold such that a departure can be released

The expected number of intervals into which one departure can be inserted is computed first. For every possible threesome of aircraft types of leading arrival, departure and following arrival, the probability of being able to insert the departure is computed. In order to insert a departure, both the departure runway occupancy time and the time for the following arrival to reach the runway threshold when it is at the minimum allowable distance from the runway must be less than the interarrival time. The most constraining of these two conditions, i.e., the one with the greatest expected value, is used in the computations.

Under the assumption that the random variables are normal, the probability that a departure is possible can be expressed as

$$Pd_{ikj} = 1 - C\left(0, \overline{IAT}_{ij} - \overline{Ra}_j - \bar{c} - \max(\overline{Rd}_k, \overline{TFA}_i), \sqrt{\sigma_{IAT_{ij}}^2 + \sigma_{Ra_j}^2 + \sigma_c^2 + \sigma_X^2}\right) \quad (19a)$$

where Pd_{ikj} is the probability of inserting a departure of type k between arrivals of type i (follower) and j (leader), TFA_i is the time for a type i aircraft to reach the runway threshold when it is at the minimum allowable distance such that a departure can be released and σ_X^2 is equal to either $\sigma_{Rd_k}^2$ or $\sigma_{TFA_i}^2$ depending on the most constraining between Rd_k and TFA_i. $C(x, \mu, \sigma)$ is the value of the normal cumulative distribution at point x when the mean is μ and the standard deviation is σ.

The distribution of TFA_i is computed based on the probability distribution of the speed of the following arrival aircraft, assumed to be a normal random variable, and the minimum distance, SD, from the runway required for the following arrival aircraft:

$$TFA_F = \frac{SD}{V_F + \delta V_F}$$

Its mean is approximated as

$$\overline{TFA}_F = \frac{SD}{V_F}$$

and its variance as

$$\sigma_{TFA_F}^2 = \frac{SD^2 \sigma_{V_F}^2}{V_F^4}$$

in a way similar to Eqs. (11a) and (16a).

After computing the probability of inserting a departure between two consecutive arrivals for all possible threesomes, the overall weighted average is computed, excluding those threesomes for which Pd_{ikj} is less than 0.5.

$$\text{Pd}_1 = \sum_{i,j,k} p_i p_j p_k \text{Pd}_{ikj} \quad \text{for all } i,j,k \text{ such that } \text{Pd}_{ikj} \geqslant 0.5 \tag{19b}$$

where Pd_1 is the overall probability to insert a departure between a pair of arrivals.

The threesomes that have Pd_{ikj} less than 0.5 are excluded because it is assumed that, for such threesomes, the air traffic controllers will not even consider the possibility of allowing a departure between two consecutive arrivals. Note that because of the assumed normality of the random variables involved, Pd_{ikj} is greater than zero for all threesomes i, k, j.

The expected number of intervals into which (at least) one departure can be inserted is then

$$\text{DI}_1 = C_{\text{arrivals}} \cdot \text{Pd}_1 \tag{19c}$$

The probability of two departures being inserted between arrival pairs (Pd_2) is computed in a similar way, also taking into account the minimum required inter-departure separations. The expected number of intervals into which two departures can be inserted is computed as

$$\text{DI}_2 = C_{\text{arrivals}} \cdot \text{Pd}_2 \tag{19d}$$

The departures capacity for Point 2 is then given by (19e). [Note that the intervals during which at least one departure can be achieved include intervals where two departures can be achieved; however, each insertion is counted only once in (19e).]

$$C_{\text{Depart Point 2.}} = \text{DI}_1 + \text{DI}_2 \tag{19e}$$

Existing separation standards in developed countries typically make it impossible to insert more than two departures between two consecutive arrivals without stretching the interarrival gap.

3.1.2.3. Point 3. Alternating arrivals and departures. In computing Point 3, the model assumes that exactly one departure is inserted between all arrival pairs, by stretching the interarrival times whenever necessary. Under this assumption, the number of arrival–departure pairs that can be achieved is computed. The required separation between successive arrivals is calculated such that there is 95% confidence that no violation of any separation requirements will occur.

The computations are performed in the same way as for Point 1, except that, in this case, the distribution of the arrival runway occupancy time of the leading aircraft is replaced with the sum of the distributions of: (1) the arrival runway occupancy time, (2) the possible communication delay between controllers and pilots, and (3) the most constraining between the departure runway occupancy time and the time it takes for the following arrival to reach the runway threshold when it is at the minimum allowable distance such that a departure can be released. In other words, Ra_L is replaced by $\text{Ra}_L + \bar{c} + \max(\text{Rd}_d, \overline{\text{TFA}_d})$ in (11), (12) and (13), and $\sigma^2_{\text{Ra}_L}$ by $\sigma^2_{\text{Ra}_L} + \sigma^2_c + \sigma^2_y$ where σ^2_y is set equal to $\sigma^2_{\text{Rd}_d}$ or $\sigma^2_{\text{TFA}_d}$ depending on the most constraining separation.

The interarrival times are then computed for all possible arrival and departure aircraft types based on Eq. (17). Finally, each of the arrivals and departures capacity (they are equal in this case) are estimated as the weighted average of the interarrival times as follows:

$$C_{\text{Point 3}} = \frac{1}{\sum_i \sum_j \sum_k p_i p_j p_k \text{IAT}_{ikj}} \tag{20}$$

3.1.2.4. Point 4. Departures only. The "all-departures capacity" is computed by the model as the weighted average of the required time separations between consecutive departures (these separations, G_{ij}, depend on the types of the leading and following aircraft and are treated here as constants) plus the communication time delay between controllers and pilots. This very simple approach corresponds to the way ATC controllers typically impose the required departure separations.

$$C_{\text{departures}} = \frac{1}{\sum_i \sum_j p_i p_j (G_{ij} + \bar{c})} \tag{21}$$

3.2. Extending the analysis to configurations of two runways

The single runway capacity model has been extended to two dependent, simultaneously active runways under a variety of geometric configurations and types of interactions between the two runways. For the capacity estimation of systems with two dependent runways, four models have been developed. The constraints related to the interactions between operations on different runways taken into account in the FAA Airfield Capacity Model (Swedish, 1981) are included in the models developed here. A description of the four models follows. We denote these as Models 2 through 5. Model 1 is considered to be the single runway model described in Section 3.1.

3.2.1. Two parallel dependent runways

In the case of a pair of parallel dependent runways, a distinction is made between the situation in which one runway is used only for arrivals and the other only for departures ("segregated operations"), and the situation in which both arrivals and departures may take place on each of the runways ("mixed operations"). Models 2 and 3 refer to the former case whereas Model 4 to the latter.

3.2.1.1. Segregated operations (Models 2 and 3). When operations are segregated, two cases can be identified. If the local ATC rules allow for independent operations on the two runways, which is often the case when two parallel runways operate under VFR (Visual Flight Rules), the model simply computes the all-arrivals capacity and the all-departures capacity of the corresponding runways (Model 2). If, on the other hand, departures and arrivals are interdependent, which is often the case when two closely spaced parallel runways operate under IFR (instrument flight rules), then the model approximates the capacity of the parallel pair by calculating the single runway capacity for arrivals only on one runway and then by adding the same number of departures for the other runway (Model 3). Note that in the case of segregated operations, the runway capacity envelope is defined by the horizontal and vertical lines drawn from the point determined by the arrival and the departure capacity of the respective runways (Fig. 6). In the case of Model 3, moreover, the arrival and the departure capacities are equal.

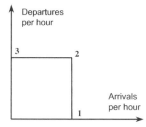

Fig. 6. Capacity envelope with three points (Models 2 and 3). In the case of Model 3 the envelope is a square.

3.2.1.2. Mixed operations (Model 4). When both runways are used for mixed operations, the most common case is that departures on each runway are independent of arrivals and departures on the other, while arrivals on the two runways are dependent. This is the situation modelled here. Specifically, an arrival on one of the runways is subject to a diagonal separation from the preceding arrival on the other runway. This is often the case when the distance between the two parallel runways is insufficient to permit independent landings on them. The required diagonal separation is specified by the rules utilized by the local ATC authorities.

As shown in Fig. 7, Model 4 examines quadruplets of arriving aircraft, with two aircraft arriving on each of the two runways. The first aircraft is arriving on one of the two runways (e.g., the "left" one), the second on the other ("right"), the third on the left runway again, and the fourth on the right. The time interval between the arrival of the first and the second aircraft is calculated based on the required diagonal separation between the two. The arrival time of the third aircraft is then constrained by its diagonal separation from the second aircraft, the miles-in-trail separation from the first aircraft, and the runway occupancy time of the first aircraft. A similar procedure is repeated for the last aircraft. As mentioned, departures are considered to be independent of operations on the other runway and are inserted between arrivals on either or both of the runways depending on the sequencing strategy in use.

The specific "algorithm" used by this model is as follows:

1. Calculate the expected interarrival time (IAT) and the standard deviation of IAT for the pair a–b (Fig. 7) using the diagonal separation requirement—instead of the miles-in-trail (MIT) separation requirement used in the computations of the single runway capacity model. Do not consider the runway occupancy time (ROT) constraint that is taken into account in the single runway capacity model.

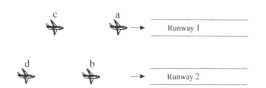

Fig. 7. A quadruplet of landing aircraft.

2. Calculate the expected IAT and standard deviation of IAT for the pair a–c in exactly the same way as for the single runway model.
3. Calculate the expected IAT and standard deviation of IAT for the pair b–c using the diagonal separation requirement instead of the MIT requirement. Again do not consider the ROT requirement.
4. Find the most constraining expected IAT for aircraft c, i.e. compute $\max(\overline{IAT}_{ac}, \overline{IAT}_{ab} + \overline{IAT}_{bc})$, the maximum of the interarrival time of aircraft a–c and of the sum of the interarrival times of aircraft a–b and b–c. Then, set $\sigma_{IAT_c} = \sqrt{(\sigma_{IAT_{ab}})^2 + (\sigma_{IAT_{bc}})^2}$, as computed in steps 1 and 3, or $\sigma_{IAT_c} = \sigma_{IAT_{ac}}$ as computed in step 2, as appropriate.
5. Calculate the expected IAT and standard deviation of IAT for the pair c–d using the diagonal separation requirement instead of the MIT requirement. As before, do not consider the ROT requirement.
6. Calculate the expected IAT and standard deviation of IAT the pair b–d in exactly the same way as in the single runway model.
7. Find the most constraining expected IAT for d by comparing $\overline{IAT}_{ab} + \overline{IAT}_{bd}$ with $\overline{IAT}_c + \overline{IAT}_{cd}$. Then, $\sigma_{IAT_d} = \sqrt{(\sigma_{IAT_{ab}})^2 + (\sigma_{IAT_{bd}})^2}$ or $\sigma_{IAT_d} = \sqrt{(\sigma_{IAT_c})^2 + (\sigma_{IAT_{cd}})^2}$.
8. Repeat steps 1–7 for all possible combinations of quadruplets of aircraft types.
9. Calculate the mean and standard deviation of the interarrival times, based on the distributions of IAT of aircraft b–d. The statistics obtained apply for arrivals on both runways. Twice the inverse of the weighted average of the interarrival time for aircraft b–d provides Point 1, i.e.,

$$C_{arrivals} = \frac{2}{\sum_i \sum_j \sum_k \sum_l p_i p_j p_k p_l \overline{IAT}(i,j,k,l)}$$

where $\overline{IAT}(i,j,k,l)$ is the mean interarrival time of the pair j–i (b–d in Fig. 7) when a quadruplet of aircraft types i, j, k, l is landing.
10. Based on the above statistics, i.e. the distributions of the interarrival times of the aircraft pairs landing on the same runway, and in a way similar to the single runway model, calculate the number of "free departures" on each runway separately, using the same procedure as in the single runway model. This provides Point 2.
11. Calculate the capacity associated with Point 3, by re-computing the interarrival separations, considering that one departure must always be inserted between successive arrivals (i.e. one departure between aircraft a–c, and one between aircraft b–d).
12. Compute the all-departures capacity as the sum of the all-departures capacity of each runway. As already noted, Model 4 assumes that departures on the two runways are independent.

Note that in this case, the runway capacity envelope will usually have a similar shape to that for the single runway case (Fig. 3).

3.2.2. Two intersecting runways (Model 5)

It is now assumed that one of the intersecting runways is used only for departures and the other only for arrivals, as is most commonly the case. The capacity is then computed on the basis of the probability of achieving one or two departures per interarrival gap. The constraints taken into

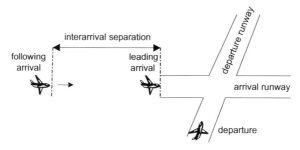

Fig. 8. Two intersecting runways.

account are (i) the time required for an arrival to clear the intersection of the two runways or to exit the arrival runway, whichever comes first, (ii) the minimum required distance of an approaching arrival from the arrival runway such that a departure can be released, (iii) the required separation between consecutive departures on the same runway and (iv) the required separation between consecutive arrivals on the same runway (Fig. 8).

Let MD_{mn} be the minimum distance that the (following) arrival, m, must be from the arrival runway such that departure n can be released. Let MT_{mn} be the corresponding time for the following arriving aircraft, m, to reach the runway threshold, and let TS_{kl} be the time interval between the instant when the leading arrival, k, crosses the threshold of the arrival runway and the instant at which a departure, l, can be released. The approach used is as follows:

Point 1

As in the single runway model, compute the "all arrivals" capacity of the single runway used for arrivals (Point 1).

Point 2

1. Compute the "all arrivals" capacity as for Point 1.
2. Calculate the mean, $\overline{MT}_{mn}$, and standard deviation, $\sigma_{MT_{mn}}$, of MT_{mn}, the time to travel the distance MD_{mn} for all possible pairs of arriving/departing aircraft types. Due to the underlying assumptions MT_{mn} is a normal random variable.
3. For all arrival pairs (i, j) and every type of departure aircraft, d_1, find the probability of being able to insert one departure between two arrivals. This is done by computing the probability that the normal random variable with mean $\mu_1 = \overline{IAT}_{ij} - \overline{MT}_{jd_1} - TS_{id_1} - \bar{c}$ and standard deviation, $\sigma_1 = \sqrt{(\sigma_{IAT_{ij}})^2 + (\sigma_{MT_{jd_1}})^2 + (\sigma_c)^2}$ takes a positive value.
4. For all arrival pairs (i, j) and every departure pair (d_1, d_2) find the probability of being able to insert two departures between two arrivals. This is done by computing the probability that the normal random variable with mean $\mu_2 = \overline{IAT}_{ij} - \overline{MT}_{jd_2} - TS_{jd_1} - DD_{d_2d_1} - 2c$, and standard deviation $\sigma_2 = \sqrt{(\sigma_{IAT_{ij}})^2 + (\sigma_{MT_{id_2}})^2 + 4(\sigma_c)^2}$ is positive, where $DD_{d_2d_1}$ is the minimum inter-departure separation.
5. Based on the results of steps 4 and 5, compute the total number of "free departures" that can be achieved in the same way as for Point 2 of the single runway model (Eqs. (19)).

Point 3

Re-compute the interarrival separations assuming that a departure must always be inserted between arrivals. The additional constraints applied now account for (1) the required distance from the runway of the next arrival if a departure is to be released, and (2) the minimum time required between the crossing of the runway threshold by the previous arrival and the instant when a departure can be released. The analysis is similar to that for Point 3 of the single runway model.

Point 4

As in the single runway model, compute the all-departures capacity (Point 4) of the single runway used for departures.

Note that for the case of intersecting runways, the runway capacity envelope will usually have a similar shape to that for the single runway case.

3.3. Other aspects of the capacity model

3.3.1. More than two simultaneously active runways

The application of analytical models to configurations involving three or more simultaneously active runways is more difficult, because of the large number of possibilities concerning the interactions among operations taking place at different runways and the complex operation-sequencing strategies that can be used. The approach taken in using MACAD for such cases is to "decompose" the set of active runways into more easily analysable components, each consisting of single- or two-runway combinations, selected from among Models 1–5 described above. The total capacity of the airport is then approximated by computing and adding together the capacities of each of these components. The decomposition most appropriate for each case will depend on the geometry of each airfield. When the runway configuration is modelled through more than one runway sets (each runway set corresponding to one of Models 1–5), the overall capacity envelope is synthesized by MACAD itself. It should also be noted that the overwhelming majority of airports in the world operate with one or two active runways at any given time.

3.3.2. Allocating capacity for arrivals versus departures

The runway capacity envelope describes, in effect, the trade-off between the maximum number of landings and takeoffs that can be achieved with any particular configuration and usage of the runway complex. For any time period of a day (e.g., a particular hour) the user of MACAD has the option of either specifying the allocation of available runway capacity between arrivals and departures or relying on MACAD's default mode to do so. The default mode is to select an allocation consistent with the mix of arrivals and departures demanded during the time period of interest (Fig. 9). Assume, for example, that in a particular hour of a day, the demand at an airport consists of 20 arrivals and 30 departures and that we wish to compute, through MACAD, the delays experienced at the runway complex by arrivals and by departures (see also Section 4). Under the default mode, MACAD will determine a "point of operation" corresponding to a line with slope 3/2 (Fig. 9) and will compute the delays for that hour using arrival and demand capacities equal to the respective co-ordinates of that point. Note that, if the delays are computed on an hourly basis, MACAD, in the default mode, will identify a point of operation for each hour, depending on the schedule of arrivals and departures during the day.

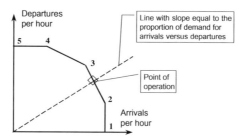

Fig. 9. Allocation of capacity to landings and takeoffs.

3.4. Estimating the capacity benefits from sequencing arrivals

In the work discussed so far, the runway capacity has been estimated based on the assumption of a first-come, first-served discipline. The objective of this section is to provide a simple methodology for evaluating a rough upper bound on the potential capacity benefits that could be obtained from sequencing landing aircraft in a manner other than first-come, first-served. Note that the probability P_{ij} of a pair of aircraft types (i,j) using the runway consecutively is given by $P_{ij} = p_i p_j$ under a first-come, first-served policy. This, however, may not be the case under other sequencing strategies.

The potential use of other sequencing strategies is motivated by the observation that disproportionately large interarrival times occur when light aircraft follow heavier aircraft. This is a result of the facts that (1) the wake vortex separation requirements that apply in such cases are more restrictive and (2) heavier aircraft are faster, and therefore, when imposing the minimum separation at the beginning of the common approach path, the distance between the aircraft will be increasing during the final approach, resulting in large interarrival times at the runway threshold.

In order to reduce the frequency of such "costly" pairs, one can encourage longer streams of aircraft of the same type, resulting in less frequent pairs of aircraft of different types landing consecutively. To achieve this, it may be necessary to delay some aircraft until they can land in a group of aircraft of the same type. Since, in practice, it is not possible to delay any aircraft for an excessive amount of time, the length of the streams of aircraft of the same type that land consecutively must be constrained. The approach described below accepts as an input a specified upper bound on the amount of time the landing of any aircraft can be delayed due to sequencing. It then computes the fraction of pairs of aircraft types landing consecutively, such that the maximum capacity can be achieved. In the following, the case in which one runway is used for arrivals only is discussed. This methodology can also be applied with Models 1, 2, 3 and 5. A quite similar approach can be applied, as well, to Model 4, where two runways are used simultaneously for arrivals.

Two steps are involved. In the first, one determines the best sequence of groups of consecutive arrivals with aircraft of the same type. In the second step, the size of each group is computed. As an example, consider the case in which three aircraft types—"light", "medium" and "heavy"—exist. In the first step it is determined whether it is best to sequence these types in the order of "a group of light aircraft, then of medium, then of heavy" or of "a group of light, then of heavy, then of medium". (As this is a cyclical process, no other sequence exists.) The second step determines the number of consecutive landings of the same aircraft type in each group.

Step 1. Find the best transition sequence involving all aircraft types.

Let n be the number of different aircraft types. Also, let $T_{1,2,\ldots,n}$ be the sum of the expected interarrival times between pairs of aircraft that generate a complete transition sequence that includes all aircraft types ("type 1 aircraft, followed by a type 2, ... followed by a type n, followed by a type 1"). We have

$$T_{1,2,\ldots,n} = \sum_{\alpha=1}^{n-1} t_{\alpha,\alpha+1} + t_{n,1}, \tag{22}$$

where $t_{i,j}$ is the expected interarrival time when a type j aircraft immediately follows a type i aircraft.

There are $(n-1)!$ possible transition sequences of the n aircraft types. Identify the one that gives the smallest sum, T', of expected interarrival times. This can be done easily through an exhaustive search because n is a small number in our case (typically 3 or 4). For example, when $n = 3$, the minimum of $(t_{21} + t_{32} + t_{13})$ and $(t_{31} + t_{23} + t_{12})$ determines the best transition sequence.

Step 2. Find the probability of pairs of consecutive arrivals.

Let x be the maximum time (in minutes) for which any aircraft can be delayed in order to be placed within a group of aircraft of the same type. (This is an externally provided "policy" requirement.) Let us divide each hour into $60/x$ equal time intervals of duration x minutes each. In order to satisfy the policy requirement, $60/x$ complete cycles of all aircraft types must take place within each hour. Then, we set

$$P_{ij} = \begin{cases} \frac{60/x}{C} & \text{for all } i \text{ and } j \text{ in the best transition sequence} \\ p_i - \frac{60/x}{C} & \text{when } i = j \\ 0 & \text{otherwise} \end{cases} \tag{23}$$

where C is the arrival capacity of the runway and p_i is the probability that a random aircraft is of type i. As a first order approximation for C, it is reasonable to use the capacity obtained under a first-come, first-served discipline.

As an example, let $n = 3$, $p_1 = p_2 = p_3 = 1/3$, $C = 36$ per hour and $x = 15$ minutes. Then, all the P_{ij} under a first-come, first-served discipline are equal to $1/9$. Let us also assume that Step 1 indicated that the best transition sequence is "1, followed by 2, followed by 3".

From (23) we would then have $P_{21} = P_{32} = P_{13} = (60/15)/36 = 1/9$, $P_{11} = P_{22} = P_{33} = 1/3 - (60/15)/36 = 2/9$, and $P_{12} = P_{23} = P_{31} = 0$.

It is worth pointing out that the maximum wait imposed on any aircraft in order to create groups of consecutive arrivals of the same type will be strictly less than the upper bound (x) since, during each time interval of length x, aircraft of all types will land, and the number of landings of each aircraft type will be proportional to the fraction of each aircraft type in the mix. Moreover, on average, the delay imposed on aircraft due to congestion of the runway complex will decrease as a result of the more efficient use of the runway system.

Once the P_{ij}'s have been determined, they can be used in (18) instead of the product $p_i p_j$. Some detailed conditions for the validity of this approach are provided in Stamatopoulos (2000).

A similar methodology is implemented for the case where two runways are used simultaneously for arrivals. The most important difference is that, instead of pairs, we now deal with quadruplets of aircraft types.

3.5. Differentiation from previous related work

As pointed out in the beginning of Section 3, the methodology of the runway capacity model proposed in this paper is based on a single-runway model previously developed at LMI (Lee et al., 1997), but differs from it in several important ways. In the model proposed here the single-runway methodology has been extended to two-runway configurations as described in Section 3.2. Other differences are summarized as follows:

1. Our runway capacity model includes an additional constraint that may prohibit a departure from being released. This constraint does not allow a departure to start to roll unless the next arrival is further than a user-specified, minimum distance from the runway threshold. This is a constraint that often plays a critical role in determining runway capacity, especially at European airports.
2. Our model calculates the expected capacity of the runway under study, i.e. the movements that can be achieved on average, as is the standard practice currently. By contrast, the LMI model computes the capacity that can be achieved 95% of the time, i.e., can be achieved with 95% confidence.
3. The LMI model uses a rather complex logic to calculate the all-departures capacity, while our model uses an entirely different and much simpler approach which computes the weighted average of inter-departure separation times.
4. We take into account the uncertainty regarding the position of the aircraft by simply adding an appropriate length to the miles-in-trail minimum separation requirements of approaching aircraft such that the controllers can be 95% confident that no violations will occur as a result of this uncertainty. In the LMI model this uncertainty is taken into account by including it in the computations of the standard deviation of the interarrival times.
5. In our model, it is assumed that controllers will not allow a departure to be inserted between arrivals, if it is projected that such an operation will violate some separation constraint with probability greater than 0.5 (see Section 3.1 for details).
6. Our model includes the methodology discussed in Section 3.4 for approximating the potential capacity benefits from sequencing arrivals.
7. Our model takes into account the possibility of two departures being inserted between a pair of arrivals.

4. Computing runway-related delays

For purposes of delay estimation the MACAD system models the runway complex as two queuing systems, one for landings and one for takeoffs. The capacities (service rates) for landings and takeoffs are computed through the runway capacity model and may vary over time. For example, if the traffic mix is different in the afternoon than in the morning, the corresponding capacities will vary accordingly. The same would be true, if due to weather conditions, noise-related policies, or other reason, the runway configuration in use changes. The demand rate for landings and takeoffs is also treated as a dynamic quantity and is assumed to be a given input. Based on the above assumptions and data requirements, the runway delay model provides an estimate of the delays incurred by aircraft on landing and takeoff as a function of time throughout the course of a day or other specified period of time.

MACAD uses an analytical queuing model, not a simulation, to estimate delays at the runways. A major problem in this respect is that the classical steady-state results of queuing theory usually cannot be applied to runway queues. During the course of a typical day demand and service rates may vary significantly over time, as just noted, and the use of steady-state expressions often yields very poor approximations (Odoni and Roth, 1983). Moreover, demand rates often exceed service rates for periods of time that may last for as long as a few hours at some major airports.

For these reasons, DELAYS, a queuing model that computes delays numerically is used in MACAD. DELAYS is based on the work of Koopman (1972), Kivestu (1976) and Malone (1995). It approximates runway systems as a queuing system with non-homogeneous Poisson arrivals and Erlang service times ($M(t)/E_r(t)/1$ in the notation of queuing theory) with the order r of the Erlang service times chosen with reference to the coefficient of variation of the service times at the runway. Beginning with a set of initial conditions at $t = 0$, DELAYS solves iteratively for t equal to $\Delta t, 2\Delta t, 3\Delta t, \ldots$ a (possibly large) set of difference equations that describe the evolution of the queuing system over the entire period of interest. The quantities computed are the probabilities, $P_n(t)$, of having n ($= 0, 1, 2, 3, \ldots$) "customers" (aircraft) in the queuing system at time t. The model adjusts internally the update interval Δt and the number of equations to be solved at each update depending on the model inputs at hand. It is extremely fast, taking advantage of an approach developed by Kivestu (1976)—for details see Malone (1995). The runway delay model incorporated in MACAD is a slightly modified version of the original DELAYS model, with increased robustness.

One major advantage of this approach is that the entire probability distribution for the number of aircraft in the queue is computed for all values of t. Thus, in addition to the usual measures of mean queue length, mean waiting time, etc., MACAD users obtain estimates of distributive measures of interest, such as, for example, the fraction of arrivals and/or departures that have to wait more than 15 minutes for access to the runway system.

5. The apron/taxiway model

5.1. Modeling the apron and taxiway area

The apron area consists of a number of elements, namely aircraft stands, apron taxiways, aircraft stand taxilanes and apron service roads. Of all those components, the apron stands most frequently pose a capacity constraint, and are the cause of significant delays. Taking this into consideration, the apron model in MACAD has as its primary objective to estimate (1) the utilization of the different categories of apron stands—categorized on the basis of the aircraft type(s) they can accept, the handler(s) that use them, and the type of flights they serve—and (2) the possible delays incurred by aircraft due to unavailability of unoccupied stands.

The taxiways are represented only in a notional way. Specifically, for each runway configuration, a probability distribution for the length of taxi-in and taxi-out times is provided as an input. For the purpose of strategic decision making, as opposed to detailed design, a more location-specific representation of the taxiway system is deemed to be unnecessary.

5.2. The simulation model

A macroscopic, discrete-event simulation model is used to represent apron/taxiway operations. It computes the utilization of the apron area and the delays due to the limitations of apron stands, taking into account most of the parameters of interest in strategic decision-making.

A flowchart of the principal operations performed by the model is shown in Fig. 10. The events that advance the "clock" and trigger the simulation are:

(a) The arrival of an aircraft in the apron buffer space. When such an event occurs, the aircraft is allocated to a stand, if one exists that can serve it. If several such stands are available, the stand that is less likely to be needed later is chosen according to a set of specified priorities.
(b) The availability of an apron stand that was previously unavailable. In this event, if an aircraft that can be served by the particular stand is waiting in the apron buffer, it will be assigned to it.

The time when an aircraft departs the stand it occupies is either the scheduled departure time or the time when apron handling is completed, whichever comes first. If the departure runway is

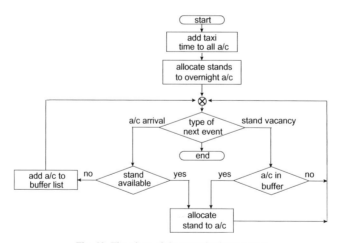

Fig. 10. Flowchart of the apron/taxiway model.

congested, the aircraft may occupy the stands for an additional amount of time, which is a user-specified input.

One practical issue of interest at some major airports is the "apron buffer space", i.e., any space in the apron or on the taxiway system where aircraft can wait temporarily until an aircraft stand becomes available, whenever all aircraft stands are occupied. Typically, the apron buffer space has considerable capacity. However there are a few airports where such space hardly exists, and there have been instances in which the landing process has been interrupted due to the unavailability of apron stands and buffer space. The simulation model identifies any periods of time during which the capacity of the apron buffer space is exceeded and modifies accordingly the landing capacity profile as described in Section 2.

6. Concluding remarks

A modelling approach has been described for estimating and assessing the capacity and level of service at the various parts of major airfields. The approach consists of a set of macroscopic models developed and utilized for the analysis of runway systems and apron areas, and a methodology for the integration of these models such that interactions among operations on the airfield are taken into account.

MACAD is sensitive to most of the major parameters that affect airfield capacity and level of service. These include airport geometry and operational characteristics, characteristics of the local air traffic control system, operational characteristics of the airside, and the characteristics of the demand for airfield access and services. All the individual models integrated into MACAD are fast, flexible and easy to use. They provide good approximations to capacity and level of service under a wide range of scenarios. These characteristics make MACAD suitable for use by decision-makers at the strategic level of planning.

MACAD has been subjected to rigorous evaluation and validation at Rome's Fiumicino Airport, one of the busiest in Europe, within the framework of the MANTEA (Management of Surface Traffic in European Airports DG XIII) project funded by the European Commission (Zografos et al., 1998). The results were very positive. For the evaluation, field data for a period of one full week of operations were used. The delays estimated by the model were very close to the observed values. Furthermore, MACAD was used as a tool for investigating a number of hypothetical scenarios about future conditions at the airport. A group of local experts also made positive comments in response to questions concerning user acceptance, cost effectiveness and potential contribution to airport planning processes. Those among them who obtained "hands-on" experience with MACAD indicated through questionnaires that the tool would help improve the quality of decisions, shorten turn-around times for analyses and reduce the cost of decision support. We have had similar experiences with informal applications of the model at a number of other airports. During 2002–03, an enhanced version of MACAD was applied with satisfactory results at six major European airports—Amsterdam, Athens, Frankfurt, Madrid, Palma de Mallorca, and Toulouse—within the framework of the OPAL (Optimisation Platform for Airports including Landside) project, funded in part by the Directorate General, Transport and Energy (DG-TREN) of the European Commission.

Acknowledgements

The work reported in this paper was supported in part by the European Commission (DG XIII) through the funding of the MANTEA (Mangement of Surface Traffic in European Airports) project.

References

Airport Council International – North America, 2001. General Information Survey: 2000, Washington, DC.
Blumstein, A., 1959. The landing capacity of a runway. Operations Research 7, 752–763.
Blumstein, A., 1960. An analytical investigation of airport capacity. Report TA-1358-G-1, Cornell Aeronautical Laboratory, Ithaca, NY.
Gilbo, E., 1993. Airport capacity: representation, estimation, optimization. IEEE Transactions on Control Systems Technology 1, 144–154.
Kivestu, P., 1976. Alternative methods of investigating the time-dependent M/G/K queue. S.M. Thesis, Department of Aeronautics and Astronautics, Massachusetts Institute of Technology, Cambridge, MA, USA.
Koopman, B.O., 1972. Air terminal queues under time-dependent conditions. Operations Research 20, 1089–1114.
Lee, D.A., Kostiuk, P.F., Hemm, R.V., Wingrove, W.E., Shapiro, G., 1997. Estimating the effects of the terminal area productivity program. NS301R3, Logistics Management Institute, VA, USA.
Malone, K., 1995. Dynamic queueing systems: behavior and approximations for individual queues and networks. Ph.D. Thesis, Operations Research Center, Massachusetts Institute of Technology, Cambridge, MA, USA.
Odoni, A.R., Roth, E., 1983. An empirical investigation of the transient behavior of stationary queueing systems. Operations Research 31, 432–455.
Odoni, A.R., 1991. Transportation modeling needs: airports and airspace. John A. Volpe National Transportation Center.
Odoni, A., Deyst, J., Feron, E., Hansman, R., Khan, K., Kuchar, J., Simpson, R., 1997. Existing and required modeling capabilities for evaluating ATM systems and concepts. International Center for Air Transportation, Massachusetts Institute of Technology, Cambridge, MA. Available from <web.mit.edu/aeroastro/www/labs/AATT/aatt.html>.
Stamatopoulos, M., 2000. A decision support system for airport strategic planning. Ph.D. Thesis, Department of Management Science and Marketing, Athens University of Economics and Business, Athens, Greece.
Swedish, W.J., 1981. Upgraded FAA airfield capacity model. Report MTR-81W16 (also Federal Aviation Administration Report FAA-EM-81-1), The MITRE Corporation, McLean, VA.
Zografos, K.G., Stamatopoulos, M.A., Odoni, A.R., Giannouli, I., Adami, S., Nicoloso, S., 1998. Verification of the airport capacity optimization tools. Technical Report – MANTEA Project (DG XIII), June 1998.

8

Marginal Cost Pricing of Airport Runway Capacity

By ALAN CARLIN AND R. E. PARK*

In an increasing number of *U.S.* cities the rapidly growing demand for use of airport runways experienced in the last decade has exceeded the available capacity, resulting in intolerably long delays to aircraft attempting to use them. Although the problem has been most acute and has received the most publicity in New York, similar problems have already arisen in Chicago and Washington and are likely to arise elsewhere in the years to come as the demand for air travel increases.

When faced with such a problem, most economists are likely to consider first the possibility of imposing marginal cost pricing or congestion tolls as a means to optimize the use of the given transportation facilities.[1] It is primarily this approach that we will explore here. Although other short-term solutions to the congestion problem are both feasible and interesting, they will be only briefly considered.

Throughout the paper our primary example will be New York's LaGuardia Airport during the period April 1967 through March 1968.[2] This is the most recent period for which data were available at the time the research was carried out.

The paper is divided into two sections. The first develops marginal delay or congestion costs for LaGuardia. The second explores the possible use of congestion tolls as a solution to the short-term congestion problem.

I. *Marginal Delay Costs*

What are the congestion costs that an additional user would impose on others? Equivalently, what would the savings to others be if one fewer plane were to use LaGuardia? In order to answer these questions, it is necessary to realize that during a period when an airport is continuously busy, each user imposes some delay on all following users until the end of the busy period. That is, an additional user shoves those following him one space back in the queue, and the effect persists until the queue dissipates.

---

* The authors are indebted to the referee for helpful suggestions. This paper is largely based on research undertaken for the Port of New York Authority, and reported more fully in our RAND memorandum. Any views expressed in this paper are those of the authors. They should not be interpreted as reflecting the views of The RAND Corporation or the official opinion or policy of any of its research sponsors.

[1] See, for example, M. Beckmann, C. B. McGuire, and C. B. Winsten, R. H. Strotz, and W. Vickrey. For a simple model that emphasizes some features of air transport, see Park. The rationale for congestion tolls is simple: A marginal user imposes congestion costs on other users, but considers only those costs that he bears himself in deciding to use a facility. A charge equal to the marginal congestion cost would internalize the external cost, so that individual decisions would lead to a socially efficient balance between use and congestion. This is clearly a partial argument. To the extent that there are offsetting external benefits from use of the facility, or that alternatives to use also involve external costs, the argument for a congestion toll is weakened. Indeed, any uncorrected departure from optimal conditions elsewhere in the economy makes it unlikely that a partially optimal congestion toll will result in a global second-best allocation. But these considerations do not rob the notion of a congestion toll of its merit. In many real cases, such as the one examined in this paper, it may be possible to say with considerable confidence that use of the facility with a congestion toll, although not globally optimal, would be more efficient than use without the toll.

[2] A similar analysis for Kennedy International Airport in New York is reported in Carlin and Park.

The Model

We seek the delay costs, C_i, imposed by a user of type i on other users at a time t when the remaining busy period equals B minutes. A type of use is defined by the type of plane and by specification as to whether it is a landing or takeoff. Thus $i=1$ may be a large jet landing, $i=4$ a light plane takeoff, and so on. Say there are m different types of use. Then if we knew the absolute service times, S_i, the number of operations of each type, N_i, that would occur from time t until the end of the busy period, and the costs per minute of delay to each type of operation, c_i, it would be easy to calculate the marginal delay costs due to an additional operation of type i as

$$(1) \quad C_i = S_i \sum_{i=1}^{m} N_i c_i$$

The operation delays each of the $N = \sum_{i=1}^{m} N_i$ operations for the length of time it takes to service it, S_i, at a cost to each of c_i per minute. But the N_i and the S_i are awkward to estimate. It is somewhat easier to estimate relative service times $s_i = S_i/S_1$, and proportions of various types of operations $n_i = N_i/N$. So we shall transform the relationship into a more usable form by introducing a second relationship. The length of the remaining busy period must just equal the sum of the time necessary to service each of the airplanes that lands or takes off before it ends:

$$(2) \quad B = \sum_{i=1}^{m} N_i S_i$$

Dividing (1) by (2), we obtain

$$(3) \quad \frac{C_i}{B} = \frac{S_i \sum_{i=1}^{m} N_i c_i}{\sum_{i=1}^{m} N_i S_i}$$

If we divide both the numerator and denominator of the right-hand expression in (3) by $S_1 N$, we obtain

$$(4) \quad \frac{C_i}{B} = s_i \cdot \frac{\sum_{i=1}^{m} n_i c_i}{\sum_{i=1}^{m} n_i s_i},$$

which conveniently expresses marginal cost per minute of the remaining busy period in terms of use proportions, relative service times, and individual costs per minute of delay.

At LaGuardia, which always operates with either a single or an intersecting runway configuration, arrivals and departures may be considered to be interdependent. In this case, we can approximate reality reasonably closely by distinguishing among four kinds of operations:

1—air carrier landings,
2—air carrier takeoffs,
3—general aviation landings, and
4—general aviation takeoffs.[3]

Since $s_1=1$, the formula for the marginal delay cost C_1 due to an air carrier landing at time t is

$$(5) \quad C_1 = \frac{n_1 c_1 + n_2 c_2 + n_3 c_3 + n_4 c_4}{n_1 + n_2 s_2 + n_3 s_3 + n_4 s_4} \cdot B(t)$$

and the costs C_i due to other types of operations are $s_i C_1$.

Empirical Estimates

The values of the n's vary throughout the day; hourly average general aviation as a percentage of total traffic on duty runways at LaGuardia varied from under 30 to over 40 percent during the busy afternoon hours.[4] So, of course, do those of the s's, in response to changing traffic mixes

---
[3] General aviation, consisting primarily of relatively small aircraft, is a category that includes air taxis, business and private planes.
[4] From an analysis of Federal Aviation Administration Runway Use Logs for 23 random sample days in 1967.

TABLE 1—PARAMETER ESTIMATES FOR LAGUARDIA

	Air Carrier Landings $i=1$	Air Carrier Takeoffs $i=2$	General Aviation Landings $i=3$	General Aviation Takeoffs $i=4$
1. Proportion of total traffic on duty runways, n_i	.32	.32	.18	.18
2. Service time relative to air carrier landings, s_i	1.00	.86	.54	.46
3a. Cost to aircraft owners (dollars per minute)	6.50	2.60	1.00	.50
3b. Passengers per operation	46.8	46.8	1.8	1.8
3c. Cost of passenger time (dollars per minute)	4.68	4.68	.36	.36
3d. Marginal cost of delays (dollars per minute), c_i	11.18	7.28	1.36	.86
4. Marginal cost of delays per minute of remaining busy period (dollars), $C_i/B(t)$	8.15	7.01	4.40	3.75

Notes on line:

1. From Carlin and Park (Table 5.1).
2. From Carlin and Park (Appendix Table C.3).
3a. From Carlin and Park (Appendix Table D.1), which also gives some cost figures for other airlines.
3b. Based on information supplied by Aviation Department, Port of New York Authority. General aviation and air carrier data are for 1965 and 1967, respectively.
3c. Assumes costs of $6 and $12 for air carrier and general aviation passenger time, respectively.
3d. Sum of lines 3a and 3c.
4. Computed using equation (5) and lines 1, 2, and 3d.

and runway configurations. And so, finally do those of the c's, primarily as a result of changing load factors throughout the day. However, to deal explicitly with all of these complexities would not, we feel, add enough precision to our estimates to be worth the large increase in computation that would be required. We thus limit our task in the next paragraphs to obtaining estimates of yearly *average* values for the quantities, other than $B(t)$, that enter expression (5) for marginal delay costs. Average values of $B(t)$ are estimated for each hour of the day.

Traffic proportions, n_i: Estimates of the n's are easily obtained from aggregate traffic statistics available for 1967, corrected to eliminate that fraction of general aviation traffic that used non-duty runways. These estimates are shown in line 1 of Table 1.[5]

Relative service times, s_i: By using the airport capacity manual prepared by Airborne Instruments Laboratory (*AIL*), it is possible to derive approximate ratios of the service times required by different classes of aircraft at LaGuardia.[6] Line 2 of Table 1 summarizes our estimates of relative service times.

Cost of delay to airplane owners and passengers, c_i: Line 3 shows our estimates of (or assumptions about) average cost of one minute delay to different kinds of operations, including both costs to the airplane owners and costs of passenger time. The estimates of air carrier costs are based on American Airlines figures for the types of planes that they operate at LaGuardia. In addition to direct variable costs of fuel, oil, and crew time, they include some allowance for indirect variable costs such as maintenance and incremental capital costs.[7] The fairly high general aviation costs reflect the fact that the average general aviation plane operating at La-

[5] For details, see Carlin and Park (p. 91).

[6] For details, see Carlin and Park (pp. 197–201). J. V. Yance performed a similar analysis for Washington National.

[7] For further details, see Carlin and Park (pp. 202–206). This also shows costs (one higher and one lower) reported by two other airlines.

Guardia is quite sophisticated. We assume $6 per hour as an average value for airline passenger time, and $12 per hour for presumably more affluent general aviation passengers.[8]

Marginal delay costs per minute of remaining busy period, $C_i/B(t)$: When the traffic proportions, the relative service times, and the delay costs per minute shown in lines 1 through 3 of Table 1 are substituted in expression (5) for marginal delay costs, the results are as shown in line 4 of that Table. These are estimates of the marginal delay costs per minute of remaining busy period that incremental operations of different types impose on other users.

Average remaining busy period, $B(t)$: To complete our estimates of marginal delay costs, we need information on the average length of remaining busy period by time of day, $B(t)$. As far as we know, this is the first time that an attempt has been made to estimate remaining busy periods. The method that we used is in principle a simple one. The basic data, kindly provided by American Airlines and United Air Lines, relate to delays experienced by individual flights. These data can be used to block out periods during which the airport was busy. For example, if an airplane that took off at 1615 was delayed for 15 minutes, this would ordinarily be an indication that the airport was busy between 1600 and 1615 on that day.[9] After busy periods were blocked out, the length of busy period remaining was tabulated at 10 minute intervals from 0700 to 2400 for each of 14 sample days and during 6 critical afternoon hours for each of 14 additional sample days. These values were averaged over all sample days to estimate expected busy period remaining by time of day. The estimates, together with standard errors, are shown in an appendix to this article which the authors will provide upon request. Hourly averages of the every-ten-minute estimates are shown in column 1 of Table 2.

Full marginal delay costs: It now remains only to multiply the costs per minute of remaining busy period shown in line 4 of Table 1 by the busy period estimates presented in column 1 of Table 2. The result-

---

cases, we based the delay estimate on the excess of actual over planned flight time, a measure that reflects other influences, such as enroute wind and weather forecast errors, in addition to terminal area delays. A random sample of about 50 flights for which both pilot-reported delays (PRD) and excess of actual over planned flight time (EFT) were recorded showed the following regression relationship:

$$PRD = .05 + .92\ EFT, \quad R^2 = .90,$$
$$(.04)$$

which we used to estimate delays when pilot reports were missing. For a few American flights, and all United flights, neither PRD nor EFT were available; there are no satisfactory delay measures in such cases. For all departures, both American and United, we calculated delays as the actual time elapsed between gate departure and takeoff, less a standard taxi time from the terminal building to the takeoff runway in use.

A second complication is that the data were occasionally contradictory. For example, one flight took off at 1615 after a calculated delay of 15 minutes, while another took off at 1610 on the same day with no delay. Much more frequently, there were gaps in the observations on individual flights. Although the observations were dense enough during some times of day to show several planes waiting for takeoff or for landing all at the same time, at other times there were periods during which no American or United flights were either waiting or operating undelayed. To resolve contradictions and fill in gaps, we made use of Federal Aviation Administration Runway Use Logs, which record the time of landing or takeoff of all planes using LaGuardia to the nearest minute, and thus provide a rough indication of whether the airport was busy or not at any particular time.

---

[8] For comparison, one study finds a value of $2.82 per hour for commuting motorists by a study of their behavior. See T. C. Thomas. Estimated marginal costs are sensitive to this assumption. Estimates for higher and lower values of passenger time are given in fn 10.

[9] In practice, there were a number of complications. In the first place, we had to use a number of different methods to calculate the delays experienced by individual flights. For some American arrivals, we had pilot reports of delays enroute and in the New York terminal area, both of which can in large part be attributed to airplane congestion at LaGuardia. For such flights we used the pilot reports as the delay measure. For some American arrivals, pilot reports were missing. In such

TABLE 2—AVERAGE REMAINING BUSY PERIOD AND FULL MARGINAL
DELAY COSTS BY HOUR OF DAY

Hour of Day	Remaining Busy Period (minutes)	Full Marginal Delay Costs ($ per incremental operation)[a]			
		Air Carrier		General Aviation	
		Arrivals	Departures	Arrivals	Departures
	(1)	(2)	(3)	(4)	(5)
0000–0700	0.0[b]	0[b]	0[b]	0[b]	0[b]
0700–0800	7.4	60	52	32	28
0800–0900	33.1	270	232	146	124
0900–1000	33.2	271	233	146	125
1000–1100	19.9	162	140	88	75
1100–1200	11.4	93	80	50	43
1200–1300	30.1	245	211	132	113
1300–1400	72.9	594	511	321	173
1400–1500	85.2	694	597	375	319
1500–1600	133.7	1090	937	588	501
1600–1700	118.2	963	829	520	443
1700–1800	96.4	786	676	424	361
1800–1900	74.5	607	522	328	279
1900–2000	44.6	364	313	196	167
2000–2100	19.5	159	137	86	73
2100–2200	7.2	59	50	32	27
2200–2300	1.7	14	12	8	7
2300–2400	.4	3	3	2	2

Notes:

[a] Computed using line 4, Table 1 and column 1, this Table.
[b] Assumed to be zero.

ing figures, shown in columns 2 through 5, are average values of the delay costs imposed on other users by incremental operations at any time of day. Some of these costs are very high. For example, it appears that an additional carrier arrival between 1500 and 1600 will, on the average, impose delay costs of over $1,000 on other users. Conversely, one less arrival during this period could be expected to reduce delay to others by the same amount. Marginal delay costs for general aviation operations during the same hour are in excess of $500.[10]

[10] If carrier and general aviation passenger time were valued at $3 and $6 per hour, respectively, the costs shown in Table 2 would be reduced by 25 percent. For $12 and $24 per hour, the costs would be increased by 49 percent.

There are apparently substantial savings to be realized by some reduction in low-value traffic at LaGuardia. Some approaches to achieving a reduction are discussed in the next section.

II. Policy Alternatives

No Change in Policy

During the study year, flight fees at LaGuardia were based on airplane weight, with a $5 minimum for each takeoff and no charge for landing. Most general aviation pays the minimum fee. Fees for carriers range from about $50 to $150, depending on the weight of the plane. Similar value-of-service fees are used at almost all major airports.

This fee structure leads to two related

inefficiencies. First, there is an inefficiently large amount of general aviation traffic. As shown in Table 1, 36 percent of all duty runway traffic at LaGuardia during 1967 was general aviation. Since most paid only $5 per landing and takeoff, and marginal congestion costs run up to on the order of 200 times that amount, one must conclude that many general aviation operations are of very low value relative to the congestion costs they impose on others.

It should be pointed out that on August 1, 1968, the Port of New York Authority raised the minimum fee to $25 for flights that land or take off between 0800 and 1000 Monday through Friday, and between 1500 and 2000 every day. This pioneering but limited step in the direction of marginal congestion cost pricing appears to have reduced significantly the amount of general aviation traffic at LaGuardia. The limited information available suggests that general aviation may have been reduced as much as 40 percent at LaGuardia during the hours when the $25 minimum applies.

Second, airline passenger loads are inefficiently low. At LaGuardia, airline load factors averaged 59.4 percent during 1967.[11] In the airline industry, competition is primarily on the basis of service rather than price.[12] One very important part of this service competition is competitive scheduling. With the present level of fares, costs are covered at fairly low load factors. The airlines tend to add flights to the same destination at roughly the same time until load factors are forced down toward these break-even levels. Although the higher frequency of service that results is not without value, it seems certain that less frequent service at higher load factors would be more efficient.

In the remainder of this section we shall

[11] Aviation Division, Port of New York Authority.
[12] For an extended discussion, see R. E. Caves (pp. 331-55).

discuss two pricing approaches to increasing the efficiency with which the runways are used.

Full Marginal Cost Pricing

One of the difficulties in making estimates of marginal costs with the intention of using them as prices is to allow for the effects that the prices themselves will have on runway use. Use of the costs shown in Table 2, for example, would not represent equilibrium conditions because their use would reduce the number of airplanes using the airport, thereby reducing marginal costs and hence the prices that should be charged. If instituted immediately such a pricing system would be less than optimally efficient by overly reducing traffic. It might even be dynamically unstable, in the sense that costs recomputed in succeeding periods and used as prices might not converge to an equilibrium level. This would be the case if, after Table 2 prices were imposed, traffic decreased so much that marginal costs fell below the level of current flight fees. Using these lower costs as prices during the following period would result in traffic above current levels, and undamped oscillations in prices and traffic would ensue.

Using Table 2 costs as prices without adjustment would clearly be unwise. On the other hand, to determine analytically a set of equilibrium prices would be an impossible task. To do so, we would need to know with some confidence and precision what the pattern of traffic would be under different sets of prices. We do not. One way to implement equilibrium marginal cost prices in light of these difficulties would be to charge an increasing percentage of the full marginal costs as recomputed after each successive increase.

Efficiency: Equilibrium marginal cost prices would result in very efficient runway use. They would obviously exclude low value general aviation traffic. They would also increase carrier load factors to a more efficient level.[13]

Practicality: Equilibrium marginal cost pricing does not appear to be a practical policy at LaGuardia. At least in the short run, airlines would be hurt by higher flight fees. The formula for calculating present airline flight fees is embodied in lease agreements between the Port Authority and the individual airlines. The airlines would therefore be able to block any move by the Port to impose higher fees.

In the longer run, there may be some offsetting considerations. For one thing, the higher flight fees would be (in principle, completely) offset by reduced operating costs as schedules were reduced and load factors increased. However, given existing airline fleet sizes and commitments for additional airplanes, it would take a long time for this adjustment to work itself out. For another thing, the increased flight fee revenues might be used by the Port Authority for capacity expansion, as Herbert Mohring suggests. However, the constraints on capacity expansion are primarily political, not financial; additional Port Authority revenue would do little or nothing to promote it.

These possible benefits are remote or uncertain enough so that short-run considerations would surely dominate. Airline opposition to full marginal cost pricing would keep it from being a practical alternative.

Proportional Marginal Cost Pricing

A more practical pricing approach is to limit total airline runway use payments to what they would be under the formulas written into the present leases, but attempt to change the basis on which fees are levied so that fees during any hour would be proportional to those that would prevail

[13] For a theoretical treatment of this latter point, see Park.

under full marginal cost pricing. Even if equilibrium marginal cost pricing were to be attempted, this would be the recommended first step toward it.

Using the full marginal costs shown in Table 2 as a basis, it is a simple step to compute what proportional fees would be on the assumption that the airlines as a group are to pay no more than they otherwise would. Using the average of September 1967 and February 1968 airline schedules, hypothetical collections with full marginal cost flight fees were computed. A percentage was then computed by dividing this number into actual airline payments to the Port Authority for runway use during the period March 1967 through February 1968. When these percentages were used to derive proportional cost fees, the prices shown in Table 3 resulted.

Practicality: Although the factors of proportionality have been chosen to keep payments by airlines as a group constant, particular airlines may pay considerably more or less under such a scheme than under the present weight-based system. Presumably the less individual airline payments exceeded present payments, the easier it would be to obtain airline agreement to such a system.

In order to explore this question, we compared what airline payments would have been using the prices shown in Table 3 and average schedule data for September 1967 and February 1968 with actual payments for the period March 1967 through February 1968. The results, shown as percentages, are presented in Table 4.

With one major exception, the calculations are fairly encouraging for airline acceptance of such a scheme at LaGuardia. The major exception is the local service airlines, particularly Allegheny and Mohawk. Because they use smaller planes which benefit from the present weight related fees, and have few flights in the

TABLE 3—PROPORTIONAL MARGINAL COST PRICES FOR LAGUARDIA
YIELDING CURRENT PORT AUTHORITY AIRLINE REVENUE
(dollars per operation)

Hour of Day	Air Carrier		General Aviation		Post-August 1968[a] Actual Minimums	
	Arrivals	Departures	Arrivals	Departures	Departures	Either[b]
0000–0700	0[c]	0[c]	0[c]	0[c]	5	
0700–0800	7	6	4	3	5	
0800–0900	30	26	16	14		25[d]
0900–1000	31	26	17	14		25[d]
1000–1100	18	16	10	9	5	
1100–1200	11	9	6	5	5	
1200–1300	28	24	15	13	5	
1300–1400	67	58	36	31	5	
1400–1500	78	67	42	36	5	
1500–1600	123	106	66	57		25
1600–1700	109	94	59	51		25
1700–1800	89	76	48	41		25
1800–1900	69	59	37	32		25
1900–2000	41	35	22	19		25
2000–2100	18	15	10	8	5	
2100–2200	7	6	4	3	5	
2200–2300	2	1	1	1	5	
2300–2400	0	0	0	0	5	

Notes:

[a] Prior to August 1968, the minimum was a uniform $5 throughout the day for departures only.

[b] For both arrival and departure if either occurs during the hours shown.

[c] Assumed to be zero.

[d] Monday through Friday only. The $5 minimum departure fee applies on other days.

Source:
Table 2.

early morning hours, they would be particularly affected by proportional cost fees. On the other hand, their higher runway use fees would be at least partially offset by reduced delay costs. Furthermore, airlines as a group would certainly be better off on balance. Since the group is a small one, one might expect informal pressures or side payments to bring about agreement by all airlines to proportional cost fees.

Efficiency: The proportional cost prices in Table 3 would do much to deter low value general aviation traffic during busy hours. The significant effect of a $25 charge for landing and takeoff combined is mentioned above. Proportional cost fees, which range up to almost five times this amount, would probably eliminate almost as much general aviation traffic as would full marginal cost prices. On the other hand, proportional prices by themselves would have little effect on inefficiently low load factors. Flight fees for carrier aircraft using La Guardia currently range from about $50 to $150 per landing and takeoff combined. If the proportional marginal cost prices of Table 3 were in effect, a carrier plane landing and taking off at peak times would pay as much as about $200. This increase is small enough so that it would probably

TABLE 4—CALCULATED AIRLINE PAYMENTS FOR LAGUARDIA RUNWAY USE USING PROPORTIONAL MARGINAL COST PRICING AS A PERCENTAGE OF ACTUAL COLLECTIONS

Trunk carriers	90
American	100
Eastern	66
National	56
Northeast	122
TWA	90
United	88
Local service carriers	230
Allegheny	263
Mohawk	242
Piedmont	142

have little influence on the schedules of the air carriers (with the possible exception of the local service carriers).

Other Alternatives

We have examined in some detail two pricing approaches to increasing the efficiency with which La Guardia's runways are used. Full marginal cost pricing is the most efficient pricing scheme, but it could not be adopted over airline opposition, and airline opposition is likely. Proportional marginal cost pricing is probably the most efficient pricing scheme with a reasonable chance of being implementable, but it does little to correct inefficiently low airline load factors. This suggests that other measures capable of affecting schedules as well as general aviation use would be even more efficient than proportional marginal cost pricing. These other alternatives include purely administrative measures and combination measures involving both pricing and administrative aspects. Although a complete discussion is beyond the scope of this paper, we shall mention a few of the possibilities here.[14]

The most efficient purely administrative measures would restrict both general aviation and air carriers to something less than their current levels of operation. One central problem in the design of an efficient administrative measure is to decide what level each should be restricted to. Another is to formulate the restrictions so as to attempt to exclude the lowest value traffic in each category. On June 1, 1969, the Federal Aviation Administration imposed limits on operations during bad weather at five busy airports, including LaGuardia. Although the limits are higher and allocate a larger share to general aviation than would be efficient, this measure is a small step toward more efficient runway use. However, bargaining among the airlines is a cumbersome way to split up the quota, and there is no guarantee that the schedules will go to the highest value users.

There are at least two combination measures that are potentially more efficient than any of the feasible "pure" alternatives. The first of these would consist of the issuance of property rights in schedule slots for particular hours in proportion to current use that could be freely traded among airport users.[15] The number of slots for each hour would be chosen administratively to approximate the efficient number. The free market in slots would then allocate them to the highest-value users. It would, of course, be permissible to subdivide the slots so that, for example, an airline might purchase the right to use a slot on Monday through Friday only. If the slots were issued to airlines in proportion to recent schedules, all would share in the gains from increased efficiency; there should be no airline opposition to overcome in introducing this measure. In theory, one could issue many small fractional slots to nonscheduled users as well, and rely on the market to allocate slots among *all* users. In practice, it would probably be

---

[14] For a more detailed discussion, see Carlin and Park (pp. 139-55).

[15] This approach was suggested by Jack Hirshleifer.

better to rely on some pricing mechanism to control nonscheduled users. As another practical matter, it would be best to issue the property rights in slots on a relatively short-term basis, say one or two years, to make it easier to adjust the number of slots or otherwise to modify the system.

The second combination measure would consist of both proportional marginal cost pricing and administrative limits on airline schedules. The proportional prices would exclude low-value general aviation users, and the schedule limits would increase airline load factors.

III. Conclusions

Because of the practical problems involved, equilibrium marginal cost pricing does not appear to be a feasible alternative for allocating runway capacity at La Guardia. The use of proportional marginal cost pricing, however, offers some of the same efficiency advantages without most of the problems. It is certainly preferable on efficiency grounds to the present weight-based, value of service pricing used at most airports. Use of administrative limits on schedules would be required in conjunction with proportional marginal cost pricing, however, to increase carrier load factors to more efficient levels.

REFERENCES

M. Beckmann, C. B. McGuire, and C. B. Winsten, *Studies in the Economics of Transportation*. New Haven 1956, pp. 80-101.

A. Carlin and R. E. Park, *The Efficient Use of Airport Runway Capacity in a Time of Scarcity*, RM-5817, The RAND Corporation. Santa Monica Aug. 1969.

R. E. Caves, *Air Transport and Its Regulators: An Industry Study*. Cambridge, Mass. 1962.

H. Mohring, "Urban Highway Investments," in R. Dorfman, ed., *Measuring Benefits of Government Investments*. Washington 1965, pp. 231-75.

R. E. Park, "Congestion Tolls for Regulated Common Carriers," P-4153, The RAND Corporation. Santa Monica Sept. 1969. Also forthcoming in *Econometrica*.

R. H. Strotz, "Urban Transportation Parables," in Julius Margolis, ed., *The Public Economy of Urban Communities*. Washington 1965.

T. C. Thomas, *The Value of Time for Passenger Cars: An Experimental Study of Commuter's Values*, Palo Alto 1967.

W. Vickrey, "Optimization of Traffic and Facilities," *J. Transp. Econ. Policy*, May 1967, *1*, 123-36.

J. V. Yance, "Movement Time as a Cost in Airport Operations," *J. Transp. Econ. Policy*, Jan. 1969, *3*, 28-36.

Airborne Instruments Laboratory *Airport Capacity*, prepared for Federal Aviation Agency and available from Center for Scientific and Technical Information as PB 181 553, New York June 1963.

Port of New York Authority, Aviation Department, *Airport Statistics*.

9

The economics of airport congestion pricing

Eric Pels and Erik T. Verhoef

Abstract

Conventional economic wisdom suggests that congestion pricing would be an appropriate response to cope with the growing congestion levels currently experienced at many airports. Several characteristics of aviation markets, however, may make naive congestion prices equal to the value of marginal travel delays a non-optimal response. This paper develops a model of airport pricing that captures a number of these features. The model in particular reflects that (1) airlines typically have market power and are engaged in oligopolistic competition at different sub-markets; (2) part of external travel delays that aircraft impose are internal to an operator and hence should not be accounted for in congestion tolls; and (3) different airports in an international network will typically not be regulated by the same authority. We present an analytical treatment for a simple two-node network and some numerical results to illustrate our findings. Some main conclusions are that second-best optimal tolls are typically lower than what would be suggested by congestion costs alone and may even be negative, and that cooperation between regulators need not be stable but that non-cooperation may lead to welfare losses also when compared to a no-tolling situation.
© 2003 Elsevier Inc. All rights reserved.

Keywords: Congestion; Market power; Networks; Airports; Airlines

1. Introduction

Many airports face capacity problems. In the US, 25 airports are classified as "severely congested" by the Federal Aviation Administration (Daniel [10]), while also in Europe many airports face congestion problems (e.g. London Heathrow, Frankfurt and Amsterdam Schiphol). This raises the economic issue of how to allocate scarce runway capacity. In the US, this is usually done on a first-come first-served principle. When capacity is limited, arriving aircraft consequently cause delays (and thus costs) for other arriving aircraft. Only four US airports (Washington Ronald Reagan, New York LaGuardia, New York Kennedy and Chicago O'Hare) are slot-constrained; with slot trading between airlines allowed (see e.g. Starkie [15]). European airports are usually slot-constrained; slots are allocated by a slot coordinator. The slot-allocation mechanism at most airports is not based on economic principles. The users of capacity (airlines) may pay less than the marginal social cost (congestion costs are not paid, entry is deterred), and are not necessarily the (potential) users that attach the highest economic value to the capacity.

Like slot trading, also airport congestion pricing aims to allocate scarce capacity to those parties that attach the highest economic value to it. Congestion pricing in aviation is, however, a relatively under-explored option in the literature. Most studies of congestion pricing in transport networks concern road traffic, and therefore consider link-based tolls. However, for aviation—and other modes—it may often be nodes, rather than links between them, that form the bottlenecks. A question that naturally arises is whether insights from studies on link-based pricing in road networks are directly transferable to node-based pricing, especially under second-best circumstances where multiple market distortions exist simultaneously. It may in particular be expected that the nature of such other market distortions, additional to congestion externalities, are different at nodes than along links. Given the substantial and growing congestion at major airports and other transport hubs throughout the world, it seems relevant to investigate the implications for congestion pricing.

An important difference between congestion on roads and in aviation is that individual road users typically do not have market power, and can thus be assumed to take travel times as given. Airports, in contrast, and especially the more congested hubs, will often have spatial monopolistic power, while their primary user(s), airlines, will often compete under oligopolistic conditions. Moreover, especially when positive network externalities (or economies of density) induce these airlines to operate hub-and-spoke networks, with different airlines using different hubs, these oligopolies may be asymmetric. A substantial share of congestion costs may then not constitute external effects, but be internal instead. That is, the travel delays imposed by one service upon other services may often concern services of the same operator, who can be assumed to take these firm internal congestion effects into account when determining profit-maximizing prices and frequencies. These firm-internal congestion costs should then not be included in congestion taxes (Brueckner [5]).

A further implication of oligopolistic competition would be that another distortion, besides congestion, is likely to be present, namely that of strategic interaction between competitors, with the result of non-competitive pricing. Absent congestion, consumer prices may then exceed marginal costs because airlines have market power, implying that an economic argument for subsidization rather than taxation would exist. As pointed out by Buchanan [8] and Baumol and Oates [1] in the context of a polluting monopolistic firm, the implication for Pigouvian externality pricing is that the second-best optimal tax would have to be below the marginal external costs, and may even become negative. This would provide a second argument, in addition to the point raised by Brueckner [5], why optimal congestion charges at a hub would be below marginal external congestion costs (if straightforwardly defined as the value of a single service's marginal delay costs for all other services).

This paper aims to investigate such issues by developing a model that considers second-best congestion pricing for incoming and outgoing flights at airports. The second-best circumstances under which congestion tolls have to be set are those just mentioned. We consider a simple network with two nodes, where both airlines and passengers suffer from congestion at airports. Three types of interacting players are present in our model: a regulatory authority, airlines, and passengers; each having their own objective. Congestion tolls can be determined by a single regulator for all airports in the network, but also by "local" regulators of specific airports. Tax competition between local regulators then becomes an issue.

As stated, airport congestion pricing has received limited attention in the literature. Carlin and Park [9] estimated the external cost of a peak-period landing at LaGuardia was $2000 (in 1969 $); about twenty times the actual landing fee, although this number should not be interpreted as an equilibrium congestion toll. Oum and Zhang [13] examine the relation between congestion tolls and capacity costs, and find that when capacity investment is lumpy, the cost recovery theorem (which states that congestion toll revenues just cover amortized capacity (expansion) costs under constant returns to scale) no longer holds. Daniel [10,11] combines stochastic queuing theory with a Vickrey-type bottleneck model. His simulation results show that congestion pricing causes a redistribution of flights over the day, where smaller aircraft may divert to other airports because they value their use less than the social cost of using the congested airport. Brueckner [5] analyzes airport congestion pricing when airlines are non-atomistic, and concludes that there may be only a limited or even no role for congestion pricing when the number of airlines using the node decreases, as the share of internalized congestion costs increases. Brueckner [6] extends the analysis of Brueckner [5] to a network setting, and finds that an airline specific toll equals the congestion damage caused by the airline, multiplied by a fraction given by one minus the airline's flight share.

This paper adds two complications to the set-up considered by Brueckner [6]. An important one is the explicit consideration of market power distortions and the effects on optimal congestion tolls. Another is that airports need not cooperate optimally to maximize joint welfare, but instead may engage in a form of tax competition in the pursuit of maximizing local rather than global welfare.

The structure of the paper is as follows. First, the notation and main assumptions are introduced in Section 2. Section 3 derives an analytical equilibrium and optimality results for a symmetric duopoly. Sections 4 presents numerical results for a symmetric and an a-symmetric duopoly. Section 5 considers tax competition between regulators. Finally, Section 6 concludes.

2. Notation and assumptions

In the model, we distinguish three different parties: an endogenous number of passengers, two airlines, and two airport authorities. Passengers wish to travel between a given city pair. To do so, the services of an airline i are necessary. The two airlines, in turn, need the services of two airports h for each service: an origin and a destination. Prices for the use of an airport may in reality be set by a profit maximizing *airport operator* or a welfare maximizing *regulatory authority*. Because we are concerned with (second-best) optimal airport prices, we will be considering a (public) regulatory authority alone. An extension of the model to four types of players (regulators, private airport operators, airlines and passengers) is considered as an interesting option for future work.

For the general specification of the model, a number of assumptions are made, that will now first be presented.

Assumption 1. A passenger return trip involves one airline only. The inverse aggregate demand is linear in form:

$$D\left(\sum_{i=1}^{2} q_i\right) = \alpha - \beta \sum_{i=1}^{2} q_i \tag{1}$$

where $\alpha > 0$ and $\beta > 0$; α represents the maximum reservation price, β is the demand sensitivity parameter, and q_i is the number of passengers transported by airline i. We consider one city pair only, served by direct flights, and the unit of analysis is return trips.

Assumption 2. An airline's frequency (in both directions) is

$$f_i = \frac{1}{\lambda_i} q_i \tag{2}$$

where λ_i is the given product of the load factor and the seat capacity, and thus gives the number of passengers per flight. Congestion occurs at nodes only (i.e., not on links; "capacity in the air" or the capacity of the air traffic control system is abundant). The average time loss per passenger or per flight due to congestion at node h, ϕ_h, is assumed to increase linearly in the total frequency at that node:

$$\phi_h = \eta_h \sum_{i=1}^{2} f_i = \eta_h \sum_{i=1}^{2} \frac{1}{\lambda_i} q_i \tag{3}$$

where η_h is the slope of the congestion function. Note that arriving and departing movements need not contribute equally to, and suffer equally from congestion. However, as we only consider return markets, we do not have to make this distinction, and ϕ_h gives the sum of time losses during departure and arrival on the airport.

The congestion term (in time units) to be included in the passengers' and airlines' (generalized) cost functions is then

$$\phi_i = \sum_{h=1}^{2} \phi_h. \tag{4}$$

Multiplying this term by the passengers' value of time (vot_p) and the airlines' value of time (vot_l) yields the monetized congestion delay cost to passengers and airlines, respectively (vot_l is assumed equal between airlines). The passengers' value of time would typically purely reflect lost time. The airline's value of time may also include additional resource costs: vot_l would capture expenditures on fuel, crew time, etc.

Assumption 3. The generalized costs for an airlines' service, as experienced by passengers, is characterized by a generalized user cost function $g_i(p_i, vot_p \times \phi_i)$ where p_i is the fare. The generalized user cost function is linearly additive in form:

$$g_i = p_i + vot_p \times \phi_i. \tag{5}$$

Assumption 4. The airline's cost per (return) passenger, c_i^q, and per (return) flight, c_i^f, are constant. The congestion toll at node h is denoted t_h and is valid for one arrival and one departure. Total operating costs for airline i are then

$$f_i \left(c_i^f + \sum_{h=1}^{2} t_h + vot_l \phi_i \right) + c_i^q q_i - F_i \tag{6}$$

which may be rewritten as

$$q_i \times \left[\frac{1}{\lambda_i} \left(c_i^f + \sum_{h=1}^{2} t_h + vot_l \phi_i \right) + c_i^q \right] - F_i \tag{6'}$$

where F_i is airline i's fixed cost.

Assumption 5. The airlines act as Cournot duopolists (i.e. they choose an optimal output (and frequency) taking the other airline's output as given). Airlines do not believe that by their actions, they can affect the regulator's tolls (i.e. regulators and airlines are playing a Stackelberg type game, the regulators being the leader). Passengers are pure price takers, who regard the airlines as pure substitutes, so that network equilibrium conditions can be represented as a Wardrop equilibrium with respect to generalized costs.

Although these assumptions may seem restrictive, many of these are quite common in the aviation economics literature. The functional form of the cost function used in this paper is similar to the one used by Brueckner and Spiller [7].[1] Combined with a linear demand curve, the Brueckner–Spiller model has been used regularly to analyze aviation networks. Despite the conceptual simplicity, recent trends in the aviation markets can easily be explained using this model; see, e.g., Brueckner [4] for an analysis of airline alliances, and Pels et al. [14] for an analysis of optimal airline networks.[2] It is not the objective of this paper to calculate exact tolls for existing airports, for which these assumptions would clearly be too restrictive. This paper aims to develop theoretical insights into the consequences of airport congestion pricing, for which these assumptions suffice.

3. The symmetric duopoly equilibrium: analytical solution

With these assumptions, we can now derive some analytical results. There are three types of players in the model, passengers, airlines and regulatory authorities, each with

---

[1] Brueckner and Spiller [7] do not include congestion in their cost function.
[2] See Brueckner [4] for additional references.

their own maximization problem. The model is solved in three steps. First, a passenger demand function for network operator i is determined. Then, using this demand function, the airline problem is specified, and the associated profit maximizing optimality conditions are derived. Finally, the regulator's problem is solved, again using the passenger demand function, and also using the operator optimality conditions as restrictions.

To determine the equilibrium, we focus in this section on a simple symmetric network, with two identical airports and two identical airlines offering services in one (direct) market only. Although these symmetry assumptions are not necessary to determine the equilibrium analytically, it greatly reduces the notation and enhances transparency. The assumption of symmetric airlines is relaxed in a numerical exercise below.

In this network, optimal congestion tolls are assumed to be the same for both airports, to reflect symmetry, but one of the two tolls could be set equal to zero without loss of generality. Moreover, the congestion toll cannot be distinguished from a subsidy necessary to counter the market-power effect. Hence, only a single toll t appears in the airline cost functions. But because both airports charge this toll, the airline pays it twice for each return flight. In more complicated networks, airline-market specific subsidies and airport specific congestion tolls will typically be necessary to achieve optimal welfare.

3.1. The passenger optimization problem

The marginal passenger's maximum willingness to pay for airline i, including monetized time costs, is given by Eq. (1), while each passenger's generalized user cost for the use of operator i are given by $g_{i,j}(\cdot)$ defined in Eq. (5). Intra-marginal passengers' net benefits are determined according to the familiar Marshallian surplus. According to Wardrop's equilibrium conditions, marginal benefits are equal to the generalized costs in equilibrium (or marginal net benefits are zero) for both airlines, so that $D(\cdot\cdot) = g_i(\cdot\cdot)$ $\forall i$ in equilibrium, while the generalized costs of an unused airline could not be lower than $D(\cdot\cdot)$ and would typically be higher.[3] Because operators incur costs for a service also when $q_{i,j} = 0$ (see (6)), an unused airline will however not survive in our model, and this possibility will be discarded. By assumption, demand and generalized cost functions are linear, so that the equilibrium condition for both airlines in the simple network implies the following fares:

$$p_1 = \alpha - \beta(q_1 + q_2) - 2\eta_h vot_p \frac{q_1 + q_2}{\lambda},$$

$$p_2 = \alpha - \beta(q_1 + q_2) - 2\eta_h vot_p \frac{q_1 + q_2}{\lambda}. \qquad (7)$$

The third RHS-term is multiplied by 2 because congestion is experienced at both airports. This operator specific inverse demand curve incorporates passengers' optimizing behavior,

---

[3] Wardrop's first principle (Wardrop [16]) is commonly used in the road pricing literature to characterize network equilibrium conditions. In short, it states that in equilibrium, the generalized user cost of all used alternatives (e.g., routes) for a given market (e.g., as defined by origin-destination pairs) must be equalized while no lower cost alternatives can be available (otherwise people would switch alternatives). With elastic demand, the resulting equilibrium average generalized user cost must in addition be equal to the marginal benefits of travel (if, for instance, the marginal benefits would be higher, additional passengers would enter the network).

and is used in the next step to maximize operator profits. Note that the arguments of this inverse demand function include the quantities sold by competing airline, and that the fares must be equal in an interior (symmetric) equilibrium.

3.2. The airline maximization problem

As stated in Assumption 5, we assume Cournot behavior in modeling airline competition. This is motivated by earlier (empirical) research.[4] In a Cournot oligopoly, excess profits can be made when the number of suppliers is finite. The current financial problems of many airlines do not mean that Cournot oligopoly modeling would not be appropriate for this sector. High fixed costs may contribute to financial problems, also under Cournot competition.

Thus, the operators in this model maximize profits with respect to q_i, taking the competitors quantities as given (note that the assumption of a fixed passenger load implies that maximization with respect to frequencies independent of passenger numbers is neither possible nor necessary). In general, the maximization problem for operator i ($i = 1, 2$) is

$$\max_{q_i} \pi_i = \left[\alpha - \beta(q_1 + q_2) - 2vot_p \eta_h \frac{q_1 + q_2}{\lambda} \right] q_i$$
$$- q_i \left[\frac{c^f + 2t + 2vot_l \eta_h (q_1 + q_2)/\lambda}{\lambda} + c^q \right] - F. \qquad (8)$$

The first-order necessary conditions for $i = (1, 2)$ are

$$\alpha - \beta(q_1 + q_2) - 2vot_p \eta_h \frac{q_1 + q_2}{\lambda} - q_i \left(\beta + \frac{2vot_p \eta_h}{\lambda} \right)$$
$$- \left[\frac{c^f + 2t + 2vot_l \eta_h (q_1 + q_2)/\lambda}{\lambda} + c^q \right] - q_i \frac{2vot_l \eta_h}{\lambda^2} = 0. \qquad (9)$$

Each additional passenger transported by airline i causes a marginal direct congestion cost $q_i 2\eta_h vot_l / \lambda^2$ for both airline i and airline $-i$, which is the increase in operating costs for other passengers transported. Likewise, a marginal congestion cost of $2\eta_h vot_p / \lambda$ is imposed on the passengers transported by both airline i and airline $-i$, which can be seen as an indirect congestion cost from an airline's perspective, in the sense that it reduces the passengers' willingness to pay for a ticket. From the first-order condition for profit maximization, it is apparent that airline i only internalizes the congestion incurred by itself and its passengers (the last LHS-term and the fourth LHS-term respectively). Because the airlines have the same outputs in the symmetric equilibrium, it follows that the airlines

---

[4] For instance, in an empirical analysis of Chicago-based airline routes involving American Airlines and United Airlines, Oum et al. [12] conclude that "the overall results indicate that the duopolists' conduct may be described as somewhere between Bertrand and Cournot behavior, but much closer to Cournot, in the majority of the sample observations." Brander and Zhang [2], using similar data, find "strong evidence... against the highly competitive Bertrand hypothesis." Brander and Zhang [2] find Cournot behavior plausible for the markets under consideration (Chicago-based routes where American Airlines and United Airlines together have a market share exceeding 75%). Based on these observations, we assume Cournot competition.

internalize half of the congestion they cause (the same result is obtained by Brueckner [5]). Solving the first-order conditions yields the following equilibrium outputs:

$$q_1 = q_2 = \frac{1}{3} \frac{\lambda[\alpha\lambda - 2t - c^f - \lambda c^q]}{\beta\lambda^2 + 2\eta(\lambda vot_p + vot_l)} \quad (10)$$

which are positive when

$$\alpha\lambda_l > 2t + c^f + \lambda c^q. \quad (11)$$

The latter condition simply states that outputs are positive when the highest reservation price (α) multiplied by the load, exceeds the average cost of the service.

From the first-order condition and the generalized cost function, we can derive the equilibrium fare:

$$p_i = \left[\frac{1}{\lambda}\left(c_i^f + 2t + 2vot_l\eta_h \frac{q_1+q_2}{\lambda}\right) + c^q\right] + q_i\left(\beta + \frac{2vot_p\eta_h}{\lambda} + \frac{2vot_l\eta_h}{\lambda^2}\right),$$
$$\forall i = 1, 2. \quad (12)$$

The first RHS-term (in square brackets) is the airline's operating cost per passenger. The second RHS-term is a mark-up consisting of two terms:

(i) $q_i(2\eta_h/\lambda)(vot_p + vot_l/\lambda)$ reflects the firm-internal direct and indirect congestion costs, and
(ii) $q_i\beta$ reflects a market power effect, which as expected increases when demand becomes less elastic (evaluated in the equilibrium).

The internalization of congestion externalities as such is consistent with efficient price setting, although the neglect of those imposed on the other airline and its passengers is not. The market power effect is not consistent with efficient pricing.

It follows from (12) that the equilibrium value for q_i is a function of the toll t. The optimal toll is determined by the regulator, and is derived in the next subsection.

3.3. The regulator's maximization problem

From the analysis in the preceding subsection, it is clear that there are potential distortions in equilibrium price setting due to non-internalized congestion externalities, and duopolistic pricing. In this section, we consider strategies for a regulator to deal with these inefficiencies.

In terms of objectives, we consider welfare-maximizing regulation. Since there is a market-power effect, which requires a subsidy when considered in isolation, the resulting optimal toll may very well be negative. Because both airlines have the same operating characteristics, and demand is shared evenly between the carriers, a regulator will set only one toll; this toll is paid by both airlines for the use of both airports. In an asymmetric equilibrium, differentiated tolls $t_{h,i}$ would typically be necessary. The same applies for non-cooperating regulators (as in Section 5).

The global regulator maximizes surplus for the entire network: the regulator considers consumer surplus and profits of both operators. It sets a common toll t for both nodes h in the system. The regulator's maximization problem is:

$$\max_{q_i} \varpi_G = \int_0^{q_1+q_2} (\alpha - \beta x)\,dx - 2(q_1+q_2)\frac{(q_1+q_2)vot_p\eta_h}{\lambda}$$
$$- (q_1+q_2)\left[\frac{1}{\lambda_i}\left(c^f + vot_l\frac{q_1+q_2}{\lambda}\right) + c^q\right]. \tag{13}$$

The first RHS-term represents total benefits (as integral of the Marshallian inverse demand function). The second RHS-term represents total generalized costs (excluding the airline fares, which cancel out against the airline revenues). The third RHS-term represents airline operating costs (excluding the expenditures on tolls, which cancel out against toll revenues). The three terms together thus give social surplus.

Comparing the first-order conditions for welfare maximization and profit maximization yields

$$\frac{\partial \varpi_G}{\partial q_i} - \frac{\partial \pi_G}{\partial q_i} = -q_{-i}\frac{2\eta_h}{\lambda}\left(vot_p + \frac{vot_l}{\lambda}\right) + q_i\beta + \frac{2t}{\lambda} \tag{14}$$

where the first RHS-term is the congestion that is not internalized by carrier i and the second RHS-term is the market power effect. The third RHS-term is the toll per passenger (for a return flight). To calculate the welfare optimizing toll, it is necessary that (14) equals zero. Solving this equation for t yields (the superscript w indicates a welfare maximizing toll)

$$t^w = \frac{\lambda}{2}\left[q_{-i}\frac{2\eta_h}{\lambda}\left(vot_p + \frac{vot_l}{\lambda}\right) - q_i\beta\right]. \tag{15}$$

In the symmetric equilibrium, $q_{-i} = q_i$, so that the first-best welfare maximizing toll is negative when the congestion effect $q_i(2\eta_h/\lambda)(vot_p + vot_l/\lambda)$ is smaller than the market power effect $q_i\beta$.

Substituting the toll rule (15) into the optimal output (10), and taking into account that $q_i = q_{-i}$ in the symmetric equilibrium, yields the optimal quantity per airline (the superscript w again indicates a welfare maximizing quantity):

$$q^w = \frac{\lambda(\alpha\lambda - c^f - \lambda c^q)}{2\beta\lambda^2 + 8\eta(\lambda vot_p + vot_l)}. \tag{16}$$

This optimal output implies the following closed-form optimal toll-level:

$$t^w = \frac{(\alpha\lambda - c^f - \lambda c^q)[2\eta_h(vot_p\lambda + vot_l) - \lambda^2\beta]}{4\beta\lambda^2 + 16\eta(\lambda vot_p + vot_l)} \tag{17}$$

which, again, is negative when the market power effect exceeds the congestion effect.

Because negative tolls (subsidies) may not be politically viable in practice, the regulator may impose a non-negativity constraint. As long as the market power effect exceeds the congestion effect, the resulting toll will equal zero. The corresponding outputs are given in (10) (with $t = 0$).

Brueckner [5] proposes another toll-rule, which we will call the 'pure congestion toll' t^c. With this toll, the airlines are charged for the congestion that is not internalized:

$$t^c = q_{-i}\eta_h\left(vot_p + \frac{vot_l}{\lambda}\right) \tag{18}$$

which is necessarily positive when $q > 0$ (i.e. when (11) holds). Substituting (18) into (10) yields

$$q^c = \frac{\lambda(\alpha\lambda - c^f - \lambda c^q)}{3\beta\lambda^2 + 8\eta(\lambda vot_p + vot_l)}, \qquad (19)$$

$$t^c = \frac{(\alpha\lambda - c^f - \lambda c^q)\eta(\lambda vot_p + vot_l)}{3\beta\lambda^2 + 8\eta(\lambda vot_p + vot_l)}. \qquad (20)$$

When we compare the welfare optimizing output in (16) with the 'congestion optimizing output' in (19), we see that the latter never exceeds the former (because the denominator is larger). Congestion, when considered in isolation, requires a positive toll to induce a reduction in the outputs; this toll is given in Eq. (18). Only when demand is perfectly elastic ($\beta = 0$), the market power effect vanishes and the toll in (18) becomes overall optimal and equal to that in (15), and also (20) and (17) become equal (i.e., $t^c = t^w$). The outputs in (10) are also adjusted accordingly (i.e. are set at the welfare maximizing level), which can be verified from the resulting equality of (19) and (16).

When the market power effect exceeds the congestion effect, a subsidy is necessary when welfare is to be maximized, so that the airlines will increase their outputs to the welfare optimizing level. When this market power effect is ignored and a positive congestion toll t^c is implemented ($t^c > 0$), outputs will be decreased rather than increased, and welfare will reduce. The toll t^c certainly becomes welfare reducing when t^w is negative. This also defines the point where a zero toll would be the optimal choice when—for political reasons—it is decided that subsidization of airlines is not warranted, and t^w would be constrained to be non-negative.

The closed-form welfare levels for the three toll levels of interest (welfare maximizing, congestion tolling and no toll) are presented in Table 1; these are obtained by substituting the associated equilibrium outputs into the welfare function.

It is straightforward that $\omega^w \geqslant \omega^c$ and $\omega^w \geqslant \omega^0$; this follows from the definition of the optimization problem. These inequalities can be shown to hold for any parameter constellation. More interesting is the comparison of ω^c and ω^0. Subtracting the two welfare levels yields (still in closed form)

$$\omega^c - \omega^0 = \frac{4}{9} \frac{(\lambda c^f + \lambda c^q - \alpha)^2 \eta(\lambda vot_p + vot_l)\Psi}{[3\beta\lambda^2 + 8\eta(\lambda vot_p + vot_l)]^2 [\beta\lambda^2 + 2\eta(\lambda vot_p + vot_l)]^2} \qquad (21)$$

Table 1
Closed-form welfare levels for different toll regimes

Toll regime	Welfare level
$t = t^w$	$\omega^w = \dfrac{1}{2}\dfrac{(\lambda c^f + \lambda c^q - \alpha)^2}{\beta\lambda^2 + 4\eta(\lambda vot_p + vot_l)}$
$t = t^c$	$\omega^c = \dfrac{(\lambda c^f + \lambda c^q - \alpha)^2[\beta\lambda^2 + 2\eta(\lambda vot_p + vot_l)]}{[3\beta\lambda^2 + 8\eta(\lambda vot_p + vot_l)]^2}$
$t = 0$	$\omega^0 = \dfrac{4}{9}\dfrac{(\lambda c^f + \lambda c^q - \alpha)^2[\beta\lambda^2 + \eta(\lambda vot_p + vot_l)]}{[\beta\lambda^2 + 2\eta(\lambda vot_p + vot_l)]^2}$

where

$$\Psi = -3\beta^2\lambda^4 - 4\lambda^2\eta(vot_k + \lambda vot_p)\beta + 8\eta^2[\lambda^2 vot_p^2 + vot_k^2 + 2\lambda vot_p vot_k]. \quad (22)$$

It is clear that $\omega^c - \omega^0 > 0$ when $\psi > 0$. Because ψ is a quadratic function of β with a negative coefficient for the squared term, $\psi > 0$ for any value of β between the two roots of ψ. Solving $\psi = 0$ for β yields the following two roots:

$$\beta_1 = 4\frac{(-\frac{1}{6} - \frac{1}{6}\sqrt{7})\eta(\lambda vot_p + vot_l)}{\lambda^2} = -2.431\frac{\eta(\lambda vot_p + vot_l)}{\lambda^2},$$

$$\beta_2 = 4\frac{(-\frac{1}{6} + \frac{1}{6}\sqrt{7})\eta(\lambda vot_p + vot_l)}{\lambda^2} = 1.097\frac{\eta(\lambda vot_p + vot_l)}{\lambda^2}. \quad (23)$$

It follows that for $\beta \in [-2.431\eta(\lambda vot_p + vot_l)/\lambda^2, \ 1.097\eta(\lambda vot_p + vot_l)/\lambda^2]$, $\omega^c - \omega^0 \geq 0$, where the lower bound is economically irrelevant (because it implies that $\beta < 0$ and hence the slope of the inverse demand function would be positive). When β is larger than the upper bound of this interval, the congestion toll leads to a welfare degradation compared to no-toll scenario.

From Eq. (17) we know that the market power effect dominates the congestion effect when $\beta > 2\eta_h(vot_p\lambda + vot_l)/\lambda^2$. We will denote this compactly as $\beta^* > 2$, with β^* defined as $\beta \cdot (\eta_h(vot_p\lambda + vot_l)/\lambda^2)^{-1}$. When this is the case, the welfare maximizing toll is negative. When the inequality is reversed ($\beta^* < 2$), the congestion effect dominates and the welfare maximizing toll is positive. For any β^* between 1.097 and 2, the welfare maximizing toll is positive, while the pure congestion toll (despite its correct sign) already leads to a welfare loss. This reflects that the welfare maximizing toll gets relatively close to zero, and relatively far below the pure congestion toll.

Figure 1 summarizes these findings. The line just above β^* shows the sign of the welfare maximizing toll t^w, and the upper line that of $\omega^c - \omega^0$.

In summary, a welfare maximizing regulator should set a toll that captures both (firm-external) congestion externalities and the market power effect. This toll can be negative. If a negative toll is not feasible, then the regulator should set a zero toll when the market power effect dominates the congestion effect ($\beta^* > 2$ in the symmetric case). The pure congestion toll t^c coincides with the optimal toll only if the market power effect vanishes ($\beta = 0$).

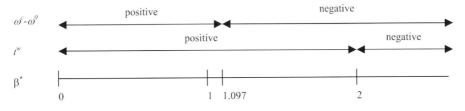

Fig. 1. Optimality of the pure congestion toll.

4. Numerical examples

This section will present some numerical results that further illustrate the comparative static properties of our model. We will begin with a symmetric case, and then move on to an asymmetric set-up.

4.1. Symmetric case

Table 2 shows the parametrization for the symmetric case. As stated, it is not the purpose of this paper to accurately describe a real-life aviation network. The parameters therefore need not correspond to real life values. However, we will calculate the equilibrium price elasticity of demand and compare this to estimates from the literature, and will check the ratio of passengers' congestion costs to generalized costs, and airlines' congestion costs to total operating costs, to confirm the plausibility of the parametrization.

Table 3 gives the no-toll equilibrium. The calculated price elasticity in equilibrium of -1.15 roughly corresponds to the value of -1.146 reported by Brons et al. [3] (the variable ε will be used to indicate the absolute value of demand elasticity with respect to generalized costs). The latter figure is the overall mean of 204 estimates from the literature. This suggests that we operate on a relevant segment of the demand curve. Passenger congestion costs are some 20% of their generalized costs, while for the airlines, congestion costs amount to some 5% of their total operating costs. Also these figures appear reasonable. The higher figure for passengers would reflect that they incur congestion costs in the terminal, in addition to those in the air.

Table 4 gives the equilibrium for the (first-best) welfare maximizing toll t^w. The toll is negative, and quite large in absolute value (compared to, for instance, the marginal cost per flight). The negative sign reflects that the market power effect in the no-toll equilibrium exceeds the congestion effect. Because the airlines receive substantial subsidies, the optimal outputs and profits are larger than in the no-toll equilibrium. Because the optimal outputs are higher, congestion costs are also higher. Without tolls, the airlines set their equilibrium outputs too low, and as a result, the congestion costs are too low in the

Table 2
Parameter values for the symmetric numerical model

Demand characteristics				Airline characteristics				Node characteristics	
α	5000	vot_p	50	c^f	100000	λ	200	η	0.5
β	1			c^q	100	vot_l	500		

Table 3
Equilibrium outputs and welfare: no toll

	q	Generalized costs		ε	Welfare effects		
		fare	congestion		consumer surplus	profits	welfare
airline 1	1162	2096	581	1.15	$1.35 \cdot 10^6$	$0.70 \cdot 10^6$	$2.05 \cdot 10^6$
airline 2	1162	2096	581	1.15	$1.35 \cdot 10^6$	$0.70 \cdot 10^6$	$2.05 \cdot 10^6$
total	2324				$2.70 \cdot 10^6$	$1.40 \cdot 10^6$	$4.10 \cdot 10^6$

Table 4
Equilibrium outputs and welfare: first-best welfare maximizing toll

	q	Generalized costs		ε	toll	Welfare effects			
		fare	congestion			consumer surplus	profits	toll revenues	welfare
airline 1	1443	1393	721	0.73	$-0.11 \cdot 10^6$	$2.08 \cdot 10^6$	$1.63 \cdot 10^6$	$-1.53 \cdot 10^6$	$2.17 \cdot 10^6$
airline 2	1443	1393	721	0.73	$-0.11 \cdot 10^6$	$2.08 \cdot 10^6$	$1.63 \cdot 10^6$	$-1.53 \cdot 10^6$	$2.17 \cdot 10^6$
total	2886	2786				$4.16 \cdot 10^6$	$3.26 \cdot 10^6$	$-3.06 \cdot 10^6$	$4.34 \cdot 10^6$

Table 5
Equilibrium outputs and welfare: pure congestion toll

	q	Generalized costs		ε	toll	Welfare effects			
		fare	congestion			consumer surplus	profits	toll revenues	welfare
airline 1	1086	2284	543	1.30	28519	$1.18 \cdot 10^6$	$0.49 \cdot 10^6$	$0.31 \cdot 10^6$	$1.98 \cdot 10^6$
airline 2	1086	2284	543	1.30	28519	$1.18 \cdot 10^6$	$0.49 \cdot 10^6$	$0.31 \cdot 10^6$	$1.98 \cdot 10^6$
total	2172					$2.36 \cdot 10^6$	$0.98 \cdot 10^6$	$0.62 \cdot 10^6$	$3.96 \cdot 10^6$

optimum. The welfare maximizing toll fixes this problem. When this welfare maximizing toll is implemented, overall welfare increases by 6% compared to the base case; this is the maximum possible increase in welfare.

The equilibrium in Table 4 may be of limited practical interest, because subsidizing airlines may be considered politically unacceptable. An alternative would then be to impose a non-negativity constraint on the toll. The result is the no-toll equilibrium in Table 3, where overall welfare (consumer surplus plus profits excluding tolls) is of course lower than in Table 4.

We have already shown that a pure congestion toll t^c is not optimal. We now determine the welfare effects of a pure congestion toll for our numerical model. Table 5 contains the relevant information.

The toll t^c is positive (as expected), and this is also reflected in consumer prices: the airlines pass the (part of) the expenditures on the toll onto the passengers. Because the fares increase, consumer surplus decreases compared to the no-toll equilibrium. Airline profits decrease, because the reduction in airline congestion costs does not outweigh the expenditures on the congestion toll. We already concluded that in the no-toll equilibrium, the airlines set their equilibrium outputs too low. The pure congestion toll causes the outputs to be even lower. The decrease in welfare is around 61% of the maximum possible increase in welfare: $\Omega^c = (\omega^c - \omega^0)/(\omega^w - \omega^0) = -0.61$ (with Ω^c denoting the relative efficiency gain due to pure congestion pricing). For the chosen parameter constellation, the welfare decrease is therefore substantial.

Because the difference between the optimal welfare toll t^w and the pure congestion toll t^c depends crucially on the elasticity of demand (as explained in Section 3), it is of interest to see how Ω^c varies with the (absolute value of) the equilibrium demand elasticity, ε. Figure 2 shows the results (which were obtained numerically by simultaneously adjusting α and β so that the same no-toll equilibrium was obtained for

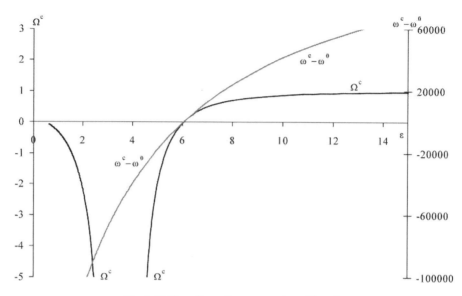

Fig. 2. Welfare effects of pure congestion tolling t^c.

each ε shown).[5] Only for rather high elasticities, above 6 in absolute value, does t^c yield a positive welfare effect (indicated by a positive value of Ω^c). This is where the congestion effect sufficiently outweighs the market power effect (compare Fig. 1). For lower elasticities, Ω^c approaches $-\infty$ for that particular combination of α and β for which both t^w and its welfare effects become zero, because the congestion effect and the market power effect exactly cancel (for ε near 3.55 in the diagram). The grey line—depicting the absolute welfare change due to t^c—shows that also at that point, substantial welfare losses due to pure congestion pricing occur, so that it is not solely a denominator-effect in Ω^c that makes t^c appear harmful to efficiency. For yet lower elasticities, their numerical values become more plausible from an empirical perspective, but Ω^c remains negative. It approaches zero from below as demand becomes perfectly inelastic, in which case symmetric tolls for symmetric duopolists will not affect symmetric demand levels, and hence congestion levels anymore.

Figure 1 implies that patterns as in Fig. 2 will be found also for other parameter constellations. In particular, note that moving from right to left in Fig. 1 means moving from left to right in Fig. 2. When doing so, we therefore always expect Ω^c to be negative near perfect inelasticity of demand (for high values of β^*, on the left end of Fig. 2 and the right end of Fig. 1), to fall to $-\infty$ when β^* falls to 2, to remain negative as long as β^* exceeds 1.097, and to increase above zero when β^* falls below 1.097—approaching unity as demand elasticity approaches infinity.

---

[5] Because the issue here is the effect of market power, and not the effect of initial demand on the optimality of the toll, the reservation price α is varied together with β so as to obtain the same no-toll equilibrium in terms of quantities q_1 and q_2. This was realized technically by treating q_1 and q_2 parametrically in Eq. (9), and solving for α as a function of β for the resulting equation (keeping all other parameters fixed).

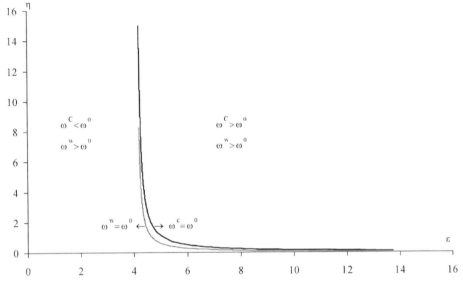

Fig. 3. Optimality of pure congestion tolling t^c.

It is of course the particular parametrization of the numerical model that causes the welfare effect of t^c to become positive only for demand elasticities above an unrealistically high value of 6 (in absolute value) in Fig. 2. Intuition suggests that when congestion would become relatively more important, one would expect this critical ε to fall (this also follows from Eq. (23) and Fig. 1). To verify this, we plot in Fig. 3 the curve $\Omega^c = 0$ (which is equivalent with $\omega^c = \omega^0$) for various combinations of values of η and ε, again such that equilibrium demand levels remain unaltered.[6] The lower curve in Fig. 3 gives the combinations of ε and η for which the market power effect equals the congestion effect (i.e. $\omega^w = \omega^0$). To the *left* of this curve, the market power effect exceeds the congestion effect ($\beta > 2\eta_h (vot_p \lambda + vot_l)/\lambda^2$), so that a subsidy is required; a pure congestion toll then cannot be optimal. From the upper curve in Fig. 3 ($\Omega^c = 0$), we may conclude that the elasticity at which a pure congestion toll is not welfare reducing decreases when congestion (η) increases.

The lower limit to the elasticity at which a pure congestion toll ceases to cause welfare losses, as discussed above, varies with η, vot_p, vot_l and λ. A decrease in λ keeping η fixed, for example, would move the two curves in Fig. 3 to the left.[7] The reason is that this is another way of making congestion relatively more important.

---

[6] Following the procedure described in footnote 4, α can be expressed in β and η. After substituting this expression for α in Ω^c, and given η, one can solve $\Omega^c = 0$ for β, which is then transformed into an elasticity.

[7] At the given parametrization (and with $\lambda = 200$), $\omega^w = \omega^0$ if $\eta = (40/21)\beta$. For $\lambda = 100$, $\omega^w = \omega^0$ if $\eta = (10/11)\beta$. This indicates that the entire curve shifts to the left when the aircraft load is reduced. For instance, at $\varepsilon = 3$, $\eta = 0.33$ when $\lambda = 100$. When $\lambda = 200$, $\eta = 0.33$ at $\varepsilon = 5.7$. To save space, no plot similar to Fig. 3 was made for $\lambda = 100$. Details are available upon request.

4.2. An asymmetric numerical model

It is interesting to briefly investigate some implications of introducing differences between airlines in the above model. As stated, this makes the analytics of the model cumbersome, but the numerical model still produces intuitive results. We increase airline 2's aircraft capacity by 10%, and we reduce airline 2's cost per passenger and flight by 10% (see Table 6). This parameter constellation more or less reflects the situation of entry of a low-cost carrier in a market that used to be served by a ("conventional") monopolist, although the increase in aircraft capacity and decrease in costs is chosen arbitrarily. Note that the airports remain identical.

The resulting equilibrium is given in Table 7. Competition combined with the passengers' equilibrium conditions forces the airlines to charge the same ticket price, despite their different cost structures. As a result, the more efficient airline 2 will enjoy a greater patronage and higher profits in equilibrium. The inefficient airline 1, however, remains in operation.

For this asymmetric case, we obtain the following equivalent of (14) for the calculation of optimal airline specific tolls:

$$\frac{\partial \varpi_G}{\partial q_i} - \frac{\partial \pi_G}{\partial q_i} = -q_{-i} \frac{2\eta_h}{\lambda_{-i}} \left(vot_p + \frac{vot_l}{\lambda_{-i}} \right) + q_i \beta + \frac{2t_i}{\lambda_i}, \tag{24}$$

from which the optimal tolls t^w can be derived as

$$t^w = \frac{\lambda_i}{2} \left[q_{-i} \frac{2\eta_h}{\lambda_{-i}} \left(vot_p + \frac{vot_l}{\lambda_{-i}} \right) - q_i \beta \right] \tag{25}$$

which is a straightforward generalization of (15). The relevant t^c can be derived from (25) by—again—removing the market power effect, and is identical to (18) with λ_{-i} substituted for λ.

The asymmetry has various consequences. First, absent congestion, only one airline would survive in the economic optimum. Starting in the no-toll equilibrium, the subsidy

Table 6
Parameter values for the asymmetric model

Demand characteristics				Airline characteristics						Node characteristics	
α	5000	vot_p	50	c_1^f	100000	c_1^f	90000	λ_1	200	vot_l	500	η	0.5
β	1			c_2^q	100	c_2^q	90	λ_2	220				

Table 7
Equilibrium outputs and welfare in the asymmetric setting: no toll

	q	Generalized costs		ε	Welfare effects		
		fare	congestion		consumer surplus	profits	welfare
airline 1	1134	2060	565	1.11	$1.35 \cdot 10^6$	$0.62 \cdot 10^6$	$1.97 \cdot 10^6$
airline 2	1240	2060	565	1.11	$1.47 \cdot 10^6$	$0.90 \cdot 10^6$	$2.37 \cdot 10^6$
total	2374				$2.82 \cdot 10^6$	$1.52 \cdot 10^6$	$4.34 \cdot 10^6$

per passenger would be larger for the larger (more efficient) airline, which would then expand services, obtain a yet larger subsidy, and so on, until the other airline is pushed out of the market. Secondly, it is very likely that with congestion, this effect is aggravated, because the larger airline will typically cause relatively low external congestion costs, as most congestion costs caused are firm-internal (only under strong asymmetries in λ might this not be the case).

With the chosen parameter values, airline 1 is indeed pushed out of business when the regulator sets welfare maximizing tolls. A first, economically irrelevant solution (which is therefore not reported) shows that the toll for airline 1 is positive, and that airline 1's resulting optimal output is negative. In other words, airline 1 pulls out of the market. Readjusting the model to the new situation results in the optimum in Table 8. Because the monopoly airline internalizes all congestion, the toll in Table 8 is solely a response to its market power.

When non-negativity constraints are imposed, airline 2's toll will be equal to 0. In that case, it sets its output below the welfare optimizing output, leaving some room for airline 1 to re-enter the market (or to remain in business). Fixing the toll for airline 2 at 0 and solving for the optimal toll for airline 1 yields a negative toll, so that also for airline 1 the non-negativity constraint becomes binding. The eventual result is the no-toll equilibrium reported in Table 7.

In this case, the relatively inefficient airline remains in business. Moreover, aggregate consumer surplus is much lower compared to Table 8, because outputs are set below the welfare economic optimum. Welfare (consumer surplus plus profits excluding tolls) is 35% higher when a welfare maximizing 'toll' is set by the regulator than without tolling.

Next, we compare the welfare economic performance of a pure congestion toll to the welfare economic performance of a zero toll. Table 9 shows that both tolls are positive, whereas welfare maximization would require one subsidized supplier. We can therefore conclude that at the chosen parameter constellation, the pure congestion toll is again welfare reducing compared to the base case of the zero toll.

Table 8
Equilibrium outputs and welfare in the asymmetric setting: first-best welfare maximizing toll

	q	Generalized costs		ε	toll	Welfare effects			
		fare	congestion			consumer surplus	profits	toll revenues	welfare
airline 2	3051	1256	693	0.64	$-0.34 \cdot 10^6$	$4.65 \cdot 10^6$	$10.52 \cdot 10^6$	$-9.31 \cdot 10^6$	$5.86 \cdot 10^6$

Table 9
Equilibrium outputs and welfare in the asymmetric setting: pure congestion tolls

	q	Generalized costs		ε	toll	Welfare effects			
		fare	congestion			consumer surplus	profits	toll revenues	welfare
airline 1	1062	2243	530	1.25	27677	$1.18 \cdot 10^6$	$0.42 \cdot 10^6$	$0.29 \cdot 10^6$	$1.89 \cdot 10^6$
airline 2	1165	2243	530	1.25	30652	$1.30 \cdot 10^6$	$0.68 \cdot 10^6$	$0.32 \cdot 10^6$	$2.30 \cdot 10^6$
total	2227					$2.48 \cdot 10^6$	$1.1 \cdot 10^6$	$0.61 \cdot 10^6$	$4.19 \cdot 10^6$

5. Variations on the regulator's optimization problem: local welfare maximization

The above analysis is based on the assumption that a single regulator regulates both airports. In reality, one may have two (national or regional) regulators, each regulating an airport. An important question then becomes how important it is that these regulators coordinate their activities, instead of pursuing local welfare maximization. For reasons of space, we will consider this issue only briefly, but find it too important to ignore altogether. We assume that both regions host one 'home airline,' and that demand is symmetric between regions (i.e., half of any equilibrium demand for return trips concerns trips by consumers from one region, and the other half from the other region). A local regulator in node h would then have the objective of maximizing local welfare as given in (26):

$$\varpi_h^L = \frac{1}{2}\left[\int_0^{q_1+q_2}(\alpha - \beta x)\,\mathrm{d}x - (q_1+q_2)[\alpha - \beta(q_1+q_2)]\right] + \pi_h + \sum_{i=1}^{2} q_i \frac{t_{h,i}}{\lambda_i}. \quad (26)$$

The first RHS-term is half of the total consumer surplus. The second RHS-term is the profit of the airline using airport h as its home airport. The third RHS-term is the total toll revenues for regulator h. It can be shown that the summation of (26) over h yields total welfare defined in (13) when tolls are undifferentiated (i.e. $t_{h,i} = t_{-h,i}$). In absence of policy coordination, we assume that the regulators take the toll of the other regulator as given, and hence exhibit Nash behavior between them (although both act as a Stackelberg leader with respect to the airlines). For reasons of transparency, we consider the symmetric case, in which airlines have the same operating characteristics, and in which the congestion impact at both airports is the same. Each airport operator then maximizes half of the total welfare, but this of course does not mean that they jointly maximize total welfare. Because the analytical expressions for the locally optimal tolls are not particularly insightful, we immediately proceed with the numerical illustration. The analytical expressions are given in Appendix A.

A first possibility we consider is when the local regulators could set differentiated tolls (for both airlines). Because the generalized price for consumers is equalized in equilibrium, consumers from both cities can be expected to use both airlines in equal proportions (there are no loyalty programs or nationalistic preferences in our model), and there is no reason to differentiate tolls over both airlines from this perspective (the first term in Eq. (26)). Likewise, toll revenues (the third term) are equally weighted, independent of which airline pays them, and also for this reason there is no reason to differentiate tolls. The middle term in (26) does provide a reason for toll differentiation: only profits for the local airline matter for local welfare.

The third column in Table 10 shows that this gives rise to a substantial toll differentiation in equilibrium: the home carrier's toll is less than 10% of the foreign carrier's toll. Both tolls are positive, and as a result, welfare deteriorates compared to the no-toll equilibrium ($\Omega = -7.09$). The closed form toll expressions in Appendix A suggest that without policy coordination, equilibrium tolls will always be positive (in symmetric equilibria), for the demand and cost functions we use. The intuition is that subsidization to correct for duopolistic pricing become less attractive from a local regulator's point of view. Only half of the resulting benefits are accounted for in (26): those accruing to the local consumers

Table 10
Local welfare levels, symmetric equilibrium

	Global welfare maximization	Zero toll	Local welfare maximization, differentiated tolls	Local welfare maximization, undifferentiated tolls
t_i	$-0.11 \cdot 10^6$	0	$0.033 \cdot 10^6$	$0.196 \cdot 10^6$
t_{-i}	$-0.11 \cdot 10^6$	0	$0.36 \cdot 10^6$	$0.196 \cdot 10^6$
ω	$2.17 \cdot 10^6$	$2.05 \cdot 10^6$	$1.20 \cdot 10^6$	$1.20 \cdot 10^6$
Ω	1	0	-7.09	-7.09

Table 11
Local welfare levels at airport 1

	Regulator 2 sets zero toll	Regulator 2 maximizes local welfare
Regulator 1 set zero toll	$2.05 \cdot 10^6$	$0.18 \cdot 10^6$
Regulator 1 maximizes local welfare	$3.78 \cdot 10^6$	$1.20 \cdot 10^6$

and airline only. But the full losses are considered: the reduction in local toll revenues. Moreover, a reason arises for further overcharging of the foreign airline, because this raises local toll revenues and indirectly increases local profits as the local airline's competitive position improves.

When the local regulators are both forced to charge the same, undifferentiated toll for both airlines, a simplistic expectation would be that this toll will be near the average of the differentiated tolls. This, indeed, turns out to be the case, with the noteworthy implication that for overall welfare, it is practically immaterial whether or not local welfare maximizers set differentiated tolls. The closed-form toll expression in Appendix A again shows that the undifferentiated toll will always be positive (and confirms its value is near the average of the undifferentiated tolls). In other words: from our results, it appears to be important whether or not airport authorities coordinate their policies when setting congestion tolls. But if they do not do so, it is relatively unimportant whether or not they charge differentiated tolls for the two airlines.

The large discrepancy between welfare under policy coordination and under policy competition makes it likely that some form of coordination would indeed arise in the context we consider. But if it does not, it will not be likely that a status quo with zero tolls would persist. Table 11 gives the relevant pay-offs to regulator 1 (due to symmetry, a similar table applies for regulator 2), and shows that, when starting with zero tolls, regulator 1 has a clear incentive to implement a local welfare maximizing toll. Regulator 2 then (still) has an incentive to do the same, and a classic prisoners dilemma arises in absence of coordination (and for a one shot game).

6. Conclusion

Conventional economic wisdom suggests that congestion pricing would be an appropriate response to cope with the growing congestion levels currently experienced at many airports. Several characteristics of aviation markets, however, may make naïve congestion prices, equal to the value of marginal travel delays, a non-optimal response. This paper has developed a model of airport pricing that captures some of these features. The model reflects that airlines typically have market power and are engaged in oligopolistic competition, and that a part of external travel delays that aircraft impose are internal to an operator and hence should not be accounted for in congestion tolls. We have also briefly considered the issue of policy coordination between airports.

Some main conclusions are that second-best optimal tolls are typically lower than what would be suggested by congestion costs alone and may even be negative, and that pure congestion tolls, even when corrected for firm-internal congestion, may cause a decrease in welfare when there is significant market power, which in itself would call for subsidization. Brueckner [5] has made clear that congestion tolls on airports may be smaller than expected when congestion costs among aircraft are internal for a firm. He also acknowledged that a pure congestion toll may not be welfare optimal, and may even lead to a welfare degradation when the market power effect exceeds uninternalized congestion (without, however, incorporating this in his analytical model). Our paper makes these welfare effects explicit, and shows that the welfare optimal toll is negative when the market power effect exceeds the welfare effect. Insofar as subsidization is considered unacceptable for whichever reason, our results suggest that the most efficient among the non-negative tolls would typically be a zero toll.

We have also seen that policy coordination between airports regulators may be important from an overall welfare perspective. The incentive to adjust tolls downwards to account for market power becomes disproportionally smaller without coordination, which may—as in our model—cause the equilibrium tolls to have the wrong sign and hence to be welfare reducing.

The model in this paper contains a few simplifying assumptions that may be relaxed in future work. Load factors and aircraft capacity are fixed in this model for simplicity. In a more advanced version of this model, load factors and aircraft capacity can be endogenized. One can also add a fourth layer to the model, describing a private airport's profit optimization problem. No distinction is made between peak and off-peak traffic in this paper. This distinction is quite common in the literature (see e.g. Brueckner [5], Daniel [10,11]) and could, as discussed, make a straightforward but important extension of our model. Furthermore, we intend to broaden our analysis to the consideration of larger (hub-and-spoke) networks, that allow consideration of the intriguing question of how congestion (pricing) and market power (regulation) interact when airlines' network configurations are endogenous.

Acknowledgments

The authors thank Jan Brueckner, two anonymous referees and the Heidezangers for excellent comments on an earlier draft. Any remaining errors or shortcomings are the authors' responsibility alone. This paper is an outflow of earlier research carried out for the research project MC-ICAM, funded by the European Commission (GRD1/2000/25475-SI2.316057). This financial support is gratefully acknowledged.

Appendix A. Analytical expressions for local optimization

Both regulators have an incentive to set differentiated tolls; one for its "home airline" (denoted by the subscript i), and a higher one for the visiting airline (denoted by the subscript $-i$). Closed-form toll levels are obtained by substituting the equilibrium q's as given in (10) (with differentiated tolls rather than the simple the t's) into (26) and maximizing over t, and read:

$$t_i^{w,l} = \frac{(\alpha\lambda - c^f - \lambda c^q) 2\eta_h (vot_p \lambda + vot_l)}{5\beta\lambda^2 + 14\eta(\lambda vot_p + vot_l)}, \tag{A.1}$$

$$t_{-i}^{w,l} = 2\frac{(\alpha\lambda - c^f - \lambda c^q)[3\eta_h (vot_p \lambda + vot_l) + \lambda^2 \beta]}{5\beta\lambda^2 + 14\eta(\lambda vot_p + vot_l)}. \tag{A.2}$$

Likewise, the following undifferentiated local toll is obtained:

$$t^{w,l} = \frac{(\alpha\lambda - c^f - \lambda c^q)[4\eta_h (vot_p \lambda + vot_l) + \lambda^2 \beta]}{5\beta\lambda^2 + 14\eta(\lambda vot_p + vot_l)}. \tag{A.3}$$

References

[1] W.J. Baumol, W.E. Oates, The Theory of Environmental Policy, 2nd Edition, Cambridge Univ. Press, 1988.
[2] J.A. Brander, A. Zhang, Market conduct in the airline industry: an empirical investigation, RAND Journal of Economics 21 (1990) 567–583.
[3] M. Brons, E. Pels, P. Nijkamp, P. Rietveld, Price elasticities of demand for passenger air travel: a meta-analysis, Journal of Air Transport Management 8 (2002) 165–175.
[4] J.K. Brueckner, The economics of international codesharing: an analysis of airline alliances, International Journal of Industrial Organization 19 (2001) 1475–1498.
[5] J.K. Brueckner, Airport congestion pricing when carriers have market power, American Economic Review 92 (2002) 1357–1375.
[6] J.K. Brueckner, Internalization of airport congestion: a network analysis, Working paper, Institute of Government and Public Affairs, University of Illinois at Urbana-Champaign, 2003.
[7] J.K. Brueckner, P.T. Spiller, Economics of traffic density in a deregulated airline industry, International Journal of Industrial Organization 37 (1991) 323–342.
[8] J.M. Buchanan, External diseconomies, external taxes, and market structure, American Economic Review 59 (1969) 174–177.
[9] A. Carlin, R. Park, Marginal cost pricing of airport runway capacity, American Economic Review 60 (1970) 310–319.
[10] J.I. Daniel, Distributional consequences of airport congestion pricing, Journal of Urban Economics 50 (2001) 230–258.
[11] J.I. Daniel, Congestion pricing and capacity of large hub airports: a bottleneck model with stochastic queues, Econometrica 63 (1995) 103–130.
[12] T.H. Oum, A. Zhang, Y. Zhang, Inter-firm rivalry and firm-specific price elasticities in deregulated airline markets, Journal of Transport Economics and Policy 27 (1993) 171–192.
[13] T.H. Oum, Y. Zhang, Airport pricing, congestion tolls, lumpy investment and cost recovery, Journal of Public Economics 43 (1990) 353–374.
[14] E. Pels, P. Nijkamp, P. Rietveld, A note on the optimality of airline networks, Economics Letters 69 (2000) 429–434.
[15] D. Starkie, Slot trading at United States airports, A report for the Director General for Transport of the Commission of the European Communities, Putnam, London, 1992.
[16] J. Wardop, Some theoretical aspects of road traffic research, Proceedings of the Institute of Civil Engineers 1 (1952) 325–378.

10

Grandfather rights in the market for airport slots

Gernot Sieg

ARTICLE INFO

Article history:
Received 17 April 2008
Received in revised form 16 April 2009
Accepted 16 April 2009

Keywords:
Airports
Grandfather rights
Use-it-or-lose-it rule
Airport slots

ABSTRACT

Grandfather rights are currently used in the European Union to allocate airport slots. This article shows that airports prefer such a use-it-or-lose-it rule to unconditional property rights. Assuming that there are informational asymmetries between airports and air carriers because air carriers have better information on passenger demand, the use-it-or-lose-it rule increases slot use when demand for air transport is low. Airport profits increase and those of the air carriers, together with social welfare, decrease. The profit-maximizing slot-use ratio is less than one.

© 2009 Elsevier Ltd. All rights reserved.

1. Introduction

As air traffic is increasing on an almost daily basis, some airports have become congested. If an airport is congested, the right to land or take-off during a well-defined time period, called a slot, becomes scarce (Jones et al., 1993). European Council Regulation No. 95/93 on the allocation of slots at Community airports defines the rules that are mandatory for coordinated airports (airports where slots are essential for use of the infrastructure). Foremost among the considerations is the fact that there are no property rights defined: neither the airport, the government, nor the air carrier owns the slot. However, there are grandfather rights: an air carrier that has used a slot in the last summer/winter period can use it in the current summer/winter period. More precisely, an alleviated use-it-or-lose-it rule holds. An air carrier only has to use the allocated slot 80% of the time to obtain the slot in the next period. Furthermore, air carriers are allowed to exchange slots. The sale of a slot is partly legal in the United States and common in the United Kingdom, but uncommon in the rest of the European Union.

History shows (Sened and Riker, 1996) that after the acquisition of governmental control over take-off and landing slots in high-density airports, the air-carrier industry has contrived to implement the current self-regulated regime of common-property ownership. Boyfield et al. (2003) discuss the endowment of individual airlines with private ownership of slots and the right to sell them. If two air carriers exchange or sell slots on a so-called secondary market, the allocative efficiency might be enhanced (Starkie, 1998). Because slots are scarce they are valuable. The initial definition of slot ownership, i.e., the allocation of slot property rights to airports, current users or the government, produces windfall profits, and therefore governments, airports, and incumbent airlines equally claim the right of property.

From a welfare economics point of view, pure property rights to slot use, without additional conditions such as a use-it-or-lose-it rule, might not be optimal. For example, if the property right is defined and allocated to an air carrier, there is no longer any need for grandfathering because the property of a slot implies that it can also be used in the next period. Airport-specific investment by an air carrier in a connection is more likely if there are grandfather rights or the air carrier owns the slot. However, if an air carrier owns a slot and does not use it to offer air transport, but merely holds it to deter competitor entry (Dempsey, 2001), a use-it-or-lose-it rule may be a welfare-enhancing proposition.

Following the arguments by Coase (1960), all firms affected by slot allocation can privately find an efficient solution. However, the longevity of the struggle in the EU to reform Regulation 793/2004 shows that transaction costs are high. Many groups are affected (Button, 2005), such as consumers, airport owners, residents and firms in the vicinity of airports, local and federal governments, and air carriers. Therefore, many different rules, such as limiting grandfather rights to a fixed period of time, returning a certain proportion of all slots, slot fees instead of landing fees, and pools for new entrants, have been proposed to improve the allocation efficiency (Boyfield et al., 2003).

The aim of this paper is to analyze the implementation of slot property rights and whether such slot ownership substitutes or complements grandfathering and the use-it-or-lose it rule. The initial step in identifying a welfare maximizing combination of rules for slot use at airports is to determine who gains and who loses when these rules are applied. Furthermore, the identification of gaining and losing groups is a prerequisite for a public choice analysis of the implementation process. This article shows that a use-it-or-lose-it rule suits the airport through maximizing profits by reducing demand fluctuations. Airports are interested in full use of slots because there are few variable costs and, in addition to take-off and landing fees, commercial revenues increase with the number of passengers using the airport. If the airport knows the approximate demand for flights, it can charge landing and take-off fees to maximize slot use. Air transport demand increases predictably during the peak season, but there are other changes in demand that are not easy to predict (Doganis, 2002, pp. 196–200). For example, when the level of disposable income of customers changes, the level of economic activity changes or travel restrictions may arise. Demand forecasting is important for air carriers, but airports are either not able to do so or it is too expensive to forecast demand. This study assumes information asymmetry between the airports and air carriers regarding the current demand status. Take-off and landing fees are set up front for a period of at least 6 months. Therefore, the airport is not able to maximize slot use by changing landing and take-off fees according to changes in demand. The airport thus needs an alternative.

This article shows that an use-it-or-lose-it provision improves slot use. Air carriers that confront temporary decreases in demand offer more flights and attract more airport customers when the use-it-or-lose-it rule holds to avoid losing the slot. This babysitting behavior decreases demand fluctuations and transfers some of the negative effects of the drop in demand from the airport to the air carriers. Airport profits increase and those of air carriers decrease. Social welfare decreases in magnitude if a use-it-or-lose-it rule holds. However, the losses are less severe if revenues from non-aviation activities are large.

The focus of the current literature on airport pricing is the internalization of congestion as well as secondary markets but not grandfathering. The improvement in efficiency of the market for airport slots by establishing a secondary market has been analyzed by Starkie (1998), Abeyratne (2000), and Barbot (2004). Auctions may improve slot allocation (Button, 2008). Boyfield et al. (2003) discuss the question of slot ownership and secondary markets in detail and provide reform options to enhance competition. They compare both gainers and losers of the current system (pp. 82–84), but do not analyze the position of airports as in the present study. The gains and losses of airports and their attitude to reforming slot property rights are essential for institutional change, as demonstrated by Riker and Sened (1991) and Sened and Riker (1996) in their analyzes of the political origin of property rights. Button (2008) analyzes the allocation of rents under different slot allocation approaches but does not analyze who gains and how social welfare is affected by grandfathering, which is addressed here.

The outline of the paper is as follows. Section 2 presents prices and quantities of slot use in the subgame perfect equilibria of the game between airport, airline and customers with and without grandfathering. In Section 3 the gainers and losers of grandfathering are identified. Section 4 analyzes social welfare and Section 5 concludes.

2. The model

For simplicity, in this model a monopolist airport sells slots to an air carrier that is a monopolistic supplier of air transport to consumers.[1] Because of changes in demand that are not easy to predict (Doganis, 2002, pp. 196–200), consumer demand is stochastic and two levels of demand, $i = l$ (low) and $i = h$ (high), occur with probability $0 < w = w_h < 1$ and $w_l = (1 - w)$, respectively. The stochastic demand for tickets x_i is represented by

$$x_i = D_i - d \cdot p_i^c,$$

where $0 < d$ is the slope of the linear demand curve and $0 < D_l < D_h$ the ordinate intercept.

This study assumes asymmetry of information between the airport and the air carrier regarding the current demand status. In contrast to the airport, the carrier knows the type of consumer demand it faces.

Airport revenues consist of the landing fee p_a charged by the airport and exogenous non-aviation revenues $s > 0$ such as rent from shops in the airport or parking fees for cars.[2] For simplicity, it is assumed as in Barbot (2004) that p_a is both the landing fee and the price-cost margin over operational costs (because they are assumed to be zero) and that the capital costs of the airport are fixed costs that do not influence the pricing strategy. The airport maximizes the expected profits

---

[1] This is a simple version of the vertical structure approach initiated by Brueckner (2002) and used by, among others, Pels and Verhoef (2004) and Zhang and Zhang (2006) and compared to the traditional approach by Basso and Zhang (2008).
[2] The landing fee p_a is usually a function of frequency and tickets x and non-aviation revenues s are a function of passengers. In this model it is assumed that tickets, non-aviation revenues and landing fees share as unit a fully booked aircraft that minimizes landing fees depending on maximum take-off weight, noise (Brueckner and Girvin, 2008), emissions, etc.

$$E\Pi = E[(p_a + s) \cdot x]$$

by charging an optimal landing fee, p_a, from the airline. Because the airport does not know whether demand is high or low, it charges p_a independently of the status of demand.

The carrier maximizes its profit knowing the demand status. For simplicity, the only costs to the carrier to operate a flight and transport a passenger are assumed to be the take-off and landing fees. Therefore, the carrier demands the ticket price p_i^c from its passengers depending on the type of demand and maximizing profits as follows:

$$(p_i^c - c) \cdot x_i(p_i^c),$$

where the constant total costs per flight c of the carrier correspond to the landing fee charged by the airport, i.e., $c = p_a$. This assumption follows the model by Zhang and Zhang (2006) but simplifies it even more by assuming that all the variable costs except for landings fees are zero.[3] If there is exactly one air carrier, as in this study, no congestion externality exists, and imposing a congestion fee cannot improve efficiency. Therefore, this study does not assume delay costs for consumers or extra costs for airlines due to congestion.

The timing of events is as follows. The airport has to determine the take-off and landing fees in advance and allocate slots at the beginning of each summer or winter period. The air carrier can decide day by day how many slots to use and what price to charge for a ticket. Therefore, the game is an sequential game and the airport is assumed to be the first mover and the air carrier the second mover, and the prices and quantities discussed in the following are results of subgame perfect equilibria determined by backward induction.

2.1. No use-it-or-lose-it rule

In the absence of a use-it-or-lose-it rule, the slot-use ratio has no effect on further possibilities for the use of slots. If there are property rights for slots, the carrier that owns the slots can use them in the future even if they are not used in the current period. The same holds true if there are no grandfather rights at all; i.e., even after 100% use the slot is not guaranteed for the next period. Therefore, the carrier optimizes its operations and profits independently of future periods.

The air carrier searches for a price vector (p_h, p_l) that maximizes profits

$$\Pi_h = (p_h - c)(D_h - dp_h) \qquad (1)$$

in the case of high demand and

$$\Pi_l = (p_l - c)(D_l - dp_l) \qquad (2)$$

when demand is low. A simple calculation shows that the optimal ticket price is

$$p_i^* = \frac{D_i + cd}{2d} \qquad (3)$$

and the derived demand for tickets is then represented by

$$x_i^* = \frac{D_i}{2} - \frac{cd}{2}. \qquad (4)$$

In contrast to the carrier, the airport does not know whether demand is high or low. The airport rationally expects the demand situation and anticipates the price decision of the carrier and the derived demand. Profit-maximization by the risk neutral airport without knowing the current demand status leads to the optimal landing fee charged to the airline:

$$p_a^* = \frac{ED}{2d} - \frac{s}{2},$$

where $ED = w_h D_h + w_l D_l$. Consequently, the airport earns the expected profit

$$\Pi = \frac{(ED + sd)^2}{8d}.$$

2.2. Airport profits with grandfather rights

Let $0 \leqslant g \leqslant 1$ be the ratio of times that the carrier has to use a slot, for example 80% in the EU, to retain the slot for itself. If the optimal quantity of slots in the event of low demand is greater than g percent of the number of slots during high demand, the carrier behaves similarly to the process outlined in the previous section. However, if the optimal slot use in the event of low demand could result in the loss of some slots, i.e., if $x_l < g \cdot x_h$, equivalently represented as

---

[3] If the carrier decides to operate a flight (even for babysitting), optimal yield management results in selling all tickets. Therefore, the total costs for a flight only operated to maintain the slot are equal to the costs of all other flights. Assuming non-zero fixed costs does not change p^* (Eq. (3)) and x^* (Eq. (4)). High fixed costs may lead to losses when babysitting a slot. In this case it could be optimal to discontinue the route. However, because the paper analyzes babysitting behavior, babysitting has to be profitable and therefore fixed costs have to be low, or as assumed in the paper, equal to zero.

$$g > 1 - \frac{2(D_h - D_l)}{2D_h - ED + ds},$$

the carrier chooses to babysit the slots if it is more profitable to do this and to hold the slots rather than use fewer slots in the event of low demand and, as a consequence, lose some slots. If $g > D_l/D_h$, then $x_l < g \cdot x_h$, and the slot-use ratio becomes large enough to be binding.

I assume that babysitting is always more profitable than not to do so.[4] This assumption holds true if it is assumed that a carrier loses all unused slots for good when it does not use the slots g percent of the time and if the lost slots are allocated to its competitors, with market entry that consequently destroys the market power of the incumbent (Dempsey, 2001). Let x_h^* be the optimal quantity when demand is high. Babysitting means that the carrier has to operate $g \cdot x_h^*$ slots in the case of low demand in order not to lose all unused slots. The optimal babysitting price for low demand sells all $(g \cdot x_h^*)$ tickets and therefore has to satisfy the following equation:

$$D_l - d \cdot p_l^* = g \cdot x_h^* \tag{5}$$

and thus the optimal price is

$$p_l^* = D_l/d - g/d \cdot D_h + g \cdot p_h^*. \tag{6}$$

If the air carrier does not babysit, it searches for a price vector (p_h, p_l) that maximizes expected profits

$$E\Pi = w_h((p_h - c)(D_h - dp_h)) + w_l((p_l - c)(D_l - dp_l)), \tag{7}$$

a problem solved in Section 2.1. However, if the air carrier does babysit, the number of high-demand slots and low-demand slots are linked (Eq. (5)). Using more slots in the high-demand case results in more slots to babysit and a lower price (Eq. (6)). Expected profits of the carrier thus are represented by

$$E\Pi = w_h((p_h - c)(D_h - dp_h)) + w_l((p_l^* - c)(D_l - dp_l^*)), \tag{8}$$

which can be simplified to

$$E\Pi = (w_h p_h + w_l p_l^* g - c\tilde{w})(D_h - dp_h) \tag{9}$$

with $\tilde{w} = w_h + g w_l$. The optimal high-demand price is

$$p_h^* = \frac{(w_h + 2w_l g^2) D_h - w_l g D_l + cd\tilde{w}}{2d(w_h + w_l g^2)},$$

and the number of tickets sold is

$$x_h^* = \frac{w_h D_h + w_l g D_l - cd\tilde{w}}{2(w_h + w_l g^2)}.$$

Therefore, a babysitting air carrier uses fewer slots under high-demand circumstances and more slots in the low-demand case than an air carrier that optimizes each demand state separately.

The airport, anticipating the pricing and babysitting policy of air carriers, maximizes its profit

$$\Pi = (p_a + s)[w_h x_h^*(p_a) + w_l x_l^*(p_a)]$$

by charging the optimal landing fee

$$p_a = \frac{\tilde{D}}{2d\tilde{w}} - \frac{s}{2},$$

where $\tilde{D} = w_h D_h + w_l g D_l$. The combination of an optimal landing fee and the air carrier's pricing policy leads to the following number of tickets sold in the high-demand case:

$$\tilde{x}_h^* = \frac{\tilde{D} + sd\tilde{w}}{4(w_h + w_l g^2)}. \tag{10}$$

To summarize, the airport earns

$$\Pi^g = (p_a + s)\tilde{x}_h^* \tilde{w} = \frac{(\tilde{D} + sd\tilde{w})^2}{8d(w_h + w_l g^2)}.$$

3. Comparison of profits

Theorem 1. *To compare profits, let the difference in profits Ψ be represented as*

---

[4] This is the case if the discounted sum of monopoly profits is higher than the discounted sum of profits when not babysitting.

$$\Psi(s) = \Pi^g - \Pi = \frac{(\tilde{D} + sd\tilde{w})^2}{8d(w_h + w_l g^2)} - \frac{(ED + sd)^2}{8d}.$$

For the function Ψ, the following results hold:

1. If
$$\frac{D_l}{D_h} < \frac{1+g}{2}$$
and $w_h > 1/2$, then $\Psi(0) > 0$;
2. $\lim_{s \to \infty} \Psi(s) = -\infty$;
3. if $D_l/D_h > g$, then $\Psi' < 0$; and
4. If $D_l/D_h < g$, then Ψ is unimodal with its maximum at $s^* = \left(\frac{D_h g - D_l}{d(1-g)}\right)$.

Proof. See the Appendix. □

The theorem shows that if s is not too large, then the airport prefers a use-it-or-lose-it rule. Because take-off and landing fees have to be paid only if the air carrier uses the slot, airport revenues are lower when demand is low. A use-it-or-lose-it rule leads to higher slot use in the event of low demand, but lower slot use during high demand. In this study the airport capacity is assumed to be endogenous. This assumption means that, in the long run, airport capacity equals slot use during high demand. However, different institutions (with or without use-it-or-lose-it stipulations) have different capacities. Therefore, the use-it-or-lose-it rule dampens demand fluctuations by inducing the air carrier to increase prices in the event of high demand and to decrease prices when there is low demand to a higher degree. As a consequence, the profits of the airport are proportionally higher if the use-it-or-lose-it rule holds validity.

If the use-it-or-lose-it rule holds, then the air carrier offers more tickets for a lower than optimal price in the event of low demand and fewer tickets for a higher than optimal price when demand is high. Therefore, the profits of the air carrier are lower for a use-it-or-lose-it rule compared to the situation for slot ownership or when grandfather rights do not exist at all. However, if this situation is compared to one in conjunction with grandfather rights, the air carriers prefer a use-it-g-percent-or-lose it rule to a pure grandfathering proposal because it is more profitable to use $g < 100\%$ of the slots than to lose all unused slots.

Airports claim the ownership of slots because they provide the infrastructure that can be used during the time slot. What type of contract would airports prefer if they really owned the slots? Because airports prefer a use-it-or-lose-it rule to a system where the air carrier has an unconditional option, especially slot ownership by air carriers, airports should not sell the slot to air carriers but should rent it out and hold on to the use-it-or-lose-it rule; the renting contract ends if slot use is not at least g percent. The status quo, grandfathering combined with a use-it-or-lose it rule, is equivalent to renting the slot for an amount equal to zero, with a user fee if the slot is used and an option for the same contract in the next period if the slot use is great enough. Therefore, the establishment of property rights for slots and their initial allocation to airports might not destroy the use-it-or-lose-it rule, and the resulting contract might be analogous to the status quo. Instead of paying take-off and landing fees, the air carrier has to pay a rental fee for a slot, independent of slot use.

Similar to the prediction of the model, the professional association of airport operators, the Airport Council International (ACI, 2007), suggests the levy of a slot reservation fee that should be accompanied by a decrease in landing and take-off charges. If the slot is used, the reservation fee should be deducted from the airport charges. If the slot is not used, the air carrier would not be reimbursed the reservation fee.

Furthermore, if an airport owns a slot and sells it to an air carrier, the possibility arises that the carrier may not use or sell the slot, but merely hold it to prevent another carrier from offering competitive flights. If a carrier owns a slot, the carrier is sure that it can use the slot in the next period even if it is not used in the current period. This effect is not modeled here because the market structure is assumed to be fixed. However, the effect supports the claim that airports are not interested in selling slots to air carriers without additional rules for slot use.

If airports can define the slot-use ratio g required for further slot use, they can demand the profit-maximizing slot-use ratio from air carriers. Because

$$\frac{\partial \Pi_g}{\partial g} = \frac{(D_l + ds - g(D_h + ds))w(1-w)[\tilde{D} + \tilde{w}ds]}{4d(w + (1-w)g^2)^2},$$

the optimal slot-use ratio is represented by the equation

$$g^* = \frac{D_l + ds}{D_h + ds},$$

subject to the condition that g is binding. The optimal g is less than 1, and therefore the optimal rule is not pure grandfathering. The reason why $g = 1$ is not optimal is the endogeneity of the airport capacity, and therefore the eventual endogeneity of the number of slots in the long run analyzed here. An air carrier that maximizes profits considers that each slot used when demand is high must be babysat while demand is low. Therefore, a higher g ratio increases the proportion of low-demand versus high-demand slot use, but might decrease high-demand slot use. In the long run, optimal slot use by air carriers during high demand is equivalent to the handling capacity of the airport. Therefore, a high g ratio decreases the airport capacity and, by implication, airport profits.

If there are no commercial revenues, i.e., if $s = 0$, then the optimal slot-use ratio is $g^* = D_l/D_h$. Because $\partial g^*/\partial s > 0$, higher commercial revenues lead to greater optimal slot-use ratios. The commercial profits of airports are increasingly projected as being more important. As the current model predicts, the professional association of airport operators, the ACI, suggests "strengthening of the use-it-or-lose-it-rule to 90/10" (ACI, 2007).

4. Comparison of social welfare

Social welfare is defined as the sum of the profits of air carriers $(E(p^c - p_a)x)$ and airports $(E(p_a + s)x)$ and the consumer rent $(E[\int_0^x \frac{D_i-q}{d} dq - (p^c + s)x])$ and equals

$$W = E\left[\int_0^x \frac{D_i - q}{d} dq\right] = E\left[\frac{2D_i x - x^2}{2d}\right]$$

because slot revenues are expenditure for air carriers but revenue for airports, and ticket revenues and non-aviation revenues are expenditure for consumers. The non-aviation good is therefore assumed to be a pure by-product of passenger transport and the price s in the competitive market equals the willingness of consumers to pay.

Without grandfather rights, $x_i = (D_i - cd)/2$ and $c = (ED - sd)/(2d)$. Therefore, $x_i = (2D_i - ED + sd)/4$. As a result,

$$W_0 = \frac{1}{d}[w_h(D_h x_h - x_h^2/2) + (1 - w_h)(D_l x_l - x_l^2/2)]$$

and therefore

$$W_0 = \frac{12(w_h D_h^2 + (1 - w_h)D_l^2) - 4ED(ED - ds) - (ED - ds)^2}{32d}.$$

If the use-it-or-lose-it rule holds true, the high-demand slot use is $\tilde{x}_h^*$, as calculated in Eq. (10), and the low-demand slot use is $g \cdot \tilde{x}_h^*$. Therefore,

$$W_g = \frac{7\widetilde{D}^2 + 6\widetilde{D}sd\widetilde{w} - (sd\widetilde{w})^2}{32d(w_h + (1 - w_h)g^2)}.$$

Theorem 2. *If $0 \leqslant s \leqslant ED/d$, then a use-it-or-lose-it rule reduces social welfare. Welfare losses decrease with increasing values of s, i.e., welfare losses are most severe when commercial revenues are small.*

Proof. See the Appendix. □

Because commercial revenue is increasingly important, losses in social welfare and therefore possible gains in efficiency predicted for abandonment of the rule decrease in theory.

If s is large, i.e., $s \geqslant \widetilde{D}/(d\widetilde{w})$, then the main source of profits is non-aviation revenue. In this case it would be optimal for the airport to pay a subsidy by levying negative take-off or landing fees to increase traffic.[5] However, this model assumes that congested airports charge positive fees. Therefore, the assumption $s < \widetilde{D}/(d\widetilde{w})$ is sensible and because $\widetilde{D}/(d\widetilde{w}) < ED/d$ the condition for Theorem 2 is fulfilled whenever an airport charges landing and take-off fees.

5. Conclusion

Comparison of a use-it-or-lose-it rule and an unrestricted slot-ownership plan revealed that the rule is profitable for airports but decreases carrier profits and social welfare. If airports owned well-defined property rights to slots, they would not sell such slots because it would be more profitable to substitute take-off and landing fees by a slot rent (independent of their use). Furthermore, the option to renew a rental agreement should depend on the effective use of slots: a use-it-g < 1-or-lose-it rule should be enforced. The model derived above shows that arrangements that increase airport profits do not necessarily improve social welfare. Therefore, the suggestions proposed by airports to reform European Council

---

[5] If the state owns the airport, subsidies may be considered as illegal state aid in the EU.

Regulation 95/93 on common rules for the allocation of slots at Community airports may or may not enhance the efficiency of airport use.

Acknowledgement

The author thanks two anonymous referees for helpful comments and Uwe Kratzsch for research assistance.

Proof of Theorem 1

1.
$$\Psi(0) > 0$$
$$\iff \tilde{D}^2 > ED^2(w_h + (1-w_h)g^2)$$
$$\iff (w_h D_h + g(1-w_h)D_l)^2 > (w_h D_h + (1-w_h)D_l)^2(w_h + (1-w_h)g^2)$$
$$\iff w_h^2 D_h^2(1 - w_h - g^2(1-w_h)) > (w_h D_h)2w_h(1-w_h)D_h D_l(w_h + g^2(1-w_h) - g)$$
$$+ (1-w_h)^2 D_l^2(w_h + g^2(1-w_h) - g^2).$$

Because $D_h > D_l$ and $w_h > 1 - w_h$, $\Psi(0)$ is positive if

$$(2w_h - 1)(1-g^2)D_h^2 > 2D_h D_l(w_h - g + g^2(1-w_h))$$
$$\iff \frac{D_h}{D_l} > \frac{2(w_h - g + g^2 - w_h g^2)}{(2w_h - 1)(1 - g^2)} = 1 + \frac{1-g}{(1+g)(2w_h - 1)}.$$

If $D_l/D_h < (1+g)/2$, then

$$\frac{D_l}{D_h} < \frac{(1+g)(2w_h - 1)}{2 + 2g - 2g} = \frac{(1+g)(2w_h - 1)}{2(1+g) - 2g} < \frac{(1+g)(2w_h - 1)}{2w_h(1+g) - 2g}$$

and therefore

$$\frac{D_h}{D_l} > 1 + \frac{1-g}{(1+g)(2w_h - 1)}.$$

2. Statement 2 holds true because $sd > sd\bar{w}$.
3. Differentiating Ψ with respect to s yields

$$\Psi' = \frac{(-1+g)(D_l - D_h g - d(-1+g)s)(-1+w_h)w_h}{4g^2(-1+w_h) - 4w_h}.$$

Therefore,

$$\Psi' < 0 \iff D_l - D_h g - d(-1+g)s > 0 \iff s > \frac{D_h g - D_l}{d(1-g)}.$$

If $D_l/D_h > g$, then $D_l > D_h g$ and $D_h g - D_l < 0 < s$. Therefore, $\Psi' < 0$ and statement 3 holds true.

Proof of Theorem 2

To compare the welfare, let

$$\Phi(s) = W_g - W_o.$$

Assume that $D_l/D_h < g$. For the function Φ, the following results hold:

1. $\Phi(0) < 0$;
2. $\Phi'(0) > 0$;
3. $\lim_{s \to \infty} \Phi(s) = \infty$; and
4. $\Phi(ED/d) < 0$.

Proof

1. $\Phi(0) < 0$ if $W_g < W_o$, and therefore, if and only if

$$12(w_h D_h^2 + (1-w_h)D_l^2) - 4ED^2 - ED^2)(w_h + (1-w_h)g^2) > 7\tilde{D}^2$$

and only if
$$12(w_h D_h^2 + (1-w_h)D_l^2) - 5ED^2)(w_h + (1-w_h)g^2) > 7w_h^2 D_h^2 + 14w_h(1-w_h)gD_h D_l + 7g^2(1-w_h)^2 D_l^2,$$
which is equivalent to
$$2D_h D_l(7g + 5g^2(1-w) + 5w) < D_h^2(5w + g^2(12-5w)) + D_l^2(7 + 5(1-w)g^2 + 5w)$$
$$\iff D_h D_l(7g + 5g^2(1-w) + 5w) + D_h D_l(7g + 5g^2(1-w) + 5w) < D_l^2(7g + 5g^2(1-w) + 5w + 7(1-g))$$
$$+ D_h^2(7g + 5g^2(1-w) + 5w + 7g^2 - 7g)$$
$$\iff D_l(7g + 5g^2(1-w) + 5w)(D_h - D_l) + D_h(7g + 5g^2(1-w) + 5w)(D_l - D_h) < D_l^2 7(1-g) + D_h^2 7g(g-1)$$
$$\iff (D_h - D_l)(D_l - D_h)(7g + 5g^2(1-w) + 5w) < 7(1-g)(D_l^2 - gD_h^2)$$
$$\iff (D_h - D_l)^2(7g + 5g^2(1-w) + 5w) > 7(1-g)(gD_h^2 - D_l^2).$$
Because $D_l/D_h < g \iff gD_h > D_l$, it follows that $D_h - D_l > D_h - gD_h = D_h(1-g)$, and therefore $W_g < W_o$ if
$$D_h^2(1-g)^2(7g + 5g^2(1-w) + 5w) > 7(1-g)(gD_h^2 - D_l^2)$$
$$\iff D_h^2(1-g)(7g + 5g^2(1-w) + 5w) > 7gD_h^2 - 7D_l^2$$
$$\iff D_h^2(1-g)(7g + 5w(1-g^2) + 5g^2) > 7gD_h^2 - 7D_l^2$$
$$\iff D_h^2(-7g + 7g - 7g^2 + (1-g)(5w(1-g^2)) + 5g^2 - 5g^3) + 7D_l^2 > 0$$
$$\iff D_h^2(-2g^2 - 5g^3 + (1-g)(5w(1-g^2))) + 7D_l^2 > 0.$$
Because $D_h > D_l/g$, it follows that $D_h^2 > D_l^2/g^2$, and therefore $W_g < W_o$ if
$$\frac{D_l^2}{g^2}(-2g^2 - 5g^3 + (1-g)(5w(1-g^2))) + 7D_l^2 > 0$$
$$\iff D_l^2\left(7 - 2 - 5g + \frac{(1-g)}{g^2}(5w(1-g^2))\right) > 0,$$
which is true.

2.
$$\Phi'(s) = \frac{3\widetilde{D}\widetilde{w} - 3ED(w + (1-w)g^2)}{16(w + (1-w)g^2)} = \frac{3(1-g)(gD_h - D_l)(1-w)w}{16(w + (1-w)g^2)} > 0.$$

3. Because $\tilde{w}^2 - (w + (1-w)g^2) = -(1-g)^2(1-w)w < 0$,
$$\lim_{s \to \infty} \Phi'(s) = -\frac{\tilde{w}^2 - (w + (1-w)g^2)}{16(w + (1-w)g^2)} > 0.$$

4. For all $0 \leqslant s < 3ED/d$, the functions $W_g(s)$ and $W_o(s)$ are monotonically increasing. Therefore,
$$\Psi(ED/d) = W_g(ED/d) - W_o(ED/d) < W_g(\widetilde{D}/(d\tilde{w})) - W_o(ED/d) = \frac{12\widetilde{D}^2}{32d(w + (1-w)g^2)} - \frac{12(wD_h^2 + (1-w)D_l^2)}{32d} < 0$$
if and only if
$$\widetilde{D}^2 - (wD_h^2 + (1-w)D_l^2)(w + (1-w)g^2) = -(gD_h - D_l)^2(1-w)w < 0,$$
which is true.

From the above statements 1–4 it follows that if $0 \leqslant s < ED/d$, a use-it-or-lose-it rule reduces social welfare. □

References

Abeyratne, R.I.R., 2000. Management of airport congestion through slot allocation. Journal of Air Transport Management 6 (1), 29–41.
ACI, 2007. ACI Europe Position on Allocation of Slots. <http://www.aci-europe.org/upload/ACI%20EUROPE%20POSITION_Slot%20allocation%20June%2007.pdf>.
Barbot, C., 2004. Economic effects of re-allocating airports slots: a vertical differentiation approach. Journal of Air Transport Management 10 (5), 333–343.
Basso, L.J., Zhang, A., 2008. On the relationship between airport pricing modes. Transportation Research Part B 42 (9), 725–735.
Boyfield, K., Starkie, D., Bass, T., Humphreys, B., 2003. A Market in Airport Slots. The Institute of Economic Affairs.
Brueckner, J.K., 2002. Airport congestion when carriers have market power. American Economic Review 92 (5), 1357–1375.
Brueckner, J.K., Girvin, R., 2008. Airport noise regulation, airline service quality, and social welfare. Transportation Research Part B 42 (1), 19–37.
Button, K., 2005. A simple analysis of the rent seeking of airlines, airports and politicians. Transport Policy 12 (1), 47–56.
Button, K., 2008. Auctions – what can we learn from auction theory for slot allocation? In: Czerny, P., Forsyth, D.G., Niemeier, H.-M. (Eds.), Airport Slots – International Experiences and Options for Reform. Ashgate, pp. 291–309.

Coase, R.H., 1960. The problem of social cost. Journal of Law and Economics 3 (1), 1–44.
Dempsey, P.S., 2001. Airport landing slots: barriers to entry and impediments to competition. Air and Space Law 26 (1), 20–48.
Doganis, R., 2002. Flying off Course – The Economics of International Airlines, 3 ed. Routledge.
Jones, I., Viehoff, I., Marks, P., 1993. The economics of airport slots. Fiscal Studies 14 (4), 37–57.
Pels, E., Verhoef, E.T., 2004. The economics of airport congestion pricing. Journal of Urban Economics 55 (2), 257–277.
Riker, W.H., Sened, I., 1991. A political theory of the origin of property rights: airport slots. American Journal of Political Science 35 (4), 951–969.
Sened, I., Riker, W.H., 1996. Common property and private property: the case of air slots. Journal of Theoretical Politics 8 (4), 427–448.
Starkie, D., 1998. Allocating airport slots: a role for the market? Journal of Air Transport Management 4 (2), 111–116.
Zhang, A., Zhang, Y., 2006. Airport capacity and congestion when carriers have market power. Journal of Urban Economics 60 (2), 229–247.

11

Allocating airport slots: a role for the market?

David Starkie

Abstract

The paper analyses the problem of allocating landing slots at congested airports from an economic perspective. First, it considers the implications of an absence of market clearing prices, after which it examines the arguments for and against a secondary market in slots particularly drawing upon evidence from US airports. It concludes that a secondary market in slots will encourage a more efficient use of scarce slots but will do little to increase service competition when capacity is scarce. In addition, it will not offset the incumbent's advantage. To address the latter an increase in landing charges is required. © 1998 David Starkie. Published by Elsevier Science Ltd. All rights reserved.

1. Introduction

It is a growing feature of modern civil aviation that many of the world's major airports suffer from inadequate runway capacity. Particular airports have become popular places to fly to and from or change planes at, but as the demand for flights has grown the expansion of runway capacity has failed to keep pace. There are a number of reasons for this. The overwhelming majority of airports are still publicly controlled utilities subject to political whims and often tight budgets, but even where such constraints apply less (as in the UK), expansion has been hampered by environmental limitations and other planning controls. Building new runways or lengthening existing ones is not impossible as London City Airport and Manchester both illustrate, but it is not an easy task.

In consequence, delays at busy airports have increased and expansion of air services has had to rely upon improvements in air traffic control technology and the adoption of new procedures to squeeze more aircraft movements through existing runways. The ability to do so has been at times remarkable. Little more than a quarter of a century ago, the (Roskill) Commission investigating locations suitable for a new international airport for London adopted the working assumption that the estimated capacity of Heathrow and Gatwick combined was 440 000 annual movements: in 1997 Heathrow *alone* handled 426 000. Nor, has the process of improving throughput slackened in recent times. Nevertheless, the salient feature remains one of severe shortages of capacity. At Heathrow the runways are operating at, or close to, declared capacity during much of the day.

2. The economics of runway congestion

The economic consequence of this can be illustrated by reference to demand and supply diagrams. The first of these – Fig. 1a – illustrates that when the demand for runway use is within declared runway capacity, the price to charge will be one that covers the cost of supply including a satisfactory return on the capital invested. In Fig. 1a, for ease of exposition, average costs are assumed to be constant across all levels of output. However, if demand continues to grow, and grows more rapidly than capacity can be expanded, maintaining the price shown in Fig. 1a will eventually result in excess demand (Fig. 1b); airlines will want to use runways more than there is capacity is available and, unless corrected, queues on the ground or in the air will develop. In these circumstances, the economically correct (or efficient) price is one that balances demand with the supply available (Fig. 1c). This is referred to as a rationing or market clearing price which, it should be noted, produces what is referred to as an economic rent, the potential for earning a return in excess of the average cost of supplying runway services. In reality, at a number of airports, not only is the price charged to the airlines less than the market clearing price but it is also, on average, less than the cost of supply. The

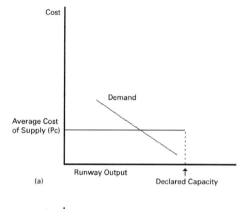
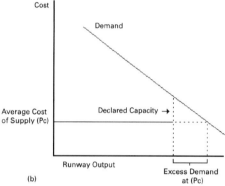
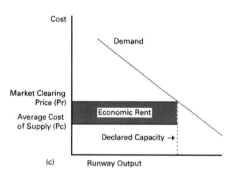

Fig. 1. Demand and supply for runway capacity.

Monopolies and Mergers Commission (MMC, 1996) in a recent report on BAA's London airports, for example, suggested that if air-side assets (runways, aprons for parking aircraft, piers and aerobridges) were to earn a 7% real rate of return, revenue from charges would need to increase by more than a third.[1]

However, and importantly, the fact that landing charges at congested airports are less than the market clearing price (and sometimes the cost of supply) does not mean that air travellers necessarily enjoy cheaper air fares. If it did, airlines, too, would have a problem of allocating an excess of demand (in this case, of passengers to seats). Instead, airlines will be inclined to charge what the market will bear and make excess profits on the use of the scarce slots. In effect, the economic rent shown in Fig. 1c is transferred to the airlines.

For Heathrow we have one indication of the size of the transfer from analysis undertaken for the 1993 RUCATSE Report. The Report suggested that the fares premium charged by airlines might be equivalent to £20 per passenger. At Gatwick, where, in contrast to Heathrow, charter traffic is important, Bishop and Thompson (1992) found that the prices charged for inclusive tours using the airport were significantly higher than prices for the same "package" at other UK airports, by a magnitude of broadly 5%.[2]

3. Administrative rationing

With the potential to charge such fare premia, naturally airlines are very keen to have slots at congested airports and, because price is not used to ration demand to the limited runway capacity available, some other rationing mechanism is needed. This mechanism is an administrative process based on guidelines laid down by the International Air Transport Association (IATA), the airline trade association. These guidelines, first and foremost, recognise the historical use of "slots" (the entitlement to use a runway at a particular time). An airline has a right to a slot if it has already made use of the runway at the same time during the preceding equivalent season.

These entitlements, known as 'grandfather rights', form the point of reference at bi-annual international conferences which take place to coordinate schedules at capacity restricted airports. At these conferences, airlines seek to modify their schedules by trading (or exchanging)

---

[1] In spite of this conclusion, the industry Regulator (the CAA) decided that charges at Heathrow and Gatwick should fall still further in real terms over the five year period starting in April 1997. The process by which such a decision is arrived at is complex and hinges on what is called the "single-till" approach. It is useful to note, however, that within the broader framework, BAA Plc does have a structure of landing fees which leads to significantly higher charges during defined peak periods. The company pioneered such a structure – still rare in world aviation – starting in the 1970s.

[2] Part of the premium might however reflect the increased costs of operating at a capacity constrained airport.

their existing rights or perhaps by trying to obtain additional slots that occasionally become available (although since 1990 the IATA rules have required a proportion of unclaimed slots to be set aside for use by new entrant carriers, defined as those with negligible or non-existent presence at the airport concerned). These basic guidelines were adopted into EU law, albeit with some minor changes, by Regulation 95/93 early in 1993.

Because the basic rules encourage airlines to exchange slots and because airlines do not even have to use their existing slots for a specific route, established carriers dominate slot-constrained airports. For example, 95% of the slots available at Heathrow for use in the Summer of 1994 went to those airlines that had made use of them in the corresponding season of the previous year. The few entrants that did commence services, did so on 'thin' routes to new destinations; there were no directly competing services introduced and those incumbent airlines that did obtain some additional slots used them to increase frequencies on their existing routes. Not surprisingly, this rule-based approach, although widely supported within the aviation industry, has been criticised by the anti-trust authorities.

4. The US approach

In the United States, for anti-trust reasons, the IATA based system does not apply; instead as a general rule airlines simply schedule their flights taking into account expected delays at the busier airports. At four major airports, however, (JFK and La Guardia in New York City, O'Hare in Chicago and Washington National), where demand for runway use is particularly high, the authorities stepped in many years ago to prescribe a limit on the number of flights during restricted hours and they have since permitted airlines to buy and sell their slot holdings at these four airports, albeit with conditions attached. The market is restricted to slots used for *domestic* services which in turn are divided into two groups: air carrier slots, and commuter slots (originally operated by aircraft with 56 or fewer seats). The latter category cannot be bought by the former and, in addition, slots used for subsidised "essential air services" are excluded from the market. The regulations stipulate that any person is entitled to purchase, sell and mortgage a slot or to lease on a temporary basis.[3] However, slots not used for a stipulated minimum of time in a two-month period have to be returned to the FAA; that is to say, carriers must "use or lose" their slot. Surrendered slots, or others becoming available, are assigned to a pool and reallocated using a lottery but with 25% initially offered to new entrants.

These basic terms were introduced in April 1986 when airlines started to buy and sell those slots which they were holding as of 16th December 1995. More recently, small amendments have been made to the regulations. From January 1993 slots have had to be used for 80% of the time in a two-month period (it was previously 65%) and the definition of those entitled to slots from the reserved pool was broadened to include incumbent carriers with few slots. In addition, restrictions were introduced to prevent slots intended for new entrants being acquired by incumbents. Other amendments have adjusted the distinction between air carrier and commuter slots, a distinction which was introduced originally in order to strike a balance between maximising the economic use of runway resources and preserving services to smaller communities. The distinction is still maintained, but the aircraft size threshold for the use of commuter slots have been increased, particularly at O'Hare.

Data on how the market has worked distinguishing between air carrier and commuter slots is available only for the first three years after its introduction. During the first six to nine months, there was an initial surge of activity as airlines acquired the slots they believed they could use best and disposed of those that could be sold profitably. Following this initial sorting out the number of outright sales declined but the number of leases grew, particularly short term leases reflecting the fact that some carriers require the use of a slot at limited times of the year only (Table 1). The distinction in the regulations between air carriers and commuters produced two separate markets and differences between them emerged. Commuter carriers have been more inclined to buy and sell, rather than lease, and some new commuter airlines took the opportunity to enter the market; as a general rule air carrier slots were traded between incumbents. An interesting feature that has emerged is that a significant number of slots is held by non-carriers. Nothing in the regulations prohibits communities from acquiring slots to enhance services to their region's airports and a number have done so. Some airlines have also mortgaged their slots to financial institutions.

Table 1
Summary of leases and sales of air carriers/*commuters* at US high density airports 1986–1988

	Leases				Sales (%)		Total transactions	
	< 6 months (%)		> 6 months (%)					
1986	26.0	*34.0*	13.0	*1.0*	61.0	*65.0*	617	*159*
1987	79.0	*13.0*	1.0	—	20.0	*87.0*	774	*23*
1988	83.0	*17.0*	8.0	—	9.0	*83.0*	734	*99*

---

[3] For further details see Starkie (1992, 1994).

5. Predation and anti-competitive behaviour

With such an interesting example of a secondary market in airport slots now more than a decade old, it is to be expected that suggestions have been made for the introduction of a similar system in Europe. At the moment, Regulation 95/93 does not allow slots at European airports to be bought and sold, although it is less clear that if money changes hands only when slots are exchanged, that this is strictly against the rules (Bass, 1994). According to press reports, however, the Transport Directorate of the European Commission favour legitimising the monetarised trading of slots in a revised regulation. Again according to press reports, this has been opposed by the Competition Directorate. The concerns of the latter appear to reflect those expressed by the US General Accounting Office (USGAO, 1996) and, more recently, the US Department of Transportation, in regard to the US secondary market. These concerns centre on the issue of dominance and predatory behaviour. Specifically, the argument is that established airlines with grandfathered rights will buy slots to keep entrants out of the market and, as a consequence, further increase their dominance at congested airports. In support of this view, both the GAO and the US DoT have pointed out that there had been few entrants into the four US airports which have a secondary market and that established airlines have increased their share of slots.[4]

This argument, that airlines with market power will engage in predatory bidding for slots, has been subject to close examination by McGowan and Seabright (1989). They accept that this is a serious objection but are of the view that, for established airlines, it is an expensive way to deter or drive out competitors. This is because at any one airport there are many slots each one of which has a large number of close or reasonably close substitutes (bearing in mind that slots are transferable between services). To keep a newcomer out of a particular market, an incumbent airlines might, therefore, have to 'overbid' on a large number of slots. In these circumstances, McGowan and Seabright argue that it is more likely that an established airlines will direct any predatory behaviour to the route (service) itself. This seems a reasonable argument, although the larger share of slots held by the dominant airline(s) the less convincing it becomes. At an airport such as O'Hare Chicago, where over 80% of all slots are in the hands of either American or United, the number of slots that these two incumbents would need to overbid on would be relatively small.[5] On the other hand, McGowan and Seabright's argument is reinforced even at airports such as O'Hare, once an additional factor is taken into account. Once a secondary market is introduced, slots, in effect, become tradable assets and, as a result, their value should be written into the balance sheet of the airlines. This value will reflect the capitalisation of the economic rent that they command, which suggests that slots will be bought when an airline is able to earn a satisfactory return on its investment in them and that they will be sold when it is unable to do so. The introduction of a secondary market, therefore, is likely to create strong pressures for under-utilised slots to be sold (even by the dominant airlines) or to be used more effectively.

Support for this view comes from an analysis of slot ownership and usage data at Chicago O'Hare (Kleit and Kobayashi, 1996). O'Hare has the most concentrated holding of slots of all the four US airports where slots are bought and sold, and it is also the one airport where airlines established before deregulation of the US domestic market have increased their slot holdings. The analysis, based on 1990 data, focused on the utilisation of slots at O'Hare, and specifically examined whether the two large dominant carriers (United and American) were using their slots more, or less, intensively than the smaller carriers: the usual market power argument would be that the dominant firm(s) have an incentive to reduce output. Slot utilisation was measured in three ways: the average rate at which slots were used; whether leased slots were used more or less intensively than owned and operated slots: and the average daily seat capacity per slot. The analysis indicated that the dominant carriers had a higher usage rate for their slots and that slots that they leased out were used at an equal or higher rate than the owned and operated slots. In other words, there was no indication that dominant carriers were hoarding poorly utilised slots, or were leasing slots to other airlines which would make little use of them. On the other hand, there was evidence that the dominant carriers were using on average smaller aircraft but it was suggested that this reflected the use of Chicago O'Hare as a regional hub by both United and American. The overall conclusion was that concentration in the slot market at O'Hare was not leading to anti-competitive behaviour. Instead, the evidence was more consistent with the hypothesis that efficiency considerations are generating concentration at O'Hare: large airlines with large networks are more likely to obtain additional value from use of the marginal slot.

6. Efficiency and equity

These processes would of course be more transparent and therefore more evident, if the price mechanism was used to balance demand with supply at popular airports. However, in the absence of the price mechanism being

---

[4] Account should also be taken of the consolidation of the US airline industry as a whole during the 1980s and of the fact that unlike in Europe, gates at US airports are often on long term exclusive leases and are difficult to obtain (see Starkie, 1992, pp. 15–16).

[5] At Heathrow, the largest airline (BA) holds less than 40% of slots and therefore McGowan and Seabright's argument is more likely to apply.

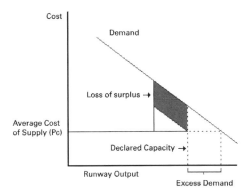

Fig. 2. Potential loss of surplus from administrative rationing.

used in this way, the conclusion from the O'Hare data supports the case for having a secondary market in slots. Such a market is likely to increase the efficient use of slots at congested airports. The point can be shown analytically if we modify the argument illustrated in Fig. 1b. This Figure showed that when prices are sub-optimal there is an excess of demand. In Fig. 2 an extreme case is assumed where the whole of the tail of excess, but low value, demand displaces an equivalent quantity of high value demand (a feasible situation when the criteria for administrative rationing emphasises historic usage). In this situation it can be seen that there is a net loss of user surplus.[6] The introduction of a secondary market in these circumstances, enables those potential users of runway capacity with high added value, to compensate through the purchase price, users with low added value; there is a net gain in welfare by, in effect, allowing the market to redistribute slots to those services from which airline passengers derive most benefit. There is, however, an interesting consequence which Fig. 2 is suggestive of. At airports which introduce secondary markets, it is quite possible that the average fare yield will increase. This is because scarce capacity is now utilised by flights from which passengers derive most benefit and airlines will be able to extract this additional economic rent in higher fare yields. This is not an adverse effect; it reflects the fact that at slot constrained airports, introducing a secondary market has added value to the network of services.

The taxing issue which follows from all this is: who should receive the economic rent? At the present time, with runway capacity priced sub-optimally, the economic rent goes to the incumbent airline which possibly obtained its slot(s) many years ago, for nothing.[7] Consequently, a secondary market in airline slots will mean that the incumbent receives a lump sum financial benefit when the slot is purchased, but this lump sum represents the present value of the scarcity rent associated with the slot.[8] The incumbent is, of course, currently receiving this scarcity value through the yield premium on fares charged to passengers. In this sense those with grandfathered rights already enjoy the "windfall" and the introduction of a formal slot market will neither add to nor subtract from this.[9]

If this situation is considered inequitable then the way forward is not to confiscate slots from incumbents and redistribute them between other airlines on the basis of criteria such as the *assumed* competitive consequences. To do so merely emphasises the arbitrary process by which the rent is "captured", and it will do little for effective competition in circumstances where there is a fundamental shortage of capacity: if one market sector, say the North Atlantic, receives a tranche of reallocated slots, this will generally be at the expense of competition in those markets from which the slots are withdrawn. A better way of approaching the problem is, clearly, to build more runways. Alternatively, if that is not possible, it is to increase the price charged for landing aircraft so that there is less of a divergence between the market clearing price and the price actually charged.[10] Increasing the price would have the effect of reducing the scarcity rent enjoyed by the incumbent airline, thus placing incumbent and entrant on a more equal footing. It does, of course, open up a range of additional issues that bear upon the regulation of airport charges such as the role of the "single-till"; the contribution made to airport finances by duty free tax concessions; and, indeed, whether there is scope for using the revenue from charges

---

[6] A legitimate question is: why do not those airlines with historic rights serving low value markets switch services to more highly valued markets? In other words, is not the division of the market portrayed here, rather artificial? The division reflects both barriers to entry associated with international air service agreements and the absence of a market in slots; airlines do not have an incentive to earn a return on assets which are freely acquired and are not fully tradable.

[7] A related issue is whether airlines enjoy any property rights to slots. Opinion is varied but the legal view is inclined to argue that airlines do not have such rights. The rule governing the US market in slots states specifically that it does not give airlines any proprietary rights.

[8] Estimates of the market price for a pair of slots at the four US airports vary from $1.0 m off-peak to in excess of $4.0 m at peak times. At Heathrow estimates vary enormously but generally start at $1.0 m for a pair of peak period slots. These values might be contrasted with the book value for aircraft. The entrant would, of course, have to finance his purchase of a slot but raising finance against the security of a slot should not be at all difficult.

[9] See Starkie and Thompson (1985) for elaboration.

[10] If charges were raised to market clearing levels, a secondary market in slots would, of course, be unnecessary. However, given the practical difficulties of determining the market clearing price (which will fluctuate between seasons) it could be argued that it is more efficient to fix landing charges conservatively and allow a secondary market to fine-tune the situation.

to compensate for environmental externalities. If increased charges were channelled into such payments there might be less resistance to the expansion of airports and building more runways might be more acceptable. But, these broader issues lie outside the compass of this paper.

Acknowledgements

I would like to thank my colleague, David Thompson, for his helpful comments.

References

Bass, T., 1994. Infrastructure constraints and the EC. Journal of Air Transport Management, September, 145–150.

Bishop, M., Thompson, D., 1992. Peak-load pricing in aviation: the case of charter air fares. Journal of Transport Economics and Policy, January, 71–82.

Kleit, A., Kobayashi, B., 1996. Market failure or market efficiency? Evidence on airport slot usage. In McMullen, B. (Ed.), Research in Transportation Economics. JAI Press, Connecticut.

McGowan, F., Seabright, P., 1989. Deregulating European Airlines. Economic Policy, October, 283–344.

MMC, 1996. BAA plc, A report on the economic regulation of the London airport companies. MMC4, CAA, London.

Starkie, D., 1992. Slot Trading at United States Airports. A Report for the DG VII, City Publications, London.

Starkie, D., 1994. Developments in transport policy: the US market in airport slots. Journal of Transport Economics and Policy, September, 325–329.

Starkie, D., Thompson, D., 1985. The airports' policy white paper: privatisation and regulation. Fiscal Studies, 30–42.

USGAO, 1996. Airline deregulation: barriers to entry continue to limit competition in several key domestic markets. Report to US Senate, United States General Accounting Office.

12

Airport terminal capacity planning

Senay Solak, John-Paul B. Clarke, Ellis L. Johnson

ARTICLE INFO

Article history:
Received 8 March 2008
Received in revised form 6 January 2009
Accepted 6 January 2009

Keywords:
Passenger terminal design
Airport planning
Capacity expansion
Multistage stochastic programming

ABSTRACT

The airport terminal capacity planning problem deals with determining the optimal design and expansion capacities for different areas of the terminal in the presence of uncertainty with regards to future demand levels and expansion costs. Analytical modeling of passenger flow in airport terminals under transient demand patterns is especially difficult due to the complex structure of a terminal. Because of this difficulty, the airport terminal capacity planning problem has not been studied in a holistic fashion, such that studies in this area either do not account for expandability or focus only on one particular area of the terminal. In this study, we consider the airport terminal capacity planning problem as a whole. In this regard, we first derive time functions to approximate maximum delays in passageways and processing stations of an airport terminal. We then use these delay functions to develop a multistage stochastic programming model based on a multicommodity flow network representation of the whole airport terminal. The solution of the model, for which we develop an efficient solution algorithm, provides optimal capacity requirements for each area in an airport terminal during the initial building phase, as well as the optimal expansion policy under stochastic future demand. The results of the study are applicable to all similar queuing networks, including other types of passenger terminals.

© 2009 Elsevier Ltd. All rights reserved.

1. Introduction

Congestion is a significant problem for the hundreds of thousands of passengers flying in and out of major airports each day. This problem has been exacerbated over the last several years by the heightened levels of security. Hence, capacity planning during the airport terminal design process is more important than ever, suggesting a need for the development of more accurate analysis methods. However, the uncertainty associated with future passenger demand levels and the complexity of the airport terminals make this a difficult task.

Several studies in the literature discuss the capacity problem at airport terminals. Hamzawi (1992) emphasizes the need for a solution to the problem of congestion caused by lack of capacity, arguing that if no remedial actions are taken, it could lead to an eventual functional breakdown of the airport system. In practice, most such actions are realized in the form of costly expansion projects, because there are limited resources available during the initial construction, and great uncertainty as to future demand. However, it is crucial that the need for expansion and the costs associated with the initial design and future expansion projects are minimized. Significant, long-lasting increases in airport terminal capacity can only be achieved through the building of new terminals that are designed to be expandable from their very conception. Considering that upwards of 20 airports may need to be built worldwide in the next two decades, there is a distinct need for new terminal designs that are efficient and flexible enough to accommodate the wide range of demand scenarios that are possible, given the significant, historically observed uncertainty in the demand for air transportation.

Most studies that consider the capacity problem are those that focus on the optimum design of airport terminals. Such studies usually include single period approaches based on short-term demand forecasts and the corresponding passenger flows within the terminal. Using this concept, Saffarzadeh and Braaksma (2000) develop a resource utilization model in which the cost of oversizing or undersizing the terminal facilities is minimized, while McCullough and Roberts (1979) present a capacity analysis model based on the study of movements within the terminal during discrete time intervals. In addition, McKelvey (1989) suggests a multi-channel queuing system approach to analyze passenger processing times under different capacity levels.

Although queuing models can be used for passenger flow analysis, a steady state assumption is not valid for airport terminals due to the high variability in the number of arrivals and departures during a typical day. Hence, the well-known steady state results for queuing systems are inapplicable. On the other hand, transient studies are generally intractable due to the complexity of flow in an airport terminal. Thus, most studies involve simulations to model this random and complex flow process. In these studies, simulation results are used to estimate the required capacity levels to make the operations more efficient. One such example is by Jim and Chang (1998), in which a simulation model is proposed to evaluate several terminal design alternatives.

None of the existing models address the airport terminal capacity problem in a truly holistic fashion, in large part because of the difficulty of modeling passenger flow in a complex terminal structure with transient demand patterns. Furthermore, expandability is never accounted for.

In this study, we assume that the level of service at airport terminals is measured by the total time a passenger spends in the system. This is consistent with the criteria used in most design applications, where capacity is measured in terms of the processing times of passengers at different service stations (Ashford, 1988). Only those processes required for arrivals or departures are considered in total time calculations, which also include walking times. To remedy the shortcomings in existing studies, we first develop time functions to approximate maximum delay in passageways and processing stations. Using the developed time functions, which are also valid for other flow networks, optimal capacities corresponding to highest possible levels of service are calculated using a stochastic programming model based on a multicommodity flow network representation of the whole airport terminal. The outputs of the model are the optimal capacity levels at the processing stations and passageways of the terminal for multiple planning periods, and the optimal expansion decisions with recourse options under the uncertainty of demand.

Hence, the contributions of this study can be summarized as follows. Focusing on passenger flow in airport terminals, closed form time functions are derived to approximate maximum delay in queuing networks where no steady state exists and transient studies are intractable. In addition, a holistic network model is developed for an airport terminal, which can also be used to model similar complex flow networks. Based on this network model, a stochastic capacity expansion problem is formulated and an efficient solution procedure is devised. The heuristic proposed as part of this solution procedure is also expected to lead to improvements in the solutions of several other capacity expansion problems in the literature.

The remainder of this paper is organized as follows. In Section 2, we describe the approximations for the time functions used in the optimization model, while the proposed multistage stochastic optimization model and a solution algorithm are discussed in Section 3. The computational results and the conclusions are presented in Section 4.

2. Approximation of maximum peak period delay

The goal of airport terminal capacity analysis is to minimize congestion related passenger delay in the terminals. Hence, approximation of walking times in passageways and delay times at processing stations as a function of capacity and flow rates is an important part of any capacity planning model. Due to the stochastic and transient nature of demand, most such estimations are based on observational data or simulation models, which do not provide appropriate inputs for optimization models. In this study, we consider the walking and processing delays separately, and develop delay time approximations for the two areas. In addition, we analyze the validity of the time functions that are developed by comparing them with simulation results.

2.1. Maximum delay in passageways

Although there have been several studies on travel time functions for vehicular traffic and general pedestrian traffic (Older, 1968; Fruin, 1971; Tanariboon et al., 1986; Virkler and Elayadath, 1994; Sarkar and Janardhan, 1997), such studies are rare for pedestrians in transportation terminals. One exception is Young (1999), in which pedestrian walking speeds are observed and analyzed in two major airport terminals. Results from this study suggest that free-flow walking speeds in airport terminals are normally distributed with a mean of 80.5 m (264 ft) per minute and a standard deviation of 15.9 m (52 ft) per minute. Regardless of domain, all of the pedestrian traffic studies include estimations of the relationship between the speed of pedestrians and the congestion levels. Using the free-flow speeds from Young (1999) to adjust the relationship suggested by Sarkar and Janardhan (1997), we derive the following linear function to represent the relation between the speed (m/s) and density (passengers/m^2) in airport terminal passageways:

$$s = -0.34\phi + 1.34 \tag{1}$$

where s represents the speed and ϕ is the density. To approximate the maximum walking time in a passageway l_ω of length L, maximum density in the passageway can be estimated using the peak flow rate f and width w of the passageway. Assuming that the peak load is instantenous and that interarrival times $I = 1/f$ are exponentially distributed, the mean and variance of the number of passengers in the passageway, N, can be obtained using the following second order approximations based upon truncated Taylor series expansions (Rice, 1995):

$$E[N] = E\left[\frac{t_o}{I}\right] = \frac{E[t_o]}{E[I]}\left(1 + \frac{Var[I]}{E^2[I]}\right) \tag{2}$$

$$Var[N] = Var\left[\frac{t_o}{I}\right] = \left(\frac{E[t_o]}{E[I]}\right)^2 \left(\frac{Var[t_o]}{E^2[t_o]} + \frac{Var[I]}{E^2[I]} - \frac{Var^2[I]}{E^4[I]}\right) \tag{3}$$

where the random variable $t_o = \frac{L}{s_o}$ is the walking time under free-flow conditions. $E[t_o]$ and $Var[t_o]$ can be estimated using similar approximations, i.e.

$$E[t_o] = \frac{L}{E[s_o]}\left(1 + \frac{Var[s_o]}{E^2[s_o]}\right) = \frac{L}{80.5}\left(1 + \frac{15.9^2}{80.5^2}\right) = 0.0130L \tag{4}$$

$$Var[t_o] = \left(\frac{L}{E[s_o]}\right)^2 \left(\frac{Var[s_o]}{E^2[s_o]} - \frac{Var^2[s_o]}{E^4[s_o]}\right) = \left(\frac{L}{80.5}\right)^2 \left(\frac{15.9^2}{80.5^2} - \frac{15.9^4}{80.5^4}\right) = 0.0024^2 L^2 \tag{5}$$

It follows from (2) and (3) that

$$E[N] = \frac{0.0130Lf}{60}(1 + 1) = 0.000433Lf \tag{6}$$

$$Var[N] = \left(\frac{0.0130Lf}{60}\right)^2 \left(\frac{0.0024^2 L^2}{0.0130^2 L^2} + 1 - 1\right) = 0.00004^2 L^2 f^2 \tag{7}$$

We assume that the distribution of N is normal, and derive a design density $\tilde{\phi}$ to approximate the maximum density in passageway l_ω based on this assumption. As normally distributed random variables do not have finite maximums, we select $\tilde{\phi}$ such that $P(\phi \leqslant \tilde{\phi}) = 1 - \varepsilon$, where ε can be defined based on the empirical rule. Hence, a typical choice for ε is 0.0027, which assumes that $\tilde{\phi} = E[\phi] + 3\sigma_\phi$. Smaller values of ε can also be used by considering higher deviations from the mean to estimate maximum passenger density. To test the validity of these assumptions and to determine the best approximation, we compare different design density levels with results from a simulation model based on the walking speed relation (1) for a single passageway. Average maximum walking times obtained through 100 replications for different flow rates and the corresponding calculated values are displayed in Fig. 1. Results from simulation studies indicate that delay times obtained using higher design densities, i.e. $4\sigma_\phi$, do not significantly differ from the $3\sigma_\phi$ case. Thus, we propose the following design density $\tilde{\phi}$ for passageway l_ω:

$$\tilde{\phi} = \frac{E[N] + 3\sigma_N}{A} = \frac{0.000553f}{w} \tag{8}$$

where $A = wL$ is the total effective area of the passageway. It then follows from (1) that the maximum walking time in a passageway can be approximated by

$$t^\omega = \frac{Lw}{-0.000188f + 1.34w} \tag{9}$$

where L and w are in meters, t^ω is in seconds, and f is given in passengers per hour. A surface plot of maximum walking times as a function of flow and passageway width is shown in Fig. 2. Although the comparisons in Fig. 1 suggest that the approximation (9) starts to overestimate the delay as flow rate increases, the estimation is accurate for flow levels up to 4000 passengers per hour, and even for higher flow levels, the absolute error is not very significant.

2.2. Maximum delay in processing stations

Most congestion at airport terminals occurs at processing stations such as security checkpoints and check-in counters. In this section, we develop relations to estimate the maximum delay at the processing stations in airport terminals as a function of flow and capacity. To this end, we consider a deterministic approximation with varying arrival rates over time and constant process rates, based on fluid approximations suggested by Newell (1982).

Passenger arrival rates, estimated from flight schedules, can be plotted against time as shown in Fig. 3. On this plot, the highest peak that can be identified is used in peak demand analysis for design purposes. A peak is defined as a period during which the arrival rate remains above the average arrival rate. We suggest three approximations that can be used to represent the shape of a peak, and use these approximations to estimate the maximum queue length. Depending on the sharpness of

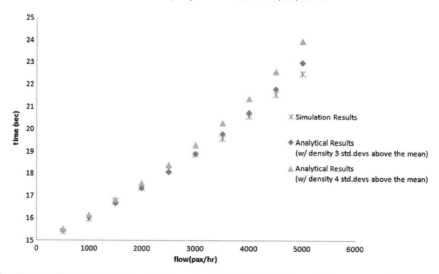

Fig. 1. Comparison of passenger walking times calculated according to relation (9) with simulation results for a passageway of length L and width w.

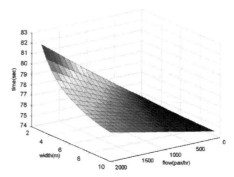

Fig. 2. Walking times as a function of flow and passageway width, as calculated from relation (9) for a passageway of length L.

the peak, we use either a triangular, parabolic or half-elliptical approximation as shown in Fig. 3. Wirasinghe and Bandara (1990) use similar approximations in airport gate position estimation. Other approximations or exact functions can also be used, if the peak can not be represented with any of these shapes.

2.2.1. Triangular peak approximation

If $f(t)$ represents the flow rate into a processing station l_p over time, then the triangular peak function can be expressed as

$$f(t) = \begin{cases} \bar{f} + a_T t & 0 \leqslant t \leqslant T_o/2 \\ \bar{f} + a_T(T_o - t) & T_o/2 < t \leqslant T_o \end{cases} \quad (10)$$

where T_o is the time when the arrival rate drops below the average arrival rate $\bar{f}$, and $a_T = \frac{2(f-\bar{f})}{T_o}$ with f representing the maximum flow rate. Assuming that queue buildup occurs only after the arrival rate exceeds the capacity u of the station, the maximum queue length can be estimated by calculating the area between the capacity line and the triangular arrival rate curve in Fig. 3. This area is equal to $\frac{(t_2-t_1)(f-u)}{2}$, where t_1 and t_2 represent the times when the arrival rate is equal to the capacity. These values can be obtained from the following relation:

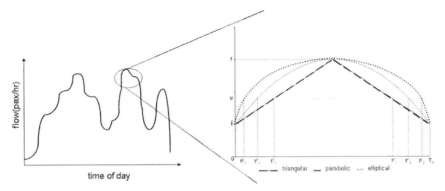

Fig. 3. Highest peak is identified and approximated by a triangular, parabolic or half-elliptical function.

$$u = \bar{f} + a_T t_1 = \bar{f} + a_T(T_o - t_2) \tag{11}$$

It follows that the maximum queue length, Q_{max}, can be expressed as

$$Q_{max} = \frac{\left(T_o - 2\left(\frac{u-\bar{f}}{a_T}\right)\right)(f-u)}{2} \tag{12}$$

Then, maximum delay t_T^ρ at a processing station with a triangular peak can be approximated by $\frac{Q_{max}}{u}$, giving the following result:

$$t_T^\rho = \frac{(u-\bar{f})^2 T_o}{2cfu} \tag{13}$$

In this expression, $c = 1 - \frac{\bar{f}}{f}$ is a constant.

2.2.2. Parabolic peak approximation

For a parabolic approximation of the peak, the arrival rate curve is

$$f(t) = f - a_P\left(t - \frac{T_o}{2}\right)^2 \tag{14}$$

where $a_P = \frac{4(f-\bar{f})}{T_o^2}$. Hence, t_1 and t_2 are the roots of the following polynomial function of the second degree:

$$f - a_P\left(t - \frac{T_o}{2}\right)^2 - u = t^2 - T_o t - \left(\frac{4u - 4f + a_P T_o^2}{4a_P}\right) = 0 \tag{15}$$

It follows that

$$t_2 - t_1 = \frac{T_o + \sqrt{T_o^2 - \frac{4u-4f+a_P T_o^2}{a_P}}}{2} - \frac{T_o - \sqrt{T_o^2 - \frac{4u-4f+a_P T_o^2}{a_P}}}{2} = T_o\sqrt{\frac{f-u}{cf}} \tag{16}$$

Similar to the triangular case, the area of the region between the capacity and parabolic arrival rate curves in Fig. 3 represents the maximum queue length. Thus, maximum time spent for the parabolic approximation of the peak at process station t_P can be expressed as follows:

$$t_P^\rho = \frac{2T_o(f-u)^{3/2}}{3u\sqrt{cf}} \tag{17}$$

2.2.3. Half-elliptical peak approximation

Another approximation can be performed assuming that the peak has a half ellipsoid shape as shown in Fig. 3. In this case, the arrival rate function can be expressed as

$$f(t) = \bar{f} + \sqrt{(f-\bar{f})^2\left(1 - \frac{(2t-T_o)^2}{T_o^2}\right)} \tag{18}$$

It follows that the queue builds up for a period of

$$t_2 - t_1 = \frac{T_o}{cf}\sqrt{(f-u)(u-f+2cf)} \tag{19}$$

Thus, the maximum delay can be estimated as

$$t_E^\rho = \frac{T_o \pi}{4cuf}(f-u)^{3/2}\sqrt{u-(1-2c)f} \tag{20}$$

2.3. Validation of the approximations

We study the accuracy of the developed approximations by comparing the analytical values with results obtained from simulation studies for different capacity/flow levels. For a processing station with a triangular peak demand curve, a comparison is shown in Fig. 4 of the approximation results with those obtained through a simulation study with Poisson arrivals and exponential processing times. As also shown numerically in Table 1, approximations for triangular peaks are accurate for all flow-capacity ratios, and appear only to include some slight underestimation. A similar observation can be made for Fig. 5, where a comparison is made between the estimates of maximum delay with simulation results for a parabolic peak demand curve. The approximations again appear to be accurate.

In addition to simulation analyses, the approximations were also compared with observed statistics at Hartsfield-Jackson Atlanta International Airport for validation purposes. For passageway delay approximation comparisons, information from Hartsfield Planning Collaborative (2001) was used, where results of a concourse circulation and level of service analysis are discussed for the six concourses at Hartsfield-Jackson Atlanta International Airport. In addition, Solak (2001) describes the results of a peak period time study for two of these concourses, providing walking time observations. The maximum walking times in two different 656-feet long passageways with effective widths of 12.5 feet were recorded as 184.2 s and 156.0 s under the peak flow rates of 5898 passengers/hour and 2802 passengers/hour, respectively. The corresponding approximations based on (9) for these two cases are 190.7 s and 166.4 s, which are very close to the actual observations. For queuing delay approximations, data for processing stations has been obtained from Hartsfield Planning Collaborative (2005). According to this study, a maximum delay of 31 min was observed at security checkpoints during a near-triangular peak demand level of 7242 passengers/hour at this station, where the average processing capacity of the security checkpoints were calculated as 3690 passengers/hour. For this setting, the triangular peak delay approximation returns an estimate of 28.3 min, thus confirming the closeness of the approximation.

However the accuracy of these approximations also need to be considered in a network structure, which is the typical environment where the approximations will be used.

2.4. Approximations in networks

The approximations above are valid when peak period analysis is performed on individual processing stations. However, in a network structure the propagation of demand has to be considered, as flow into downstream processes will be affected by the capacity of preceding processes. The effect of the capacity on the departure process from a service station is illustrated in Fig. 6. As seen in this plot, the departure rate curve has a flat peak due to the capacity of the station. Hence, assuming the

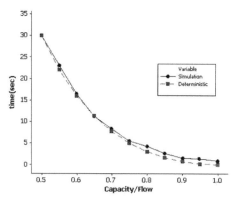

Fig. 4. Comparison of delay approximations with simulation results for a processing station with a triangular peak.

Table 1
Comparison of analytical and simulation results for triangular and parabolic peaks.

Capacity/Flow	Triangular peak		Parabolic peak	
	Avg. Max. Delay in Sim.	Approx.	Avg. Max. Delay in Sim.	Approx.
0.50	30.10	30.00	40.00	40.00
0.55	23.10	22.09	30.90	31.05
0.60	16.40	16.00	24.20	23.85
0.65	11.20	11.31	17.80	18.02
0.70	8.40	7.71	13.20	13.28
0.75	5.49	5.00	9.75	9.43
0.80	4.27	3.00	7.17	6.32
0.85	2.60	1.59	4.47	3.87
0.90	1.53	0.67	2.77	1.99
0.95	1.35	0.16	1.61	0.67
1.00	0.82	0.00	0.91	0.00

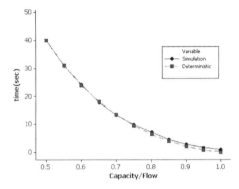

Fig. 5. Comparison of delay approximations with simulation results for a processing station with a parabolic peak.

same peak shape for downstream processes could lead to the underestimation of the actual arrival pattern at these service stations. A better approximation can be obtained through the half-ellipse approximation. Hence, given any arrival curve at a station, the arrival rates for all downstream processes can be approximated by using the time functions obtained for the half-elliptical peak. The validity of this assumption was tested by comparing results from a simulation study with the approximations for each shape studied. The simulation study was conducted by considering only the departing passengers on the simplified network representation of an airport terminal shown in Fig. 7. In this representation, passengers are assumed to arrive at the Terminal Entry node, who then proceed to the Gate nodes via the check-in and security checkpoint stations. Gate-to-gate and gate-to-baggage claim arcs were not considered in this set of simulations. Different capacity/flow ratios for the security checkpoints were used in the simulations, where the flow rates were determined by the sum of the processing rates at the preceding stations and the rate of passengers going directly to the checkpoints. Each capacity/flow level was simulated for 100 replications, and average maximum delay at the security checkpoints have been recorded and compared with the results from delay approximations for each shape.

Fig. 6. Effect of the capacity on the departure process from a service station.

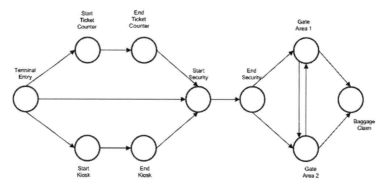

Fig. 7. A simplified network representation of an airport terminal.

Comparisons of the triangular and half-ellipsoid approximations with simulation results at the security checkpoints are shown in Fig. 8. As seen in this figure, as well as in Table 2, although the approximations for the triangular and parabolic peak assumptions underestimate the actual maximum delay, as hypothesized, it is observed that the half-elliptical approximation is fairly accurate. Thus, arrivals at downstream processes need to be studied according to a half-elliptical peak assumption. However, in all cases, it is possible to analyze the functions individually, possibly through observations or simulation studies, and determine the best approximating shape. In the following section, we use these general findings to develop an optimization model for capacity planning at airport terminals, in which the objective is to minimize a weighted sum of the delay functions above.

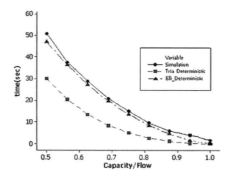

Fig. 8. For downstream processes, the peaks are best approximated by a half-elliptical shape as observed from the comparison of triangular and elliptical approximations with the simulation results on a network.

Table 2
Comparison of analytical and simulation results for networks.

Capacity/Flow	Simulation	Triangular peak approx.	Parabolic peak approx.	Half-elliptical peak approx.
0.500	51.10	30.00	40.00	47.10
0.563	37.50	20.42	29.10	36.35
0.625	29.00	13.50	20.78	27.36
0.688	21.00	8.52	14.37	19.85
0.750	15.10	5.00	9.42	13.60
0.813	9.64	2.60	5.65	8.48
0.875	5.85	1.07	2.85	4.45
0.938	3.92	0.25	0.94	1.52
1.000	1.66	0.00	0.00	0.00

3. The multistage stochastic optimization model

For analysis purposes, we consider the terminal as a network, in which passengers with different origin destination pairs move between nodes following pre-determined demand patterns. Let $G(\mathscr{V},\mathscr{A})$ denote this directed network, where $\mathscr{V} = \{v_1, v_2, \ldots, v_n\}$ is its set of nodes and $\mathscr{A} = \{a_1, a_2, \ldots, a_m\}$ is its set of arcs. Each node $v_i \in \mathscr{V}$ represents either a physical location in the terminal or the arrival and departure events at a service station, such as the ticket counters or the security checkpoints. Let $\mathscr{A} = \mathscr{A}_w \cup \mathscr{A}_p$ such that $\mathscr{A}_w$ is the set of arcs between location nodes and $\mathscr{A}_p$ is the set of arcs connecting the service arrival and departure nodes. If $\mathscr{K}$ represents the set of passenger types, we assume two subsets of $\mathscr{K}$ such that $\mathscr{K} = \mathscr{K}_d \cup \mathscr{K}_p$, where $\mathscr{K}_d$ contains types of passengers that do not go through a process station to reach their destination, and $\mathscr{K}_p$ contains those that need to go through a process station. Furthermore, $\widetilde{\mathscr{K}}_l$ is a subset of $\mathscr{K}_p$, which contains all passenger types that can be processed at process station $l \in \mathscr{A}_p$.

For each passenger type $k \in \mathscr{K}$, a set of nodes $\mathscr{O}^k$ contains all nodes that passenger type k can originate from and a singleton set $\mathscr{D}^k = \{v^k\}$ represents the destination, while d_i^k denotes the peak arrival rate into a node $i \in \mathscr{O}^k$. Passengers of type $k \in \mathscr{K}_d$ are defined such that they have a unique origin and destination pair, so $\mathscr{O}^k$ is also a singleton set for $k \in \mathscr{K}_d$. We also define $\mathscr{R}$ as the set of process completion nodes in the network. Furthermore, $\mathscr{R}^k$ is the set of process completion nodes that passengers of type k can visit as the last process node before arriving at their destination.

In addition, let u_l denote the service capacity of a process represented by arc $l \in \mathscr{A}_p$. Similarly, let w_l be the width of a passageway represented by arc $l \in \mathscr{A}_w$. Furthermore, f_l represents the peak flow rate on arc $l \in \mathscr{A}$, while x_l^k is the flow of passenger type k on arc l. For each arc $l \in \mathscr{A}$, let t_l correspond to the maximum time spent by any passenger on that arc, which, due to congestion, varies with the amount of flow on the arc according to results obtained in Section 2. A simplified sample network representation of an airport terminal is shown in Fig. 7. In this sample network, five passenger types can be considered. $\mathscr{K}_p$ contains two types with Gate Area1 and Gate Area2 as destinations, while $\mathscr{K}_d$ contains four passenger types with unique origin destination pairs of Gate Area1-Gate Area2, Gate Area2-Gate Area1, Gate Area1-Baggage Claim and Gate Area2-Baggage Claim.

The described network is similar to a multicommodity flow network, in which different types of passengers correspond to different commodities. Several objective functions can be considered for this flow model. An objective could be to find a routing for passengers through the network in such a manner that the maximum total time a passenger spends in the system for the worst case scenario is minimized for all routes. Another similar objective could be the minimization of maximum delay on each passageway and processing station. Consistent with the system equilibrium concept of Wardrop (1952), we assume that during peak demand periods, passenger flow is distributed optimally among alternate routes within the airport terminal. In the proposed model, minimization of maximum delay on each arc is chosen as the objective, and a weight factor corresponding to the arc flow rate f_l is introduced in the objective function of the model for each arc travel time function to approximate this behavior. These delay functions depend on the capacity levels, which are maximized in the optimization model given a budget B.

Expandability and the decisions on when to expand play an important role in the determination of the optimal capacity levels for a terminal building. These expansions can be realized by building a separate terminal building or by expanding the existing one to accommodate increased demand. In any case, a fixed cost β_l and a variable cost α_l will be incurred for each unit of added capacity ϵ_l on the component of the terminal represented by arc l. Assuming several planning epochs $i, i = 0, 1, 2, \ldots, T$, a multiperiod decision model based on the network structure described above can be formulated as the airport terminal capacity planning problem. On the other hand, such a model also has to consider the variation in demand forecasts, as the randomness associated with demand forecasts may play a significant role in the cost-effectiveness of an expansion policy. Hence, we account for these factors by considering the described model in a stochastic setting. One observation on the complexity of the airport terminal capacity planning problem is that the deterministic version of the problem is NP-hard, as it can easily be shown that it contains the integer knapsack problem as a special case. Thus, the stochastic version of the airport terminal capacity planning problem is also NP-hard.

Stochastic programming approaches to capacity planning problems are common in the literature (Eppen et al., 1989, Berman et al., 1994, Swaminathan, 2000, Riis and Andersen, 2004, Ahmed et al., 2003, Barahona et al., 2005). Other than Ahmed et al. (2003), all such studies either consider linear problems or present two-stage integer stochastic models. In this study, we propose a multistage stochastic integer programming model with nonlinear costs for the capacity planning problem at airport terminals. We assume that decisions on initial design capacities u_l^o for service stations and w_l^o for passageways with associated unit costs α_l^o are made while the specific scenario to occur is unknown. Expansion decisions at future planning periods are made after the realization of demand, providing recourse options.

Suppose that demand levels $d = \{d^k, k = 1, 2, \ldots, K\}$ between consecutive planning periods occur at one of multiple levels, i.e. low, medium and high, for each scenario. Hence, a scenario tree $\mathscr{T}$, reflecting possible realizations of demand levels over the planning periods can be constructed. Each node n of the tree corresponds to a state at some planning epoch $i = 0, 1, 2, \ldots, T$. The probability of being in state n is given as p_n, and let the subscript n refer to the values of all other parameters at state n. Furthermore, let $\mathscr{P}(n)$ represent a path from the root node 0 in the scenario tree to node n, and let $\mathscr{N}$ denote the set of non-leaf nodes. If v_{nl} is a boolean variable denoting whether an expansion on arc l is realized at the planning epoch corresponding to node n, and ϵ_{nl} is the amount of expansion, then the following stochastic program can be used to obtain the optimal capacity expansion policy under stochastic demand:

Airport Terminal Capacity Planning Problem (ATCAP):

$$\text{minimize} \quad z = \sum_{n \in \mathcal{F}} \sum_{l \in \mathcal{A}_p} p_n f_{nl} t_{nl}^{\rho}(\cdot) + \sum_{n \in \mathcal{F}} \sum_{l \in \mathcal{A}_w} p_n f_{nl} t_{nl}^{\omega}(\cdot) \qquad (21)$$

s.t.

$$\sum_{j \in \mathcal{V}:(i,j) \in \mathcal{A}} x_{n,ij}^k - \sum_{j \in \mathcal{V}:(j,i) \in \mathcal{A}} x_{n,ji}^k = 0 \quad \forall n, k, \forall i \notin \{\mathcal{O}^k \cup \mathcal{D}^k \cup \mathcal{R}\} \qquad (22)$$

$$\sum_{j \in \mathcal{V}:(i,j) \in \mathcal{A}} x_{n,ij}^k = d_{in}^k \quad \forall n, k, \forall i \in \mathcal{O}^k \qquad (23)$$

$$\sum_{j \in \mathcal{V}:(j,i) \in \mathcal{A}} x_{n,ji}^k = \sum_{i' \in \mathcal{O}^k} d_{i'n}^k \quad \forall n, \forall k \in \mathcal{K}_d, \forall i \in \mathcal{D}^k \qquad (24)$$

$$\sum_{j \in \mathcal{V}:(j,i) \in \mathcal{A}} x_{n,ji}^k = \sum_{i' \in \mathcal{R}^k} \sum_{j' \in \mathcal{V}:(i',j') \in \mathcal{A}} x_{n,i'j'}^k \quad \forall n, \forall k \in \mathcal{K}_p, \forall i \in \mathcal{D}^k \qquad (25)$$

$$\sum_{j \in \mathcal{V}:(i,j) \in \mathcal{A}} x_{n,ij}^k - u_{n,i'i} \frac{\sum_{j \in \mathcal{O}^k} d_{jn}^k}{\sum_{k' \in \widetilde{\mathcal{K}}_{i'i}} \sum_{j \in \mathcal{O}^{k'}} d_{jn}^{k'}} = 0 \quad \forall n, \forall (i',i) \in \mathcal{A}_p, \forall k \in \widetilde{\mathcal{K}}_{i'i} \qquad (26)$$

$$u_l^o + \sum_{m \in \mathcal{P}(n), m \neq n} \epsilon_{ml} = u_{nl} \quad \forall n, \forall l \in \mathcal{A}_p \qquad (27)$$

$$w_l^o + \sum_{m \in \mathcal{P}(n), m \neq n} \epsilon_{ml} = w_{nl} \quad \forall n, \forall l \in \mathcal{A}_w \qquad (28)$$

$$\epsilon_{nl} - M_{nl} v_{nl} \leqslant 0 \quad \forall n \in \mathcal{N}, n \neq 0, \forall l \qquad (29)$$

$$\sum_{l \in \mathcal{A}} (\alpha_{nl} \epsilon_{nl} + \beta_{nl} v_{nl}) \leqslant B_n \quad \forall n \in \mathcal{N}, n \neq 0 \qquad (30)$$

$$\sum_{l \in \mathcal{A}_w} \alpha_l^o u_l^o + \sum_{l \in \mathcal{A}_p} \alpha_l^o w_l^o \leqslant B^o \qquad (31)$$

$$\sum_{k \in \mathcal{K}} x_{nl}^k = f_{nl} \quad \forall n, l \qquad (32)$$

$$u_{nl} - f_{nl} \leqslant 0 \quad \forall n, \forall l \in \mathcal{A}_p \qquad (33)$$

$$(1 - c_{nl}) f_{nl} - u_{nl} \leqslant 0 \quad \forall n, \forall l \in \mathcal{A}_p \qquad (34)$$

$$Q(x_{nl}^k, u_{nl}, f_{nl}, \epsilon_{nl}) \leqslant 0 \quad \forall n, k, l \qquad (35)$$

$$x_{nl}^k, u_{nl}, f_{nl}, \epsilon_{nl}, u_l^o, w_l^o \geqslant 0 \quad \forall n, k, l \qquad (36)$$

$$v_{nl} \in \{0, 1\} \quad \forall n \in \mathcal{N}, n \neq 0, \forall l \qquad (37)$$

where $t_{nl}^{\rho}(\cdot)$ and $t_{nl}^{\omega}(\cdot)$ in (21) represent the time function associated with each process and passageway arc in the network, respectively. Constraints (22)–(26) are node balance constraints, where (25) and (26) capture the transient behavior at process arcs during peak load periods, assuming that the departure rate from a process station is equal to the service rate of that station. Hence, f_l in the time functions of downstream arcs is determined by a proportion of the departure rate from the preceding process arcs. This proportion is defined according to the ratio of demand levels for each passenger type. In addition, (27) and (28) ensure that the total available capacity is equal to the sum of expansions made up to the current planning epoch. Constraints (29) limit the amount of expansion to M_{nl} and ensure that no expansion is made when $v_{nl} = 0$. Constraints (30) and (31) are the budget constraints, where initial budget B^o in (31) is defined such that fixed costs are deducted from it. Constraints (33) and (34) ensure that the capacity of a process station lies between the average and maximum flow rates into that station, which is a required assumption for the validity of the delay approximations used in (21). The constants c_{nl} can be estimated as $c_{nl} = 1 - \left(\sum_{k \in \widetilde{\mathcal{K}}_l} \sum_{i \in \mathcal{O}^k} \bar{d}_{in}^k \right) \big/ \left(\sum_{k \in \widetilde{\mathcal{K}}_l} \sum_{i \in \mathcal{O}^k} \bar{d}_{in}^k \right)$, which follows from the assumption that $\left(\sum_{k \in \widetilde{\mathcal{K}}_l} \sum_{i \in \mathcal{O}^k} \bar{d}_{in}^k \right) \big/ \left(\sum_{k \in \widetilde{\mathcal{K}}_l} \sum_{i \in \mathcal{O}^k} d_{in}^k \right) = \bar{f}_{nl}/f_{nl}$. Finally, (35) refers to a vector of additional constraints imposed on the flows and capacities. These additional constraints may include minimum flow and capacity requirements or those that require simultaneous expansions in different areas of the terminal. Moreover, an important result is that the objective function is convex for the developed approximations, which we prove in Appendix A.

Inputs to the above model are the peak inflow rates d_{in}^k for each level of demand realization, the cost terms α_{nl} and β_{nl}, and the arc time function expressions $t_{nl}^{\rho}(\cdot)$ and $t_{nl}^{\omega}(\cdot)$, which are discussed in detail in Section 2. Depending on the shape of the peak demand curve, the model can be implemented with any of the processing delay approximations, while the half-ellipsoid approximation must be used in downstream process arcs. Regardless of the delay function used, the developed model serves as a general framework for capacity planning problems in networks, where the objective function can be modified by substituting the described approximations with some different cost or delay measure. For all cases, ATCAP is a multistage stochastic integer program with linear constraints and a nonlinear objective function, which is convex under the developed maximum delay time approximations.

Since there are no practical general purpose algorithms for multistage stochastic integer programming problems, most efforts to solve such problems have been problem specific, and are based on decomposition procedures through column generation (Lulli and Sen, 2004; Shiina and Birge, 2004). Although the deterministic equivalent of a stochastic integer problem can be solved by branch and bound methods, for most problem formulations the multistage structure leads to a large number of integer variables, which makes the problem difficult to solve. On the other hand, for *ATCAP*, the number of stages is limited, since the planning periods are usually 4–5 years long and passenger demand forecasts exist usually for 15–20 years into the future. Thus, the number of discrete variables will not be so large as to prevent the solution of the deterministic equivalent of the proposed stochastic model in reasonable time. Nonetheless, efficiency of any implemented solution procedure is important. In the following section, we propose a branch and bound algorithm, which is significantly efficient when compared to standard branch and bound procedures used by general purpose mixed integer nonlinear programming (MINLP) solvers. Our branch and bound algorithm relies on the implementation of an effective upper bounding heuristic at each node of the branch and bound tree.

3.1. An efficient branch and bound algorithm for ATCAP

A lower bound for *ATCAP* can be obtained by solving the nonlinear programming (NLP) relaxation of the problem obtained by relaxing the binary capacity expansion decision variables. Since all the constraints in the model are linear, an optimal solution to this relaxed problem can be obtained in a relatively easy fashion. This lower bound can be used to obtain tight upper bounds during the branch and bound algorithm.

The solution to the NLP relaxation provides initial capacities as well as flow and capacity levels in future time periods. Although a rounding procedure can be implemented to obtain a feasible integer solution, the quality of this solution is likely to be poor. A tighter upper bound can be obtained through better heuristics. Given the solution to the NLP relaxation of *ATCAP*, we propose a heuristic based on solving a relaxed multiple choice knapsack problem. In our proposed heuristic, it is assumed that the flow levels and initial capacities are fixed according to the relaxed MINLP solution, and a feasible integer solution is obtained by determining an expansion policy that aims to maximize capacity at each node of the scenario tree, while remaining feasible according to other constraints involving capacity levels. We let $\mathscr{S}_t$ and $\mathscr{S}^n_{t+1}$ represent the set of nodes in scenario tree $\mathscr{T}$ that correspond to time stage t, and the set of child nodes of node n, respectively. Furthermore, we let P_n represent the parent node of node n and G be a user defined scalar. Then, the following algorithm provides a feasible integer solution for *ATCAP*:

Algorithm 1 (*Procedure ATCAP upper bound*). Given a scenario tree $\mathscr{T}$, feasible flow **F**, arc capacities **U** and arc widths **W** for relaxed *ATCAP*

    for $t = 1$ to T
        for each $n \in \mathscr{S}_t$
            for each $l \in \mathscr{A}$
                Step 1. Set $\underline{\epsilon}_{nl}$ and $\overline{\epsilon}_{nl}$ to be the minimum and maximum possible expansion levels
                if $l \in \mathscr{A}_p$
                    $\underline{\epsilon}_{nl} = \max\{0, \max_{n' \in \mathscr{S}^n_{t+1}} \{(1 - c_{nl})f_{n'l} - u_{nl}\}\}$
                    $\overline{\epsilon}_{nl} = \min\{M_{nl}, \min_{n' \in \mathscr{S}^n_{t+1}} \{f_{n'l} - u_{nl}\}\}$
                  if $\overline{\epsilon}_{nl} < \underline{\epsilon}_{nl}$
                    Set $t = t - 1, n^o = n, n = P_n$
                    Repeat Step 1 by replacing $\underline{\epsilon}_{nl} = \max\{0, \max_{n' \in \mathscr{S}^n_{t+1}} \{f_{n'l}/2 - (u_{nl} + \underline{\epsilon}_{n^ol} - \overline{\epsilon}_{n^ol})\}\}$
                endif
                else
                  if $l \in \mathscr{A}_w$
                    $\underline{\epsilon}_{nl} = 0$
                    $\overline{\epsilon}_{nl} = M_{nl} - w_{nl}$
                  endif
                endif
                for $g = 0$ to G
                    $\epsilon^g_{nl} = \frac{(\overline{\epsilon}_{nl} - \underline{\epsilon}_{nl})g}{G} + \underline{\epsilon}_{nl}$
                endfor
            endfor
        Step 2. Solve the LP relaxation of the following optimization problem:

minimize $z = \delta_n$ (38)

s.t.

$$\sum_{l \in \mathscr{A}} \sum_{g: \epsilon^g_{nl} \neq 0} (\alpha_{nl} \epsilon^g_{nl} + \beta_{nl}) y^g_{nl} + \delta_n = B_n \quad (39)$$

$$\sum_{g=0}^{G} y_{nl}^{g} = 1 \qquad (40)$$

$$y_{nl}^{g} \in \{0, 1\} \qquad (41)$$

    for each $l \in \mathscr{A}$
      for each g such that $y_{nl}^{g*} \neq 0$
        if $y_{nl}^{g*} = 1$
          $\epsilon_{nl} = \epsilon_{nl}^{g}$
        else
          if $0 < y_{nl}^{g*} < 1$
            $\epsilon_{nl} = \max_{g} \{\epsilon_{nl}^{g} : \sum_{g': 0 < y_{nl}^{g'*} < 1} (\alpha_{nl} \epsilon_{nl}^{g'} + \beta_{nl}) y_{nl}^{g'*} \geq \alpha_{nl} \epsilon_{nl}^{g} + \beta_{nl}\}$
          endif
        endif
      endfor
      for each $n' \in \mathscr{S}_{t+1}^{n}$
        $u_{n'l} = u_{nl} + \epsilon_{nl}$ **if** $l \in \mathscr{A}_{p}$
        $w_{n'l} = w_{nl} + \epsilon_{nl}$ **if** $l \in \mathscr{A}_{w}$
      endfor
    endfor
  endfor
endfor
endprocedure

The procedure above results with a feasible solution for *ATCAP*, which can be used to obtain an upper bound for the optimal objective function value. Assuming that flow levels at each time stage and initial capacities are fixed, Step 1 determines the minimum and maximum expansion levels such that the resulting capacities will be feasible at each node of the scenario tree. Since, any expansion will be between these bounds, this interval is divided into discrete values which are candidate expansion levels. The number of these discrete values, G, can be determined by considering the computational burden and the level of accuracy desired in the heuristic. In Step 2, a modified relaxed version of the multiple choice knapsack problem is solved which ensures that maximum capacity expansion is achieved given the available budget. The integer variables in the optimal solution of this subproblem indicate the level of expansion on an arc for the considered node. The fractional decision variables in the solution are considered together, and the portion of budget used for these variables in the optimization problem is reallocated so that the resulting expansion policy is feasible. Capacities for the child nodes of the current node are determined by adding the expansion level on each arc to the capacity available at this node. These procedures are performed for all nodes in the scenario tree. If the maximum expansion level possible at a node is not sufficient to ensure feasibility at a child node, then the procedure backtracks to the parent node and resolves the expansion problem after updating the minimum expansion level at the parent node accordingly. If necessary, this process is iterated so that feasibility is always maintained.

4. Computational results

Computational studies were conducted using the simplified network representation of an airport terminal in Fig. 7, as well as the larger network in Fig. 9, which is based on the configuration of the South Terminal at Hartsfield-Jackson Atlanta International Airport. Despite several simplifications of actual passenger flow, this larger network contains 59 passageway arcs and 6 processing arcs. Nine terminal entry points are assumed for departing passengers with a single destination node representing the completion of security screening. For arriving passengers, a single node represents the origin, while three destinations corresponding to three different terminal exit points are assumed.

In the first test model, only unidirectional flow was assumed between arcs. However, bidirectional flow was integrated into the larger model by approximating the delay times using the speed density relation (1) and assuming that density is based on flow in both directions. An arrival rate curve similar to Fig. 3 was assumed to be available for each customer type, and lengths of passageways were assumed to be fixed constants. The demand curves in the initial processing stations were assumed to be of triangular shape, while for the downstream processing stations a half-elliptical peak was used. The process delay times were estimated using the approximations in Section 2.2. Other input parameters were determined based on actual measured peak demand levels and forecasts at Hartsfield-Jackson Atlanta International Airport, and multistage models of up to five stages were studied. Implementation of a standard branch and bound procedure as well as the improved method with the upper bounding heuristic was performed using the GAMS/SBB MINLP solver. Computations were performed on a PC with an Intel Pentium 4 1.4 GHz processor and 512 MB of internal memory. A relative tolerance of 0.0001 was used, while a time limit of 1 h was imposed on the computations. The improvements in the solution times when the upper bounding heu-

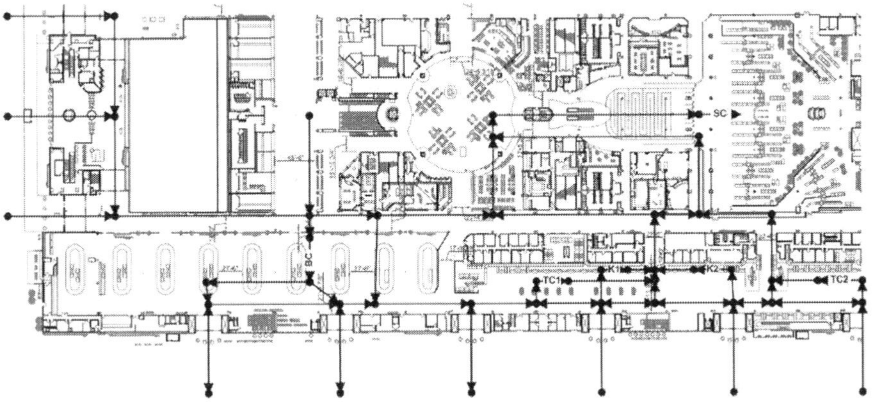

Fig. 9. The network model based on the configuration of the South Terminal at Hartsfield-Jackson Atlanta International Airport.

Table 3
Performance of the upper bounding heuristic.

$|E|$	$|\mathcal{F}|$	Standard B&B			B&B with heuristic		
		Nodes	CPUs	Gap (%)	Nodes	CPUs	Gap (%)
14	4	2	0.05	–	0	0.05	–
14	13	36	3.75	–	2	0.29	–
14	40	5538	3600	8.8	63	24.83	–
14	121	2017	3600	14.4	83	639.4	–
65	4	5	0.09	–	0	0.12	–
65	13	71	10.1	–	6	3.14	–
65	40	428	1885	–	20	496.6	–
65	121	672	3600	0.8	49	2020	–

ristic is used are shown in Table 3. In this table, the first column represents the number of edges in the test problem networks, while the second column is the number of nodes in the scenario tree. Standard branch and bound implementation did not produce an optimal solution within the 1 h time limit for three and four stage problems on the small network, as well as the four stage problem on the larger network. Although the running time of the heuristic increases with increasing problem size and complexity, in all instances the improved branch and bound procedure performs significantly better than the standard solution approach. The results suggest that the developed upper bounding heuristic performed well under all scenarios, including those scenarios where the inflow rates have been the highest. This can be seen by considering the relatively small number of branch and bound nodes used by the devised algorithm, especially in the five stage instances, where scenarios with highest demand levels were considered. Since the demand levels in the test models were based on actual 20-year traffic forecasts at one of the busiest airports in the world, it can be concluded that the heuristic is applicable to all realistic scenarios, and is not sensitive to higher arrival rates. Hence, the only limitation of the algorithm is the increase in required computational time for larger problem instances. On the other hand, this is not a significant limitation, as realistic test instances could still be solved within desired timeframes and much faster than standard methods for this important decision making problem.

Overall, results for the test problems with a different number of stages suggest that the proposed model is an innovative and powerful tool that can be used in capacity planning at airport terminals. For given budgets and other feasibility constraints, the solutions provide an optimal expansion policy for an airport terminal such that the resulting configurations account for the uncertainty of future demand and minimize the expected amount of congestion over the planning horizon. For example, for the large network based on the South Terminal at Hartsfield-Jackson Atlanta International Airport, the solutions provide information on how much capacity addition must be made in each area of the terminal so that the overall congestion is minimized. This is a significantly improved approach, since current practice is to consider each area individually for any type of expansion.

Furthermore, the results from the computational studies were analyzed to determine how the solutions alter airports over time, and whether the solutions suggest any intuitive rules for airport expansion. To this end, we tried to gain insights on the following issues related to capacity expansion decisions at airport terminals:

1. Can a conclusion be drawn on the relationship between the optimal expansion decisions and the expected future demand at a given decision point?
2. Is it possible to conclude on a prioritization of passageway versus processing station expansions, i.e. should one have a priority over the other?
3. Is it possible to conclude on a prioritization of upstream versus downstream expansions?

The analysis of issue (1) involved a comparison of capacity expansions at the nodes of the corresponding scenario tree for each test instance, and then relating these decisions to the expected peak demand at these nodes. In practice, an intuitive approach to capacity planning may involve the consideration of expected demand for the periods ahead, and make expansion decisions based on these expectations. We tried to determine whether such an intuitive proportional relationship existed, which could be used as general guideline in capacity expansion decisions. More specifically, the analysis considered whether it was possible to have an optimal policy in which the capacity increase for a low expected demand scenario is larger than for a scenario with high expected demand. Despite the intuition, computational tests show several instances where the optimal solution consists of higher capacity additions for low expected peak demand levels. This situation is demonstrated in Fig. 10 by an example over three decision periods, where a ranking of the expected demands and capacity expansions are compared pairwise for a processing station, namely the security checkpoints in the large network example. In this figure, demand and capacity levels are defined as low, medium, high, corresponding to levels 1,2, and 3, respectively. It is seen for instance that Scenario A has the highest expected future demand in period 2, but the optimal capacity level in that period is the lowest, when compared with other scenarios that have lower expected future demand in period 2. Hence, optimal capacity policies are not myopic, and expansion decisions at a stage are not based on the expectation of the stochastic parameters at that stage. As a result, policies based on expected demand levels are likely to be suboptimal. This conclusion demonstrates the value of the developed stochastic programming model, as it accounts for the costs associated with any recourse actions that can be taken under different future demand realizations, and takes advantage of this additional information in determining optimal expansion decisions.

For issues (2) and (3), we studied results from several instances to see if a trend could be identified suggesting that expansion of one specific area in the terminal should have priority over other areas. This involved comparisons of passageway and processing station expansions, as well as expansion decisions for upstream and downstream locations. Analytical comparisons for these are not tractable, due to the interaction between the capacity of a processing station and the downstream flow of passengers. For comparison purposes, we standardized resource allocation decisions for each area by assuming equal cost structures. We then considered the total resource allocation for each area type at different decision epochs for all test instances by only considering the expansion amounts that are greater than the minimum required capacity levels. For processing stations, these minimum levels are defined by the assumption that the capacity of a station is greater than the average flow into that station. For passageways, we assumed a minimum width of 3 m.

It was observed at the nodes of the corresponding scenario trees in these instances with equal cost structures that the total investment in processing station expansions beyond the required minimum capacity levels was always higher than total investment for similar passageway expansions. This implies that under equilibrium of passenger flow, if the decision to be made is to increase the capacity of either a passageway or a processing station but not both, then the expansion should be made at the processing station. Further, under the above conditions, if both types of areas can be expanded simultaneously, then the resource allocation for expansion should be such that the allocation for capacity increase in processing stations is greater than or equal to the allocation for passageway expansions.

This conclusion is in line with intuitive analysis that the bottlenecks in passenger terminals are mostly processing stations, and therefore there would be more value in adding to the capacity of a processing station than that of a passageway. However, it must also be noted that this result only suggests a relative importance of one area over the other in terms of passenger service, and does not imply a distinct prioritization, where processing station expansions are made up to the maximum possible level, and then the remaining resources are used for passageway expansions. In an optimal policy, overall

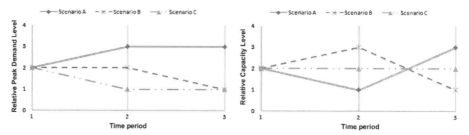

Fig. 10. Optimal capacity levels are not dependent on the expected future demand at a decision epoch.

service level is typically maximized by simultaneous expansions in different areas of an airport terminal according to available budget and cost structures.

The comparison of upstream and downstream stations in terms of relative importance was conducted similar to the above analysis. However, no conclusions could be drawn as to the relative importance or priority of either of these areas. It was observed that the ratio of the allocated resources for each area varied at the nodes of the scenario tree in all test instances. Hence, from a policy perspective, both types of stations should be treated as equally important, as the solutions suggested that optimal expansions were made such that the flow balance in the system was maintained based on the model setup.

5. Conclusions

To the best of our knowledge, our model is the first holistic model for airport terminals. Given the inefficiency and congestion associated with current airport designs, it is essential that accurate capacity planning is performed for new airport designs using concepts such as those that have been proposed in this study. The results of the study are also applicable to existing airports. Current configurations of these airports can be modified according to the results to maximize efficiency. By adding feasibility constraints, the model can be configured to determine whether it is optimal to build a new terminal building rather than expanding the existing one. In all cases, by minimizing the need for expansion and optimizing expansion schedules for airports, significant cost reductions can be achieved.

In the theoretical context, the peak period approximations derived for airport terminals are applicable to any other traffic flow network or queuing system where steady state is not attained and transient analysis is intractable. Furthermore, the upper bounding heuristic that has been developed can be used and tested on other capacity expansion models in the literature.

Several extensions to the study are possible. One such area is the modification of the model to incorporate the uncertainties associated with expansion costs and budgets, as well as risks of disruptions in the normal operation of an airport terminal. In addition, more efficient solution procedures can be developed either by improving the proposed method or through new approaches that would account for the highly nonlinear and nonconvex structures that would arise after including stochastic corrections to the deterministic approximations. Another extension is possible by integrating the model with the airside of an airport, thus forming a global capacity planning model for airports, and possibly for the national airspace system.

Appendix A

In this appendix, we provide the proof that the objective function proposed for ATCAP is convex for almost all practical instances. As described in Section 3, the objective function is expressed using the passageway maximum delay estimations and the approximations provided for processing station maximum delays. We first show that each component in the summation defining the objective function is convex in the decision variables:

Lemma 1. *The weighted function of maximum passageway delay in the objective function of ATCAP is convex for all $f > 0, w > 1$, and $f < 7127.66w$.*

Proof. The corresponding function is given by:

$$\frac{Lfw}{-0.000188f + 1.34w} \tag{A.1}$$

Since L is a constant, we consider the function $g(f,w) = \frac{fw}{-0.000188f + 1.34w}$, and show that the Hessian $H_g(f,w)$ for this function is positive semidefinite for all values of $f > 0$ and $w > 1$, such that $f < 7127.66w \cdot g(f,w)$ is twice differentiable, and $H_g(f,w)$ is given by:

$$\begin{pmatrix} a_{11} & a_{12} \\ a_{21} & a_{22} \end{pmatrix}$$

where

$$a_{11} = \frac{-2.68f}{(-0.000188f + 1.34w)^2} + \frac{3.5912fw}{(-0.000188f + 1.34w)^3}$$

$$a_{12} = a_{21} = \frac{1}{-0.000188f + 1.34w} + \frac{0.000188f - 1.34w}{(-0.000188f + 1.34w)^2} - \frac{0.00050384fw}{(-0.000188f + 1.34w)^3}$$

$$a_{22} = \frac{0.000376w}{(-0.000188f + 1.34w)^2} + \frac{7.0688 * 10^{-8}fw}{(-0.000188f + 1.34w)^3}$$

Note that since $t^\omega \geqslant 0$, then clearly $-0.000188f + 1.34w > 0$, implying that $f < 7127.66w$. It follows that $a_{11} > 0$ and $a_{22} > 0$ for $f > 0$ and $w > 1$. Further, it can easily be shown by algebraic manipulation that $|H_g(f, w)| = 0$. Thus, the Hessian $H_g(f, w)$ is positive semidefinite and the function (A.1) is convex. □

Lemma 2. *The weighted function of maximum processing station delay based on the triangular peak assumption in the objective function of ATCAP is convex for all $f > 0, u > 0$, and $f > u$.*

Proof. The corresponding function is given by:

$$\frac{f(u-f)^2 T_0}{2cfu} = \frac{T_0}{2c} \frac{(u-f)^2}{u} \tag{A.2}$$

Since $\frac{T_0}{2c}$ is a constant, it suffices to show that $\frac{(u-f)^2}{u}$ is convex in u and f. Note that

$$\frac{(u-f)^2}{u} = \frac{u^2}{u} - \frac{2uf}{u} + \frac{f^2}{u} = u - 2f + \frac{f^2}{u}$$

Clearly, the terms u and $2f$ are linear functions. Further, $\frac{f^2}{u}$ is convex as it is the ratio of a quadratic and linear function. Thus, $\frac{(u-f)^2}{u}$ is a sum of convex functions, and is also convex. □

Lemma 3. *The weighted function of maximum processing station delay based on the parabolic peak assumption in the objective function of ATCAP is convex for all $f > 0, u > 0$, and $f > u$.*

Proof. The corresponding function is given by:

$$\frac{2f(f-u)^{3/2} T_0}{3u\sqrt{cf}} \tag{A.3}$$

Hence, we consider the Hessian $H_{g'}(f, u)$ of $g'(f, u) = \frac{f(f-u)^{3/2}}{u\sqrt{cf}}$, and show that it is positive semidefinite. $H_{g'}(f, u)$ can be calculated as:

$$\begin{pmatrix} b_{11} & b_{12} \\ b_{21} & b_{22} \end{pmatrix}$$

where

$$b_{11} = \frac{0.75f}{\sqrt{(f-u)}u\sqrt{cf}} + \frac{3f\sqrt{(f-u)}}{u^2\sqrt{cf}} + \frac{2f(f-u)^{3/2}}{u^3\sqrt{cf}}$$

$$b_{12} = b_{21} = \frac{-1.5\sqrt{(f-u)}}{u\sqrt{cf}} - \frac{0.75f}{\sqrt{(f-u)}u\sqrt{cf}} + \frac{0.75cf\sqrt{(f-u)}}{u(cf)^{3/2}} - \frac{(f-u)^{3/2} + 1.5f\sqrt{(f-u)}}{u^2\sqrt{cf}} + \frac{cf(f-u)^{3/2}}{2u^2(cf)^{3/2}}$$

$$b_{22} = \frac{3\sqrt{(f-u)}}{u\sqrt{cf}} - \frac{c(f-u)^{3/2} + 1.5cf\sqrt{(f-u)}}{u(cf)^{3/2}} + \frac{0.75f}{\sqrt{(f-u)}u\sqrt{cf}} + \frac{0.75c^2 f(f-u)^{3/2}}{u(cf)^{5/2}}$$

Clearly, $b_{11} > 0$, as all of its components are positive. To show that $b_{22} \geqslant 0$ also holds, we first consider the difference $\frac{3\sqrt{(f-u)}}{u\sqrt{cf}} - \frac{1.5cf\sqrt{(f-u)}}{u(cf)^{3/2}}$, which can be shown to be positive as follows:

$$\frac{3\sqrt{(f-u)}}{u\sqrt{cf}} - \frac{1.5cf\sqrt{(f-u)}}{u(cf)^{3/2}} = \frac{3\sqrt{(f-u)}}{u\sqrt{cf}} - \frac{1.5cf\sqrt{(f-u)}}{ucf\sqrt{cf}} = \frac{1.5\sqrt{(f-u)}}{u\sqrt{cf}}$$

Then, we consider the summation

$$\frac{0.75c^2 f(f-u)^{3/2}}{u(cf)^{5/2}} + \frac{0.75f}{\sqrt{(f-u)}u\sqrt{cf}} - \frac{c(f-u)^{3/2}}{u(cf)^{3/2}}$$

which reduces to

$$\frac{0.75c(f-u)^{3/2}}{u(cf)^{3/2}} + \frac{0.75f}{\sqrt{(f-u)}u\sqrt{cf}} - \frac{c(f-u)^{3/2}}{u(cf)^{3/2}} = \frac{0.75f}{\sqrt{(f-u)}u\sqrt{cf}} - \frac{0.25c(f-u)^{3/2}}{u(cf)^{3/2}} = \frac{0.75cf^2 - 0.25c(f-u)^2}{\sqrt{(f-u)}u(cf)^{3/2}}$$

Clearly, $f^2 > (f-u)^2$, implying that $\frac{0.75cf^2 - 0.25c(f-u)^2}{\sqrt{(f-u)}u(cf)^{3/2}} > 0$, and thus $b_{22} > 0$. Further, it can be shown by algebraic manipulation that $|H_{g'}(f, u)| = 0$. Hence, $H_{g'}(f, u)$ is positive semidefinite, and the corresponding term in the objective function is convex. □

Lemma 4. *The weighted function of maximum processing station delay based on the half-elliptical peak assumption in the objective function of ATCAP is convex for all $f > 0, u > 0, f > u$, and $c \geqslant \max\left\{\frac{4f^3 - u^3 - 4uf^2 + u^2 f}{8f^3 - 4uf^2 - u^2 f}, \frac{2.5(f-u)}{5f - 3.5u}\right\}$.*

Proof. The corresponding function is given by:

$$\frac{T_0\pi(f-u)^{3/2}\sqrt{u-(1-2c)f}}{4cu} \tag{A.4}$$

Hence, to show convexity, it suffices to show that $\frac{(f-u)^{3/2}\sqrt{u-(1-2c)f}}{u}$ is convex. The Hessian $H_{g''}(f,u)$ of this function can be calculated as:

$$\begin{pmatrix} c_{11} & c_{12} \\ c_{21} & c_{22} \end{pmatrix}$$

where

$$c_{11} = \frac{0.75\sqrt{u-f+2cf}}{u\sqrt{f-u}} - \frac{1.5\sqrt{f-u}}{u\sqrt{u-f+2cf}} + \frac{3\sqrt{f-u}\sqrt{u-f+2cf}}{u^2} - \frac{0.25(f-u)^{3/2}}{u(u-f+2cf)^{3/2}}$$
$$- \frac{(f-u)^{3/2}}{u^2\sqrt{u-f+2cf}} + \frac{2(f-u)^{3/2}\sqrt{u-f+2cf}}{u^3}$$

$$c_{12} = c_{21} = \frac{-0.75\sqrt{u-f+2cf}}{u\sqrt{f-u}} - \frac{1.5(c-1)\sqrt{f-u}}{u\sqrt{u-f+2cf}} - \frac{0.25(f-u)^{3/2}(-1+2c)}{u(u-f+2cf)^{3/2}}$$
$$- \frac{1.5\sqrt{f-u}\sqrt{u-f+2cf}}{u^2} - \frac{0.5(f-u)^{3/2}(-1+2c)}{u^2\sqrt{u-f+2cf}}$$

$$c_{22} = \frac{0.75\sqrt{u-f+2cf}}{u\sqrt{f-u}} + \frac{1.5(-1+2c)\sqrt{f-u}}{u\sqrt{u-f+2cf}} - \frac{0.25(-1+2c)^2(f-u)^{3/2}}{u(u-f+2cf)^{3/2}}$$

We first show that c_{11} and c_{22} are always nonnegative under the given conditions. For c_{11}, we rewrite the corresponding function using the common denominator $u^3(u-f+2cf)^{3/2}\sqrt{f-u} > 0$, and the numerator

$$c_{11}^{num} = 0.75u^2(u-f+2cf)^2 - 1.5u^2(f-u)(u-f+2cf) + 3u(f-u)(u-f+2cf)^2 - 0.25u^2(f-u)^2$$
$$- u(f-u)^2(u-f+2cf) + 2(f-u)^2(u-f+2cf)^2$$

To show that $c_{11}^{num} \geq 0$ always holds, we first observe that $-1.5u^2(f-u)(u-f+2cf) - 0.25u^2(f-u)^2 \leq -1.75u^2(f-u)(u-f+2cf)$. It follows that:

$$c_{11}^{num} \geq (u-f+2cf)[0.75u^2(u-f+2cf) - 1.75u^2(f-u) + 3u(f-u)(u-f+2cf) - u(f-u)^2 + 2(f-u)^2(u-f+2cf)] \tag{A.5}$$

We then consider the cases $c > \frac{1}{2}$ and $c \leq \frac{1}{2}$ separately. For $c > \frac{1}{2}$, we have $u - f + 2cf > f - u > u$, and thus the right hand side of (A.5) always evaluates to a value greater than zero. However, if $c \leq \frac{1}{2}$, then $f - u \leq u - f + 2cf \leq u$, and $c_{11}^{num} \geq 0$ holds only when $c \geq \frac{4f^3 - u^3 - 4uf^2 + u^2f}{8f^3 - 4uf^2 - u^2f}$. Note that this is not an important restriction on the value of c, as by definition $c \geq \frac{f-u}{f}$ and in most cases the latter lower bound is larger.

We show that $c_{22} \geq 0$ also holds, by rewriting the corresponding function as:

$$c_{22} = \frac{0.75(u-f+2cf)^2 + 1.5(-1+2c)(f-u)(u-f+2cf) - 0.25(-1+2c)^2(f-u)^2}{u\sqrt{f-u}(u-f+2cf)^{3/2}} \tag{A.6}$$

For $c > \frac{1}{2}$ (A.6) is positive, as $u - f + 2cf \geq f - u$ and $0 < (-1+2c) \leq 1$. On the other hand, for $c \leq \frac{1}{2}$, $-1 \leq (-1+2c) \leq 0$, and (A.6) is positive, only if $c \geq \frac{2.5(f-u)}{5f-3.5u}$, which again in most cases is less than the defined bound of $\frac{f-u}{f}$.

Finally, it can also be shown by algebraic manipulation that the determinant $|H_{g'}(f,u)|$ is equal to 0 for the Hessian $H_{g''}(f,u)$. It follows that (A.4) is convex under the given conditions. □

Theorem 1. *The objective function of ATCAP is convex for almost all practical instances.*

Proof. The result follows from Lemmas 1–4, as the objective function of *ATCAP* consists of the summation of the functions discussed in these lemmas. □

References

Ahmed, S., King, A.J., Parija, G., 2003. A multistage stochastic integer programming approach for capacity expansion under uncertainty. Journal of Global Optimization 26 (1), 3–24.
Ashford, N., 1988. Level of service design concept for airport passenger terminals – A European view. Transportation Planning and Technology 12 (1), 5–21.
Barahona, F., Bermon, S., Gunluk, O., Hood, S., 2005. Robust capacity planning in semiconductor manufacturing. Naval Research Logistics 52 (5), 459–468.

Berman, O., Ganz, Z., Wagner, J.M., 1994. A stochastic optimization model for planning capacity expansion in a service industry under uncertain demand. Naval Research Logistics 41 (4), 545–564.
Eppen, G.D., Martin, R.K., Schrage, L., 1989. A scenario approach to capacity planning. Operations Research 37 (4), 517–527.
Fruin, J.J., 1971. Designing for pedestrians: a level-of-service concept. Highway Research Record 355, 1–15.
Hamzawi, S.G., 1992. Lack of airport capacity: exploration of alternative solutions. Transportation Research Part A 26 (1), 47–58.
Hartsfield Planning Collaborative, 2001. Hartsfield-Jackson Atlanta International Airport Peak Week Survey Results, Atlanta.
Hartsfield Planning Collaborative, 2005. Hartsfield-Jackson Atlanta International Airport Peak Week Survey Results, Atlanta.
Jim, H.K., Chang, Z.Y., 1998. An airport passenger terminal simulator: a planning and design tool. Simulation Practice and Theory 6 (4), 387–396.
Lulli, G., Sen, S., 2004. A branch-and-price algorithm for multistage stochastic integer programming with application to stochastic batch-sizing problems. Management Science 50 (6), 786–796.
McCullough, B.F., Roberts, F.L., 1979. Decision tool for analysis of capacity of airport terminal. Transportation Research Record 732, 41–54.
McKelvey, F.X., 1989. Use of an analytical queuing model for airport terminal design. Transportation Research Record 1199, 4–11.
Newell, G.F., 1982. Applications of Queuing Theory. Chapman and Hall, London.
Older, S.J., 1968. Movement of pedestrians on footways in shopping streets. Traffic Engineering and Control 10 (4), 160–163.
Rice, J., 1995. Mathematical Statistics and Data Analysis. Duxbury Press, Belmont.
Riis, M., Andersen, K.A., 2004. Multiperiod capacity expansion of a telecommunications connection with uncertain demand. Computers and Operations Research 31 (9), 1427–1436.
Saffarzadeh, M., Braaksma, J.P., 2000. Optimum design and operation of airport passenger terminal buildings. Transportation Research Record 1703, 72–82.
Sarkar, A.K., Janardhan, K.S., 1997. A Study on Pedestrian Flow Characteristics. Presented at Transportation Research Board Annual Conference, Washington, DC.
Shiina, T., Birge, J.R., 2004. Stochastic unit commitment problem. International Transactions in Operational Research 11 (1), 19–32.
Solak, S., 2001. Hartsfield-Jackson Atlanta International Airport Departing/Arriving Passenger Airport Transit Time Study, Atlanta.
Swaminathan, J.M., 2000. Tool capacity planning for semiconductor fabrication facilities under demand uncertainty. European Journal of Operational Research 120 (3), 545–558.
Tanariboon, Y., Hwa, S.S., Chor, C.H., 1986. Pedestrian characteristics study in Singapore. Journal of Transportation Engineering 112 (3), 229–235.
Virkler, M.R., Elayadath, S., 1994. Pedestrian speed-flow-density relationships. Transportation Research Record 1438, 51–58.
Wardrop, J.G., 1952. Some theoretical aspects of road traffic research. Proceedings of the Institute of Civil Engineering 2 (1), 325–378.
Wirasinghe, S.C., Bandara, S., 1990. Airport gate position estimation for minimum total costs-approximate closed form solution. Transportation Research Part B 24 (4), 287–297.
Young, S.B., 1999. Evaluation of pedestrian walking speeds in airport terminals. Transportation Research Record 1674, 20–26.

Part IV:

Scheduling

13

Airline Schedule Planning: Accomplishments and Opportunities

Cynthia Barnhart

Amy Cohn

Plagued by high labor costs, low profitability margins, airspace and airport congestion, high capital and operating costs, security and safety concerns, and complex and large-scale management and operations decisions, the airline industry has armed its planners with sophisticated optimization tools to improve decision making and increase airline profits. In this paper, we describe optimization approaches for airline schedule planning, demonstrating how optimization can facilitate the management of a diverse and finite set of expensive, highly constrained resources. We focus on the art and science of modeling and solving these problems, providing illustrative examples of the associated impacts and challenges, and highlighting effective techniques that might be applicable to problems arising in other industries.

Key words: airline scheduling; network design; large-scale optimization

1. Introduction: Optimization and the Airline Industry

Driven by competitive pressures, low profit margins, and complex operations involving expensive assets and crews, the airline industry has been a leader in the development and application of operations research methods. As a case in point, in the late 1970s, when the U.S. domestic airline industry was deregulated, existing U.S. airlines were threatened by intense competition from low-cost, new entrants such as People's Express and Southwest Airlines. The existing airlines faced the grim choice of matching the fares charged by the new entrants and losing money, or not matching the new entrant fares and losing market share. Either choice produced the same end result—The existing airlines faced elimination. Instead, a number of airlines turned to operations research for an alternative. The answer was revenue management. By creating multiple fares and allocating seat inventory among the fare classes, existing airlines could match the low-cost carrier fare for a portion of their seat inventory and charge higher fares for high-value customers (typically business travelers). Because the new entrants did not have the operations research and information technology expertise needed to design and implement revenue management systems, existing carriers were able to survive deregulation and the challenge of low-cost entrants.

Revenue management represents only one of many operations research success stories for airlines. Another is airline schedule planning. Schedule planning involves designing future airline schedules to maximize airline profitability. In designing schedules, the airline answers questions of which origin-destination markets to serve, with what frequency, and over which hubs. Moreover, the airline determines the departure time and aircraft type for each of these flights. With thousands of flights per day; hundreds of aircraft of differing types; hundreds of airports and multiple hubs; constraints related to gates, airport slots, air traffic control, curfews, maintenance, and crews; and complex issues involving competition, demand forecasting, pricing, and revenue management, schedule planning poses daunting challenges for the schedule planner. Applying sophisticated forecasting and optimization tools is critical. American Airlines claims that their schedule-planning system generates over $500 million in incremental profits annually. This impact is deeply significant when you consider that without revenue management and schedule-planning systems in the period 1990–2000, American Airlines would have been profitable in only one year, an all-time record year for profitability (Cook 2000). Other testimonials to the impact of optimization of the airline industry can be found in Yu et al. (2003), Butchers et al. (2001), Wiper et al. (1994), Smith et al. (1992), and Patty et al. (1991).

In this paper, we describe the state-of-the art and practice in airline schedule planning optimization. While this focused topic does not provide a comprehensive view of the operations research challenges faced by airlines, it does provide insights into the design of effective optimization approaches for airline planning, and their impacts on the industry. Our goal is to illustrate effective techniques for modeling and solving airline scheduling problems that might be applicable to other industries.

In §2, we describe the schedule-planning problems airlines face, overview various modeling approaches, and highlight the impacts and challenges associated with these efforts. In §3, we focus on the blend of art and science needed to solve these large-scale, complex schedule-planning models, again highlighting effective approaches, impacts, and challenges. Finally, in §4, we describe future research opportunities and challenges.

2. Scheduling Problems

Before an airline begins operation, it has to resolve a number of questions, including:

(1) *Schedule Design*. Which markets to serve and with what frequency, and how to schedule flights to meet these frequencies.

(2) *Fleet Assignment*. What size aircraft to assign to each flight.

(3) *Aircraft Maintenance Routing*. How to route aircraft to ensure the satisfaction of maintenance requirements.

(4) *Crew Scheduling*. Which crews to assign to each flight so that crew costs are minimized.

Collectively, these problems are characterized by numerous and well-defined constraints, a large number of interrelated decisions, and nonlinear cost structures. To illustrate this, consider that (1) revenues associated with assigning an aircraft to one flight leg often cannot be computed without knowing the types of aircraft assigned to *several other* flight legs in the network (because passenger itineraries often include multiple flights) and (2) for a particular flight leg, the cost of the assigned crew depends on which *other* flight legs are assigned to that crew (and thus the amount of time spent on the ground between flights). To model the interdependencies and nonlinearities of the above problems, very large-scale linear programs with integer variables have been developed, typically containing *at least* thousands of constraints and billions of decision variables. The combination of problem complexity and size often renders decision makers ineffective in producing cost-effective solutions, despite their wealth of intuition and experience. The airlines have thus turned to optimization techniques.

To date it has been impossible to construct and solve a single optimization model that alone can answer this myriad of questions. One key difficulty stems from model size: A single model is simply too large, containing many billions of decision variables and constraints. Airlines have instead employed a decomposition approach, breaking up the large problem into a set of smaller problems and then solving them sequentially. Even these smaller *core* problems, resulting from the sequential solution approach, present significant modeling and solution challenges, as discussed below.

2.1. The Core Problems

Schedule planning at airlines is typically broken into a set of four core problems, each solved sequentially. These problems, depicted in Figure 1, are *schedule design, fleet assignment, aircraft maintenance routing,* and *crew scheduling*.

2.1.1. Schedule Design.
The flight schedule, containing the flight legs to be flown and the departure time of each flight leg, is the single most important product of an airline. It largely defines the market share an airline will capture, and hence is a key

Figure 1   Aircraft and Crew Schedule Planning

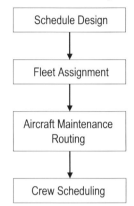

determinant of airline profitability. Designing a flight schedule to maximize profitability is extraordinarily complex, with essentially all elements of the airline (and competing airlines as well) linked to the flight schedule design decisions. One leading industry executive (Cook 2000) remarked, "The network planners are usually the smartest people in an airline."

Impacts and Challenges. Operations researchers, armed with optimization models and methods, have not fully met the challenges posed by the size and complexity of airline schedule design, for reasons including:

(1) *Complexity and Problem Size.* Decisions involving schedule design are integrally tied to the assignment of aircraft and crews to the flight legs. Incorporating crew, fleeting, and schedule design decisions into a single model, however, involves numerous flight-leg options and complex constraints and interdependencies. Moreover, such a model would be intractable, containing many billions of constraints and variables.

(2) *Data Availability and Accuracy.* Critical inputs for designing the flight schedule include the airline's expected *unconstrained market demands* and *average fares*, two particularly challenging forms of data.

• The airline's unconstrained market demand is defined as the maximum demand the airline will experience for an origin-destination market, independent of the capacity provided in that market. Unconstrained demand data are critical to developing a good flight schedule, but extremely difficult to estimate accurately. The first issue is that unconstrained demands cannot be directly observed. The second is that the demand an airline will experience in a given market is a function of the airline's schedule in that market, with greater frequency of service typically leading to greater market share. This relationship creates a chicken-and-egg effect, with demand for airline service a function of the airline schedule and the optimal airline schedule a function of market demand. Moreover, an airline's demand is influenced by the schedule of competing airlines, again inducing a chicken-and-egg effect, with competing airlines adjusting their schedules as an airline makes changes to its own schedule. Air carrier demand research appears in Proussaloglou and Koppelman (1995, 1999).

• Average fares are another core element of the input data for schedule design. (Because an airline offers an enormous number of fares, models are typically based on *average* fares.) Average fares are affected by complex pricing and revenue management systems, the order in which customers request tickets for a flight, and the demand and capacity in a market—which are themselves dependent on the flight schedule. Further complicating the estimation of fares are the competitive pressures in the industry that force airlines to adjust their fare structures dynamically, reacting to pricing changes made by their competition. Industry executives lament that an airline's pricing strategy can be only as good as its worst competitor.

These compounding difficulties have contributed to the current, typical airline practice of designing flight schedules manually, with limited optimization. However, by limiting the complexity and scope of models, recent progress has been made in applying optimization to schedule design problems. Researchers have focused on determining incremental changes to flight schedules, producing a new schedule by applying a limited number of changes to the existing schedule. Generally, the approach is to cast these problems as network design models, with the objective of maximizing the incremental profits of the new schedule.

In their incremental optimization approach, Lohatepanont and Barnhart (2001) select flight legs to include in the flight schedule and simultaneously optimize aircraft assignments to these legs. Using their approach—an extension of the fleet assignment models and algorithms in the following sections—they demonstrate potential improvements in aircraft utilization and significant increases in revenue, with an estimated impact exceeding $200 million at one major airline. Other recent research efforts to optimize airline schedule design are described in Armacost et al. (2002) and Erdmann et al. (1999).

2.1.2. Fleet Assignment. Once the flight schedule has been specified, the next step in schedule planning is *fleet assignment*. The fleet assignment problem is to assign a particular *fleet* (equipment) type to each flight leg so as to minimize *operating* and *spill* costs. Operating costs vary by aircraft type and represent the cost of flying a flight leg with an aircraft of that type. Spill costs represent the revenue lost when passenger demand for a flight leg exceeds the assigned aircraft's seating capacity, resulting in *spilled demand* (that is, passengers turned away by the airline) and lost potential revenue.

At first glance, the approach to determining optimal fleet assignments appears straightforward—simply match as closely as possible flight demand with assigned aircraft seating capacity. The optimal solution is complicated, however, by the interactive nature of the flight network. Specifically, assigning an aircraft to one leg of the network impacts the feasible assignments of aircraft to other flight legs. This occurs both because the airline has a limited number of aircraft of each type and because assignments of aircraft to flight legs must be balanced, with the number of aircraft of a particular type arriving at a location equal to the number departing that location.

Modeling Approach. To capture these considerations, fleet assignment models have historically been cast as multicommodity network flow problems with side constraints (Hane et al. 1995). The underlying network (see Figure 2 for an illustration) is a *time-line network*, with

(1) Nodes corresponding to the times and locations of flight departures and arrivals.

(2) Two types of arcs, *flight arcs* and *ground arcs*. Flight arcs represent the schedule's flight legs, with arrival times adjusted to include the minimum amount of time aircraft must remain on the ground.

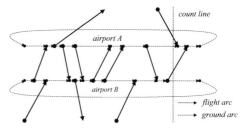

Figure 2   A Time-Line Network Involving Two Airports

This time is needed for tasks such as disembarking and embarking passengers, unloading and loading baggage, and refueling. Ground arcs represent aircraft on the ground between flights.

Each aircraft type is a commodity, and the objective is to flow each commodity through the network feasibly and with minimum cost, such that each flight leg is assigned to exactly one aircraft type. For each feasible assignment of a fleet type to a flight leg, the decision of whether or not to make that assignment is represented by a binary variable.

Impacts and Challenges. Fleet assignment models are widely used by the industry in making their fleeting decisions and are credited with contributing to significant cost savings, measuring in the millions of dollars annually. For example, Rushmeierf and Kontogiorgis (1997) state that at USAir, an audit based on *actual* results indicates savings of at least $15 million annually. Using fleet assignment models, Wiper et al. (1994) report annual savings of $100 million at Delta Airlines, and Abara (1989) reports a 1.4% improvement in operating margins at American Airlines. In addition to providing economic benefits, research on fleet assignment problems, such as that presented in Hane et al. (1995), led to advanced techniques for solving large-scale linear programs. Many of these techniques have been generalized and incorporated into commercial solvers, allowing more efficient solution of large-scale optimization problems.

These impressive results notwithstanding, there remain several critical challenges in fleet assignment. Many of these challenges stem from modeling assumptions that include:

(1) Many fleet assignment models assume that the flight schedules repeat daily, even though most airlines operate different schedules on the weekend.

(2) Most fleeting models assume flight-leg demand is known and does not vary by day of week, but historical data clearly show that day-to-day demand variations are present.

(3) Flying times and ground times are typically assumed to be deterministic in fleet assignment models; however, historical data show large variations in flight and ground times, caused by factors including congestion on the ground and in the air, weather conditions, and new security practices.

(4) Most fleet assignment models assume that the number of spilled passengers, and their associated spill costs, can be computed per *flight leg*. In fact, passenger demand, spill, and the revenue associated with each passenger is *itinerary* specific, not *flight-leg* specific. Hence, obtaining unconstrained demand and average fare for each *flight leg* in order to compute spill costs poses challenges, as described in the next section.

Estimates of Spill Costs. Greatly limiting the accuracy of many fleet assignment models is the fact that spill costs must be estimated for each *flight leg*, and not for each *itinerary*. To achieve this, itinerary fares must be allocated to flight legs so that the total resulting leg-based spill costs equal total spill costs over all itineraries. One allocation rule satisfying this criterion is to allocate an itinerary's fare to its flight legs such that their sum equals the total fare of the itinerary. While necessary, this rule is not sufficient to ensure that the spill costs of a particular fleet assignment will be correctly computed. The issue stems from the multileg nature of some itineraries.

Consider, for example, an airline that operates a network consisting of flight legs X–Y and Y–Z, serving two nonstop origin-destination markets X–Y and Y–Z, and one connecting market X–Z, with flight legs X–Y and Y–Z. Table 1 shows unconstrained market demands and average fares for these markets. Assume that the airline operates two aircraft types, one with 100 seats and the other with 200 seats. Further assume that the scheme to allocate itinerary fares

Table 1 **Demand and Fare Data**

Market	Itinerary (Sequence of Flight Legs)	Number of Passengers	Average Fare ($)
X–Y	1	75	200
Y–Z	2	150	225
X–Z	1–2	75	300

to flight legs results in the following spill costs:

(1) $200 for the X–Y market on the X–Y flight leg.
(2) $225 for the Y–Z market on the Y–Z flight leg.
(3) $150 for the X–Z market on the X–Y flight leg.
(4) $150 for the X–Z market on the Y–Z flight leg.

Consider the assignment of the 100-seat aircraft to both flight leg 1 (X–Y) and flight leg 2 (Y–Z). Given these allocated costs, the optimal spill and its associated cost for each flight leg can be characterized as:

Flight Leg 1. Spill 50 X–Z passengers, for a total associated spill cost of $50 * \$150$.

Flight Leg 2. Spill 50 Y–Z passengers and 75 X–Z passengers on flight leg 2, for a total spill cost of $50 * 225 + 75 * 150$.

This simple example illustrates the inconsistencies that result with a leg-based approach to fleet assignment; namely, spill costs are computed using the assumption that spill on each leg can be optimized without regard to other flight legs in the network. In this example, all 75 passengers from X–Z are spilled from flight leg 2, but only 50 are spilled from flight leg 1. Clearly, this results in an underestimation of true spill—passengers do not travel on only a portion of their desired itineraries.

Another issue of this leg-based approach is that spilling passengers in an optimal manner on each *flight leg* based on the allocated spill costs does not result in an optimal spill solution. Again, with 100-seat aircraft assigned to both flight legs 1 and 2, the true optimal spill is 75 Y–Z passengers and 50 X–Z passengers. It is cost effective to displace from flight leg 2 a Y–Z passenger with allocated spill cost of $225 and replace that passenger with an X–Z passenger with allocated spill cost of $150 because the X–Z passenger also has allocated cost of $150 on flight leg 1. A leg-based approach cannot recognize such a solution as optimal, because it does not capture these network interdependencies. In fact, Barnhart et al.

(2002b) show that there is no single scheme for allocating itinerary fares to flight legs that can always guarantee an optimal fleet assignment.

To overcome the inaccuracies of leg-based models, more recent modeling efforts have introduced itinerary- or origin-destination-based fleet assignment models (Barnhart et al. 2002b, Erdmann et al. 1999, Jacobs et al. 1999). In Barnhart et al. (2002b), the fleet assignment model described above is expanded to include path variables that represent the assignment of passengers to itineraries, obviating the need to allocate itinerary fares to flight legs. The passenger flow variables are linked to the aircraft assignment variables through the capacity constraints, ensuring that the number of available seats is not exceeded by the number of assigned passengers. In a case study involving a major U.S. airline, they report that fleet assignments using network-based models with passenger itineraries improve upon leg-based fleeting solutions significantly, with estimated savings ranging from 30 million to over 100 million dollars annually.

2.1.3. Aircraft Maintenance Routing. Once the fleet assignment decisions have been made, the flight network decomposes into subnetworks, each one associated only with the aircraft of a particular fleet type. The aircraft-maintenance-routing and crew-scheduling steps of the schedule-planning process, therefore, require the solution of much smaller problems, one for each aircraft type.

Given the subnetwork of flight legs assigned to a particular aircraft type, the assignment of *individual* aircraft to these flight legs occurs in the *aircraft-maintenance-routing* step. The goal of aircraft maintenance routing is to determine *routings*, or *rotations*, for each aircraft in a fleet. A routing is a sequence of flight legs, with the destination of one flight leg the same as the origin of the next leg in the sequence. A rotation is a routing which starts and ends at the same location. Each aircraft's rotation is mandated to visit, at regular intervals, airports that serve as maintenance stations for that aircraft type. This mandate is motivated by regulatory restrictions requiring aircraft to undergo maintenance checks between blocks of flying time, not to exceed a specified limit. Detailed descriptions of the maintenance-routing problem are contained in Gopalan and Talluri (1998) and Clarke et al. (1996b).

Modeling Approach. The aircraft-maintenance-routing problem can be modeled as a *network circulation problem* with side constraints. The decision variables correspond to sequences (*strings*) of flight legs, with the sequence (1) beginning and ending at a maintenance station and (2) satisfying the rules governing the maximum time between maintenance. If a string is included in the solution, a single aircraft flies each flight in the sequence and then undergoes maintenance. Side constraints, beyond the flow circulation constraints ensuring aircraft balance, include *cover constraints* and *count constraints*. Cover constraints ensure that each flight leg is contained in exactly one selected string, and count constraints limit the number of assigned aircraft to the number available. Additional details are provided in Barnhart et al. (1998a).

The primary objective of the aircraft-maintenance-routing problem is to find a *feasible* solution, one ensuring sufficient maintenance opportunities for each aircraft. Historically, another objective has been to determine routings that maximize *through revenue*. Through revenue is the incremental fare airlines charge passengers for the convenience of staying on the same aircraft between flights. When computer reservation systems (*CRSs*) were the primary distribution channel, prior to the use of the Internet as a way to purchase tickets, *through itineraries* (with passengers staying on the same aircraft between flights) were given priority in CRS displays over connecting itineraries (with passengers changing aircraft between flights). Not surprisingly, the order in which an itinerary appeared on a CRS display was correlated with the number of sales of that itinerary, with itineraries appearing first having the highest booking levels. Using the Internet, airline passengers are increasingly aware of available itineraries and their associated fares. Arguably, given the price sensitivity of many passengers, this diminishes the relevance of through revenues. Moreover, because of disruptions, aircraft rotations are often altered during operations and passengers who were booked on through itineraries are in fact required to change planes to connect. These factors suggest that in modeling today's aircraft-maintenance-routing problems, the objective might best be cast as one only of achieving a feasible maintenance routing.

Impacts and Challenges. Barnhart et al. (1998) note that aircraft-routing problems of major U.S. airlines, containing up to 200 flight legs and over 400 million string variables, can often be solved on workstation-class computers, typically requiring less than 10 hours of computation time. This suggests that feasible solutions can be found, *when they exist*. Feasibility is not guaranteed, however, given the sequential approach of first solving the fleet assignment problem and then solving the resulting aircraft-routing problems. Barnhart et al. (1998) found the likelihood of a fleet assignment solution yielding maintenance-feasible aircraft routings to be a function of the structure of the flight network.

Sequential Solution and Network Structure. In *hub-and-spoke networks*, the effects of a sequential approach are mitigated by the existence of *banks*, that is, times at which many aircraft are on the ground at a hub airport to allow passengers to connect between flights. With many aircraft of a given type at the same location at roughly the same time, banks provide aircraft with many possible routings. This is in contrast with *point-to-point networks*, especially international networks with low frequencies. Separating the fleet assignment and aircraftrouting decisions in this latter case can often result in fleetings without maintenance-feasible aircraft routings.

The likelihood that the fleet assignment solution yields maintenance-infeasible aircraft routings is reduced by incorporating approximate maintenance constraints, called *pseudomaintenance constraints*, into the fleet assignment model. Ensuring that sufficient numbers of aircraft of each type are located at maintenance stations nightly, these constraints are straightforward to include in fleet assignment models. However, they cannot guarantee that each *individual* aircraft will have sufficient maintenance opportunities. Instead, pseudomaintenance constraints enforce *aggregate* requirements on the number of aircraft that must be maintained daily. Indeed, one aircraft might be maintained every night while another is never maintained.

To guarantee the satisfaction of *individual* aircraft maintenance requirements, the fleet assignment model must be altered dramatically, with decision variables based on strings (as in aircraft-routing models). Expanding the model in this manner, effectively integrating the fleet assignment and aircraft-routing models, increases the number of variables dramatically and introduces tractability issues (Barnhart et al. 1998c).

For hub-and-spoke airlines, this added complexity is rarely warranted. Including pseudomaintenance constraints in the fleet assignment models is almost always sufficient to ensure a feasible maintenance routing. For point-to-point airlines, however, the altered model is often necessary to ensure that the fleeting solution is maintenance feasible. Additional detail about the integrated fleet assignment and aircraft routing problem is provided in §2.2.

Euler-Tour Requirement. An interesting twist often applied to aircraft routings in U.S. domestic networks is the *Euler-tour requirement*. In order to ensure equal wear and tear on their aircraft, several airlines require that *all* aircraft of a particular type fly all flight legs assigned to that aircraft type. This requirement can be formulated as the problem of finding one maintenance-feasible rotation containing each flight leg exactly once (an Euler tour) and requiring no more than the number of aircraft of that fleet type to fly all flight legs daily. Again, the difficulty of satisfying this particular constraint is a function of the network structure of the flight schedule.

In hub-and-spoke networks, this restriction is typically easily satisfied through a sequential solution approach, first solving fleet assignment with pseudomaintenance constraints and then solving aircraft routing with Euler-tour constraints. In contrast, to ensure feasible solutions in point-to-point networks, it is often necessary to build integrated models capturing the fleeting, maintenance routing, and Euler constraints simultaneously. For a more detailed discussion of this topic, the reader is referred to Barnhart et al. (1998c).

2.1.4. Crew Scheduling. Airlines typically partition their crew-scheduling problem into two categories. *Cabin crews* (flight attendants) are responsible for the comfort and safety of the passengers, and *cockpit crews* (pilots) are responsible for operating the aircraft and executing the flight leg. Most optimization research on airline crew scheduling has focused on the pilot problem, primarily because cockpit crews are paid substantially more than cabin crews. The cockpit crew problem is also smaller and simpler in structure than the cabin crew problem, for reasons including:

(1) Cockpit crews, unlike cabin crews, stay together throughout the workday, allowing crews, instead of individuals, to be modeled.

(2) For each flight leg, the size and composition of the cockpit crew is known a priori, based upon the defined requirements for each aircraft. The cabin crew size, however, varies as a function of the number of passengers on the flight leg.

(3) Cockpit crews have fewer options: They can be assigned only to those flight legs with assigned aircraft types that they are qualified to fly. Cabin crews have much more flexibility, with only limited restrictions on the type of aircraft to which they are assigned.

For both cockpit or cabin crews, the crew-scheduling problem itself is usually solved sequentially. First, a set of minimum-cost work schedules (*pairings*) typically spanning one to five days is determined. Feasible pairings are constrained by a host of work rules imposed by regulatory agencies and collective bargaining agreements. Rules include restrictions on the maximum number of work hours in a day, the minimum number of hours of rest between work periods, the maximum time away from home, etc. These restrictions notwithstanding, the number of possible pairings often numbers in the billions for major U.S. carriers. Further complicating the problem is the cost of a pairing, usually represented as a nonlinear function of flying time, total elapsed work time, and total time away from home.

The second step in solving crew-scheduling problems is to assemble pairings into monthly work schedules, called *bidlines* or *rosters*, and to assign them to individual crew members. With rostering, a practice commonly used outside the United States, schedules are constructed for and assigned to specific individuals, taking into consideration their particular needs or requests. This is in contrast to bidline generation—a practice more commonly used in the United States. With bidline generation, schedules are generated but not for specific individuals.

The cost-minimizing subset of schedules is selected, and individual employees reveal their relative preferences for these schedules through a *bidding* process. The airline then makes the specific assignment of schedule to employees based on individual priority rankings—rankings that are often related to seniority. More details on the bidline and rostering problems can be found in Kohl and Karisch (2002), Cappanera and Gallo (2001), Caprara et al. (1998), Christou et al. (1999), Dawid et al. (2001), Day and Ryan (1997), and Gamache et al. (1998).

In addition to the complexity already described, crew-scheduling models must also incorporate a host of other constraints, including crewbase requirements, work balance concerns, etc. Moreover, depending on whether the flight schedule is domestic or international, different modeling and solution techniques are required. Detailed descriptions of the airline crew-scheduling problem are included in the survey papers by Barnhart et al. (2003), Clarke and Smith (2000), and Desaulniers et al. (1998).

Modeling Approach. The crew-pairing, bidline, and rostering problems can all be cast as *set-partitioning problems*. While simple in form, the set-partitioning model is a powerful one in this context. To illustrate, we focus on the crew-pairing problem. Construct one binary decision variable y_p for each pairing $p \in P$ (where P is the set of all feasible pairings), and define δ_{fp} to be an *indicator variable*, with value one if pairing p contains flight $f \in F$ (where F is the set of all flight legs) and zero otherwise. The crew-pairing problem is then formulated as

$$\min \sum_{p \in P} c_p y_p, \quad (1)$$

$$\text{subject to} \sum_{p \in P} \delta_{fp} y_p = 1 \quad \forall f \in F \quad (2)$$

$$y_p \in \{0, 1\} \quad \forall p \in P. \quad (3)$$

The objective (1) minimizes the cost of the chosen set of pairings. The cover constraints (2) and integrality constraints (3) require that for each flight f, exactly one pairing is chosen containing that flight.

By defining variables to correspond to *sequences of flight legs*, only *feasible* pairings are considered and explicit representation of complicated work rules is unnecessary. Moreover, nonlinear costs associated with a day of work are captured by a *single quantity* representing pairing cost. The result is a crew-pairing model with simple form, containing a linear objective function and binary decision variables. With its advantages, however, comes one major disadvantage—namely, the huge number of possible crew pairings (often, numbering in the billions or more). Hub-and-spoke network structures, in particular, exacerbate this issue. With many aircraft on the ground at the same time and location, a huge number of crew connections, and hence pairings, is possible. In §3, we present some of the specialized algorithmic approaches used to overcome this obstacle.

Impacts and Challenges. Airline crew scheduling has garnered the most attention of optimizers, with research spanning decades. Crew-scheduling problems, with their numerous, complex rules and well-defined costs, are particularly amenable to optimization. Because there are so many possible decisions, it can be difficult to find feasible—let alone close to optimal—solutions manually. Moreover, crew costs represent the airlines' second-highest operating cost after fuel, so even slight improvements in the utilization of crews can translate into significant savings.

For these reasons, most major airlines use optimization tools to generate part or all of their crew schedules. As is the case with aircraft-scheduling tools, crew-scheduling optimization systems are either developed in-house by the airline's operations research group (often in collaboration with researchers from academia), or purchased from companies with expertise in airline optimization, including other airlines. Optimization has had a significant economic impact on crew scheduling. A decade ago solutions to crew-pairing problems were typically 10%–15% above the lower bound of flying cost, compared to today's solutions which typically are within at most 1%–2% of the lower bound. This improvement in solution quality translates to savings on the order of $50 million annually for a large airline (Barnhart et al. 2003).

In addition to these economic benefits, crew-pairing optimization can be a useful negotiation tool, helping airlines to quantify the impacts of proposed changes in cost structures, benefits, and work rules proposed by their labor unions. The economic impact of each proposed change can be evaluated precisely by changing selected inputs to the crew-pairing model, and re-running the optimization procedure.

While significant, the effects of optimization on crew scheduling are nonetheless limited by the sequential nature of the solution process. Once the flight schedule, the fleet assignments, and the aircraft-routing decisions have been made, the range of crew possibilities is significantly narrowed. Although researchers have been unsuccessful to date in modeling and solving the fully integrated schedule-planning problem, they are developing models that integrate pieces of the overall problem, as described in the next section.

Another issue associated with optimized crew schedules (and, in fact, with optimized fleet assignments and maintenance routings as well) is that the true impact of optimization is not exactly known. One reason for this is that the optimized solutions are rarely executed as planned. Crew sickness, vacation, and training periods, as well as mechanical failures and adverse weather conditions, result in necessary changes, often leading to significantly increased costs. Moreover, a finely tuned, optimized solution achieves increased utilization through the removal of slack, providing crews with less time to connect between flights and aircraft with less time on the ground between flying. Less slack time, although economical in theory, can translate in practice into less robustness and increased costs. In §4, we further discuss this important issue.

2.2. Integrating Core Models

After decades of research, *opportunities* to improve core problem models still exist, but *improvements*, especially significant ones, are increasingly difficult to achieve. Some researchers have thus turned their attention to modeling integrated core problems, in an attempt to ameliorate some of the drawbacks of a sequential solution approach. Because a tractable model integrating *all* decisions is not currently attainable, researchers have adopted alternative strategies. These strategies achieve *partial integration* of the core problems either by:

(1) Merging two core problem models to create an integrated model that fully captures the two problems or

(2) Enhancing a core problem model by incorporating into it some of the key elements of another core problem model.

EXAMPLE 1: THE INTEGRATED FLEET ASSIGNMENT AND AIRCRAFT-MAINTENANCE-ROUTING PROBLEM. Barnhart et al. (1998c) ensure that fleet assignment decisions guarantee maintenance feasibility by merging the fleet assignment and aircraft-routing models. Their model contains one core aircraft-routing model for each aircraft type, along with the fleet assignment constraints requiring that each flight leg be assigned to exactly one aircraft type. They show that for a set of problems based on an international flight schedule containing more than 1,000 flight legs and nine fleet types, five out of nine had no maintenance-feasible solution when the fleeting and routing problems were solved sequentially. Their integrated model, however, produced near-optimal fleeting and feasible routing solutions in less than six hours, using a workstation-class computer.

EXAMPLE 2: THE INTEGRATED AIRCRAFT-MAINTENANCE-ROUTING AND CREW-PAIRING PROBLEM. In the sequential solution approach, the aircraft-routing solution imposes limitations on the possible crew-scheduling opportunities, resulting in potentially significant increases in crew costs. To understand the connection between the two problems, it is important to understand that crews and aircraft are independent. A crew connecting between two flights might stay on the same aircraft, or might transfer between two different aircraft, depending on the aircraft routings. Transferring between different aircraft requires more time (thereby introducing inefficiencies) than staying with the same aircraft. Hence, the set of feasible crew solutions changes as aircraft rotations change. Specifically, a crew cannot be assigned to a *short connect* (a flight connection with less than the minimum required crew connection time) unless both of the flights in the connection are assigned to the same aircraft. This highlights one of the key issues of sequential solution: The aircraft-routing solution is optimized without consideration of associated crew costs, yet crew costs are the airline's second-largest operating costs.

Klabjan et al. (2002) address this by solving the crew-pairing problem *before* the maintenance-routing problem, and provide computational results demonstrating the degree to which choosing the "wrong" maintenance-routing solution can impact the quality of the crew solution. Although this approach has the benefit of focusing on minimizing crew costs, it does not ensure that a maintenance-feasible solution will be found. To guarantee compatible solutions, Cordeau et al. (2000) directly integrate the basic maintenance-routing and crew-scheduling models. As an alternative approach, Cohn and Barnhart (2003) achieve improved crew-scheduling solutions by integrating *key elements* of the maintenance-routing and crew-scheduling problems. In their work, the crew-pairing problem and maintenance-routing problems are merged, but the aircraft-routing model is significantly modified to contain only decisions that (1) are relevant to the crew-pairing problem, and (2) assure a feasible maintenance-routing solution. We provide added discussion of this problem in §3.

EXAMPLE 3: ENHANCED FLEET ASSIGNMENT TO CAPTURE THE IMPACT ON CREW COSTS. In a sequential solution approach, crew-pairing problems decompose by aircraft type, allowing one problem to be solved independently for each type. Merging the crew-pairing and fleet assignment models, however, results in an integrated and *intractable* model that includes *all* crew pairings for *all* fleet types. Nonetheless, airline schedule planners have keen interest in improving upon the sequential solution approach, with its costly impact on crew scheduling.

Clarke et al. (1996a) and Barnhart et al. (1998a) have taken steps towards integrating fleet assignment and crew scheduling by modifying fleet assignment models to account for some of the downstream effects on crews. Clarke et al. (1996a) include *bonuses* for fleet assignments that allow crews to stay with the same aircraft. This reduces the occurrence of extended periods of crew rest between flights (the fleet assignment objective indirectly works to achieve solutions with high aircraft utilization), thereby eliminating unnecessary crew inactivity and costs.

In Barnhart et al. (1998a) crew costs are more explicitly incorporated into the fleet assignment model by adding decision variables representing *partial* crew pairings, with *approximate* costs. Solving their enhanced model using data from a long-haul airline, they achieve a reduction in crew costs of over 7% with a corresponding increase in fleeting costs of just over 1%, for a total decrease in combined crew and fleeting costs of over 3%.

EXAMPLE 4: ENHANCED FLEET ASSIGNMENT TO INCLUDE SCHEDULE DESIGN DECISIONS. Because the core schedule design problem has not been successfully modeled in all its complexity, researchers have focused on determining incremental changes to flight schedules to allow a better matching of flight schedules and fleetings. In one such approach, proposed by Rexing et al. (2000), the fleet assignment model is modified to allow small retimings of flight-leg departures (on the order of 5 to 20 minutes). This retiming can allow additional aircraft assignments. To understand how, consider a spoke station with only two flights, one inbound and the other outbound, throughout the day. If the scheduled arrival time of the inbound flight and the scheduled departure time of the outbound flight are separated by only 25 minutes, these two legs might require different aircraft. If so, the two aircraft assigned to these legs will be severely underutilized, requiring them both to spend significant amounts of time (almost an entire day) on the ground at the spoke station. Long ground times can be eliminated, and aircraft utilization and productivity can be enhanced, by delaying the flight-leg departing the spoke by 5 to 10 minutes. This could allow sufficient time for a *single* aircraft to perform both the inbound and outbound legs. While a planner can readily recognize the value of a single retiming such as this, an optimization approach is required to track its networkwide effects and to determine the optimal set of retimings.

Rexing et al. (2000) show that allowing scheduled departures to be retimed within 20-minute intervals results in significantly improved fleetings, saving $20 to $50 million annually for one major airline. Interestingly, the economic gains come both from increased revenues achieved through a reduction in spill costs, and increased aircraft productivity. The retimings provide more fleeting options and, hence, achieve a better overall match between flight-leg demand and assigned capacity.

Incorporating into one core problem some of the key elements of another core problem involves both *art and science*, balancing the types of information and the level of detail necessary to maintain tractability and achieve the maximum impact on solution quality. While these enhancement efforts and the core-model mergers do not integrate the schedule design and fleet assignment problems fully, they do provide additional options and better coordination between decisions in the sequential solution process. The results are improved resource utilization and reduced costs, leading to vastly improved solutions.

2.3. Modeling for Solvability

Advanced fleet assignment, schedule design, and integrated schedule-planning models, by their nature, often take the form of network design models, with one set of decision variables assigning supply to the network and another assigning demand to the network. An example of this is the integrated *fleet assignment and passenger flow problem*, involving two types of decision variables: the assignment of aircraft types (the *supply* of seats) and the assignment of passengers to flight legs (the *demand* for seats). In basic fleet assignment models, revenue associated with demand and costs associated with supply are bundled together in the cost coefficient for each decision variable. In the integrated model, revenues are associated with demand variables and costs are associated with supply variables. This separation of costs and revenues leads to fractional aircraft decisions in the linear programming (LP) relaxation of the integrated model. This results in highly fractional solutions and large branch-and-bound trees. The weak LP relaxations of the integrated model pose major solution challenges.

One approach to resolving these challenges is to exploit the fact that there are many different, yet *equivalent*, formulations for mixed-integer problems. Equivalent formulations contain the same set of *optimal* solutions, but possibly very different sets of solutions to their associated LP relaxations. This difference is relevant to a branch-and-bound solution process: The LP bounds associated with equivalent models can vary—often dramatically.

Modeling to achieve tight relaxations is a rich research area, with substantial literature (see for example, Vanderbeck 2000 and Martin 1999). In schedule planning, research has demonstrated that models with tight LP relaxations can be achieved through an *expansion in the set of decisions represented by a variable*.

Even without the consideration of LP bounds, variable expansion has been used extensively in modeling airline-scheduling problems. In modeling core and integrated problems, expanded variables allow complex, nonlinear constraints and costs to be modeled exactly using linear constraints and a linear objective function. A case in point is the crew-pairing problem in which complex constraints are implicitly satisfied by each pairing variable, and the nonlinear crew cost structure can be represented as a linear function of the pairing variables. The fact that variable expansion can also lead to improved LP bounds—and hence improved tractability—is an added benefit.

Determining which decisions to group together within a single variable, however, is a tremendous challenge. Finding the most appropriate variable definition, capturing the complexities of the problem while allowing tractability, is very much an art. At one extreme, variables can be associated with the most elemental of decisions, such as the assignment of a crew to a flight leg, or an aircraft type to a flight leg. Such models typically have relatively small numbers of decision variables, but often suffer from factors such as weak LP relaxations, nonlinearities, and very large sets of constraints. At the other extreme, a variable can be defined that encompasses *all* decisions. The model is then structurally and algorithmically trivial—it contains one constraint requiring the greedy selection of the best solution. The difficulty with this model is, of course, its enormous number of variables. In solving scheduling problems, researchers have experimented with various expanded variable definitions to find the right balance among these alternatives.

An example can be found in the fleet assignment and passenger mix model developed by Barnhart et al. (2002). Instead of defining a fleet assignment variable as an assignment of *an aircraft type* to a *flight leg*, they expand the definition to an assignment of aircraft *types* to a *subnetwork* of flight legs. Although the expansion is motivated by the need to capture spill costs accurately, they prove that another effect of the variable expansion is that the resulting LP relaxation can provide better bounds. They illustrate, with a problem instance drawn from one major airline, that the gap between the initial LP solution and the optimal solution was just 0.3% of that for models without variable expansion. Similar findings are reported by Armacost et al. (2002) for an application involving airline schedule design for express parcel delivery, and by Cohn and Barnhart (2003) for a service parts logistics application.

This tightening of the LP relaxation bound comes at the cost, however, of increased formulation size, with many more decision variables in the expanded-variable formulation. The effect, then, is that the expanded-variable formulation can enhance tractability with its associated improved LP relaxations, but at the same time can hamper tractability with its significantly increased model sizes. These same effects are observed in using expanded variables to model the integrated problems of aircraft routing and crew scheduling (Cohn and Barnhart 2003) and fleet assignment and schedule design (Lohatepanont and Barnhart 2001, Rexing et al. 2000).

3. Solving Scheduling Problems

As seen in §2, careful model selection can reduce complex airline planning problems to classical, well-known problems (sometimes with added side constraints) such as *set partitioning* (crew scheduling), *multicommodity flow* (fleet assignment), or *network design* (flight schedule design). These classical problems have been extensively studied and are well understood, with a sizeable body of associated literature. Even so, airline schedule-planning models present formidable solution challenges, primarily because of their immense size.

Given this, schedule-planning solution approaches prior to the 1990s focused on heuristic methods to achieve solutions. Many of the heuristics involved finding a subset of variables that could produce a quality solution, without requiring all variables to be considered explicitly. Examples of this strategy can be found in Anbil et al. (1991), Gershkoff (1989), and Hoffman and Padberg (1993). While producing improved solutions compared to earlier results, these heuristic strategies lacked the ability to indicate how much was lost in solving the models heuristically rather than exactly.

In the 1990s, with advances in computing and optimization, and motivated by the observation that even slight improvements in aircraft utilization and crew efficiency often produced significant cost savings, researchers shifted their focus to optimization-based approaches to generate provably near-optimal solutions.

3.1. Problem-Size Reduction Methods

To manage problem size, the primary hurdle in solving airline planning models, *problem-size reduction methods* have proven essential. These techniques diminish problem size through *variable elimination*, *exploitation of dominance*, and *variable disaggregation*.

Variable Elimination. Recall that the network representation of airline flight schedules gives rise to two variable types in fleet assignment models, those corresponding to the assignment of aircraft to ground arcs and those to flight arcs. Because aircraft assignments must satisfy conservation of flow, one constraint is needed for each network node. Many of these constraints, however, are redundant. Consider the scenario, as is often the case when flights are scheduled into banks at hubs, in which an uninterrupted set of arrivals is followed by an uninterrupted set of departures. Clearly, any aircraft landing during the arrival bank will remain on the ground at least until the first departure in the departure bank. This implies that the decision variables associated with the assignment of aircraft to ground arcs within the arrival bank are unnecessary; they are fully specified by the flight-leg assignment variables corresponding to the arrival bank. Removal of the superfluous ground arc decision variables, referred to as *node consolidation*, is just one example of variable elimination techniques used in modeling and solving airline problems. Related techniques, including *arc consolidation* and *islands*, have been identified in Hane et al. (1995) and Rexing et al. (2000). Applying such reduction techniques to an extended fleet assignment model, Rexing et al. (2000) reduced their model size by more than 40%, allowing formerly intractable problem instances to be solved.

Dominance. The effectiveness of solution algorithms often depends on their ability to eliminate *dominated* variables. Shortest-path algorithms, for example, eliminate from consideration all subpaths to a node except the shortest one. Like solution algorithms, the tractability of optimization models is inextricably linked to the degree to which the principles of dominance are exploited in formulating the problem.

For example, in modeling the integrated problem of aircraft routing and crew scheduling, Cohn and Barnhart (2003) defined variables representing *complete, feasible solutions to the maintenance-routing problem*, rather than strings representing partial aircraft routings. By doing so, they replace the set of maintenance-routing constraints with a single constraint requiring the selection of a single maintenance-routing solution. In addition to eliminating a large block of constraints, their approach results in an LP relaxation that is tighter than one based on directly integrating the crew and maintenance-routing problems. The key drawback to this approach, however, is the enormous number of new variables—one per feasible maintenance-routing solution. This drawback can be overcome, though, by exploiting the fact that the only components of a maintenance-routing solution relevant to crew scheduling are the short connects it contains. (Recall that a short connect in an aircraft-routing solution is a pair of flights, assigned in succession to the same aircraft, with elapsed time between the two flights allowing sufficient time for crews to connect *only* because they stay on the same aircraft.) Short connects, when used in the crew-pairing solution, reduce crew ground time and potentially result in reduced crew costs.

The problem of finding feasible aircraft routings and minimum-cost crew solutions can therefore be thought of as finding the aircraft-routing solution and its corresponding set of short connects that allows crew costs to be minimized. Conceptualizing the problem in this way, each maintenance-routing solution can be represented by the set of *short connects* it contains. Cohn and Barnhart (2003) reported that in their experiments, a single set of short connects often represented *numerous* different aircraft-routing solutions. The result was that many of the aircraft-routing variables were redundant and could be eliminated, dramatically reducing the size of their model and allowing them to establish tractability.

The number of dominated variables is greatly influenced by variable definition. As the number of decisions encapsulated in a single variable increases, the number of variables increases and the effects of dominance become more pronounced. To illustrate this, again consider the shortest-path problem. Often, shortest-path problems are formulated using "arc-based" variables specifying whether or not an arc is included in a shortest path. An alternate formulation based on subpaths would define variables specifying whether or not a subpath is included in the shortest path. Clearly, the subpath formulation has many more variables than the arc-based formulation. Because any subpath variable except the shortest is dominated, however, the effects of dominance are much more pronounced in the subpath formulation.

Variable Disaggregation. While *aggregated decision variables* arguably are an important mechanism for building tractable schedule-planning models, model tractability is enhanced if these aggregated variables can be *disaggregated* into variables encompassing fewer decisions.

For example, in the enhanced fleet assignment model of Barnhart et al. (2002a), decision variables correspond to subnetworks of flight legs and their assigned fleetings. The subnetworks are constructed to allow an accurate accounting of spill costs, computing spill costs as a function of itinerary flows rather than simply single flight-leg flows. The minimal subnetwork needed to compute spill costs accurately depends on the assignments of fleet types to the flight legs in that subnetwork. For example, if aircraft with relatively many seats are assigned to each flight leg, no spill results and hence spill costs can be computed exactly with subnetworks containing only a single flight leg. Thus, the minimal subnetwork size, and hence the minimal variable size needed to accurately compute spill costs, varies with the fleeting assignment over the subnetwork. Barnhart et al. (2002a) use this observation in developing a variable disaggregation scheme that allowed the elimination, for one test instance, of over 90% of the variables in their enhanced fleet assignment model. This reduction in problem size allowed a previously intractable model to be solved.

3.2. Branch-and-Price Algorithms

Even with variable elimination, disaggregation, and dominance strategies, the number of remaining variables in schedule-planning models is often too large for explicit enumeration. A typical instance of the crew-pairing problem for the domestic operations of major U.S. airlines, for example, will contain *hundreds of billions* of feasible pairings. In such a case, just the enumeration of the variables alone is intractable. Remarkably, *branch-and-price* algorithms, developed specifically for huge integer programs, can be applied successfully to solve to near-optimality even these problems in which complete variable enumeration is not practical.

Like branch-and-bound, branch-and-price is a smart enumeration strategy in which LP relaxations are solved at each node of a branch-and-bound tree to generate bounds on the optimal solution value. What makes branch-and-price particularly well suited to solving airline scheduling problems is the fact that the LPs are solved with a specialized solution approach called *column generation*. Column generation allows very large LPs to be solved without explicitly enumerating all of the variables. With advancements in both optimization techniques and computing capabilities, branch-and-price and column generation algorithms have been widely applied in the past several years, making it possible to consider very large problems in application areas such as transportation, scheduling, and combinatorial optimization (for a survey, see Barnhart et al. 1998b).

Often the strategy is to infuse the optimization process with heuristics. One commonly applied heuristic is to use column generation to solve the root node LP relaxation, and branch-and-bound to solve the *restricted* integer program (IP) containing only the subset of columns generated in solving the LP relaxation. This approach has been applied in solving the international crew-pairing problem studied by Barnhart et al. (1994) and the rostering problem considered by Ryan (1992). Although useful, and sometimes even necessary, this strategy suffers from a major shortcoming; namely, there is no guarantee that a good solution, or even a feasible solution, exists among the subset of columns producing a good LP solution.

Branch-and-price algorithms avoid this pitfall, providing a framework for finding optimal solutions to these large-scale problems. Although theoretically straightforward, the implementations of branch-and-price algorithms are nontrivial, as highlighted in the following sections.

3.2.1. Bounding: Solving the Linear Programming Relaxation.
In branch-and-price, the LP relaxations are solved using *column generation*, a technique

that *implicitly*, rather than explicitly, considers all variables (often referred to as *columns*). Instead of directly solving the *master problem* (the problem with all possible columns), a *restricted master problem* containing only a subset of the original variables is solved. After solving this much smaller problem, the resulting dual information is used to identify columns with negative reduced cost to add to the restricted master problem. The restricted master problem is then re-solved, and the process repeats until no negative reduced-cost columns can be found, and the algorithm terminates with an optimal solution to the master problem.

The key steps of column generation are:

Step 1: Solve the Restricted Master Problem. Find the optimal solution to the current restricted master problem.

Step 2: Solve the Pricing Problem. Generate one or more columns with negative reduced cost. If no columns are found, STOP: The LP relaxation is solved.

Step 3: Construct a New Restricted Master Problem. Add the columns generated in Step 2 to the restricted master problem and return to Step 1.

Solution times for this algorithm are particularly sensitive to both the *number* of iterations of each step and the amount of *time* needed for each iteration. The number of iterations required in turn depends on the set of columns included in the initial restricted master problem as well as the number of columns added at each iteration. Experience shows that jump-starting the solution algorithm with a set of columns corresponding to a good heuristic solution can substantially reduce the number of required iterations. Adding many negative-reduced-cost columns at Step 3, rather than only adding the single most negative-reduced-cost column, typically leads to reductions in the number of iterations as well.

With respect to the amount of time needed to solve each step, significant gains have been made in the past few decades in reducing the times associated with Steps 1 and 3, both of which can be accomplished using standard optimization software. Lustig and Bixby (2001) detail recent advances. In contrast, solving the pricing problem (Step 2) is typically very sensitive to the models and algorithms used to solve it. Often, without tailoring the pricing-problem model and algorithm to exploit special problem structure, even solving the root node LP with column generation can be intractable.

EXAMPLE 5: THE CREW-PAIRING PRICING PROBLEM. In the case of the crew-pairing problem, it *is* in fact possible to identify negative-reduced-cost variables without explicitly pricing them all out. This is done by formulating the pricing problem as a *multi-label shortest-path problem*, with minimum-cost pairings corresponding to shortest paths in an appropriately constructed network. (For a detailed exposition of multilabel shortest-path problems, see Desrochers and Soumis 1988.) Using shortest-path algorithms that exploit dominance characteristics, the shortest paths can be identified without examining all paths, and hence, the minimum reduced-cost pairings can be identified without considering all the pairings.

Although each crew pairing is represented by a network path, only a subset of paths satisfy all of the work rules and thus correspond to feasible pairings. To identify the subset of paths representing pairings, labels are used in the shortest-path algorithm. For example, a label is maintained to track the number of hours of flying in the current day's work and dynamically disallow connections to flights that violate the maximum allowed. For applications of column generation to airline crew scheduling, see Barnhart et al. (1994), Desaulniers et al. (1998), Desrosiers et al. (1991), Gamache and Soumis (1993), Lavoie et al. (1988), Ryan (1992), and Vance et al. (1997).

Even with the shortest-path framework, there are many design decisions to consider. For example, different network representations, such as arcs representing flights or arcs representing sequences of flights comprising a day of work (called a *duty period*), lead to large differences in network sizes and in the number of labels needed in the multilabel shortest-path algorithm. While more compact, networks with flight arcs (Desrosiers et al. 1995) require many more labels than duty period networks (Lavoie et al. 1988, Barnhart et al. 1994, Marsten 1994, Vance et al. 1997). In solving shortest paths in duty period networks, because only *feasible* duty periods are included, all shortest-path labels designed to ensure duty period feasibility are redundant and can be eliminated. The network representation leading to the fastest multilabel shortest-path algorithm will vary, depending on problem size and complexity of work rules.

3.2.2. Branching: Generating Integer Solutions.
The need to blend art with science extends beyond the column generation element of branch-and-price. It is also essential in developing branching strategies that maintain tractability and allow quality integer solutions to be found within reasonable run times.

A particular challenge in branch-and-price algorithms is that the standard branching rule based on variable dichotomy is often difficult to implement. The issue is that once a branching decision is taken, *all* subsequent columns generated in solving the pricing problem *must satisfy* the branching decision. This requires the pricing-problem algorithm to enforce the branching rule. If this can be done without altering the pricing algorithm, then the branching decision and the algorithm are said to be *compatible* and the efficiency of the column generation algorithm is not compromised.

Unfortunately, often the standard branching strategy based on variable dichotomy is NOT compatible with the pricing algorithm. Moreover, the number of branching decisions to prove optimality often is excessive for airline planning problems. To remedy this, just as in the case of column generation, researchers have embedded heuristics within the branch-and-price optimization process. An example is the *variable fixing* approach described in Marsten (1994). To reduce the number of branching decisions taken, variables with fractional values close to one are *fixed* to one sequentially. Marsten (1994) shows that by reducing the number of LPs solved in generating integer solutions, improved solutions can be generated with significantly less computing time and memory.

EXAMPLE 6: A BRANCHING RULE FOR THE CREW-PAIRING PROBLEM. Again consider the crew-pairing problem. Using branching on variable dichotomy, when a pairing variable is set to zero, it cannot be generated by the pricing algorithm, even if its reduced cost is negative. To ensure this, the multilabel shortest-path algorithm must be altered to allow for nondominated paths in the event that the dominant paths have been excluded. This alteration has deep consequences because, in the worst case, *all* pairings have to be generated, leading to an intractable pricing problem.

Instead of branching based on variable dichotomy, the branching rule most commonly used is referred to as *branch-on-follow-ons*, derived from Ryan and Foster (1981). For crew assignment problems, the branching rule is based on pairs of flights, with one flight immediately following the other. One branching decision requires pairings containing either flight to contain *both* flights, and the other decision disallows pairings that contain both flights, with one after the other. Unlike the decisions forcing a pairing in or out of the solution, branch-on-follow-on decisions can be enforced without adversely affecting the performance of the pricing algorithm. Because the decisions are based on pairs of flights, corresponding to arcs in the network, the branching decisions can be enforced by eliminating arcs in the network. This differs from the variable dichotomy branching that affects pairings, or paths in the network. While network arcs can be easily eliminated, network paths cannot.

The branch-on-follow-on decisions are generalizable, as illustrated in Vance et al. (1994) for binary cutting-stock problems, in Savelsbergh (1997) for generalized assignment problems, in Desrochers and Soumis (1989) for urban transit crew-scheduling problems, in Desrosiers et al. (1995) and Savelsbergh and Sol (1995) for vehicle routing and scheduling problems, and in Mehrotra and Trick (1996) for graph-coloring problems.

4. Future Research and Challenges
Notwithstanding the enormous progress made in recent decades in solving the airline problems of schedule design, fleet assignment, maintenance routing, and crew scheduling, significant work remains. Research opportunities that we have identified include the following.

4.1. Core Problems
The development and application of optimization techniques to the problem of flight schedule design has immense potential, but also has equally large modeling and algorithmic challenges. More accurately, modeling the revenue function in fleet assignment problems, and more extensively adapting and applying crew-scheduling approaches to the cabin crew problem, the crew training schedule problem, and the problem of *optimizing* work rules and labor agreements, are additional, important core problem research topics that could lead to improved resource utilization.

4.2. Integrated Scheduling

Integrating crew and fleeting decisions, influencing schedule decisions based on aircraft and crew resources and constraints, and expanding planning models to include other decisions and processes, such as pricing and revenue management, could all have tremendous impacts on airline resource utilization, revenue attainment, and overall profitability. In developing these integrated models, the critical challenge is to find the appropriate balance between model solvability and model scope and realism.

4.3. Robust Planning and Plan Implementation

Thus far, the majority of airline research has focused on developing efficient plans. Even a fully integrated plan, however, can be expected to be suboptimal in practice. This is because plans are based on input data that is assumed to be known and fixed. Weather conditions, mechanical problems, personnel delays and absences, and a host of other unplanned events can lead to disruptions. Moreover, because resources are in most cases highly utilized and interdependent, substantial "snowballing" effects can result from even the smallest disruptions. A delayed flight leg not only impacts subsequent legs scheduled to use the same aircraft, but future flight legs scheduled to use that flight's crew members and passengers on affected flight legs. Thus, one disruption can lead to many downstream disruptions.

Nevertheless, airline plans are typically developed so as to maximize resource utilization. The cost of aircraft implicitly suggests the value of having minimal "ground time" between flights. Similarly, flight crews are paid such that excess time between flights increases costs. An "optimal" airline plan, therefore, is typically one with very limited slack. This lack of slack makes it difficult for disruption to be absorbed in the schedule and limits the number of options for recovery.

It is therefore reasonable to ask "Are optimal plans optimal in practice?" A number of researchers have begun to consider this question, so far with limited results. Before answering this question and identifying the *most robust* minimum-cost solution to a planning problem (that is, the solution that will perform with least cost operationally), researchers must determine the best strategy for quantifying schedule robustness and comparing two plans. This often involves capturing how airlines recover from disruptions—another important question facing both the industry and the OR community.

Given its complexity and size, robust planning is a problem rich in opportunity and potential impact. Most successful work to date focuses on isolating causes of disruption and/or downstream effects, and incorporating within the objective function the goal of decreasing such conditions. One example is the work of Ageeva (2000), who modifies the fleet assignment problem to reward opportunities for swapping planes. Such opportunities can help to localize the impact of a disruption caused by an unavailable aircraft. Another approach to developing more robust fleet assignments is seen in Rosenberger et al. (2001a). They seek to develop solutions containing many short cycles of flights, allowing an airline to limit the number of flights cancelled when a cancellation is necessary. In crew scheduling, Klabjan and Chebalov (2003), similar to Ageeva select crew pairings with crew-swapping opportunities. Schaefer et al. (2001) and Yen and Birge (2001) take a different approach and use stochastic programming to seek more robust crew schedules.

4.4. Operations Recovery

Closely related to the issue of robustness is the airline schedule recovery problem. Given a plan and one or more disruptions, the question is how to recover in an optimal manner. Such problems are, of course, particularly challenging, involving all resources (aircraft, crew, passengers, etc.), and requiring a global view of the system. Moreover, recovery decisions often need to be made in a matter of minutes. Nonetheless, the most technologically advanced airlines have implemented the information infrastructure needed to track all resources and accommodate real-time decision making. This infrastructure, together with progress made to date, suggests that with additional research, the optimization community will be able to deliver fast, high-quality solutions consistently for the integrated aircraft, crew, and passenger recovery problem.

A number of researchers have made initial attempts at addressing this problem, typically considering only a subset of the resources involved in the disruption. Jarrah et al. (1993) consider those schedule disruptions caused by aircraft shortages. Stojkovic et al.

(2002) propose a model that allows for flight delays but not cancellations. Thengvall et al. (2000) propose a multicommodity flow model that permits both delay and cancellation decisions for aircraft recovery. Clarke (1997) proposes a similar multicommodity flow model that focuses on ensuring crew and aircraft maintenance feasible. Rosenberger et al. (2001b) propose an optimization model for aircraft recovery that partially captures passenger connections as well. Yu et al. (2003) have developed an approach to generate near-optimal crew recovery solutions.

Notwithstanding this important body of literature, much important research still remains to be done in this area, as the research community struggles to address the needs of passengers, crews, and aircraft simultaneously, while rapidly determining low-cost solutions.

4.5. Operations Paradigms

Just as deregulation in the 1970s led to significant changes in airline practices (for example, revenue management), the industry continues to face upheavals that necessitate reexamination. Even in the past 12–18 months, major events such as the terrorist attacks of September 11, 2001, and the recent economic downturn, have a wide array of impacts. Changes in security procedures, increasing costs, changing patterns of business passenger willingness to pay, and growth of low-cost competitors, all of these issues affect airline strategy and operations.

Evidence of this can be seen by recent changes to bank structures within hub-and-spoke networks. To increase aircraft and crew utilization, several airlines are considering—or have already shifted to—*depeaked* flight schedules, spreading out the arrivals and departures of aircraft at hubs over time. A depeaked schedule allows more efficient utilization of aircraft (with less time spent waiting on the ground for connecting passengers, and shorter arrival and departure queues on the ground) and spreads the workload of ground personnel and equipment more evenly throughout the day, thereby eliminating the need for additional resources during peak periods. The disadvantage of this strategy is less coordinated, longer average passenger connection times at hubs. Related research questions involve restructuring of the revenue model to account for schedule performance, both planned and operational. Optimization is playing, and can continue to play, an important role in assessing the systemwide cost and service impacts of this, and numerous other, operating paradigm shifts.

References

Abara, J. 1989. Applying integer linear programming to the fleet assignment problem. *Interfaces* **19**(4) 20–28.

Ageeva, Y. 2000. Approaches to incorporating robustness into airline scheduling. MIT thesis, Cambridge, MA.

Anbil, R., E. Gelman, B. Patty, R. Tanga. 1991. Recent advances in crew-pairing optimization at American Airlines. *Interfaces* **21** 62–74.

Armacost, A., C. Barnhart, K. Ware. 2002. Composite variable formulations for express shipment service network design. *Transportation Sci.* **36**(1) 1–20.

Barnhart, C., A. Farahat, M. Lohatepanont. 2002a. Airline fleet assignment with enhanced revenue modeling: An alternative model and solution approach. Working paper, Operations Research Center, MIT, Cambridge, MA.

Barnhart, C., T. Kniker, M. Lohatepanont. 2002b. Itinerary-based airline fleet assignment. *Transportation Sci.* **36**(2) 199–217.

Barnhart, C., F. Lu, R. Shenoi. 1998a. Integrated airline scheduling. G. Yu, ed. *Operations Research in the Air Industry*. International Series in *Operations Research and Management Science*, Vol. 9, 384–403.

Barnhart, C., E. Johnson, R. Anbil, L. Hatay. 1994. A column generation technique for the long-haul crew assignment problem. T. Ciriano, R. Leachman, eds. *Optimization in Industry: Vol. II*. Wiley, New York, 7–22.

Barnhart, C., E. Johnson, G. Nemhauser, M. Savelsbergh, P. Vance. 1998b. Branch-and-price: Column generation for solving huge integer programs. *Oper. Res.* **46**(3) 316–329.

Barnhart, C., N. Boland, L. Clarke, E. Johnson, G. Nemhauser, R. Shenoi. 1998c. Flight string models for aircraft fleeting and routing. *Transportation Sci.* **32**(3) 208–220.

Barnhart, C., A. M. Cohn, E. L. Johnson, D. Klabjan, G. L. Nemhauser, P. H. Vance. 2003. Airline crew scheduling. Randolph W. Hall, ed. *Handbook of Transportation Science*, 2nd ed. Kluwer Academic Publishers, Norwell, MA.

Butchers, E. R., P. R. Day, A. P. Goldie, S. Miller, J. A. Meyer, D. M. Ryan, A. C. Scott, C. A. Wallace. 2001. Optimized crew scheduling at Air New Zealand. *Interfaces* **31** 30–56.

Cappanera, P., G. Gallo. 2001. On the airline crew rostering problem. Technical Report TR-01-08, Department of Computer Science, University of Pisa, Italy.

Caprara, A., P. Toth, M. Fischetti, D. Vigo. 1998. Modeling and solving the crew rostering problem. *Oper. Res.* **46** 820–830.

Christou, I. T., A. Zakarian, J. Liu, H. Carter. 1999. A two-phase genetic algorithm for large-scale bidline-generation problems at Delta Air Lines. *Interfaces* **29** 51–65.

Clarke, L., C. Hane, E. Johnson, G. Nemhauser. 1996a. Maintenance and crew considerations in fleet assignment. *Transportation Sci.* **30**(3) 249–260.

Clarke, L., E. Johnson, G. Nemhauser, Z. Zhu. 1996b. The aircraft rotation problem. *Ann. Oper. Res.* **69** 33–46.

Clarke, M. 1997. Development of heuristic procedures for flight rescheduling in the aftermath of irregular operations. Working paper, Department of Aeronautical/Astronautical Engineering, MIT, Cambridge, MA.

Clarke, M., B. Smith. 2000. The impact of operations research on the evolution of the airline industry: A review of the airline planning process. Research paper, Sabre Inc., Dallas, TX.

Cohn, A., C. Barnhart. 2002. Composite-variable modeling for service parts logistics. Submitted to *Ann. Oper. Res.*

Cohn, A., C. Barnhart. 2003. Improving crew scheduling by incorporating key maintenance routing decisions. *Oper. Res.* **51** 387–396.

Cook, T. 2000. Creating competitive advantage using model-driven support systems. Presentation in the *MIT Global Airline Indust. Study Distinguished Speaker Sem. Ser.*, Cambridge, MA.

Cordeau, J., G. Stojkociv, F. Soumis, J. Desrosiers. 2000. Benders decomposition for simultaneous aircraft routing and crew scheduling. Technical Report G-2000-37, GERAD, École Polytechnique de Montréal, Québec, Canada.

Dawid, H., J. König, C. Strauss. 2001. An enhanced rostering model for airline crews. *Comput. Oper. Res.* **28** 671–688.

Day, P. R., D. M. Ryan. 1997. Flight attendant rostering for short-haul airline operations. *Oper. Res.* **45** 649–661.

Desaulniers, G., J. Desrosiers, M. Gamache, F. Soumis. 1998. Crew scheduling in air transportation. T. Crainic, G. Laporte, eds. *Fleet Management and Logistics*. Kluwer Academic Publishers, Boston, MA, 169–185.

Desrochers, M., F. Soumis. 1988. A generalized permanent labeling algorithm for the shortest path problem with time windows. *INFOR* **26** 191–212.

Desrochers, M., F. Soumis. 1989. A column generation approach to the urban transit crew scheduling problem. *Transportation Sci.* **23** 1–13.

Desrosiers, J., Y. Dumas, M. M. Solomon, F. Soumis. 1995. Time constrained routing and scheduling. *Vehicle Routing*, North-Holland, Amsterdam.

Desrosiers, J., Y. Dumas, M. Desrochers, F. Soumis, B. Sanso, P. Trudeau. 1991. A breakthrough in airline crew scheduling. Report G-91-11, GERAD, Montréal, Canada.

Erdmann, A., A. Noltemeier, R. Schrader. 1999. Modeling and solving the airline schedule generation problem. Technical Report zpr99-351, ZAIK, University of Cologne, Germany.

Gamache, M., F. Soumis. 1993. A method for optimally solving the rostering problem. Les Cahier du GERAD, G-90-40, École des Hautes Études Commerciales, Montréal, Canada.

Gamache, M., F. Soumis, D. Villeneuve, J. Desrosiers, E. Gélinas. 1998. The preferential bidding system at Air Canada. *Transportation Sci.* **32** 246–255.

Gershkoff, I. 1989. Optimizing flight crew schedules. *Interfaces* **19** 29–43.

Gopalan, R., K. Talluri. 1998. The aircraft maintenance routing problem. *Oper. Res.* **46** 260–271.

Hane, C. A., C. Barnhart, E. L. Johnson, R. E. Marsten, G. L. Nemhauser, G. Sigismondi. 1995. The fleet assignment problem: Solving a large-scale integer program. *Math. Programming* **70** 211–232.

Hoffman, K. L., M. Padberg. 1993. Solving airline crew-scheduling problems by branch-and-cut. *Management Sci.* **39** 657–682.

Jacobs, T. L., E. L. Johnson, B. C. Smith. 1999. O&D FAM: Incorporating passenger flows into the fleeting process. *AGIFORS Sympos.*, New Orleans, LA.

Jarrah, A., G. Yu, N. Krishnamurthy, A. Rakshit. 1993. A decision support framework for airline flight cancellations and delays. *Transportation Sci.* **27**(3) 266–280.

Klabjan, J., S. Chebalov. 2003. Robust airline crew pairing optimization. *FAA-NEXTOR–INFORMS Sympos.*, Falls Church, VA.

Kohl, N., S. E. Karisch. 2002. Airline crew rostering: Problem types, modeling, and optimization. Working paper, Carmen Consulting, Copenhagen, Denmark.

Lavoie, S., M. Minoux, E. Odier. 1988. A new approach for crew pairing problems by column generation with an application to air transportation. *Eur. J. Oper. Res.* **35** 45–58.

Lohatepanont, M., C. Barnhart. 2001. Airline schedule planning: Integrated models and algorithms for schedule design and fleet assignment. *Transportation Sci.* Forthcoming.

Lustig, I., R. Bixby. 2001. A historical perspective on linear programming performance. http://www.ilog.com/products/optimization/times_winter2001/tech_historical.cfm.

Marsten, R. 1994. Crew planning at Delta Airlines. *Math. Programming Sympos. XV*, Ann Arbor, MI.

Martin, R. C. 1999. *Large Scale Linear and Integer Optimization: A Unified Approach*. Kluwer Academic Press, Norwell, MA.

Mehrotra, A., M. A. Trick. 1996. A column generation approach for exact graph coloring. *INFORMS J. Comput.* **8** 344–354.

Patty, B., E. Gelman, R. Tanga, R. Anbil. 1991. Recent advances in crew-pairing optimization at American Airlines. *Interfaces* **21** 62–74.

Proussaloglou, K. E., F. S. Koppelman. 1995. Air carrier demand: An analysis of market share determinants. *Transportation* **22** 371–388.

Proussaloglou, K. E., F. S. Koppelman. 1999. The choice of carrier, flight and fare class. *J. Air Transport Management* **5**(4) 193–201.

Rexing, B., C. Barnhart, T. Kniker, A. Jarrah, N. Krishnamurthy. 2000. Airline fleet assignment with time windows. *Transportation Sci.* **34**(1) 1–20.

Rosenberger, J., E. Johnson, G. Nemhauser. 2001a. A robust fleet assignment model with hub isolation and short cycles. Working paper, SISE, Georgia Institute of Technology, Atlanta, GA.

Rosenberger, J., E. Johnson, G. Nemhauser. 2001b. Rerouting aircraft for airline recovery. Working paper, SISE, Georgia Institute of Technology, Atlanta, GA.

Rushmeier, R., S. Kontogiorgis. 1997. Advances in the optimization of airline fleet assignment. *Transportation Sci.* **31**(2) 159–169.

Ryan, D. M. 1992. The solution of massive generalized set partitioning problems in air crew rostering. *J. Oper. Res. Soc.* **43** 459–467.

Ryan, D. M., B. A. Foster. 1981. An integer programming approach to scheduling. A. Wren, ed. *Computer Scheduling of Public Transport Urban Passenger Vehicle and Crew Scheduling*. North-Holland, Amsterdam, The Netherlands, 269–280.

Savelsbergh, M. W. P. 1997. A branch-and-price algorithm for the generalized assignment problem. *Oper. Res.* **45** 831–841.

Savelsbergh, M. W. P., M. Sol. 1995. The general pickup and delivery problem. *Transportation Sci.* **29** 17–29.

Schaefer, A., E. Johnson, A. Kleywegt, G. Nemhauser. 2001. Airline crew scheduling under uncertainty. Working paper, SISE, Georgia Institute of Technology, Atlanta, GA.

Smith, B. C., J. F. Leimkuhler, R. M. Darrow. 1992. Yield management at American Airlines. *Interfaces* **22** 8–31.

Stojkovic, G., F. Soumis, J. Desrosiers, M. Solomon. 2002. An optimization model for a real-time flight scheduling problem. *Transportation Res.* **36A** 779–788.

Thengvall, B., G. Yu, J. Bard. 2000. Balancing user preferences for aircraft schedule recovery during irregular airline operations. *IIE Trans.* **32** 181–193.

Vance, P. H., C. Barnhart, E. L. Johnson, G. L. Nemhauser. 1994. Solving binary cutting stock problems by column generation and branch-and-bound. *Comput. Optim. Appl.* **3** 111–130.

Vance, P. H., C. Barnhart, E. L. Johnson, G. L. Nemhauser. 1997. Airline crew scheduling: A new formulation and decomposition algorithm. *Oper. Res.* **45** 188–200.

Vanderbeck, F. 2000. On Dantzig-Wolfe decomposition in integer programming and ways to perform branching in a branch-and-price algorithm. *Oper. Res.* **48** 111–128.

Wiper, D. S., J. D. Quillinan, R. Subramanian, R. P. Scheff, Jr., R. E. Marsten. 1994. Coldstart: Fleet assignment at Delta Air Lines. *Interfaces* **24** 104–120.

Yen, J., J. Birge. 2001. A stochastic programming approach to the airline crew scheduling problem. Submitted to *Oper. Res.*

Yu, G., M. Argüello, G. Song, S. McCowan, A. White. 2003. A new era for crew recovery at Continental Airlines. *Interfaces* **33** 5–22.

14

Daily Aircraft Routing and Scheduling

Guy Desaulniers • Jacques Desrosiers • Yvan Dumas
Marius M. Solomon • François Soumis

In this paper we consider the daily aircraft routing and scheduling problem (DARSP). It consists of determining daily schedules which maximize the anticipated profits derived from the aircraft of a heterogeneous fleet. This fleet must cover a set of operational flight legs with known departure time windows, durations and profits according to the aircraft type. We present two models for this problem: a Set Partitioning type formulation and a time constrained multicommodity network flow formulation. We describe the network structure of the subproblem when a column generation technique is applied to solve the linear relaxation of the first model and when a Dantzig-Wolfe decomposition approach is used to solve the linear relaxation of the second model. The linear relaxation of the first model provides upper bounds. Integer solutions to the overall problem are derived through branch-and-bound. By exploiting the equivalence between the two formulations, we propose various optimal branching strategies compatible with the column generation technique. Finally we report computational results obtained on data provided by two different airlines. These results show that significant profit improvement can be generated by solving the DARSP using our approach and that this can be obtained in a reasonable amount of CPU time.
(*Air Transportation; Routing; Scheduling; Column Generation; Dantzig-Wolfe Decomposition; Multicommodity Network*)

1. Introduction

In this paper, we consider the problem faced by an airline needing to construct daily schedules for a heterogeneous aircraft fleet. An aircraft schedule consists of a sequence of flight legs to be carried out by an aircraft (the routing aspect) and the exact times at which these flight legs must start and end (the scheduling aspect). This daily aircraft routing and scheduling problem (DARSP) is very important for an airline since a fleet schedule determines a large part of the airline cost estimates including the fixed cost for each aircraft, the cost of the fuel consumed and the salaries of the crew members. Furthermore, the total revenue of the airline derived from a given fleet schedule can also be estimated if a demand function is known for each flight leg to be flown.

Obviously, different aircraft schedules lead to different costs and revenues for the airline. For example, a flight leg that can be flown by two aircraft of different capacities can result in a loss of revenue if the smaller aircraft is chosen when the demand for the leg exceeds the smaller aircraft's capacity. There can be a significant difference in profits between two daily schedules that require different aircraft fleet sizes since the fixed cost of an aircraft is very high. Therefore, substantial cost reductions and revenue increases can be achieved by optimally solving the DARSP. Such a superior profit position is an immediate necessity for any airline participating in today's extremely competitive market. Nevertheless, as the DARSP is a highly complex problem, its optimal solution and the benefits stemming from it cannot be achieved without the use of sophisticated mathematical programming tools as the ones we are about to develop in this paper.

1.1. Problem Description

The definition of the DARSP varies across the literature because many factors influence the costs and revenues of a fleet schedule and numerous types of constraints can be taken into account while constructing such a schedule. An extended version of the problem can include the selection of the flight legs to fly, their frequency and departure times, as well as the collective agreements which regulate the salaries of the crew members and, consequently, affect the costs of a fleet schedule. Unfortunately, such a version is very unlikely to be solved even for small airlines since the combinatorial aspect of the problem plays a highly significant role. In this paper, we will consider the following definition of DARSP:

Given a heterogeneous aircraft fleet, a set of operational flight legs over a one-day horizon, departure time windows, durations and costs / revenues according to the aircraft type for each flight leg, find a fleet schedule that maximizes profits and satisfies certain additional constraints.

A solution to this problem specifies the aircraft type and the departure time for each operational flight leg. It also provides the routing for each aircraft consisting of a sequence of flight legs and ground connections. Generally, when significant changes are made to flight departure times, there is an impact on the demand for those flights and consequently on the revenue. However, when flight departure time window width remains fairly narrow, it is realistic to assume that this will not impact demand. We make this flight departure time independence assumption throughout the paper.

The revenue derived from a flight leg also depends on the aircraft capacities of connecting legs. For example, if a small aircraft is assigned to a leg, this may reduce the number of passengers on the subsequent connecting legs and hence lower the revenues derived from these. Taking into account this type of dependence, Farkas and Belobaba (1995) obtained additional profit improvements of about 1% for fixed time-tabled flights.

Although this aspect of the problem is interesting, it will not be considered in this paper as it creates difficulties that cannot be addressed with current techniques.

Some additional constraints that can be considered in the DARSP are: the number of available aircraft for each type, the restrictions on certain aircraft types at certain times and stations (e.g., curfews), the required thrus (i.e., connections between two flight legs imposed by the airline) and the limits on daily service at certain stations. The problem may also include the possibility of using shorter than normal connection times between two flight legs and the possibility of adding flight legs selected from a set of potential flight legs to daily schedules.

If the set of flight legs is balanced (i.e., at each station there are as many arrivals as there are departures of the same type), one can further impose at each station the availability of an equal number of aircraft of each type at the beginning and at the end of the day. However, because of time window width, these conditions do not ensure a periodic schedule, i.e., replicable every day. Consider for example, a flight leg that spans part of two consecutive days, i.e., it is in progress at the time junction of these two days. Even though at the end of the first day, the set of flight legs is balanced, this leg may still not be able to depart due to a deficit of aircraft. This is created by another leg which, while arriving in its time window, does so later than the departure time of the first leg. Since passenger demand varies daily and the flights offered depend on the day of week, we do not impose that the schedule be periodic. The periodic daily aircraft routing and scheduling problem is much more difficult as it will be seen from the brief discussion given in §6.

1.2. Literature Review

The literature on the DARSP and related problems dates back to the early 1960s. Most of the papers until the early 1980s have considered small airline problems or parts of the extended version of the problem such as determining the flights to be flown, or their frequency, or scheduling the aircraft using predetermined routes. Furthermore, most of these papers do not consider multiple aircraft types, departure time windows or the additional constraints of the DARSP mentioned above. They use heuristic solution approaches since computers were much less powerful at that time. The survey of Etschmaier and Mathaisel (1984) provides a good review of these papers.

Levin (1971) was the first to have proposed a model for the DARSP that included variable departure times for the flight legs. The departure times could only take the finite number of values obtained by discretizing the time windows of the corresponding flight legs. The problem was formulated as an integer linear program with bundle constraints. An interesting aspect of this formulation is that the linear relaxation resulted in an integer solution most of the time. However, this model does not consider multiple aircraft capacities, nor the additional constraints of the DARSP. Agin and Cullen (1975) have treated transportation routing and vehicle loading problems. They presented a mixed integer programming model, similar to a multicommodity network flow model, that can be adapted to DARSP using a discretization of the time windows. It is solved using a heuristic based on Dantzig-Wolfe decomposition. For each aircraft, there is one subproblem that generates promising routes; when such a route is added to the master problem, the previous route of the corresponding aircraft is deleted. Hence, the integrality requirement that a single route be assigned to each aircraft is always satisfied.

Recently, Abara (1989) has proposed an integer linear programming approach to solve the DARSP with fixed flight departure times. The model is a multicommodity network flow problem with additional constraints to limit, for example, the number of aircraft overnighting or the number of slots used at a station. The author does not specify the technique used to solve this large integer program, but reports good results for real-life problems at American Airlines.

Hane et al. (1995) have also presented a multicommodity network flow model to solve the DARSP without departure time windows. Their model used an aggregation of the flow variables of Abara's model (see §4) and hence is adequate to determine the aircraft type assigned to each flight leg. Their approach consists of a cost perturbation strategy, an interior point LP algorithm and a heuristic branch-and-bound procedure based on a generalized upper-bound dichotomy branching rule. The interior point algorithm is only used to solve the linear relaxation of the problem at the root node of the search tree. The authors report successful computational experience on instances of the DARSP containing more than 2,500 flight legs. Similar model and solution approach have also been used by Subramanian et al. (1994).

The problem instances we consider cannot be directly compared in size to those treated by Hane et al. (1995) since departure times are variable in this paper and fixed in their approach. Moreover, Hane et al. have taken advantage of the hub-and-spoke network underlying their problems. Such a network structure permits to fix many connections a priori, thus reducing the size of the problem to optimize. This structure is not present in the instances considered hereafter.

1.3. Overview and Contribution of the Paper

We present two equivalent formulations for the DARSP. Both integer programming models are solved by branch-and-bound. In the first model, we define a binary variable for each possible schedule for an aircraft type giving rise to a large Set Partitioning type problem (§2). To obtain upper bounds, we optimally solve its linear relaxation using a column generation approach. For each type of aircraft, there is one subproblem that generates promising schedules. The subproblem's solution is obtained by solving a longest path problem with time windows. We describe the underlying time-space network in detail in §3.

In the second model, a binary variable represents a possible connection between two flight legs performed by a particular aircraft. For each aircraft type, we define these variables on a time-space network identical to the one used in the column generation solution approach of the first model. This second formulation gives rise to a multicommodity network flow model with the usual flow variables and also time variables (§4). Abara (1989) and to some extent, Hane et al. (1995) have developed special cases of this generalized model. Our model can include all constraints considered to date in addition to flexible departure times.

The second formulation also provides the fundamental concepts necessary to develop optimal branching strategies compatible with the column generation solution approach used for the first model (§5). This mechanism is not well known in the literature as noted, for example, by Chvàtal (1983, pp. 197–198) in the context of the Cutting-Stock problem. As shown in the survey by Desrosiers et al. (1995), multicommodity network flow type models can also be used for many other fixed or variable time constrained vehicle routing and crew scheduling problems. In this regard, we consider some important extensions of the DARSP model in §6. Finally, §7 presents the computational results we have obtained on real-world test problems and §8 presents our conclusions.

2. A Set Partitioning Type Formulation

In this section, we formulate the DARSP as a Set Partitioning problem with additional constraints. We also propose a solution strategy to solve the linear relaxation of this formulation.

2.1. Notation

Let N be the set of operational flight legs and K the set of aircraft types. Denote by n^k the number of available aircraft of type $k \in K$. Define Ω^k, indexed by p, as the set of feasible schedules for aircraft of type $k \in K$ and let index $p = 0$ denote the empty schedule for an aircraft. Next associate with each schedule $p \in \Omega^k$ the value c_p^k denoting the anticipated profit if this schedule is assigned to an aircraft of type $k \in K$ and a_{ip}^k a binary constant equal to 1 if this schedule covers flight leg $i \in N$ and 0 otherwise. Furthermore, let S be the set of stations and $S^k \subseteq S$ the subset having the facilities to serve aircraft of type $k \in K$. Then, define o_{sp}^k and d_{sp}^k to equal to 1 if schedule p, $p \in \Omega^k$, starts and ends respectively at station s, $s \in S^k$, and 0 otherwise.

Denote by θ_p^k, $p \in \Omega^k \setminus \{0\}$, $k \in K$, the binary decision variable which takes the value 1 if schedule p is assigned to an aircraft of type k, and 0 otherwise. Finally, let θ_0^k, $k \in K$, be a nonnegative integer variable which gives the number of unused aircraft of type k.

2.2. Formulation

Using these definitions, the DARSP can be formulated as:

$$\text{Maximize} \sum_{k \in K} \sum_{p \in \Omega^k} c_p^k \theta_p^k \quad (1)$$

subject to:

$$\sum_{k \in K} \sum_{p \in \Omega^k} a_{ip}^k \theta_p^k = 1 \quad \forall i \in N, \quad (2)$$

$$\sum_{p \in \Omega^k} (d_{sp}^k - o_{sp}^k)\theta_p^k = 0 \quad \forall k \in K, \forall s \in S^k, \quad (3)$$

$$\sum_{p \in \Omega^k} \theta_p^k = n^k \quad \forall k \in K, \quad (4)$$

$$\theta_p^k \geq 0 \quad \forall k \in K, \forall p \in \Omega^k, \quad (5)$$

$$\theta_p^k \text{ integer} \quad \forall k \in K, \forall p \in \Omega^k. \quad (6)$$

The objective function (1) states that we wish to maximize the total anticipated profit. Constraints (2) require that each operational flight leg be covered exactly once. Constraints (3) correspond to the flow conservation constraints at the beginning and the end of the day at each station and for each aircraft type. Constraints (4) limit the number of aircraft of type $k \in K$ that can be used to the number available. Finally, constraints (5) and (6) state that the decision variables are nonnegative integers. This model is a Set Partitioning problem with additional constraints.

2.3. Solution Strategy

We have chosen a branch-and-bound approach. Branching strategies will be explored in detail in §5. Upper bounds are obtained by utilizing a column generation technique to solve the linear relaxation (1)–(5) of this problem (see Lasdon 1970). The technique consists of dividing a linear program into a restricted master problem and a subproblem. The role of the restricted master problem, consisting in the present case of the linear program (1)–(5) defined over a relatively small number of feasible schedules, is to find a current optimal solution and to compute the dual variables associated with this current solution. It can be solved using the simplex algorithm.

On the other hand, the subproblem is used to test whether the current solution is optimal over all possible schedules, i.e., over $\bigcup_{k \in K} \Omega^k$. The subproblem is a longest path problem with time windows which uses the dual variables of the current optimal solution of the master problem. If the current solution is not optimal, the subproblem must provide a new feasible schedule to be added to the restricted master problem. The subproblem can be solved using dynamic programming (Desrosiers et al. 1983, Desrochers and Soumis 1988a, b).

For additional applications of the column generation technique to various vehicle routing and crew scheduling problems, the reader is referred to the survey paper by Desrosiers et al. (1995).

3. The Subproblem Network Structure

A specific network $G^k = (V^k, A^k)$, where V^k is the set of nodes and A^k is the set of arcs, is used for each aircraft type $k \in K$ to generate feasible schedules. The same networks will also be used later for the time constrained multicommodity network flow model. Each network contains five node types and seven arc types as illustrated in Figure 1.

3.1. The Nodes

The five node types in V^k are: *source, sink, initial station, final station* and *flight*. There is a single source node $o(k)$ and a single sink node $d(k)$. These two nodes represent the start and the end, respectively, of all paths corresponding to the schedules for aircraft type $k \in K$. An initial station node $s \in S^k$ and a final station node $t \in S^k$ indicate the stations where a schedule starts and ends, respectively. The sets of initial and final station nodes are denoted by S_1^k and S_2^k, respectively. Remark that these two sets contain the same stations due to the flow conservation constraints for each aircraft type at each station. Finally, a flight node i ($i \in N^k \subseteq N$) simply represents an operational flight leg to be flown. There can be several nodes representing the same flight leg in different networks when this leg can be flown by different types of aircraft. To summarize, the set of nodes in G^k is given by:

$$V^k = N^k \cup S_1^k \cup S_2^k \cup \{o(k), d(k)\}.$$

3.2. The Arcs

The seven arc types in A^k are: *empty, source, sink, schedule start, schedule end, turn* and *short turn*. There is a single empty arc $(o(k), d(k))$ which represents an empty aircraft schedule. This arc forms the set OD^k. Note that this empty arc $(o(k), d(k))$ can be removed from A^k since the corresponding empty schedule variable θ_0^k can be introduced with cost c_0^k in the restricted master problem prior to the column generation process. A source arc $(o(k), s)$, $s \in S_1^k$, part of the arc set denoted by OS_1^k, goes from the source node to an initial station node. A sink arc $(s, d(k))$, $s \in S_2^k$, belonging to the arc set S_2D^k, links a final

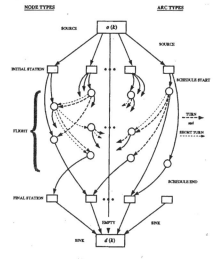

Figure 1. The Nodes and the Arcs of Network G^k

station node to the sink node. A schedule start arc (s, j), $s \in S_1^k$, $j \in N^k$, part of the arc set S_1N^k, begins at an initial station node and ends at a flight node whose origin is station s. Similarly, a schedule end arc (i, s), $i \in N^k$, $s \in S_2^k$, belonging to the arc set NS_2^k, goes from a flight node to the final station node where this flight leg ends. A turn arc (i, j), i and $j \in N^k$, included in the arc set NN^k, links two flight nodes and simply represents a normal connection between these two flight legs. Such an arc exists between two flight nodes if the flight legs can be flown consecutively by the same aircraft while respecting the time windows of each flight leg and the normal connection time of the aircraft at the connecting station. Formally, let a_i^k be the earliest time at which leg i can start, b_j^k the latest time at which leg j can start, l_i^k the duration of leg i, and t_{ij}^k the normal connection time between legs i and j. Then, there exists a turn arc between flight nodes i and j in G^k if $a_i^k + l_i^k + t_{ij}^k \leq b_j^k$, and the arrival station of leg i is the same as the departure station of leg j. Finally, short (or quick) turn arcs, belonging to the arc set denoted by NQN^k, are turn arcs involving a connection time s_{ij}^k that is shorter than normal, i.e., $s_{ij}^k < t_{ij}^k$. Such an arc exists if $a_i^k + l_i^k + s_{ij}^k \leq b_j^k$. This may be the only arc between nodes i and j, or a turn arc may also exist. Note that if $b_i^k + l_i^k + t_{ij}^k \leq a_j^k$, there is no need to include a short turn arc because a normal connection always fits. Since normal connection times are preferable to short connection times, short turn arcs incur penalty costs. To conclude, the set of arcs in G^k is given by:

$$A^k = OD^k \cup OS_1^k \cup S_1 N^k \cup NN^k$$
$$\cup NQN^k \cup NS_2^k \cup S_2 D^k.$$

A schedule generated by the subproblem must meet two requirements: it must be feasible and its marginal profit must be positive. To test whether these requirements are satisfied, information is kept on each arc concerning the duration of the activities on the arc and the costs/revenues related to these activities.

3.3. Schedule Feasibility

The feasibility of a schedule is tested in the longest path algorithm using constrained time variables representing the departure times of the flight legs. To be feasible, schedules must satisfy time window constraints concerning the departure times. That is, for each flight leg j, the value of the corresponding time variable must be within the time window $[a_j^k, b_j^k]$. Hence, to compute the values of the time variables and test schedule feasibility, we are required to know the duration of the activities (flight legs and connections) on each arc of the network. We have chosen to place the duration of a flight leg on the arc leaving the flight node. Table 1 summarizes the duration of each arc type and the additional information described below.

3.4. The Cost/Revenue Structure

The longest path algorithm finds a feasible schedule with the largest marginal profit. The marginal profit is calculated using the revenue and cost of each activity and the dual variables associated with the current optimal solution of the restricted master problem. The anticipated cost of an empty schedule for a type k aircraft is e_o^k, so the profit coefficient on arc $(o(k), d(k))$ is $-e_o^k$, $k \in K$. Next, the profit of flight leg j is placed on every arc leaving flight node j. This profit is equal to $r_i^k - e_i^k$, where r_i^k and e_i^k are the anticipated revenue and cost, respectively, if flight leg $i \in N^k$ is assigned to an aircraft of type $k \in K$. To favor normal connections between flight legs, a penalty q_{ij}^k is imposed on the arc between legs i and j in G^k if this is a short turn arc. Finally, to minimize the number of aircraft required to cover all operational flight legs, a large fixed cost M is placed on every source arc. For a fixed fleet, the source arcs are assigned a zero profit.

In addition to revenues and costs, the dual variables must be placed on the appropriate arcs in the network. Let α_i, σ_s^k, and β^k, $\forall i \in N$, $\forall k \in K$, and $\forall s \in S^k$, be the dual variables associated with constraints (2), (3), and (4), respectively. The marginal profit $\bar{c}_p^k$ of a schedule $p \in \Omega^k$ is calculated as:

$$\bar{c}_p^k = c_p^k - \sum_{i \in N^k} \alpha_i a_{ip}^k - \sum_{s \in S^k} \sigma_s^k (d_{sp}^k - o_{sp}^k) - \beta^k, \quad (7)$$

where c_p^k, the anticipated profit of schedule p, is equal to the sum of the profits on the arcs forming the path corresponding to schedule p. Consequently, to correctly compute the marginal profit of a schedule $p \in \Omega^k$ using a longest path algorithm, the following values must be assigned to the appropriate arcs of G^k: $-\alpha_i$, $i \in N^k$, on all arcs leaving flight node i, $-\beta^k$ on all source arcs and

Table 1   The Information Associated with Each Arc in A^k

Arcs	Type	Set	Duration	Profit	Dual Variables
$(o(k), d(k))$	Empty	OD^k	0	$-e_o^k$	$-\beta^k$
$(o(k), s)$, $s \in S_1^k$	Source	OS_1^k	0	$-M$ or 0	$-\beta^k$
(s, j), $s \in S_1^k$, $j \in N^k$	Schedule Start	$S_1 N^k$	0	0	σ_s^k
(i, j), i and $j \in N^k$	Turn	NN^k	$f_i^k + t_{ij}^k$	$r_i^k - e_i^k$	$-\alpha_i$
(i, j), i and $j \in N^k$	Short Turn	NQN^k	$f_i^k + s_{ij}^k$	$r_i^k - e_i^k - q_{ij}^k$	$-\alpha_i$
(i, s), $i \in N^k$, $s \in S_2^k$	Schedule End	NS_2^k	f_i^k	$r_i^k - e_i^k$	$-\alpha_i - \sigma_s^k$
$(s, d(k))$, $s \in S_2^k$	Sink	$S_2 D^k$	0	0	0

on the empty arc, $-\sigma_s^k$, $s \in S_2^k$, on all final station arcs entering the final station node s, and σ_s^k, $s \in S_1^k$, on all initial station arcs leaving the initial station node s.

3.5. Specialized Representations

The definition of a flight leg can be extended to include sequences of consecutive operational flight legs that must be assigned to the same aircraft as required by the airline. Such a sequence is called a thru and only one covering constraint (2) is necessary in the Set Partitioning type formulation of §2 to account for all operational flight legs in it. Similarly, if such a thru can be assigned to an aircraft of type $k \in K$, then only one flight node is necessary to represent it in G^k.

In this paper, we assume that the networks G^k, for all $k \in K$, are acyclic since time windows of relatively small width are considered. If this was not the case, any G^k could be transformed into an acyclic network by dividing the time windows of the nodes included in cycles and creating a distinct node copy for each subdivision. This is equivalent to having several time windows for the service at customers in the time constrained vehicle routing problem (Desrochers et al. 1992).

Other network representations such as time-line networks described in Barnhart et al. (1991) for crew scheduling problems and in Hane et al. (1995) for aircraft routing problems can be equivalently used. The network defined in this section was preferred over the others because it simplifies the presentation of the following multicommodity network flow formulation.

4. A Time Constrained Multicommodity Network Flow Formulation

This section formulates the DARSP as a time constrained multicommodity network flow formulation. First we introduce the notation which is followed by the formulation. Next we discuss a solution strategy to solve it. In the next section, we will refer to this formulation to design branching strategies for the Set Partitioning type formulation (1)–(6).

4.1. Notation

First, let X_{ij}^k be the integer flow variable corresponding to type k aircraft, $k \in K$, on the arc $(i, j) \in A^k$. This variable indicates the number of type k aircraft using arc (i, j). Next, let T_i^k, $k \in K$, be a time variable defined at node $i \in V^k$. If $i \in N^k$, this variable is the departure time of flight leg i within the time interval $[a_i^k, b_i^k]$. Otherwise, it is fixed at 0 for all source and initial station nodes and corresponds to the latest arrival time at all final station and sink nodes. Denote by d_{ij}^k the duration of the activities on arc $(i, j) \in A^k$ depending on the aircraft type $k \in K$. These arc durations have already been presented in Table 1.

4.2. Formulation

The proposed time-constrained multicommodity network flow formulation is given by:

$$\text{Maximize} \sum_{k \in K} \sum_{(i,j) \in A^k} c_{ij}^k X_{ij}^k \quad (8)$$

subject to:

$$\sum_{k \in K} \sum_{j:(i,j) \in A^k} X_{ij}^k = 1 \quad \forall i \in N, \quad (9)$$

$$\sum_{i:(i,s) \in NS_2^k} X_{is}^k - \sum_{j:(s,j) \in S_1 N^k} X_{sj}^k = 0 \quad \forall k \in K, \forall s \in S^k, \quad (10)$$

$$\sum_{s \in S_1^k} X_{o(k),s}^k + X_{o(k),d(k)}^k = n^k \quad \forall k \in K, \quad (11)$$

$$\sum_{i:(i,j) \in A^k} X_{ij}^k - \sum_{l:(j,l) \in A^k} X_{jl}^k = 0$$

$$\forall k \in K, \forall j \in V^k \setminus \{o(k), d(k)\}, \quad (12)$$

$$\sum_{s \in S_2^k} X_{s,d(k)}^k + X_{o(k),d(k)}^k = n^k \quad \forall k \in K, \quad (13)$$

$$X_{ij}^k \geq 0 \quad \forall k \in K, \forall (i,j) \in A^k, \quad (14)$$

$$a_i^k \leq T_i^k \leq b_i^k \quad \forall k \in K, \forall i \in V^k, \quad (15)$$

$$X_{ij}^k (T_i^k + d_{ij}^k - T_j^k) \leq 0 \quad \forall k \in K, \forall (i,j) \in A^k, \quad (16)$$

$$X_{ij}^k \text{ integer} \quad \forall k \in K, \forall (i,j) \in A^k. \quad (17)$$

The objective function (8) maximizes the total profit made from daily schedules. Relations (9) require that each operational flight leg be covered exactly once. Relations (10) represent the flow conservation constraints for each aircraft type at each station, i.e., the number of aircraft of type $k \in K$ at station $s \in S^k$ must be the same at the beginning and at the end of a day. Relations (11) ensure that a maximum of n^k schedules be assigned to aircraft of type $k \in K$. Relations (12) are the usual network flow conservation constraints. Given (11) and (12), relations (13) are redundant. Together, these constraints describe a path structure with n^k units flowing from $o(k)$ to $d(k)$. Relations (14) are the nonnegativity constraints. Relations (15) define the time window constraints. Relations (16) ensure the compatibility between the flow and the time variables. Finally, integrality constraints on the flow variables are given by relations (17).

Removing the coupling constraint set (10) and adding capacity constraints, the above model becomes the vehicle routing problem with time windows. Two successful solution approaches have been described for this problem: Desrochers, Desrosiers and Solomon (1992) have proposed a column generation based scheme while Kohl and Madsen (1997) have used a Lagrangean Relaxation method.

4.3. Solution Strategy

The previous time constrained multicommodity network flow model can be solved using a decomposition technique such as Dantzig-Wolfe or Lagrangean relaxation embedded in a branch-and-bound search tree. Using the former, formulation (8)–(17) is divided into a master problem, consisting of the objective function (8) and the constraint sets (9) and (10), and a subproblem which considers the relations (11)–(17) and a modified objective function involving dual variables. The master problem retains the flight covering constraints and the flow conservation constraints for each type of aircraft at each station. The subproblem, which is separable by aircraft type k, is a longest path problem with time windows and a supply of n^k units at the source node of G^k.

4.4. Models for Fixed Time-Tabled Flights

By removing relations (15) and (16) which concern the time dimension, the above model becomes an Abara (1989) type model. On the other hand, by defining additional variables as:

$$X_i^k = \sum_{j:(i,j) \in A^k} X_{ij}^k, \quad \forall k \in K, \forall i \in N^k,$$

one can recognize the structure of the model of Hane et al. (1995). The new variables determine if the aircraft type k is assigned to flight leg i. Their objective function can be obtained using these new variables if short connection times are not considered in our model. In fact, the cost coefficients in (8) can be rewritten as $c_i^k = r_i^k - e_i^k$, $k \in K$, $i \in V^k$, instead of c_{ij}^k, $k \in K$, $(i,j) \in A^k$ when short connection times are forbidden. The flight covering constraints can be obtained directly. The other constraints of their formulation (availability of aircraft and flow conservation) are not identical to ours as they defined the flow variables on a time-line network and also considered periodic schedules.

5. Branch-and-Bound Strategies

In the time constrained multicommodity network flow formulation (8)–(17), the branching decisions used to obtain integer solutions must naturally be taken on the flow or the time variables. This is also the case if a Lagrangean relaxation scheme is applied to (8)–(17).

On the other hand, if the Set Partitioning type model (1)–(6) is used, the path variables θ_p^k, $p \in \Omega^k$, $k \in K$, may be considered for branching decisions. A fractional variable θ_p^k, $0 < \theta_p^k < 1$, can easily be set to 1: it consists of deleting all the flight legs covered by the corresponding path in all networks G^k, $k \in K$, as well as their corresponding flight covering constraints in the master problem, and in adjusting the other constraints accordingly. On the other hand, setting θ_p^k to 0 is useless since its corresponding path will be generated again in the optimal solution of the linear relaxation. Therefore the branching decisions cannot be taken directly on the path variables. However there exist several ways to transfer the effects of these decisions to the subproblem variables. For example, setting $\theta_p^k = 0$ is equivalent to fixing at 0 one or many of the flow variables on the corresponding path, leading to several branches in the branching tree (Desrosiers et al. 1984).

Alternatively, knowing the values of the path variables, one can evaluate the network flow variables. Indeed, for single- and multicommodity network flow problems, it is well known that the integer node-arc and node-path formulations are equivalent (see Ahuja et al. 1993). However it is much less known that the node-path formulation can be obtained from the node-arc formulation by applying a Dantzig-Wolfe decomposition, even if such a result dates back to the sixties (see Tomlin 1965, and Jarvis 1969). In our case, the time constrained multicommodity network flow formulation is decomposed as follows: the constraints (9)–(10) involving several commodities are kept in the master problem, while the local path constraints (11)–(17) involving a single commodity appear in the subproblems.

Therefore, even if the Set Partitioning type model is used, optimal branching decisions can be taken on the X_{ij}^k variables restricted to integer values. These flow variables appear in both the subproblem structure of the column generation scheme and the multicommodity flow model. This fundamental observation allows us to develop branching strategies compatible with the column generation technique.

In addition to branching decisions taken on the flow variables, one can take binary decisions on linear combinations of them such as

$$X_{ij} = \sum_{k \in K} X_{ij}^k, \quad i,j \in N^k, \text{ and} \quad (18)$$

$$X_i^k = \sum_{j:(i,j) \in A^k} X_{ij}^k, \quad k \in K, i \in N^k. \quad (19)$$

A decision to set X_{ij} at 1 in (18) imposes a connection between flight legs i and j whatever the aircraft type. Setting $X_i^k = 1$ in (19) forces the assignment of aircraft type k to flight leg i.

Another useful set of variables is

$$X_{o(k)}^k = \sum_{s \in S_1^k} X_{o(k),s}^k, \quad k \in K \quad (20)$$

where each variable counts the number of aircraft of type k used in the current solution. This number is restricted to take integer values and hence any branching decision can easily be incorporated by defining two-side inequalities in (4) or (11).

Other branching strategies based on the variables of the multicommodity network flow model can also be conceived. Not only flow variables can be used in numerous ways, but also time variables can lead to several appealing branching rules (Gélinas et al. 1995).

6. Extensions

In this section, we discuss how to modify the two formulations presented in §§2 and 4 to account for several interesting extensions of the DARSP.

6.1. Potential Flight Legs

Situations arise where in addition to N, the set of flight legs to cover, there exists a set of potential flight legs from which it is possible to select additional flight legs to be flown. Denote by P this set of potential flight legs which contains different subsets, $P^k \subseteq P, k \in K$, for each type of aircraft. For each potential flight leg in P^k, $k \in K$, create a new potential flight node in $G^k = (V^k, A^k)$ where

$$V^k = N^k \cup P^k \cup S_1^k \cup S_2^k \cup \{o(k), d(k)\},$$

and link it to the other nodes with schedule start, schedule end, turn and short turn arcs so that A^k is appropriately defined. To ensure that these potential flight legs are not covered more than once, the only new constraints that must be introduced are:

$$\sum_{k \in K} \sum_{p \in \Omega^k} a_{ip}^k \theta_p^k \leq 1 \quad \forall i \in P, \text{ in model (1)–(6), and}$$

$$\sum_{k \in K} \sum_{j:(i,j) \in A^k} X_{ij}^k \leq 1 \quad \forall i \in P, \text{ in model (8)–(17).}$$

6.2. Time Dependent Flight Legs

The problem treated here can be extended to consider departure time dependent flight legs. This would require the solution of a stochastic nonlinear multicommodity integer program over the probability distribution of flight demands defined on the flights' departure time windows. An approximate solution to such a clearly nontractable program could be obtained by partitioning the departure time windows into a certain number of very narrow time intervals. We assume that demand remains constant within each of the time intervals of the partition. For each node, we define as many copies of it as there are time windows in the partition. Constraint set (2) or (9) will ensure that the model will choose exactly one among these.

6.3. Periodic Daily Schedule for Fixed Time-Tabled Flights

Given a set of flight legs balanced over a daily horizon, i.e., for each station, there are as many departures as there are arrivals, there could be a need to construct periodic daily schedules to be repeated day after day. This periodic daily schedule problem without time windows has been solved by Abara (1989) and by Hane et al. (1995).

Consider a horizon of two consecutive days. Since the daily schedule is replicable day after day, the deployment of the airline fleet with respect to aircraft types must be identical each of the two days. That is, if t is a given time of the first day and D a 24-hour duration constant, then at time t and $t + D$ there must be the same number of aircraft of each type at each station, and the aircraft types assigned to the flight legs in progress must also be the same. From this observation, we infer that the specific time where we start the schedule might be selected arbitrarily. Let t_0 be this time. If no flight legs are in progress at time t_0 then the models presented in §§2 and 4 without time constraints are suitable for the periodic daily schedule problem.

On the other hand, if there are some flight legs in progress at time t_0, then the networks G^k must be modified. Observe that these legs are divided in two parts, one after t_0 and the other before t_0. The aircraft assigned to the first part is not necessarily the same as the one assigned to the second; however, they must be of the same aircraft type. All aircraft assigned to the legs in progress must be taken into account as they might be assigned to subsequent flight legs.

Therefore, instead of associating a single flight node with a leg in progress, we associate two. The first node corresponds to the second part of the leg which occurs after t_0 while the second node represents the first part which takes place before $t_0 + D$. Let N_1^k and N_2^k be the sets of first and second nodes associated with legs in progress, respectively. The nodes in N_1^k and N_2^k are linked to the other nodes of G^k in the same manner as the initial station and the final station nodes, respectively. For each leg in progress two additional arcs must be added. One between the node in N_1^k corresponding to this leg and the final station node in S_2^k where this leg ends. The other connects the initial station node in S_1^k where this leg begins with the node in N_2^k associated with this leg. These additional arcs allow us to consider schedules containing only a single leg in progress.

In the formulations presented in §§2 and 4, the nodes in N_1^k and N_2^k can be included either in N^k or in S_1^k and S_2^k, respectively. If they are included in N^k (that is, $N^k := N^k \cup N_1^k \cup N_2^k$), then Equations (2) or (9) ensure the covering of the two parts of the flight legs in progress. However, an additional flow conservation constraint for each aircraft type and for each pair of corresponding nodes in N_1^k and N_2^k must be added to the two formulations to ensure that these nodes are covered by the same aircraft type. On the other hand, if the nodes are included in S_1^k and S_2^k (that is, $S_1^k := S_1^k \cup N_1^k$ and S_2^k

$:= S_2^k \cup N_2^k$), then covering constraints for the flight legs in progress must be added to the two models. In this case, Equations (3) or (10) ensure that the two parts of a flight leg in progress are covered by the same aircraft type. Note that in both cases only one covering constraint is necessary for each pair of corresponding nodes in N_1^k and N_2^k, since the flow conservation constraints ensure that if one of them is covered then the other will be as well.

6.4. Periodic Daily Schedule for Flexible Time-Tabled Flights

In addition to the above modifications needed for the periodic daily schedule problem for fixed time-tabled flights, the flexible version may require additional constraints to ensure that the departure time of a flight leg in progress before t_0 is the same as the departure time of this leg the next day. If no flight legs are in progress at time t_0, then the models presented in §§2 and 4 with time constraints are suitable for this flexible periodic daily schedule problem.

On the other hand, if there are some flight legs in progress at time t_0, let $[a_i^k, b_i^k]$ be the time window of flight leg $i \in N_2^k$. Define then $[a_i^k - D, b_i^k - D]$ as the time window on the corresponding leg $i \in N_1^k$. The time windows on the source node $o(k)$, the initial station nodes in S_1^k, the final station nodes in S_2^k and the sink node $d(k)$ are replaced by the value $a^k = \min_{i \in N_1^k} a_i^k$. They become $[a^k, a^k]$, $[a^k, a^k]$, $[a^k, \infty]$ and $[a^k, \infty]$, respectively.

Furthermore, the time window constraints (15) for flight legs $i \in N_1^k \cup N_2^k$ are modified to

$$a_i^k \left(\sum_{j:(i,j) \in A^k} X_{ij}^k \right) \le T_i^k \le b_i^k \left(\sum_{j:(i,j) \in A^k} X_{ij}^k \right)$$

$$\forall k \in K, \forall i \in N_1^k \cup N_2^k.$$

In the optimal solution, if $i \in N_1^k \cup N_2^k$, $k \in K$, then due to constraints (9), (14) and (17), $\sum_{j:(i,j) \in A^k} X_{ij}^k$ is restricted to be binary, i.e., it is equal to 1 if an aircraft of type k visits node i, and 0 otherwise. Therefore, the time variables belong to $[a_i^k, b_i^k]$ if node i is covered, and equal 0 otherwise.

Denote by $(u, u') \in N_1^k \times N_2^k$ the pair of nodes corresponding to a flight leg in progress performed by an aircraft of type k. The compatibility of the departure times of this leg in progress is then ensured by the constraint:

$$T_u^k + D = T_{u'}^k, \quad (u, u') \in N_1^k \times N_2^k,$$

which can also be written as:

$$T_u^k - a_u^k = T_{u'}^k - a_{u'}^k, \quad (u, u') \in N_1^k \times N_2^k.$$

Since the aircraft type which will cover this leg is unknown and the value of $T_u^k - a_u^k(\Sigma_{j:(u,j)\in A^k} X_{uj}^k)$ is equal to 0 if leg $u \in N_1^k \cup N_2^k$ is not covered by an aircraft of type $k \in K$, the equations ensuring the compatibility of the departure times of the legs in progress are:

$$\sum_{k \in K} \left(T_u^k - a_u^k \left(\sum_{j:(u,j) \in A^k} X_{uj}^k \right) \right)$$

$$= \sum_{k \in K} \left(T_{u'}^k - a_{u'}^k \left(\sum_{j:(u',j) \in A^k} X_{u'j}^k \right) \right)$$

$$\forall (u, u') \in N_1^k \times N_2^k. \quad (21)$$

Constraints (21) are coupling constraints and hence cannot be considered in the subproblem. Note that these coupling constraints include both time and flow variables. However, if $a_u^k = a_u$, $\forall k \in K$ and $\forall u \in N_1^k \cup N_2^k$, then the flow variables can be removed from (21) since $\Sigma_{k \in K} \Sigma_{j:(u,j) \in A^k} X_{uj}^k = 1$ by the covering constraints (9). One can observe that the subproblem retains only the local time constraints, i.e., the time window on a single path, while the coupling constraints (21) permit us to link the time variables on two different paths. When these coupling constraints are relaxed in a Lagrangean relaxation (or kept in the restricted master problem of a Dantzig-Wolfe decomposition), the time variables appear in the objective function together with dual multipliers. In this case, the marginal profit of a new schedule varies with the marginal cost of the arcs and also with the visit times of nodes in $N_1^k \cup N_2^k$. This problem is much more difficult and requires a different time constrained optimization path algorithm (Ioachim et al. 1997).

7. Computational Results

All the test problems presented in this section were solved using the GENCOL software, developed at the GERAD research center, which relies on the optimizer CPLEX (CPLEX 1993) to solve linear programs. This software package consists essentially of a branch-and-bound algorithm where the upper bound at each node is obtained by solving the linear relaxation (1)–(5) of the Set Partitioning type formulation using the column generation technique described in §2.

7.1. Solution Strategies

The branching decisions were taken on the following linear combination of the flow variables: $X_{ij} = \Sigma_{k \in K} X_{ij}^k$, where i and $j \in N$. Fixing the binary variable X_{ij} at 1 corresponds to imposing a connection between flight legs i and j. A depth first strategy was used. Although optimal solutions can be obtained through an exhaustive exploration of the branch-and-bound search tree, a heuristic procedure has been used to limit the computational time. The following rules were applied: 1) stop prematurely the solution process of the restricted master problem at a branching node if there is no improvement over the last 10 iterations; 2) fix at 1 the path variables that have a value very close to 1, i.e., greater than or equal to 0.95; and 3) fathom a pending node if the difference between its upper bound and the best integer solution found so far is less than $2,000.

Two series of test problems were solved by GENCOL. The information concerning the size of these problems is summarized in Table 2.

7.2. North American Carrier Test Problems

The first set of data corresponds to a typical weekday for a medium haul fleet of a North American airline. There are 204 flow conservation constraints for each aircraft type at each station in addition to the 383 flight covering constraints of the master problem. The objective is first to minimize the number of aircraft utilized to cover all the flight legs and then to maximize the anticipated profit. Four scenarios, differing in terms of the flexibility of the flight departure times, were solved using GENCOL. The first considered fixed departure

Table 2 Size Information for the Test Problems

	North American Carrier	European Carrier
Number of Flight Legs	383	252
Number of Aircraft	91	51
Number of Types	9	6
Number of Stations	33	44
Short Turn Arcs	yes	no

times while the other three considered departure time windows (centered at the fixed departure times of the first scenario) of width ±10, ±20 and ±30 minutes. The ±30 minutes scenario is presented primarily for numerical interest. One would expect that in practice, time windows of such width would begin to affect demand and therefore the objective function.

The airline who supplied these data also provided a solution for the fixed departure time case utilizing the 91 aircraft. However, comparisons between their solution and the solutions obtained by GENCOL cannot be made since they also considered a cargo transportation component which was not described in the data. Nevertheless the following results show the usefulness and the efficiency of the column generation approach in this case.

Table 3 presents the results obtained by GENCOL for the four scenarios. Each column corresponds to a scenario. The rows of the table are divided in four parts. The first part specifies the size of the subproblem timeline network. The second part gives information about the solution process of the linear relaxation problem. It indicates the value z_{LP}^H of the heuristic solution (which has been verified, for each of these four scenarios, to be equal to the value z_{LP}^* of the optimal solution), the number of aircraft utilized in this solution, the number of iterations (i.e., the number of calls to the restricted master problem) performed to obtain this solution, the CPU times to solve the subproblem and the restricted master problem as well as the total CPU time on a HP 9000/735 workstation (86.7 Specfp92, 52.0 Specint92). The third part gives the value of the heuristic integer solution (z_{IP}^H) and the numbers of aircraft and short time connections utilized in this solution. It also specifies the number of nodes explored in the branch-and-bound search tree. Finally, in addition to the overall CPU times, the global information part indicates the numbers of iterations and columns generated during the overall solution process, as well as the absolute and relative integrality gaps between the optimal linear relaxation solution and the heuristic integer solution, i.e., $z_{LP}^* - z_{IP}^H$ and $(z_{LP}^* - z_{IP}^H)/z_{LP}^*$, respectively.

Observe that the number of nodes and arcs of the subproblem network increases with the width of the time windows. This comes from the duplication of certain flight nodes which is required whenever a flight leg can be connected to a subsequent leg if the departure time of the first leg is early enough, but cannot be connected to that same leg if this departure time occurs too late in the time window.

The linear relaxation part shows that the anticipated profit and the number of aircraft utilized decrease as the time windows become wider. The decrease in the number of aircraft is due to the fact that more schedules are feasible as the flexibility of the departure times is increased. Since the main objective is to minimize the number of aircraft utilized, a larger set of feasible schedules leads to a reduction in the number of aircraft utilized. Compared to the scenario without time window flexibility which requires 79 aircraft, the ±10, ±20 and ±30 minutes scenarios lead to a decrease of 3.8%, 8.9% and 13.9% in the number of aircraft utilized, respectively. Along with this reduction, a decrease in the anticipated profit can occur since fewer aircraft are used to cover all flight legs and the number of short turns is variable. Notice that the number of iterations performed increases slowly over the four scenarios and that the

Table 3 GENCOL's Results on the North American Carrier Data

	±0 min	±10 min	±20 min	±30 min
Network Information				
Number of Nodes	2,070	2,118	2,617	2,765
Number of Arcs	4,070	4,345	5,500	6,498
Linear Relaxation:				
$z_{LP}^H (=z_{LP}^*)$	$301,410	$302,040	$293,350	$271,830
Number of Aircraft	79	76	72	68
Number of Iterations	77	95	127	135
CPU_{SP}	90	109	59	75
CPU_{MP}	106	131	246	292
CPU_{TOT}	196	240	305	367
Integer Solution:				
z_{IP}^H	$301,410	$302,040	$292,520	$270,470
Number of Aircraft	79	76	72	68
Number of Short Turns	11	8	14	34
Number of B&B Nodes	2	0	8	14
Global Information				
Number of Iterations	177	95	380	708
Number of Columns	20,644	15,467	72,238	171,050
CPU_{SP}	195	109	367	947
CPU_{MP}	234	131	1,102	2,561
CPU_{TOT}	429	240	1,469	3,508
Absolute Integrality Gap	$0	$0	$830	$1,360
Relative Integrality Gap	0%	0%	0.28%	0.5%

heuristic linear relaxation solution is obtained quite rapidly (in less than 7 minutes).

Similar observations on the anticipated profit and the number of aircraft can be made about the integer solution part. Moreover, observe that the number of short time connections used is reasonable and that the number of branch-and-bound nodes is relatively small for each scenario. The latter can be explained by the fact that the solution to the linear relaxation of the Set Partitioning formulation provides an excellent bound for vehicle routing problems, which are similar to the DARSP, leading to an efficient branch-and-bound algorithm (Bramel and Simchi-Levi 1993).

Finally, the global information part shows the efficiency of the solution process. The test problems were solved in reasonable times. The solutions of the first two scenarios are optimal with respect to both the number of aircraft and the anticipated profit. For the last two scenarios, they are optimal with respect to the number of aircraft and show small integrality gaps on the anticipated profit (less than 0.5%).

7.3. European Carrier Test Problems

The second set of data presented in Table 2 corresponds to a typical weekday for a medium haul fleet of a European airline. The objective is to maximize the anticipated profit. The total CPU times to solve the test problems vary between 10 and 45 minutes on a HP 9000/720 workstation (66.1 Specfp92, 38.5 Specint92).

The tests were separated into three parts. In the first part, two scenarios with the same aircraft availability as the airline's solution were solved. The first of these scenarios considered fixed departure times while the second considered departure time windows of ±10 minute width. In the second part, several scenarios were solved with departure time windows of ±10 minute width and a total number of 51 available aircraft, but with different aircraft type availability. The goal of the last part was to optimize the fleet composition of the airline. A single scenario with departure time windows of ±10 minute width was solved where the total number of available aircraft was fixed at 51 and the number of available aircraft of each type was unconstrained.

Figure 2 shows the profit improvement over the airline's solution of the different scenarios solved by GENCOL. The first column gives the aircraft types while the second indicates the number of aircraft of each type utilized in the airline's solution. The other columns present profit improvements obtained with GENCOL when the fleet size varied. For each scenario, the width of the departure time windows is given in the last row. The fleet size changes are provided in the corresponding aircraft type row (for example, a +2 in the B737 row of a scenario column means that 11 + 2 aircraft of type B737 are available for this scenario while a −2 in the A320 row means that 23 − 2 aircraft of type A320 are available). The last column corresponds to the fleet composition optimization scenario and the number of aircraft of each type utilized in the GENCOL solution is given directly on each row.

As illustrated in Figure 2, solving the problem with GENCOL using the same fleet as the one for the airline's solution and fixed departure times has led to a profit improvement of 6.8%. When allowing for flexible departure times (that is, departure time windows of ±10 minute width), the improvement increases to 11.2%. The second part of the tests presents similar profit improvements (between 10.9% and 16.1%) when the composition of the fleet is modified slightly. Finally, the last scenario shows the influence of the fleet composition

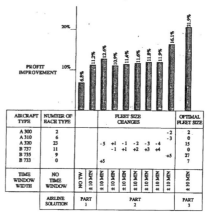

Figure 2   GENCOL's Results on the European Carrier Data

on the profit improvement. For departure time windows of ±10 minute width, the profit improvement increases from 11.2% to 21.9% when GENCOL was allowed to determine the fleet composition.

8. Conclusions

In this paper we have studied the daily aircraft routing and scheduling problem (DARSP) which consists of finding a fleet schedule that maximizes profits given a heterogeneous fleet of aircraft, a set of operational flight legs over a one-day horizon, departure time windows, durations and profits according to the aircraft type for each flight leg. We have presented two equivalent formulations for this problem: a multicommodity network flow formulation previously described in the DARSP literature and a Set Partitioning type formulation recently utilized in the context of the vehicle routing problem with time windows. We have described the network structure of the subproblem when a column generation technique is applied to solve the linear relaxation of the Set Partitioning type formulation or a Dantzig-Wolfe decomposition approach is used to solve the linear relaxation of the time constrained multicommodity network flow formulation.

We have used a branch-and-bound algorithm to obtain integer solutions. We have presented optimal branching strategies compatible with the column generation technique. These strategies were developed by exploiting the relationship between the two formulations. Finally, computational results obtained on real data provided by two airlines, one North American and the other European, have shown that branching on flow variables was very effective. They have also illustrated that the Dantzig-Wolfe decomposition or the column generation technique can be used to solve real-world problems in reasonable computational times, leading to substantial profit improvements.[1]

[1] This research was supported by the Quebec Government (Programme Synergie du Fonds de Développement Technologique) and by the Natural Sciences and Engineering Council of Canada. Marius M. Solomon was partially supported by the Patrick F. and Helen C. Walsh Research Professorship. We would also like to thank the management of Ad Opt Technologies, in particular Pierre Trudeau, and the programming team from GERAD consisting of Johanne Gilbert and Ianick Gentes. Finally, the authors wish to thank the Editor, the Associate Editor and two referees whose suggestions have improved the paper.

References

Abara, J., "Applying Integer Linear Programming to the Fleet Assignment Problem," *Interfaces*, 19 (1989), 20–28.

Agin, N. and D. Cullen, "An Algorithm for Transportation Routing and Vehicle Loading," in M. Geisler (Ed.), *Logistics*, North-Holland, Amsterdam, 1975, 1–20.

Ahuja, R. K., T. L. Magnanti, and J. B. Orlin, *Network Flows*, Prentice Hall, Englewood Cliffs, NJ, 1993.

Barnhart, C., E. Johnson, R. Anbil, and L. Hatay, "A Column Generation Technique for the Long-Haul Crew Assignment Problem," in T. A. Ciriani and R. Leachman (Eds.), *Optimization in Industry 2: Mathematical Programming and Modeling Techniques in Practice*, John Wiley and Sons, New York, 1991, 7–22.

Bramel, J. and D. Simchi-Levi, "On the Effectiveness of Set Partitioning Formulations for the Vehicle Routing Problem," Working Paper, Graduate School of Business, Columbia University, New York, 1993.

Chvàtal, V., *Linear Programming*, W.H. Freeman and Company, New York, 1983.

CPLEX Reference Manual, *Using the CPLEX Callable Library and CPLEX Mixed Integer Library*, CPLEX Optimization, Inc., Incline Village, NV, 1993.

Desrochers, M., J. Desrosiers, and M. M. Solomon, "A New Optimization Algorithm for the Vehicle Routing Problem with Time Windows," *Oper. Res.*, 40 (1992), 342–354.

——— and F. Soumis, "A Generalized Permanent Labeling Algorithm for the Shortest Path Problem with Time Windows," *INFOR*, 26 (1988a), 191–212.

——— and ———, "A Reoptimization Algorithm for the Shortest Path Problem with Time Windows," *European J. Oper. Res.*, 35 (1988b), 242–254.

Desrosiers, J., Y. Dumas, M. M. Solomon, and F. Soumis, "Time Constrained Routing and Scheduling," in M. Ball, T. Magnanti, C. Monma, and G. Nemhauser (Eds.), *Handbooks in Operations Research and Management Science*, Volume 8, Network Routing, Elsevier Science Publishers B.V., Amsterdam, 1995, 35–139.

———, F. Soumis, and M. Desrochers, "Routing with Time Windows by Column Generation," *Networks*, 14 (1984), 545–565.

———, P. Pelletier, and F. Soumis, "Plus Court Chemin avec Contraintes d'Horaires," *RAIRO*, 17 (1983), 357–377 (in French).

Etschmaier, M. M. and D. F. X. Mathaisel, "Aircraft Scheduling: The State of the Art," *AGIFORS*, 24 (1984), 181–225.

Farkas, A. and P. P. Belobaba, *Leg Dependence in Aircraft Assignment Decisions*, paper presented at the INFORMS National Meeting, October 29–November 1, New Orleans, LA, 1995.

Gélinas, S., M. Desrochers, J. Desrosiers, and M. M. Solomon, "A New-Branching Strategy for Time Constrained Routing Problems with Application to Backhauling," *Ann. Oper. Res.*, 61 (1995), 91–109.

Hane, C., C. Barnhart, E. L. Johnson, R. Marsten, G. L. Nemhauser, and G. Sigismondi, "The Fleet Assignment Problem: Solving a Large-Scale Integer Program," *Math. Programming*, 70 (1995), 211–232.

Ioachim, I., S. Gélinas, J. Desrosiers, and F. Soumis, "A Dynamic Programming Algorithm for the Shortest Path Problem with Time Windows and Linear Node Costs," *Networks* (1997) (forthcoming).

Jarvis, J. J., "On the Equivalence Between the Node-Arc and Arc-Chain Formulations for the Multi-Commodity Maximal Flow Problem," *Naval Res. Logistics Quarterly*, 16 (1969), 525–529.

Kohl, N. and O. B. G. Madsen, "An Optimization Algorithm for the Vehicle Routing Problem with Time Windows Based on Lagrangean Relaxation," *Oper. Res.* (1997) (forthcoming).

Lasdon, L. S., *Optimization Theory for Large Systems*, Macmillan, New York, 1970.

Levin, A., "Scheduling and Fleet Routing Models for Transportation Systems," *Transportation Sci.*, 5 (1971), 232–255.

Subramanian, R., R. P. Scheff, J. D. Quillinan, D. S. Wiper, and R. E. Marsten, "Coldstart: Fleet Assignment at Delta Air Lines," *Interfaces*, 24, 1 (1994), 104–120.

Tomlin, J. A., "Minimum-Cost Multicommodity Network Flows," *Oper. Res.*, 14 (1966), 45–51.

15

The fleet assignment problem: solving a large-scale integer program [1]

Christopher A. Hane, Cynthia Barnhart, Ellis L. Johnson,
Roy E. Marsten, George L. Nemhauser, Gabriele Sigismondi

Abstract

Given a flight schedule and set of aircraft, the fleet assignment problem is to determine which type of aircraft should fly each flight segment. This paper describes a basic daily, domestic fleet assignment problem and then presents chronologically the steps taken to solve it efficiently. Our model of the fleet assignment problem is a large multi-commodity flow problem with side constraints defined on a time-expanded network. These problems are often severely degenerate, which leads to poor performance of standard linear programming techniques. Also, the large number of integer variables can make finding optimal integer solutions difficult and time-consuming. The methods used to attack this problem include an interior-point algorithm, dual steepest edge simplex, cost perturbation, model aggregation, branching on set-partitioning constraints and prioritizing the order of branching. The computational results show that the algorithm finds solutions with a maximum optimality gap of 0.02% and is more than two orders of magnitude faster than using default options of a standard LP-based branch-and-bound code.

Keywords: Linear programming; Mixed-integer programming; Large-scale optimization; Airline fleet assignment

1. Introduction

Given a flight schedule and set of aircraft, the fleet assignment problem is to determine which type of aircraft should fly each flight segment. The specific fleet assignment problem studied here is a daily, domestic one, where domestic refers to the US cities together with a few other North American cities served by the airline. The domestic

---

[1] This work was supported by NSF and AFORS grant DDM-9115768 and NSF grant SES-9122674.

problem is differentiated from the intercontinental one by a daily schedule (with exceptions) and a clearly defined period of inactivity during which maintenance is routinely performed, usually in the late evening to early morning.

Among the factors considered in assigning a fleet to a flight leg are passenger demand (both point-to-point and continuing service), revenue, seating capacity, fuel costs, crew size, availability of maintenance at arrival and departure stations, gate availability, and aircraft noise. Many of these factors are captured in the objective coefficient of the decision variable, others are captured by constraints. For example, the potential revenue generated by a flight is determined by forecasting the demand for seats on that flight and multiplying the minimum of it and the seat capacity by the average fare.

The fleet assignment solution must satisfy balance constraints that force the aircraft to circulate through the network of flights. The balance constraints are enforced by modeling the activity at each station with a time line for each fleet, see Fig. 1. This time line has entries designating the arrivals and departures from the station for each fleet. Each departure (arrival) from the station splits an edge and adds a node to the time line at the departure (arrival + refueling/baggage handling) time. The nodes created at the arrival city and departure city are connected by the decision variable representing the assignment of that fleet to that flight. Thus, the balance of aircraft is enforced by the conservation of flow equations for a time-expanded multi-commodity network. We make the time line a cycle, which forces the solution to be a circulation through the network. The circulation arises from the balance constraints and the lack of source or sink nodes in the network. Since the network has a time span of 24 hours, the circulation defined by the solution defines a daily schedule.

The time line's purpose is to preserve aircraft balance, but it also must allow the proper aircraft flight connections. Therefore, the placement of the arrival end of the flight arc must coincide with the time when the aircraft is ready to takeoff. Any earlier placement could violate the feasibility of having a single aircraft fly two consecutive flights. In Fig. 1, if flight C were put in the time line at its arrival time, it would precede flight B. Then if the only flights assigned to this fleet are C and B, any sequence of flights would violate the minimum ground time, or remain more than 24 hours on the ground (which requires an extra aircraft). We use the term "ready time" to indicate the time at which the arriving flight is ready to takeoff. Ready time is fleet- and city-dependent because larger aircraft and busier cities require more time.

The next section gives a mathematical formulation of the basic fleet assignment model. The formulation is similar to Abara's [1] and Berge and Hopperstad's [2]. Abara's model uses extra variables to compute the sequence of flights individual aircraft will

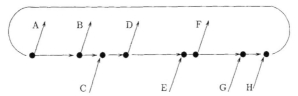

Fig. 1. A city-fleet time line.

fly, in addition to determining the fleeting decision. These variables cause a tremendous growth in model size as the number of flights increase. Berge and Hopperstad's model is part of a dynamic fleet assignment system which is constrained by equal ready times across the fleets and the inability to handle maintenance and crew issues. This model is called basic because it does not contain constraints on such factors as maintenance and crew planning considerations that are needed to get an implementable solution. These model enhancements are discussed briefly in Section 5.1 of this paper and are developed in detail in the subsequent paper [3].

The main contribution of this paper is a case study in the solution of a very large mixed-integer program. Using standard default options of a mathematical programming system, we could not come close to solving problems of the size that are required. The solution methodology developed in this paper solves a 150-city, 2500-flight, eleven-fleet daily fleet assignment problem routinely in less than one hour.

In Section 2, we give the mathematical model. Sections 3 and 4 discuss the computational history, including the difficulties encountered and the remedies applied to improve the computational efficiency of the model for both the mixed-integer program and its linear programming relaxations. Section 5 summarizes the results and describes possible enhancements.

2. Mathematical model

The set of cities serviced by the schedule is denoted by C, the set of available fleets by F and the number of aircraft in each fleet is $S(f)$ for $f \in F$. The set of flights in the schedule is denoted by L, with elements $\{i\}$, or $\{odt\}$, with $o, d \in C$ and t a time. The set of flight arcs $O(f)$, for $f \in F$ denotes the arcs whose time span contains 3am EST. The actual time is arbitrary but picking an early morning time reduces the cardinality of $O(f)$. Additionally, there is a set of marketing constraints that fix certain pairs of flights to be connected. These constraints preserve one-stop service in markets where there is a significant amount of incremental revenue gained by having one-stop instead of connecting flights. These connections are called "required throughs". The set of required throughs is denoted by H, with elements (i, j) with i and $j \in L$. Also, the schedule may need to violate the minimum ready times for some flights because of fleet size restrictions. These special short ready times are also modeled as required throughs.

The nodes N in the network are enumerated by $\{fot\}$, with $f \in F$, $o \in C$ and t a time of a takeoff or landing at o. We use t^- to denote the time preceding t and t^+ the following time. When arrivals and departures occur simultaneously, arrivals precede departures in the time line. The last node in a time line is $\{fot_n\}$, the node that precedes 3am EST; its successor is $\{fot_1\}$.

The decision variable X_{fodt}, also written as X_{fi}, has value 1 if fleet f flies the flight leg from o to d departing at time t, and 0 otherwise. The other variables that appear in the model are "ground arcs" which count the number of aircraft on the ground at each station at every point in time for each fleet. These ground arc variables are Y_{fott^+}

with $f \in F$, $o \in C$, and $[t, t^+]$ the time interval covered by the arc. They are defined as continuous variables because once all flight variables are integral the flows on the ground arcs are forced to be integral as well. The basic model is the following integer programming formulation of basic fleet assignment model:

$$\min \sum_{i \in L} \sum_{f \in F} c_{fi} X_{fi},$$

$$\sum_{f} X_{fi} = 1, \quad \text{for all } i \in L, \tag{1}$$

$$\sum_{d} X_{fdot} + Y_{fot^-t} - \sum_{d} X_{fodt} - Y_{fott^+} = 0, \quad \text{for all } \{fot\} \in N, \tag{2}$$

$$X_{fi} - X_{fj} = 0, \quad \text{for all } (i, j) \in H, \tag{3}$$

$$\sum_{i \in O(f)} X_{fi} + \sum_{o \in C} Y_{fot_n t_1} \leqslant S(f), \quad \text{for all } f \in F, \tag{4}$$

$$Y_{fott^1} \geqslant 0, \quad \text{for all } \{fott^+\} \in N, \tag{5}$$

$$X_{fi} \in \{0, 1\}, \quad \text{for all } i \in L \text{ and } f \in F. \tag{6}$$

The objective coefficient c_{fi} represents the cost of assigning fleet type f to flight i. The positive part of the projected demand for seats minus the seating capacity of the aircraft is called the "spill". These passengers may wait to catch the next flight of the same airline in which case they are "recaptured", or they are lost to another airline. Given the projected demand, recapture rate for a flight, fare structure and available seats, a cost for spilled passengers for each (flight, fleet) pair is computed. This cost is combined with the operating costs to make the objective coefficient.

The cost portion of the objective function can be as difficult to determine as the profit side. Some easy parts of the cost are fuel, and an estimate of crew costs (the number of crew members multiplied by the flying time and pay rate). However, the cost of introducing a fleet to a city where that fleet currently does not operate is difficult to estimate. It contains many fixed components, such as maintenance crew training or relocation and spare parts inventory.

There are four main sets of constraints in the basic model. The first set is the cover rows, forcing each flight leg to be flown by exactly one fleet. Thus, the solution cannot eliminate unprofitable flight legs, or relocate aircraft on nonscheduled flights.

The second set of constraints is the "balance" constraints. These are the flow conservation equations for the nodes of each fleet that force the flow to be a circulation.

The third set of constraints enforces the flight legs of each required through to be flown by aircraft of the same fleet. As long as the first leg's ready time is adjusted to be the departure time of the paired flight, this formulation is sufficient to guarantee that there exists a sequencing of individual aircraft which can fly these legs consecutively.

The final set of constraints in the basic model is the fleet size constraints which count the number of aircraft of each fleet used by the solution. These constraints are captured by slicing each fleet network at 3am EST and counting the flow across this cutset.

The four sets of constraints described above are present in the models used in the computational results that follow. The model enhancements only modify the representation of these constraints. While this model does not address all the issues in the fleeting decision, its solution is fundamental to more advanced models.

3. Computational history

This section follows the chronological history of the solution strategy for solving the basic fleet assignment problem. The data for these tests was provided by Delta Air Lines, Inc. and represents six schedules for the period September 1991–June 1992. These schedules have approximately 2500 flights serving almost 150 cities with eleven fleet types. The number in the problem name refers to the schedule, the letter designates the fleets used in the model, i.e., 1E and 2E are problems from different schedules but the same fleets are present. Table 1 shows the initial sizes of the problems we considered.

Subproblems were necessary to test solution and modeling methods because the full problem was initially too large to solve in a reasonable amount of time. Creating good subproblems is nontrivial. The main obstacle is making a subproblem that is balanced, i.e., has the same number of arrivals and departures at each station, and does not use more than the allowable number of aircraft. Delta personnel provided us with a current fleeting of the schedule to allow this subproblem development. By selecting only the flight legs currently assigned to some subset of fleets, a balanced subproblem could be made with only those legs and that subset of the fleets. For example, if a subproblem

Table 1
Problem sizes

Name	Fleets	Flights	Integer variables	Rows	Columns	Nonzeros
1A	2	158	312	914	544	1504
1B	2	1201	2126	3211	3598	10038
1C	4	239	869	1911	1485	4075
1D	4	1605	5861	13103	16299	40216
1E	7	2320	12504	29629	37993	92018
2A	2	161	301	1299	909	2205
2B	2	1260	2235	5998	6441	15853
2C	4	261	943	3221	2843	6833
2D	4	1709	6236	13689	17148	42371
2E	7	2376	12851	30018	38638	93769
1	11	2559	22679	47994	65254	159064
2	11	2637	23512	48982	66942	163472
3	11	2627	23118	48674	66429	161751
4	11	2588	22737	48159	65202	159282
5	11	2590	22745	48204	65213	159357
6	11	2589	22746	48109	65164	163472

containing only wide-bodied aircraft was desired, only the flights currently assigned to wide-bodies are in the problem formulation. The feasibility of the current assignment guarantees that the flights selected are balanced and can be flown by the available aircraft. Proper construction of subproblems allowed various size problems to be generated and provided early feedback to validate the data and the model.

3.1. Aggregation

There is an obvious change in our network model that removes thousands of rows and columns from the problem formulation. The time line's purpose is to preserve aircraft balance and allow proper connections. However, the model does not care if an arrival occurs at 10:00am or 10:05am as long as there is no departure between these two times. Thus, there is no benefit for placing arrivals in the time line earlier than the next departure. Similarly, there is no benefit for placing departures in the time line later than the previous arrival. An alternative view of this argument is that a node spans a time interval which begins with consecutive arrivals followed by consecutive departures.

In Fig. 1 only three nodes are required, one for C and D, one for E and F, and the last for G, H, A and B. Note that C can never be consolidated into the same node as B, an earlier departure. If this were to happen, an arrival to C could travel back in time to depart via B.

In addition to these network based reductions, reductions relying on the algebra of the constraints can also be exploited. This algebraic preprocessing is an option in some optimization codes. The purpose of this preprocessing is to reduce the size of the model by substituting out variables whose values are fixed by other variables, e.g., the constraints $\sum_i a_i X_i = Y_j$, $a_i, Y_j, X_i \geq 0$, allow Y_j to be substituted out of the problem, along with this row. Preprocessing can also identify empty rows or columns, and eliminate redundant rows. We use the term aggregation to refer to both node consolidation and algebraic preprocessing.

3.2. Initial runs

The initial solution strategy focused on solving the linear programming relaxation of the basic model. Table 2 lists the comparison between model size and primal simplex solution time for problems with and without the node consolidation and algebraic preprocessing. These runs were performed on an IBM RS/6000 Model 320 with OSL Release 2. Tables 4–12 show results using an IBM RS/6000 Model 550 which is approximately twice as fast as the Model 320.

Table 2 shows that even with the aggregation, the number of primal simplex iterations is increased by a factor of 4 to 8 when the model is expanded from two to four fleets and about 400 flight legs are added. The eleven-fleet model with 2500 flights would clearly take an exorbitant amount of computation.

All the remaining runs are performed with node consolidation done in the model generation followed by algebraic preprocessing.

Table 2
Aggregation comparison

Problem name		Rows	Columns	Simplex iterations	CPU-seconds
1A	No aggregation	914	544	786	7.2
	Aggregation	212	357	407	1.6
1B	No aggregation	3211	3598	4519	165.5
	Aggregation	987	1860	1966	32.6
1C	No aggregation	1911	1485	2359	59.1
	Aggregation	734	1319	1807	25.4
1D	No aggregation	13103	16299	35467	8250.2
	Aggregation	5297	8968	16742	1879.6
2A	No aggregation	1299	909	1156	15.2
	Aggregation	235	376	408	1.8
2B	No aggregation	5998	6441	9227	710.1
	Aggregation	1359	2290	3045	63.1
2C	No aggregation	3221	2843	4734	189.0
	Aggregation	963	1636	2472	50.0
2D	No aggregation	13689	17148	39429	10094.6
	Aggregation	5579	9508	18975	2381.4

Our next step in improving the solution of the initial LP relaxation focused on tuning the primal simplex solution parameters and investigating if decomposition, dual simplex or interior-point methods would achieve better results. More will be said about the simplex method in Section 3.6.

The "tuned" version of the primal simplex algorithm selected Devex pricing [4,6,9], and "crashing" to a basis while trying to maintain dual feasibility. This crash procedure begins with an all artificial basis and pivots in columns with few nonzeros and zero objective coefficient. The dual feasible basis crash works very well since the ground arcs have zero objective coefficients and most appear in only two rows. These simplex results are shown in Table 3. Compared to the results in Table 2, Table 3 shows that selecting the proper parameters for OSL's primal simplex algorithm has a significant impact on the solution time. The larger problems, 1D and 2D, show a speedup of 146% and 140%, respectively, without a comparable reduction in the iteration count. At this time, other simplex based tests were not encouraging. The dual simplex method always used fewer iterations to find the optimal solution, but it invariably required more time. The decomposition strategy used OSL's LP decomposition routine to exploit the staircase structure of the model. This method did not improve on the primal simplex solution times.

After testing primal and dual simplex methods, we turned to interior-point algorithms. We hoped that these algorithms would fare significantly better than the simplex methods because of the severe degeneracy of the problems (only 20% to 40% of basic variables are nonzero). After obtaining an optimal LP solution from an interior-point algorithm, it is necessary to find an optimal basis before proceeding to the branch-and-bound phase of the algorithm.

The problem of moving from an optimal solution to an optimal basis is referred to as the "crossover problem". An interior-point method converges to the optimal face of the polyhedron. Thus, the crossover problem is to find a basic solution on the optimal face, starting from an arbitrary point on that face. Neither the interior optimal solution nor an optimal basic solution have many nonzeros. Thus, the problem of selecting a basis from the interior-point solution is to select which variables at value 0 should be basic and which $X_{fi} = 1$ should be nonbasic. (The X_{fi} are binary, so upper bounds are automatically added by OSL.)

The initial run using the primal–dual predictor–corrector routine of OSL to solve problem 2E took only 26 minutes to find an optimal (nonbasic) solution versus the two-hour simplex time. Table 3 compares the interior-point efficiency to the fine tuned primal simplex algorithm for aggregated problems. The rows labelled "Primal" show the time and iterations required to solve the problem from scratch. The rows labelled "PD-PC" show the number of iterations and time required by the primal–dual predictor–corrector method and also the simplex time to move from the optimal interior-point solution which was not basic to an optimal basis. (OSL provides a parameter for its simplex algorithm which allows it to begin with a nonbasic solution.)

The main insight obtained from Table 3 is that the interior-point algorithm for the larger problems is much faster than the simplex, and that the time spent in getting an optimal basis after obtaining an optimal solution is in some cases greater than the time required to find that optimal solution. Also, the improvement in solution time grows with problem size. For more information on implementations of the primal–dual interior-point method, see [7, 10, 12].

3.3. Crossover time

Since OSL performs perturbation automatically when it encounters degeneracy, we did not specifically address primal degeneracy. However, we perturbed the cost coefficients of the ground arcs by small uniform random deviates to reduce dual degeneracy and the dimension of the optimal face. Since the range of coefficients on the flight arcs is 1000–50 000, this small change in objective value should not change the optimal solution significantly. Note, however, that if the perturbation is done prior to finding the interior-point solution, the decrease in dimension of the optimal face may increase the number of iterations required to find an optimal solution. Therefore, we initially perturbed the cost coefficients after finding an optimal interior solution and before calling the simplex algorithm.

Perturbing costs prior to the interior-point algorithm always adversely affected the number of interior-point iterations required. In some cases this increase in interior iterations was offset by finding an optimal basis more quickly. However, extensive tests of perturbing the ground arc costs, either prior to or after the interior-point algorithm, showed that perturbation had little effect or increased the time to obtain an optimal basis. In retrospect this negative result should have been anticipated because regardless of the dimension of the optimal face, the initial step in solving the crossover problem is adding at least a partial basis of artificial variables. The number of artificial variables added is independent of the dimension of the optimal face. Furthermore, the crossover

Table 3
Simplex vs. primal–dual predictor–corrector

Problem name		Interior iterations	Interior time (sec)	Simplex iterations	Simplex time (sec)	Total time (sec)
1A	Primal	–	–	260	1.4	1.4
	PD-PC	11	1.3	234	< 1	< 2.3
1B	Primal	–	–	1409	29.2	29.2
	PD-PC	14	8.5	1195	8.8	17.3
1C	Primal	–	–	753	12.6	12.6
	PD-PC	15	6.1	1012	10.3	16.4
1D	Primal	–	–	8031	762.8	762.8
	PD-PC	28	201.2	6695	380.2	581.4
1E	Primal	–	–	31674	8114.2	8114.2
	PD-PC	40	1899.0	17215	1331.9	2230.9
2A	Primal	–	–	228	1.3	1.3
	PD-PC	10	1.2	225	< 1	< 2.2
2B	Primal	–	–	1545	34.0	34.0
	PD-PC	17	11.0	862	7.6	18.6
2C	Primal	–	–	968	18.8	18.8
	PD-PC	14	6.9	1194	14.0	20.9
2D	Primal	–	–	9407	991.6	991.6
	PD-PC	32	213.3	5873	284.0	497.3
2E	Primal	–	–	30508	7277.2	7277.2
	PD-PC	37	1580.5	11740	1540.0	3120.5

problem ends as soon as any nonartificial basis is reached and there is no reason to expect the effort should vary with the dimensionality of the optimal face.

Perturbation of the ground arc costs reduced the pure simplex algorithm time by fifty minutes (38%) for problem 1E and had an average speedup of 19% for all the problems. The anomaly of the perturbation helping the simplex algorithm when it is used alone, but adversely affecting the combined interior-point/simplex algorithm, regardless of whether it is done before or after the interior-point solution is obtained, is surprising. In fact, for many problems the number of simplex iterations in the crossover problem is still at least 50% of the number of simplex iterations to solve the problem from scratch, and for problems 1C and 2C, the number of simplex iterations for the crossover problem exceeded the number used in solving the entire problem. However, if one uses Megiddo's algorithm for obtaining an optimal basis from an interior-point solution, then the number of steps, each with at most the amount of work as a simplex iteration, is bounded by the number of rows and columns in the problem [11]. We did not have an implementation of this algorithm, but felt that we required a method better than straightforward simplex for getting an optimal basis from the interior-point solution. Fortunately, these experiments with perturbation of the ground arc costs led to other insights as the next section demonstrates.

3.4. Fixing variables

Preliminary investigations in solving small fleet assignment problems to integrality showed that the gap between integer and fractional optimal objective values is much less than 1%. This small gap encouraged us to pursue a strategy of fixing variables from the optimal fractional *interior* solution before entering the branch-and-bound phase.

Each flight variable whose value is greater than 0.99 is fixed to 1. We also force the integer solution to select a fleet which has seat capacity within the range of capacities indicated by the fractional solution, i.e., we sort the fleets by seat capacity and if, for example, $X_{3i} = X_{5i} = 0.5$, then we restrict the integer program to select between fleets 3, 4 and 5 by setting the upper bound of the others to zero. Fixing to 0 generalizes fixing to 1, since a cover row with only one nonzero has that variable fixed to 1 when the others are fixed to 0.

In some integer programming applications, the reduced cost of a nonbasic variable can be large enough so that changing it from its current value is clearly not optimal. If, for example, a variable has value 0 and its reduced cost is greater than a known bound on the IP-LP gap, then it cannot be positive in an optimal solution. Unfortunately, the reduced costs of the individual flight variables are not large enough to support any such fixing argument. Other fixing strategies and avoiding fixing that leads to infeasibility are discussed in Section 5.2.

After fixing, the problem is aggregated again using the optimizer's algebraic preprocessor. For each flight arc fixed to one, at least one cover row and all its entries are removed from the problem, resulting in a "crushed" model. The success of this approach depends on the interior-point solution having enough variables near their upper bound, and feasibility of the crushed problem. At first we were concerned that the interior-point solution would be very fractional in comparison with an optimal basic solution. Surprisingly however, the interior-point solution is not significantly more fractional than a basic solution.

In the last section, we demonstrated that perturbing the objective coefficients of the ground arcs did not improve the solution time. However, if we fix variables near 1 to 1, then the number of variables near 1 becomes important for both feasibility and computational speed. Fortunately, the perturbation of costs before solving the LP relaxation with the interior-point method forces many more X variables to take values near 1. For example, for problem 2D the difference is 500 (48%) more integral X variables in the interior-point solution. One explanation for this phenomenon is the optimal face is of lower dimension, so the interior-point solution is a convex combination of fewer extreme points. This extra integrality translates to the removal of at least as many cover rows, many other balance rows and many integer variables. Note that this perturbation is performed even though it increases the number of interior-point iterations required for solution of the initial LP.

Table 4 shows the reduction of problem size achieved by fixing X variables from the interior-point solution. Those problems with an "R" appended to the name have the ground arc costs perturbed before finding the interior-point solution. No results are

Table 4
Fixing 0/1 variables after interior solution

Problem name	Original		# X's fixed = 1	# X's fixed = 0	Crushed	
	Rows	Columns			Rows	Columns
1C	819	1399	193	306	125	191
1C-R			230	282	31	80
1D	5521	9146	1538	2118	213	415
1D-R			1536	2082	241	687
1E	10382	19434	1774	6648	1740	3047
1E-R			2033	6481	1063	2182
2C	870	1529	199	343	170	258
2C-R			258	309	15	66
2D	5789	9661	1049	2735	1863	2680
2D-R			1562	2247	522	1056
2E	10601	19877	1992	6780	1296	2472
2E-R			2003	6672	1365	2524

shown for the two-fleet problems since all were aggregated to a unique solution, i.e., fixing the variables at 1 removed every column from the problem. This is very common with two-fleet problems since the cover row $X_{1i} + X_{2i} = 1$ is always removed and the substitution $X_{1i} = 1 - X_{2i}$ is performed prior to solving the LP relaxation.

The simplex times for the crushed problems are significantly smaller than the problems without variable fixing. Table 5 shows the solution times for obtaining an optimal LP basis when variables are fixed by the optimal interior solution values and perturbation is performed prior to the interior-point algorithm. Comparing Tables 3 and 5, we see that the improvements in the interior times can be accounted for largely by the faster computer, but the dramatic improvements in simplex crossover times cannot begin to be accounted for by the difference in computers. For the larger problems, the simplex crossover times went from 1332 and 1540 seconds to an astonishingly fast 9.7 and 9.4 seconds.

This application of fixing variables to their bounds and aggregating again *before* finding a basis was a clear breakthrough. It has a tremendous impact on reducing the time required in solving the crossover problem but does not increase the objective value of the crushed problem in comparison with the original problem, or adversely affect integer feasibility.

Table 5
LP times with fixing and perturbed ground arc costs

Problem name	Interior iterations	Simplex iterations	Interior time	Simplex time	Total time
1C	17	121	3.9	0.1	4.0
1D	30	214	124.7	0.7	125.4
1E	36	3412	859.9	9.7	869.6
2C	16	72	3.7	0.0	3.7
2D	38	930	157.0	2.2	159.2
2E	41	1383	1058.0	9.4	1067.4

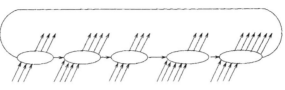

Fig. 2. A hub's time line.

3.5. Islands and connections

This section describes how to exploit the topology of the fleet assignment network to reduce the size of the model beyond what was achieved from the aggregation.

Since deregulation of the airline industry, the airlines have changed their schedules to a "hub-and-spoke" network. This topology concentrates the majority of flights at hubs with periodic feeder activity to and from the spokes and almost no activity from spoke to spoke. Another feature of the schedule at a hub is its decomposition into "complexes", a period of arrivals followed by departures separated by very little or no activity, see Fig. 2. These complexes are arranged to allow passengers the maximum opportunity to make connections to other spokes or hubs. In fact, the sparsity of the network forces the airlines to have complexes at hubs in order to provide adequate service to their passengers.

The spoke's time line differs from that of the hub in more than just volume of activity. The morning activity at a spoke is flights to the hubs, whereas the hub's initial complex consists of the arrivals from the spokes and subsequent departures. Also, the mid-day complexes at spokes consist typically of a few arrivals and a few departures. This sparsity of activity can be exploited by forcing the minimum number of aircraft to be used at that city and avoiding having unnecessary aircraft on the ground overnight. If there are no aircraft at a spoke at some time t, then after an equal number of arrivals and departures following t there will be no aircraft on the ground. Since there are no aircraft on the ground, the ground arcs in the model corresponding to these times can be removed. This removal of ground arcs yields a time line that consists of "islands", where an island is an interval of time where there exists at least one aircraft on the ground. Since there are no aircraft on the ground before an island, the number of arrivals and departures during the island must be equal. A complex itself may be an island; however complexes need not be balanced so an island may contain many complexes.

Of particular interest are islands with one arrival and one departure. These islands indicate that the aircraft that arrives must depart on the next flight, otherwise it violates the zero aircraft count assumption. This implies that the pair of the corresponding X variables in the original formulation can be combined into one variable which now represents flying the pair of flights. In other words, there is no longer any decision to make regarding the fleeting of the outbound flight; it is completely dependent on the decision made for the inbound flight. The third and fourth nodes in Fig. 3 show the forced connections that result from deleting the ground arcs between islands. These forced connections can extend through a sequence of spoke cities until a flight arrives

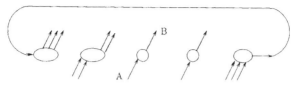

Fig. 3. A spoke's time line.

at a busier city. Many of these paths are sequences of 3–5 flights. Since these paths are the same across fleets, cover rows for each flight leg are no longer necessary but are replaced with one cover row for each path of flights. Also, the required through constraints are removed and replaced by variables indicating the fleeting for the pair of flights. Thus, X_{fi} now refers to assigning fleet f to "flight path" i which consists of one or more consecutive flights.

Another implication of island analysis is determining missed connections. Each fleet in the model has its own ready-time. Therefore, the island structure across fleets may differ. Fig. 4 shows the same time line as Fig. 3 except one arrival misses a connection. This situation often occurs for wide-body aircraft that have significantly longer ready times. In this case, we argue that no aircraft of this fleet would fly either flight A or B of the missed connection. If an aircraft of this fleet flies one of those legs, it must overnight at this station or another fleet would have to cover the paired flight. However, the only way another fleet can cover flight A or B without covering both is to use an additional aircraft.

This missed connection argument is not entirely based on the fact that there must be zero aircraft on the ground at some time. (Fig. 4 still shows zero planes on the ground during the missed connection.) Instead, it relies on the fact that if the missed connection is flown by an undesirable fleet, an extra aircraft must overnight at this city. This is seen by noting the differences in the durations of the islands in Figs. 3 and 4. The model generator identifies these missed connections and forbids both flights from the fleets that miss the connections. This removes two 0/1 variables for each fleet that misses the connection.

It is impossible to force this minimum aircraft assumption across all cities because the interactions among flights, fleets and ready times may not allow this lower bound on total aircraft to be achieved. The question of where to enforce this assumption, which greatly reduces model size, especially the number of integer variables, is a delicate one and depends on the schedule. Clearly, enforcing islands at too many cities will make the problem infeasible, or yield a poor solution. The busiest cities should be excluded from the island construction for they have the most potential to profit by using more

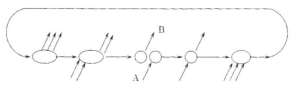

Fig. 4. A missed connection.

Table 6
Island and connection preprocessing

Problem name	Flights	Additional connections	Missed connections	Ground arcs removed	0/1 variables removed
1	2559	482	1022	8466	7162
2	2637	496	961	8524	7355
3	2627	487	888	8464	7016
4	2588	475	868	8434	7246
5	2590	482	881	8451	7339

than their minimum number of aircraft.

We have analyzed the LP solutions to problems solved with and without islands to identify cities where the LP solution violates the island assumption. An automatic method of determining which cities should have islands enforced can be based on the total duration of all ground arcs which connect islands. The shorter this excess ground time the less likely the city should have islands enforced. These cities together with the hubs do not have the minimum aircraft count enforced by the islands. This analysis was needed to ensure that imposing the island structure would not adversely affect the solution quality.

Table 6 shows the reduction in model size for five eleven-fleet problems. These problems are based on three schedules, with problems 3, 4 and 5 being variants of one schedule. Table 7 shows the dramatic improvement in LP solution times by using the island structure for the two seven-fleet problems solved by the interior-point algorithm and fixing variables before calling the simplex algorithm. The total time contains only LP time, not I/O times. This table also shows the initial LPs of the eleven-fleet problems for these schedules have reasonable solution times of less than forty minutes. All of the preprocessing work, node consolidation, islands, and missed connections reduced the size of problem 2 from 48 982 by 66 942 to 7703 by 20 464.

Even though the eleven-fleet problems can be solved in less than forty minutes, there is an order of magnitude difference between those times and those of the seven-fleet problems. Table 8 shows the change in model parameters for the seven- and eleven-

Table 7
Islands and connections

Problem name		Interior		Simplex		Total time
		Iterations	Time	Iterations	Time	
1E	No islands	36	859.9	3412	9.7	869.6
	Islands	32	135.5	1224	3.7	139.2
2E	No islands	41	1058.0	1383	9.4	1067.4
	Islands	36	141.6	885	4.0	145.6
1	Islands	36	2206.9	3149	110.3	2317.2
2	Islands	35	2573.0	938	25.3	2598.3
3	Islands	37	2199.3	2010	63.3	2262.6
4	Islands	40	1756.1	4455	165.2	1921.3
5	Islands	39	1685.6	4171	155.7	1841.3
6	Islands	38	1611.4	2559	86.2	1697.6

Table 8
Model parameters with islands

Problem	Rows	Columns	$|A|$	$|L|$	$|A|$/columns	$|A|$/rows	$|L|/|A|$
1E	4392	10230	29523	365983	2.886	6.722	12.397
2E	4505	10482	30304	363779	2.891	6.727	12.004
1	7299	19430	55690	2504575	2.866	7.630	44.974
2	7703	20464	58438	2731498	2.856	7.586	46.742
3	7707	20317	58039	2589310	2.857	7.531	44.613
4	7332	19521	55923	2106975	2.865	7.627	37.676
5	7206	19369	55547	2083972	2.868	7.708	37.517
6	7179	19361	55580	2088080	2.871	7.742	37.569

fleet problems with islands. The columns $|A|$ and $|L|$ show the number of nonzeros in the model after aggregation and in the Cholesky factorization, respectively. While the average number of nonzeros per column has remained the same, the average number of nonzeros per row has increased. This foreshadows the drastic increase in number of nonzeros in the Cholesky factor. The rate of increase in Cholesky nonzeros is much greater than the rate of increase in nonzeros in the model.

3.6. Dual steepest edge

After this work was completed, OSL introduced a new steepest edge simplex pricing routine based on [5,8]. At the suggestion of Robert Bixby, we now compared simplex methods to the interior point to be sure that the change in model structure and size did not change the performance of the methods. Unexpectedly, the changes made the dual simplex method with steepest edge pricing the fastest method for the eleven-fleet problems.

Table 9 shows the results for the simplex variants on these problems. The times and iterations represent the computation required to get the optimal basis to the unperturbed problem. This means that we are first solving the perturbed problem, removing the perturbation, then reoptimizing. The dual method was much faster than the primal on the eleven-fleet problems. This again is the reverse of the behavior for seven-fleet

Table 9
Simplex pricing performance

Problem	Primal Devex		Primal SE		Dual SE	
	Iterations	Time	Iterations	Time	Iterations	Time
1E	13519	571.2	12573	557.1	9623	536.8
2E	13833	646.8	13848	660.8	8385	469.9
1	33101	3257.5	32097	3194.5	15408	1431.8
2	29031	2785.3	32934	3256.3	14302	1554.8
3	25888	2328.5	26528	2471.7	15714	1623.9
4	34903	3369.3	31244	3099.8	15231	1513.4
5	34800	3363.1	31342	3090.8	16012	1536.6
6	29463	2779.9	32811	3199.1	14954	1461.5

problems without islands where primal simplex was faster. The problems also possess the interesting behavior that when the objective coefficients are perturbed, Devex and steepest edge pricing in the primal simplex method obtain the optimal solution in a comparable number of iterations, as seen in Table 9. Although the detailed computational results are not provided here, perturbation of the objective coefficients of all variables by uniform deviates helps the dual steepest edge method as well.

These results run counter to some widely held beliefs in computational linear programming. Usually, when faced with severely degenerate problems, the more effort that is put into pricing, the greater the reduction in the number of simplex iterations. For these problems, Devex and steepest edge pricing perform comparably in primal simplex.

Computational results for interior-point algorithms seem to suggest that the efficacy of these methods grows with problem size. Clearly, our results show that size must be measured in terms of the nonzeros in the Cholesky factor, which is quite sensitive to the number and structure of nonzeros in the model. Furthermore, common measures of sparsity, like nonzeros per column, must be viewed with care when used in arguments for interior-point methods because nonzeros per row is an equally good measure which can lead to different conclusions.

We conclude this section by noting that the interior-point method is better than the dual steepest edge simplex for the seven-fleet problems, but worse for the eleven-fleet problems. The only explanation we have for this change is the explosive growth of the number of nonzeros in the Cholesky factor. In fact, the problems with largest $|L|/|A|$ are the ones for which the dual steepest edge simplex method showed the largest improvement over the interior-point method.

3.7. Summary of LP algorithm

In Fig. 5 we summarize the algorithm developed for solving the initial LP for the eleven-fleet problems. The three main model enhancements developed are: node consolidation, island construction and eliminating missed connections. These procedures are all part of the program which constructs the matrix describing the basic model. Within the optimization system, we perturb all costs, then aggregate using the optimizer's algebraic preprocessor, and solve this problem with the dual simplex method using steepest edge

Solution steps:
   (1) Aggregate using optimizer's algebraic preprocessor.
   (2) Perturb all costs.
   (3) Dual steepest-edge simplex.
   (4) Remove perturbation.
* (5) Reoptimize.
   (6) Disaggregate.
   (7) Fix X variables with value $\geqslant 0.99$ to 1.
   (8) Aggregate again without harming the cover rows to get crushed problem.
   (9) Dual steepest edge simplex.
  (10) Branch and Bound

Fig. 5. Dual steepest edge algorithm for fleet assignment.

Solution steps:
(1) Aggregate using optimizer's algebraic preprocessor.
(2) Perturb all ground arc costs.
(3) Primal-dual predictor-corrector.
(4) Remove perturbation.
(5) Disaggregate.
(6) Fix X variables with value $\geqslant 0.99$ to 1.
(7) Aggregate again without harming the cover rows to get crushed problem.
(8) Dual steepest edge simplex.
(9) Branch and Bound

Fig. 6. PD-PC algorithm for fleet assignment.

pricing. The solution obtained is then unperturbed, reoptimized and used to fix variables yielding a crushed problem. The crushed problem is then solved by dual steepest edge simplex to obtain an optimal basis, which is then passed on to the branch-and-bound phase. Note the algebraic preprocessor that exploits the fixed variables must not change the structure of the cover rows, which is needed in the branch-and-bound phase.

For the seven-fleet problems the interior-point method with fixing prior to obtaining an optimal basis is much faster than the dual steepest edge method. The model parameters given in Table 8 can be used to decide upon the proper algorithm at run time. Fig. 6 shows the interior-point version of the algorithm. The main difference between the two methods, in addition to the LP algorithm, is that the interior-point version is forced to fix X's to 1 from an optimal perturbed LP solution and the simplex version reoptimizes after removing the perturbation, then fixes.

4. Branch and bound

With any large integer programming model that is designed to be part of an ongoing decision support system, a significant effort must be made to achieve robustness in the solution methodology. This section focuses on the branch-and-bound enhancements that have been implemented in order to control the growth of the tree.

After solving an LP relaxation at a node of the branch-and-bound tree, we must decide which branching constraints should be added and which relaxation to evaluate next. We implemented two modifications of OSL's default branching rule by branching on the cover rows in a specialized way and reordering the selection of branches.

Given a fractional LP solution, a cover row

$$\sum_f X_{fi} = 1,$$

which in OSL terminology is an SOS type-3 constraint, is selected for branching. First, the variables in the cover row are partitioned into two sets $\{I_1, I_u\}$ each containing some fractional X's. The constraint on one branch is then

$$\sum_{f \in I_1} X_{fi} = 0,$$

and on the other branch is

$$\sum_{f \in I_u} X_{fi} = 0.$$

These branches give a much more balanced tree than the usual branches, $X_{fi} = 0$ or 1.

4.1. Branching strategies

In OSL, each cover row is a set and possesses a priority either by default, or defined by the user. The easiest way to change the branch-and-bound strategy is to change the priorities among the sets. We use objective information about the flights to determine the priorities. The rules selected order the sets based on a measure of the variability among the objective coefficients. The larger the variability in the objective coefficients, the greater the impact of imposing a constraint on that set and the more likely that the LP values will change significantly on both branches.

The first method calculates the initial priority of a flight leg as the sum of the absolute value of the differences in the objective coefficients of the X's covering that leg, e.g.,

$$\sum_f |c_{f^-,i} - c_{f,i}| = \text{Priority}(i),$$

where f^-, i is the fleet with next smaller seating capacity compared to f allowed on leg i and the sum begins with the second fleet allowed on i. Since the fleets are sorted by seat capacity, this sum measures the spread of the objective values. The second method sets the initial priority of the leg to the difference between the maximum and minimum objective coefficients of X's covering that leg. We chose these surrogates for variance to avoid having to loop over the columns twice. With either method, after computing this variability for each set, sets with nearly equal variance are placed in the same priority class. We used five classes in our computations. With this grouping, OSL still has flexibility to use its own heuristic rules to choose the branch.

In OSL, the default branching rule is implemented in the following manner. First, an estimate of the objective value change (the degradation) is computed for each of the branching constraints that could be added. The chosen branch is the one among all sets with highest priority that has the minimum maximum degradation [4]. This branch is estimated to harm the objective function the least. The node selection strategy prefers more recent nodes if there is no integer feasible solution, or selects the node with the best estimated solution.

4.2. Branch-and-bound results

Table 10 gives the IP computational results for the eleven-fleet problems solved in the earlier sections. These runs began with the optimal bases from the crushed problem obtained from the interior-point algorithm in Fig. 6. The last column (Time in B&B) is the CPU-time measured after an optimal basis to the initial LP was obtained until

Table 10
Branching strategy results

Problem	Branching rule	Nodes in B&B	Node of first	Node of optimal	# 0/1 solutions	Time in B&B
1	Default	2000+	87	220	5	6743.3
	Absolute difference	46	8	8	1	258.9
	Range	96	24	53	3	591.2
2	Default	74	4	14	2	67.9
	Absolute difference	68	10	50	5	254.9
	Range	46	8	45	4	178.0
3	Default	1763	7	780	4	3600.1
	Absolute difference	30	6	11	2	180.6
	Range	42	7	37	5	266.3
5	Default	2000+	23	566	6	6744.0
	Absolute difference	47	13	44	3	349.0
	Range	167	15	57	3	883.2
6	Default	499	36	345	5	809.3
	Absolute difference	141	11	123	4	703.2
	Range	60	11	41	3	249.3

the optimal IP solution was found or 2000 nodes were exhausted in B&B. The column designated "Node of first" reports the node at which the first integer solution is found. The column designated "Node of optimal" reports the node at which the best integer solution is found. This is the optimal integer solution to the crushed problem even for those problems that reached the 2000 node limit. The difference between the nodes in B&B and nodes to the optimal solution indicate how quickly the B&B tree is being pruned.

The objective function branching criteria performed significantly better than the default method. On two problems the default method exhausted the 2000 node limit, and for each of these problems the objective function based criteria performed quite well. These two problems also show the default method required the most effort *after* it had found the optimal solution. Also note that the absolute difference criteria performed best on the problems for which the default criteria required an excessive number of nodes. The CPU-time reported in branch-and-bound includes writing out all the integer feasible solutions, thus problem 2 shows the default method being much faster than the others, but requiring more nodes in the B&B tree.

Based on these runs, the absolute difference criteria has the lowest average number of nodes explored in B&B, and is the most robust branching rule of the three tested.

5. Conclusions

The formulation and solution procedure perform very well for the basic model. Table 11 shows the full results of the most robust solution method described in Fig. 5 for the eleven-fleet problems. Table 12 shows the same results for the interior-point algo-

Table 11
Full results of dual SE algorithm

Problem name	Dual SE simplex		B&B		% IP-LP gap	Total time
	Iterations	Time	Nodes	Time		
1	15 351	1501.8	500+	3360.8	0.020	5027.9
2	13 691	1394.6	10	47.6	0.004	1633.4
3	15 087	1529.9	6	103.6	0.002	1807.2
4	14 052	1392.2	111	947.9	0.005	2506.1
5	14 753	1422.0	10	184.5	0.006	1771.9
6	14 177	1376.0	103	636.5	0.012	2176.3

rithm applied to the eleven-fleet problems. Overall, the LP and IP performances have improved by using the dual steepest edge algorithm with only problem 1 suffering from the change. The simplex iterations and time reported in Table 11 include that required to unperturb the solution. The total time reflects time in the entire program including I/O.

The differences in the branch-and-bound results are due to the reoptimization of the LP after removing the perturbation on the costs when using the dual steepest edge method. This prevents the fixing from making some "mistakes" and yields smaller IP-LP gaps. However, in spite of the small gap for problem 1, we were unable to prune its tree in 500 nodes.

As more constraints are added to the model, the formulation and solution procedure will undergo revisions. A drawback of the current method is the need to fix many variables from the optimal LP solution before proceeding to branch-and-bound. This fixing may not work so well as more nonnetwork constraints are added to the model, which is likely to increase the possibility of having more fractional variables in the optimal linear programming solution that cannot be fixed to 1.

5.1. Model enhancements

The basic model is easily adapted to contain such varied constraints as limiting noise at airports, providing extended uninterrupted periods of time with aircraft out of service for pilot training or maintenance; limiting the total flying hours assigned to a class of crew compatible fleets; or enforcing limits on the number of wide-bodied aircraft that may be at an airport at any time. More complex constraints, like providing a solution which minimizes bad situations for crew planning, are also within the scope

Table 12
Full results of interior-point algorithm

Problem name	Interior		Simplex		B&B		% IP-LP gap	Total time
	Iterations	Time	Iterations	Time	Nodes	Time		
1	38	2141.8	3022	15.33	46	258.93	0.013	2551.6
2	35	2346.4	1777	7.90	68	254.94	0.010	2747.7
3	38	2578.9	3178	32.14	30	180.60	0.221	2933.3
5	40	1812.3	3734	8.17	47	349.03	0.005	2328.6
6	39	2205.2	3739	27.11	141	703.21	0.012	3069.4

of the model. However, these goals require additional variables as well as many more constraints to capture crew movements within the fleet assignment model. These model enhancements and their computational consequences are discussed in [3].

The solution to the basic model cannot be implemented without intervention from the analysts in the operations department. The major drawbacks to its implementation are aircraft sequencing and exception handling. The first of these issues arises from the fact that the fleet assignment model does not assign aircraft to flights, rather it assigns aircraft types to flights. Because the model does not know the previous or next flights to which the aircraft will connect (excepting connections derived from required hookups or islands), many decisions needed to implement a schedule are postponed. Among these postponed decisions is scheduling 4–5 hour maintenance opportunities that should take place every 2–4 days. Exception handling refers to the problem arising from the use of a daily model when actual schedules differ from day to day. It may also be the case that profit may be improved by using different fleeting for some days of the week.

5.2. Solution enhancements

The initial results from modifying the branch-and-bound method are encouraging. However, fixing all the variables near 1 to 1 in more complex models may lead to infeasibility. In this situation the fixing of variables to zero, and allowing at least two fleets per flight leg can help prevent creating an infeasible IP. A better method is finding cycles of flow at value 1 in the LP solution, and to fix flows along these cycles. If not enough variables are fixed in this manner, then paths of flow from hub to hub could be fixed. The hub to hub restriction puts the endpoints of the paths at busy airports where there is a greater opportunity to find other flights with which to connect.

The realization that the dual simplex algorithm with steepest edge pricing is superior to interior-point methods for some classes of fleet assignment problems implies we are no longer forced to fix variables due to difficulties arising from the crossover problem. This will allow us more flexibility in pursuing other strategies for the IP and is a current research area.

Other branching strategies could include flying time information. Assigning an aircraft to a long duration flight removes an aircraft from the pool of available aircraft for a large part of the day. Therefore, branching on these paths early in the tree will cause the relaxation objective values to change more quickly.

5.3. Final remarks

While the advent of workstations and optimization libraries has advanced mathematical programming capabilities enormously, such advances do not imply that users can naively apply this technology to construct effective decision support systems for hard problems. This paper demonstrates that the optimization library, while greatly simplifying the task, does not replace the effort of the analyst that goes into making a robust solution algorithm.

Acknowledgements

We wish to thank the employees of Delta Air Lines, Inc., especially Joe Davis, Dave Caldwell and Richard Scheff, who contributed to our understanding of the issues involved in the fleet assignment problem.

References

[1] J. Abara, "Applying integer linear programming to the fleet assignment problem," *Interfaces* 19 (1989) 20-28.
[2] M.A. Berge and C.A. Hopperstad, "Demand driven dispatch: a method for dynamic aircraft capacity assignment, models and algorithms," *Operations Research* 41 (1993) 153-168.
[3] L.W. Clarke, C.A. Hane, E.L. Johnson and G.L. Nemhauser, "Modeling issues in fleet assignment," *Transportation Science*, to appear.
[4] J. Druckerman, D. Silverman and K. Viaropulos, *IBM Optimization Subroutine Library, Guide and Reference, Release 2*, Document Number SC230519-02, IBM, Kingston, NY (1991).
[5] J.J. Forrest and D. Goldfarb, "Steepest-edge simplex algorithms for linear programming," *Mathematical Programming* 57 (3) (1992) 341-374.
[6] J.J.H. Forrest and J.A. Tomlin, "Implementing the simplex method of the Optimization Subroutine Library," *IBM Systems Journal* 31 (1992) 11-25.
[7] J.J.H. Forrest and J.A. Tomlin, "Implementing interior point linear programming methods in the Optimization Subroutine Library," *IBM Systems Journal* 31 (1992) 26-38.
[8] D. Goldfarb and J.K. Reid, "A practicable steepest-edge simplex algorithm," *Mathematical Programming* 12 (3) (1977) 361-371.
[9] P.M.J. Harris, "Pivot selection methods of the Devex LP code," *Mathematical Programming* 5 (1) (1973) 1-28; reprinted in: *Mathematical Programming Study* 4 (1975) 30-57.
[10] I.J. Lustig, R.E. Marsten and D.F. Shanno, "On implementing Mehrotra's predictor-corrector interior point method for linear programming," *SIAM Journal on Optimization* 2 (1992) 435-449.
[11] N. Megiddo, "On finding primal- and dual-optimal bases," *ORSA Journal on Computing* 3 (1991) 63-65.
[12] S. Mehrotra, "On the implementation of a primal-dual interior point method," *SIAM Journal on Optimization* 2 (1992) 575-601.

16

IMPROVING CREW SCHEDULING BY INCORPORATING KEY MAINTENANCE ROUTING DECISIONS

AMY MAINVILLE COHN

CYNTHIA BARNHART

Crew costs are the second-largest operating expense faced by the airline industry, after fuel. Thus, even a small improvement in the quality of a crew schedule can have significant financial impact. Decisions made earlier in the airline planning process, however, can reduce the number of options available to the crew scheduler. We address this limitation by delaying some of these earlier planning decisions—specifically, key maintenance routing decisions—and incorporating them within the crew scheduling problem. We present an *extended crew pairing model* that integrates crew scheduling and maintenance routing decisions. We prove theoretical results that allow us to improve the tractability of this model by decreasing the number of variables needed and by relaxing the integrality requirement of many of the remaining variables. We discuss how to solve the model both heuristically and to optimality, providing the user with the flexibility to trade off solution time and quality. We present a computational proof-of-concept to support the tractability and effectiveness of our approach.

Subject classifications: Programming, integers, branch and bound; branch and price. Transportation, models, assignment: crews and aircraft.

1. INTRODUCTION

The airline planning process is made up of many large and complex problems. Of these, crew scheduling is of particular importance. Crew costs are the second-largest operating expense faced by the airlines, after fuel; thus, improving the quality of the crew schedule by even a small amount can have significant financial benefits (Anbil et al. 1993, 1991, Gershkoff 1989, Graves et al. 1993).

A key step in solving the crew scheduling problem is to select a minimum cost set of *crew pairings*—sequences of flights that can be flown by a single crew. This step is known as the *crew pairing problem*. The chosen pairings are then combined to form complete schedules for individual crews. The quality of the crew schedule therefore depends on the set of feasible crew pairings. This feasible set can be impacted significantly by decisions made earlier in the planning process.

One restriction on a valid pairing is that two sequential flights cannot be assigned to the same crew unless the time between these flights (known as *connection* or *sit time*) is sufficient for the crew members to travel through the terminal, from the arrival gate of one flight to the departure gate of the next. This minimum connection time can be relaxed if both flights have been assigned to the same aircraft, because the crew remains with the aircraft. We use the term *short connect* to refer to a connection which is feasible for a crew only if the two sequential flights comprising that connection have been assigned to a common aircraft.

The assignment of aircraft to flights occurs in the *maintenance routing problem*, which typically precedes crew scheduling in the airline planning process. In the maintenance routing problem, aircraft are assigned to strings of flights so as to ensure that every aircraft will have adequate opportunity to receive maintenance. This assignment of aircraft to flights determines the set of short connects in the network, thereby impacting the set of feasible pairings permitted in the subsequent crew scheduling problem. Given that the maintenance routing problem does not consider the impact of short connects on the crew scheduling problem, solving the maintenance routing and crew scheduling problems sequentially can result in a suboptimal solution. The goal of our research is to address this limitation.

Prior works by Klabjan et al. (1999) and Cordeau et al. (2000) demonstrate the impact of short connect selection on crew scheduling, and present models for addressing this limitation. Klabjan et al. (1999) reverse the order in which they consider the maintenance routing and crew pairing problems. They solve the crew pairing problem first, assuming all short connects to be valid. They next solve the maintenance routing problem, in which all short connects used in the crew pairing solution are required to be included in the maintenance routing solution. This approach yields significant improvements for many real-world problem instances. It does not guarantee maintenance feasibility, however, and nonpathological instances exist for which the short connects in a crew pairing solution lead to maintenance infeasibility.

Cordeau et al. (2000) present an integrated approach with approximate crew costs, in which they link maintenance routing and crew pairing models by a set of additional constraints. There is one constraint for each short connect, which enforces the rule that we can choose a crew pairing containing that short connect only if we also choose a maintenance routing string containing it. They present a Benders decomposition approach, consisting of a maintenance routing master problem and a crew pairing subproblem, along with a heuristic branching strategy. They present computational results for a number of problem instances and compare the quality of their heuristic to a more basic approach.

In our research, we have developed an *extended crew pairing model (ECP)* which further contributes to this literature. We have focused on three key objectives:
• First, we want to guarantee a maintenance-feasible crew pairing solution;
• Second, we want to provide the user with the flexibility to trade off solution time and quality. When solved completely, our model yields an exact solution to the integrated maintenance routing and crew pairing problem. Alternatively, our approach can be used heuristically to find quality solutions more quickly while still guaranteeing maintenance feasibility;
• Third, we want to leverage the fact that only a fraction of the decisions made in the maintenance routing phase impact the crew pairing problem. By including in the extended crew pairing model only those maintenance decisions which are relevant, we can reduce the size of the model significantly.

The remainder of the paper is structured as follows. In §2 we present the extended crew pairing model. We prove theoretical results that allow us to improve the tractability of this model by eliminating a large number of variables and by relaxing the integrality requirement of many others. In §3 we discuss implementation details associated with *ECP*. In §4 we discuss an alternative approach, the *constrained crew pairing problem*, which can be solved in parallel to *ECP* for improved performance. We provide our conclusions and suggested areas for future research in §5.

2. THE EXTENDED CREW PAIRING MODEL

Before introducing the extended crew pairing model, we briefly review the crew pairing and maintenance routing problems.

2.1. The Crew Pairing Problem

The crew pairing problem is typically formulated as a *set partitioning problem*, in which we want to find a minimum cost set of feasible crew pairings such that every flight is included in exactly one pairing.

We define the following notation:
• P is the set of feasible pairings;
• F is the set of flights;
• c_p is the cost of pairing p;
• δ_{fp} is an indicator variable that has value 1 if flight f is included in pairing p and 0 otherwise;
• y_p is the binary decision variable associated with pairing p. If $y_p = 1$, then pairing p is included in the solution; otherwise, $y_p = 0$.

Given this, we write the crew pairing problem (*CP*) as:

$$\min \sum_{p \in P} c_p y_p \tag{1}$$

st

$$\sum_{p \in P} \delta_{fp} y_p = 1 \quad \forall f \in F \tag{2}$$

$$y_p \in \{0, 1\} \quad \forall p \in P. \tag{3}$$

The objective (1) minimizes the cost of the chosen set of pairings. The cover constraints (2) and integrality constraints (3) state that, for each flight f, the number of chosen pairings containing that flight must be exactly one. This formulation eliminates the need to incorporate complicated feasibility rules. It also allows us to linearize the cost function, because the cost associated with each pairing is computed "offline." Note, however, that the number of variables (that is, the number of feasible pairings in the flight network) is exponentially large—often exceeding hundreds of millions. The literature on solving this large-scale integer program includes Anbil et al. (1992), Ball and Roberts (1985), Beasley and Cao (1996), Chu et al. (1997), Crainic and Rousseau (1987), Desaulniers et al. (1997), Hoffman and Padberg (1993), Klabjan et al. (1999), Klabjan and Schwan (1999), Lavoie et al. (1988), Levine (1996), and Vance et al. (1997).

2.2. The Maintenance Routing Problem

As is the case with crew pairing, a string-based approach is often used in formulating the maintenance routing problem (for example, see Barnhart et al. 1998).

We define the following additional notation:
• R is the set of feasible route strings;
• c_r is the cost of route string r;
• α_{fr} is an indicator variable that has value 1 if route string r contains flight f and 0 otherwise;
• d_r is the binary decision variable associated with route string r. If $d_r = 1$, then route string r is included in the solution; otherwise, $d_r = 0$;
• N is the set of nodes which represent points in space and time at which route strings begin or end (and thus, aircraft are needed or become available);
• g_n^- and g_n^+ are the ground arc variables representing the number of aircraft on the ground at station s immediately prior to and immediately following time t, given a node n that represents time t at station s;
• R^T is the set of route strings that span time T, an arbitrary time known as the *countline*;
• N^T is the set of nodes with corresponding ground arcs g_n^+ spanning the countline;
• K is the available number of aircraft.

Given this, we write the maintenance routing problem (*MR*) as:

$$\min \sum_{r \in R} c_r d_r, \tag{4}$$

st

$$\sum_{r \in R} \alpha_{fr} d_r = 1 \quad \forall f \in F, \tag{5}$$

$$\sum_{\substack{r \text{ ends at} \\ \text{node } n}} d_r + g_n^- - \sum_{\substack{r \text{ starts at} \\ \text{node } n}} d_r - g_n^+ = 0 \quad \forall n \in N, \tag{6}$$

$$\sum_{r \in R^T} d_r + \sum_{n \in Z^T} g_n^+ \leqslant K, \tag{7}$$

$$d_r \in \{0, 1\} \quad \forall r \in R, \tag{8}$$

$$g_n^+, g_n^- \geqslant 0 \quad \forall n \in N. \tag{9}$$

The objective function (4) minimizes the cost of the chosen route strings—we set the coefficients c_r to zero, given that we are concerned only with finding a feasible solution. The first set of constraints (5) are cover constraints, which state that each flight must be included in exactly one chosen route string. The second set of constraints (6) are *balance constraints*. They ensure that the flow on route strings and ground arcs forms a circulation. The balance constraint for a specific node n states that the number of aircraft on route strings terminating at n plus the flow on the ground arc into n must equal the number of aircraft on route strings originating at n plus the flow on the ground arc out of n. Constraint (7) ensures that the total number of aircraft in use at time T (and thus at any point in time, given that the flow forms a circulation) does not exceed the number of aircraft in the fleet. Finally, note that although the route string variables are required to be binary (8), the integrality of the ground arc variables can be relaxed (9), as discussed in Hane et al. (1995).

As in the crew pairing problem, maintenance routing is complicated by an exponentially large number of valid route strings. Barnhart and Talluri (1997) provide a survey of the solution literature.

2.3. The Basic Integrated Model

In the crew pairing problem, we want to select a minimum cost set of feasible pairings such that every flight is included in exactly one pairing. Solving this problem after solving the maintenance routing problem can be suboptimal, because the maintenance routing solution can limit the set of feasible pairings from which we can choose. We can therefore improve the quality of the crew scheduling solution by solving the crew pairing and maintenance routing problems simultaneously.

One way to do this is to integrate the existing basic models. To provide as many feasible pairings as possible, we include all short connects in the crew pairing network. We then insure maintenance compatibility by adding one constraint per short connect. This constraint states that we cannot choose a crew pairing containing that short connect unless we also choose a maintenance routing string containing that short connect.

We define the following additional notation:
- C is the set of short connects;
- ϑ_{cr} is an indicator variable that has value 1 if route string r contains short connect c and 0 otherwise;
- η_{cp} is an indicator variable that has value 1 if pairing p contains short connect c and 0 otherwise.

Given this, we write the *basic integrated model (BIM)* as:

$$\min \sum_{p \in P} c_p y_p, \tag{10}$$

st

$$\sum_{p \in P} \delta_{fp} y_p = 1 \quad \forall f \in F, \tag{11}$$

$$\sum_{r \in R} \alpha_{fr} d_r = 1 \quad \forall f \in F, \tag{12}$$

$$\sum_{\substack{r \text{ ends at} \\ \text{node } n}} d_r + g_n^- - \sum_{\substack{r \text{ starts at} \\ \text{node } n}} d_r - g_n^+ = 0 \quad \forall n \in N, \tag{13}$$

$$\sum_{r \in R^T} d_r + \sum_{n \in Z^T} g_n^+ \leqslant K, \tag{14}$$

$$\sum_{r \in R} \vartheta_{cr} d_r - \sum_{p \in P} \eta_{cp} y_p \geqslant 0 \quad \forall c \in C, \tag{15}$$

$$d_r \in \{0, 1\} \quad \forall r \in R, \tag{16}$$

$$g_n^+, g_n^- \geqslant 0 \quad \forall n \in N, \tag{17}$$

$$y_p \in \{0, 1\} \quad \forall p \in P. \tag{18}$$

Objective Function (10) and Constraint Sets (11) and (18) are the same as in the *CP* model. Constraint Sets (12), (13), (14), (16), and (17) are the same as in the *MR* model. These two models are linked together by Constraint Set (15), which states that we cannot choose a pairing containing a short connect unless we also choose a maintenance solution containing that short connect.

2.4. The ECP Formulation

The basic integrated model has two important deficiencies—its large size and its weak LP relaxation—leading to intractability for many problem instances. To address this, we present an alternative model called the *extended crew pairing model (ECP)*. In this model, we start with the basic crew pairing model and add a collection of variables, each of which represents a *complete solution* to the maintenance routing problem. Thus, we can eliminate all the constraints associated with the original maintenance routing problem, replacing them with a single *convexity constraint*. This constraint ensures that we select exactly one maintenance routing solution. We ensure compatibility between this maintenance routing solution and the chosen crew pairings by including one constraint for each short connect, which specifies that we cannot choose a pairing containing that short connect unless we also choose a maintenance routing solution containing it.

We define the following additional notation:
- S is the set of feasible maintenance routing solutions;
- β_{cs} is an indicator variable that has value 1 if short connect c is included in maintenance solution s and 0 otherwise;
- x_s is the binary decision variable associated with maintenance solution s. If $x_s = 1$, then maintenance solution s is chosen; otherwise, $x_s = 0$.

Given this notation, we write the extended crew pairing model (*ECP*) as:

$$\min \sum_{p \in P} c_p y_p, \quad (19)$$

st

$$\sum_{p \in P} \delta_{fp} y_p = 1 \quad \forall f \in F, \quad (20)$$

$$\sum_{s \in S} \beta_{cs} x_s - \sum_{p \in P} \eta_{cp} y_p \geq 0 \quad \forall c \in C, \quad (21)$$

$$\sum_{s \in S} x_s = 1, \quad (22)$$

$$x_s \in \{0, 1\} \quad \forall s \in S, \quad (23)$$

$$y_p \in \{0, 1\} \quad \forall p \in P. \quad (24)$$

The objective (19) and the cover constraints (20) are the same as in the basic crew pairing model. Constraint (22), in conjunction with (23), ensures the selection of exactly one solution to the maintenance routing problem. Constraint Set (21) eliminates pairings that contain short connects not included in this selected maintenance solution.

This model yields an optimal integrated solution if all maintenance routing solutions are included. Furthermore, if only a subset of the maintenance solutions are considered (including that which would have been provided from the sequential approach currently used in practice), we are still guaranteed a feasible solution to the integrated model, which is at least as good as that found using the sequential approach.

Associated with this model, however, are a number of concerns regarding tractability. How many maintenance solutions will be needed in this new model? How can they be identified? Will the new model have too many binary variables? We address these concerns in the remainder of this section.

2.5. Reducing Problem Size Through Variable Elimination

We can solve *ECP* to optimality by including one column for every feasible maintenance routing solution. In practice, however, this is usually not an option, given that the number of feasible maintenance solutions is an exponential function of the number of flights. In this section we leverage the fact that only certain key maintenance routing decisions impact the crew pairing problem, thereby allowing us to significantly decrease the number of maintenance variables required to ensure an optimal solution.

In our initial description of the *ECP* model, we referred to maintenance routing solution variables. An examination of the constraint matrix, however, highlights the fact that most maintenance routing decisions are implicit in the variable definition, with only short connect information stated explicitly. In other words, we can think of a maintenance column not as a full-blown specification of a feasible solution to the maintenance routing problem, but as a *short connect set for which a feasible maintenance routing solution exists*. We refer to this as a *maintenance-feasible short connect set*. This has important ramifications for the size and structure of *ECP*, because there may be many different feasible maintenance routing solutions associated with a given set of short connects. In particular, when solving the crew pairing model for a given short connect set, it is not relevant to crew scheduling *how* the aircraft are routed, but rather that a feasible routing exists.

We claim that in order to guarantee an optimal solution to *ECP*, it is not necessary to include one column for each feasible maintenance routing solution. Instead, it is sufficient to include one column for each *unique and maximal (UM)* maintenance-feasible short connect set. We define this terminology in the following sections.

2.5.1. Uniqueness. Consider a basic example with six flights (A, B, C, D, E, and F) and one short connect (A–B). Suppose that there are two feasible maintenance solutions of two route strings each (A–B–C and D–E–F or A–B–F and D–E–C). Note that these two solutions will result in identical columns in *ECP*, with 1s in the row for short connect A–B and in the convexity constraint, and 0s throughout the rest of the column. We need to include only one of these two columns in *ECP*—both solutions define the same set of feasible crew pairings.

We refer to this potential for reducing the required number of columns in *ECP* as *uniqueness*. In other words, we need only one column for each unique maintenance-feasible short connect set, rather than one per distinct maintenance routing solution. To gain some sense of the impact of this reduction, we selected a set of short connects from an actual airline problem instance and began generating distinct feasible maintenance routing solutions, requiring each to contain exactly these selected short connects. We found over 8,700 distinct solutions, all of which could be represented by a single column in *ECP*. Because the number of potential short connects is typically only a small fraction of the number of possible aircraft connections in the network, we believe that similar reductions in the number of required maintenance columns will be found in most real-world instances.

2.5.2. Maximal Sets. We take the notion of uniqueness one step further by defining the concept of a *maximal set*. Consider the case where one maintenance solution contains three short connects, denoted by U–V, W–X, and Y–Z. Another solution contains short connects U–V and Y–Z only. Clearly, any crew pairing that is feasible for the second maintenance routing solution is also feasible for the first solution. Therefore, we can discard the second column. In doing so, we do not eliminate from *ECP* any feasible crew pairing solutions, because the chosen maintenance solution tells us which short connects are *permissible* for the crews, not *required*. More generally, we note that it is necessary only to include columns that correspond to *maximal sets*—that is, columns representing maintenance-feasible short connect sets for which adding any additional short connects would result in maintenance infeasibility.

By considering only those maintenance solution columns with *UM* short connect sets, we dramatically reduce the number of columns required in our model. In another example, we looked at a problem instance containing over 25,000 distinct solutions to the maintenance routing problem. Only *four* of these solutions corresponded to unique and maximal short connect sets.

Given the complete set of maintenance routing solutions, we can remove any column that does not correspond to a *UM* short connect set without eliminating any feasible crew pairing solutions. Therefore, it is sufficient to include in *ECP* only those columns that represent unique and maximal maintenance-feasible short connect sets.

2.6. Identifying UM Columns

It is not sufficient that the number of required maintenance columns be small. We must also be able to identify these columns in a reasonable fashion—for example, we don't want to have to generate *all* 25,000 feasible maintenance routing solutions from our earlier example in order to isolate those four which contain unique and maximal short connect sets. We can identify *UM* maintenance routing solutions by solving a series of maintenance routing problems with side constraints and a modified objective function.

We begin by solving the maintenance routing problem defined by (5), (6), (7), (8), and (9), with the objective of maximizing the total number of short connects included in the solution. We associate with each route string r a coefficient c_r, the number of short connects included in route string r. Our objective function is then

$$\min \sum -c_r d_r,$$

where d_r is the binary decision variable associated with route string r.

Clearly, a solution to this problem yields a *UM* set of short connects. Let C^1 represent the set of short connects included in the solution to this first iteration of the modified maintenance routing problem. We then add a constraint to the modified maintenance routing problem of the form

$$\sum_{c \in C \setminus C^1} \sum_{r \in R} \vartheta_{cr} d_r \geq 1.$$

This constraint states that the solution to the next iteration must include at least one route string containing a short connect which is *not* in C^1. We then re-solve and generate a new solution with a new corresponding set of short connects C^2. This set will be *UM*, because it is the largest cardinality set which is not a subset of another solution. We can continue to iterate, adding cuts for each newly generated solution and re-solving the model until all *UM* short connect sets have been identified.

Thus, it is possible to generate n *UM* columns in at most the amount of time it takes to solve n maintenance routing problems. In fact, it may take significantly less time, because at each iteration we can use the previous iteration's maintenance routing solution as an advanced start.

2.7. Structural Properties of ECP

2.7.1. Relaxing the Integrality of the Maintenance Variables. Even a relatively small number of additional binary variables can have significant impact on the tractability of a model. This is one of the challenges posed by the *BIM* model—in addition to all the binary crew pairing variables, we add one binary variable for each route string as well. For the *ECP* model, however, Cohn (2002) proves that the binary constraints on the maintenance solution variables can be relaxed. That is, we can replace the integrality constraints with nonnegativity constraints—once we have fixed the crew pairing variables to binary values, the resulting polyhedron will have integer extreme points. This is in contrast to the *BIM* model, where we may have to branch not only on crew pairing variables, but on maintenance routing variables as well. The result is that *the ECP model has no more integer variables than the original crew pairing model by itself*. Moreover, this property holds true even if the maintenance routing problem is posed as an optimization problem, contributing to the objective function, rather than as a feasibility problem.

2.7.2. Quality of the LP Relaxation. The *ECP* model not only has fewer integer variables than the basic integrated model, but has a provably tighter linear programming relaxation as well. To see this, we first note that any solution to the LP relaxation of *ECP* has a corresponding solution to the LP relaxation of *BIM* with the same cost. To construct this corresponding solution, consider each maintenance routing solution column x_s in the solution to the LP relaxation of *ECP* with strictly positive value. By definition, each of these columns must correspond to at least one feasible maintenance routing solution. Choose one feasible maintenance solution for each such s—we denote this by X_s—and assign the value x_s to each of the variables in *BIM* which correspond to the route strings in the set X_s. Using a one-to-one mapping of crew pairing variables, it is clear that the constructed solution is feasible for *BIM* and has the same cost as the *ECP* solution. Thus, the LP relaxation of *ECP* is at least as tight as the LP relaxation of *BIM*. An example is provided in Cohn (2002) to show that the *ECP* LP relaxation can produce strictly tighter bounds than that of *BIM*.

3. IMPLEMENTING ECP

The extended crew pairing model is an extension of the basic crew pairing model, a problem that is itself computationally challenging. The crew pairing problem is often solved using a *branch-and-price* solution approach (Barnhart et al. 1998), in which column generation is used to solve the LP relaxations at nodes of the branch-and-bound tree. The branch-and-price approach to solving crew pairing problems can be extended quite easily to incorporate the added variables and constraints associated with the maintenance routing decisions in *ECP* (see Figure 1). In the sections that follow, we discuss the details of the implementation.

Figure 1. *ECP* Branch-and-price algorithm.

(1) Initialize root node
   (a) Set lower bound to $-\infty$.
   (b) Set upper bound to ∞.
   (c) Create initial set of crew pairings.
   (d) Create initial set of maintenance solutions.
(2) Choose a pending node and solve.
   (a) Solve current LP and compute dual values.
   (b) For each crew base, look for a negative reduced cost crew pairing.
   (c) Look for a negative reduced cost maintenance solution.
   (d) If any new columns are identified, add to the current LP and return to Step 2a.
(3) Update lower bound.
(4) If solution is fractional:
   (a) If objective value is not strictly less than upper bound, discard the node.
   (b) If objective value is stricly less than upper bound, create two new nodes.
(5) If solution is integer:
   (a) If objective value is strictly less than upper bound, update upper bound.
   (b) Discard the node.
(6) If pending nodes exist, return to Step 2.

3.1. Initializing the Root Node

In solving the basic crew pairing problem, we begin by creating an initial set of feasible pairings. In *ECP*, we must also generate an initial set of feasible maintenance solutions. We can generate one such feasible solution by solving the original maintenance routing problem. Note that if we were to include only this column in *ECP*, we would achieve the same result as that found using the sequential solution process currently employed by many airlines.

To identify additional maintenance columns, we can follow the steps described in §2.6. Note that n iterations of this process will yield the n *UM* short connect sets of largest cardinality. As illustrated in the proof-of-concept later in this section, even a small number of such *UM* columns can have a significant impact on the quality of the solution. Users may also choose to provide some additional columns based on their knowledge of the problem domain. For example, they might choose to include columns associated with the maintenance routing solutions implemented over the past several planning periods, or choose to seek maintenance solutions that contain short connects known to be beneficial to the crew schedule.

3.2. Generating Crew Pairings

To see how crew pairings can be generated in *ECP*, we first review how pairings are generated in the basic crew pairing model. In *CP*, the reduced cost of a pairing is the cost of the pairing minus the sum of the duals associated with the flights contained in it. If we denote the dual variable associated with the cover constraint for flight f by π_f, then we can write the *pricing problem* (that is, the optimization problem used to identify the most negative reduced cost variables) as:

$$\min c_p - \sum_{f \in F} \delta_{fp} \pi_f,$$

st

$$p \in P.$$

Barnhart et al. (1999) provide a survey of techniques used in solving such problems. Typically, a crew pairing network is defined, for example, with nodes representing flights and arcs representing feasible flight connections. Specialized algorithms are then used to find the shortest path in this network, where side constraints ensure that a path corresponds to a feasible pairing and the length of a path is equivalent to the reduced cost of the pairing.

In the extended crew pairing model, we must also take into account the dual variables associated with the short connect linking constraints. If we denote by γ_c the dual variable associated with short connect c, then the reduced cost of a pairing becomes

$$c_p - \sum_{f \in F} \delta_{fp} \pi_f + \sum_{c \in C} \eta_{cp} \gamma_c.$$

By assigning the dual values associated with short connects to the corresponding connection arcs in the crew pairing network, we can solve this pricing problem using the same techniques as those used when solving the basic crew pairing problem. In other words, by simply modifying some of the input parameters, we can use the same pairing generator for both the basic and the extended crew pairing models.

3.3. Generating Maintenance Columns

Column generation may also be used to identify additional maintenance solution columns. If we denote by σ the dual variable associated with the convexity constraint, then the reduced cost of a maintenance column is

$$-\sum_{c \in C} \beta_{cs} \gamma_c - \sigma.$$

(Recall that the cost of a maintenance column in *ECP* is 0.) The pricing problem can thus be written as

$$\min -\sum_{c \in C} \beta_{cs} \gamma c,$$

st

$$s \in S.$$

If the optimal solution to this pricing problem has objective value less than σ, then we have identified a new negative reduced cost column. Otherwise, we have established that no new negative reduced cost maintenance columns exist for the current dual values.

Let $R(s)$ denote the set of route strings found in maintenance routing solution s. Then,

$$-\sum_{c \in C} \beta_{cs} \gamma_c = \sum_{r \in R(s)} \left(-\sum_{c \in C} \vartheta_{cr} \gamma_c \right).$$

We can therefore formulate the maintenance pricing problem as a basic maintenance routing problem in which the cost coefficient c_r associated with route string r is

$$-\sum_{c \in C} \vartheta_{cr} \gamma_c.$$

We can enhance this pricing problem by adding an appropriately small constant Δ to each of the duals γ_c. This ensures that if the short connects associated with one feasible solution are a subset of the short connects in another feasible solution, then the second solution will have an objective value that is lower than that of the first. (This addresses the case where some of the dual values are zero; note that the Δs must be removed from the duals before comparing the optimal solution to σ.) Thus, any solution to the maintenance pricing problem will be *UM*.

3.4. Branching Strategy

As discussed in §2.7.1, the maintenance variables are guaranteed to take integer values once the crew pairing variables have been fixed to integer values. We can therefore directly apply the branching strategy used in basic crew pairing solvers.

3.5. Proof-of-Concept

Given that a significant optimality gap has been shown to exist between the sequential and integrated approaches (Cordeau et al. 2000), we wanted to get some sense of how difficult it is to capture a significant portion of this potential for improvement using *ECP* heuristically. To test the efficacy of our approach, we performed a limited experiment on two small test examples. We considered two actual airline problem instances, both containing approximately 125 flights. We used the following strategy for generating maintenance columns in both instances. First, we generated the 10 *UM* maintenance-feasible short connect sets of largest cardinality. Then, we identified those short connects that were not part of any of these columns. For each of these short connects, we generated the largest cardinality *UM* maintenance-feasible short connect set that contains it, thereby ensuring that each short connect had the potential to be included in a crew pairing. As a result of this approach, problem instance *A* had 16 maintenance columns and problem instance *B* had 20 maintenance columns. We then solved *ECP*, completely enumerating all feasible pairings, but not generating any further maintenance variables.

In order to analyze the quality of our solution, we generated a lower bound by computing the optimal crew pairing solution when all short connects are permitted.

As shown in Table 1, with no more than 20 maintenance solution columns we generate a solution at most 2% away from optimal in both problem instances. We believe that this is largely due to the fact that the number of short connects used in an optimal integrated solution is often much smaller than the total number of short connects. For example, problem instance A had 58 possible short connects.

Table 1. Proof-of-Concept.

Problem Instance	ECP Solution	Lower Bound	Optimality Gap
A	31,396.10	31,396.10	0.0%
B	25,498.60	25,076.60	1.7%

The 16 short connect columns that we generated contained on average just over 38 short connects each. The optimal solution used only 9 short connects. In problem instance B there were 68 possible short connects. The 20 short connect columns generated contained on average 37 short connects each. The optimal solution used only 10. This indicates that with *UM* columns of maximal cardinality, we may capture the optimal set of short connects even with only a small number of short connect columns.

4. The Constrained Crew Pairing Model

One benefit of the *ECP* model is that it can either be solved to optimality or it can provide a feasible solution in less time if we limit the number of maintenance routing solutions from which to choose. This is an advantage over the approach of Klabjan et al. (1999), which may result in an infeasible solution. On the other hand, the Klabjan approach has the benefit of quickly finding an optimal solution in those instances where the optimal crew pairing problem is in fact maintenance feasible. In contrast, the *ECP* model may take much longer to solve such problem instances if an appropriate maintenance solution is not included in the model at an early iteration.

To address this drawback, we present an alternative approach, which we call the *constrained crew pairing model (CCP)*. In this approach, we start off by solving the unconstrained crew pairing problem (that is, the crew pairing problem in which all potential short connects are permitted). If the short connects used in the solution are maintenance feasible, we have an optimal solution and the algorithm terminates. If not, we add a cut to the crew pairing problem ruling out the current infeasible solution, and we reiterate.

This approach can require many iterations, each of which requires us to solve an instance of the crew pairing problem (with side constraints) and an instance of the maintenance routing problem. Another drawback is that this approach does not provide us with a feasible solution until we reach the optimal solution. To remedy these issues we suggest solving this model *in parallel* to *ECP*, as discussed in the sections that follow.

4.1. Implementing CCP

To solve *CCP*, we begin by solving the basic crew pairing problem in which *all* potential short connects are permitted. Given the resulting set of short connects used, denoted F^0, we then solve a maintenance routing problem modified to ensure that all short connects in F^0 are included in the solution. For example, if short connect *A–B* appears in a crew pairing in the current solution, we do not permit route strings which contain flight A followed by any flight other than B. Note that this actually simplifies the maintenance problem by restricting the set of feasible strings.

If we are able to find a feasible solution to this maintenance routing problem, we have an optimal solution to the crew pairing problem and the algorithm terminates. Otherwise, we have a lower bound which we can use in the *ECP* branch-and-bound algorithm. (Note that *ECP* also generates alternative lower bounds based on its LP relaxation.)

If the current crew solution is maintenance infeasible, we proceed by: 1) adding a cut to the crew pairing model to prohibit the current solution, and 2) re-solving the modified crew pairing problem. For example, if the current optimal solution is Y^0 and this solution uses N^0 pairings, then we add a cut of the form

$$\sum_{p \in P : y_p^0 = 1} y_p \leq N^0 - 1. \qquad (25)$$

These cuts are not very efficient, however. For example, when we solve the $i+1$th iteration of *CCP*, the new solution might contain a different set of pairings from the ith iteration but the same maintenance-infeasible set of short connects. Thus, a better cut would be one that prohibits the short connect set F^i rather than the set of pairings Y^i. Such a cut can be written as

$$\sum_{p \in P} \sum_{c \in F^i} \eta_{cp} y_p \leq |F^i| - 1. \qquad (26)$$

One inefficiency associated with Cut (26) is that we might generate several "nested" solutions in successive iterations that are all infeasible. For example, consider the case where $F^i = \{A, B, C, D\}$. Perhaps this solution is maintenance infeasible because short connects A and B are incompatible. These two short connects might be desirable to the crew pairing problem, however. Our next three iterations might therefore yield solutions containing short connect sets $\{A, B, C\}$, $\{A, B, D\}$, and then $\{A, B\}$, all of which are maintenance infeasible.

We can bypass these intermediate iterations by prohibiting short connect set $\{A, B\}$ rather than the original set $\{A, B, C, D\}$. More generally, we want our cuts to represent *minimally infeasible* subsets $F^{i'}$ of F^i; that is, $F^{i'}$ is also maintenance infeasible, but any proper subset of $F^{i'}$ is maintenance feasible. The new cut is then written as:

$$\sum_{p \in P} \sum_{c \in F^{i'}} \eta_{cp} y_p \leq |F^{i'}| - 1.$$

Just as we want maintenance-feasible short connect sets corresponding to columns in *ECP* to be as *large* as possible, we want maintenance-infeasible short connect sets corresponding to constraints in *CCP* to be as *small* as possible. In the same way that using maximal short connect sets allows us to minimize the number of maintenance columns needed in *ECP*, using minimally infeasible short connect sets in *CCP* allows us to minimize the number of maintenance cuts needed.

4.1.1. Generating Minimally Infeasible Short Connect Sets. Given a short connect set F^i from the ith iteration of *CCP*, we first solve a variation of the maintenance routing problem in which our objective is to maximize the number of short connects in F^i included in the solution. If the optimal objective value to this problem contains all the short connects in F^i, then the crew pairing solution is maintenance feasible and therefore optimal for *ECP*. Otherwise, the short connect set is infeasible and we seek the smallest maintenance-infeasible subset of F^i to generate a new cut for *CCP*—we refer to this problem as the *minimally infeasible set problem (MIS)*.

Consider a minimally infeasible subset $F^{i'}$. For every feasible solution to the maintenance routing problem, there must be at least one element of $F^{i'}$ *not* included in that solution; otherwise there would be a maintenance solution containing all short connects in $F^{i'}$. To model *MIS*, we let f_c be a binary decision variable indicating whether or not $c \in F^i$ is part of the minimally infeasible set, and use $C(s)$ to denote the set of short connects occurring in maintenance solution s. We can then formulate *MIS* as:

$$\min \sum_{c \in F^i} f_c,$$

st

$$\sum_{c \in F^i \setminus C(s)} f_c \geq 1 \quad \forall\, s \in S,$$

$$f_c \in \{0, 1\} \quad \forall\, c \in F^i.$$

For example, if the initial infeasible short connect set is $F^i = \{A, B, C, D\}$ and the maintenance routing problem has three feasible solutions, containing short connects $\{A, C\}$, $\{B, C, D\}$, and $\{A, C, D\}$, respectively, then the minimally infeasible set problem would be:

$$\min f_A + f_B + f_C + f_D,$$

st

$$f_B + f_D \geq 1, \qquad (27)$$
$$f_A \geq 1, \qquad (28)$$
$$f_B \geq 1, \qquad (29)$$
$$f_A, f_B, f_C, f_D \in \{0, 1\}. \qquad (30)$$

The optimal solution to this is $\{A, B\}$, and thus we add the cut

$$\sum_{p \in P} \sum_{c \in \{A, B\}} \eta_{cp} y_p \leq 1$$

to eliminate any crew pairing solutions containing both short connects A and B.

Note that Constraint (27) is redundant—it is dominated by Constraint (29). Note also that Constraints (28) and (29) correspond to short connect sets $\{B, C, D\}$ and $\{A, C, D\}$, which are both maximal. This demonstrates the fact that in the *MIS* model, we need only include one constraint for each maximal short connect set. This fact is important from an implementation standpoint, as it can significantly decrease the number of constraints required in the model.

Another way to improve performance is to use *cut generation* in solving *MIS* itself. In this approach, we begin by solving a restricted version of *MIS* which contains just the set of constraints corresponding to the *UM* columns currently included in the *ECP* model. Given the solution to *MIS*, we solve a maintenance routing problem attempting to identify a *UM* maintenance solution containing this short connect set. If we find such a *UM* maintenance solution, the short connects in the restricted *MIS* solution are maintenance feasible and we identify a violated inequality. We add the cut corresponding to this *UM* short connect set to our restricted *MIS* and repeat. Note that we can also add a new column to *ECP*, as we have found a *UM* maintenance solution not currently contained in the restricted master.

If we *do not* find a *UM* short connect set containing the short connects in the current solution to the restricted *MIS*, this solution to the restricted *MIS* is also optimal for the original *MIS*. Thus, we have found a minimally infeasible short connect set. We add the corresponding cut to *CCP* and solve to find a new lower bound on *ECP*.

We summarize the steps to *CCP* as follows:

Step 1. Initialize *CCP* as the basic crew pairing model, in which all short connects are assumed to be feasible crew connections.

Step 2. Solve the current version of *CCP*; the optimal objective value provides an updated lower bound on *ECP*. Let F^i denote the short connects used in this solution.

Step 3. Solve a maintenance routing problem to find the *UM* short connect set using the maximum number of elements from F^i. If all elements from F^i are included, the current crew pairing solution is optimal and the algorithm terminates. Otherwise, we have established that F^i is a maintenance-infeasible short connect set, and we can construct a new cut for *CCP*.

Step 4. Initialize an instance of *MIS*, corresponding to F^i, to contain one constraint for every *UM* short connect set in *ECP*.

Step 5. Solve the current version of *MIS*; denote the solution by $F^{i'}$.

Step 6. Solve a maintenance routing problem to find the *UM* short connect set using the maximum number of elements from $F^{i'}$. If one or more elements from $F^{i'}$ *are not* included, then $F^{i'}$ is maintenance infeasible and thus a minimally infeasible short connect set has been identified. Add the cut corresponding to $F^{i'}$ to *CCP* and return to Step 2.

Step 7. If all elements from $F^{i'}$ *are* included in the maintenance routing solution, then we have identified a violated cut for *MIS*. We add this cut to the restricted *MIS* and return to Step 5. We also add the maintenance routing solution to *ECP*, given that it is a *UM* short connect set not currently included in *ECP*.

4.2. Synergies Between *ECP* and *CCP*

It is interesting to note the synergies between *ECP* and *CCP*. We demonstrate this in Figure 2. This figure presents the output of each of the subproblems that we have described and how this output may be used. *ECP* and *CCP* generate increasingly tighter upper and lower bounds, respectively, allowing us to determine when the optimality gap is sufficiently small to terminate the algorithm. Crew

Figure 2. Model synergy.

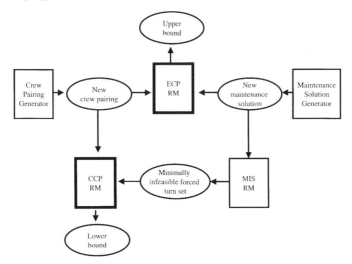

pairings generated when solving *ECP* can also be added to the restricted master for *CCP* and vice versa. Maintenance solutions generated for *ECP* lead to new cuts for *MIS*, and new cuts for *MIS* lead to new columns for *ECP*. In addition, solutions to *MIS* lead to new cuts for *CCP*. Finally, note that the user can control how to best utilize this collection of models.

5. CONCLUSIONS

In this paper we present the extended crew pairing model and solution approach. This new approach solves the important real-world problem of integrating the maintenance routing and crew scheduling problems. We have advanced the existing research in this area by focusing on three main goals: guaranteeing maintenance feasibility, providing user flexibility to trade off solution time and quality, and leveraging the fact that only a fraction of the maintenance routing decisions are relevant to the crew pairing problem. We have satisfied these goals in a model that has no more binary decision variables than the basic crew pairing model alone. Furthermore, this model is flexible in that it can directly incorporate new advances in maintenance solvers and pairing generators and it can be used in a column generation framework. We have also demonstrated that the LP relaxation of *ECP* is tighter than that of the basic integrated approach. We have proposed an alternative approach, *CCP*, that can work in parallel with *ECP*, in some cases more quickly identifying an optimal solution and in others providing useful information in the form of increasingly tight lower bounds and additional maintenance routing solution variables. Finally, we believe that our model has greater potential for extendibility to include additional airline planning decisions.

ACKNOWLEDGMENTS

This research is supported in part by a National Science Foundation Fellowship, a United Airlines research grant, and the Alfred P. Sloan Foundation research grant establishing the MIT Global Airline Industry Program.

REFERENCES

Anbil, R., R. Tanga, E. Johnson. 1992. A global approach to crew-pairing optimization. *IBM Systems J.* **31** 71–78.

——, E. Gelman, B. Patty, R. Tanga. 1991. Recent advances in crew-pairing optimization at American Airlines. *Interfaces* **21** 62–74.

——, C. Barnhart, L. Hatay, E. Johnson, V. Ramakrishnan. 1993. Crew-pairing optimization at American Airlines decision technologies. T. Ciriano, R. Leachman, eds. *Optimization in Industry: Mathematical Programming and Modeling Techniques in Practice*. John Wiley and Sons, Chichester, U.K., 31–36.

Ball, M., A. Roberts. 1985. A graph partitioning approach to airline crew scheduling. *Transportation Sci.* **19** 107–126.

Barnhart, C., K. Talluri. 1997. Airline operations research. Arthur McGarity, Charles ReVelle, eds. *Design and Operation of Civil and Environmental Engineering Systems*. John Wiley and Sons, New York, 435–469.

——, E. Johnson, G. Nemhauser, P. Vance. 1999. Crew scheduling. Randolph W. Hall, ed. *Handbook of Transportation Science*. Kluwer Academic Publisher, Norwell, MA, 493–521.

——, ——, ——, M. Savelsbergh, P. Vance. 1998. Branch-and-price: Column generation for solving huge integer programs. *Oper. Res.* **46** 316–329.

——, N. Boland, L. Clarke, E. Johnson, G. Nemhauser, R. Shenoi. 1998. Flight string models for aircraft fleeting and routing. *Transportation Sci.* **32** 208–220.

Beasley, J., B. Cao. 1996. A tree search algorithm for the crew scheduling problem. *Eur. J. Oper. Res.* **94** 517–526.

Chu, H., E. Gelman, E. Johnson. 1997. Solving large scale crew scheduling problems. *Eur. J. Oper. Res.* **97** 260–268.

Cohn, A. M. 2002. Composite-variable modeling for large-scale problems in transportation and logistics. Working paper, Massachusetts Institute of Technology, Cambridge, MA.

Cordeau, J., G. Stojković, F. Soumis, J. Desrosiers. 2000. Benders decomposition for simultaneous aircraft routing and crew scheduling. Technical Report G-2000-37, GERAD, École Polytechnique de Montréal, Montréal, Quebec, Canada.

Crainic, T., K. Rousseau. 1987. The column generation principle and the airline crew scheduling problem. *INFOR* **25** 136–151.

Desaulniers, G., J. Desrosiers, Y. Dumas, S. Marc, B. Rioux, M. Solomon, F. Soumis. 1997. Crew pairing at Air France. *Eur. J. Oper. Res.* **97** 245–259.

Gershkoff, I. 1989. Optimizing flight crew schedules. *Interfaces* **19** 29–43.

Graves, G., R. McBride, I. Gershkoff, D. Anderson, D. Mahidhara. 1993. Flight crew scheduling. *Management Sci.* **39** 736–745.

Hane, C., C. Barnhart, E. Johnson, R. Marsten, G. Nemhauser, G. Sigismondi. 1995. The fleet assignment problem: Solving a large-scale integer program. *Math. Programming* **70** 211–232.

Hoffman, K., M. Padberg. 1993. Solving airline crew scheduling problems by branch-and-cut. *Management Sci.* **39** 657–682.

Klabjan, D., K. Schwan. 1999. Airline crew pairing generation in parallel. Technical Report TLI/LEC-99, Georgia Institute of Technology, Atlanta, GA.

——, E. Johnson, G. Nemhauser. 1999. Solving large airline crew scheduling problems: Random pairing generation and strong branching. Technical Report TLI/LEC-99-11, Georgia Institute of Technology, Atlanta, GA.

——, ——, ——, E. Gelman, S. Ramaswamy. 1999. Airline crew scheduling with time windows and plane count constraints. Technical Report TLI/LEC-99-12, Georgia Institute of Technology, Atlanta, GA.

Lavoie, S., M. Minoux, E. Odier. 1988. A new approach for crew pairing problems by column generation with an application to air transportation. *Eur. J. Oper. Res.* **35** 45–58.

Levine, D. 1996. Application of a hybrid genetic algorithm to airline crew scheduling. *Comput. Oper. Res.* **23** 547–558.

Vance, P., C. Barnhart, E. Johnson, G. Nemhauser. 1997. Airline crew scheduling: A new formulation and decomposition algorithm. *Oper. Res.* **45** 188–200.

Part V:

Safety and Security

17

An assessment of risk and safety in civil aviation

Milan Janic

Abstract

Risk and safety have always been important considerations in civil aviation. This is particularly so under current conditions of continuous growth in air transport demand, frequent scarcity of airport and infrastructure capacity, and thus permanent and increased pressure on the system components. There is also the growing public and operators' awareness of these and other system externalities such as air pollution, noise, land use, water/soil pollution and waste management, and congestion. This paper offers an assessment of risk and safety in civil aviation. It deals with general concept of risk and safety, describes the main causes of aircraft accidents and proposes a methodology for quantifying risk and safety. © 2000 Elsevier Science Ltd. All rights reserved.

Keywords: Risk; Safety; Civil aviation; Externalities

1. Introduction

Society faces important challenges in how best to manage modern technology. There is a need to efficiently and safely use and manage existing technologies; and then how to make progress by introducing new technologies. Introducing new technologies is usually expected to provide social benefits through improved efficiency and safety. There is, however a need for care and awareness of the negative impacts of any technology on the environment, in its broadest sense, that can offset at least some of the gains from modernization and the introduction of new innovations. Optimization involves the assessment of such risk and ultimately the setting of standards to maximize society's utility from new technologies.

There are different definitions of risk. It may be defined as the probability of occurrence of a hazardous event in given period. Second, it may be considered as the possibility that an individual or group be impaired through the effects of specific actions in a more or less random manner. Third, risk can be related to a statistically expected value of loss (i.e., the statistical likelihood of a randomly exposed individual being affected by some hazardous event). In this case risk involves a measure of probability of severity of adverse impacts. In addition, there are very general classifications of risk (Evans, 1996; Kanafani, 1984; Kuhlmann, 1981; Sage and White, 1980).

Risk may be voluntary or involuntary. Voluntary risk is the risk that individuals elect to assume which is not so with involuntary risk. Travelling by air represents voluntary exposure to risk of death or injury while living near a nuclear power plant or airport where some uncontrollable radiation or aircraft accident may happen, represents involuntary exposure to risk. Risk may involve objectively or subjectively known or assumed exposure probabilities in relation to space, population and time dependency. Generally, spatial characteristic of exposure probability range from quite localized to global hazards. For many types of risks there are groups of the population that bear specific risk. Dependent on whether a hazard exists over a substantial time horizon and whether the effects or separate exposures to hazard are cumulative or not, dependent exposure probability to risk may be continuous, periodic and cumulative.

Four types of societal risk can also be identified (Sage and White, 1980):

- Real risk to an individual, which may be determined on the basis of future circumstances after their full development;
- Statistical risk, which may be determined by the available data on the incidents and accidents in question;
- Predicted risk, which may be predicted analytically from the models structured from relevant historical studies; and
- Perceived risk, which may intuitively be felt and thus perceived by individuals.

Civil aviation is an activity where all four types of risk are present. To companies providing insurance for airlines flying constitutes a known statistical risk of the occurrence of an accident. For passengers who purchase their insurance while on the ground, flying represents a perceived risk that usually exceeds statistical risk. To air traffic control authorities, anticipated changes in traffic patterns and equipment involve predicted risk. These changes may be sufficiently good approximations of future real risk assessments that they are incorporated in decisions on the introduction of new ATC technology.

Aircraft accidents often have specific features that can distinguish them from accidents associated with other modes:

- Because flying may take place over long distances, accidents may occur at any point in time or space. Hence, there is exposure to individual and global hazard.
- Passengers and aircraft crews are primal target groups exposed to risk of an accident but there are individuals on the ground who may be exposed to the same accidents albeit at a lower probability.
- Although being a rare event in an absolute sense, aircraft accidents can have severe implications.
- Conditionally, any aircraft movement is an inherently risky event, then, according to probability theory, aircraft accidents may be classified as highly unlikely (although possible) events.
- With respect to time dependency, risk is always present during given time and space horizons (i.e., whenever a flight takes place). The effect is non-cumulative and particularly related to the separate exposures of the people on board.

A practical problem in air transport is how to manage risk and safety. Typically, this has been resolved by investigations of causes of fatal accidents, assessment of their risk and setting-up a risk standards consistent with society's preference function (Sage and White, 1980). Assessment of the risk of aircraft accidents may be carried out in different ways, from highly intuitive to very formal and analytical but is usually partitioned into sub-tasks:

- Risk determination relates to the risk identification involving new risk and changes in the risk parameters. The latter involves determining the probability of occurrence of risky events and the likely consequences of their outcome.
- Risk evaluation may be decomposed into risk aversion and risk acceptance.
- Risk measurement involves quantification. One convenient measure of risk is the number of accidents per unit of a system's output. Air accidents have normally be viewed in terms of fatal events with the system's output defined as the number of aircraft kilometers, passenger kilometers and/or aircraft departures over a given period. This is useful for comparing risk and the level of safety of different transport modes, including civil aviation, as well as for monitoring sustainability[1] of the sector. There are a number of ways of modeling and statistically examining these data (Ang and Tang, 1975; Johnston et al., 1989).

2. The safety record

In the late 1990s the world's airline fleet consists of more than 15 000 aircraft flying a network of approximately 15 million kms and serving nearly 10 000 airports. The sector directly employs more than 3.3 million people, with over 1.4 million in USA (Air Transport Action Group, 1996). Some 12 billion people and 23 million tonnes of freight are being moved per annum. The freight figure represents approximately one third of value of the world's manufactured exports.

Total accidents are closely related to the scale of civil aviation operations. A variety of international institutions, organisations and agencies deal with forecasting future trends, including International Civil Aviation Organization (ICAO) and International Air Transport Association (IATA). The airspace manufacturers such as Airbus Industry, Boeing and Rolls Royce also make projections. Some idea of projected growth can be seen in Table 1 (International Civil Aviation Organization, 1994). The broad range of predicted growth rates vary between 5 and 6.5% across particular forecasters with the exception of the low figure from Fokker.

Historically, when there has been relatively rapid growth in air transport, it has often been followed by a series of accidents. The occurrence of such events has stimulated the introduction of technical and operational measures. As a result, overall safety has improved over time. ICAO, for example, has shown the fatality rate for international and domestic schedule aviation operations has been consistently decreasing over time. Between 1970 and 1993 the fatality rate fell from 0.18 to 0.04 fatalities per 100 million passenger kilometers with particularly marked reductions recorded between 1970 and 1977. During the period 1984–1993, the trend was relatively stable. The same analysis indicates that the number of fatal accidents during this 23-yr period varied between 16 and 31/yr. The average number of accident per annum was 25 and the average annual number of passenger

---

[1] In this context, 'sustainable' development can be defined as the development in which the system's output increases and its negative impacts on the environment stagnate or decrease. The sustainable development of aviation sector can be evaluated through externalities such as safety, air pollution, noise and congestion (Janic, 1999).

Table 1
Example of air traffic forecasts[a]

Forecaster	Period	Average annual growth Rate (pkm)[1] (%)
Airbus Industry	1992–2001	5.8
	2002–2011	5.1
Boeing	1993–2013	5.2
Rolls-Royce	1993–2012	5.2
AcDonnell Douglas	1990–2000	6.5
Fokker	1994–2013	3.5
ICAO	1992–2003	5.0

[a] *Source:* International Civil Aviation Organisation (1994); Air Transport Action Group (1996).

fatalities was 741/anuum.[2] At the same time the output of the sector rose from 1971 to 389 billion passenger-kilometers which is over a 500% increase (International Civil Aviation Organization, 1992,1994). Some are arguing that the scope for further improvements in safety are becoming exhausted implying that if the accident rate remains the same, while air travel increases, the number of accidents will inevitably rise (Cole, 1997).

3. Factors causing fatal air accidents

Investigating causes of fatal aircraft accidents is difficult because they generally stem from a complex system of mutually dependent, sequential factors (Owen, 1998). These factors can be classified in several ways. First, according to the current state-of-knowledge they can be categorized into known and avoidable and unknown and unavoidable causes. The former should be considered conditionally in the sense that immediately after an accident the real causes are seldom fully known but as the investigation progresses they become known and avoidable. The causes of some accidents are never uncovered. Second, with respect to accident type, the main causes of air accidents can conditionally be classified into human errors, mechanical failures, hazardous weather, and sabotages and military operations.

- Most accidents can be attributed to human error combined with other factors. Human errors have been present in the production, maintenance and operation of aviation hardware ranging through aircraft, airports and air traffic control facilities and equipment. Human operational errors can come about when workloads exceed work ability, e.g., in stressful situations. In aviation, working capacity primarily depends on the ability to receive, select, process and distribute information on an on-line and off-line basis in the control of individual aircraft or air traffic. Long exposition to heavy mental workloads causes stress that can lead to fatigue and deterioration in work performance. Under stressful conditions, diminished performance may cause conscious or unconscious risky and unsafe behavior and generate errors that may result in fatal accidents. The most common types of such accidents are mid-air collisions and aircraft flying into terrain.
- Mid-air collisions have mainly been caused by air traffic controller errors usually involving a failure to maintain prescribed separation minima between aircraft. For example, the mid-air collision between BEA and Inex-Adria aircraft on 10 September 1976 over Zagreb was caused by an error of air traffic control. The investigation discovered that the controller had been working for a long period under stress caused by traffic overloading and weaknesses in the monitoring equipment that left it unable to safely support existing volumes of traffic. In the accident 176 people lost their lives. It initiated improvements to the air traffic monitoring procedures at the location and hastened the development of airborne anti-collision equipment (Stewart, 1994).
- Collisions of aircraft with terrain are mostly associated with pilot-error, a cause identified with many other unexplainable air accidents. One example of air accidents caused by pilot error was the crash of a British Midland B737 near East Midlands Airport (UK) on 8 January 1989. Forty-one passengers were killed and 79 survived the accident. The inquiry found that the crew made a series of mistakes caused by confusion in reading instruments in an emergency approach following an engine failure (Owen, 1998). Another example of pilot error involved an American Airlines B727 on 8 November 1965 near Cincinnati (US). In this case, the crew made mistakes in setting the altimeter and in determining the vertical position of the aircraft while approaching the airport in rainy weather (Stewart, 1994; Owen, 1998).
- Crew inexperience can also cause air accidents. Inexperience may lead to pilot-error, that together with other factors may cause an accident with fatal outcome. One of the examples is a crash of Air Florida B737 on 13 January 1982 just after take-off from Washington National Airport (US). Seventy five passengers and crew were killed and only five survived. The investigation indicated that the main cause of the accident was the accumulation of ice on the aircraft wings and fuselage. The crew, who were inexperienced in cold weather flying, had not operated the anti-icing system prior to before take-off and did not apply full engine take-off power, which

---

[2] The data exclude accidents in the former USSR and the events involving unlawful interference with aviation.

could save the aircraft despite severe icing (Owen, 1998).³
- Strictly, mechanical failures result from human errors made whilst constructing, producing and maintaining the equipment. Such errors can accelerate metal fatigue and other failures in aircraft components. The crashes of Comets are one example (Owen, 1998) and another was the problem of an Aloha Airlines B737 in 1988 when the aircraft suddenly lost part of its cabin roof and sides during flight. In this latter case, investigators found the main cause of cabin crack was metal fatigue due to the frequency of take-offs and landings of the aircraft and corrosion due to frequent flying in salt air. Design problems lead to modifications in equipment. The main cause of a crash of a DC-10 near Paris in 1974 that killed 346 people was weakness in the aircraft's doors and difficulties in to checking if they were closed. The result was stronger and better designed doors. The crash of a DC-10 at Chicago in 1979 happened due to engine failure. The event resulted in stricter rules and procedures covering engine maintenance and a review of take-off speeds (Stewart, 1974).
- The root-cause of many disasters originates in maintenance workshops and in the factories where vital components and systems have been produced. An example fire on a British Airtours B737 at Manchester Airport in 1985. Thermal fatigue, or weakening of the metal by constant heating and cooling during an engine's life produced a crack in the combustion during the take-off. The section separated from the engine and hit the port wing fuel tank spilling of fuel on a hot engine. Subsequently, cracks were found in other engines of this type (Owen, 1998).
- Hazardous weather such as thunderstorms and frontal systems can cause troublesome winds, rain, snow, fog, and low ceilings that may pose safety concerns at all stages of a flight. In particular, strong windshear developing near airports can make flying difficult because of its rapid change in speed and direction and because of a loss of lift in certain conditions. The crash of an Eastern Airlines B727 during approach at New York's Kennedy Airport in June 1975 offers a case study of the dangers involved. During the period 1970–1987 the US National Transportation Safety Board identified low-altitude wind shear as the factor causing or contributing to 18 commercial aircraft accidents; seven were fatal resulting in the loss of 575 lives. The development of sophisticated weather reporting, forecasting and detecting systems, onboard and ground-based, have reduced this type of threat.
- Terrorist actions are highly correlated with political and economic tensions in the world. A typical example was the crash of a B747 on 23 June 1985 due to a suspected bomb explosion. After the crash security measures at high risk airports were strengthened. Such acts have also initiated the introduction of new technologies and security procedures that are intended to prevent an illegal entry onto the aircraft and to detect the presence of weapons being taken onboard. (Rosenberg, 1987).
- Military and semi-military operations have also resulted in accidents. One example was the crash of a Korean B-747 over Sakhalin Inland killing 269 people. Due to navigational error the aircraft deviated from its prescribed course and entered Soviet airspace and flew over a prohibited area. After several warnings, the aircraft was shot down by a Soviet missile. The event stimulated improved coordination of civil and military aviation (Stewart, 1994).

Human errors can be reduced by training and the structuring of air traffic patterns so as to avoid excess stress. Factors such as hazardous weather, mechanical faults, sabotages and military operations would seem to be more random and less easily dealt with. This does not mean the system is unsafe. Safety should be considered with respect to the base causes of accidents. If accidents occur due to known and avoidable factors, the system should be considered as unsafe. Otherwise, if accidents occur for unknown and unavoidable reasons, the system should be considered as safe.

4. A methodology for assessing the risk and safety

In civil aviation, risk has been assessed as the probability of the occurrence of an air accident in terms of two aggregate indicators, the accident rate and the fatality rate. The probability of an air accident is very low making it a difficult and complex task to properly explain, locate, and manage overall aviation safety. There is also the need to consider the impact of policy on different impacted groups such as users, service operators (airlines, airports, air traffic control), aviation and non-aviation professional and non-professional organizations and public (Kanafani, 1984).

Two approaches for assessing risk and safety are considerd. The causal approach looks at the number of accidents and number of fatalities, the scale of the system's output during a given period and other relevant characteristics that are seen as relevant causal variables. The number of accidents, deaths and injuries per unit of

---
³ This example illustrates the importance of experience and training in reducing the probability of an accident (Kuhlmann, 1981). However, education and training of aviation staff is expensive which poses problems at time when airlines are under pressure to control costs (Dose, 1995).

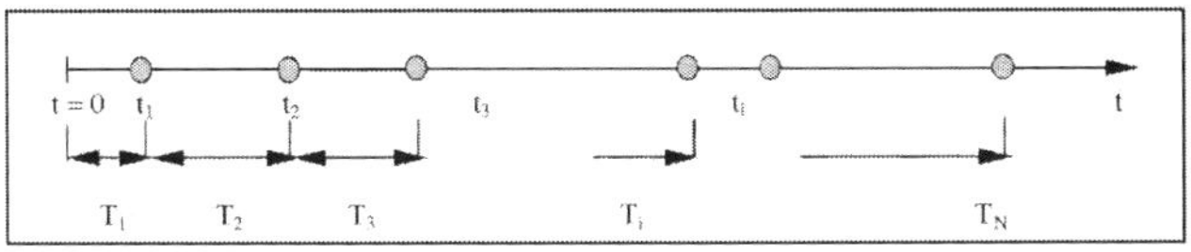

Fig. 1. Scheme of a Poisson-type events (process).

air transport output over time offers an indicator of whether the sector's safety is improving.[4]

The second approach involves the statistical modeling the occurrence of air accidents over time; a Poisson sequence or Poisson process is often deployed. Such a process is based on the following assumptions (Ang and Tang, 1975):

- An event can occur at random and at any time or any point in space. Past aircraft accidents have possessed this characteristic. They occurred in a random manner in different parts of the world.
- The occurrence of an event in a given time or space interval or segment is independent on what happened in any other non-overlapping intervals or segments. Air accidents, except very rare mid-air collisions, have occurred as the series of independent events in time and space.
- The probability of an event occurring in a small interval Δt is proportional to Δt and can be estimated by $\lambda \Delta t$ where λ is the mean rate of occurrence of the event. It is assumed constant and equal to $\lambda = 1/T_a$, where T_a is the average time interval between consecutive events. The probability of two or more occurrences in Δt is negligible (of higher order of Δt). From empirical evidence, as Δt is assumed to be a sufficiently short period, the probability of an occurrence of more than one aircraft accident will normally be negligible.

Fig. 1 illustrates a scheme of a Poisson process that commences at time $t = 0$ and at random times $t_1, t_2, t_3, \ldots, t_i, \ldots, t_N$, the Poisson-type events occur.

In Poisson processes the time intervals between successive events is exponentially distributed, indicating no-memory property in the process. This means that future events do not depend on the number or time of previous events. This would logically seem to be the case with air accidents. Mathematically, let T be the random variable representing the time between any two consecutive events. This variable is exponentially distributed. The probability that no accident will occur in time period t is

$$P(T > t) \simeq P(X_t = 0) = e^{-\lambda t}, \quad (1)$$

[4] Besides national aviation authorities and airlines, ICAO providing the data on safety.

where, X_t is the number of air accidents in time t and λ is the average accident rate. Similarly, the probability of the occurrence of at least one event in time t is

$$P(T \leq t) = 1 - P(T > t) = P(X_t \neq 0) = 1 - e^{-\lambda t} \quad (2)$$

5. Application of the methodology

5.1. Causal assessment

Causal assessment considers risk at the global level, the level of airlines and level of particular aircraft type. At the global level the number of deaths per passenger-kilometer is taken as the dependent variable GF_R. This is then regressed on the number of fatalities per aircraft accident and the annual volume of passenger-kilometers denoted by N_D and PKM_A, respectively. Data for period 1981–1996 are used for estimation (International Civil Aviation Organization, 1994) in the following specification (Janic, 1999):

$$GF_R = 3.801 \times 10^{-10} + 4.196 \times 10^{-11} N_D$$
$$\quad (2.983) \quad\quad\quad (10.674)$$
$$\quad - 2.095 \times 10^{-16} PKM_A.$$
$$\quad (3.446)$$

$$R_{\text{adj}}^2 = 0.901; F = 69.296; DW = 1.617; N = 16. \quad (3)$$

The overall regression is significant at the 1% level with significant coefficients (t-statistics are in parenthesis). It also has a relatively high explanatory power without first order auto-correlation problems (Johnston et al., 1989). The fatality rate increases with the number of people killed per crash and decreases with the increase in the level of output. The risk of crashes has significantly fallen despite more flying.

The safety of airlines is assessed by regressing the number of accidents per million flights by an airline, A_R, on the its number of flights, F. Fig. 2 illustrates the trend. The accident rate per airline has decreased more than proportionally with the cumulative number of flights. Since larger airlines have performed a larger number of these flights they would seem less risky than smaller ones. US and European airlines have much lower accident rates per total number of flights than other carriers.

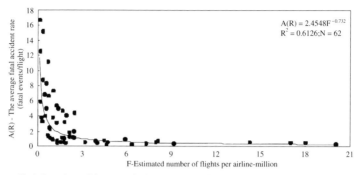

Fig. 2. Dependence of the average fatal accident rate on the number of airline flights (1970–1997).
Source of data: Internet (1998).

The risks associated with different aircraft types are found by regressing the number of accidents per aircraft type AR_A, on the number of flights per aircraft type F_A, and the average age of particular aircraft type E_A. The data cover the period from the entry into service of a particular aircraft type to 1992. The aircraft types covered are Fokker F28, Fokker F70/F100; Airbus A300, A310, A320; Lockheed L1011; British Aerospace BAe146; Boeing B727, B737-1/200, B737-3/4/500, B747, B757, B767; McDonnell Douglas DC9, MD80 (Internet, 1998; Walder, 1991). The equation used is

$$AR_A = 1.206 + 1.743 F_A + 0.900 E_A$$
$$\quad\quad (0.692) \quad (6.355) \quad\quad (3.887),$$
$$R^2 = 0.929; F = 84.640; DW = 1.823; N = 16. \quad (4)$$

The overall equation and individual coefficients are significant at the 1% level. The equation may offer an explanation of the past but this information was not available in advance to those involved. The equation indicates that the cause of air accidents could stem from the existence of geriatric factors that escalated faster as aircraft are utilized more and age. Because the operational hypothesis is that aircraft accidents happen as random events, the equation does not imply that more used and older aircraft have been less safe. It indicates that the risk of traveling in these aircraft is higher.

5.2. Probabilistic assessment

The probabilistic assessment of accidents uses a sample of 259 accidents over the period 1965–1998. The distribution of time intervals between these events is shown in Fig. 3.[5] A simple calculation provides an estimate of the average accident rate: $\lambda \cong 7.818$ accidents per year or $\lambda \cong 0.020$ accidents per day. An analysis of the time intervals between accidents, independent of aircraft type, indicates they have been independent and exponentially distributed (a χ^2 test confirms the hypothesis matching the empirical and theoretical data, Ang and Tang, 1975). This offers confirmation that the observed pattern of accidents can be treated as Poisson process. Using the exponential distribution seen in Fig. 3, it is possible to assess the probability of an occurrence of an air accident. If there is unlikely to be any improvement in safety features then this distribution can be used for assessing the probability of future events. Fig. 4 illustrates the probability of the occurrence of at least one air accident per period t. This probability rises over time until the event. For example, the probability of at least one accident by the following day from now is about 0.02, by next month 0.45, by six months 0.97, and by next year 0.999.

5.3. Assessment of deaths and injuries

To complete the analysis of past accidents, the distributions of air accidents, fatalities and survivors per aircraft category can be separated. Aircraft can be treated as turbojets, turbo-props and piston-engine; see Table 2. The largest number of accidents involved turbo-prop aircraft but the greatest number of people involved in

---
[5] The accidents involved aircraft types, Boeing B727, B737, B747, B757, B767, B777 (no event); MD80, DC10, MD11; Lockheed L1011, Airbus A300, A310, A320, A330 (no events), A340 (no events); Fokker F28, F100; British Aerospace BAe 146; Embraer EMB-110 Bandeirante, EMB-120 Brasilia; Dorrnier 228; and Saab 340.

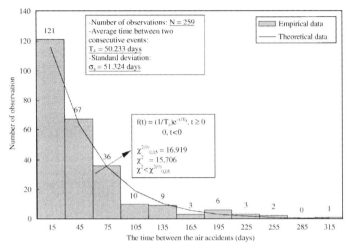

Fig. 3. Distribution of time intervals between consecutive air accidents (1965–1998). *Source of data*: Internet (1998).

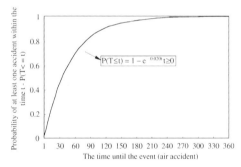

Fig. 4. Dependence of the probability of the occurrence of at least one air accident within time period t (*according to the distribuion shown in Fig. 3*).

accident were on turbojet aircraft because the latter can carry more passengers.

Regarding the number of deaths per accident (1965–1998), there were 130 events involving no survivors implying an overall probability of death during an air accident of about 50%. In the absolute numbers, the analysis shows that the average number of deaths per accident has been $N_d = 76$ ($\sigma_d = 81$) and the total number of people onboard on the aircraft when the accident happened is $N_a = 103$ ($\sigma_a = 88$). By further elaborating the above figures, it can be seen that about 73% of passengers and crews have been killed during the aircraft accident (although some survivors have been severely injured).

6. Conclusions

This paper has presented a methodology for assessment risk and safety in civil aviation. The outcomes confirm that the accident and fatality rates have decreased in line with increases in the volume of the sector's output. The accident rate has been more frequent at more heavily used and older aircraft which supports ideas of permanent monitoring, detecting and remedying such things as metal fatigues.

Air accidents belong to a class of extremely rare events in the context of the volume and intensity of the operations and activities involved. Some of the most recent evidences indicates that despite positive past trends, it seems that it will be difficult to continue to reduce risks. The implications of this is an absolute increase in the number of fatalities and accidents. ICAO's long-traffic forecasts indicate that if the rate of accidents stays stable until 2003, the number of fatalities will increase by about 75% with the number of fatal accidents rising to 40/yr, respectively (Corrie, 1994). This poses a range of problems for policy makers. High numbers of accidents will inevitably attract considerable media attention but aviation is the safest mode of transport. Transferring resources to continually reduce the average risk of an accident or fatality from other, much more dangerous modes of transport or from other sectors, such as health

Table 2
Characteristics of fatal accidents by aircraft category[a]

Aircraft category	Fatal accidents per type of aircraft (%)	Killed people per aircraft (%)	Survived people per aircraft (%)	Number of people died per aircraft	Number of survived people per aircraft
Turbojet	34.2	69.6	86.5	56	41
Turbo-prop	48.5	28.1	11.4	16	4
Piston-engine	17.3	3.3	2.1	5	2

[a]*Source:* International Civil Aviation Organization (1992); Internet (1998).

care or support of the elderly, will inevitably cause even more deaths in society as a whole.

References

Ang, H-S.A., Tang, H.W., 1975. In: Probability Concepts in Engineering Planning and Design: Vol. I – Basic Principles. Wiley, New York.

Air Transport Action Group, 1996. The Economic Benefits of Air Transport. ATAG, Geneva.

Cole, J., 1997. Overview of aviation safety issues, Paper presented at The Seventh Annual Aviation Forecast Conference. NATCA-National Air Traffic Controllers Association, Washington.

Corrie, S.J., 1994. Potential growth in air travel demands renewed effort to improve safety record. International Civil Aviation Organisation, Montreal, Canada, ICAO Journal 7–9.

Dose, A., 1995. Safety is best served by paying close attention to the key elements in its management. ICAO Journal 20–21.

Evans, A.W., 1996. Risk assessment by transport organisations. Transport Reviews 17, 145–163.

International Civil Aviation Organisation, 1992. Investment requirements for aircraft fleets and for airport and route facility infrastructure to the year 2010. Circular 236, ICAO, Montreal.

International Civil Aviation Organisation, 1994. ICAO projects long-term moderate traffic growth of 5 per cent per year. ICAO Journal 20–21.

Internet, 1998. Safety information for airline passengers. http://airsafe.com/airline.htm.

Janic, M., 1999. Aviation and externalities: the accomplishments and problems. Transportation Research D 4, 159–180.

Johnston, A.C., Johnston, M.B., Buse, R.C., 1989. Econometrics: Basic and Applied. McMillan, New York.

Kanafani, A., 1984. The analysis of hazards and the hazards of analysis: reflections on air traffic safety management. Institute of Transportation Studies, University of California, Berkeley, Working paper, UCB-ITS-WP-84-1.

Kuhlmann, A., 1981. Introduction to Safety Science. Springer, New York.

Owen, D., 1998. Air Accident Investigation: How Science Is Making Flying Safer. Patrick Stephens Limited, Yeovil.

Rosenberg, B., 1987. Air safety: the state of art. Aviation Week and Space Technology 51–66.

Sage, A.P., White, E.B., 1980. Methodologies for risk and hazard assessment: a survey and status report. IEEE Transaction on System, Man, and Cybernetics SMC-10, 425–441.

Stewart, S., 1994. Air disasters: dialogue from the black box. The Promotional Reprint Company Limited, Leicester.

Walder, R., 1991. Ageing aircraft programme entails major effort and expense. ICAO Journal 6–8.

18

The Evolution of Crew Resource Management Training in Commercial Aviation

Robert L. Helmreich, Ashleigh C. Merritt, and John A. Wilhelm

In this study, we describe changes in the nature of Crew Resource Management (CRM) training in commercial aviation, including its shift from cockpit to crew resource management. Validation of the impact of CRM is discussed. Limitations of CRM, including lack of cross-cultural generality are considered. An overarching framework that stresses error management to increase acceptance of CRM concepts is presented. The error management approach defines behavioral strategies taught in CRM as error countermeasures that are employed to avoid error, to trap errors committed, and to mitigate the consequences of error.

The roots of crew resource management training in the United States are usually traced back to a workshop, *Resource Management on the Flightdeck* (Cooper, White, & Lauber, 1980)[1] sponsored by the National Aeronautics and Space Administration (NASA) in 1979. This conference was the outgrowth of NASA research into the causes of air transport accidents. The research presented at this meeting identified the human error aspects of the majority of air crashes as failures of interpersonal communications, decision making, and leadership. At this meeting, the label *Cockpit Resource Management* (CRM) was applied to the process of training crews to reduce "pilot error" by making better use of the human resources on the flight deck. Many of the air carriers represented at this meeting left it committed to developing new training programs to enhance the interpersonal aspects of flight op-

---

[1] In Europe, the research of Elwin Edwards (1972) was translated into human factors training at KLM Royal Dutch airlines in the late 1970s.

erations. Since that time, CRM training programs have proliferated in the United States and around the world. Approaches to CRM have also evolved in the years since the NASA meeting. The focus of this article is on the generations of CRM training that reflect this evolution and on the problems that have been encountered in changing the attitudes and behavior of flight crews. CRM training in the military has followed its own path of growth and evolution and will not be addressed here (for a discussion of military CRM programs, see Prince & Salas, 1993).

We use the term *evolution* in describing the changes in CRM over the last two decades. Evolution, as formally defined, refers to the process of growth and development, a description that aptly fits CRM. Similarly, the very different content and foci of programs called CRM justifies defining them in terms of generations (although temporally a CRM generation is closer to that of the Drosophila than the human). Our focus is on the most recent approaches to CRM training. Early generations are described briefly to show their context and emphases (for a more complete description of early programs, see Helmreich & Foushee, 1993).

FIRST GENERATION COCKPIT RESOURCE MANAGEMENT

The first comprehensive U.S. CRM program was initiated by United Airlines in 1981. The training was developed with the aid of consultants who had developed training programs for corporations trying to enhance managerial effectiveness. The United program was modeled closely on a form of training called the "Managerial Grid" developed by psychologists Robert Blake and Jane Mouton (1964). The training was conducted in an intensive seminar setting and included participants' diagnoses of their own managerial style. Other airline programs in this era also drew heavily on management training approaches. These programs emphasized changing individual styles and correcting deficiencies in individual behavior, such as a lack of assertiveness by juniors and authoritarian behavior by captains. Supporting this emphasis, the National Transportation Safety Board (NTSB, 1979) had singled out the captain's failure to accept input from junior crew members (a characteristic sometimes referred to as the "Wrong Stuff") and a lack of assertiveness by the flight engineer as causal factors in a United Airlines crash in 1978. First generation courses were psychological in nature, with a heavy focus on psychological testing and such general concepts as leadership. They advocated general strategies of interpersonal behavior without providing clear definitions of appropriate behavior in the cockpit. Many employed games and exercises unrelated to aviation to illustrate concepts.[2] It

---

[2]As an example, one of the most widely used exercises or games was called "Lost on the Moon"—requiring participants to prioritize supplies necessary for survival. Another game was called "Win as Much as You Can."

was also recognized that CRM training should not be a single experience in a pilot's career, and annual recurrent training in CRM became part of the program. In addition to classroom training, some programs also included full mission simulator training (Line Oriented Flight Training [LOFT]) in which crews could practice interpersonal skills without jeopardy. However, despite overall acceptance, many of these courses encountered resistance from some pilots, who denounced them as "charm school" or attempts to manipulate their personalities.

SECOND GENERATION CREW RESOURCE MANAGEMENT

NASA held another workshop for the industry in 1986 (Orlady & Foushee, 1987). By this time, a growing number of airlines in the United States and around the world had initiated CRM training, and many reported on their programs. One of the conclusions drawn by working groups at the meeting was that explicit (or stand alone) CRM training would ultimately disappear as a separate component of training when it became embedded in the fabric of flight training and flight operations.

At the same time, a new generation of CRM courses was beginning to emerge. Accompanying a change in the emphasis of training to focus on cockpit group dynamics was a change in name from cockpit to crew, making the new name Crew Resource Management. The new courses, typified by the program developed by Delta Airlines (Byrnes & Black, 1993) dealt with more specific aviation concepts related to flight operations and became more modular as well as more team oriented in nature. Basic training conducted in intensive seminars included such concepts as team building, briefing strategies, situation awareness, and stress management. Specific modules addressed decision-making strategies and breaking the chain of errors that can result in catastrophe. Many of the courses still relied on exercises unrelated to aviation to demonstrate concepts. Participant acceptance of these courses was generally greater than that of the first generation, but criticism that the training was heavily laced with "psycho-babble" continued (for example, the notion of "synergy" in group dynamics was often condemned by participants as representative of irrelevant jargon). Second generation courses continue to be used in the United States and other parts of the world.

THIRD GENERATION CRM: BROADENING THE SCOPE

In the early 1990s, CRM training began to proceed down multiple paths. Training began to reflect characteristics of the aviation system in which crews must function, including such multiple input factors as organizational culture that determine safety. At the same time, efforts began to integrate CRM with technical training and to focus on specific skills and behaviors that pilots could use to function more effectively. Several airlines began to include modules addressing CRM issues in the use of flight deck automation. Programs also began to address the recognition and assessment of human factors issues.[3] Accompanying this was the initiation of advanced training in CRM for check airmen and others responsible for training, reinforcement, and evaluation of technical and human factors.

Accompanying this greater specificity in training for flight crews, CRM began to be extended to other groups within airlines, such as flight attendants, dispatchers, and maintenance personnel. Many airlines began to conduct joint cockpit–cabin CRM training. A number of carriers also developed specialized CRM training for new captains to focus on the leadership role that accompanies command.

Although third generation courses filled a recognized need to extend the concept of the flight crew, they may also have had the unintended consequence of diluting the original focus on the reduction of human error.

FOURTH GENERATION CRM: INTEGRATION AND PROCEDURALIZATION

The Federal Aviation Administration (FAA) introduced a major change in the training and qualification of flight crews in 1990 with the initiation of its Advanced Qualification Program (AQP; Birnbach & Longridge, 1993). AQP is a voluntary program that allows air carriers to develop innovative training that fits the needs of the specific organization. In exchange for this greater flexibility in training, carriers are required to provide both CRM and LOFT for all flight crews and to integrate CRM concepts into technical training. Most of the major U.S. airlines and several regional carriers are transitioning into AQP from the older model expressed in Federal Aviation Regulations, Parts 121 and 135. To complete the shift to AQP, carriers are required to complete detailed analyses of training requirements for each aircraft and to develop programs that address the human factors (CRM) issues in each aspect of training. In addition, special training for those charged with certification of crews and formal evaluation of crews in full mission simulation are required (Line Operational Evaluation [LOE]).

As part of the integration of CRM, several airlines have begun to proceduralize the concepts involved by adding specific behaviors to their checklists. The goal is to ensure that decisions and actions are informed by consideration of "bottom lines" and that the basics of CRM are observed, particularly in nonstandard situations.

---

[3]By assessment, we mean understanding how well specific behaviors are enacted not formal evaluation of human factors skills.

On the surface, the fourth generation of CRM would seem to solve the problems of human error by making CRM an integral part of all flight training. It would also appear that the goal of making explicit CRM training "go away" is starting to be realized. Although empirical data are not yet available, there is general consensus among U.S. airlines that the AQP approach yields improvements in the training and qualification of flight crews. However, the situation is more complex and the resolution not so straightforward. Before considering the latest iteration of CRM, it may be valuable at this point to pause and examine what has been accomplished in the past two decades of CRM training.

SUCCESSES AND FAILURES OF CRM TRAINING

Validation of CRM

The fundamental question of whether CRM training can fulfill its purposes of increasing the safety and efficiency of flight does not have a simple answer. The most obvious validation criterion, the accident rate per million flights, cannot be used. Because the overall accident rate is so low and training programs so variable, it will never be possible to draw strong conclusions about the impact of training during a finite period of time (Helmreich, Chidester, Foushee, Gregorich, & Wilhelm, 1990). In the absence of a single and sovereign criterion measure, investigators are forced to use surrogate criteria to draw inferences more indirectly (Helmreich & Foushee, 1993; Helmreich & Wilhelm, 1991). Reports of incidents that do not result in accidents are another candidate criterion measure. However, incident reporting is voluntary, and one cannot know the true base rate of occurrences, which is necessary for validation. We will discuss new developments in incident reporting later.

The two most accessible and logical criteria are behavior on the flight deck and attitudes showing acceptance or rejection of CRM concepts. Formal evaluation during full mission simulation (LOE) is a start. However, the fact that crews can demonstrate effective crew coordination while being assessed under jeopardy conditions does not mean that they practice these concepts during normal line operations. We feel that the most useful data can be obtained from line audits in which crews are observed under nonjeopardy conditions (Helmreich & Merritt, 1998; Hines, 1998). Data from such audits have demonstrated that CRM training that includes LOFT and recurrent training does produce desired changes in behavior (Helmreich & Foushee, 1993). This finding is congruent with participant evaluations of training. Crews completing course evaluations report that it is effective and important training (Helmreich & Foushee, 1993).

Attitudes are another indicator of effect as they reflect the cognitive aspects of the concepts espoused in training. Although attitudes are not perfect predictors of behavior, it is a truism that those whose attitudes show rejection of CRM are unlikely to follow its precepts behaviorally. The attitudes that have been measured to assess the impact of CRM were ones identified as playing a role in air accidents and incidents (Helmreich & Foushee, 1993; Helmreich, Merritt, Sherman, Gregorich, & Wiener, 1993). Data from a number of organizations show that attitudes about flight deck management change in a positive direction (Helmreich & Wilhelm, 1991).

CRM Does Not Reach Everyone

From the earliest courses to the present, a small subset of pilots have rejected the concepts of CRM (Helmreich & Wilhelm, 1991). These CRM failures are found in every airline and are known to their peers and to management. Any chief pilot can identify these individuals, who have come to be known by a variety of names—*Boomerangs, Cowboys*, and *Drongos* to mention a few.[4] Efforts at remedial training for these pilots have not proved particularly effective.

Although CRM is endorsed by the majority of pilots, not all of its precepts have moved from the classroom to the line. For example, a number of airlines have introduced CRM modules to address the use of cockpit automation. This training advocates verification and acknowledgment of programming changes and switching to manual flight rather than reprogramming Flight Management Computers in high workload situations or congested airspace. However, a significant percentage of pilots observed in line operations fail to follow these precepts (Helmreich, Hines, & Wilhelm, 1996).

Acceptance of Basic Concepts May Decay Over Time

We have surveyed pilots in a number of organizations several years after they received initial CRM training. A disturbing finding from this research is a slippage in acceptance of basic concepts, even with recurrent training (Helmreich & Taggart, 1995). Figure 1 shows shifts in CRM-related attitudes over time within two airlines.[5] The reasons for the decay in attitudes are not immediately apparent, but it is possible to speculate about likely causes. One candidate is a lack of management support for CRM and a failure by such evaluators as line check airmen to reinforce

---

[4]The Drongo label comes from Australia and is perhaps the most appealing. A Drongo is a small bird that flies around and defecates on the heads of unsuspecting passersby.

[5]The data are also interesting in showing the impact of initial training. The airlines from which data are shown did not stress the effects of stress on behavior, and the scores stayed relatively flat across the measurement period.

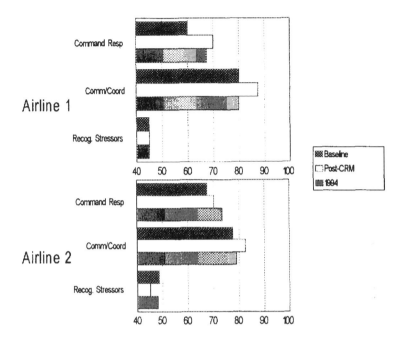

FIGURE 1 Changes in Crew Resource Management attitudes over time at two major U.S. airlines.

its practice. Another is the broadening of training to include flight attendants and other personnel, because a program stretched to fit all groups may lack the specificity needed to change behavior.[6] As training has evolved from one generation to the next, the original, implicit goal of managing error may have become lost. Proceduralizing CRM (i.e., formally mandating the practice of CRM precepts) might also obscure the purpose of the behavior.[7] Support for this view comes from informal interviews of crews asked "What is CRM?" A typical response is "Training to make us work together better." Although this is certainly true, it represents only part of the story. It seems that in the process of teaching people how to work together, we may have lost sight of why working together well is important. The overarching rationale for CRM, reducing the frequency and severity of errors that are crew-based, has been lost.

---

[6]We strongly endorse joint training as a means of enhancing overall performance. Our concern is with the dilution of meaning.

[7]This is not a criticism of proceduralizing CRM, which can aid in making the practices part of the culture.

CRM Did Not Export Well

As first and second generation CRM training programs began to proliferate, many airlines in the United States and around the world began to purchase courses from other airlines or training organizations. Even in the United States, courses imported from other organizations had less impact than those that were developed to reflect the organizational culture and operational issues of the receiving carrier. The situation was much worse when training from the United States was delivered in other nations. In many cases, the concepts presented were incongruent with the national culture of the pilots.

The Dutch scientist, Geert Hofstede (1980), defined dimensions of national culture, several of which are relevant to the acceptance of CRM training. High Power Distance cultures, such as China and many Latin American countries, stress the absolute authority of leaders. Subordinates in these cultures are reluctant to question the decisions and actions of their superiors because they do not want to show disrespect. Exhortations to junior crew members to be more assertive in questioning their captains may fall on deaf ears in these cultures. Many cultures that are high in Power Distance are also collectivist. In collectivist cultures, in which emphasis is on interdependence and priority for group goals, the concept of teamwork and training that stresses the need for effective group behavior may be readily accepted. In contrast, highly individualistic cultures, such as the United States, stress independence from the group and priority for personal goals. Individualists may cling to the stereotype of the lone pilot braving the elements and be less attuned to the group aspects of flight deck management. A third dimension, Uncertainty Avoidance, refers to the need for rule-governed behavior and clearly defined procedures (Merritt, 1996). High Uncertainty Avoidance cultures, such as Greece, Korea, and many Latin American countries, may be much more accepting of CRM concepts that are defined in terms of required behaviors. The United States is low in Uncertainty Avoidance, which is reflected operationally in greater behavioral flexibility, but also weaker adherence to Standard Operating Procedures (Helmreich, Hines, & Wilhelm, 1996). Management of cockpit automation is also influenced by national culture. Pilots from high Power Distance or Uncertainty Avoidance cultures show more unquestioning usage of automation, whereas those from cultures low in Power Distance or Uncertainty Avoidance show a greater willingness to disengage (Sherman, Helmreich, & Merritt, 1997). The low Uncertainty Avoidance of U.S. pilots may account, in part, for frequent failure to complete checklists and the imperfect acceptance of proceduralized CRM in this country.

There is a growing trend for carriers outside the United States to include national culture as part of CRM training and to customize their programs to achieve harmony with their own culture. This is an important development that should enhance the impact of CRM in those organizations. Malaysian Airlines, for example, has made national culture a part of its program (Helmreich & Merritt, 1998).

Considering both the observed limitations of CRM in the United States and the differing reactions to the training in other cultures, let us now turn to the fifth generation of CRM training—one that we believe addresses the shortcomings of earlier training approaches.

FIFTH GENERATION CRM: SEARCH FOR A UNIVERSAL RATIONALE

We have been searching for a rationale for CRM training that could be endorsed by pilots of all nations—including the Drongos. Returning to the original concept of CRM as a way to avoid error, we concluded that the overarching justification for CRM should be error management (Helmreich & Merritt, 1998; Merritt & Helmreich, 1997b). In reaching this position, we were much influenced by the work of Professor James Reason (1990, 1997). Although human error was the original impetus for even the first generation of CRM, the realization and communication of this was imperfect. Even when the training advocated specific behaviors, the reason for utilizing them was not always explicit. What we advocate is a more sharply defined justification that is accompanied by proactive organizational support.

CRM as Error Management

Underlying the fifth generation of CRM is the premise that human error is ubiquitous and inevitable—and a valuable source of information. If error is inevitable, CRM can be seen as a set of error countermeasures with three lines of defense. The first, naturally, is the avoidance of error. The second is trapping incipient errors before they are committed. The third and last is mitigating the consequences of those errors that occur and are not trapped. This error management troika is shown in Figure 2. The same set of CRM countermeasures apply to each situation, the difference being in the time of detection. For example, consider an advanced technology aircraft that experiences a controlled flight into terrain (CFIT) because an improper waypoint is entered into the Flight Management Computer (FMC). A careful briefing on approach procedures and possible pitfalls, combined with communication and verification of FMC entries would probably avoid the error. Cross-checking entries before execution and monitoring of position should trap erroneous entries. Finally, as the last defense, inquiry and monitoring of the position should result in mitigating the consequences of an erroneously executed command before CFIT.

To gain acceptance of the error management approach, organizations must communicate their formal understanding that errors will occur and should adopt a nonpunitive approach to error. (This does not imply that any organization should

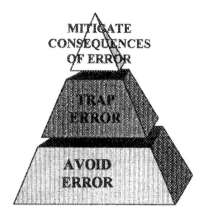

FIGURE 2 The error troika.

accept willful violation of its rules or procedures.) In addition to normalizing error, organizations need to take steps to identify the nature and sources of error in their operations. The U.S. FAA has announced a new initiative, Aviation Safety Action Programs, to encourage incident reporting within organizations to deal with safety issues proactively (FAA, 1997). For example, American Airlines is participating in the program with the cooperation of the pilots' union and the FAA. This confidential, nonjeopardy reporting system allows pilots to report safety concerns and errors. The program has proved to be a resounding success, with nearly 6,000 reports received in a 2-year period. Data generated by this system allow the company to take steps to prevent or minimize the recurrence of incidents.

Considerations for Fifth Generation CRM

Instruction in the fifth generation has at its aim the normalization of error and the development of strategies for managing error (Helmreich, 1997). Its basis should be formal instruction in the limitations of human performance. This includes communicating the nature of cognitive errors and slips as well as empirical findings demonstrating the deleterious effects of such stressors as fatigue, work overload, and emergencies. These topics, of course, require formal instruction, indicating that CRM should continue to have its own place in initial and recurrent training. These can be dramatically illustrated with examples from accidents and incidents in which human error played a causal role. Indeed, the analysis of human performance is common to all generations of CRM training. We would argue, however, that even more powerful learning may result from the use of positive examples of how errors are detected and managed.

Pilots from all regions of the world have been found to hold unrealistic attitudes about the effects of stressors on their performance—the majority feel, for example, that a truly professional pilot can leave personal problems behind while flying and that their decision-making ability is the same in emergencies and normal operations (Helmreich & Merritt, 1998; Merritt & Helmreich, 1997b). This attitude of personal invulnerability is a negative component of the professional culture of pilots and physicians (Helmreich & Merritt, 1998).[8] Training that demonstrates that these are erroneous or overconfident beliefs and that every individual is subject to stress can foster more realistic attitudes by reducing the onus attached to personal vulnerability. In turn, pilots who recognize the performance degradation associated with stress should more readily embrace CRM training as an essential countermeasure.

In theory, the error management approach should provide a more compelling justification for CRM and human factors training, but the impact remains to be evaluated empirically. Continental Airlines has refocused both the basic awareness and recurrent components of CRM as error management. As part of their commitment to this approach, all pilots were given the new basic course. Data on the outcomes of this program should help determine the effectiveness of the fifth generation approach. At the same time that error management became the primary focus of CRM training, Continental introduced a new program to train instructors and evaluators in the recognition and reinforcement of error management (Tullo & Salmon, 1997). This training stresses the fact that effective error management is the hallmark of effective crew performance, and the well-managed errors are indicators of effective performance.

As part of our development of strategies for using the line audit as an organizational assessment strategy, we have modified the Line/LOS Checklist, which is used to measure team performance, to include data on error types and error management (Helmreich, Butler, Taggart, & Wilhelm, 1994). In preliminary observations at a U.S. airline, we found that observers could readily identify errors, their sources, and management strategies. Examples were found of errors avoided, errors trapped, and errors mitigated. Instances of errors never detected by crews and errors whose consequences were exacerbated by crew action were also found. We feel that a focus on error management both in LOFT, LOE, and in line checking can provide valuable feedback and reinforcement for crews.

HOW DOES ERROR MANAGEMENT CRM RELATE TO EARLIER GENERATIONS?

Fifth generation CRM is compatible with earlier generations. Special training in the use of automation and the leadership role of captains as highlighted in the third generation can be neatly subsumed under this model. The error management focus

---

[8]There are many positive aspects of pilots' professional culture, such as pride in job and motivation, that contribute strongly to safety.

should strengthen the AQP approach to training by providing an all-important demonstration of the reasons for stressing CRM in all aspects of flight training. In the same vein, the integration of CRM into technical training and the proceduralization of CRM also fit under this umbrella and are likely to be better understood and accepted when the goals are clearly defined and organizationally endorsed. Pilots should also be better able to develop effective strategies for error management in situations in which procedures are lacking and provide a focal point for CRM skills that are not amenable to proceduralization.[9]

Such training modules as situation awareness and the nature and importance of briefings can be seen as basic error management techniques. Similarly, joint training of cabin and cockpit crews can be seen as extending the scope of error management to all employees in a safety culture (Merritt & Helmreich, 1997a). Finally, clarification of the basic goals of CRM training may be the best way to reach the Drongos who should find it difficult to deny the importance of error management.

CRM IN CONTEXT

CRM is not and never will be the mechanism to eliminate error and assure safety in a high-risk endeavor such as aviation. Error is an inevitable result of the natural limitations of human performance and the function of complex systems. CRM is one of an array of tools that organizations can use to manage error.

The safety of operations is influenced by professional, organizational, and national cultures and safety requires focusing each of these toward an organizational "safety culture" that deals with errors nonpunitively and proactively (Helmreich & Merritt, 1998). When CRM is viewed in the context of the aviation system, its contributions and limitations can be understood. What we do know is that the rationale for human factors training is as strong now as it was when the term CRM was first coined.

REFERENCES

Birnbach, R., & Longridge, T. (1993). The regulatory perspective. In E. Wiener, B. Kanki, & R. Helmreich (Eds.), *Cockpit resource management* (pp. 263–282). San Diego, CA: Academic.

Blake, R. R., & Mouton, J. S. (1964). *The managerial grid.* Houston, TX: Gulf.

Byrnes, R. E., & Black, R. (1993). Developing and implementing CRM programs. In E. Wiener, B. Kanki, & R. Helmreich (Eds.), *Cockpit resource management* (pp. 421–446). San Diego, CA: Academic.

---

[9]Leadership represents a critical area in which training can be effective, but a set of rote procedures will not lead to optimum performance (Pettitt & Dunlap, 1997).

Cooper, G. E., White, M. D., & Lauber, J. K. (1980). *Resource management on the flightdeck: Proceedings of a NASA/Industry Workshop* (Rep. No. NASA CP–2120). Moffett Field, CA: NASA–Ames Research Center.

Edwards, E. (1972). Man and machine: Systems for safety. In *Proceedings of the British Airline Pilots Association Technical Symposium* (pp. 21–36). London: British Airline Pilots Association.

Federal Aviation Administration. (1997). *Aviation safety action programs* (Advisory Circular No. 120–66). Washington, DC: Author.

Helmreich, R. L. (1997, May). Managing human error in aviation. *Scientific American*, 62–67.

Helmreich, R. L., Butler, R. E., Taggart, W. R., & Wilhelm, J. A. (1994). *The NASA/University of Texas/FAA Line/LOS Checklist: A behavioral marker-based checklist for CRM skills assessment* (NASA/UT/FAA Tech. Rep. No. 94–02; revised 12/8/95). Austin: The University of Texas.

Helmreich, R. L., Chidester, T. R., Foushee, H. C., Gregorich, S. E., & Wilhelm, J. A. (1990). How effective is Cockpit Resource Management training? Issues in evaluating the impact of programs to enhance crew coordination. *Flight Safety Digest, 9*(5), 1–17.

Helmreich, R. L., & Foushee, H. C. (1993). Why crew resource management? Empirical and theoretical bases of human factors training in aviation. In E. Wiener, B. Kanki, & R. Helmreich (Eds.), *Cockpit resource management* (pp. 3–45). San Diego, CA: Academic.

Helmreich, R. L., Hines, W. E., & Wilhelm, J. A. (1996). *Common issues in human factors and automation use: Data from line audits at three airlines* (NASA/UT/FAA Tech. Rep. No. 96–1). Austin, TX: University of Texas.

Helmreich, R. L., & Merritt, A. C. (1998). *Culture at work in aviation and medicine: National, organizational, and professional influences*. Aldershot, England: Ashgate.

Helmreich, R. L., Merritt, A. C., Sherman, P. J., Gregorich, S. E., & Wiener, E. L. (1993). *The Flight Management Attitudes Questionnaire (FMAQ)* (NASA/UT/FAA Tech. Rep. No. 93–4). Austin: The University of Texas.

Helmreich, R. L., & Taggart, W. R. (1995). CRM: Where are we today? In *Proceedings of the CRM Industry Workshop*. Washington, DC: Air Transport Association.

Helmreich, R. L., & Wilhelm, J. A. (1991). Outcomes of Crew Resource Management training. *International Journal of Aviation Psychology, 1*, 287–300.

Hines, W. E. (1998). *Teams and technology: Flightcrew performance in standard and automated aircraft*. Unpublished doctoral dissertation, The University of Texas, Austin.

Hofstede, G. (1980). *Culture's consequences: International differences in work related values*. Beverly Hills, CA: Sage.

Merritt, A. C. (1996). *National culture and work attitudes in commercial aviation: A cross-cultural investigation*. Unpublished doctoral dissertation, The University of Texas, Austin.

Merritt, A. C., & Helmreich, R. L. (1997a). Creating and sustaining a safety culture: Some practical strategies. In B. Hayward & A. Lowe (Eds.), *Applied aviation psychology: Achievement, change, and challenge* (pp. 135–142). London: Avebury Aviation.

Merritt, A. C., & Helmreich, R. L. (1997b). CRM: I hate it, what is it? (Error, stress, culture). In *Proceedings of the Orient Airlines Association Air Safety Seminar* (pp. 123–134). Jakarta, Indonesia: Association of Asia Pacific Airlines.

National Transportation Safety Board. (1979). *Aircraft accident report: United Airlines, Inc., Douglas DC–8–54, N8082U, Portland, Oregon, December 28, 1978* (NTSB–AAR–79–7). Washington, DC: Author.

Orlady, H. W., & Foushee, H. C. (1987). *Cockpit resource management training* (NASA CP–2455). Moffett Field, CA: NASA–Ames Research Center.

Prince, C., & Salas, E. (1993). Training and research for teamwork in the military aircrew. In E. Wiener, B. Kanki, & R. Helmreich (Eds.), *Cockpit resource management* (pp. 337–366). San Diego, CA: Academic.

Reason, J. (1990). *Human error*. New York: Cambridge University Press.

Reason, J. (1997). *Managing the risks of organizational accidents.* Aldershot, England: Ashgate.

Sherman, P. J., Helmreich, R. L., & Merritt, A. C. (1997). National culture and flightdeck automation: Results of a multi-nation survey. *International Journal of Aviation Psychology, 7,* 311–329.

Tullo, F., & Salmon, T. (1997). The role of the check airman in error management. In R. S. Jensen (Ed.), *Proceedings of the Ninth International Symposium on Aviation Psychology* (pp. 511–513). Columbus: The Ohio State University.

19

Wildlife collisions with aircraft: A missing component of land-use planning for airports

Bradley F. Blackwell, Travis L. DeVault, Esteban Fernández-Juricic, Richard A. Dolbeer

ARTICLE INFO

Article history:
Received 28 January 2009
Received in revised form 28 May 2009
Accepted 6 July 2009
Available online 7 August 2009

Keywords:
Airport planning
Aviation hazard
Bird strike
Land use
Risk
Wildlife strike

ABSTRACT

Projecting risks posed to aviation safety by wildlife populations is often overlooked in airport land-use planning. However, the growing dependency on civil aviation for global commerce can require increases in capacity at airports which affect land use, wildlife populations, and perspectives on aviation safety. Our objectives were to (1) review legislation that affects airports and surrounding communities relative to managing and reducing wildlife hazards to aviation; (2) identify information gaps and future research needs relative to regulated land uses on and near airports, and the effects on wildlife populations; and (3) demonstrate how information regarding wildlife responses to land-use practices can be incorporated into wildlife-strike risk assessments. We show that guidelines for land-use practices on and near airports with regard to wildlife hazards to aviation can be vague, conflicting, and scientifically ill-supported. We discuss research needs with regard to management of stormwater runoff; wildlife use of agricultural crops and tillage regimens relative to revenue and safety; the role of an airport in the landscape matrix with regard to its effects on wildlife species richness and abundance; and spatial and temporal requirements of wildlife species that use airports, relative to implementing current and novel management techniques. We also encourage the development and maintenance of datasets that will allow realistic assessment of wildlife-strike risk relative to current airport conditions and anticipated changes to capacity. Land uses at airports influence wildlife populations, and understanding and incorporating these effects into planning will reduce risks posed to both aviation safety and wildlife species.

Published by Elsevier B.V.

Contents

1. Introduction 2
2. Legislation 3
3. Information gaps 4
   - 3.1. Stormwater management 4
   - 3.2. Land cover 4
   - 3.3. Natural areas 5
4. Land use and wildlife-strike risk 6
5. Conclusions 7
   - Acknowledgements 7
   - References 7

1. Introduction

Safety and revenue are critical factors to the ability of civil aviation to meet the demands of global commerce. However, aircraft collisions with birds and other wildlife (wildlife strikes) pose an increasing safety and financial threat to the civil aviation industry worldwide (Allan, 2002; Dolbeer and Eschenfelder, 2002; Dolbeer and Wright, 2008). The estimated cost (direct and indirect expenses) to civil aviation worldwide is over U.S. $1.2 billion annually (Allan, 2002). Wildlife strikes have claimed over 219 lives and over 200 aircraft (military and civil) since 1988 (Richardson and West, 2000; Thorpe, 2003, 2005; Dolbeer and Wright, 2008). In the USA, 82,057 wildlife strikes (97.5% involving birds) were reported to the Federal Aviation Administration (FAA; 1990–2007) and represent at least U.S. $628 million annually in direct and indirect losses (Dolbeer and Wright, 2008). Importantly, these wildlife-strike statistics reflect an increasing risk (i.e., likelihood of harm) to aviation safety (Dolbeer, 2006a).

Air traffic has increased markedly with the post-World War II advent and growth of the civil aviation industry (Kelly and Allan, 2006). By the 1960s, airframes were larger and turbine power was replacing piston-powered engines. Both trends contributed to a higher likelihood of wildlife strikes, because the greater surface area of an aircraft and the vacuum associated with jet engines represent a larger area to avoid for any animal in the flight path (Solman, 1973). Further, there is a greater probability for jet engines, versus piston-powered engines, to suffer damage upon ingestion of an animal (Solman, 1973). Also, air carriers recently have replaced four-engine aircraft with two-engine designs that markedly reduce the noise of their predecessors, which is suspected to reduce the distance at which animals can detect and react to aircraft (Solman, 1976; Kelly et al., 2001; Kelly and Allan, 2006). Another factor contributing to the observed increase in bird strikes is population growth of some species (e.g., Rusch et al., 1995; Waller and Alverson, 1997; Blackwell et al., 2007), especially larger animals (>2 kg) that present substantial hazards to aviation safety (Dolbeer et al., 2000; Dolbeer and Eschenfelder, 2002; Dolbeer and Wright, 2008).

Analysis of strike data indicates that habitat management on and near airports plays a significant role in the frequency of wildlife strikes (Cleary and Dolbeer, 2005; DeVault et al., 2005; Blackwell and Wright, 2006; Dolbeer, 2006b). Specifically, wildlife (particularly birds) use of habitats within approach and departure zones increases the likelihood of wildlife strikes because of the altitudes in which aircraft operate within those areas. For example, Dolbeer (2006b) found that 95% of bird strikes reported to the FAA (1990–2004) occurred at <1067 m above ground level (AGL), altitudes for which aircraft on approach and departure would be within 18.5 km of major airports (those that serve at least 5 million passengers annually; FAA, 2008a). For strikes >152 m AGL, waterfowl (Anatidae), gulls/terns, passerines, and vultures were the species groups most frequently struck. Song-birds (Passerines), gulls/terns (Laridae), doves (Columbidae), and raptors (including vultures) were the species groups most frequently struck at altitudes $\leq$152 m AGL. Notably, for strikes resulting in substantial damage to the aircraft (Dolbeer et al., 2000; Dolbeer and Wright, 2008), 66% occurred at $\leq$152 m AGL (Dolbeer, 2006b). In general, an aircraft descending on a 3° glideslope would be $\leq$152 m AGL at 3 km from the runway (Flight Safety Foundation, 2000).

Therefore, measures to reduce wildlife hazards to aviation on airport property can be augmented by land-use management involving municipalities in surrounding areas (Rao and Pinos, 1998; Sodhi, 2002). Such collaboration is more pressing now with the anticipated demands on airports both for revenue and capacity (the maximum number of flights that an airport can routinely accept per hour). For example, to accommodate demands for airport development and growth (e.g., runway designs for larger aircraft, as well as new gate, taxiway, and apron configurations) worldwide through 2010, Humphreys et al. (2001) estimated a cost at U.S. $350 billion. By 2017, the FAA anticipates a 45% increase in passengers accompanied by a 33% increase in air carrier operations (FAA, 2008b). Through 2025, the U.S. civil fleet is anticipated to grow by 2.5% annually to accommodate increased demand, with the narrow-body fleet (i.e., aircraft with fuselage diameter from 3–4 m) projected to grow by 117 aircraft annually; the wide-body fleet (fuselage diameter $\geq$5 m) is projected to grow by 40 aircraft annually as the Boeing 787 and Airbus A350s enter existing fleets (FAA, 2008b). This increase in air carrier operations and aircraft size at the busiest airports will warrant development of additional runways to increase capacity. Globally, 9 billion passengers are expected by 2025, and the number of annual aircraft movements anticipated is 120 million (Aaronson, 2007). Planning for increasing airport capacity includes not only infrastructure, but potential economic linkages with surrounding communities, flight safety, and environmental concerns (Kelly and Allan, 2006).

For example, Graham and Guyer (1999), referring to projected growth of air transport within the European Union, suggested that planners must consider environmental capacity, which comprises infrastructure, sources of pollution, and visual amenity. Similarly, Abeyratne (2000) argued that effective expansion and management of airport capacity includes environmentally sustainable development (as outlined in the Rio Declaration on Environment and Development, United Nations Conference on Environment and Development). Vreeker et al. (2002) developed an evaluation process for airport expansion planning that includes safety (defined as a qualitative factor) and environment considerations, such as natural conservation areas and anticipated disturbance of fauna habitats. Lee and Yang (2003) examined strategies that would enable the incremental development of a "winged city", thus advocating the commercial linkage of an airport to off-airport enterprises (see also Reiss, 2007). The establishment of these economic linkages between an airport and community could prove critical to national economies, particularly given the current global economic downturn (e.g., Butterworth, 2008; Weikel, 2008; Airport Technology, 2009). We note, also, that planning for airport capacity changes is affected by regional perspectives that are separate from economic concerns. For example, environmental considerations figure prominently in the urban planning process in Europe (see European Union, EU, 2001) and could easily run counter to opinions favoring an increase to an airport's capacity. However, notably absent from much of the commentary on airport planning considerations, even work specifying safety and environmental concerns, is guidance on land use to minimize wildlife strikes (e.g., Abeyratne, 2000; but see Khalafalla and El-Rayes, 2006).

A wildlife perspective in airport planning is important because it can influence aviation safety (e.g., Kelly and Allan, 2006). In this study, we (1) review legislation that affects airports and surrounding communities relative to managing and reducing wildlife hazards to aviation; (2) identify information gaps and future research needs relative to regulated land uses on and near airports, and the effects on wildlife populations; and (3) demonstrate how information regarding wildlife responses to land-use practices can be incorporated into wildlife-strike risk assessments. We focus primarily on aviation in the USA, particularly in our reference to the FAA National Wildlife Strike Database as a basis for the development of the risk assessment. Our ultimate purpose is to stimulate collaborative efforts to more accurately assess how changes in capacity needs, considerations for revenue-producing land uses, and goals for resource sustainability on airport properties can affect wildlife hazards and, subsequently, risk posed to aviation safety. Our approach offers an exciting opportunity to integrate different disciplines (wildlife management, landscape ecology, conservation biology, geography, and sensory ecology) into the airport planning process.

2. Legislation

The primary body providing oversight and guidance to the civil aviation industry on a worldwide basis is the International Civil Aviation Organization (ICAO). The ICAO is a United Nations Specialized Agency whose mission is to achieve safe, secure, and sustainable development of civil aviation through cooperation among its 190 member states. In 1990, the member states of ICAO adopted, in Annex 14 to the Convention on Civil International Aviation, the following practices regarding bird hazards to aviation: (1) assess the extent of the risk posed by birds on and in the vicinity of airports; (2) take necessary action to decrease the number of birds; and (3) eliminate or prevent the establishment of any site in the vicinity of the airport which might serve as an attraction to birds and thereby present a danger to aviation. Member states voted to make these recommended practices into ICAO Standards, effective November 2003. This action makes these practices a mandatory component of the operation standards at airports within those member states (see Kelly and Allan, 2006; Dolbeer, 2007).

The guidance provided by the ICAO relative to wildlife hazards to aviation safety is found in the Airport Services Manual (ICAO, 1991) and the Airport Planning Manual (ICAO, 2002). Guidance on environmental management and modifications to airport property is found in the Airport Planning Manual and pertains broadly to modifications that might offer food, water, or shelter to wildlife, and primarily birds. Land uses considered as contributing to wildlife hazards on or near (i.e., within 13 km) airports are fish-processing operations; agriculture; livestock feed lots; refuse dumps and landfills; factory roofs; parking lots; theaters and food outlets; wildlife refuges; artificial and natural lakes; golf and polo courses, etc.; animal farms; and slaughter houses. In addition, the ICAO grades land uses as to whether they are acceptable within radii from the airport center of 3 and 8 km (ICAO, 2002). However, by changing from broad guidance to more specific instructions for land uses near airports, and without discussion of potential implications, some ICAO recommendations can be conflicting or misleading. Food-waste disposal, for example, is discouraged within both the 3- and 8-km zones, but non-food garbage is permissible within each zone. However, traditional landfills are generally not food-free and, subsequently, require netting or other management to reduce use by birds. Also, the guidelines recommend that "grass" areas on airports be maintained at 20 cm or more because "birds do not have good visibility and feeding is hindered" (ICAO, 1991). Such specific guidance, particularly to member states that span bioclimatic and geographic zones, ignores the myriad of factors that might contribute to avian use of grasslands. We suggest, therefore, that contact information be provided for member states that have active wildlife management programs at their airports, including grassland-management protocols. Further, if these management protocols are based on research examining avian foraging and antipredation behaviors in managed grasslands, appropriate references should be included in the ICAO guidelines.

Clearly, the necessity of some land uses at airports, such as parking lots, requires consistent management to deter use by loafing birds. However, other land uses within the ICAO 13-km siting criterion offer opportunities to increase revenue for the airport or other property owners without increasing attraction to wildlife. For example, land not used for airport operations is often leased for agricultural production to generate revenue and minimize maintenance (e.g., mowing costs; ICAO, 1991, 2002). The need to understand which land-cover types might attract hazardous birds is noted. But, there is also opportunity for the ICAO to lead in the dissemination of information or discussion among its member states (e.g., via the web) regarding the use of land covers to reduce use by hazardous wildlife while realizing revenue opportunities or conservation objectives (see Kelly and Allan, 2006).

For airports in the USA, the FAA exerts regulatory control over certification and operation via Title 14 Code of Federal Regulations (CFR), Federal Aviation Regulations, Part 139–*Certification of Airports*. In general, certificated airports are those facilities that receive scheduled passenger-carrying operations with >9 seats or unscheduled passenger-carrying operations with >30 seats (CFR §139.1). Currently, there are approximately 570 airports certificated under Part 139. In addition, there are about 2860 non-certificated airports that are organized under the *National Plan of Integrated Airport Systems* (NPIAS; FAA, 2006). These NPIAS airports are eligible to receive FAA funding under the *Airport Improvement Program* and, therefore, are encouraged to observe regulations in CFR Part 139.

Regulations concerning wildlife hazards to aviation are found in CFR 139. §139.337–*Wildlife Hazard Management*. These regulations state that each certificate holder must take *immediate* action to alleviate wildlife hazards whenever they are detected and ensure that a wildlife hazard assessment (see Cleary and Dolbeer, 2005) is conducted when any of the following events occur on or near the airport: (1) an air carrier experiences multiple wildlife strikes (a strike might involve multiple birds; see also 4, below); (2) an air carrier experiences substantial damage (damage or structural failure adversely affecting strength, performance, or flight) from striking wildlife; (3) an air carrier experiences engine ingestions of wildlife; or (4) wildlife of a size, or in numbers, capable of causing a strike (as defined above) is observed to have access to any airport flight pattern or aircraft movement area. Further, the wildlife hazard assessment must contain at least the following: (1) analysis of events or circumstances that prompted assessment; (2) identification of wildlife species observed, numbers, locations, movements, and daily and seasonal occurrences; (3) identification and location of features on and near the airport that attract wildlife; (4) a description of wildlife hazards to air carrier operations; and (5) recommended actions for reducing identified wildlife hazards to air carrier operations. However, because wildlife populations on and near airports are not static, but change in response to local land use, management policies (including control strategies), season, and climatic conditions (Cleary and Dolbeer, 2005), the FAA provides additional guidance to both certificated and non-certificated airports via the Advisory Circular (AC) 150/5200-33B–*Hazardous Wildlife Attractants On Or Near Airports*. Specifically, the AC provides airport operators and those with whom they cooperate guidance to assess and address potentially hazardous wildlife attractants when locating new facilities and implementing certain land-use practices on or near public-use airports. However, with the exception of the siting of new waste disposal operations (FAA AC 150/5200-34–*Construction or Establishment of Landfills Near Public Airports*), the FAA's regulatory role over land uses off of airport property is limited. Thus, communication and collaboration between airport operators, other U.S. Federal agencies, municipal governments, and developers is encouraged (see AC 150/5200-33B).

Also, the FAA recognizes that most public-use airports have large tracts of open, undeveloped land that provide added margins of safety and noise mitigation. However, these areas also can pose hazards to aviation if they attract wildlife to an airport's approach or departure airspace or air operations area (AOA). The AOA refers to areas on the airport designated for takeoff, landing, and surface maneuvers of aircraft (CFR Part 139, Subpart D) and within FAA siting criteria for certificated airports (i.e., within 1.5-km of a runway for airports servicing piston-powered aircraft only and within 3.0 km of a runway for airports servicing turbine-powered aircraft). For all airports, the FAA recommends a distance of 5 statute miles (8 km) between the farthest edge of the airport's AOA and the hazardous wildlife attractant if the attractant could contribute to wildlife movement into or across the approach or departure airspace.

In addition, AC 150/5200-33B states that constructed or natural areas, such as poorly drained locations, detention/retention ponds, roosting habitats on buildings, landscaping, odor-causing rotting organic matter (putrescible waste) disposal operations, wastewater treatment plants, agricultural or aquaculture activities, surface mining, or wetlands can provide wildlife with habitat for foraging, loafing, breeding, and escape from predators. Also, facilities such as restaurants, taxicab staging areas, rental car facilities, aircraft viewing areas, and public parks are included in the AC because they frequently serve as sources of food for wildlife. However, like the ICAO (1991, 2002) recommendations, guidance relating wildlife use of airport facilities or undeveloped areas to aspects of facility design and area, proximity to other habitat features, site-specific operational and management procedures, or land-cover types and seasonality is absent. Instead, both the AC 150/5200-33B and the FAA Airport Wildlife Hazard Mitigation (WHM) homepage (http://wildlife-mitigation.tc.faa.gov/public_html/index.html) provide links to agency, university, and international information for management of hazardous wildlife. However, the FAA does not include in its AC or WHM homepage a selection of references from the peer-reviewed literature pertaining directly or indirectly to the various areas of on-going research pertaining to wildlife strikes.

With regard to the management of airport properties, the airport must be considered a component of the landscape and, therefore, contributing to and subject to local- and landscape-level factors affecting wildlife populations. Inherent to successful management of wildlife hazards to aviation at local and landscape levels is collaboration within municipal, state, and provincial governments, and internationally. The ICAO guidelines establish a foundation for such collaboration, and the EU is moving toward mandatory reporting of wildlife strikes to the ICAO (EU, 2003). In the USA, groundwork for such collaborative efforts is exemplified by the 2003 Memorandum of Agreement between the FAA, U.S. Air Force, the U.S. Army, U.S. Environmental Protection Agency, U.S. Fish and Wildlife Service, and the U.S. Department of Agriculture to address "aircraft-wildlife strikes"; the 2005 Memorandum of Understanding (MOU) between the U.S. Department of Transportation, FAA, and the U.S. Department of Agriculture for mitigating wildlife hazards to aviation (No. 12-34-71-0003-MOU); and the 2006 MOU between the National Association of State Aviation Officials and the U.S. Department of Agriculture (APHIS 06-7100-0202-MU) to seek a mutual goal of alleviating wildlife hazards to aviation. Finally, airport managers also must adhere to national legislation affecting wildlife populations (e.g., the U.S. Endangered Species Act of 1973) and international treaties (e.g., the Migratory Bird Treaty Act of 1918 between the USA, Canada, Japan, Mexico, and Russia; the International Union for Conservation of Nature).

3. Information gaps

Quantifying wildlife hazards to aviation safety is critical to airport planning, particularly evaluations of future capacity needs. However, data are generally lacking with regard to the contribution to wildlife hazards posed by specific land uses, particularly within airport approach/departure zones. In the following sections we address research needs for three prominent land-use practices on or near airports relative to wildlife use: (1) stormwater management, (2) land covers, and (3) natural areas. We also discuss how data on land use and wildlife species can be integrated into airport planning. Again, our focus is primarily on aviation in the USA.

3.1. Stormwater management

Unlike other land uses on and near airports, the containment of stormwater is necessary for safe operations on runways, taxiways, and aprons, but also as a means to control the entry of contaminants into natural water systems (AC 150/5200-33B, ICAO 2002). However, the containment of stormwater runoff can also create a wildlife attractant. For U.S. airports, the AC 150/5200-33B addresses this issue by suggesting that water runoff be held for a maximum of 48 hrs by use of *detention* ponds. A detention pond is designed to temporarily hold a maximum amount of water while draining to another location. In contrast, a *retention* pond is designed to hold a set amount of water indefinitely. Various other methods of covering standing water are offered in the AC as management options. In addition, sub-surface flow (SSF) wetlands for runoff treatment are in use at some airports (Higgins and Liner, 2007), thus removing the attractant. However, SSF designs do not necessarily supplant the need for surface containment. Design considerations for above-ground stormwater-management facilities to reduce use by wildlife are not outlined by the FAA or ICAO; only recently has this issue been addressed relative to aviation safety (Blackwell et al., 2008).

Blackwell et al. (2008) monitored avian use of 30 stormwater-management ponds in Washington (USA), over one year and evaluated the fit of six *a priori* models relative to pond use by 13 avian groups. Their findings indicate that the primary focus in minimizing bird use should be on reducing pond perimeter via circular or linear designs. The authors also recommend that ponds should be located so as to maximize the distance between stormwater-management ponds and other water resources, particularly within 1 km of a planned stormwater facility. Based on this study, new research is underway to quantify avian use of stormwater-management facilities found within the approach/departure zones of other U.S. airports (J. Armstrong, Auburn University, School of Forestry and Wildlife Sciences, Auburn, AL, USA, personal communication). Researchers on a companion study are investigating physical modifications to stormwater-management ponds, biotic and synthetic water-treatment methods, and hydrology scenarios to effectively treat runoff while minimizing use by birds (C.E. Boyd, Auburn University, Dept. of Fisheries and Allied Aquacultures; K.H. Yoo, Auburn University, Dept. of Biosystems Engineering, personal communication). In addition, there is a critical need for benefit:cost assessments with regard to retrofitting existing stormwater facilities on an near airports with synthetic liners (to control emergent vegetation), covers, netting, or grid systems to reduce use by birds.

3.2. Land cover

The choice of land cover at airports usually depends on air-operations safety regulations, economic considerations, location, and wildlife-hazard management. From an air-operations perspective, land cover should prevent soil erosion and blowing dust and debris, require little maintenance, and provide a firm braking surface near runways for aircraft during emergencies (Blokpoel, 1976). Wildlife managers must work under these constraints when contemplating land-cover types that will not attract hazardous wildlife. Historically, the principal land cover at airports has been turf grass, even though large expanses of turf grass can attract various hazardous bird species (e.g., European starlings [*Sturnus vulgaris*], Canada geese [*Branta canadensis*], and various gulls [*Larus* spp.]), and there is no consensus regarding the species composition and height of grass that best reduces wildlife hazards (Mead and Carter, 1973; Brough and Bridgman, 1980; Seamans et al., 2007; Washburn and Seamans, 2007; Washburn et al., 2007). However, regardless of species composition and height, turf-grass maintenance at airports is expensive (ICAO, 1991, 2002). An attractive alternative to turf grass on some portions of airport properties would be the establishment of land-cover types that generate income rather than consume resources (ICAO, 2002). Such land-cover options would be especially beneficial for smaller airports that operate on limited budgets (Dolbeer et al., 2008).

An obvious alternative to turf grass is agriculture, and in an era when plant agriculture includes food crops, landscaping vegetation, and crops for biofuels, potential revenue-producing land covers for airports abound. However, the ICAO and FAA recommend against using airport property for most types of agriculture because of the potential to attract hazardous wildlife (ICAO, 1991; AC 150/5200-33B). Specifically, the AC 150/5200-33B instructs certificated airports to refrain from using airport land for agriculture unless "...the airport has no financial alternative to agricultural crops to produce income necessary to maintain the viability of the airport". Should an airport consider agriculture for revenue, crop-distance guidelines are provided in AC 150/5300-13–*Airport Design, Appendix 17, Minimum Distances between Certain Airport Features and Any On-Airport Agricultural Crops*. Notably, these minimum-distance rules for agriculture operations are not based on research characterizing wildlife use of specific crops. Further, despite the hazards ostensibly inherent to agriculture at airports, many small airports in the USA which are not regulated by the FAA lease substantial portions of airport properties for agricultural production. In a recent study of 10 small airports in Indiana, USA, row-crop fields (corn and soybeans) covered approximately 20% of the combined airport properties, and some row-crop fields were within 20 m of active runways (DeVault et al., 2008).

To begin consideration of the types of agriculture that might be compatible with airport operations from a wildlife–hazard perspective, one must consider recognized wildlife–habitat relationships in agricultural landscapes. Many farmland bird populations have declined in recent decades because of agricultural intensification in Europe (Donald et al., 2001, 2002; Benton et al., 2003) and the USA (Blackwell and Dolbeer, 2001; Murphy, 2003; Peterjohn, 2003; Krapu et al., 2004). Increases in average field size, enhanced weed and invertebrate pest control, and the shift from agricultural mosaics to monocultures of row crops has resulted in the homogenization of agricultural landscapes (Arnold, 1983; Benton et al., 2003). The reduction in available nesting habitats (Best et al., 1995; Blackwell and Dolbeer, 2001), invertebrate populations (Wilson et al., 1999), weed seeds (Wilson et al., 1999; Krapu et al., 2004), and waste grain (Krapu et al., 2004) all have contributed to reduced bird diversity and population sizes in present-day agricultural landscapes (Benton et al., 2003; Tscharntke et al., 2005; however, see reference to the wood pigeon *Columba palumbus* in Raven et al., 2007).

Even in relatively diverse agricultural landscapes, birds use row-crop fields infrequently compared to adjacent habitat types. Birds are generally more abundant in wooded fence rows, grassed waterways, and woodlots, where nesting locations and food resources are more abundant (Blokpoel, 1976; Best et al., 1995, 2001; Patterson and Best, 1996; McMaster and Davis, 2001). Frequent anthropogenic disturbance, low plant species diversity, and the use of pesticides contribute to the relative lack of birds found in row-crop fields (Best et al., 1995). In a review of habitat use by farmland birds in the midwestern USA, only red-winged blackbirds (*Agelaius phoeniceus*) were considered "very abundant" in any agricultural habitat (grass hayfields), and no species were considered "very abundant" or "abundant" in pastures or row crops (Best et al., 1995). Furthermore, relatively few species nest in row-crop fields compared to grassland habitats (Patterson and Best, 1996). Most species use row-crop fields only for foraging, preferring to nest in adjacent habitats (Best et al., 1990, 1995; Murphy, 2003).

Furthermore, agricultural fields also serve as avian foraging habitat during winter (Wilson et al., 1996; Perkins et al., 2000). Fields that are completely plowed under after harvest ("conventional tillage") usually undergo a high incidence of bird use for a short period of time, because of attraction to seeds and invertebrates brought to the surface (Wilson et al., 1996). Fields that are partially tilled or not tilled at all ("conservation tillage"), thereby leaving some crop residue on the soil surface (Best, 1986), generally attract more birds throughout the winter period than conventional tillage (Flickinger and Pendleton, 1994; Butler et al., 2005; but see Perkins et al., 2000). However, as is the case during the growing season, grass fields generally are preferred by invertebrate-feeding birds over crop fields during winter due to decreased invertebrate abundances in crop fields (Tucker, 1992).

Although birds are generally less abundant in crop fields than in adjacent habitat types, over 50 bird species have been documented using row-crop fields during the breeding season in the midwestern USA (Best et al., 1995). Further, extensive work has been directed at bird damage to agriculture (e.g., blackbird [Icteridae] damage to corn (Dolbeer et al., 1984), sunflowers (Blackwell et al., 2003; Peer et al., 2003), and vegetables (Mott et al., 1972); waterfowl damage to cereal grains (Mott et al., 1972), and European starling damage to fruits (Feare, 1985; Stevens, 2008)). In a review of studies documenting bird damage to crops in the USA, Sterner et al. (1984) found damage reported for grains, seeds, and silages (18 of 24 crop types), vegetables (15 of 25), fruits (17 of 20), and nuts (5 of 6). However, Sterner et al. (1984) found no studies documenting bird damage to cotton, cottonseed, dry edible beans, hops, sweet potatoes, soybeans, and several types of fruits and vegetables. Sixty-nine species of birds were reported to damage crops, although blackbirds were the most frequently cited species linked to crop damage. Blackbirds are likely the most economically important bird-species group affecting agriculture in the USA (Sterner et al., 1984; Conover, 2002; Blackwell et al., 2003). Interestingly, despite the abundance of soybean fields in the USA, soybeans are not a preferred food for birds (Krapu et al., 2004), and birds rarely cause damage in soybean fields (Sterner et al., 1984; Humberg et al., 2007). It is worth noting, however, that birds often forage for invertebrates in fields where no wildlife damage occurs (Best et al., 1990; Krapu et al., 2004; Humberg et al., 2007).

Because all crops do not attract birds equally, the opportunity exists to identify revenue-producing crops and practices (e.g., irrigation requirements) that are compatible with minimizing wildlife hazards at airports. However, airport environments differ from rural landscapes, offering grassland, pavement, and structural habitats. Thus, studies are needed to understand how hazardous bird species use crop fields and various tillage regimens in airport environments. Movement patterns and home ranges of hazardous birds in airport environments will likely be important in determining potential use of airport crop fields. Further, nesting locations of these species in airport habitats should be identified so they can be eliminated or altered to be unattractive. In addition, little is known concerning wildlife use of non-traditional field crops (e.g., meadowfoam [*Limnanthes alba*]; Alternative Field Crops Manual, 1989), some of which might prove suitable for use on airports. It is also important to note that agriculture at airports has implications for mammalian (e.g., white-tailed deer [*Odocoileus virginianus*]) as well as bird hazards, especially at small airports where funding is often limited and fending inadequate (DeVault et al., 2008; Dolbeer et al., 2008).

3.3. Natural areas

Various types of human disturbance have been shown to have negative effects on wildlife (e.g., Canaday, 1996; Reed and Merenlender, 2008), particularly in highly urbanized landscapes (Fernández-Juricic, 2000a). However, airports have relatively low levels of at least one type of human disturbance (e.g., recreational activities) due to heightened security. Minimal pedestrian disturbance can enhance the suitability of different habitat types (forests, grasslands, water sources) in terms of foraging and breeding opportunities (Fernández-Juricic, 2002). Furthermore, the diversity of habitats at airports (Baker and Brooks, 1981) might exceed that found in other landscape elements, like urban parks or residential areas. For example, raptors exploit the availability of open foraging areas (often with higher densities of small mammals), perch availability, and nesting habitats on airports (Baker and Brooks, 1981; Linnell et al., 1996; Kelly, 1999; Avery and Genchi, 2004; Blackwell and Wright, 2006). Airports also provide some of the only remaining extensive areas of grassland habitat in heavily urbanized regions like the northeast USA, and some contend that these habitats should be managed for nesting avifauna (Osborne and Peterson, 1984; Vickery et al., 1994; Houston and Bowen, 2001; see also Kershner and Bollinger, 1996).

However, simply setting aside undeveloped areas as natural areas on airports can pose negative effects for aviation safety and wildlife species. For example, there is a general presupposition of a direct relationship between the local density of a given species of bird (whether hazardous to aviation or not) and the rate of bird strikes (Sodhi, 2002). Empirical evidence supports this association in some species (e.g., Linnell et al., 1996; Belant, 1997; Byron and Downs, 2002; Baxter and Allan, 2008). Further, airports can function as ecological traps (Kokko and Sutherland, 2001) for some endangered or threatened species due to direct collisions with aircraft (e.g., lappet-faced vulture [*Torgos tracheliotus*], black-footed albatross [*Phoebastria nigripes*], Townsend's shearwater [*Puffinus auricularis*]; Dolbeer and Wright, 2008) or indirect effects of wildlife-control programs targeting other species. Also, some locally protected species may be affected negatively by air traffic through indirect effects. For instance, military aircraft have been shown to disturb grey heron (*Ardea cinerea*) adults incubating and feeding young, and ultimately facilitating the access to nest predators (Kitowski, 2001). Thus, to safely and effectively incorporate biodiversity and conservation efforts into airport-planning models, information is needed on the direct effects of airport operations and potential indirect effects on species populations that use airport habitats.

Unfortunately, we know little about how species abundance/richness varies between airports and other landscape elements. For example, species richness can differ considerably across various urban landscape elements (Fernández-Juricic, 2000b; Sandstrom et al., 2006). If an airport acts as a population sink, it is likely that individuals from source areas (either of the same or related species) might reoccupy the vacated niches (Brown et al., 2001b), which may require reducing the accessibility of those individuals to the airport to control the population. On the other hand, if airports act as sources (Brown et al., 2001a), control of breeding populations on the airport could be opposed, especially for species of concern (e.g., bald eagle [*Haliaeetus leucocephalus*] nesting at Orlando International Airport, Florida, USA; see Metcalf, 2007). Also, severe local control of population growth (on or near an airport) could reduce the dispersal of individuals into other populations and potentially affect the regional persistence of a species. This latter scenario could require carefully planned reintroduction efforts.

Successful planning and management for select, non-hazardous wildlife species on airport properties must, therefore, consider inter-specific variations in some processes that can affect local populations, such as density-dependence, behavioral responses to aircraft or aversive methods (speed of reaction, sensitization, habituation, etc.), and movement between suitable patches within and surrounding an airfield. We suggest that planners consider implementing the concept of buffer areas, which has been used in conservation biology and wildlife management (Wells and Brandon, 1993; Shafer, 1999a). This concept has been applied both at the landscape scale (hereafter, landscape buffer areas) and at the patch scale (hereafter, patch buffer areas). A landscape buffer area (also known as a buffer zone) is an area surrounding critical habitat for a population or a community that also can serve as an environmental "cushion" to minimize external disturbances (Sayer, 1991; Shafer, 1999b). Similarly, a patch buffer area (also known as a set-back zone) denotes a minimum area of critical habitat for an individual or a group of individuals concentrated in space (breeding colony, roost; Vos et al., 1985; Fox and Madsen, 1997; Fernández-Juricic et al., 2005).

The delineation of a landscape buffer area is based on a threshold distance from a source of disturbance at which the density of a species or species richness increases substantially (Reijnen et al., 1995; Miller et al., 1998; Sinclair et al., 2005). Usually, this threshold distance establishes a minimum width of habitat required for protection (Palomino and Carrascal, 2007).

Conceptually, the establishment of patch buffer areas is related to the theory of anti-predator behavior (Lima, 1998), because it assumes that individuals perceive humans (or human-related activities) as threats and respond to them by becoming alert and eventually fleeing (Frid and Dill, 2002). Subsequently, estimation of patch buffer areas is based on the distance at which animals become fearful of humans (Knight and Skagen, 1988; Knight and Temple, 1995; Richardson and Miller, 1997). First, minimum approaching distances (minimum horizontal distance of non-intrusion by humans that would preclude disturbance; Rodgers and Smith, 1995; Rodgers and Schwikert, 2002) are calculated. Second, patch buffer areas are estimated using the minimum approaching distance as the radius of a circular area (Fox and Madsen, 1997). In a conservation context, patch buffer areas have helped limit the amount of disturbance to wildlife through a reduction in detection and avoidance behavior by birds (Rodgers and Schwikert, 2002). This concept can be reversed for bird-aircraft scenarios so that management techniques can be applied within patch buffer areas to enhance the probability of aircraft detection and avoidance. However, the assertion that wildlife respond to human activities (e.g., aircraft) in similar ways to those of predators is a key assumption that requires empirical testing across a wide range of species to establish models for bird-strike research (e.g., Blumstein et al., 2003, 2005; Blackwell and Bernhardt, 2004; Blackwell et al., 2009).

In summary, landscape buffer areas offer opportunities for sustainable development on and near airports without necessarily enhancing wildlife hazards. Patch buffer areas would allow us to better define the proportional area of airports in which birds (as well as other wildlife) and aircraft overlap, and consequently the spatial range of certain wildlife management control techniques. Overall, the adoption of the buffer-area approach into airport planning offers a means of targeting select, nonhazardous species and their habitats for conservation in planning models, and with regard to aviation safety.

4. Land use and wildlife-strike risk

As the footprint of an airport on local habitats changes (via operations, land management, expansion, etc.), the wildlife communities using those habitats are necessarily affected in richness and abundance (e.g., Fernández-Juricic, 2004; Chace and Walsh, 2006). Further, though airport development often degrades ecosystems, some species respond positively to human-induced changes to the landscape. Thus, airport planners must weight designs affecting functionality of the airport (e.g., stormwater systems), novel revenue-producing land uses, and considerations for biodiversity and species conservation relative to potential wildlife-strike hazards.

Schafer et al. (2007) noted that effective prioritization of species management on airports entails an assessment of the realistic potential for damage associated with wildlife strikes, and suggested the implementation of risk assessment that reflects an index of species frequency within critical locations on and near the airport and associated strike-damage metrics. A risk assessment has two basic phases (Graham et al., 1991): (1) a conceptual understanding of the sources of the problem (e.g., factors contributing to wildlife hazards to aviation), realistic endpoints or potential events (e.g., a hull loss; see Dolbeer et al., 2000; Dolbeer and Wright, 2009), and mechanisms by which the sources contribute to the defined endpoints; and (2) a spatiotemporal estimate of exposure to the problem sources and a quantification of potential effects. In the context of an airport, seasonal demographic cycles of species using particular habitats could be evaluated relative to species abundance estimates within critical airspace (e.g., agriculture near an airport; Baxter and Robinson, 2007; runway protection zones; Schafer et al., 2007) to better discern the contribution of land use to wildlife-strike risk. Thus, the wildlife-strike risk assessment should include land-use data and, at minimum, species relative abundance estimates and strike statistics. Other components include data on aircraft types serviced by the airport and number of movements relative to seasonal abundance estimates of hazardous species. Conceptually, these data components would be maintained within a single database, such as the FAA National Wildlife Strike Database (NWSD).

In 1995, the FAA, through an interagency agreement with the U.S. Department of Agriculture, Wildlife Services (WS), initiated a project to obtain more objective estimates of the magnitude and nature of the national wildlife strike problem for civil aviation. This effort involves the (1) editing of all strike reports (FAA Form 5200-7, Birds/Other Wildlife Strike Report) received by the FAA since 1990; (2) entering strike data into the NWSD; (3) supplementing FAA-reported strikes with additional, non-duplicated strike reports from other sources; and (4) assisting the FAA with the production of reports summarizing the results of analyses of these data. The analyses conducted by WS on strike data focus on the economic costs of wildlife strikes, the magnitude of safety issues, wildlife species involved, types of damage, height and phase of flight during which strikes occur, and seasonal patterns (Dolbeer and Wright, 2008; see also Dolbeer et al., 2000; DeVault et al., 2005; Blackwell and Wright, 2006; Dolbeer, 2006b).

However, the NWSD contains no current land-use data for the airport or within the FAA separation distances. For example, the location of strikes occurring within the approach/departure zones (e.g., the 8-km separation for airports receiving turbine-powered aircraft) is assigned as that of the airport. Without data on the landscape matrix surrounding an airport and wildlife use of these habitats, the necessary covariates for assessing wildlife-strike risk associated with current or planned land uses are limited. In the absence of site-specific data, we suggest use of frequency distributions reflecting species seasonal occurrence in similar habitats or long-term data sets reflecting species trends (e.g., Breeding Bird Survey; Sauer et al., 2008), as well as consideration of wildlife-strike statistics for geographically similar locations. We note, also, that climate-induced changes in migration and nesting phenology of some bird populations could affect local population dynamics (e.g., Crick, 2004; Johnson et al., 2005; Both et al., 2006) and, subsequently, species-specific strike risk. Estimates of species-specific damage resulting from wildlife strikes are available from the NWSD (see Dolbeer and Wright, 2008) and could be used as surrogate data for similar species.

5. Conclusions

Collaborative efforts to more accurately assess goals for airport capacity needs, revenue, and sustainability in light of risks posed to aviation safety by wildlife populations are needed. International legislation guiding airport land-use planning recognizes wildlife hazards to aviation, but the recommendations are often general and in some cases conflicting. Further, with a world-wide focus on wildlife strikes and on-going international research, we encourage a proactive communication between the ICAO and aviation organizations within its member states (e.g., the FAA), such that science-based management protocols form the foundation for guidelines to reduce wildlife hazards to aviation. Moreover, we suggest that an airport is a component of the landscape and, therefore, contributes to and is subject to local- and landscape-level factors that affect wildlife populations. In turn, those same wildlife populations pose a level of risk to aviation safety. We, therefore, encourage continued and new research in four types of land use that affect airport operations in the USA and internationally: (1) management of stormwater on and near airports so as to meet local and national requirements for water treatment, while reducing use by species documented as hazardous to aviation; (2) wildlife (particularly bird) use of agricultural crops and various tillage regimens, as well as the periodicity and seasonality of use relative to other landscape uses, such as turf grass; (3) quantification of species richness and abundance relative to elements within and between landscapes, so as to better understand the role of the airport as a component of the landscape in explaining species population dynamics; and (4) use of buffer areas in planning for sustainable development on and around airports. Finally, we encourage the development and maintenance of datasets that will allow realistic assessment of wildlife-strike risk relative to current airport conditions as well as to anticipated increases in capacity.

Acknowledgements

The U.S. Department of Agriculture, Animal and Plant Health Inspection Service, Wildlife Services, National Wildlife Research Center supported this research. The authors received salary and logistical support from their respective institutions. In addition, we thank A. de Hoon and E. Poggiali for logistical assistance. We greatly appreciate reviews of earlier drafts of this manuscript by T.W. Seamans and L.A. Yako.

References

Aaronson, R.J., 2007. Leadership and action: a winning combination. ICAO J. 5, 36.
Abeyratne, R.I.R., 2000. Management of airport congestion through slot allocation. J. Air Transport Manage. 6, 29–41.
Airport Technology, 2009, 23 February. Expansion bucks the economic trend. Web site: http://www.airport-technology.com/features/feature49850/.
Allan, J.R., 2002. The costs of bird strikes and bird strike prevention. In: Clark, L., Hone, J., Shivik, J.A., Watkins, R.A., Vercauteren, K.C., Yoder, J.K. (Eds.), Human Conflicts with Wildlife: Economic Considerations, Proceedings of the Third NWRC Special Symposium. National Wildlife Research Center, Fort Collins, CO, USA, pp. 147–153.
Alternative Field Crops Manual, 1989. University of Minnesota CAPAP, MN, USA.
Arnold, G.W., 1983. The influence of ditch and hedgerow structure, length of hedgerows, and area of woodland and garden on bird numbers on farmland. J. Appl. Ecol. 20, 731–750.
Avery, M.L., Genchi, A.C., 2004. Avian perching deterrents on ultrasonic sensors at airport wind-shear alert systems. Wildl. Soc. Bull. 32, 718–725.
Baker, J.A., Brooks, R.J., 1981. Distribution patterns of raptors in relation to density of meadow voles. Condor 83, 42–47.
Baxter, A.T., Allan, J.R., 2008. Use of lethal control to reduce habituation to blank rounds by scavenging birds. J. Wildl. Manage. 72, 1653–1657.
Baxter, A.T., Robinson, A.P., 2007. Monitoring and influencing feral Canada goose (Branta canadensis) behaviour to reduce birdstrike risks to aircraft. Int. J. Pest Manage. 53, 341–346.
Belant, J.L., 1997. Gulls in urban environments: landscape-level management to reduce conflict. Landscape Urban Plan. 38, 245–258.
Benton, T.G., Vickery, J.A., Wilson, J.D., 2003. Farmland biodiversity: is habitat heterogeneity the key? Trends Ecol. Evol. 18, 182–188.
Best, L.B., 1986. Conservation tillage: ecological traps for nesting birds? Wildl. Soc. Bull. 14, 308–317.
Best, L.B., Bergin, T.M., Freemark, K.E., 2001. Influence of landscape composition on bird use of rowcrop fields. J. Wildl. Manage. 65, 442–449.

Best, L.B., Freemark, K.E., Dinsmore, J.J., Camp, M., 1995. A review and synthesis of habitat use by breeding birds in agricultural landscapes of Iowa. Am. Midl. Nat. 134, 1–29.

Best, L.B., Whitmore, R.C., Booth, G.M., 1990. Use of cornfields by birds during the breeding season: the importance of edge habitat. Am. Midl. Nat. 123, 84–99.

Blackwell, B.F., Avery, M.L., Watts, B.D., Lowney, M.S., 2007. Demographics of black vultures in North Carolina. J. Wildl. Manage. 71, 1976–1979.

Blackwell, B.F., Bernhardt, G.E., 2004. Efficacy of aircraft landing lights in stimulating avoidance behavior in birds. J. Wildl. Manage. 68, 725–732.

Blackwell, B.F., Dolbeer, R.A., 2001. Decline of the red-winged blackbird population in Ohio correlated to changes in agriculture (1965–1996). J. Wildl. Manage. 65, 661–667.

Blackwell, B.F., Fernández-Juricic, E., Seamans, T.W., Dolans, T., 2009. Avian visual configuration and behavioural response to object approach. Anim. Behav. 77, 673–684.

Blackwell, B.F., Huszar, E., Linz, G., Dolbeer, R.A., 2003. Lethal control of red-winged blackbirds to manage damage to sunflower: an economic evaluation. J. Wildl. Manage. 67, 818–828.

Blackwell, B.F., Schafer, L.M., Helon, D.A., Linnell, M.A., 2008. Bird use of stormwater-management ponds: decreasing avian attractants on airports. Landscape Urban Plan. 86, 162–170.

Blackwell, B.F., Wright, S.E., 2006. Collisions of red-tailed hawks (*Buteo jamaicensis*), Turkey (*Cathartes aura*), and black vultures (*Coragyps atratus*) with aircraft: implications for bird strike reduction. J. Raptor Res. 40, 76–80.

Blokpoel, H., 1976. Bird Hazards to Aircraft. Clarke, Irwin & Company Limited.

Blumstein, D.T., Anthony, L.L., Harcourt, R., Ross, G., 2003. Testing a key assumption of wildlife buffer zones: is flight initiation distance a species-specific trait? Biol. Cons. 110, 97–100.

Blumstein, D.T., Fernandez-Juricic, E., Zollner, P.A., Garity, S.C., 2005. Inter-specific variation in avian responses to human disturbance. J. Appl. Ecol. 42, 943–953.

Both, C., Bouwhuis, S., Lessells, C.M., Visser, M.E., 2006. Climate change and population declines in a long-distant migratory bird. Nature 441, 81–83.

Brough, T.E., Bridgman, C.J., 1980. An evaluation of long-grass as a bird deterrent on British airfields. J. Appl. Ecol. 17, 243–253.

Brown, K.M., Erwin, R.M., Richmond, M.E., Buckley, P.A., Tanacredi, J.T., Avrin, D., 2001b. Managing birds and controlling aircraft in the Kenney Airport-Jamaica Bay wildlife refuge complex: the need for hard data and soft opinions. Environ. Manage. 28, 207–224.

Brown, K.M., Tims, J.L., Erwin, R.M., Richmond, M., 2001a. Changes in the nesting populations of colonial waterbirds in Jamaica Bay Wildlife Refuge, New York, 1974–1998. Northeastern Nat. 8, 275–292.

Butler, S.J., Bradbury, R.B., Whittingham, M.J., 2005. Stubble height affects the use of stubble fields by farmland birds. J. Appl. Ecol. 42, 469–476.

Butterworth, M., 2008, 19 November. UK economy will suffer due to insufficient air links, BA chief warns. Telegraph, London, UK. Web site: http://telegraph.co.uk/finance/financetopics/recession/3484184/UK.

Byron, J., Downs, C.T., 2002. Bird presence at Oribi Airport and recommendations to avoid bird strikes. S. African J. Wildl. Res. 32, 49–58.

Canaday, C., 1996. Loss of insectivorous birds along a gradient of human impact in Amazonia. Biol. Conserv. 77, 63–77.

Chace, J.F., Walsh, J.J., 2006. Urban effects on native avifauna: a review. Landscape Urban Plan. 74, 46–69.

Cleary, E.C., Dolbeer, R.A., 2005. Wildlife Hazard Management at Airports, second ed. Federal Aviation Administration, Office of Airport Safety and Standards, Airport Safety and Compliance Branch, Washington, DC, USA.

Conover, M.R., 2002. Resolving Human–Wildlife Conflicts. Lewis, Boca Raton, FL, USA.

Crick, H.Q., 2004. The impact of climate change on birds. Ibis 146, 48–56.

DeVault, T.L., Kubel, J.E., Glista, D.J., Rhodes Jr., O.E., 2008. Mammalian hazards at small airports in Indiana: impact of perimeter fencing. Human–Wildl. Confl. 2, 240–247.

DeVault, T.L., Reinhart, B.D., Brisbin Jr., I.L., Rhodes Jr., O.E., 2005. Flight behavior of black and turkey vultures: implications for reducing bird–aircraft collisions. J. Wildl. Manage. 69, 592–599.

Dolbeer, R.A., 2006a. Birds and aircraft are competing for space in crowded skies. ICAO J. 3, 21–24.

Dolbeer, R.A., 2006b. Height distribution of birds as recorded by collisions with civil aircraft. J. Wildl. Manage. 70, 1345–1350.

Dolbeer, R.A., 2007. Managing the risks of bird strikes. Int. Airport Rev. 2, 61–64.

Dolbeer, R.A., Begier, M.J., Wright, S.E., 2008. Animal ambush: the challenge of managing wildlife hazards at general aviation airports. Corp. Aviat. Saf. Sem. 53, 1–12.

Dolbeer, R.A., Eschenfelder, P., 2002. Population increases of large birds, airworthiness standards and high-speed flight: a precarious combination. In: Proceedings of the 55th International Air Safety Seminar, Dublin, Ireland. Flight Safety Foundation, Alexandria, VA, USA, pp. 273–281.

Dolbeer, R.A., Woronecki, P.P., Stehn, R.A., 1984. Blackbird (*Agelaius phoeniceus*) damage to maize: crop phenology and hybrid resistance. Prot. Ecol. 7, 43–63.

Dolbeer, R.A., Wright, S.E., 2008. Wildlife strikes to civil aircraft in the United States, 1990-2007. U.S. Department of Transportation, Federal Aviation Administration, Office of Airport Safety and Standards, Serial Report No. 14, Washington, DC, USA, 57 pp.

Dolbeer, R.A., Wright, S.E., 2009. Safety management systems: how useful will the FAA National Wildlife Strike Database be? Human–Wildl. Confl. 3, 167–178.

Dolbeer, R.A., Wright, S.E., Cleary, E.C., 2000. Ranking the hazard level of wildlife species to aviation. Wildl. Soc. Bull. 28, 372–378.

Donald, P.F., Green, R.E., Heath, M.F., 2001. Agricultural intensification and the collapse of Europe's farmland bird populations. Proc. Royal Soc. Lond. B 68, 25–29.

Donald, P.F., Pisano, G., Rayment, M.D., Pain, D.J., 2002. The common Agricultural Policy, EU enlargement and the conservation of Europe's farmland birds. Agric. Ecosystems Environ. 89, 167–182.

European Union, 2001. Directive 2001/42/EC of the European Parliament and of the Council on the Assessment of the Effects of Certain Plans and Programmes on the Environment, Luxembourg.

European Union, 2003. Directive 2003/42/EC of the European Parliament and of the Council of 13 June 2003 on occurrence reporting in civil aviation, Luxembourg.

Feare, C.J., 1985. The Starling. Shire Publications, Princes Risborough, United Kingdom.

Federal Aviation Administration, 2006. Report to Congress. National Plan of Integrated Airport Systems (NPIAS) 2007–2011.

Federal Aviation Administration, 2008a. Procedures for handling airspace matters. Section 2. Class B Airspace Standards. Order JO 7400.2G.

Federal Aviation Administration, 2008b. FAA aerospace forecast fiscal years (2008–2025). Web site: http://www.faa.gov/data_statistics/aviation/aerospace_forecasts/2008-2025/.

Fernández-Juricic, E., 2000a. Local and regional effects of pedestrians on forest birds in a fragmented landscape. Condor 102, 247–255.

Fernández-Juricic, E., 2000b. Avifaunal use of linear strips in an urban landscape. Conserv. Biol. 14, 513–521.

Fernández-Juricic, E., 2002. Can human disturbance promote nestedness? A case study with birds in an urban fragmented landscape. Oecologia 131, 269–278.

Fernández-Juricic, E., 2004. Spatial and temporal analysis of the distribution of forest specialists in an urban-fragmented landscape (Madrid, Spain): implications for local and regional bird conservation. Landscape Urban Plan. 69, 17–32.

Fernández-Juricic, E., Venier, P., Renison, D., Blumstein, D.T., 2005. Sensitivity of wildlife to spatial patterns of recreationist behavior: a critical assessment of minimum approaching distances and buffer areas for grassland birds. Biol. Conserv. 125, 225–235.

Flight Safety Foundation, 2000. Flight Safety Foundation approach-and-landing accident reduction briefing note 4.2—energy management. Flight Saf. Digest. August–November, 75–80.

Flickinger, E.L., Pendleton, G.W., 1994. Bird use of agricultural fields under reduced and conventional tillage in the Texas Panhandle. Wild. Soc. Bull. 22, 34–42.

Fox, A.D., Madsen, J., 1997. Behavioural and distributional effects of hunting disturbance on waterbirds in Europe: implications for refuge design. J. Appl. Ecol. 34, 1–13.

Frid, A., Dill, L.M., 2002. Human-caused disturbance stimuli as a form of predation risk. Cons. Ecol. 6 (11), Web site: http://www.consecol.org/vol6/iss1/art11.

Graham, B., Guyer, C., 1999. Environmental sustainability, airport capacity and European air transport liberalization: irreconcilable goals? J. Air Transp. Geog. 7, 165–180.

Graham, R.L., Hunsaker, C.T., O'Neil, R.V., Jackson, B.L., 1991. Ecological risk assessment at the regional scale. Ecol. Appl. 1, 196–206.

Higgins, J., Liner, M., 2007. Engineering runoff solutions. Airport Business 21 (3), 22–25.

Houston, C.S., Bowen Jr., D.E., 2001. Upland sandpiper (*Bartramia longicauda*). In: Poole, A. (Ed.), The Birds of North America, No. 580. Cornell Lab of Ornithology, Ithaca, NY.

Humberg, L.A., DeVault, T.L., MacGowan, B.J., Beasley, J.C., Rhodes Jr., O.E., 2007. Crop depredation by wildlife in northcentral Indiana. Proc. Natl. Wild Turkey Symp. 9, 199–205.

Humphreys, I., Francis, G., Fry, J., 2001. Lessons from airport privatization, commercialization, and regulation in the United Kingdom. Transp. Res. Rec. 1744, 9–16.

International Civil Aviation Organization, 1991. Bird control and reduction. Airport Services Manual, Doc 9137-AN/898, Part 3.

International Civil Aviation Organization, 2002. Land use and environmental control. Airport Planning Manual, Doc 9184 AN/902, Part 2.

Johnson, W.C., Millett, B.V., Gilmanov, T., Voldseth, R.A., Guntenspergen, G.R., Naugle, D.E., 2005. Vulnerability of northern prairie wetlands to climate change. BioSci. 55, 863–872.

Kelly, T.A., 1999. Seasonal variation in birdstrike rate for two North American raptors: Turkey Vulture (*Cathartes aura*) and red-tailed Hawk (*Buteo jamaicensis*). J. Raptor Res. 33, 59–62.

Kelly, T.C., Allan, J., 2006. Ecological effects of aviation. In: Davenport, J., Davenport, J.L. (Eds.), The Ecology of Transportation: Managing Mobility for the Environment. Springer, The Netherlands, pp. 5–24.

Kelly, T.C., O'Callaghan, M.J.A., Bolger, R., 2001. The avoidance behaviour shown by the rook (corvus frugeilegus) to commercial aircraft. In: Pelzc, H.-J., Cowan, D.P., Feare, C.J. (Eds.), Advances in Vertebrate Pest Management, pp. 291–299.

Kershner, E.L., Bollinger, E.K., 1996. Reproductive success of grassland birds at east-central Illinois Airports. Am. Midl. Nat. 136, 358–366.

Khalafalla, A., El-Rayes, K., 2006. Optimizing airport construction site layouts to minimize wildlife hazards. J. Manage. Engrg. 22, 176–185.

Kitowski, I., 2001. Military impact on a colony of Grey Heron Ardea cinerea protected in the nature reserve. Ekológia (Bratislava) 20, 191–197.

Knight, R.L., Skagen, S.K., 1988. Effects of recreational disturbance on birds of prey: a review. In: R.L. Glinski, et al. (Eds.), Proceedings of the Southwest Raptor Management Symposium and Workshop, Inst. Wild. Res., Natl. Wildl. Fed. Sci. Tech. Ser. No. 11, pp. 355–359.

Knight, R.L., Temple, S.A., 1995. Wildlife and recreationists: coexistence through management. In: Knight, R.L., Gutzwiller, K.J. (Eds.), Wildlife and

Recreationists: Coexistence Through Management and Research. Island Press, Washington, pp. 327–333.

Kokko, H., Sutherland, W.J., 2001. Ecological traps in changing environments: ecological and evolutionary consequences of a behaviourally mediated Allee effect. Evol. Ecol. Res. 3, 537–551.

Krapu, G.L., Brandt, D.A., Cox Jr., R.R., 2004. Less waste corn, more land in soybeans, and the switch to genetically modified crops: trends with important implications for wildlife management. Wildl. Soc. Bull. 32, 127–136.

Lee, H., Yang, H.M., 2003. Strategies for a global logistics and economic hub: Incheon International Airport. J. Air Transp. Manage. 9, 113–121.

Lima, S.L., 1998. Non-lethal effects in the ecology of predator–prey interactions. BioSci. 48, 25–134.

Linnell, M.A., Conover, M.R., Ohashi, T.J., 1996. Analysis of bird strikes at a tropical airport. J. Wildl. Manage. 60, 935–945.

Mead, H., Carter, A.W., 1973. The management of long grass as a bird repellent on airfields. J. Br. Grassland Soc. 28, 219–221.

Metcalf, J.C., 2007. Bald eagle nest removal: making a case and building consensus among various agencies and organizations for amicable removal. In: Bird Strike Committee Proceedings, Bird Strike Committee USA/Canada, 9th Annual Meeting, Kingston, Ontario.

McMaster, D.G., Davis, S.K., 2001. An evaluation of Canada's permanent cover program: habitat for grassland birds? J. Field Ornithol. 72, 195–325.

Miller, S.G., Knight, R.L., Miller, C.K., 1998. Influence of recreational trails on breeding bird communities. Ecol. Appl. 8, 162–169.

Mott, D.F., West, R.R., DeGrazio, J.W., Guarino, J.L., 1972. Foods of the red-winged blackbird in Brown County, South Dakota. J. Wildl. Manage. 36, 983–987.

Murphy, M.T., 2003. Avian population trends within the evolving agricultural landscape of eastern and central United States. Auk 120, 20–34.

Osborne, D.R., Peterson, A.T., 1984. Decline of the upland sandpiper (*Bartramia longicauda*) in Ohio: an endangered species. Ohio J. Sci. 84, 8–10.

Palomino, D., Carrascal, L.M., 2007. Threshold distances to nearby cities and roads influence the bird community of a mosaic landscape. Biol. Conserv. 140, 100–109.

Patterson, M.P., Best, L.B., 1996. Bird abundance and nesting success in Iowa CRP fields: the importance of vegetation structure and composition. Am. Midl. Nat. 135, 153–167.

Peer, B.D., Homan, H.J., Linz, G.M., Bleier, W., 2003. Impact of blackbird damage to sunflower: bioenergetic and economic models. Ecol. Appl. 13, 248–256.

Perkins, A.J., Whittingham, M.J., Bradbury, R.B., Wilson, J.D., Morris, A.J., Barnett, P.R., 2000. Habitat characteristics affecting use of lowland agricultural grassland by birds in winter. Biol. Conserv. 95, 279–294.

Peterjohn, B.G., 2003. Agricultural landscapes: can they support healthy bird populations as well as farm products? Auk 120, 14–19.

Rao, A., Pinos, A., 1998. Bird strike threat is best countered by effective wildlife control augmented by land-use management. ICAO J. 53 (8), 5–6, 25.

Raven, M.J., Noble, D.G., Baillie, S.R., 2007. The Breeding Bird Survey 2006. BTO Research Report 471. British Trust for Ornithology, Thetford, United Kingdom.

Reed, S.E., Merenlender, A.M., 2008. Quiet, nonconsumptive recreation reduces protected area effectiveness. Conserv. Lett. 1, 146–154.

Reijnen, R., Foppen, R., Ter Braak, C., Thissen, J., 1995. The effects of car traffic on breeding bird populations in woodland. III. Reduction of density in relation to the proximity of main roads. J. Appl. Ecol. 32, 187–202.

Reiss, B., 2007. Maximizing non-aviation revenue for airports: developing airport cities to optimize real estate and capitalize on land development opportunities. Airport Manage. 1, 284–294.

Richardson, C.T., Miller, C.K., 1997. Recommendations for protecting raptors from human disturbance: a review. Wildl. Soc. Bull. 25, 634–638.

Richardson, W.J., West, T., 2000. Serious birdstrike accidents to military aircraft: updated list and summary. In: Proceedings of the 25th International Bird Strike Committee Meeting, Amsterdam, Netherlands, pp. 67–98.

Rodgers Jr., J.A., Smith, H.T., 1995. Set-back distances to protect nesting bird colonies from human disturbance in Florida. Conserv. Biol. 9, 89–99.

Rodgers Jr., J.A., Schwikert, S.T., 2002. Buffer zone distances to protect foraging and loafing waterbirds from disturbance by personal watercraft and outboard-powered boats. Conserv. Biol. 16, 216–224.

Rusch, D.H., Malecki, R.E., Trost, R.E., 1995. Canada geese in North America. In: LaRoe, E.T., Farris, G.S., Puckett, C.E., Doran, P.D., Mac, M.J. (Eds.), Our Living Resources: A Report to the Nation on the Distribution, Abundance, and Health of U.S. Plants, Animals, and Ecosystems. U.S. Department of the Interior, National Biological Service, Washington, DC, pp. 26–28.

Sandstrom, U.G., Angelstam, P., Mikusinski, G., 2006. Ecological diversity of birds in relation to the structure of urban green space. Landscape Urban Plan. 77, 39–53.

Sauer, J.R., Hines, J.E., Fallon, J., 2008. The North American Breeding Bird Survey, Results and Analysis 1966–2007, Version 5.15.2008, USGS Patuxent Wildlife Research Center, Laurel, MD.

Sayer, J., 1991. Rainforest Buffer Zones: Guidelines for Protected Area Managers, IUCN, Morges, Switzerland.

Schafer, L.M., Blackwell, B.F., Linnell, M.A., 2007. Quantifying risk associated with potential bird-aircraft collisions. In: Irwin, C.L., Nelson, D., McDermott, K.P. (Eds.), Proceedings of the International Conference on Ecology and Transportation. Center for Transportation and the Environment, North Carolina State University, Raleigh, NC, pp. 56–63.

Seamans, T.W., Barras, S.C., Bernhardt, G.E., Blackwell, B.F., Cepek, J.D., 2007. Comparison of two vegetation-height management practices for wildlife control at airports. Human–Wildl. Confl. 1, 97–105.

Shafer, C.L., 1999a. U.S. national park buffer zones: historical, scientific, social and legal aspects. Environ. Manage. 23, 49–173.

Shafer, C.L., 1999b. National park and reserve planning to protect biological diversity: some basic elements. Landscape Urban Plan. 44, 123–1153.

Sinclair, K.E., Hess, G.R., Moorman, C.E., Mason, J.H., 2005. Mammalian nest predators respond to greenway width, landscape context and habitat structure. Landscape Urban Plan. 71, 277–293.

Sodhi, N., 2002. Competition in the air: birds versus aircraft. Auk 119, 587–595.

Solman, V.E.F., 1973. Birds and aircraft. Biol. Conserv. 5, 79–86.

Solman, V.E.F., 1976. Aircraft and birds. Bird Control Sem. Proc. 7, 83–88.

Sterner, R.T., Elias, D.J., Garrison, M.V., Johns, B.E., Kilburn, S.R., 1984. Birds and airport destruction in the conterminous United States: a review of literature. In: Office of Airport Standards, Wildlife Hazards to Aircraft Conference and Training Workshop, DOT/FAA/AAS, Washington, DC.

Stevens, J., 2008. Foraging success of adult and juvenile starlings *Sturnus vulgaris*: a tentative explanation for the preference of juveniles for cherries. Ibis 127, 341–347.

Thorpe, J., pp. 85–113 2003. Fatalities and destroyed aircraft due to bird strikes, 1912–2002. In: Proceedings of the 26th International Bird Strike Comm. Meeting, Warsaw, Poland.

Thorpe, J., pp. 17–24 2005. Fatalities and destroyed aircraft due to bird strikes, 2002–2004 (with an appendix of animal strikes). In: Proceedings of the 27th International Bird Strike Comm. Meeting, Athens, Greece.

Tscharntke, T., Klein, A.M., Kruess, A., Steffan-Dewenter, I., Thies, C., 2005. Landscape perspectives on agricultural intensification and biodiversity–ecosystem service management. Ecol. Lett. 8, 857–874.

Tucker, G.M., 1992. Effects of agricultural practices on field use by invertebrate-feeding birds in winter. J. Appl. Ecol. 29, 779–790.

Vickery, P.D., Hunter Jr., M.L., Melvin, S.M., 1994. Effects of habitat area on the distribution of grassland birds in Maine. Conserv. Biol. 8, 1087–1097.

Vos, D.K., Ryder, P.A., Graul, W.D., 1985. Response of breeding great blue herons to human disturbance in northcentral Colorado. Col. Waterbirds 8, 13–22.

Vreeker, R., Nijkamp, P., Ter Welle, C., 2002. A multicriteria decision support methodology for evaluating airport expansion plans. Transp. Res. Part D 7, 27–47.

Waller, D.M., Alverson, W.S., 1997. The white-tailed deer: a keystone herbivore. Wildl. Soc. Bull. 25, 217–226.

Washburn, B.E., Seamans, T.W., 2007. Wildlife responses to vegetation height management in cool-season grasslands. Rangel. Ecol. Manage. 60, 319–323.

Washburn, B.E., Barras, S.C., Seamans, T.W., 2007. Foraging preferences of captive Canada geese related to turfgrass mixtures. Human–Wildl. Confl. 1, 188–197.

Weikel, D., 2008, 30 November. John Wayne airport to run with expansion plan. Los Angeles Times, Los Angeles, CA, USA, 30 November. Web site: articles.latimes.com/2008/nov/30/local/me-jwa30.

Wells, M.P., Brandon, K.E., 1993. The principles and practice of buffer zones and local participation in biodiversity conservation. Ambio 22, 157–162.

Wilson, J.D., Morris, A.J., Arroyo, B.E., Clark, S.C., Bradbury, R.B., 1999. A review of the abundance and diversity of invertebrate and plant foods of granivorous birds in northern Europe in relation to agricultural change. Agric. Ecosyst. Environ. 75, 13–30.

Wilson, J.D., Taylor, R., Muirhead, L.B., 1996. Field use by farmland birds in winter: an analysis of field type preferences using resampling methods. Bird Study 43, 320–332.

20

Learning and Policy Improvement After Disaster

The Case of Aviation Security

THOMAS A. BIRKLAND

This article considers whether policy makers in the aviation security field have learned from actual or apparent aviation security breaches in the late 1980s through 2001. The author finds that the loss of Pan Am Flight 103 in 1988 and of TWA Flight 800 in 1996 did lead to greater policy-making attention to a relatively narrow range of issues raised by these events. The author also finds that the September 11 terrorist attacks led to a comprehensive search for improved policy tools to prevent a recurrence of the attacks. The author argues that this post–September 11 search would not have been possible without the debates on aviation safety that accompanied the earlier events.

Keywords: terrorism; aviation security; policy change; policy learning; agenda setting; policy process; September 11 attacks

Among the many issues and challenges highlighted by the September 11 attacks is the challenge of keeping commercial aviation safe from terrorist and criminal attacks.[1] In this article I consider the following three major aviation security events: the Pan Am Flight 103 (PAA 103) bombing over Lockerbie, Scotland, in 1988; the loss of TWA Flight 800 (TWA 800) off Long Island, New York, in 1996 (which was not as it turned out the result of terrorist action); and the clearly important September 11 hijackings and attacks. As I will show, prima facie evidence of some sort of learning (May, 1992) is evident in all three of these cases, and learning that derives from direct experience is evident after both PAA 103 and September 11. In particular, I show that policy-making activity after the 1988 and 1996 events provided the raw material for many of the debates surrounding policy change following the September 11 hijackings and attacks. Although I do not claim that this prior experience was necessary to achieve policy change after September 11—and whereas it is clear that these events were insufficiently compelling to create much change before September 11—I do argue that these events and the debate in the weeks after the loss of TWA 800 contributed to federal policy makers' ability to quickly change law and regulations in an attempt to address the policy failures that allowed four airliners to be hijacked nearly simultaneously and deliberately crashed into targets on the ground.

Like all policy inspired by "focusing events" (Birkland, 1997), the "window of opportunity" (Kingdon, 1995) for policy change in aviation disasters is rather short after a large, attention-grabbing event. This may be possible, as we will see, for two reasons. First, the initial enthusiasm for the issue—among the media (which can serve as a proxy for public attention) and policy makers—is likely to be quite short-lived, even for as important an issue as the September 11 attacks. Second, as I will discuss, the "easy" solutions are often engaged and adopted first in order to do "something" after a focusing event. Ideas engaged later are often more controversial, and advocates for these policies face a policy environment in which urgency has waned and opponents to further change argue that new solutions have already been explored and need time to work.

But going beyond the obvious notion of a focusing event as a wake-up call, we can view the PAA 103 and TWA 800 events as rehearsals for the comprehensive policy making that followed the September 11 attacks. This is true for two reasons. First, the mode of attack—the commandeering of airplanes for use as guided missiles—was novel to most policy makers.[2] But the intentional destruction of aircraft in flight is not novel in the United States; according to the database maintained at www.airdisaster.com, at least four U.S. civil airliners have been bombed in American airspace, and at least one was crashed due to the actions of a disgruntled former pilot. In recent years, policy makers in the aviation security domain could draw on experience in policy making that followed the PAA 103 and TWA 800 events, both of which were characterized both by advocacy for greater aviation security and by arguments about cost-benefit analysis, the actual risk of terrorism, and the appropriate role of government in what was at least believed to be a private industry (substantial government subsidies notwithstanding). All these arguments were revisited after September 11.

The second reason why we can argue that the PAA and TWA events were rehearsals for post–September 11 policy is the incremental nature of aviation safety and security policy. Aviation safety and security policy does not change in leaps and bounds. Rather, because of the rapid accumulation of knowledge about major and minor operational issues and problems in aviation (Perrow, 1999), operators and regulators are able to rather quickly learn from and address problems as experience is gained. Criminal and terrorist threats to aviation are also dealt with incrementally as policies were enacted to address the most recent sort of threats, from criminal hijackings of airplanes for transportation purposes, to terrorist attacks for extortion and blackmail (St. John, 1989), to the current environment of bombings and suicide attacks that use planes as weapons in pursuit of political goals.

So, although September 11 created sweeping change in aviation security policy, it is, as I will show here, safe to say that post–September 11 policy making could draw on a rich history of efforts to improve policy and a history of incremental policy that in some ways improved security and in other ways failed to do so, as evidenced by the attacks themselves.

FOCUSING EVENTS, POLICY FAILURE, AND LEARNING IN PUBLIC POLICY

In my book *After Disaster* (Birkland, 1997), I outlined how focusing events (Kingdon, 1995) can attract attention to major public problems and lead to searches for solutions. This search begins because focusing events can be used to demonstrate the existence of policy failure; that is, participants in policy making can reasonably argue that a focusing event would not have happened or would not have been so severe "if only" something had been done. Other times, focusing events serve groups that were already warning of the existence of a problem; these events are what we might call "I-told-you-so" events that are seized on by those who have long argued that some sort of action should be taken to address a problem. For example, well before the September 11 hijackings and attacks, there were many voices calling for greater attention to the aviation security threats confronting the United States.[3] And it is therefore reasonable to posit the argument that aviation security policies and practices failed to prevent the hijackings of the planes.

With the argument for policy failure comes a search for answers and in particular, an attempt to apply these so-called lessons of an event[4] to mitigate the impacts of future such events. But what does learning look like in the policy process, particularly when such learning is triggered by disasters? Important to this investigation is an understanding of how the so-called lessons—like the problems that lead to learning—are socially constructed—are derived and advocated as part of strategic efforts to advance a particular set of policies that may or may not be objectively related to the event itself.

As I review in this article, an important part of agenda setting is not merely attention to the problem but attention to particular aspects of a problem or indeed, the various different ways to define what the problem "really" is. The definition of an issue or problem is itself contentious, and the definition of a problem often prejudges the solutions to the claimed problem (Hilgartner & Bosk, 1988; Rochefort & Cobb, 1994). Thus, the definition of possible policy solutions can be very contentious, with organized interests engaging in sometimes fierce political battles to advance their problem definition and achieve their policy goals.

Thus, the sort of learning that happens after a major focusing event is not necessarily learning about what went wrong or how best to fix the problems most clearly revealed by the event. Rather, we will find evidence of learning about why an event happened, how policy can prevent or mitigate future similar events, and how advocates for new policies can better hone their arguments to advance their policy preferences.

This article will not provide a comprehensive review of the literature on learning; this literature is rich, complex, and has yet to reach any consensus on the nature of learning. Indeed, Levy (1994) called this research a "conceptual minefield." Who learns, what is learned, and how learning is employed have been defined differently by students of the policy process (Bennett & Howlett, 1992). The main controversy in the debate over who learns is whether nonhuman entities such as institutions or organizations can learn or whether only individuals learn. Many scholars (Busenberg, 2001; Levy, 1994; May, 1992; Sabatier, 1988) deal with this problem by assuming that individuals—agency heads, interest group leaders, academics, journalists, and so on—are the key objects of learning. Indeed, Sabatier (1987) argued that learning at the level of groups and organizations is largely metaphorical because organizations do not have the cognitive capacity to learn.

Thus, Busenberg (2001) provided a simple and elegant definition of learning as "a process in which individuals apply new information and ideas to policy decisions" (p. 173). And Levy (1994) provided an equally parsimonious definition of "experiential learning" as "a change in beliefs (or the degree of confidence in one's beliefs) or the development of new beliefs, skills, or procedures as a result of the observation and interpretation of experience" (p. 283). Levy explicitly noted that his definition of learning does not require actual policy change but merely requires "an improved understanding of the world, or an increasingly complex cognitive structure" (p. 283). In this article however, I use evidence of policy change, or at least movement in the direction of policy change, to reflect how some sort of learning may have occurred.

Focusing events cause individual actors to react to the event in certain ways. A focusing event will lead to the obvious response to the event itself—providing relief, recovery, and security services after a terrorist attack or a natural disaster, for example—but the reactions I study here are policy reactions contained within what Busenberg (2001) called the "learning process." In the end, I argue that one should be able to find evidence of learning from a focusing event. The evidence of this learning is found at the institutional level. By studying the outputs of institutions—debates, news stories, proposed laws and regulations, enacted laws and regulations, and so on—we can gain insight on whether and to what extent the key participants in these institutions have learned.

Learning from disasters can be rapid or slow. Disasters create learning opportunities because they create "cognitive openness" to change (Stern, 1997). But whether that change happens soon after the event or some time later is variable and requires analysis. Certainly, many events will lead to rapid and immediate changes, whereas the same events will lead to other changes that have to be made deliberately. In fact, if change happens too slowly after an event, it is difficult to claim whether and to what extent learning was the result of a particular event or whether and to what extent other intervening factors, such as the accumulation of experience from later events or changes in the governing coalition or national mood, were the "real" causes of learning and change.

POLICY LEARNING AND POLICY FAILURE

Peter May (1992) argued that policy failure inspires three different kinds of learning; it is this link between events and failure on the one hand and failure and learning on the other that suggests a connection between events and learning. May divided learning into the following three categories: instrumental policy learning, social policy learning, and political learning. In all three types of learning, policy failure—politically and socially defined—provides a stimulus for learning about how to make better policy.

- Instrumental policy learning concerns learning about "viability of policy interventions or implementation designs." This sort of learning centers on implementation tools and techniques. When feedback from implementation is analyzed and changes to the design are made that improve its performance, then this suggests that learning has happened and was successful.
- Social policy learning involves learning about the "social construction of a policy or program." This type of learning goes beyond simple adjustments to program management and goes to the heart of the problem itself, including attitudes toward program goals and the nature and appropriateness of government action. If successfully applied, social policy learning can result in better understanding of the underlying causal theory of a public problem, leading to better policy responses. Prima facie indicators of social learning involve "policy redefinition entailing changes in policy goals or scope—e.g., policy direction, target groups, rights bestowed by the policy" (p. 336).
- Political learning is considerably different from instrumental and social learning. Political learning is involved with learning about "strategy for advocating a given policy idea or problem," leading potentially to "more sophisticated advocacy of a policy idea or problem." Political learning can be assumed to have occurred when advocates for or against policy change alter their strategy and tactics to conform to new information that has entered the political system.

In the ideal case, learning reflects the accumulation and application of knowledge to lead to better policies. However, policy makers and their supporters may support policy change that is not objectively related to the actual problems revealed by the event. May (1992) called mimicking or copying policy without assessment or analysis superstitious instrumental learning. For example, merely introducing a new aviation security bill that is a rehash of previously failed legislation without providing any sort of rationale for why the tools contained in the bill are now relevant may be seen as mimicking across time rather than across place.

May's (1992) article lists what he called prima facie evidence of these various forms of learning. What constitutes evidence of such learning and other features of each type of learning are shown in Table 1. In the conclusion of this

TABLE 1: Policy Learning and Failure

	Policy Learning			Political Learning
	Instrumental	*Social*		*Political Learning*
Entails learning about	Viability of policy interventions or implementation designs	Social construction of a policy or problem		Strategy for advocating a given policy idea or problem
Foci	Policy instruments or implementation designs	Policy problem, scope of policy, or policy goals		Political feasibility and policy processes
May lead to	Understanding of source of policy failure or improved policy performance in reaching existing goals	Changed expectations concerning existing goals or redefinition of policy goals		More sophisticated advocacy of a policy idea or problem
Requisite conditions	Improved understanding of policy instruments or implementation based on experience or formal evaluation	Improved understanding or alteration of dominant causal beliefs about a policy problem or solution within the relevant policy domain		Awareness of political prospects and factors that affect them
Prima facie indicators	Policy redesign entailing change in instruments for carrying out the policy, for example, inducements, penalties, assistance, funding, timing of implementation, and organizational structures	Policy redefinition entailing change in policy goals or scope, for example, policy direction, target groups, rights bestowed by the policy		Policy advocates change in political strategy, for example, shifting arenas, offering new arguments, employing new tactics for calling attention to a problem or idea
Potentially confused with	Superstitious learning involving presumed superiority of a given instrument; mimicking behavior	Policy redefinition unrelated to change in dominant causal beliefs within a policy domain		Haphazard change in political strategy unrelated to understanding of political dynamics
Requires evidence of	Increased understanding of policy instruments or implementation	Change in dominant causal beliefs within the relevant policy domain		Awareness of relationship between political strategy and political feasibility within a given advocacy coalition

SOURCE: May (1992).

article, I will provide a preliminary assessment of whether and to what extent a prima facie case for learning can be made about the September 11 attacks and their effects on aviation security policy.

THREE INCIDENTS AND THEIR OUTCOMES—
A SUMMARY OF AVIATION SECURITY EFFORTS
IN THE UNITED STATES

Aviation security is an important part of the history of civil aviation. The number of airliner bombings, hijackings, suicide attacks, and other crimes against commercial aviation is striking both in terms of the lengthy history of these attacks and the relative newness of the policy responses to these threats. The first attempted hijacking occurred in 1931, but the most public manifestation of the problem came with the rash of hijackings of planes to Cuba in the 1960s and early 1970s. A particularly sensational tale of hijacking was the 1972 hijacking of a domestic flight by "D. B. Cooper," who collected ransom for the plane and jumped out the back stairs of a 727 flying over rugged land between Seattle and Portland, never to be seen again (although his money washed up years later). And, according to Court TV's *Crime Library*, at least one individual survived a jump from a hijacked plane with ransom money, although he was found and convicted after the crime.[5] Hijackings in other nations also occurred for political or other reasons, and we are now in an era where most attacks against commercial aviation are made for political reasons by terrorists (St. John, 1989).

For the purposes of this article, I focus on the following three aviation security events: PAA 103, TWA 800, and the September 11, 2001, hijackings. Of these events, only the 2001 events were actual hijackings in U.S. airspace—the TWA crash was ultimately not attributed to terrorism, and the PAA 103 bombing happened in foreign airspace. But all three of these events led to fairly extensive legislative and regulatory activity if not outright change. And as I will show, the changes that resulted are on their face at least reasonably related either to the most immediate event on the agenda or to issues that are important within the domain in general. As I discuss later, there is relatively little peripheral attention to unimportant issues.

The details of these events are well known and have been covered in other contexts, so I will not delve into the details.[6] Rather, I summarize these events in Table 2 so as to focus on the following four key elements of each event: the facts of the event itself, a description of the ultimate cause as generally agreed on by elite decision makers and mainstream journalists, a summary of alternate theories of events (which are often merely conspiracy theories), and key to this discussion, a summary of the policy responses to these events.

Table 2 shows the key causal features of these crashes and the ensuing reaction to them. To lay the foundations for this discussion, I will review how these

TABLE 2: Key Aviation Security Events

Event	What Happened	Dominant Causal Story	Alternate Causal Stories	Policy Responses
Pan Am 103, December 21, 1988	Pan Am Boeing 747 bound for New York explodes over Lockerbie, Scotland, killing all aboard and 11 on the ground	Bomb planted by two members of the Libyan secret services, perhaps in retaliation against Anglo-American strikes on Libya in 1996	Syrian terrorists	Aviation Security Improvement Act, November 16, 1990; led to increased attention to explosives detection, changes in organization of Department of State and Federal Aviation Administration (FAA) regarding intelligence information
TWA Flight 800, July 16, 1996	TWA Boeing 747 explodes minutes after leaving JFK Airport bound for Paris	Empty center fuel tank, full of fumes and overheated from sitting on the ground on a hot day and from nearby air conditioning unit, explodes when a spark is introduced into the tank, possibly from fuel-level equipment	Terrorist bomb; terrorist missile; errant U.S. Navy missile	Federal Aviation Authorization Act of 1996; required FAA to implement explosives detection, baggage matching, and passenger profiling systems
September 11, 2001, terrorist attacks	Four cross-country flights—one out of Newark, NJ, one out of Dulles International Airport, and two out of Boston—are hijacked; one crashes into Pentagon, two into the World Trade Center, utterly destroying that facility, and one crashes in Pennsylvania as a result of passengers rising against hijackers	Hijackers introduced weapons onto planes, somehow passing through security; hijackers seized control of planes and crashed them; hijackers part of the al-Qaida terrorist organization led by Osama bin Ladin	Few serious alternative theories were offered that were taken seriously; some conspiracy theories about Israel and so on	Aviation and Transportation Security Act; comprehensive change in a wide array of aviation security policies (see narrative)

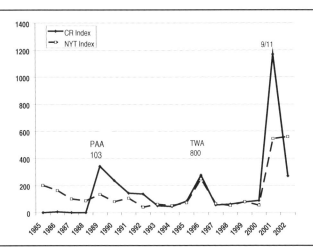

Figure 1: The Aviation Security Agenda, 1985-2002
NOTE: Index = mean number of news stories or *Congressional Record* entries on the term *aviation security* each year from 1985 to 2000 equals 100.

events have influenced the media, legislative, and regulatory agendas. The agenda discussion will consider the volume of discourse on the agenda as well as the nature of that debate. I will then turn to a discussion of the ideas described in that debate as the ideas are narrowed down from the broader media agenda to the more narrowly focused institutional agendas. What I will show is that the ideas for dealing with the greatest threats to aviation safety have been on various agendas since at least the PAA 103 disaster but that September 11 was such a spectacular and, to many, shocking event that it was the only one of the three events studied here that led to sweeping change.

AGENDA CHANGE AND SECURITY INCIDENTS

That these events influenced the agenda is well known intuitively, but it remains useful to understand just how much these events influenced the media, regulatory, and legislative agendas. Figure 1 shows how the issue of aviation security behaved on the agenda for both *The New York Times* and the *Congressional Record*. For both sources, data were gathered via computer searches on the term *aviation security* in the Lexis-Nexis and THOMAS[7] databases. Using these two sources allows us to compare key institutional agendas—that of the media and Congress. For comparison purposes, the yearly number of news stories or *Congressional Record* entries is indexed to the mean number of annual stories or entries in each source from 1985 to 2000. The index therefore excludes the largest event to show the contrast between the normal levels of discussion of this issue and the most important aviation security event in our history.

That the September 11 attacks show the greatest attention in these domains is unsurprising. And the data suggest that Congress tends to react most dramatically to the event, in large part because the agenda space available to Congress for any one issue is considerably more constrained than the space available to the *Times* in covering the issue, as evidenced by the *Times*'s low but fairly persistent level of coverage of aviation security until the TWA incident versus Congress's almost total inattention to the issue before 1989. Congress by contrast became deeply involved in aviation security—among other homeland security aspects—after the September 11 attacks.

THE COMPOSITION OF THE AGENDA

The actual composition of the agenda is at least as important as its sheer size because the examination of how various issues are treated by key actors reveals a great deal about the politics that follow a major event. On the one hand, Birkland (1997) appeared to argue that focusing events create a more sharply defined set of issues surrounding an event. Lawrence (2000) on the other hand argued in what she called "event centered problem definition" that events can lead to a remarkable wave of different and often competing causal stories (see also Stone, 1997). Much as Hilgartner and Bosk (1988) argued that agenda setting is the competition of various issues in a particular institutional venue, Lawrence and Birkland (2000) argued that various definitions of the same problem will vie for attention as it becomes clear that (a) the issue itself will gain great attention and (b) the policy outcomes that result from this attention will in large part flow from how the problem and the solutions are constructed.

Figures 2, 3, and 4 track the relative position on the agenda of the following three key aspects of aviation security since 1997: explosives detection (a key issue in the wake of PAA 103 and TWA 800), passenger screening, and cockpit security. Cockpit security in particular was a very heavily discussed issue after September 11; before September 11, interest in the security of the cockpit was relatively low and was driven by a few incidents of drunken passengers or "air rage." In these figures, I collected data from *The New York Times, The Washington Post*, and all articles in the aviation and aerospace industry sector of the business news items contained in the Lexis-Nexis database.

Interest in all these aspects grew dramatically after September 11. A primary reason for the success of the September 11 hijackings was the ability of the hijackers to get legal and illegal weapons through the passenger checkers at Dulles, Logan, and Newark airports. Although cockpit security became a high priority issue in the September 11 attacks, one can argue convincingly that had screening worked, the weapons would not have been brought aboard the planes, there would have been no breach of the cockpit, and the hijackings would not have occurred. In other words, screening is one of several lines of possible defense, ranging from passenger profiling at one end of the process to onboard

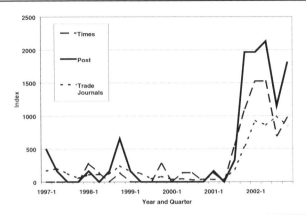

Figure 2: Attention to Explosives Detection, *The New York Times*, *The Washington Post*, and Aviation Trade Press, 1997 to 2002
NOTE: Index = mean number of stories in each quarter from the first quarter 1997 to the second quarter of 2001 equals 100.

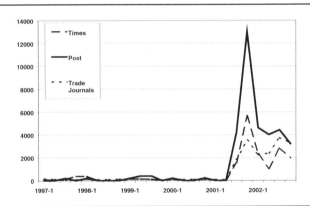

Figure 3: Attention to Screeners and Screening, *The New York Times*, *The Washington Post*, and Aviation Trade Press, 1997 to 2002
NOTE: Index = mean number of stories in each quarter from the first quarter 1997 to the second quarter of 2001 equals 100.

security at the other. But as practice in the United States, aviation security largely focused on the carriage of weapons by potential attackers on planes.

Attention to the screener issue was quite high, although the index value of attention was not as high as for cockpit security, owing largely to the almost total novelty of cockpit security as an issue in the field. But the essential point is this: The September 11 attacks yielded increased attention to a broad range of issues surrounding aviation security. Put more starkly, it is fair to say that the September 11 attacks laid bare the entire aviation security system in the United States and opened it to claims that it had failed or was likely to fail again in the future.

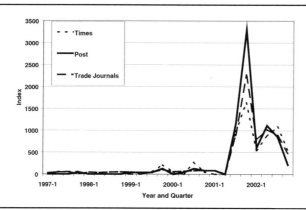

Figure 4: Attention to Cockpit/Cockpit Security, *The New York Times,* *The Washington Post,* **and Aviation Trade Press, 1997 to 2002**
NOTE: Index = mean number of stories in each quarter from the first quarter 1997 to the second quarter of 2001 equals 100.

DID DOMINANT ISSUES MATCH THE "REAL" PROBLEM?

Although there is a great deal of attention to a range of issues following the September 11 attacks, it is important to ask a broader question: Did the sorts of problems that emerged as the dominant subject of discussion after PAA 103, TWA 800, and September 11 reasonably relate to the putative cause of the accident? The three most important issues in each domain are shown in Table 3.

The key issues related to the PAA and September 11 disasters can fairly be said to be related to the actual likely cause of these incidents. And the snap conclusions reached by Congress and the media after TWA 800 are certainly understandable—after all, the loss of TWA 800 looked eerily similar to the destruction of PAA 103. However, there was relatively little discussion of TWA 800 as a security problem because the investigation moved reasonably quickly to the conclusion that TWA 800 was lost due to a mechanical fault rather than human intention, even though the FBI continued to seek evidence of terrorism after the fuel tank theory began to dominate professional investigators' theories of the accident (Negroni, 2000). Thus, the TWA event may have had more of an influence on the aviation safety agenda.

PRELIMINARY CONCLUSIONS: AVIATION SECURITY INCIDENTS AS REHEARSALS FOR POST–SEPTEMBER 11 POLICY DEBATE

Thus far, this article has demonstrated that two aviation security breaches and one suspected breach gained considerable attention on the agenda, that the substance of that attention can be reasonably related to the most likely cause of these disasters. The central question in this article then is whether the experience

TABLE 3: Most Important Issues on Various Agendas Related to Particular Aviation Security Events

Pan Am 103		TWA 800		September 11 Attacks	
The New York Times	Congressional Record	The New York Times	Congressional Record	The New York Times	Congressional Record
Explosives and explosives detection	Explosives and explosives detection	Explosives and explosives detection	Explosives and explosives detection	Passenger screening	Passenger screening
Passenger profiling	Passenger screening	Passenger profiling	Passenger screening	Air marshals	Air marshals/new organization
Airport access control and passenger screening (tie)	Modify existing organizations	Airport Access control and bag matching (tie)	Performance standards for screening companies	Cockpit security	Performance standards for screening companies

amassed in the United States after the first two of these events—PAA 103 and TWA 800—provided in effect a rehearsal for the policy making that followed September 11. That is, were advocates for improved policy after these events able to use the results of the pre-September 11 debates to press their arguments?

To assess this question, it is useful to track whether issues that arose before the September 11 attacks were revisited during the debate over the September 11 attacks and their relationship with aviation security. I considered this question by reviewing both *Congressional Record* and *The New York Times* coverage of the 26 subtopics that were identified under the aviation security rubric. I found in the *Times* coverage that 23 subtopics arose in the aviation security domain that specifically related to the September 11 attack and that of those 23 subtopics, 20 had arisen in the aftermath of either TWA 800 or PAA 103. Also, 14 of these 26 subtopics have arisen in all three disasters.

We can conclude then that the previous aviation security measures provided a rich variety of policy ideas and options from which to choose and that at least from an aviation security perspective, the September 11 attacks did not raise a set of novel aviation security issues. Rather, it reinvigorated the debate over an existing set of issues. Policy makers could—and did—draw on a rich body of material that aided in post–September 11 policy making, and this material was useful in drafting legislation and regulations to address the threats revealed on September 11.

ACTUAL POLICY CHANGE IN THE WAKE OF SEPTEMBER 11

Given the number of overseas security breaches in the 1980s coupled with PAA 103 and the reinforced specter of disaster raised by TWA 800, one might suspect that substantive policy change should be the result of these events and that such policy changes were designed to respond to the threats revealed by these incidents. Indeed, four aviation security bills were enacted into law in 1990 and 2000. These laws are summarized in Table 4 by the issues they covered. This table also includes key post–September 11 legislation.

Clearly, the September 11 attacks led to a comprehensive review of and change in national aviation security policy. The Aviation and Transportation Security Act of 2001 (ATSA) was the most sweeping measure of the six laws summarized here, encompassing 17 policy issues, nearly twice as many as any other bill. And although the agenda data showed that the most important issues on the agenda could be reasonably related to the cause of the event to which discussion most obviously responded, the September 11 attacks thoroughly opened up the whole range of issues for review. As Cobb and Primo (2003) noted,

> There was [after September 11] a marked effect on the aviation industry. Security procedures in the airports and on planes came into question. All aspects of the

TABLE 4: Key Issues Addressed in Aviation Security Legislation

Topic	Aviation Security Improvement Act of 1990	Federal Aviation Authorization Act of 1996	Federal Aviation Administration Authorization Bill	Airport Security Improvement Act of 2000	Aviation and Transportation Security Act	Homeland Security Act of 2002
Airport access control	•				•	
Baggage matching	•	•			•	
Background checks of employees	•	•			•	
Cargo and mail security		•		•	•	
Cockpit security					•	
Employee ID systems	•				•	
Explosives and explosives detection	•	•	•		•	•
Create or restore air marshals	•	•			•	
Modify existing organizations						•
Create new organizations						•
Passenger profiling	•				•	
Allow pilots to carry fatal weapons						•
Allow pilots to carry nonfatal weapons					•	
Certification of screening companies		•			•	
Require screening personnel be U.S. citizens					•	
Require all airport personnel be screened (including flight crews)					•	•
Screeners—general issues	•				•	
Make screeners federal employees		•			•	
Provide security training to the aircrew					•	
Provide security training to pilots					•	
Total	7	8	1	1	17	5

security process were reexamined, severely affecting airline travel.... Many policy changes in aviation safety were unprecedented in their scope and in the speed at which they were enacted, but none of the issues was new to the political agenda. (p. 120)

Indeed, even the relatively novel issue of cockpit security had arisen before, albeit in the context of passenger unruliness rather than hijacking. We can therefore understand the debate and legislation before the ATSA as in a sense rehearsals for the big legislative action. This argument is plausible for two reasons.

First, as Cobb and Primo (2003) noted, aviation safety and security policy making is reflective of the incrementalism said to characterize American policy making (Lindblom, 1959, 1979). Because aviation security and safety is very much driven by learning from prior events, because there are many opportunities for learning as relatively small technical problems arise, and because this learning is well institutionalized in agencies such as the Federal Aviation Administration (FAA) and National Transportation Safety Board as well as among airlines and pilots' unions (Perrow, 1999), the accretion of knowledge about aviation security has steadily led to some policy change and improvement. As I discuss later, it is certainly true however that such learning was not successful in devising policies and systems to prevent the September 11 hijackings.

Second, in the earlier legislation it is clear that many members of the legislative branch and interest group communities sensed that whatever good was accomplished by this legislation, there was still work yet do be done. Ultimately, to a greater extent than the ATSA, prior aviation security legislation was a compromise between airline interests, which sought to keep costs down, and advocates for greater security, both in the private sector and in government, who sought more stringent safety regimes, often without regard to costs.

MOMENTUM FOR CHANGE IN
THE IMPLEMENTATION PROCESS

If PAA 103, reinforced by TWA 800, led to a reasonably broad range of legislative solutions to address aviation security lapses, how could September 11 have happened? A large body of evidence exists that outlines the failure of responsible agencies—most notably, the FAA—to fully implement recommendations from presidential commissions or the demands of federal laws. A plausible argument could be made that the September 11 attacks would have been much more difficult to achieve had these pre-September 11 recommendations been adopted and if federal law had been fully enforced by the FAA. Students of the policy process have found that policy implementation is often where attention to issues flags and where problems arise that diminish the high hopes raised when legislation is passed (Nice & Grosse, 2001). Often, the passage of legislation removes an issue from the immediate congressional agenda, and journalists pay less attention to the issue as it moves from lurid front-page headlines to the more mundane aspects of daily administration. And the literature is replete with examples of legislators and executives with too high expectations (both in terms of management techniques and the application of technology), with examples of funding and other resources failing to match the perceived needs addressed by the legislation, and in particular, an increase in conflict among the most directly influenced parties after legislation is passed and implementation begins.

The aviation security domain is not immune from such implementation shortcomings or failures (depending on one's perspective). Between 1987 and 2003, the General Accounting Office (GAO) of the Congress issued 52 reports on various aspects of aviation security, most of them addressing the key aspects of aviation security discussed in this article and particularly emphasizing screeners and explosives detection. These reports are generally balanced and do when warranted, recognize FAA efforts to improve security. But these efforts were in the 1990s generally weak and ineffective, and congressional mandates were largely ignored, leading GAO to issue reports with titles such as

- *Aviation Security: Corrective Actions Underway, but Better Inspection Guidance Still Needed* (1988);
- *Aviation Safety and Security: Challenges to Implementing the Recommendations of the White House Commission on Aviation Safety and Security* (1997);
- *Aviation Security: Implementation of Recommendations Is Under Way, but Completion Will Take Several Years* (1998);
- *Aviation Security: Slow Progress in Addressing Long-Standing Screener Performance Problems* (2000);
- *Aviation Security: Vulnerabilities Still Exist in the Aviation Security System* (2000);
- *Aviation Security: Terrorist Acts Illustrate Severe Weaknesses in Aviation Security* (September 2001).

These reports often highlighted the failure of the FAA and other responsible parties to implement these changes. For example, in a 1998 report, GAO found that of three recommendations made in the Gore Commission report, only one relating to sharing of intelligence information had been implemented in 1997, whereas one other was partially implemented and the other was not near implementation. And GAO found,

> FAA has made progress but encountered delays in implementing the five recommendations made by the Commission and the similar mandates contained in the Reauthorization Act. These delays have occurred, in large part, because the recommendations involve new technologies and, in some cases, require FAA to issue regulations. (GAO, 1998, p. 3)

This latter point is important: Recent aviation security policy often turned on the belief that the passage of legislation would spur the rapid adoption of new technology. But the deployment of explosives detection technology has been more costly, controversial, and technically difficult than lawmakers envisioned, and this aspect of aviation security stalled as a result.

To attribute delay in responsive policy change to FAA's need to issue regulations is interesting. Rulemaking is admittedly time consuming given public comment and other sunshine law requirements. But is delay necessarily related to procedural requirements? Or to conflict between interests that occurs in implementation (Nice & Grosse, 2001) and that manifests itself in the delays in rulemaking, such as extensions of time for final comments? This is deserving of further research, but GAO's dismissal of this time problem is curious at best.

There are two ways in which we can explain why aviation security efforts have not met the expectations of legislative drafters. First, implementation of policy changes will become more difficult as the low-hanging fruit is picked. There is already evidence of this effect in the post–September 11 aviation security environment as the more easily implemented features were addressed. The ATSA required among other things much more stringent passenger screening, inspection of luggage, more restrictions on the sorts of things that could be carried aboard aircraft, and in particular, the federalization of the passenger screening workforce to ensure that weapons would be detected. Although many of the screening processes and training for screeners had been improved shortly after the enactment of ATSA, Kenneth Mead, the inspector general of the Department of Transportation, noted in January 2002 that "while progress has been made, clearly the heavy lifting (installing explosives detection systems to screen all checked baggage and hiring a workforce) lies ahead."[8] And explosives detection machinery in particular was not installed rapidly after passage of ATSA, owing to technological and practical considerations—the machines were quite large, and airports were not designed to accommodate them.

Another reason why the screening changes, including the deployment of TSA employed screeners, were accomplished quickly is that they were very symbolically important measures designed both to add some measure of security (although not of course total security) while at the same time reassuring the traveling public that something was being done—and the urge to do something or anything is often quite strong after focusing events (Cobb & Primo, 2003; Nice & Grosse, 2001).

Second, conflict will arise over implementation even when a dramatic event seems to create greater pressure for some sort of change. One might assume that the September 11 attacks were so large and important that they so altered the balance of power in aviation security policy that industry would find it difficult to oppose any potential policy change. Opposition might even be seen as heartless or even unpatriotic. Although this may be true in the most visible areas of aviation security, such as passenger screening and explosives detection (where measures to address the issue had to be taken quickly for both substantive and symbolic reasons), the more esoteric aspects of the lessons learned from September 11 are still prone to conflict.

One such example is the debate over whether the transponders on airplanes should be able to, with one quick action by a member of the flight crew, transmit a signal to air traffic control (ATC) that the plane has been hijacked. A transponder is a radio device on an airplane that transmits the plane's flight number, position, speed, and altitude to ATC so that controllers need not rely solely on the radar echo produced by ATC's radar transmitters. Under international rules, code 7500 is transmitted by the transponder when a crew member wishes to use the transponder to signal that the plane has been hijacked. The intent of the new transponder rules being issued and considered by the FAA is to make it easier for crews to indicate that they are being hijacked and to ensure that the transponder transmits continuously (and is not shut off, as they were on the four September 11 flights), thereby alerting controllers that there is a problem on board the plane and giving the time needed to notify relevant authorities and to respond to the hijacking. In the post–September 11 environment, one of those options would be to shoot down a hijacked plane if the hijacking appears to be intended to convert the plane into a guided missile in the manner of the September 11 attacks. The FAA has begun the process to require the continuous operation of a transponder broadcasting the 7500 code and to make it impossible for a hijacker to turn off the transponder, as occurred on three of the four September 11 flights.

The Air Transport Association—an interest group representing the major U.S. air carriers—opposes those changes on the grounds that these measures are "too costly," ineffective, or that the cost burden properly belongs to the federal government, not the airline industry (Bond, 2003). But one cannot simply dismiss this as yet another example of industry resistance to security measures. Although an argument can be made that in the history of aviation security cost considerations have been at least equal to if not superior to security effectiveness, the arguments against continuous transponder operation may be compelling. These arguments include cost, the possibility of false alarms with no way to rescind the false alarm, and the fact that such a rule may not be necessary because already enacted requirements regarding cockpit door strength and ground screening of passengers may prevent anyone from doing something untoward on the plane in the first place (Learmount, 2003). In essence, one can argue that this change is more difficult to make than the other more obvious changes, in part because this particular problem with the transponder was more recently recognized than were the more familiar problems of securing airports and in particular, airplanes. Thus, experience with any sort of transponder problem has failed to accumulate.

CONCLUSIONS

The aviation security domain shows considerable prima facie evidence of learning from prior disasters. I summarize this learning in terms of Peter May's (1992) three categories of learning in Table 5.

TABLE 5: Evidence of Learning in Aviation Security

	Policy Learning					
	Instrumental	Evidence of Instrumental Learning	Social	Evidence of Social Learning	Political Learning	Evidence of Political Learning
Requisite conditions	Improved understanding of policy instruments or implementation based on experience or formal evaluation	Accumulation of knowledge about implementation failure based on the results of attacks	Improved understanding or alteration of dominant causal beliefs about a policy problem or solution within the relevant policy domain	Accumulation of information about terrorist attacks on airliners	Awareness of political prospects and factors that affect them	Aviation interests learned that change was inevitable after September 11; strategy shifted to making these changes economically acceptable
Prima facie indicators	Policy redesign entailing change in instruments for carrying out the policy, for example, inducements, penalties, assistance, funding, timing of implementation, and organizational structures	Changes in policy foci in response to recent threats; examples include explosives detection in PAA 103 and TWA 800 and attention to screeners and screening after September 11	Policy redefinition entailing change in policy goals or scope, for example, policy direction, target groups, and rights bestowed by the policy	Learning that ultimate target of policy is terrorists, not hijacking for transportation or ransom; redefinition of hijackings from a transportation problem to a national security problem	Policy advocates change in political strategy, for example, shifting arenas, offering new arguments, and employing new tactics for calling attention to a problem or idea	Shift in tactics from opposition to security to support for security coupled with aid to airlines

Requires evidence of	Increased understanding of policy instruments or implementation	Expert demands for change, presidential commissions, and legislative change encompassing some of these recommendations all with an eye toward policy refinement	Change in dominant causal beliefs within the relevant policy domain	Evidence of change in attitudes toward hijackers as likely to be terrorists; terrorists now assumed to be potentially suicidal	Awareness of relationship between political strategy and political feasibility within a given advocacy coalition	Evidence of awareness that the previous arguments would be hard to defend

SOURCE: Modified from May (1992); see also Table 1.

Evidence of instrumental learning most clearly includes the substantive policy change that has followed the major aviation security incidents in the late 1980s through the 2001 attacks. These changes include changes to policy instruments to address more clearly emerging threats from explosives and after September 11 to address the flaws in passenger screening systems that allowed the terrorists to commandeer the four airplanes. Evidence of social policy learning includes in particular the shift in treatment of aviation security from a problem of the transportation sector to a national security problem, with national consequences for policy design and implementation. Even if it emerges that in the end aviation security is viewed as less a national security issue than it was immediately after September 11, one can discern a shift from treating aviation security as a private good to be paid for and enjoyed only by the traveling public and the airlines to one paid for and enjoyed by all Americans because as was learned after September 11, one need not be on board an airplane to be a victim of a hijacking. And political learning was manifest after the event as the airline industry very quickly learned that it would be unable to oppose major overhauls of aviation security policy and would instead have to seek some sort of compromise in an environment that was very much biased in the direction of policy change.

Future research will be needed to provide a sense of whether the events that preceded September 11 provided dress rehearsals for proponents and opponents of more stringent security to devise policy ideas, develop favored problem definitions, and develop political strategies to promote or retard new policies. But the evidence presented here strongly suggests that post–September 11 policy is in part a product of all the experience with aviation security that had been amassed before these attacks. Future research may need to consider whether the ATSA would have been developed and passed in its current form had it not been for prior experience with aviation security. Given the incrementalist nature of public policy generally and of aviation security policy in particular, it is hard to imagine that the sweeping changes made after September 11 would have been possible without having had a foundation of other policies laid before.

NOTES

1. Aviation security policy involves policies and practices designed to protect commercial aircraft, airports, and related facilities from criminal and terrorist attacks. I define *commercial aviation* as aviation operations that are conducted under the provisions of Title 49 parts 121 and 135 of the Code of Federal Regulations.

2. This is not to say that no one had contemplated the possibility of attacks of this sort. For example, a 1999 report prepared by the Federal Research Division of the Library of Congress noted:

> Al-Qaida's expected retaliation for the U.S. cruise missile attack against al-Qaida's training facilities in Afghanistan on August 20, 1998, could take several forms of terrorist attack in the nation's capital. Al-Qaida could detonate a Chechen-type building-buster bomb at a federal building. Suicide bomber(s) belonging to al-Qaida's Martyrdom

Battalion could crash-land an aircraft packed with high explosives (C-4 and semtex) into the Pentagon, the headquarters of the Central Intelligence Agency (CIA), or the White House. Ramzi Yousef had planned to do this against the CIA headquarters. (Hudson, 1999)

3. There have been many conspiracy theories published on the downing of TWA Flight 800 (TWA 800); a search on the term *TWA 800* at amazon.com will find many such books on the subject. These treatments obliquely acknowledge the need for greater security but at the same time attribute TWA 800 to a number of implausible causes. Mary Schiavo's (1997) book *Flying Blind, Flying Safe* attracted considerable attention but was also criticized in the aviation community because of several fundamental errors in the book regarding safety, security, and operations. After Pan Am Flight 103, a group called Families of Pan Am 103 appeared before congressional hearings to discuss shortcomings in aviation security, particularly related to threats to flights outside the United States. The most comprehensive documentation of the failures of aviation security policy came from more than 50 reports issued by the U.S. General Accounting Office. These reports are available at http://www.gao.gov/airptsec.html.

4. Throughout this article, I use the term *event* to mean any sort of focusing event. *Event* is a more neutral term than *accident, disaster, calamity, tragedy*, or other terms often used to describe large, injurious events. Clearly, whether an event is a mere *incident* or a *tragedy* is often strongly contested, and these terms are chosen by their users for the greatest rhetorical effect. I avoid taking sides by sticking with the neutral—if passionless—*event*.

5. See http://www.crimelibrary.com/criminal_mind/scams/DB_Cooper/9.html?sect=27.

6. For summaries of these incidents, refer to the narrative in Rubin, Cumming, Tanali, and Birkland (2003). A reasonably balanced journalistic account of the TWA 800 accident is provided by Negroni (2000).

7. Maintained by the Library of Congress and accessible at http://thomas.loc.gov.

9. Statement of Kenneth Mead, "Challenges Facing TSA in Implementing the Aviation and Transportation Security Act," Committee on Transportation and Infrastructure, Subcommittee on Aviation, U.S. House of Representatives, January 23, 2002, http://www.house.gov/transportation/aviation/01-23-02/mead.html.

REFERENCES

Bennett, C. J., & Howlett, M. (1992). The lessons of learning: Reconciling theories of policy learning and policy change. *Policy Sciences, 25*, 275-294.

Birkland, T. A. (1997). *After disaster: Agenda setting, public policy and focusing events*. Washington, DC: Georgetown University Press.

Bond, D. (2003). No longer needed? Airlines say the FAA fumbled the analysis of benefits, cost and feasibility for the transponder hijack rule. *Aviation Week and Space Technology, 158*(18), 46.

Busenberg, G. J. (2001). Learning in organizations and public policy. *Journal of Public Policy, 21*, 173-189.

Cobb, R. W., & Primo, D. M. (2003). *The plane truth: Airline crashes, the media, and transportation policy*. Washington, DC: Brookings Institution.

Hilgartner, J., & Bosk, C. (1988). The rise and fall of social problems: A public arenas model. *American Journal of Sociology, 94*, 53-78.

Hudson, R. A. (1999). *The sociology and psychology of terrorism: Who becomes a terrorist and why*. Retrieved July 20, 2004, from http://www.loc.gov/rr/frd/pdf-files/Soc_Psych_of_Terrorism.pdf

Kingdon, J. W. (1995). *Agendas, alternatives and public policies* (2nd ed.). New York: HarperCollins.

Lawrence, R. G. (2000). *The politics of force: Media and the construction of police brutality*. Berkeley: University of California Press.

Lawrence, R. G., & Birkland, T. A. (2000, September). *The politics of event driven problem definition: School violence, media frames, and policy responses.* Paper presented at the meeting of the American Political Science Association, Washington, DC.

Learmount, D. (2003). Hijack transponder "no longer needed;" pilots may be reluctant to use emergency code says AEA. *Flight International*(March 4), 5.

Levy, J. (1994). Learning and foreign policy: Sweeping a conceptual minefield. *International Organization, 48,* 279-312.

Lindblom, C. E. (1959). The science of "muddling through." *Public Administration Review, 19,* 79-88.

Lindblom, C. E. (1979). Still muddling, not yet through. *Public Administration Review, 39,* 517-526.

May, P. J. (1992). Policy learning and failure. *Journal of Public Policy, 12,* 331-354.

Negroni, C. (2000). *Deadly departure: Why the experts failed to prevent the TWA Flight 800 disaster and how it could happen again.* New York: Cliff Street/HarperCollins.

Nice, D. C., & Grosse, A. (2001). The evolution of emergency management in America: From a painful past to promising but uncertain future. In A. Farazmand (Ed.), *Handbook of crisis and emergency management* (pp. 55-67). New York: Marcel Dekker.

Perrow, C. (1999). *Normal accidents: Living with high-risk technologies.* Princeton, NJ: Princeton University Press.

Rochefort, D. A., & Cobb, R. W. (1994). Problem definition: An emerging perspective. In D. A. Rochefort & R. W. Cobb (Eds.), *The politics of problem definition* (pp. 1-31). Lawrence: University Press of Kansas.

Rubin, C. B., Cumming, W. B., Tanali, I. R., & Birkland, T. A. (2003, March). *Major terrorism events and their U.S. outcomes (1988-2001).* Retrieved July 20, 2004, from http://www.colorado.edu/hazards/wp/wp107/wp107.html

Sabatier, P. A. (1987). Knowledge, policy-oriented learning, and policy change. *Knowledge: Creation, Diffusion, Utilization, 8,* 649-692.

Sabatier, P. A. (1988). An advocacy coalition framework of policy change and the role of policy-oriented learning therein. *Policy Sciences, 21,* 129-168.

Schiavo, M. (1997). *Flying blind, flying safe.* New York: Avon Books.

Stern, E. (1997). Crisis and learning: A conceptual balance sheet. *Journal of Contingencies & Crisis Management, 5*(2), 69-86.

St. John, P. (1989). The politics of aviation terrorism. In P. Wilkinson & B. M. Jenkins (Eds.), *Aviation terrorism and security* (pp. 27-49). London: Frank Cass.

Stone, D. (1997). *Policy paradox: The art of political decision making.* New York: Norton.

U.S. General Accounting Office. (1998). *Aviation security: Implementation of recommendations is under way, but completion will take several years.* Washington, DC: Author.

21

Surveillance at the airport: surveilling mobility/mobilising surveillance

Peter Adey

Abstract. In this paper the author is concerned with the relationship between mobility and practices of surveillance, examining their interconnections within the modern airport. Recent deliberations about airports define these spaces as free, empty of power and social relationships—open to mobility. The author questions these assumptions and explores the surveillance practices that work to control and differentiate movement, bodies, and identities within the airport. Four examples are discussed, ranging from techniques that ignore mobile passengers towards those that simulate them. The airport is argued to offer perhaps a blueprint for public space, intensifying the surveillance of movement through mobilised and combined forms of monitoring. The author concludes the paper by reflecting upon the implications for the mobility and identity of the passenger as spaces such as airports become increasingly reflexive.

1 Introduction

Mobility is something we have always found difficult to see; slipping and evading our grasp—its forms liquefy into ebbs and flows (Bauman, 2000; Urry, 2000). Technologies such as CCTV (closed-circuit television), tagging, and smart roads are all designed to 'keep tabs' on us. Indeed, John Torpey (2000) has suggested that states have authority over the legitimate 'means of movement'—they say who goes where and who does not. The need for states to identify illegitimate or threatening movements has contributed to an increasing identification of individuals (see Salter, 2004) whereby identities are made more legible by issuing and requiring passports and visas and, more recently, by retina scans. This is central to the 'embracing' of mobile populations. And yet, since the 9/11 terrorist attacks on New York, transgressions of state and national boundaries pose new kinds of problems, intensifying our suspicion of movement. Indeed, it has been argued that a new architecture of governance is evolving to protect us from these mobile threats that transcend the traditional dangers to states (Carter, 2002). The border zones through which people must move are, then, the likely candidates for the focus of new and intensified forms of surveillance and control. However, it is not just our own movements that succumb to this gaze but the 'threat vectors' (NRC, 1999) of our luggage and personal possessions. Our identities, history, and past finances are additionally subjects of surveillance. This is nowhere truer than at the airport.

And yet studies have remained largely concerned with transnational mobilities, examining the international regulation of migration. Little research has been completed on the control of the microscale movements that occur in border zones and airports. This lack of enquiry is somewhat paradoxical given that the control of international mobilities that cross *through* airports and border zones are effectively managed, filtered, and screened *within* these sites. Questions should be asked of how these techniques imagine passengers. How are identities, bodies, and movements treated in these spaces?

In this paper I explore these questions and examine a politics to this control through a number of surveillance practices. The new dangers that face international security since 9/11 have provided the stimulus for the intensification and concentration of a number of these techniques (Carter, 2002; Flynn, 2002; Gormley, 2002; Jenkins, 2002; Lyon, 1994; 2001; 2002a).

The paper is broadly divided into three sections. Initially, in section 2, I examine a body of literature from disciplines such as cultural studies, sociology, and popular philosophical commentaries that discuss the airport. These writings conceptualise airports as free from control—as sites of freedom. I then go on, in section 3, to discuss surveillance at and of the airport, focusing particularly on a range of techniques that are inexorably tied to the control of movement. I have grouped these into four sections according to several different ways that identity and the mobile body have been treated in airport surveillance. In section 3.1, I examine the *disappearance* of the passenger and individual identities through practices of passenger management and airport planning. Such approaches, as a precursor to airport operation methods, have been attempts to manage movement through the terminal in the most efficient way. I then discuss the dominant policies of airport surveillance in the Netherlands (section 3.2) and in the United States (section 3.3). I illustrate how passengers *reappear* to be identified and *read* through biometrics (section 3.2) and are *inscribed* by passenger profiling systems (section 3.3). Last, airports are increasingly born and nurtured on the computer screen. Through interviews and questionnaires with various airport software engineers, I examine, in section 3.4, how the newest software technologies are used to design the airport terminal, facilitating the planning and running of this space—making simulated passengers become real. I conclude the paper, in section 4, by reflecting upon the future of these surveillance techniques for the control of mobility and the future of public space. I suggest that airports are spaces of complete control, mobilising and recombining forms of 'everyday' surveillance (see Lyon, 2001).

2 Airports and surveillance

Marc Augé's (1995) concept of 'non-place' has become synonymous with airports and other spaces of transportation. The central tenet of nonplace follows that airports are places stripped of any meaning and social interaction. His argument suggests that spaces where we move—from one place to another—are proliferating, becoming emblematic of our 'supermodern' age. Others, such as Manuel Castells (1996), draw a similar conclusion from the sociology of Madrid airport. For Castells, the airport is a *space of flows*—characterised by a vacuous and desolate sociality (see also Gottdeiner, 2001). Furthermore, the geographer Edward Relph (1976) morally positions airports as placeless, analogous to sites such as the motorway.

Texts such as Augé's and that of others conceptualise airports in placeless terms—where place is imagined as both rigid and fixed. Mobility becomes a characteristic of the other side of the dichotomy, as the source of broken social relationships and severed ties. This way of thinking may be labelled a 'sedentary metaphysics' (Cresswell, 2001). That said, as a starting point, they are useful in order to understand the airport as a space where people and things flow—where mobility is most active. In contrast to scholars proposing the 'nonplace' arguments, others have perceived the mobility of the airport in less negative and dystopic terms. Instead, the architect Hans Ibelings perceives the airport to be the perfect illustration of our globalised world—invoking a more mobile sense of place. For Ibelings:

"it is now the airport that is the focus of interest. Mobility, accessibility and infrastructure are seen as fundamental themes of the age, unlimited access to the world as the ideal of the moment" (1998, page 79).

Just as Deyan Sudjic writes:
> "the airport is a hybrid kind of space, one for which there are next to no conceptual frameworks, just the pragmatic expediencies of keeping traffic moving" (1993, page 166).

But this discussion of physical movements must not forget the immaterial. In his book, *Angels*, Michel Serres (1995) used the airport as a metaphor to discuss the connectivity of humans and nonhumans or actants. The writings of Ian Chambers (1990; 1994) and Rosi Braidotti (1994) also represent a generation of theory for which, as with Serres, the airport becomes a metaphor. Here, the airport has become symbolic of a utopia of free-flowing fluid and mobile identities that are posed in opposition to centred and masculine ways of being.

Yet, in some ways, these texts go too far. They romanticise the airport, becoming in themselves celebrations of postmodernity (for a critique, see Crang, 2002). The airport is rendered as a site of freedom, where the pressures of the world slip away, where equal and undisturbed mobilities and identities form irrespective of the uneven relationships that go on outside. Little attention is paid to where a person may go, what borders they may cross. This is most evident in the work of the novelist J G Ballard (1997):

> "Visiting London, I always have the sense of a city devised as an instrument of political control, like the class system that preserves England from revolution. The labyrinth of districts and boroughs, the endless columned porticos that once guarded the modest terraced cottages of Victorian clerks, together make clear that London is a place where everyone knows his place. By contrast, at an airport such as Heathrow the individual is defined, not by the tangible ground mortgaged into his soul for the next 40 years, but the indeterminate flicker of flight numbers trembling on an annunciator screen. We are no longer citizens with civic obligations, but passengers for whom all destinations are theoretically open, our lightness of baggage mandated by the system.... Air travel may well be the most important civic duty that we discharge today, erasing class and national distinctions and subsuming them within the unitary global culture of the departure lounge."

In stark contrast to Ballard and others, Justine Lloyd (2002) has suggested that social and class differences are perhaps most evident within the airport. The airport is presented by Lloyd to be a place of 'uneven' global flows (Lloyd, 2002). What is needed, therefore, is an adequate historicising, contextualisation, and specific qualitative examination of these spaces to problematise fully Lloyd's proposition and to question the 'romanticised invocations' (Crang, 2002) that characterise so much written on these spaces. Instead, we must be critical of tendencies to valorise an inherent liberation in movement that is often found within promotions of nomadism—or a 'nomadic metaphysics' (Cresswell, 1997; 2001). Within this paper, I attempt to fulfil this aim in one respect, by grounding the airport in terms of the specific surveillance practices that facilitate its control and uneven flows.

Surprisingly, airports have rarely featured in studies of surveillance. Scholars have examined how CCTV has transformed the means by which our streets, offices, and public areas may be policed (Norris and Armstrong, 1999; Norris et al, 1999). Others have explored methods, such as data surveillance (Agre, 1994; Clarke, 1994), the design of buildings (Foucault, 1977), electronic tagging (Richardson, 1999), and so forth, but only a few authors have begun to examine the interstitial spaces of airports, border zones, and ports, where surveillance is becoming increasingly potent (Lyon, 2003; Salter, 2003; 2004). Particular surveillance practices have been argued to ignore mobility and to focus instead upon fixed locations, 'you are where you live' being the mantra of the marketing geodemographic systems that model the consumer.

And yet these practices are changing. Geodemographics systems are increasingly able to profile people according to their mobility. Indeed, road transport informatics (RTI) now allows an understanding of the individual under the premise 'you are what you drive' (Bennett et al, 2002). These identification systems, it seems, increasingly understand the means by which we become mobile as opposed to their sedentary predecessors. The mechanisms of surveillance are also becoming more mobile. For David Lyon (2001), surveillance resembles creeping plants, spreading into the nooks and crannies of disorder. Accordingly, these means are also increasingly decentralised and peripheral. Kevin Haggerty and Richard Ericson argue:

"surveillance is driven by the desire to bring systems together, to combine practices and technologies and integrate them into a larger whole. It is this tendency which allows us to speak of surveillance as an assemblage, with such combinations providing for exponential increases in the degree of surveillance capacity" (2000, page 610).

Multiple and mobile systems of surveillance are therefore combining.

Yet, despite the obvious role of the airport as a place in which mobility and control are paramount, this has only recently been recognised within surveillance studies (Lyon, 2001; 2002a). What is clear from this discussion is that, for whatever reason, we seem to lack knowledge of airport surveillance practices. Writings are filled with romanticism, empty of detailed empirical analysis. Others may concentrate upon global mobilities of migrants and refugees, or the surveillance of cities, shopping malls, and now border zones. In section 3.1 I begin to contribute to such a study by discussing a surveillance technique that was used to understand and optimise the efficiency of passenger movement within airport spaces.

3 Surveillance at and of the airport
3.1 Disappearing passengers

The growth of air transport is a relatively recent phenomenon. The airports we know today have become necessary only since the development of mass air transportation in the late 1960s. Before the introduction of wide-body jets, airports and planes were filled by upper-class and business passengers. Air travel was still heroic and romantic. Since then, the passenger has become ever more complex and difficult to predict, with the introduction of a spectrum of society to flight. For airports to plan and manage passenger movement effectively, passenger mobility had to be known and understood. To keep passengers happy, meet passenger demand and safety, and to ensure profits airports have taken steps to improve their knowledge of passenger movements (Tosic, 1992). Although attempts to understand and track passengers within airports have become increasingly automated in recent years, initial techniques utilised a variety of approaches from operational and management research.

One such method for the surveillance of passenger mobility was the use of card-punching techniques, pioneered by the late John Braaksma (1976; 1977; Braaksma and Shortreed, 1971). Passengers were required to have their cards punched in order to monitor the time taken to walk between different vicinities of the airport and to pinpoint areas of slow-moving traffic. This technique was also closely tied to a form of management called critical path analysis (CPA), which was used to understand better these movements (see Sealy, 1966; 1976). CPA resembles the scientific management techniques that have been used to watch and rationalise the body's movement in modernity (Lyon, 1994; also, see Bahnisch, 2000).

The CPA approach was developed at the Central Electricity Generating Board (CEGB) in Great Britain in 1958. Other variations on this method were developed at DuPont de Nemours Corporation in France, and, significantly, at the US Naval Special

Projects Office for the development of the Polaris submarine missile system. Consequently, other terms such as critical path management (CPM) and program evaluation and review technique (PERT) have been used (see Battersby, 1964; Lockyer, 1969). CPA techniques were implemented to develop more efficient management and planning structures by breaking down and analysing activities. They worked by determining the sequence of events within a process and calculating the longest time in which this could be completed—the *length* of the path. The *critical* path is then the longest path in the network (see also Battersby, 1964; Wiest and Levy, 1969). If this is not feasible within the given time constraints, then the critical path method analyses the areas that need to become redefined and more efficient, thereby shortening the length of the path.

Airport engineers could now *see* passenger movement, or at least an abstracted visualisation of it through link-and-node diagrams that demonstrated passengers' paths through airport processing. It was hoped that mobility could then be better understood and more efficiently managed. However, this technique also enabled the surveillance of mobility in a way that was commensurable and thus comparable with any other airport. This allowed movement to be transformed into tangible, understandable information, which could then be abstracted into tables and charts of processing efficiency and passenger speed.

Parallels to the 'science of work', or the scientific management of work, resonate strongly with these studies (Rabinbach, 1992). Here, time is of the essence, and space, along with all the actions that go on within it, become reduced and broken up into 'tabulated space' (Foucault, 1973). Such a synoptic perspective (see Scott, 1998) eases the surveillance of movement by transforming mobility and the body into legible material for the overlooking gaze of the airport engineer. So that movement might be rationalised and standardised, bodies were therefore made invisible, marginalised, as Jonathan Crary puts it: "into a phantom in order to establish a space of reason." (1992, page 41). This trend has also been argued to be taking place through surveillance techniques that employ the latest telecommunication technologies (Lyon, 2001). Other work within disability studies has proffered ways in which the body is seen to vanish (Imrie, 2000). Here, an able-bodied or disembodied persona becomes privileged within transportation policy or architecture (Imrie, 2003; Law, 1999).

This early stage of airport surveillance is illustrative of approaches that show a disinterest in the micromobility of people, identity, and the body. CPA is perhaps the highest level of abstraction, where individual differences become dissolved by the premise of a 'universal disembodied subject' (Imrie, 2000) or passenger. The technique may be attributed to the lack of a need to distinguish one passenger from another, airport planners being interested only in the generalisation of passenger movement (Horonjeff and Mckelvey, 1993).

In section 3.2, shifts in these trends become evident. The CPA practice to capture and abstract *movement* into information can be seen to have shifted to methods that pinpoint individual *bodies*. Through biometrics, bodies become read and consequently inscribed with particular categories, making passengers not only understandable but also manipulable.

3.2 Reappearing bodies
The use of body surveillance, according to Lyon (2001) is as old as history itself (through tagging, marking, and so forth). Images and descriptions of bodies have been recorded in passports. However, as air travel and aviation terrorism have developed, airlines and governments can no longer be so sure of paper documents (Salter, 2004). Surveillance is now being focused with greater intensity upon the body of the individual, the body becoming the stable token of identity. With the progression of a

technology known as biometrics, moving passengers' bodies may now be captured by technologies that scan eyes, hands, and faces to discover a person's identity. This form of surveillance is discrete, moving away from well-known examination procedures enacted by security personnel towards the silent preemption and categorisation of people before they even set foot in the airport (Salter, 2004).

Within this section and section 3.3 I will discuss issues surrounding biometrics and profiling procedures within airports. These practices are shown to transform *bodies* (rather than mobility) into data as a means of surveilling and identifying individuals—which might be called *dataveillance* (Clarke, 2003). They also inscribe particular categories that differentiate and sort passengers along the framings of neoliberal ideological formations of statehood and citizenship. This follows the work of Mathew Sparke (2004) concerning fast border-crossing systems known as PACE (Peace Arch Crossing Entry) and NEXUS that facilitate the Cascadia postnational concept regulating US–Canadian border crossing.

The artist and cultural critic Martha Rosler aligns airport surveillance practices to the social control of the airport. She writes:

> "information manipulation—which includes the construction and dissemination of social narratives as well as covert surveillance and other forms of data gathering and management—has come into focus as the most visible and consistent form of social control. This impulse to control is part and parcel of the air transport system" (1998, page 32).

Perhaps biometrics is the most obvious form of Rosler's proposal. Most biometric techniques in use at airports identify specific body parts, such as faces, eyes, and palms, which are unique to every individual (Agre, 2001). This information about a person's identity is kept on databases stored on either a card or a computer system so that the recorded biometric information may be compared with that on a secure database, thereby confirming a person's identity. This process is known as authentication. These technologies are not restricted to airports, for they can also be found in border zones, as Irma van der Ploeg (1999) discusses in her work on the Eurodac. In this form of biometrics, an illegal migrant may be 'identified' out of thousands of records. Biometrics can now be seen at Heathrow Airport, for example, which has just finished trials of an eye-recognition scanner. Already in place at Schiphol Amsterdam, the Privium system allows fast border passage for business travellers. Indeed, topical uses of biometrics can be seen in the publicity surrounding the remote thermo-imaging systems used to scan body temperatures for signs of severe acute respiratory syndrome (SARS) at Singapore airport. Biometrics has also become one of the priorities for groups such as the International Air Transport Association (IATA). The programme Simplifying Passenger Travel (SPT) aims: "to measurably improve the passenger experience and enable security enhancements by: implementing biometrics and other new technologies" (SPT, 2003).

Examining the justification for biometrics reveals a politics of mobility and technology that underlines its neoliberal framings. Indeed, biometrics is often portrayed as a magical solution to improve passenger experience yet enabling security. Such a framing works to quiet the apparent intrusion into the body that biometrics involves and concerns over what use the personal data are put to (Agre, 2001; van der Ploeg, 1999). However, the effects of these systems upon the microscale mobility of passengers are often overlooked. For instance, Sparke (2004) highlights the ideological values that underlie the processing of mobility on the US–Canadian border. Here, practices such as biometrics facilitate the ease of speed for trusted, 'good' and economically sound business travellers and yet impede the flow of 'bad guys' or secondary processing—where officers 'really don't care how long it takes' to process their entry.

The Privium biometric scheme provides an appropriate example within the space of Schiphol airport. The Privium scheme employs retina scanning for 'known travellers'. The outcomes of such schemes for mobility are not subtle. The differentiation of speeds and access to areas of the airport is something perhaps many of us have felt. Ultramobile travellers might best be considered as the 'kinetic elite' (Graham and Marvin, 2001; Wolf, 2000). For the cost of membership and a short interview, Privium members may check in late at close parking facilities, removing the hassle of pulling up in a carpark far away from the terminal. They enjoy increased velocities through security and immigration checks and enjoy VIP lounges with air-side access to their flights. Effectively, elite passengers may 'tunnel through' the airport from beginning to end (Andreu, 1998). The 'privileged' business passengers of the Privium scheme may therefore buy their speedy global–local citizenship.

The improved mobility of these Privium cardholders is therefore paired with the promise that illegal aliens and potential terrorist threats will be deterred. The argument follows that more airport staff are then available for greater scrutiny of other passengers who are not members of the scheme. Freedom of movement and national affiliation, then, seems to rest upon the interests of economics: a 'citizenship as entrepreneurial calculation' (Sparke, 2004).

However, for biometrics to be successful, it is also necessary for passenger information to be shared between multiple sources. Indeed, it is this sharing of information within airport systems and other agencies that has become essential to the perception of a secure airport and a secure nation. A common critique of biometrics is that these perceptions are rarely questioned. Biometrics thus creates a new body ontology that "redefines bodies in terms of, or in terms as, information" (van der Ploeg, 2002, page 64). The body is effectively transformed into text so that it may be read (Torpey, 2000). These techniques bring up issues of bodily interrogation that are of obvious concern to issues of privacy (see Gibson, 2001; van der Ploeg, 2002). The testing of technologies that may X-ray people in order to identify the possibility of concealed weapons is a similar and perhaps more obvious example of this invasion. Here, surveillance effectively breaks down the barriers of the clothing and individual (NRC, 1996, page 18), although in the case of X-raying the purposes of identifying a threat become less about the identity of the passenger and more about the particular object that may cause a particular danger.

My concern here, however, is also the way by which targeted biometric data are passed and interconnected to other sources within the surveillance assemblage of airport security. For example, the insufficiency of data sharing is seen by many to pose limits to the effectiveness of biometrics (see Thalheimer, 2002). As such, information sharing is argued to be key to a 'smart border'. Combined with software operation suites marketed by those such as SITA, packages such as 'Airport in a Box' boast the overall control and connection of information, bringing multiple systems together. Others, such as Imaging Automation, offer a similar integration and the proposition of connecting to many other organisations. The integration of information about passengers, combined with financial and marketing records, staff details, work schedules, and passenger flows within these systems, resonates strongly with visions of the surveillance assemblage.

In contrast to the surveillance of movement within the CPA studies, biometrics records bodies, fixing the body to passenger identities and their movements, which are then deemed acceptable, or otherwise, by the state. It appears that passengers' bodily and personal boundaries must be crossed as they themselves traverse state and physical borders. Unease over the penetrating gaze of biometrics and its appropriation of bodies is becoming one source of critique. Moreover, the conversion of passengers' bodies and movements into readable information, accessible across connected networks, is clearly an example of the surveillance assemblage and the 'phenetic' 'urge' or 'fix' at work (Lyon, 2002b; Phillips and Curry, 2002), and this has drawn the most concern. In section 3.3 I focus upon the further manipulation and categorisation of passenger information into profiles. These are characterised by the prediction of particular types of behaviour that then work to classify groups of passengers, inscribing particular categories upon the mobile body.

3.3 Profiled passengers

As airports have increased in size and value it has been found that retail space provides an additional profitable use of the airport. Shops also add extra activities for bored passengers who may wish to relieve the anxiety of flight. Indeed, most international airports have become vast shopping malls, advertising themselves as retail destinations (Gottdeiner, 2001). It is somewhat ironic and perhaps comes as no surprise that airports and airlines are now employing similar strategies to retailers in an attempt to better sort and categorise customers and passengers.

The ability of surveillance to sort and categorise data has been well documented (Lyon, 2002a). Sometimes posited as surveillance simulations (Graham, 1998) or the simulation of surveillance (Bogard, 1996), models are constructed that preempt risk and particular behaviour patterns—separating people based upon their identity. This 'panoptic sort' (Gandy, 1993) began in consumer-profiling techniques and geodemographic systems that target consumers based on demographic statistics and buying habits. This form of surveillance is now finding its way into transportation systems (see Lyon, 2002a).

At airports, the growth in numbers of those wishing to fly has meant that airlines and airports cannot so easily recognise suspicious or potentially threatening travellers. These concerns have led airports to force passengers into two journeys through the airport, "one of which is overt, 'the sunlit trip', and the other which is covert, an odyssey controlled by the authorities through 'categories and definitions and foreign languages'" (Pascoe, 2001, page 202). The emergence of profiling—the categorisation of passengers—has become one of the most controversial methods of airport surveillance, where passengers must unwittingly journey through the 'covert trip'. In this section, the emerging screening policies of the USA are discussed.

Since the TWA flight crash in 1996, the United States has imposed a computer assisted passenger prescreening system, or CAPPS (FAA, 1999), as a temporary measure while explosive detection systems (EDSs) are being installed to scan the bag of every passenger. Introduced by the Israeli airline El Al, automated passenger profiling has meant that selected passengers may be profiled automatically so that 'trusted travellers' are then distinguished from others who might be chosen to have additional scans. The profiles are based on information known about the passenger collated from airlines, immigration, and US Federal Aviation Authority (FAA) intelligence. However, reports of the implementation of an updated CAPPS, CAPPS 2, have disturbed those worried about the increasing availability of information accessible to the state and the possible discrimination against particular profiled groups (Delio, 2003). As part of President Bush's renamed Terrorist Information Awareness programme (http://www.epic.org/privacy/profiling/tia/), CAPPS 2 is reported to use information from multiple databases of government organisations building risk-assessment profiles for all passengers. This rhizomatic interconnection between multiple databases and sources of information leads Bill Thalheimer to suggest:

"Information will be obtained from multiple sources—local, regional, federal and international—and the database will contain text as well as biometric identifiers.... For effective use, the database will require interoperability between various agencies" (2002).

In Europe, advanced passenger screening (APS), a variant on CAPPS, has emerged, in which computers retrieve data about a passenger in order to reduce the time and the number of questions asked at immigration checkpoints (Yates, 1999).

The creation of passenger profiling aims to model the characteristics and possible behaviour patterns of passengers. In essence, norms and values of behaviour become inscribed upon the passenger's identity. Questions must then be asked about the categories into which people are placed, about how these categories are constructed, about what they will mean for passenger mobility, and about what, if any, control we have over such categories. Such concerns have led to debate and a recent ruling by the European Parliament on 13 March 2003 that blocks an agreement made by the European Commission sanctioning the transfer of passengers' personal information from European airlines to US customs. The ease with which personal information can be made mobile and shared is of serious concern to proponents of privacy and human rights. As such, the Senator for Oregon, Ron Wyden, on 13 March 2003 proposed an amendment, which has meant that the Secretary of Homeland Security will have to present a report to Congress addressing the privacy and civil liberties issues CAPPS 2 will meet (Wyden, 2003). Until recently, very little was known about the categories and assumptions passenger profiling is based upon. Indeed, suggestions have been made over the possible discrimination of passengers from Arab nations. Giving transparency to CAPPS is clearly important to resolve these issues.

The construction of these practices and technologies is also important. Again, as with biometrics, profiling has become aligned to neoliberal technocratic solutions. Conceptions of CAPPS within FAA documents remain embedded in constructions of technology as neutral and value free. Threats to privacy are said to be human, not inherent to the technology. For example, the FAA-proposed rule-making on CAPPS suggests that:

> "Because manual screening allows for more extensive human interaction between passengers and air carrier employees, it carries the potential that, even though the factors used in conducting manual screening are not biased, an employee's personal bias can be evident, regardless of whether a given passenger is a selectee or not" (FAA, 1999, pages 10–11).

The assumptions behind screening may embody particular and biased beliefs concerning the likelihood of a threat; however, this is quickly side-stepped by claims that problems are attributable solely to 'human factors' (NRC, 1999) rather than the system itself. In effect, profiling software systems may become legitimised by their apparent externality to the social world.

Again, the rhetoric surrounding profiling, as with biometric authentication schemes, emphasises the ability to speed up the mobility of those within the terminal—reemphasising the coupling of increased mobility to some passengers. Immigration officers are then given more time to perform checks on other passengers outside of the scheme or those who fit higher risk profiles. Speed of movement within the terminal becomes the most obvious differentiation of these passengers (Virilio, 1986). Indeed, it may be possible for potential 'selectees' to be plagued continually by airport security, as recommendations suggest that this status is to remain for the duration of a passengers' journey (NRC, 1999). Such treatment allows not only greater speed for first-class and business passengers but also more time to have their bodies taken care of. In opposition to the disembodied treatment of coach passengers, who may feel like 'cattle' shunted through airports and squashed in a tight seat, the 'kinetic elites' are treated as embodied—able to enjoy a shower, a large seat, and a glass of champagne. The categories, information, and profiles that we relinquish control over and our identities, bodies, and movements have become, it seems, inextricably linked.

3.4 Simulated passengers

Profiling risk and projected passenger behaviour is not the only use for models and simulations within airport surveillance. Developments in computing technology (for a review, see Tosic, 1992) allow simulations accurately to model and predict movements within whole environments as opposed to the simplifications of the early CPA models I have discussed (see Batty, 2001; Helbing et al, 2001). Their application for use in airports cannot be underestimated given the continual development of these spaces [often referred to as 'constant building sites' (Sudjic, 1993)]. The simulations allow changes to be tested and experienced before they are built.

In passenger-flow simulations, virtual passenger movements may be tracked from check-in to boarding, before airspace simulations take over. Although these simulations do not offer the perfect 'Mirror Worlds' that have been projected by some (Gelernter, 1992), they place greater emphasis on how people use airports rather than how long it takes to travel through them. These systems do not necessarily present themselves as surveillance systems; however, they may be used as another arm of airport security and can be interpreted as such. They focus, again, upon the movement of passengers within the airport and, in some cases, from the perspective of the passenger.

Simulation engineers use three-dimensional (3D) visualisations to attempt to predict more closely what is happening within the terminal from the embodied perspective of the passenger. Therefore, in several systems 3D animations have been built of passengers moving through airport environments and undergoing airport processing. One simulation engineer commented:[1]

> "With the help of 3D animation, you can *see* what will happen. Animation gives a great insight in processes, capacity, waiting times, and queue lengths" (respondent A, December 2002).

3D animation therefore allows the simulation engineers to effectively experience the airport system. However, 3D animation is also a fuzzy point within airport simulations, as some see this as a gadget or gimmick. For one engineer 3D visualisations:

> "are more cool than useful, you must have them or else you are not 'serious'" (respondent B, December 2002).

3D simulations are increasingly becoming utilised to attempt to understand the microscale movements of passengers within airports. These visualisations reembody the surveillance of the airport from the perspective of the traveller, airport security guard, or airline worker. Planners and managers of airports can see how the airport may be negotiated and how threats can be better predicted and prevented. Moreover, simulations are now being used to aid in risk assessments in terms of the surveillance of passengers in the evacuation of an airport. Modelling simulations perhaps offer new forms of surveillance. Where technologies have been argued to 'sever' surveillance vision from the human eye (see the discussion by Thrift, 1994) these simulations allow a virtual reembodiment of this perspective.

Simulation models are therefore becoming of interest to state security services. The recent Aviation and Transportation Security Act (2001), which established the Transportation Security Administration (TSA) under the new Department for Homeland Security (DHS) in the USA, has led to calls for innovation in modelling simulations. The TSA states:

> "Simulation models offer the opportunity to estimate the operational impact of new security equipment and procedures, and also provide a *non-intrusive* way to examine the complex interdependencies of the airport environment" (TSA, no date, emphasis added).

[1] The following quotes are from telephone interviews and questionnaires conducted by the author in December 2002 with a number of airport simulation engineers.

In December 2001, the head of the DHS, Tom Ridge, and Canadian Deputy Prime Minister, John Manley, signed the 'Smart Border' Declaration, to ensure the secure flow of people and goods across US–Canadian borders (Sparke, 2004). The development of simulations is one of the priorities for predicting the impact of the 'Smart Border' measures. Although simulation as a nonintrusive technique may take place on a computer screen, the material changes made to passengers may well be real as such techniques are being increasingly used in airport and border security.

Where simulations have increasingly become used within the planning of airport terminals they are also finding their way into the everyday running of the airport. Some simulations may connect with other data inputs such as flight schedules and check-in data to model dynamically the movement of passengers. The resulting synchronicity allows airlines to predict carefully when staff should work and where they should be so that they may avoid the passenger frustration of queues, delays, and bottlenecks. Simulations enable the connection of staff rosters and schedules that automatically denote and 'pencil in' how many staff are needed. Airline management of staff and passengers can then be preempted by these surveillant simulations. They are also used more overtly for security purposes. For example, simulations used at Schiphol airport predict how many passport control agents should be allocated during the day after queue build-ups are predicted (respondent A, December 2002). Indeed, the RAND Corporation (Kauvar et al, 2002) has suggested that simulations are to be used to predict the impact of EDSs upon the airport.

A predominant use for simulation is therefore in the design of the processing facilities of airports. As we have seen, airports are now planned and run to encourage optimal flows and the most efficient security measures. And yet the usage of simulations can also be more trivial and subversive than this. Work in pedestrian analysis has illustrated how simulations may be used to design the optimum layout of airports, encouraging passengers to arrive in the doorway of a retail outlet (Lemos, 1997). Terminal shops have been found to earn double those on the high street (Edwards, 1998), where research has shown that an increase in 'dwell time' encourages people to part with their money through boredom, adding a much needed revenue source for airports (Rowley and Slack, 1999). Surveillance simulations are clearly also good for airport economics.

4 Reflections and conclusions
In this paper I have provided an account of some of the multiple, connected, and different practices and technologies that watch, predict, and enable the control of an airport. In opposition to the literature discussed in section 2 it is obvious that airports are not spaces of equal movement and flow but are places imbued with power and control. Whereas surveillance at the border once relied upon a single security guard and the display of particular documents (Edmunds, 2001; Fussell, 1982) the airport is now a surveillance machine—an assemblage where webs of technology and information combine. Movement and, increasingly, the body, identity, and objects are made legible, momentarily fusing with technology and virtual realms. Passengers crossing boundaries and state territories then endure the crossing of their own bodily and personal boundaries by the authorities to allow permission to access aircraft and country. Many of these techniques, particularly those employed by the United States, have proved to be of concern in the sharing of private information and to distinguish high-risk from low-risk travellers.

Some further reflections and possible implications can also be drawn from airport surveillance. First, airports may mark the future of what is to come within public spaces. Paul Virilio has already suggested that airports:

"were turned into theatres of necessary regulation ... they also became breeding and testing grounds for high-pressured experiments in control and aerial surveillance" (1997, page 381).

Other border zones offer similar, though perhaps not as extensive, efforts of surveillance. Roads are increasingly surveilled through CCTV and software simulations and are sorted through profiles. Shopping malls also offer an example of monitoring through CCTV, mobility monitoring, and so forth. Could it be that the union of surveillance practices at the airport will occur elsewhere? The argument that nonplaces might be proliferating has been made by Augé (1995; Bauman, 2000), and Georges Benko has suggested that "never before in the history of the world have non-places occupied so much space" (1997, page 23). I have attempted to illustrate the oversimplification of Augé's argument in this paper. And yet his central proposition—that transport places are proliferating through the growth and spread of international travel—is unavoidable. Combined with heightened security measures, business kinetic-elite programmes, and postnational citizenship schemes, perhaps we will see similar 'airport-style' surveillance practices drifting into other spaces and places.

What will this then mean for mobility? This control of mobility has been shown to be distinctly ideological; the airport has become a significant expression of the governance of mobility. Henk van Houtem and Ton van Naerssen suggest:

"it is at borders where normative values of differential social systems meet. Borders function as spatial mediators of often latent power and governance discourses and practices of places in society" (2002, page 129).

Under the guise of an improved travel experience, scientific and technological solutions are often employed for the imperatives of economic efficiency and security. Mobility is stratified into fast-moving low-risk business travellers, to slower travellers and to high-risk threats. Differences in the speed of passengers' movement may seem insignificant. Does it matter if some people move slower than others? Kinetic-elites enjoy VIP lounges, saunas, and showers and glide through the airport in stark contrast to the busy immigration, security procedures, and long queues that await other passengers of the kinetic underclasses. In essence, these trends in airport security and business schemes may be emblematic of a societal move not to price people out of access to mobility but out of access to speed. Passengers who may be unable to afford the mobility of business schemes become slowed down. This form of dromological exclusion has also been felt within other border zones and, most recently, on motorways, where access to vital infrastructure and virtual mobility is prioritised in favour of premium customers rather than to the 'less desirables' (Graham and Marvin, 2001).

Another point that can be made about these forms of surveillance is the way in which environments such as airports are developing a greater reflexivity. As airport surveillance and control become more sophisticated, airports are becoming more automated, integrating software programs with electronic data and monitoring technologies. Spaces such as airports, roads, and shopping malls are not inert but instead react to the chaotic hustle and bustle of people. The airport environment is an example of this cyborgic dynamism, where signs and symbols change on video display units, and even doors can be programmed to act in different ways (Yates, 1999). Automated archway detection metres (ADMs) project infrared beams that count the number of passengers passing through a doorway when breached. In London Gatwick Airport, the number of passengers on a train station platform are automatically calculated, thereby managing the connector train for efficient usage. As discussed, most of the surveillance measures are therefore automatic in their recognition of 'high-risk' identities; surveillance simulations may become self-fulfilling prophecies reproducing themselves in the terminal. What remains to be seen are the possible impacts upon the self and upon human relationships.

For some, the effects of these technologies are not consciously recognised (Clough, 2000; Thrift and French, 2002). Within airports in particular, passengers have been described as passive and machine-like, leading David Pascoe to suggest:

> "the systems of modern airspace silently compromise freedom of choice. Hence, the traveller 'unwittingly' comes to a decision, oblivious to the fact that his liberties are being taken ... the individual is assailed by the devices of circulation, process and containment" (2001, page 202).

In many ways, the passenger becomes, in Augé's (1995, page 103) words, "no more than what he does". A passenger becomes reduced to the term 'pax' (the reductionist label that airports give to passengers) and enters airport processing to be modelled by software such as 'Airport Machine'. The automated systems of surveillance take over; passengers are scanned like a bar code and are silently organised and processed through the airport. These questions clearly need attention. However, according to Elizabeth Stanley (2000), perhaps passengers might be more responsive than we think. Stanley, in her study of audits, argues that people perform roles that are expected of them. They are not unaware of expectations but act, in some cases, accordingly to make life easier. Similarly, for Auge, passengers enjoy:

> "like anyone who is in possession—the passive joys of identity-loss, and the more active pleasure of role-playing" (1995, page 103).

Perhaps we can think of people as actors performing this role of a docile and simple traveller. They fit the identities and 'learn the lines' of the categories and profiles they are placed into merely to ease their passage through the airport. Salman Rushdie articulates his own performance of border crossing:

> "At the frontier our liberty is stripped away—we hope temporarily—and we enter the universe of control .... These people, guarding these lines must tell us who we are. We must be passive, docile... .This is where we must present ourselves as simple, as obvious: I am coming home. I am on a business trip. I am visiting my girlfriend ... I am one-dimensional. Truly. I am simple. Let me pass" (2002, page 412).

But the issue remains that those who create the profiles are those in control. Therefore: "people who are judged against the profile are found wanting or not, and not the other way round" (Stanley, 2000, page 51).

Continued enquiry into the impacts of these surveillance systems is needed, along with an examination of the assumptions and underlying concepts that frame them. These practices must become transparent if we are to evaluate critically the politics of mobility at the airport. And yet it is somewhat ironic that the increasing intensity of these techniques will almost certainly provide the foremost threat to this ambition.

Acknowledgements. Many thanks must go to Tim Cresswell, Jon Anderson, Paul Bevan, Suzie Watkin, and three anonymous referees for their advice and comments. I am also grateful to correspondence from John Shortreed for pointing out the work he and J P Braaksma carried out on airport passenger mobility.

References
Agre P, 1994, "Understanding the digital individual" *The Information Society* **10** 73–76
Agre P, 2001, "Your face is not a bar code: arguments against automatic face recognition in public places" *Whole Earth* **106** 74–77
Andreu P, 1998, "Tunnelling", in *Anyhow* Ed. C Davidson (MIT Press, Cambridge, MA) pp 58–63
Augé M, 1995 *Non-places: Introduction to an Anthropology of Supermodernity* (Verso, London)
Aviation and Transportation Security Act, 2001, S.1447, Public Law 107-71 (US Government Printing Office, Washington, DC)
Bahnisch M, 2000, "Embodied work, divided labour: subjectivity and the scientific management of the body in Frederick W. Taylor's 1907 'Lecture on Management'" *Body and Society* **6** 51–68

Ballard J G, 1997, "Airports: going somewhere?" *The Observer: The Week in Review* 14 September, page 11

Battersby A, 1964 *Network Analysis for Planning and Scheduling* (Macmillan, London)

Batty M, 2001, "Agent-based pedestrian modeling" *Environment and Planning B: Planning and Design* **28** 321–326

Bauman Z, 2000 *Liquid Modernity* (Polity Press, Cambridge)

Benko G, 1997, "Introduction: modernity, postmodernity and the social sciences", in *Space and Social Theory: Interpreting Modernity and Postmodernity* Eds G Benko, U Strohmayer (Blackwell, Oxford) pp 1–27

Bennett C, Raab C, Regan P, 2002, "People and place: patterns of individual identification within intelligent transportation systems" *Surveillance as Social Sorting: Privacy, Risk, and Digital Discrimination* Ed. D Lyon (Routledge, London) pp 153–176

Bogard W, 1996 *The Simulation of Surveillance: Hypercontrol in Virtual Societies* (Cambridge University Press, Cambridge)

Braaksma J P, 1976, "Time-stamping: a new way to survey pedestrian traffic in airport terminals" *Transportation Research Record*, number 588, 27–34

Braaksma J P, 1977, "Reducing walking distances at existing airports" *Airport Forum* **7** 135

Braaksma J P, Shortreed J H, 1971, "Improving airport gate usage with critical path method" *ASCE Transportation Engineering Journal* **97** 187–203

Braidotti R, 1994 *Nomadic Subjects: Embodiment and Sexual Difference in Contemporary Feminist Theory* (Columbia University Press, New York)

Carter A B, 2002, "The architecture of government in the face of terrorism" *International Security* **26** 5–23

Castells M, 1996 *The Rise of the Network Society—Volume 1. The Information Age: Economy, Society and Culture* (Blackwell, Oxford)

Chambers I, 1990 *Border Dialogues: Journeys in Postmodernity* (Routledge, London)

Chambers I, 1994 *Migrancy, Culture, Identity* (Routledge, London)

Clarke R, 1994, "The digital persona and its application to data surveillance" *The Information Society* **10** 77–92

Clarke R, 2003, "Biometrics in airports—how to, and how not to, stop Mahommed Atta and friends", available at http://www.anu.edu.au/people/Roger.Clarke/DV/BioAirports.html

Clough P T, 2000 *Autoaffection: Unconscious Thought in the Age of Technology* (University of Minnesota Press, Minneapolis, MN)

Crang M, 2002, "Between places: producing hubs, flows, and networks" *Environment and Planning A* **34** 569–574

Crary J, 1992 *Techniques of the Observer: On Vision and Modernity in the Nineteenth Century* (MIT Press, Cambridge, MA)

Cresswell T, 1997, "Imagining the nomad: mobility and the postmodern primitive", in *Space and Social Theory: Interpreting Modernity and Postmodernity* Eds G Benko, U Strohmayer (Blackwell, Oxford) pp 360–379

Cresswell T, 2001, "The production of mobilities" *New Formations* **43** 11–25

Delio M, 2003, "Traveling? Take big brother along" *Wired News* 4 April, available at http://www.wired.com/news/privacy/0,1848,58344,00.html

Edmunds P, 2001 *Vivat Heathrow! Airport Life Unwrapped* (Cirrus, Gillingham, Kent)

Edwards B, 1998 *The Modern Terminal: New Approaches to Airport Architecture* (Routledge, London)

European Parliament, 2003, "Transfer of personal data by airlines to the US immigration service", P5_TA-PROV(2003)0097, http://www.europarl.eu.int/comparl/libe/elsj/events/hearings/20030506/p5_ta-prov(2003)0097_en.pdf

FAA, 1999, "Security of checked baggage on flights within the United States", Notice of Proposed Rule Meeting, Docket FAA-1999-5536, Notice 99-05; Federal Aviation Administration, http://dmses.dot.gov/docimages/pdf37/57279_web.pdf

Flynn S E, 2002, "Transforming border management in the post September 11th world", in *Governance and Public Security* Ed. A Roberts (Campbell Public Affairs Institute, New York) pp 37–52

Foucault M, 1973 *The Order of Things: An Archaeology of the Human Sciences* (Vintage Books, New York)

Foucault M, 1977 *Discipline and Punish* (Penguin Books, Harmondsworth, Middx)

Fussell P, 1982 *Abroad: British Literary Travelling Between the Wars* (Oxford University Press, Oxford)

Gandy O H, 1993 *The Panoptic Sort: A Political Economy of Personal Information* (Westview Press, Boulder, CO)

Gelernter D, 1992 *Mirror Worlds: or: The Day Software Puts the Universe in a Shoebox... How it Will Happen and What it Will Mean* (Oxford University Press, Oxford)

Gibson M, 2001, "The truth machine: polygraphs, popular culture and the confessing body" *Social Semiotics* **11** 61 – 73

Gormley W T Jr, 2002, "Reflections on terrorism and public management", in *Governance and Public Security* Ed. A Roberts (Campbell Public Affairs Institute, New York) pp 1 – 16

Gottdeiner M, 2001 *Life in the Air: Surviving the New Culture of Air Travel* (Rowman and Littlefield, Oxford)

Graham S, 1998, "Spaces of surveillant simulation: new technologies, digital representations, and material geographies" *Environment and Planning D: Society and Space* **16** 483 – 504

Graham S, Marvin S, 2001 *Splintering Urbanism: Networked Infrastructures, Technological Mobilities and the Urban Condition* (Routledge, London)

Haggerty K, Ericson R, 2000, "The surveillant assemblage" *British Journal of Sociology* **51** 605 – 622

Helbing D, Molnár P, Farkas I J, Bolay K, 2001, "Self-organizing pedestrian movement" *Environment and Planning B: Planning and Design* **28** 361 – 383

Horonjeff R, McKelvey F X, 1993 *Planning and Design of Airports* 4th edn (McGraw-Hill, New York)

Ibelings H, 1998 *Supermodernism: Architecture in the Age of Globalization* (Netherlands Architecture Institute, Rotterdam)

Imrie R, 2000, "Disability and discourses of mobility and movement" *Environment and Planning A* **32** 1641 – 1656

Imrie R, 2003, "Architects' conceptions of the human body" *Environment and Planning D: Society and Space* **21** 47 – 65

Jenkins D, 2002, "Airport security", in *Governance and Public Security* Ed. A Roberts (Campbell Public Affairs Institute, New York) pp 69 – 83

Kauvar G, Rostker B, Shaver R, 2002, "Safer skies: baggage screening and beyond", RAND white paper, http://www.rand.org/publications/WP/WP131/WP131.pdf

Law R, 1999, "Beyond 'women and transport': towards new geographies of gender and daily mobility" *Progress in Human Geography* **23** 567 – 588

Lemos P, 1997, "Relieving you of the stress... along with your cash", unpublished MSc thesis, Bartlett School of Architecture, University College London, London

Lloyd J, 2002, "Departing sovereignty" *Borderlands e-journal* **1**(2), available at http://www.borderlandsejournal.adelaide.edu.au/vol1no2_2002/lloyd.departing.html

Lockyer K G, 1969 *An Introduction to Critical Path Analysis* (Pitman, London)

Lyon D, 1994 *Electronic Eye: The Rise of the Surveillance Society* (Polity Press, Cambridge)

Lyon D, 2001 *Surveillance Society: Monitoring Everyday Life* (Open University Press, Milton Keynes, Bucks)

Lyon D, 2002a *Surveillance as Social Sorting: Privacy, Risk, and Digital Discrimination* (Routledge, London)

Lyon D, 2002b, "Surveillance studies: understanding visibility, mobility and the phenetic fix" *Surveillance and Society* **1** 1 – 7, http://www.surveillance-and-society.org/articles1/editorial.pdf

Lyon D, 2003 *Surveillance After September 11th* (Polity Press, Cambridge)

Norris C, Armstrong G, 1999 *The Maximum Surveillance Society: The Rise of CCTV* (Berg, Oxford)

Norris C, Moran J, Armstrong G, 1999 *Surveillance, Closed Circuit Television and Social Control* (Ashgate, Aldershot, Hants)

NRC, 1996 *Airline Passenger Security Screening: New Technologies and Implementation Issues* Committee on Commercial Aviation Security, Panel on Passenger Screening, National Materials Advisory Board (NMAB), Commission on Engineering and Technical Systems, National Research Council (NRC), publication NMAB-482-1 (National Academy Press, Washington, DC)

NRC, 1999 *Assessment of Technologies Deployed to Improve Aviation Security: First Report* Panel on Assessment of Technologies Deployed to Improve Aviation Security, National Materials Advisory Board (NMAB), Commission on Engineering and Technical Systems, National Research Council (NRC), publication NMAB-482-5 (National Academy Press, Washington, DC)

Pascoe D, 2001 *Airspaces* (Reaktion, London)

Phillips D, Curry M, 2002, "Privacy and the phenetic urge: geodemographics and the changing spatiality of local practice", in *Surveillance as Social Sorting: Privacy, Risk, and Digital Discrimination* Ed. D Lyon (Routledge, London) pp 137 – 153

Rabinbach A, 1992 *The Human Motor: Energy, Fatigue, and the Origins of Modernity* (University of California Press, Berkeley, CA)

Relph E, 1976 *Place and Placelessness* (Pion, London)

Richardson F, 1999, "Electronic tagging of offenders: trials in England" *The Howard Journal of Criminal Justice* **38**(2) 158 – 172
Rosler M, 1998 *In the Place of the Public: Observations of a Frequent Flyer* (Cantz Verlag, Frankfurt)
Rowley J, Slack F, 1999, "The retail experience in airport departure lounges: reaching for timelessness and placelessness" *International Marketing Review* **16** 363 – 375
Rushdie S, 2002 *Step Across this Line* (Jonathan Cape, London)
Salter M B, 2003 *Rights of Passage: The Passport in International Relations* (Lynne Rienner, Boulder, CO)
Salter M B, 2004, "Passports, mobility, and security: how smart can the border be?" *International Studies Perspectives* **5**(1) 71 – 91
Scott J C, 1998 *Seeing Like a State: How Certain Attempts to Improve the Human Condition Have Failed* (Yale University Press, New York)
Sealy K R, 1966 *The Geography of Air Transport* (St Martins Press, London)
Sealy K R, 1976 *Airport Strategy and Planning* (Oxford University Press, London)
Serres M, 1995 *Angels: A Modern Myth* (Flammarion, Paris)
Sparke M, 2004, "Passports into credit cards: on the borders and spaces of neoliberal citizenship", in *Boundaries and Belonging* Ed. J Migdal (Cambridge University Press, Cambridge) forthcoming
SPT, 2003, "SPT vision" *Simplifying Passenger Travel*, http://www.simplifying-travel.org/public/pub.php?id_page=11
Stanley L, 2000, "From 'self-made women' to 'women's made-selves'? Audit selves, simulation and surveillance in the rise of public woman", in *Feminism and Autobiography: Texts, Theories and Methods* Eds T Cosslett, C Lury, P Summerfield (Routledge, London) pp 40 – 61
Sudjic D, 1993 *The 100 Mile City* (Flamingo, London)
Thalheimer B, 2002, "The new paradigm of border control" *Security Products Magazine* October, http://www.secprodonline.com/stevens/secprodpub.nsf/PubArchive?openview
Thrift N, 1994, "Inhuman geographies: landscapes of speed, light and power", in *Writing the Rural: Five Cultural Geographies* Eds P J Cloke, M Doel, D Matless, M Phillips, N Thrift (Paul Chapman, London) pp 191 – 248
Thrift N, French S, 2002, "The automatic production of space" *Transactions of the Institute of British Geographers, New Series* **27** 309 – 335
Torpey J, 2000 *The Invention of the Passport: Surveillance, Citizenship and the State* (Cambridge University Press, Cambridge)
Tosic V, 1992, "A review of airport passenger terminal operations: analysis and modelling" *Transportation Research A* **26** 3 – 26
TSA, no date, "Security technologies—modeling/simulation", Transportation Security Administration, http://www.tsa.gov/public/display?theme=86&content=09000519800318da
Urry J, 2000 *Sociology Beyond Societies: Mobilities for the 21st Century* (Routledge, London)
van der Ploeg I, 1999, "The illegal body: 'Eurodac' and the politics of biometric identification" *Ethics and Information Technology* **1** 295 – 302
van der Ploeg I, 2002, "Biometrics and the body as information: normative issues of the socio-technical coding of the body", in *Surveillance as Social Sorting: Privacy, Risk, and Digital Discrimination* Ed. D Lyon (Routledge, London) pp 57 – 75
van Houtem H, van Naerssen T, 2002, "Bordering, ordering and othering" *Tijdschrift voor Economische en Sociale Geografie* **93** 125 – 136
Virilio P, 1986 *Speed and Politics: An Essay on Dromology* (Semiotext(e), New York)
Virilio P, 1997, "The overexposed city", in *Rethinking Architecture: A Reader in Cultural Theory* Ed. N Leach (Routledge, London) pp 381 – 390
Wiest J D, Levy F K, 1969 *A Management Guide to PERT/CPM* (Prentice-Hall, Englewood Cliffs, NJ)
Wolf G, 2000, "Exploring the unmaterial world" *Wired* June; available at http://www.wired.com/wired/archive/8.06/koolhaas.html
Wyden R, 2003, "Wyden wins Commerce Committee approval to require oversight of CAPPS II airline passenger screening system—now part of Air Cargo Security Bill, Wyden language requires focus on privacy, civil liberties", news release, 13 March; http://wyden.senate.gov/media/2003/03132003_capps.html
Yates C, 1999 *Airport Security: Standards and Technology* (Jane's Information Group, Coulsdon)

Part VI:

Disruption Management and Resilience

22

Airline disruption management—Perspectives, experiences and outlook

Niklas Kohl, Allan Larsen, Jesper Larsen, Alex Ross, Sergey Tiourine

Abstract

Since the deregulation of many markets, airlines have become more concerned with developing an optimal flight schedule, allowing little slack to accommodate variations from the optimal solution. During operation, the planned schedules often have to be revised because of disruptions caused by severe weather, technical problems and crew sickness. Thus, airline disruption management techniques have emerged. The purpose is, first to offer an introduction to airline disruption management, provide a description of the planning processes, and deliver a detailed overview of the numerous aspects of airline disruption management. Second, it is to report on experiences from a development project on airline disruption management that is the first prototype of a multiple resource decision support system at the operations control center in a major airline to be implemented.
© 2007 Elsevier Ltd. All rights reserved.

Keywords: Airline operation; Real-time decision support; Irregular operations

1. Introduction

The principal resources used to supply an air service are crew and aircraft. Together with the passengers they constitute the three main elements that must be planned and monitored to obtain operational efficiency. During the planning process crew, aircraft and passengers are typically seen as separate entities, which can be scheduled and optimized more or less independently. Given the timetable and fleet assignment (allocation of aircraft type to the flights) the planning processes run in parallel.

Crew scheduling consist of two problems: crew pairing and crew rostering. In the crew pairing phase, anonymous pairings (trips), starting and ending at a home base, are constructed. In total, the pairings must cover all positions to be covered in the flights defined by the timetable. The purpose of crew rostering is to assign all pairings and possibly other activities (e.g. stand-by duties) to named individuals. The crew scheduling must be completed several weeks before the day of operations and the resulting personalized rosters often span a time period of about 1 month. Later changes, i.e. due to changes in the timetable or in crew availability, are handled in the roster maintenance phase.

Tail assignment, the assignment of actual aircraft individuals (tail numbers) to flights (and consequently the routing of aircraft individuals), is typically done a few days before the day of operations. Revenue management, adjustment of prices and seat availability, is carried out over the entire period from the publication of the timetable to day of operations (Fig. 1.)

Before the day of operations the scheduling of crew, aircraft and passengers is only loosely connected. In some cases crew pairings or passenger connections will depend on a particular aircraft connection, e.g., the same aircraft may carry out two particular flights in sequence. This can be modeled as a fixed link constraint for the tail assignment and routing problem, but apart from that, there are no significant dependencies. On the day of operations, crew, aircraft and passengers interact closely with each other in case the planned crew or aircraft schedule cannot be

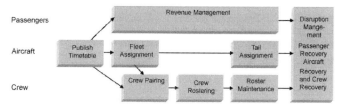

Fig. 1. A simplified illustration of the scheduling of passengers, aircraft and crew.

executed. Every change to the timetable (e.g. cancellation, flight retiming, or aircraft fleet type change) must be feasible for crew as well as aircraft and should preferably minimize passenger inconvenience. We denote the process of monitoring and scheduling the resources close to the day of operations as Disruption Management. Another commonly used term to describe this problem is operations control.

The focus here is on disruption management within the airline industry. Similar problems occur for other modes of transportation such as railways and urban transportation. In addition, also within production planning settings the problem of being able to recover from schedule disturbances or disruptions must be dealt with. For a more general introduction to disruption management (Clausen et al., 2001).

Even though crew, aircraft and passengers are the most important aspects of airline disruption management, other resources need consideration, including ground staff (check-in staff, gate staff, ramp staff, and luggage staff), catering, and gates, but these resources are generally more flexible and less expensive than crew and aircraft and will only be considered briefly.

2. Airline practice

Most commercial airlines operate according to a published schedule that typically optimizes revenue and with resources allocated within the schedule with the least possible cost. When nothing prevents an airline operating to the schedule as planned, it will maximize profits. There are, however, many external events that can disrupt smooth execution. The most common are aircraft mechanical problems, inclement weather, airport congestion, and industrial action. In reaction to these events, airlines have to adjust their schedules and the corresponding resource allocation. The ability of an airline to respond to unexpected events depends on a variety of factors. In the following sections, we discuss the most important factors influencing airline operational stability and describe the current business practices of dealing with them.

2.1. Network structure

The two most common types of route networks are point-to-point and hub-and-spoke. In the hub-and-spoke network airports are partitioned in two sets, called hubs and spokes. Most spoke airports are served from only one hub and hubs are connected by regular flights. The vast majority of mainstream airlines operate hub-and-spoke networks, which is considered to be the most cost effective way of linking a large number of destinations. A typical passenger itinerary in the hub-and-spoke network consists of two or three legs. To optimize passenger connections at hubs, most North American airlines operate so-called banks, a bank is an arrival wave followed directly by a departure wave. The banks create huge peaks on demand for airport facilities that reduces operational stability. In the aftermath of the events of 11 September 2001 and increased security checks the airlines are studying the possibility of de-banking their operation.

Low cost airlines favor point-to-point networks. These networks directly link economically attractive pairs of destinations, providing little or no connecting possibilities. This type of operation is less dependent on overcrowded hubs and therefore is less sensitive to major operational disruptions that are usually associated with hubs. The main remaining challenge, however, is to manage resources across the network to reduce impact of smaller disruptions, like aircraft unavailability or crew sickness.

Aircraft manufactures express their views of the future development of airline network structures in their strategic plans. So, the fortunes of the huge Airbus A380 depend on the future growth of long haul hub-and-spoke networks. On the other hand, Boeing is betting on the increasing importance of point-to-point traffic for its somewhat smaller 787 Dreamliner. This also reflects differing views on how airlines will cater for the growing demand for air transport. From the passengers perspective, frequent flights with rather small aircraft are ideal but the congested airspace, limited capacity at major airports and operational costs suggest increased use of larger aircraft.

2.2. Resource planning and recovery strategies

During the past decade the airline industry has optimized its planning processes. Most airlines nowadays perform their key planning process, including revenue management and aircraft and crew scheduling, aided with sophisticated software tools. Although further improvements of the planning processes are possible, the focus now is seemingly shifting towards trying to ensure that the planned can be maintained through to the day of operation and can be executed smoothly in operation i.e. that optimized resource plans are robust and allow for efficient recovery.

Usually, a disruption situation originates in a local event such as an aircraft maintenance problem, a flight delay, or an airport closure. Ideally, most disruptions should also be resolved locally using only resources directly affected by the event and within the timeframe of the event itself. In reality, disruptions tend to extend far beyond the events that originated them. For example, a small delay in the morning may trigger a cancellation in the evening. How does this happen? Part of the answer is that the resource plans tend to be optimized to a degree where no slack is available to accommodate for even a small unexpected event. Therefore even a small event can trigger a significant disruption in the airline schedule.

All airlines try to anticipate the unexpected and to build some flexibility into their schedules. This flexibility can be used in recovering from unexpected events. Commonly used techniques include:

- *Add slack in the plans*: For each aircraft and crew rules state a minimum turn time. Instead of operating all day at a minimum turn time slack is incorporated into the plans such that each line of work has some degree of self-recovery.
- *Crew follows each other and the aircraft*: This technique makes monitoring of operations easier. It also allows for a simple recovery strategy that preserves some of the properties of the original schedule. However, due to the fact that rules applicable to various resources are very different, the most constrained resource will determine the structure of the plan. Also, the resulting plan can potentially be very tight for this one resource, which could make the entire plan unstable. Continental Airlines has implemented this technique in full. Most other airlines use some elements of it.
- *Out and back*: If an aircraft flies from a hub to a spoke and back to the same hub, these two flights can be cancelled without affecting the rest of the aircraft schedule. If the same crew is planned for these two flights, the cancellation will not affect the rest of the crew schedule either. In the perfect hub-and-spoke network all flights are either in- or outbound from a hub. A pool of resources available at a hub allows for replanning in an event of disruption.
- *Stand by crew and aircraft*: A spare crew or an aircraft are valuable but very costly resources that can be used in case of disruption.
- *Extra buffers added to turnaround times*: Extra buffers are often added after frequently delayed flights, but they also provide slack in the schedule that can be used in recovery.
- *Increased cruise speed*: Aircraft have an interval of possible cruise speeds. Airlines will typically operate aircraft at the most economic speed that will always be lower than top speed. Speed-ups represent an additional cost due to increase fuel burn, but it may avoid higher costs in itinerary repair for aircraft, crew and passengers. This tool is more effective the longer the flight is.

2.3. Organization of operations control

Most large airlines operate operation control centers (OCC) to perform on-the-day coordination of schedule execution. Their purpose is to monitor the progress of operations, to flag actual or potential problems, and to take corrective actions in response to unexpected events. Representatives of key airline functions work together to ensure smooth schedule execution. The most common support roles in airline operations control are:

- *Flight dispatch and following*: This is a prominent role in North America. The flight dispatcher shares responsibility for flight safety, follows preparation and progress of a number of flights and raises alerts with other areas when problems occur. In Europe, the aircraft control role usually performs the task of flight following, while flight planning and dispatch is often performed outside of the operations control area.
- *Aircraft control*: Besides managing the aircraft resource, this is often the central coordination role in operations control. In Europe it is divided in long and short haul, in North America the most common division is according to geographical regions like North West, South West, etc.
- *Crew tracking*: The crew-tracking role is responsible for the staffing of flights. Crew check-ins must be monitored and crew pairings must be changed in case of delays or cancellations. The stand-by crew resource must be dispatched and perhaps reserve crew must be called in. In most airlines crew tracking is divided into cockpit and cabin crew.
- *Aircraft engineering*: Aircraft scheduling is responsible for unplanned service and maintenance of the aircraft as well as the short-term maintenance scheduling. Changes to the aircraft rotations may impact on short-term maintenance e.g. because maintenance cannot be done at all stations.
- *Customer service*: Decisions taken in the OCC will typically affect passengers. The responsibility of the customer service role in the OCC is to ensure that passenger inconvenience is taken into consideration in these decisions. Delays and cancellations will affect passengers who need to be informed and in some cases rebooked or provided with meals or accommodation. However, customer service is mainly provided at the gates and in customer service centers that are not a part of the OCC.
- *Air traffic control (ATC) coordination*: The ATC role is not a part of the OCC as it is common for all airlines and operated by a public authority, for example the

Federal Aviation Administration (FAA) in the US and EuroControl in Europe. However, the ATC coordination becomes more and more important in North America, as airlines can actively participate in air traffic management through the Ground Delay Program by the FAA based on the collaborative decision-making (CDM) initiative (Chang et al., 2001). In Europe, aircraft control typically takes this role.

Successful operation of an airline depends on coordinated actions of all supporting functions. However, each group typically operates under its own directive, with its own budget and performance measures. The most challenging job in the OCC is the one of a duty manager[1] who is responsible for the overall coordination of operations, ensuring that all groups act as one team and strive towards common objectives. Exactly how the duty manager should perform the task, most of airlines leave up to the duty manager.

Currently, there are two alternative trends in operational management at the OCC. We will denote them consolidation and cooperation. In consolidation, the duty manager and representatives of a few key-supporting functions essentially work at the same desk, thereby ensuring that all-important decisions are taken by this team. In cooperation, a framework for cooperation between supporting functions can be established, promoting structured communication about the current operational situation, disruptions and available options. Both approaches provide a way of dealing with complexity, i.e. communication between decision makers, high degree of uncertainty and high volume of information. In the consolidation approach, the first two issues are addressed directly in one team.

For the stakeholders in the day-of-operations process up-to-date information is crucial. Especially for crew controllers and the aircraft controllers'online information is vital in the effort to master last minute changes. A wealth of relevant data is stored in the data warehouses of large airlines, and by displaying the right information as quickly as possible substantial support can be given to the controllers.

Most often aircraft controllers have access to Gantt charts that display important information like status of the flight and changes as they happen. The system updates as new information about the flights become available, thereby helping the controller to track the current status of his/her fleets. For trans-Atlantic flights, satellite navigation can help the aircraft controller in keeping track of the current position of the flights. This is generally not part of the aircraft system, but rather a separate program on the desktop of the controller. For busy airports like London Heathrow, a useful tool for the aircraft controllers is to listen in on the communication between ATC and the aircraft. This can identify the position of an aircraft in the holding pattern, thereby making it possible for the aircraft controller to come up with qualified estimates of a possible arrival time.

Other groups like crew and passenger controllers are often left with a lesser alternative. They can receive updated information but only by querying the information systems themselves hence the controller will send querying-commands to the relevant system to obtain the information needed.

In some cases, identical information is not always measured in the same way. Thereby data such as departure time for crew and aircraft can seem inconsistent although the crew was on that aircraft. In day-of-operations this poses a challenge to the work of the controllers as they might have to act on last minute information. Also while information from engineering is typically available for the OCC, information from less critical functions like catering, cargo and gate staff is not. Here, communication between relevant departments has to be established manually.

3. Problem definition and objectives

3.1. The disruption management process

Disruption management is seen as an ongoing process rather than a single problem that can be formulated explicitly (Fig. 2). Airlines constantly monitor their operations. The state of operations is defined by the planned events (time table, fleet and tail assignment, crew scheduling, etc.) and the actual events. The actual events are often recorded in an on-line message stream and the average message density is often more than one message per second. Some actual events will indicate a discrepancy between plans and operation and raise question whether it is necessary to do something. This question could also be raised by the lack of an expected event, say a crew member who did not report for duty, or by the need for taking a decision, such as to call in additional stand-by crew, before a given point in time. These are time triggers, because the possible need to do something is driven by the time rather than by an unexpected event.

It is unnecessary to act on all unexpected events or even time triggers. Some unexpected events, such as minor delays, do not require changes of plans and cause limited inconvenience for passengers. Other events may be quite serious but it may not be possible to do anything about them. In case it is necessary to do something about the event or time trigger, we will denote it a disruption. First it is necessary to identify the possible actions and to evaluate these. The evaluation will involve evaluations from the passenger, crew and aircraft perspective and possibly even from other perspectives. These evaluations may result in proposed changes to the option. From the passenger perspective it may, for example, make sense to delay an outbound flight (i.e. a flight out of an airlines hub) to ensure that passengers on a delayed inbound flight will be able to make their connection. This option must then be evaluated from the crew and aircraft perspective. In

---
[1] In North America often called sector manager or SOC director.

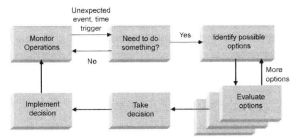

Fig. 2. High-level view of the disruption management process.

principle, this process can continue, until an option that is legal and acceptable from all perspectives, has been found.

Based on the agreed option, one can decide whether it is necessary to do something now or whether we can postpone the final decision, i.e. plan, but not commit to the plan yet. This is dependent on the actions considered. If we intend to change the schedule of a crew-member, a 2 h notice may be required whereas a crew member on standby could be assigned with a 1 h notice. In any case, we will try to avoid to committing the resources earlier than necessary. Once a decision has been taken it must be implemented and the monitoring must continue.

At this level of abstraction, the disruption management process differs from most control processes in complex systems involving humans. The most important distinct features are the very broad array of potential options and the computational complexity of assessing the impact of each of these options.

3.2. The objectives of disruption management

One of the difficult aspects of disruption management is to specify the objectives. Objectives fall in three broad categories: Deliver the customer promise (i.e. get passengers and their luggage to their destination) on-time with the booked service level, minimize the real costs including excess crew costs, costs of compensation, hotel and accommodation to disrupted passengers and crew, and tickets on other airlines, and get back to the plan as soon as possible.

The first two objectives are quite easy to agree on and can be quantified and, in principle, be measured in the same units. Even though there is a lot of judgment involved in quantifying the soft cost of a passenger delay, it is clear there is a distinct trade-off between delivering the customer promise and keeping costs down. The third objective is harder to quantify and the motivation underlying it is also more debatable.

Getting back to plan is conventional airline wisdom. In some cases it is necessary because it may not be possible to change crew schedules without long notice. It may for example, be essential to ensure that a crew member can fly the rest of the pairings on her monthly roster even if the current pairing is disrupted. Getting back to plan may also make disruption management easier in the sense that it is easier to decide what actions to take. The complexity of the problem is reduced. This might also be a drawback in getting back to plan. The original plan was (hopefully!) optimal in the situation before the disruption occurred, but in case of a major disruption it may be relevant to completely discard the old plan—at least for the resources where this does not cause major inconvenience to humans. Aircraft tail assignment and routing as well as gate allocation are examples.

3.3. To what extent can disruption management be automated?

Due to the complexity of disruption management, there is little reason to believe disruption management can in the foreseeable future be automated to the same extent as crew and fleet scheduling. Realistic approaches to disruption management must involve humans in the key parts of the process, in particular:

- In many cases, humans must determine whether a particular event or sequence of events should be characterized as a disruption one must act upon. Typically this will be triggered by a message from computerized systems consolidating operational data, but the role of the human is to determine whether events are sufficiently serious to require an action and also to define the scope of the disruption. Several apparently unrelated events may for example be relevant to be treated together as one disruption because the same resources are likely to be involved in the resolution of the disruption.
- Humans must be involved in the actual decision-making and determination of when decisions must be taken. This is partly because humans will be responsible for the consequences of the decision but also because the decision in many cases will be partly dependent on

information and judgments that will not exist in computer systems.
- In the foreseeable future the implementation of a decision will require human communication.

The main roles for computer systems in disruption management would seem to be, to process the large amounts of operational data and present potentially critical events for a human, and to generate and evaluate possible actions for a well-defined disruption.

3.4. Proactive decision-making and disruption management

In disruption management we try to solve the disruptions when they have occurred. The aim of proactive decision-making is partly to avoid disruptions in the first place, partly to limit the impact of disruptions when they occur. There are several ways of practicing proactive decision-making. Some of the most important include:

- *Robust planning*: Slack should be built into the plan where it is known to be particularly vulnerable to disruptions.
- *Avoiding operational complexity*: An airline that operates a point-to-point network with one class of service with one fleet and flight and cabin crew that follow the aircraft as much as possible can limit the impact of disruptions much more than an airline with a complex route network, many fleets, several classes of service and highly optimized crew and fleet scheduling.
- *Exploit probability of events*: Probability of events can be utilized as well in planning as in disruption management. The cost of a pairing could for example be viewed as the expected cost of executing the pairing rather than the cost of executing it as planned.
- *Planning for alternative scenarios*: One could, for example, plan which flights one would cancel if it for some reason would be necessary to reduce capacity by, say, 50% the next day. Here, the advantage is that there is more time to do computations now rather than tomorrow when the decision may have to be taken within the next few minutes.

Robust planning and avoiding operational complexity are well-known techniques. Planning with probabilities and planning for alternative scenarios are not yet in widespread use.

3.5. Recent work

Most work on disruption management in airlines have focused on resolving conflicts for a single resource at a time, and cooperation between airlines have not be covered at all. For an in-depth and theoretical description of the academic research within disruption management we refer to the review by Clausen et al. (2005). Another review can be found in Kohl et al. (2004). Generally, in the disruption management literature passengers are given a low priority.

Multiple resources are considered for the first time by Teodorovic and Stojkovic (1995). Their approach considers crew and maintenance in an iterative manner where a heuristic first generates a new crew schedule and then a new aircraft schedule and finally checks for maintenance feasibility. There is, however, no thorough testing of the approach.

Lettovsky (1997) presents a framework for an integrated approach although it has not been completely tested. A mathematical model is developed aimed at solving the integrated problem of crew and aircraft. The MIP model is very large and computational intractable for anything but unrealistically small problems. Therefore Lettovsky suggests solving the problem using a decomposition scheme controlled by a master problem denoted the Schedule Recovery Model. It provides a cancellation and retiming plan. Thereafter the sub-problems for crew, aircraft, passenger etc. can be solved separately given a solution to the master problem. The solution algorithm applies Benders' decomposition to a MIP formulation of the master problem. Based on nine computational experiments from the method appears effective (Lettovsky et al., 2000).

A more recent contribution by Bratu and Barnhart (2003) describes two models for integrated recovery. The models are focused on passenger recovery but also incorporate rules and regulations on aircraft and crew. Two models are developed. In the passenger delay metric (PDM) model delay costs are more accurately computed by explicitly modeling passenger disruptions, recovery options and delay costs then in the disrupted passenger metric model (DPM). Both models have an objective function incorporating operation costs and passenger recovery costs. The models are solved using OPL Studio. Multi-day test cases are presented using an Operations Control Center simulator. Airline data represents a domestic US operation involving 302 aircraft (divided into four fleet types), 83,869 passengers on 9925 itineraries a day, 74 airports and three hubs. Scenarios based on the level of disruptions are presented. Execution times are in the range of 200–5000 s each time one of the models needs to be solved. Conclusions are the PDM cannot be used in a real-time environment, whereas DPM is fast enough to be used in a recovery situation.

Clarke (1997a, b) presents a model and algorithms for the airline schedule recovery problem, i.e. the problem of aircraft reassignment for all operational aircraft in a fleet in the aftermath of irregularities. The model is an integer program and solution strategies are discussed and tested. Flights can be cancelled or delayed and a number of constraints are introduced to ensure feasibility with respect to aircraft maintenance, accommodation of passengers, crew availability, slot allocation and gate allocation. Hence, the model captures a very large number of resources, but has a rather simplistic model of all resources but aircraft. The model and algorithms have been tested

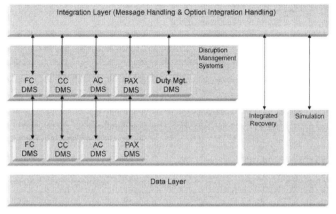

Fig. 3. Overview of the architecture of the Descartes system. *Notes*: FC is flight crew, CC is cabin crew, AC is aircraft, DMS is disruption management system, DCR is dedicated crew recovery, DAR is dedicated aircraft recovery, and DPR is dedicated passenger recovery.

and validated on operational data from a major US domestic carrier.

4. The Descartes project

The Descartes (DEcision Support for integrated Crew and AiRcrafT recovery) project involving British Airways (BA), Carmen Systems, and the Technical University of Denmark ran from 2000 to 2003.[2] Its main objective was to develop a disruption management system based on a holistic approach. The system should integrate the decisions of the resources in one integrated feasible decision. The focus was on the four key resources involved namely aircraft, flight and cabin crew, and passengers.

4.1. The Descartes architecture

The Descartes system is build as a suite of systems (Fig. 3) consisting of:

- *Dedicated solvers*: These systems are only able to handle single resources like aircraft or flight crew. During the project solvers for aircraft, crew and passengers denoted dedicated aircraft recovery system, dedicated crew recovery system and dedicated passenger recovery system were developed.
- *Integrated recovery*: Based on solutions from the dedicated solvers, integrated recovery constructs an integrated solution. This is done via a messaging system specifying single resource problems, that needs to be solved by one or more of the dedicated solves.

[2]The project was supported by the European Union and a detailed description can be found in the Descartes Consortium (2003).

- *Integration layer*: All systems are integrated with the managers' view of the operation by the communication architecture known as the umbrella. Communication to and from the dedicated solvers is processed via the disruption management systems.
- *Simulation*: Simulation makes it possible on a step-by-step basis to monitor the operation and thereby verify the robustness and attractiveness of the plans.

One of the advantages of this approach is the possibility of including existing dedicated solvers into the Descartes system. If the airline already has developed or purchased dedicated solvers they can replace the solvers developed in the Descartes project and be incorporated into the Descartes system through an API. The prototypes for the Descartes passenger recovery system, the Descartes aircraft recovery system the Descartes crew recovery system and the integrated system have all been tested using business experiments. The experiments were conducted by developing realistic scenarios (showing differing levels of disruption) in cooperation with operations control business experts at BA. These scenarios were based on the Operations Controllers' experience and knowledge. The scenarios were then solved both manually (by an Operations Controller) and automatically (using a solver) and the results compared.

4.2. Dedicated passenger recovery system

The purpose of the dedicated passenger recovery solver (DPR) is to evaluate possible recovery options (that may be generated manually or automatically by one of the other dedicated solvers in the Descartes architecture) from the perspective of the passengers and to propose an optimal rebooking plan. For each recovery option to be evaluated the DPR calculates the passenger inconvenience cost plus any real costs associated with this recovery option by finding an optimal rebooking plan for the recovery option. The optimal rebooking scenarios are created based on the following metrics:

- *The cost of passenger delays.* The cost depends on the delay at the final destination of the passenger. This is not the traditional way to measure delay in airlines, but we find this is a more relevant measure than the delay of the aircraft compared to schedule. The delay cost calculation also takes into consideration the commercial value of the passenger—for example based on the booked fare class and frequent flyer information. It is a subjective issue how to derive a formula for the cost of passenger delays, but it is well established that there is a long-term cost associated with delaying passengers.
- *The cost of passenger off loads.* There may be several real costs as well as loss of goodwill associated with offloading a booked passenger.
- *The cost of meals and hotel accommodation for severely disrupted passengers.* In many cases the airline is required to or volunteers to provide passengers with meals and accommodation in case of disruptions. A recent initiative of the European Parliament have made such services mandatory within the European Union.
- *The cost of passenger upgrades and downgrades.* These costs are partly real costs for upgraded catering and downgrade compensation, but there is also loss of goodwill costs associated with downgrades.

These costs determine how much, in monetary terms, the disruption from a passenger perspective is costing. In the experiments carried out with BA data the dominating factor was passenger delays, but for a no-frills airline the unavoidable real costs would probably dominate.

In its most general form the passenger recovery problem can be formulated as a multi-commodity flow problem, where each passenger is represented as a resource. For a discussion of the multi-commodity model and solution approached we refer to Ahuja et al. (1993). A flight is represented by a start and end node connected by a capacity constrained arc, whereas possible connections between flights are represented as asymptotic arcs. The start and end of each passenger's itinerary are represented with nodes. Special offload arcs are introduced to ensure feasibility of the model.

The four cost components discussed above can with small approximation be associated with arcs in the outlined network. The cost of passenger delays can all be associated with arcs terminating in the end destination of a commodity, as delays are only measured at the passengers' destination. Passenger offload costs are associated with the offload arcs. Meal and accommodation costs will always be associated with connections between flights or a delayed initial flight and can therefore be associated with arcs. Upgrades and downgrades represent a slightly more difficult problem, depending on the configuration of the aircraft. There are three cases to consider:

- The number of seats in the classes is fixed. This is typically the case for long-haul aircraft, where the first class cabin, the business class cabin and the tourist class cabin are physically separate units that cannot be enlarged or reduced. Each cabin can be treated as a separate flight arc in the network and upgrade and downgrade costs can be modeled correctly.
- Seats can be converted from one class to another at a one to one ratio, i.e. a tourist class seat can be converted to a business class seat and vise versa. This is sometimes the case in short-haul operations. The flight is modeled with one arc where the resulting number of tourist and business class seats is a simple consequence of which passengers the flight carries in the optimal solution. In practice it is only possible to convert rows of seats (by moving the curtain), but this cannot be captured within the multi-commodity flow model. This approximately amounts to a possibly additional upgrade of part of one row worth from tourist passengers to business class—i.e. a close approximation.
- Seats can be converted from one class to another but not at a one to one ratio. Frequently a row of five or six seats in tourist class will convert into four seats in business class. This cannot be captured within the multi-commodity flow model and either the model must be extended or the curtain positioning problem must be solved as a separate optimization problem.

The multi-commodity flow problem presents particular challenges and within the project simplifications are adopted. Similar passengers can be aggregated and this reduces the number of commodities while parts of the network can be optimized separately reducing the size of the optimization problem. Depending on the extent of the approximation, the problem may be reduced to variants of the easily solvable single commodity flow problem. Fortunately the BA route network is quite simple with virtually all flights originating or terminating in London making a number of simplifications tenable.

The DPR developed in the Descartes project have been benchmarked against the current practice at BA at which staff produced a number of scenarios reflecting the types of everyday disruption problems. These scenarios ranged from the simple disruptions to more complex problems where several flights had to be cancelled. These were entered into the DPR as they were given to the customer service recovery manager (CSRM), ensuring that both received the same information. This was as close to simulating the live operational environment as possible, without actually running the system within the operation. The outcomes were then compared and analyzed. The solutions proposed by the CSRM and the DPR, were compared with respect to the agreed cost function as well as the solution time.

In all cases the CSRM used approximately 45 min to solve the problem whereas the DPR used less than 1 s for the simplest cases and almost 10 s on the most complex ones. In the former the proposed solutions were identical, but in the more complex cases the DPR solutions were either better or much better. The differences in the proposed solutions were analyzed and it was found that DPR solutions were superior offering a more exact assessment of the total commercial value of the passengers and a better analysis of the rebooking possibilities, especially regarding connecting passengers.

The Descartes work found the DPR experimental results extremely encouraging. This is due to the vast time savings using the DRP compared to manual analysis and also to the documented improved solution quality. As a conclusion of these results, the DPR as a stand-alone tool is believed to bring business benefit and add value to decision-making.

4.3. Dedicated aircraft recovery (DAR) solver

The objective of the DAR solver prototyping work was to develop an automatic decision-support tool capable of proposing alternative action plans to recover an infeasible aircraft schedule back to feasibility. DAR is capable of employing any combination of the key schedule recovery techniques used in practice, namely flight delays, cancellations, aircraft type changes and aircraft registration (tail number) changes within a fleet. Each of these actions incur a user-specified penalty in DAR and the objective for DAR is to consider these factors together with other relevant criteria such as passenger loads and values, plan quality criteria, resource constraints, etc. and return multiple, feasible, low-cost solution options. The scope of DAR developed within the Descartes project was defined as the BA London Heathrow short-haul operation.

The DAR solver developed in the Descartes project is based on an extension of the local search heuristic of Løve et al. (2002). A heuristic approach was chosen due to the time requirements. The solver should be able to generate recovery options within 2–3 min. The model used is an extension on the time-line network proposed in Cao and Kanafani (1997a, b). The network consists of nodes that represent the aircraft, flights and standby aircraft with sink nodes that indicate the end of a link of flights. The network also holds a number of cancellation nodes that are used in cases of cancel flights. The arcs that connect the aircraft and the flight nodes represent the aircraft assigned to the flight to which it is connected. The heuristic generates a feasible flight schedule by changing these assignments through simple swaps and allows retimings, cancellations and fleet swaps. Swaps within a single fleet or between fleets can be handled. The model maximizes the sum of revenues of the flights flown minus the costs of delays and those associated with cancellations.[3]

Before any experiments were performed, the DAR constraints and costs were calibrated to reflect current decision-making policies within the OCC at BA. A number of disruption scenarios were prepared and analyzed with experienced aircraft controllers and the model parameter settings adjusted until DAR returned the types of solution options expected in all scenarios. DAR can potentially be useful for business purposes. Therefore the experiment was broken down into three fundamental components, to estimate the value of DAR:

- Real-time, on-line decision-support tool to aid effective recovery from schedule disruption on the day of operation.
- Support tool to aid schedule planners make effective, tactical schedule change decisions up to a few days before the day of operation.
- The decision-making core of a simulation tool capable of flying through a day of operation, thus allowing off-line investigation of the impact of schedule design and/or delivery policies on schedule delivery key performance indicators.

Experiment 1 – Evaluation of DAR as an on-line decision support tool for disruption recovery on the day of operation. As DAR should be capable of solving any type of disruption to the aircraft schedule, the objective of this experiment was to compare the quality (and, to a lesser extent, response time) of solution options produced by DAR and by experienced aircraft controllers across a cross-section of realistic, standalone disruption scenarios ranging from very minor disruption to mass disruption at the hub airport (Fig. 4).

As it was impossible technically to provide the aircraft schedulers with the drag-and-drop Gantt editing functionality of their live schedule editing tool in the experimental setting, they were required to solve disruptions using a static view of the schedule and no playground facility. This meant that it was significantly more difficult for controllers to solve disruptions in the experimental setting than in the real world and this is recognized in the experimental findings.

Five medium-sized disruption scenarios were prepared. Both the disruption scenarios and proposed solutions to those scenarios were specified by an experienced aircraft controller in advance and the scenarios were then run through DAR to compare the quality of its results with manual expectations. The experiment indicated that the DAR was able to produce the same solution as the aircraft controller within at most 2 min compared to manual solution times of up to 1 h. In addition, it produced a number of other solutions that were inferior in terms of the

---
[3] A description of the model and the results of the initial testing can be found in Løve et al. (2002).

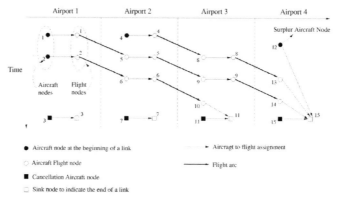

Fig. 4. The network of the heuristic approach.

DAR objective, but that potentially could be better from the perspective of the crew resource or passengers.

Experiment 2—Evaluation of DAR as an on-line decision support tool for tactical schedule change prior to the day of operation. As DAR should be capable of solving any type of real schedule change request received by operations scheduling, the objective of this experiment was to compare the quality (and, to a lesser extent, response time) of solution options produced by DAR and by an experienced aircraft scheduler, across a cross-section of realistic, tactical schedule change request scenarios. A set of 17 tactical schedule change requests and proposed solutions was created by an aircraft scheduler and these scenarios were then run through DAR to compare the quality of DAR results with manual expectations. The following types of schedule changes were considered:

- Insert extra activities into the aircraft schedule (e.g. charter flights, additional maintenance activities).
- Change duration of existing schedule activities (e.g. lengthen a maintenance activity).
- Complex cancellations (e.g. cancel an outbound and inbound leg where the legs are scheduled on aircraft types).
- Move specified schedule activities to a specific aircraft type (e.g. upgrade particular flight numbers to a 767 aircraft, move some maintenance from A320 to A319 aircraft, etc.).
- Retime specific schedule activities to occur later than planned.
- Multiple change requests entailing combinations of the above types of request (e.g. add a new 757 charter, move some flying from 737 to A320, extend a maintenance activity on 737, etc.).

For simple change requests, DAR found the simple (and best) solutions that were also found by the scheduler. In more complex change requests where a solution option was not obvious to the scheduler, DAR again returned the types of option expected by the scheduler. Finally, the schedulers were particularly keen on the DAR functionality that allows them to restrict the types of options searched for by DAR. For example, schedulers can specify that DAR must not cancel or retime any activity or change certain, specified activities or aircraft at all (this is useful for protecting standby aircraft). If no good solution options are found by DAR then the schedulers would realize that some of the restrictions then need to be relaxed.

Experiment 3—Evaluation of DAR as the core of an operational simulation tool: The capability to use planned schedule and disruption probability distributions (or specific disruption events) as input and automatically simulate through a day(s) of operation is considered to be very powerful as it facilitates, in a safe environment, investigation into relationships between schedule attributes and/or delivery policies and key performance indicators for schedule delivery. This, in turn, can help shape fundamental schedule design, management and delivery policies.

A simulation framework was built around DAR thus creating a tool that generates disruption events, invokes DAR to solve them, updates the schedule with the best DAR solution, and generates more disruption events and so on. Rather than solving each single disruption in turn, DAR solves all disruption occurring during a specific time window (usually 1 h) and then the simulation clock is advanced by an amount of time equal to the time window.

Prior to the DAR experiment, BA had already undertaken a manual tabletop exercise that comprised experimenters providing aircraft controllers with a snapshot of the planned aircraft schedule for a particular day and then playing through the day, informing the controller that the current time of day is now x, disruption y has occurred and requires to be solved, etc. The purpose of this manual exercise was to help estimate the impact that new types of schedules and delivery policies are likely to have on various schedule delivery key performance indicators. It was decided to use this tabletop output as a manual benchmark with which to compare the output produced by DAR after simulating through exactly the same disruption events on exactly the same schedule.

The base experiment involved the entire BA 757 and A319 fleets. The result produced by the DAR had 30% lower costs, as defined by the agreed cost metric, than the manual benchmark. The solution reduced the number of cancellations from seven to five but increased total delay from 292 to 430 min. Cancellation of five or seven flights is rather extreme at BA and the reported saving may therefore not be representative for the typical day of operations. Other experiments, with other assumptions were also carried out.

These simulation runs verified the capability of the Descartes simulation framework to play through a day of operation successfully. In addition, they also demonstrated the value of DAR as an on-line, hands-on tool for Aircraft Controllers (i.e. using DAR to manage the tabletop day of operation rather than manual methods resulted in a significant disruption saving at the end of the day). The simulations do however not quantify the value of having a "What if?" simulation capability available at BA to evaluate various schedule creation, management and delivery policies and initiatives. The value of such a capability is very difficult to quantify but some real applications within the business have already been identified (e.g. DAR is being used to aid an OR investigation into how the business could better plan and deliver international domestic aircraft connections in the schedule).

Firstly, the experiments demonstrate that, given a real schedule and realistic disruption situations, the DAR model recommends consistently the same recovery plan as the one suggested by an experienced aircraft controller. We believe, therefore, that the model contains all the correct business constraints and preferences and that the parameters governing the types of solution options generated (i.e. cost of delay and cost of cancellation) have been calibrated correctly. There is evidence in the stand-alone scenario experiments that DAR is capable also of identifying good potential recovery solutions that are difficult to spot manually, especially in situations of mass disruption, but it is difficult to quantify this accurately given the fact that controllers did not have available their usual schedule-editing tools when creating manual solutions. More conclusive evidence that DAR is capable, in some situations, of identifying better solutions than can be found manually is found in the simulation experiment, although a direct comparison between manual tabletop and simulation results is difficult due to slight differences in the environment/rules. The capability of the mechanism to play through a day of operation, making valid recovery proposals at each decision-point has been demonstrated. Furthermore, there is a business benefit in having this type of off-line simulation tool to aid policy evaluation, etc. Some additional simulation runs have been carried out to demonstrate the capability to vary parameters and observe the effect on schedule delivery key performance indicators (e.g. What if there were more/less standby aircraft available?, What if we were prepared to cancel flights more/less readily in disruption?, What if schedule stability was more important on the day of operation?, etc.). It is difficult to quantify the size of this business benefit financially.

4.4. Dedicated crew recovery (DCR) solver

The DCR solver was designed to be a useful decision support tool for crew controllers and duty managers within operations control. The aim of the DCR was to use the available crew resource more effectively in a disruptive situation (i.e. to make better use of standby crew and improve re-assignment of disrupted crew members to alternative duties).

In the current, manual environment within BA, uncovered flights resulting from a disruption would usually be covered by crew members allocated from the pool of standby crew. However, the DCR provides functionality to re-allocate the disrupted crew members to alternative flights (with a later departure) whereas the flights subsequent to the disrupted flights will be crewed by the crew that has been de-allocated from the former flights. The re-allocation procedure is known as re-linking and is only possible within certain regulatory constraints. If re-linking is not feasible in the given situation, the delayed crew will usually be relieved from the duty and the subsequent flights operated by crew members called from standby duty.

The DCR developed during the Descartes project focused solely on the cabin crew resource and the rules and techniques used to manage these accordingly. However, the same methodology could easily be adjusted to manage disruption on flight crew also, as there is principally another rule set to build the model and parameters around. Furthermore, as the dimensions of the flight crew recovery problem are smaller than those of cabin crew, this means that being able to solve the latter also suggests that one should be able to solve the former problem.

The DCR employs various techniques to generate recovery options. This includes relinking, allocating crew from standby, up- and down-grading crew (i.e. for instance letting a standard cabin crew member work as a purser whenever appropriate) and pre-empting the problem (i.e. finding a solution in advance of the problem hitting the control center). The solver uses a mix of these techniques to try to come up with structurally differing recovery options.

The DCR is based on a differential column-generation technique to find legal roster changes to each crew member involved in the disruption. The legal roster changes are included in a constrained integer optimization problem

(IP). The problem is then solved multiple times. For each option generated, an additional constraint forbidding the new option is added. A sequence of options with increasing costs are found that together constitute a set of best solution options. The ability to produce multiple recovery options is the real strength of the DCR as the controller can use experience and intuition to pick the option best suited for implementation.

The DCR was tested on a number of scenarios provided by the business team at BA. These scenarios were inspired by real, historic disruptions from the past.

A group of crew controllers were selected to produce manual solutions to the same scenarios as were used to test the DCR. After the tests the results were analyzed by an expert user to determine whether the solutions were feasible in an operational environment. The data that were used for the experiments were captured from the BA crew control systems prior to the experiment.

The DCR solver was tested on a number scenarios that were structurally different. One of these was the scenario described below. This scenario consisted of 5 delayed flights that were fed into the system simultaneously to evaluate the impact of the full scenario:

Date	Flight	Origin	Destination	Departure	Arrival	Delay (mins.)
12 Aug	BA-941	DUS	LHR	14:45	16:10	60
12 Aug	BA-970	LHR	HAM	13:20	14:55	90
12 Aug	BA-309	CDG	LHR	10:25	11:35	65
12 Aug	BA-393	BRU	LHR	10:50	12:00	110
12 Aug	BA-1446	LHR	EDI	13:00	14:15	60

A total of 21 crew members were involved in the delay scenario. The results below demonstrate how the DCR tool solved this disruption. In this scenario, the flight delays caused conflicts in the continuing duties of the crew members involved. The primary problem was a violation of the minimum time required to connect from the delayed flight to the crew member's next flight. Generally, the minimum connection time rule is a hard constraint within the crewing rule set that under no circumstances can be broken.

The recovery option generated by the DCR involved standby crew from both the London Heathrow (LHR) central base station as well as the Glasgow (GLA) base. The breakdown of crew involved was as follows:

9 crew used from standby duties;

2 crew used from standby duty who were Glasgow based, who were not originally part of the problem but were re-assigned from their original rostered duty to allow other permutations to occur;

Upgrades of pursers to work as customer service directors (CSD) positions and CSD's were removed from the trips.

The total recovery option involved 20 flights and 30 crew members. This is a substantial increase to the number of flights and crew initially affected in the initial disruption. This is due to the fact that the DCR breaks up a number of the crew rosters to use these in the re-assignment of disrupted crew. However, this also underlines one of the drawbacks of the re-linking and re-allocation schemes used in the DCR; the solver does not minimize the number of disrupted crew. At BA, the quality of life of the crew members is considered to be very important and should be protected also in disruption, i.e. the recovery options produced should minimize the number crew members involved in the solution to protect the lifestyle of the crew members. The DCR, however, did use a greater number of crew to suggest a solution. A production quality version of the DCR should address this issue.

The rule sets for BA crew are restrictive in terms of what BA can and cannot do with the crew on the day of operation. Emphasis is placed upon crew quality of lifestyle and that limits changes. To make best use of a crew recovery tool BA would need to look at the possibilities of changing the cabin crew restrictions during unplanned operations. If it were not to do this then the benefits from manpower savings would be minimal. Capability to re-link crew could potentially save a number of standby crew on the day of operation, but current rules states that crew members must be off duty not more than a short time later than their original planned arrival.

During the development of the DCR, a simulation study was performed to investigate the potential savings in standby usage offered by the re-linking technique based on 4000 scenarios holding randomly generated, small disruptions in which an average of 10% of the flights were delayed from 15 to 120 min. The initial findings suggested that the re-linking feature could generate substantial savings in cases of small disruptions.

The initial results thus indicated that the DCR would bring benefits to the operations control environment. By using this tool, crew controllers and duty managers could make more complex decisions in a shorter time with savings from better crew utilization. However, the DCR developed within the project still needs some further to take account of the quality of life aspect when generating feasible recovery options. Furthermore, the options generated by the prototype did not take robustness into consideration and further delays could make the proposed option infeasible.

4.5. Integrated recovery

Integration in the disruption management process can be handled in two ways; by developing stand-alone tools for each of the relevant resources and then using these tools as components in an integrated system, or by designing a system that determines solutions in an integrated fashion using concurrent access to available information for each of the resources. The first system type is integrated sequential recovery (ISR), while the other is tailored integrated recovery (TIRS).

ISR uses the subsystems for single resources as black boxes for solution generation and evaluation and allows a stepwise development in terms of standalone systems for each of the resources. It therefore also allows the possibility of early business benefits based on single resource systems and it is not necessary to handle integrated information. Data for the subsystems may be handled independently for each subsystem, e.g. for aircraft recovery problems, knowledge of the current crew situation is only necessary when a feasible solution from the aircraft point of view has to be evaluated with respect to crewing. On the other hand, the process of generating solutions of high quality with respect to all resource areas is a challenge. The integrated recovery system must be able to control the dedicated solvers by putting very specific queries to them.

The potential advantage of TIRS is the ability to steer the solution process based on information on all resources. Ideally, this corresponds to having a mathematical model incorporating all resource areas rather than having a model for each resource area. Solutions generated are generally better balanced across the resource areas than solutions initially proposed because of their quality for one particular resource area. The tailored integrated approach, however faces two major problems: the data issue becomes more complicated as aircraft, crew and passenger data needs to be integrated and the complexity of an integrated model virtually rules out the possibility of attacking the problem in a real-time setting based on optimization methods.

The core of ISR is an intelligent messaging system that integrates all available recovery subsystems. Integration is based on the principle of encapsulating each area's specific data and rules in dedicated recovery modules. Modules communicate by exchanging suggestions on schedule changes. Each dedicated recovery module is capable of evaluating the impact of a schedule change on its corresponding area of operations. Some modules are designed to generate schedule change suggestions, referred to as options. Currently, aircraft and crew recovery modules are able to suggest schedule changes to other subsystems. The challenge is to be able to generate options that are good from the overall business perspective. For this purpose, dedicated systems are designed to be able to consider constraints and objectives from other areas.

The development of TIRS is based on the time-band network of Argüello (1997), a variant of the time-line networks used in many fleet assignment methods. To decrease the complexity of the problem, the time line is subdivided into intervals that, together with schedule information, form the basis of the recovery method. The current TIRS-version builds a time-band network both with respect to aircraft and with respect to crew. A path in the aircraft network corresponds to the line of work of an aircraft and a path in the crew network corresponds to the line of work of a crew member. In the initial investigation, a full crew is considered as one unit. The basic idea is now, in case of a disruption, to represent a solution by a modified crew schedule and a modified aircraft schedule and to let the development of these two schedules take place concurrently. During the solution process, each schedule is therefore influenced not only by what is good in the context of aircraft with respect to crew, but also by the difference to that schedule, that is currently under consideration for the other resource. Time-band networks for crew and aircraft are then constructed and a basic heuristic local search (based on simulated annealing) has been implemented.

5. Conclusions

An operations control center is required to make important operational decisions with potentially significant operational and commercial ramifications and often under extreme time pressure and sometimes without complete information. Manual methods often mean that only one or two possible solution options can be considered with the prospect that a solution far from optimal across all the key areas may be implemented. As a result of the sequential nature of manual processes, implemented for one resource might very well have a profound impact on other areas. Research for IT-supported decision support tools is often, however, characterized by single resource systems and a rather academic approach. The Descartes project discussed here aimed at developing a system spanning multiple resources method integrating data sources. It was demonstrated that the system improves the quality of decision-making. The focus of the system is not to generate the optimum solution in the strict academic sense, but rather to provide flexible tools that can add value to the business process of operations control at various airlines.

Acknowledgments

The work forming the basis of the paper was supported by European Union contract IST-1999-14049. The authors gratefully acknowledge the recommendations of the journal's editor-in-chief that helped to improve the quality of the paper.

References

Ahuja, R.K., Magnanti, T.L., Orlin, J.B., 1993. Network Flows: Theory, Algorithms, and Applications. Prentice-Hall, Upper Saddle River.

Argüello, M.F., 1997. Framework for Exact Solutions and Heuristics for Approximate Solutions to Airlines' Irregular Operations Control Aircraft Routing Problem. Ph.D. Thesis, The University of Texas at Austin.

Bratu, S., Barnhart, C., 2003. Flight operations recovery: new approaches considering passenger recovery. Working Paper, Massachusetts Institute of Technology.

Cao, J.-M., Kanafani, A., 1997a. Real-time decision support for integration of airline flight cancellations and delays. Part I: mathematical formulation. Journal of Transportation Planning and Technology 20, 183–199.

Cao, J.-M., Kanafani, A., 1997b. Real-time decision support for integration of airline flight cancellations and delays. Part II: algorithm and computational experiments. Transport Planning and Technology 20, 201–217.

Chang, K., Howard, H., Oiesen, R., Shisler, L., Tanino, M., Wambganss, M.C., 2001. Enhancements to the FAA ground-delay program under collaborative decision making. Interfaces 31, 57–76.

Clarke, M.D.D., 1997a. The airline schedule recovery problem. Working Paper, International Center for Air Transportation, Massachusetts Institute of Technology.

Clarke, M.D.D., 1997b. Development of heuristic procedures for the flight rescheduling in the aftermath of irregular airline operations. Working Paper, International Center for Air Transportation, Massachusetts Institute of Technology.

Clausen, J., Larsen, A., Larsen, J., 2005. Disruption management in the airline industry—review of models and methods. Technical Report, Department of Informatics and Mathematical Modelling, Technical University of Denmark.

Clausen, J., Hansen, J., Larsen, J., Larsen, A., 2001. Disruption management—operations research between planning and execution. OR/MS Today 28 (5), 40–43.

Descartes Consortium—British Airways Plc, Carmen Systems AB, The Technical University of Denmark, 2003. EU-project IST-1999-14049. Descartes Final Report. Can be downloaded from Carmen Systems Web-site at: ⟨http://www.carmen.se/research_development/descartes.htm⟩.

Kohl, N., Larsen, A., Larsen, J., Ross, A., Tiourine S., 2004. Airline disruption management—perspectives, experiences and outlook. Technical Report 2004–16. Department of Informatics and Mathematical Modelling, Technical University of Denmark.

Lettovsky, L., 1997. Airline operations recovery: an optimization approach. Ph.D. Thesis, Georgia Institute of Technology, Atlanta.

Lettovsky, L., Johnson, E.L., Nemhauser, GL., 2000. Airline crew recovery. Transportation Science 34, 337–348.

Løve, M., Sørensen, K.R., Larsen, J., Clausen, J., 2002. Disruption management for an airline—rescheduling of aircraft. In: Cagnoni, S., Gottlieb, J., Hart, E., Middendorf, M., Raidl, G.R. (Eds.), Applications of Evolutionary Computing, volume 2279 of Lecture Notes in Computer Science. Springer, New York.

Teodorovic, D., Stojkovic, G., 1995. Model to reduce airline schedule disturbances. Journal of Transportation Engineering 121, 324–331.

23

Disruption management in the airline industry—Concepts, models and methods

Jens Clausen, Allan Larsen, Jesper Larsen, Natalia J. Rezanova

ARTICLE INFO

Available online 7 April 2009

Keywords:
Disruption management
Crew recovery
Aircraft recovery
Passenger recovery
Integrated recovery
Airline optimization
Network models

ABSTRACT

This paper provides a thorough review of the current state-of-the-art within airline disruption management of resources, including aircraft, crew, passenger and integrated recovery. An overview of model formulations of the aircraft and crew scheduling problems is presented in order to emphasize similarities between solution approaches applied to the planning and recovery problems. A brief overview of research within schedule robustness in airline scheduling is included in the review, since this proactive measure is a natural complement to disruption management.

© 2009 Elsevier Ltd. All rights reserved.

1. Introduction

The airline industry is one of the most successful examples of applying operations research methods and tools for the planning and scheduling of resources. Optimization-based decision support systems have proven to be efficient and cost-saving for the scheduling of aircraft and crew, not to mention the short term re-scheduling problems, where modifications to the initial plans are required before the final schedules can be executed.

On the day of operation carefully planned crew and aircraft schedules can become infeasible due to external disruptions and internal failures. To date, no planning tools have been able to cope with the complexity of re-planning all airline operations at the same time during disruptions. Despite the increasing power of hardware and sophisticated solution methods, there is still a gap between the reality faced in airlines' operations control and the decision support offered by the commercial IT-systems targeting the recovery of aircraft, crew and passenger itineraries in one integrated system. However, substantial achievements have been made in developing solution methods that support the stand-alone recovery of aircraft and crew since the mid 1980s, and a few prototype systems for integrated airline recovery have been presented in the operations research literature. The majority of the mathematical models and solution methods for solving the airline recovery problems are similar to the methods applied for planning purposes. Tools for planning as well as for recovery are, in most research cases, based on a network representation that describes how flights can be sequenced either in a rotation or in a crew pairing. In the remainder of this section we present an overview of the most commonly used network models for airline optimization problems and a short description of the planning process used by major airlines today. Section 2 describes aircraft, crew, and integrated and passenger recovery as presented in the literature, while Section 3 briefly discusses robustness in relation to disruption management. Finally, Section 4 contains discussions of future prospects for disruption management systems in the airline industry.

1.1. Airline planning process

Prior to the departure of an aircraft, a sequential planning approach takes place. First, the flight schedule is determined, based on forecasts of passenger demand, available slots at the airports and other relevant information. Thereafter, specific types of aircraft are assigned to individual flights in the schedule, and sequences of flights are generated within each fleet—these processes are called fleet assignment and aircraft routing, respectively. Aircraft rotations must respect various types of constraints as e.g. maintenance and night curfews. In the subsequent crew scheduling phase, flight crew and cabin crew are assigned to all flights based on the already determined aircraft rotations. Individual flights are grouped to form anonymous crew pairings. Each pairing starts and ends at the same crew base and has a typical length of three–four days. Afterwards, pairings are grouped to form personnel rosters, which are lines of work typically for 14 days or one month, including rest periods, vacations and training. Finally, physical aircraft from a given fleet are assigned to flights in the tail assignment process. The complete planning process is illustrated in Fig. 1.

The planning process is very complex since numerous restrictions and rules have to be considered. For aircraft, rules on maintenance, differences between various aircraft types, etc. must be taken into

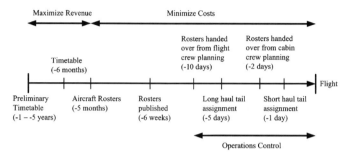

Fig. 1. The time line for the operation of a major European airline.

the planning. Also, characteristics of each individual airport have to be respected. For crew, there are regulations on flying time, off-time, etc., based on international and national rules, as well as regulations originating in agreements with unions, specific to each airline. Changes in plans due to e.g. crew sickness, aircraft breakdowns and changes in passenger forecasts take place in the tracking phase of the planning process. This phase normally resides with the planning department of the airline.

The plans for aircraft and crew assignments are handed over from the planning department to the operations control center (OCC) a few days ahead of the day of operation. It now becomes the responsibility of the OCC to maintain all resources so that the flight schedule is feasible as an integrated entity. Events like acute crew unavailabilities and delayed flights have to be handled. Not only the immediately affected flights, but also knock-on effects in other parts of the schedule can cause serious problems. Generally, a disrupted situation (often just denoted a disruption) is a state during the execution of the current operation, where the deviation from the plan is sufficiently large to impose a substantial change. This is not a very precise definition; however, it captures the important point that a disruption is not necessarily the result of one particular event.

The generation of recovery plans is a complex task, since many resources (crew, aircraft, passengers, slots, catering, cargo etc.) have to be re-planned. When a disruption occurs on the day of operation, large airlines usually react by solving the problem in a sequential fashion with respect to the problem components. First, infeasibilities in the aircraft schedule are resolved, then crewing problems are addressed. Afterwards, ground problems are tackled, and finally, the impact on passengers is evaluated. Sometimes, the process is iterated with all stakeholders until a feasible plan for recovery is found and can be implemented. As a rule, determining the quality of a recovery option is a difficult task. The objective function can be composed of several conflicting and sometimes non-quantifiable goals. Examples of objectives are minimizing the number of passenger delay minutes, returning to the plan as quickly as possible, minimizing passenger dissatisfaction, minimizing the cost of the recovery operation, etc. In most airlines, controllers performing the recovery have only limited IT-based decision support to help them construct recovery options or evaluate the quality of the recovery action they are about to implement. Often, controllers are content with only producing one viable recovery plan since there is no time to consider alternatives.

1.2. Models for airline optimization problems

The majority of airline recovery models are formulated and solved similar to the corresponding planning problems, using the same

Table 1
A sample schedule for Sample Air with aircraft rotations.

Aircraft	Flight	Origin	Destination	Departure	Arrival	Flight time
AC1	11	OSL	CPH	14:10	15:20	1:10
	12	CPH	AAR	16:00	16:40	0:40
	13	AAR	CPH	17:30	18:10	0:40
	14	CPH	OSL	18:50	20:00	1:10
AC2	21	CPH	WAV	14:30	15:30	1:00
	22	WAV	CPH	15:50	16:50	1:00
	23	CPH	WAV	17:30	18:30	1:00
	24	WAV	CPH	18:50	19:50	1:00
AC3	31	AAR	OSL	15:00	16:20	1:20
	32	OSL	AAR	17:00	18:20	1:20

network representations to model the schedules. However, there are also some differences between the modelling approaches. In order to draw a parallel between recovery models and optimization problems occurring during the planning phase, we briefly present the aircraft routing and the crew scheduling problem formulations, as well as their substantial differences from the recovery models.

1.2.1. Network representations

The three most commonly used network representations for airline planning and recovery problems are time-line networks, connection networks and time-band networks. In order to illustrate the networks, consider a small flight schedule of an artificial airline Sample Air shown in Table 1, where flights connecting Copenhagen (CPH), Oslo (OSL), Aarhus (AAR), and Warsaw (WAV) are given. Assume that the turn-around-time for an aircraft is 40 min in CPH and OSL and 20 min in AAR and WAV.

A *connection network* is an activity-on-node network, where flight legs correspond to nodes in the network and connections between flight legs correspond to directed edges (arcs) between the nodes. A flight leg is given by its origin, destination, departure time and date and arrival time and date. A node i, representing the flight leg l_i, is connected by a directed edge (i,j) to a node j, which represents the flight leg l_j, if it is feasible to fly l_j immediately after l_i using the same aircraft with respect to turn-around-times and airport. In addition, there is a set of origin and destination nodes indicating possible positions of aircraft in a fleet at the beginning and at the end of the planning horizon, respectively. A path in the network from an origin to a destination node corresponds to a sequence of flights feasible as part of a rotation. Schedule information is not represented explicitly in the network, but is used when generating the nodes in the network. Maintenance restrictions can be easily incorporated through the concept of a maintenance feasible path,

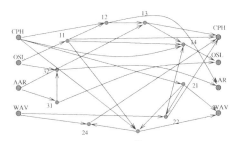

Fig. 2. The sample schedule shown as a connection network. The rotation for AC1 shown in Table 1 corresponds to the path OSL-11-12-13-14-OSL.

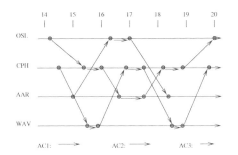

Fig. 3. The sample schedule shown as a time-line network. The rotation for AC1 shown in Table 1 corresponds to the AC1 path.

which is a path providing sufficient extra time with the required intervals at a node corresponding to a station, where maintenance can take place. Note that the number of feasible paths may be very large—it grows exponentially with the planning time horizon. The Sample Air flight schedule represented as a connection network is shown in Fig. 2.

The idea of a *time-line network* is to represent the possible schedules in a natural way from the time-and-station point of view, which is not possible when using a connection network. A time-line network has a node for each event, an event being an arrival or a departure of an aircraft at a particular station. Time-line networks are activity-on-edge networks, where directed edges correspond to activities of an aircraft, and schedule information is represented explicitly by the event nodes. All event-nodes of a particular station are located on a time line corresponding to that station. The length of the time line corresponds to the planning horizon. There is a directed edge from one event-node to another, if the two events may follow each other in a sequence in a schedule of the same aircraft. Edges connecting nodes on the time lines for different stations correspond to flights feasible with respect to flying time, while edges connecting nodes on the time line for a particular station correspond to grounded aircraft. In the same way as for the connection network, a direct path is possible rotation for an aircraft. The time-line network for Sample Air is shown in Fig. 3. Notice that ground arcs that are not used in the aircraft schedule presented in Table 1 are omitted from the network for simplicity.

When network representations are used in the recovery context, a network is usually built for shorter time periods, beginning at a time of disruption and limited by the time when the schedule is expected to be recovered. The source nodes in the network represent the exact positions of the aircraft at the time of disruption, while the sink nodes represent the expected positions of the aircraft at the end of the recovery. The schedules within the recovery time window are then re-planned in order to repair infeasibilities caused by disruptions, while the schedules outside of the recovery time window are not changed.

A *time-band network* is proposed by Argüello [7] in order to model the aircraft schedule affected by disruptions, and is used in the context of aircraft recovery. The network can be constructed dynamically as disruptions occur, for a certain recovery time period. There is a set of station-time nodes and a set of station-sink nodes. A station-time node represents activities at a particular airport aggregated within a certain discrete time interval, called a time band. The time label of a station-time node corresponds to the availability time (the arrival time plus the turn-around time) of the first available aircraft in the time band. A station-sink nodes represent the end of the recovery period at each station. The edges in the network represent the flights. A scheduled flight from station A to station B has an emanating edge for each A-time node, in which there is an aircraft available, and for which the flight can be flown within the recovery period. Each of these edges will end in the B-time node corresponding to the time when the aircraft becomes available at B. The number of emanating edges is the same for all station-time nodes corresponding to the same station. Finally, there are edges connecting each station-time node to the station-sink node for the relevant airport. A recovery solution corresponds to a flow in the network. Edges of the originally scheduled flights, which carry no flow, correspond to cancelled flights, and re-timings of flights correspond to the flow on the "new" flight edges, indicating that flights are flown at a later time than scheduled. Fig. 4 shows the time-band network model for the Sample Air schedule, where aircraft AC2 is out of service from 14:00 to 21:00 due to an unexpected maintenance, and with time bands of 30 min. The network is constructed in a stepwise fashion in order to avoid generating time-station nodes with no aircraft availability. Two flows in this network, one starting in OSL and another in AAR, and ending in either OSL or AAR, determine the way to use the two remaining aircraft, AC1 and AC3.

1.2.2. Aircraft routing

An *aircraft routing problem* (also called *aircraft rotation problem*) determines the optimal set of routes flown by all aircraft in a given fleet, given that the fleet assignment is already performed. There are two general formulations of the aircraft routing problem: a set partitioning model and a multicommodity network flow model. The connection network and the time-line network can both be used to represent the schedule.

In a multicommodity network flow formulation of the aircraft routing problem non-negative integer decision variables x_{ij} represent the flow on arc (i,j) of the network, each unit of flow representing one aircraft in a given fleet. Flow balance constraints of the problem at each node of the network ensure that each flight leg is covered by exactly one aircraft and that the balance of grounded aircraft at each station is ensured. This also ensures that the number of rotations in the network is less than or equal to the number of aircraft in a given fleet.

The aircraft routing problem can also be formulated as a set partitioning problem. Let F be the set of available aircraft in a fleet. For each aircraft $f \in F$, an origin o^f and a destination d^f relative to the planning horizon is given. Given a connection network with a set of flight nodes N, origins o^f and destinations d^f, P^f denotes the set of feasible paths between o^f and d^f in the network. If maintenance is to be taken into account, only maintenance feasible paths are considered. The relations between the flights and the paths are given

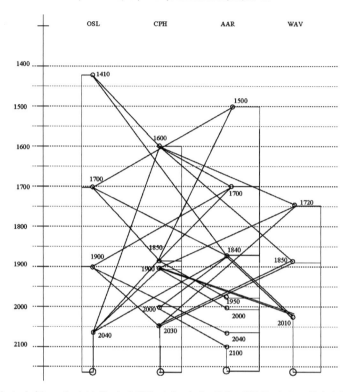

Fig. 4. The time-band network of the sample schedule. The aircraft AC2 is out of service from 14:00 to 21:00. Time bands are 30 min. A feasible recovery rotation for AC1 is OSL-11-21(delayed 1.5 h)-22(delayed 1.5 h)-14(delayed 10 min)-OSL. This rotation corresponds to the path OSL(1400-1429)-CPH(1600-1629)-WAV(1700-1729)-CPH(1900-1929)-OSL(2030-2059)-OSL(sink).

by binary parameters a_{ip}, which are equal to one if flight leg i is on path p. To determine which aircraft are to fly the scheduled flights, we define binary decision variables x_p^f, which are equal to one if and only if the flight legs on the path p with cost c_p^f are flown by aircraft f. The constraints of the problem ensure that each flight leg is contained in exactly one of the selected paths, and that only one path must be chosen for each aircraft:

Minimize $\sum_{f \in F} \sum_{p \in P^f} c_p^f x_p^f$

subject to $\sum_{f \in F} \sum_{p \in P^f} a_{ip} x_p^f = 1 \quad \forall i \in N,$

$\sum_{p \in P^f} x_p^f = 1 \quad \forall f \in F,$

$x_p^f \in \{1, 0\} \quad \forall f \in F, \; p \in P^f.$

The aircraft recovery model can be formulated similar to the above aircraft routing problem, with extra binary decision variables determining if flight f is to be cancelled or not in the recovery solution, and expressing the costs of delays and cancellations in the objective function.

1.2.3. Crew scheduling

On passenger aircraft there are two types of crew: flight (cockpit) crew responsible for flying the aircraft and cabin crew who service the passengers. Each of the crew groups are further divided by rank. A crew will typically get a plan of work for a two or four-week period. The task of assigning crew to itineraries is generally very complex. It is therefore split into two stages: *crew pairing* and *crew assignment* (also known as *crew rostering*). Both problems are usually formulated as generalized set partitioning or set covering problems with one constraint for each task to be performed. In the crew pairing problem the task is a flight to be covered and in the crew assignment problem the task is a pairing/other work to be covered. For an exhaustive description of airline crew scheduling problems and solution methods refer to Barhnart et al. [12].

The objective of the crew pairing problem is to find a minimum cost subset of feasible pairings such that every flight is covered by exactly one selected pairing. Let F be the set of flights to be covered and P the set of all feasible pairings. Decision variable y_p is equal to one if pairing p is included in the solution and zero otherwise. The relation between pairing p and flight i is given by a parameter a_{ip}, which is equal to one if p contains i and zero otherwise. The cost of a pairing is denoted c_p and includes allowances, hotel and meal costs, ground transport costs and paid duty hours.

$$\text{Minimize} \quad \sum_{p \in P} c_p y_p$$
$$\text{subject to} \quad \sum_{p \in P} a_{ip} y_p = 1 \quad \forall i \in F,$$
$$y_p \in \{1, 0\} \quad \forall p \in P.$$

Generation of pairings can be done using one of the two network representations presented earlier: the flight connection network (mainly used for domestic and short-haul operations) or the duty time-line network (mainly appropriate for international and long-haul operations). A pairing is a path from the source to the sink, usually represented by crew bases. However, not all paths represent legal pairings since duty rules, like maximum flying hours, etc., are not explicitly expressed in the network. These rules must be checked for each path in order to ensure legality.

In order to solve the crew pairing problem one possibility is to construct all legal pairings. The challenge is that the number of legal pairings can be extremely large, typically varying from 500,000 for a minor airline to billions of pairings for major airlines. For smaller problems all legal pairings can be generated a priori. For larger problems, a limited a priori generation can be used as a heuristic, finding a good solution without guaranteeing optimality. Another approach is to generate the pairings as they are needed in a dynamic column generation process. The problem of generating the pairings then becomes a variant of the shortest path problem.

The crew assignment (rostering) problem is solved for each crew type, i.e. captain, first officer, etc. Each crew member should be assigned to exactly one work schedule, while each pairing from the crew pairing solution must be contained in the appropriate number of selected work schedules, depending on how many crew members of each type are required for a given pairing. Let K be the set of crew members of a given type and let P be the set of pairings to be covered. For each crew member k the set of feasible work schedules is denoted S^k. n_p is the minimum number of crew members needed to cover pairing p and γ_p^s is equal to one if pairing p is included in schedule s and zero otherwise. c_s^k is the cost of schedule s for crew k. Decision variables are x_s^k, taking the value of one if schedule $s \in S^k$ is assigned to crew $k \in K$ and zero otherwise.

$$\text{Minimize} \quad \sum_{k \in K} \sum_{s \in S^k} c_s^k x_s^k$$
$$\text{subject to} \quad \sum_{k \in K} \sum_{s \in S^k} \gamma_p^s x_s^k \geq n_p \quad \forall p \in P,$$
$$\sum_{s \in S^k} x_s^k = 1 \quad \forall k \in K,$$
$$x_s^k \in \{1, 0\} \quad \forall s \in S^k, \ k \in K.$$

The network representation for the crew assignment problem is similar to the pairing problem, but instead of defining a path of flights as in the pairing problem the path consists of pairings. The problem can be solved with the same solution methods as the crew pairing problem, e.g. column generation.

The crew recovery problem formulations presented in the Operations Research literature are similar to the crew scheduling models, but often other decision variables are added, representing the decisions to be taken in order to recover disrupted situations. For instance, a binary decision variable z_i can determine if flight leg i is cancelled or not, or an integer decision variable s_i can decide the number of crew deadheading (flying as a passenger for re-positioning reasons) on flight leg i. By introducing a cost in the objective function corresponding to decision variables responsible for recovery and adding the variables to the problem constraints, an optimal re-scheduling solution can be found with respect to the objectives specified for recovering a particular disruption.

2. Disruption management

Clarke [20] provides the first overview of the state-of-the-practice in operations control centers in the aftermath of irregular operations. The overview is based on field studies at several airlines. The author provides an extensive review of the literature within the airline disruption management and proposes a decision framework that addresses how airlines can re-assign aircraft to scheduled flights after a disruptive situation. Kohl et al. [33] provide a general introduction to the airline disruption management and include a description of the planning processes in the airline industry. The paper reports on the experiences obtained during the large-scale airline disruption management research and development project DESCARTES, supported by European Union. A survey incorporating issues from the point of view of airports can be found in Filar et al. [25], and a small section devoted to disruption management is included in Yu and Yang [77].

The book by Yu and Qi [76] considers disruption management from a more general perspective. It includes chapters on disruption management for flight and crew scheduling for airlines as well as chapters on disruption management for a number of other applications, e.g. machine scheduling and supply chain coordination. Due to the general view on disruption management taken by the authors, the chapters on disruption management for airlines are not particularly detailed with respect to methodology. Ball et al. [10] give insight into the infrastructure and constraints of airline operations, as well as the air traffic flow management methods and actions. Simulation and optimization models for aircraft, crew and passenger recovery are also discussed. Furthermore, the authors give an excellent survey of the airline schedule robustness as a proactive alternative to recovery, including model descriptions and a literature review.

2.1. Aircraft recovery

The initial research within disruption management focused on aircraft recovery, possibly due to the fact that the number of aircraft is much smaller than the number of crew members, and the rules for aircraft scheduling are less complex. Teodorović and Guberinić [63] are the pioneers of the aircraft recovery research, their research is extended by Teodorović and Stojković [64,65]. Since the complexity and the size of problem instances are not as challenging as for crew, many solution approaches to aircraft recovery are to a larger extent based on the original planning models. Jarrah et al. [31], Rakshit et al. [48], Mathaisel [44], Yan and Yang [73], Cao and Kanafani [14,15] formulate the aircraft recovery problem as a minimum cost network flow problem and use network flow algorithms to solve it. Argüello et al. [8,9], Løve et al. [40], Andersson [5], and Liu et al. [37,38] apply metaheuristics, while the vast majority of the publications use integer programming solution methods to solve the aircraft recovery problem. We group the latter by the network representations used by the authors for formulating the IP models, i.e. the time-line network, the time-band network and the connection network. Finally, Table 2 gives a summary of the aircraft recovery literature in a chronological order.

2.1.1. Initial efforts

One of the first studies of the airline recovery problem is presented in the paper from 1984 by Teodorović and Guberinić [63]. Here, one or more aircraft are unavailable and the objective is to minimize the total passenger delays by reassigning and re-timing the flights. The authors devise a heuristic that sequentially constructs the chain of flights to be flown by each aircraft. Their solution assumes a single fleet type and ignores all maintenance constraints.

Table 2
Overview of proposed methods for the aircraft recovery problem.

Authors	Year	Network	Functionality			Data	Dimensions			Solution time	Objectives
			Cancel	Retime	Multi-fleet		AC	Fleets	Flights		
Teodorović and Guberinić [63]	1984	CN	No	Yes	No	G	3	1	8	NA	Delay minutes
Teodorović and Stojković [64]	1990	CN	Yes	Yes	No	G	14	1	80	180	Canx and delay minutes
Jarrah et al. [31], Rakshit et al. [48]	1993/6	TLN	Yes	Yes	No	RL	NA	9	NA	0–30	Delay, swap and ferrying
Teodorović and Stojković [65]	1995	CN	Yes	Yes	No	G	NA	1	80	140	Canx and delay minutes
Mathaisel [44]	1996	TLN	Yes	Yes	No	NA	NA	NA	NA	NA	Revenue loss, operating cost
Talluri [61]	1996	CN	No	No	Yes	G	NA	NA	NA	10	Swaps when changing AC type
Yan and Yang [73]	1996	TLN	Yes	Yes	No	RL	17	1	39	49	Costs minus revenue
Clarke [18,19]	1997	CN	Yes	Yes	Yes	RL	177	4	612	NA	Costs minus revenues
Yan and Tu [72]	1997	TLN	Yes	Yes	Yes	RL	273	3	3	1800	Costs minus revenue
Cao and Kanafani [14,15]	1997	TLN	Yes	Yes	No	G	162	1	504	869	Revenue minus costs
Luo and Yu [41]	1997	NA	No	Yes	NA	RL	NA	NA	71	15	Number of delayed flights
Argüello et al. [8]	1997	TBN	Yes	Yes	Yes	RL	16	1	42	2	Route cost and cancellation cost
Luo and Yu [42]	1998	NA	No	Yes	NA	RL	NA	NA	71	15	Delayed flights
Thengval et al. [66]	2000	TLN	Yes	Yes	No	RL	27	1	162	6	Revenue minus cost
Thengval et al. [67,68]	2001/3	TLN	Yes	Yes	Yes	RL	332	12	2921	1490	Revenue minus cost
Bard et al. [11]	2001	TBN	Yes	Yes	No	RL	27	1	162	750	Delay and canx
Rosenberger et al. [50]	2003	CN	Yes	Yes	No	G	96	1	407	16	Delay and canx
Andersson and Värbrand [6]	2004	CN	Yes	Yes	Yes	RL	30	5	215	10–1100	Cancellations, swap and fleet swap
Løve et al. [40]	2005	TLN	Yes	Yes	No	RL	80	1	340	6	Revenue minus costs
Andersson [5]	2006	–	Yes	Yes	Yes	RL	30	5	215	10[a]	Cancellations, swap and fleet swap
Liu et al. [37,38]	2006/8	–	No	Yes	No	RL	7	1	70	NA	Delay, cancellations and assignment
Eggenberg et al. [23]	2007	TBN	Yes	Yes	No	RL	10	1	240	29	Flight, delay, plus maintenance cost
Zhao and Zhu [80]	2007	–	Yes	Yes	No	G	6	1	20	NA	Cost

Model types: connection network (CN), time-line network (TLN) or time-band network (TBN). Data types: generated (G) or real-life (RL) instances. Solution times are in seconds. Luo and Yu [43] is not mentioned since it is identical to Luo and Yu [41]. Yan and Lin [71] and Yan and Young [74] are not mentioned since the papers are very similar to Yan and Young [73] and Yan and Tu [72].

[a]This is the running time of the tabu search which is superior to the simulated annealing algorithm of the same paper.

The authors present a very simple example with only eight flights. Teodorović and Stojković [64] extend this work to also consider airport curfews. The described method is tested on a small example of 14 aircraft and 80 flights. Teodorović and Stojković [65] further extend their model to also include crew considerations. The proposed method is tested on 240 different randomly generated numerical examples.

2.1.2. Solution approaches based on network flow algorithms

Jarrah et al. [31] present two network flow models for solving the aircraft recovery problem: one for cancellation and one for re-timing. The models are based on the successive shortest path method presented by Gershkoff [28]. The major disadvantage of their approach is that the methods do not allow for a trade-off between cancelling and delaying in a single decision process. To evaluate the cost of delaying or cancelling the aircraft the authors construct a disutility function, which depends on the total number of passengers, the number of passengers with a down-line connection, lost crew time and disruption of maintenance. The three test scenarios in the paper are based on United Airlines' B737 fleet and a regional subdivision of the United States. In both cases, running times of the models are sufficiently small to allow their use in a real-time implementation. The solution method was successfully implemented in a decision support system at United Airlines. The impact of this implementation is reported in Rakshit et al. [48]. The papers by Cao and Kanafani [14,15] are basically extensions of this work. A quadratic zero-one programming model is presented in which the flight revenue subtracted swap and delay costs are maximized. Their model allows for a solution combining delays and cancellations. Furthermore they also take into account the issues of *ferrying* (flying an empty aircraft to an airport to cover open flights from that airport) as well as multiple aircraft type swapping. The algorithm is tested on a set of randomly generated scenarios with 20–50 airports, 30–150 aircraft, 5–12 surplus aircraft, 65–504 flights, and approximately 25% delayed aircraft. The work by Løve and Sørensen [39], in which a reproduction of the results is attempted, suggests that the description of the model is not complete.

Mathaisel [44] describes the business process as well as the IT challenges faced in the design and implementation of a decision support system for airline disruption management. The system described is based on a network of workstations; one of them working as a server, the remaining ones as clients. The author mentions that several optimization methods are embedded in the environment. The network flow model for aircraft rerouting in case of disruptions is presented, and the out-of-kilter network flow algorithm on a time-line network is used to solve the problem. The model is capable of using cancellation as well as re-timing. However, the paper does not discuss multiple types of aircraft, crew considerations, or solution times.

2.1.3. Solution approaches based on time-line networks

Another approach that has received significant attention is the representation introduced by Yan and Yang [73]. The framework is based on the classical time-line network with flight arcs, ground arcs, and overnight arcs. The final, and most general, model is derived step-by-step, so the paper essentially encompasses four models. Arcs for ferrying are added to the model. Furthermore, in order to allow for delays, time-shifted copies of the "original" flights are also added to the network. An extra set of constraints is added to the model in order to make sure that at most one of the copies is used in a solution. The model is based on a single fleet set up with no maintenance or crew scheduling considered. The authors consider the case where only one aircraft is disrupted. While the first two models of the paper are pure network flow models, the latter two are the network flow models with side constraints which are difficult to solve. In order to obtain solutions fast, all side constraints are relaxed, and the resulting model is solved using Lagrangian relaxation with the subgradient method. A feasible solution is derived from this using a Lagrangian heuristic. Near-optimal solutions were generated within a few minutes on practical problems of a considerable size. Yan and

Tu [72] describe similar methods (much of the text in the papers is in fact identical), except the models are extended to multi-fleet problems. Yan and Lin [71] looks at the case of the temporary closure of airports, but the paper remains very similar to Yan and Yang [73] and Yan and Tu [72]. Finally, Yan and Young [74] possesses identical text to the three aforementioned papers and merely adds multi-stop flights to the method. Though the modelling framework and the solution methods are identical, the proposed strategies for solving the perturbation problem are slightly different.

Thengvall et al. [66] use the model proposed in Yan and Yang [73] and adds protection arcs as well as through-flight arcs. In the evaluation of a proposed recovery schedule, such arcs make it possible to prioritize the deviation from the original schedule by giving special emphasis to flying all legs in a flight with several stops by the same aircraft. Like the previous time-line network models, this model can handle swaps, delays and cancellations. However, it does not take crew nor maintenance into consideration. The LP relaxation of the integer programming model is solved. If the solution is fractional, a heuristic is used to produce an integer solution based on the LP relaxation optimum. The approach is tested on real-life data from Continental Airlines (B757 schedule with 16 aircraft and 13 stations, and B737-100 with 27 aircraft and 30 stations). Results indicate that the approach clearly allows the construction of different recovery schedules corresponding to changes in priorities between delay minute costs, cancellation costs and the cost of deviation from the original schedule. Computing times are sufficiently small to allow it to be used in real-time. Thengvall et al. [67,68] extend the work of Thengvall et al. [66] to consider the closure of a hub, as well as multiple fleets. Three mixed-integer programming models are introduced: two so-called preference models, which are based on time-line networks for every subfleet, and a model based on time-bands, as introduced in Argüello [7].

2.1.4. Solution approaches based on time-band networks

Bard et al. [11] present an aircraft recovery model based on the *time-band network*, introduced in the Ph.D. thesis of Argüello [7]. The idea is to represent the schedule on a time-line network, leaving out all arcs except those corresponding to the flights of the schedule. No ground arcs are included. The resulting model is an integer minimum cost flow model with additional constraints that ensure each flight is either cancelled or flown by a unique aircraft. The model is also described by the same authors in Argüello et al. [9]. During the initialization step of the solution method the time-band network is generated using the original flight schedule and the predetermined time-bands. The integer programming formulation is derived from the network. Based on the optimal LP-solution, an integer-valued solution that represents the final schedule is derived. The cost is calculated and compared to the lower bound provided by the LP-relaxation. The approach is tested on a Continental Airlines B737-100 fleet schedule with 162 flights covering 30 stations and serviced by 27 aircraft. Four hundred and twenty seven test cases are reported: 27, in which one aircraft is grounded, and 100 cases for each case of two, three, four and five aircraft grounded. The time-bands are varied from 5 to 30 min, and this also allows variations between hub and spoke stations. Using the lower bounds derived and the actual cost of the solutions, the quality of the solutions can be assessed. The results depend on the time-band resolution, and are generally encouraging with respect to quality.

Eggenberg et al. [23] use a decomposed problem structure of the aircraft recovery problem, where a generalized set partitioning problem is the master problem and a resource constrained shortest path problem is a subproblem. An independent recovery network is constructed for each aircraft. Having independent time-band networks for each aircraft makes it easy to incorporate maintenance constraints through the introduction of maintenance arcs in the network for a given aircraft. In order to keep the problem small only a subset of recovery plans are considered. Data from a practical instance with up to 10 aircraft and a recovery period up to 7 days produce instances with up to 250 flights. Only larger instances require branching, while the remaining are solved in the root node. Running times suggest that the method is able to recover the proposed disruption scenarios.

2.1.5. Set partitioning models formulated on connection networks

Another approach is to formulate the aircraft recovery problem as a set partitioning model on a connection network, traditionally used for tactical planning problem formulation. Rosenberger et al. [50] formulate the aircraft recovery problem as a set partitioning model with additional time slot and capacity constraints, ensuring the airport capacity restrictions during irregular operations. The objective of the recovery is to minimize the cost of cancellations and re-routing of aircraft, and it is the responsibility of the controllers to define the parameters accordingly. For each disrupted aircraft, a preprocessing heuristic determines a number of non-disrupted aircraft with routes allowing a swap with the disrupted aircraft. The legs of these routes are included in the route generation procedure. The generated routes form the columns in the set partitioning model, which is solved with CPLEX 6.0. This approach results in running times between 6 and 16 s for three real-size problem instances. The paper reports an impressive testing using SimAir, Rosenberger et al. [49], simulating 500 days of operations for the three fleets ranging in size from 32 to 96 aircraft servicing 139–407 flights.

Using the connection network as the underlying network, Andersson and Värbrand [6] base their approach on the set packing problem with generalized upper bound (GUB) constraints, which ensure that each aircraft is assigned exactly one route. The problem is solved with a Lagrangian relaxation-based heuristic and a method based on the Dantzig–Wolfe decomposition. Two of the three approaches implemented in Andersson [4]. The subproblem is a shortest path problem with time windows and linear node costs. To ensure fast convergence a heuristic is developed to solve the subproblem. Computational results are based on data from a domestic Swedish carrier that operates five fleets with a total of 30 aircraft. Instances consist of 98–215 flights and 19–32 airports. Smaller instances can be solved with the solution method based on the Dantzig–Wolfe decomposition, while the running times are excessive on the larger instances. Comparable results are also achieved for the Lagrangian relaxation-based heuristic.

It should be mentioned that the working papers by Clarke [18,19] also propose a column generation model based on a generalized set partitioning model, and a substantial number of extra constraints is added to incorporate crew availability, slot allocation and maintenance. The objective sums the cost associated with reassigning flights, operating costs, predetermined passenger revenue spill costs and operating revenue. A tree-search heuristic and a set packing-based optimal solution method are proposed. Each of the developed methods is based on a three-phase procedure: first, potential flight sequences adhering to all operational constraints are generated, second, the sequences are assigned to operating aircraft, and finally, the structure of the problem is revised. The case studies have multiple aircraft types, 35–177 aircraft, 180–612 flights and 15 or 37 airports.

2.1.6. Metaheuristic approaches

As the field of aircraft recovery became more popular, contributions based on metaheuristics began to appear. Argüello et al. [8] describe a heuristic approach based on a Greedy Randomized Adaptive Search Procedure (GRASP) for the reconstruction of aircraft routes when one or several aircraft are grounded. Maintenance is not considered and the method is only made for a single fleet recovery situation. An initial solution based on the cancellation of the affected flight is altered using three different neighborhood operations: flight route augmentation, partial route exchange and simple circuit cancellation. The method is tested on B757 fleet data from Continental Airlines with 16 aircraft and 42 flights. The results obtained by the proposed method are clearly superior to just cancelling the flights serviced by the grounded aircraft.

Optimization methods based on local search are presented in Løve et al. [40], based on the master thesis by Løve and Sørensen [39]. The heuristics are based on a network formulation, where nodes are either aircraft or flights. Assigning an aircraft to a given flight is done by selecting the edge connecting the aircraft and flight for the solution. Based on this representation the existing solution is altered by swaps that exchange flights between two aircraft. Using the so-called "ghost aircraft", ferrying and cancellations can be incorporated. The actions are weighted in the objective function, which makes it possible to obtain solutions with different characteristics by changing the weights accordingly. Although "true" weights are difficult to assess, this approach has been used by several researchers, e.g. Andersson [5]. For more on the estimation of passenger delay costs, fuel burn, etc. see Cook et al. [22]. The data used in Løve et al. [40] are randomly generated. However, a feasibility study on real data from British Airways with 80 aircraft, 44 airports, and 340 flights has been carried out as part of the DESCARTES project described in Kohl et al. [33]; this confirmed the results from the randomly generated data.

The issue of generating multiple solutions with different characteristics is embedded in both the tabu search and simulated annealing metaheuristics presented in Andersson [5]. Both metaheuristics are based on a local search subroutine that allows flights to be delayed or cancelled and planes to be swapped. The representation of the solution is quite similar to Argüello et al. [8]. The neighborhood is defined by first selecting two aircraft and then adding their flights to the cancelled flights to form a pool. From this pool a new route for each aircraft is generated. The heuristics in the paper produce a set of ranked, structurally different (non-dominated) solutions. Tests are carried out on instances originating from a Swedish domestic carrier. Both methods produce encouraging results, although the tabu search consistently produces better results for the same computing resources. For both methods good solutions are often found in less than 60 s, sometimes even below 15 s.

Liu et al. [37] use multi-objective evolutionary algorithms to construct new feasible aircraft routings. The method only considers a single fleet. The options are to swap flights between aircraft or delay flights. Cancellation is not allowed, nor is ferrying. The objective function consists of three terms: delay costs, swap costs and a cost of assigning a given aircraft to a specific flight. The chromosome in the algorithm represents the allocation of flights to specific aircraft. The developed algorithm was tested on the flight schedule of a Taiwan domestic airline consisting of seven aircraft and 70 flights. No running times are given. In Liu et al. [38], the approach is extended to a multi-fleet airline. It is, however, difficult to extract the extensions made to accommodate multiple fleets. In the flight schedule used as a test case, the problem is decomposed into separate problems for each fleet.

2.1.7. Special cases

The problem of optimizing under the Ground Delay Program (GDP) of the US aviation authorities (FAA) addressed in Luo and Yu [41–43] can be considered a special case of the aircraft recovery. The problem can be defined as follows. Given a set of arriving flights and a set of landing slots provided by the FAA, the landing of the incoming flight must be adjusted in order to minimize the maximum delay of outgoing flights. The problem is modelled as an assignment problem with side constraints. The authors develop valid inequalities to further strengthen the formulation, and a heuristic based on solving the landing assignment problem is developed. The two papers Luo and Yu [41,43] are identical.

The paper Talluri [61] investigates a special case of changing the assignment of equipment type for a specified leg while maintaining feasibility of the schedule. Central to the approach is the *swap opportunity* which is defined as change of equipment type where the new assignment is also valid. The method is based on classifying swap opportunities based upon the number of overnight equipment changes involved in the swap. The paper proposes a polynomial time algorithm for solutions with same-day swaps. Testing is very limited and only documented by a single instance.

A grey programming approach is presented by Zhao and Zhu [80]. Grey programming is a part of the grey system theory, where a system is called "white" when the system information is fully known, "black" when the system information is unknown, and "gray" when the system information is partially known. The authors transform the model of Jarrah et al. [31] to the concepts of grey programming. The approach includes surplus aircraft and the possibility of delays and cancellations. Testing is only done on one very small case of six crew members and 20 flights. Two schedule solutions to the test problem are presented, without describing the essence of the disruption or the computational details.

A view which is seldom adopted in the recovery literature is the view of the airport. The paper by Filar et al. [26] describes techniques that enhance the utilization of airport capacities. In addition, methods that limit damage or provide recovery in disruptive situations are reviewed. The paper describes methods involving the traffic management, airport authorities and airlines.

2.2. Crew recovery

The majority of publications formulate the crew recovery problem under assumption that the flight schedule is recovered before the crew re-scheduling decisions are made, thereby following the hierarchical structure of the disruption recovery in practice. These publications include Wei et al. [69] and Song et al. [57], which are almost identical, Stojković et al. [60], Guo [29], Nissen and Haase [47], and Medard and Sawhney [45]. When the flight schedule is fixed, the crew recovery problems can be formulated as tactical crew pairing or rostering models. Other authors extend the classical crew scheduling formulation of the recovery problem by adding a set of decision variables, which allow to cancel flight legs. This formulation is presented in Johnson et al. [32], Lettovsky et al. [36] and Yu et al. [78]. Finally, problem formulations of the crew recovery problem, which explicitly account for departure delays, are reported in Stojković and Soumis [58,59], Abdelgahny et al. [1] and Zhao et al. [81]. Each minute of departure delay is given a cost in the objective function, while the flight precedences and delay limitations are ensured by constraints in the models.

The real-time nature of the recovery problems requires short computation times, which can be achieved by reducing the dimensions of optimization problems. Two general methods for reducing the problem space are used by various authors. First, the *time window technique* is applied. A part of the flight schedule used in the recovery problem is limited by a time window, which spans from the time the disruption occurs up to a certain number of hours into the future. The length of the time window varies from a few hours until the rest of the day of operation. Second, the number of crew members included into the recovery is limited by only including the *affected crew members* and a number of selected *candidate crew members*. The set of candidate crew members is necessary in order to expand the solution space and ensure that a high quality solution can be found. An example of reducing the recovery problem space is shown in Fig. 5, following the notation of Medard and Sawhney [45]. The authors refer to the fixed part of the schedule before and after

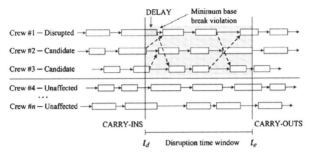

Fig. 5. Reducing the problem space of a crew recovery problem.

the disruption as the *carry in* and the *carry out* flights, respectively. In the given example a single crew member is delayed on the second flight leg of the day. The disruption leaves the schedule infeasible, since the rule that specifies the minimum duration of a break at the base station is violated. The time window is then defined from the time of the disruption, t_d, until the end of the day of operation, t_e. Two candidate crew members are used to construct the recovery solution, whereas the remaining crew rosters are left unaffected by the disruption.

In the remaining part of this section we review literature contributions dedicated to the recovery of crew resources, with or without a possibility to alter the flight schedule by delays or cancellations. The proposed methods are summarized in Table 3, where the publications are listed in order of appearance in the literature.

2.2.1. Crew recovery with fixed flight schedules

Wei et al. [69] and Song et al. [57] model the crew pairing repair problem as an integer multicommodity network flow problem on a connection network. The challenge is to repair the pairings that are broken and the objective is to return the entire system to its original schedule as soon as possible while minimizing the operational cost. The authors use the time window technique including only a fraction of the full schedule into the recovery problem. The problem is formulated as a generalized set covering problem, which is solved using a depth-first branch-and-bound search algorithm.

Stojković et al. [60] use the time window technique and the set of crew candidates in order to limit the solution space of the crew recovery. The problem is formulated as an integer nonlinear multicommodity network flow problem, which is decomposed into a set partitioning master problem and a shortest path with resource constraints subproblem. A column generation procedure within a branch-and-bound tree is used to obtain integer solutions, and an early branching strategy is applied to accelerate the solution process. Solutions to the one-day period test scenarios were found within half a minute, while the seven-days period test scenarios took between 4 and 20 min to resolve.

Medard and Sawhney [45] stress that the crew recovery problem is structurally different from the crew pairing and rostering problems because contrary to the planning phase, these two subproblems have to be solved at the same time in the recovery phase. This means that both rules on the pairing and the rostering level have to be respected. Thus, the recovery challenge is to merge the pairing characteristics into a rostering problem which is modelled at the flight level. The authors propose an optimization model which is the flight-based equivalent to the original pairing-based rostering model, where the re-assigned flights replace the pairings. The optimization model is formulated as a set covering model, which is solved using column generation. The columns are generated by finding shortest paths using either a depth-first search strategy or a reduced cost column generator. The latter approach performs worse than the depth-first search method due to a large overhead for setting up the duty network, and the authors conclude that the column generation framework has to be refined. Single base test problems are resolved within approximately one and a half minute, while the multi-base test problems could take several minutes to be resolved.

Nissen and Haase [47] propose a duty-based formulation for the crew recovery problem, which is different from the earlier published modelling approaches. This modelling approach is especially well suited for solving the crew disruption for European airlines, as these, contrary to the North American airlines, employ fixed monthly crew rates, which should be taken into consideration when solving a crew disruption. The duty-based approach means that the disruption is resolved within each duty period. This implies shorter recovery horizons which leads to a reduction of the problem size. The authors propose a branch-and-price-based solution method using a set covering formulation as the master problem and a resource constrained shortest path as the pricing problem. The approach is tested on a number of scenarios covering realistic disruptions from the delay of single flight to a several hour long closure of a hub airport. The authors conclude that the running times are acceptable for operational environment for the best choice of carefully tested model parameters, e.g. the length of the recovery period.

Guo [29] presents a decision support framework for recovering airline crew rosters, which is also reported in Guo [30]. The crew recovery problem is formulated as a set partitioning problem, aimed at minimizing the modifications from the planned schedule. Two solution methods are implemented, a standard column generation with LP relaxation of the set partitioning problem and a heuristic method based on a hybrid of a genetic algorithm with a local search. At the preprocessing step, a solution strategy is chosen using the *strategy mapping*, which is the main focus of the article. The strategy mapping provides a method to prioritize alternative solution methods for solving the crew recovery problem by evaluating different criteria, such as additional cost for recovering the schedule, solution time, the number of crew members that need to be notified, the period of time starting from the first updated flight to the last one, and the number of disturbances to crew. A solution strategy is a combination of solution methods (column generation and genetic algorithm) and relevant parameters, as for instance the length of the recovery period. A case study containing data from a European airline with several home bases is presented. The disruption involves two delayed flights, one cancelled flight, two new flights, 188 crew members and 85 daily flights on average during a five days recovery period. The authors present the way to compare three chosen

Table 3
Overview of proposed methods for the crew recovery problem.

Authors	Year	Functionality			Data	Dimensions		Solution time	Objectives
		Canx	Retime	Indiv. roster		Crew	Flights		
Johnson et al. [32]	1994	Yes	No	No	NA	NA	NA	NA	Pairing, stand-by, deadheading costs
Wei et al. [69]	1997	No	No	No	G	18	51	6	Pairing cost
Stojković et al. [60]	1998	No	No	Yes	RL	32	210	1200	Pairing, deadheading, undercovering costs
Lettovsky et al. [36]	2000	Yes	No	No	RL	38	122	97	Pairing, cancel flight costs
Stojković and Soumis [58]	2001	No	Yes	Yes	RL	59	190	13	Modifications, uncovered flights, flight delays.
Yu et al. [78]	2003	Yes	No	No	RL	NA	40	321	Deadheading, modifications, uncovered flight costs
Guo [29]	2004	No	No	Yes	NA	NA	NA	NA	Stand-by, modifications, operating costs
Abdelgahny et al. [1]	2004	No	Yes	Yes	RL	121	NA	2	Deadheading, stand-by, swap, flight delay costs
Stojković and Soumis [59]	2005	No	Yes	Yes	RL	177	190	5105	Modifications, uncovered flights, flight delays
Nissen and Haase [47]	2006	No	No	Yes	RL	NA	860	345	Modifications to original schedule
Medard and Sawhney [45]	2007	No	No	Yes	NA	885	NA	840	Illegal crew, uncovered flights, and affected crew
Castro and Oliveira [16]	2007	No	No	Yes	RL	NA	NA	25	Crew cost
Zhao et al. [81]	2007	No	Yes	Yes	G	6	20	NA	Crew, flight delay cost

Solution times are in seconds.

criteria in order to choose between two solution method strategies, and conclude that in the presented case study the genetic algorithm solution method is preferred to the column generation method, and produces an acceptable solution within approximately 3 min.

An implementation of the distributed multi-agent system (MAS) represents the operations control center of an airline is presented in two very similar publications by Castro and Oliveira [16,17]. The MAS includes a crew recovery agent, an aircraft recovery agent and a passenger recovery agent. The papers are focused on the architecture and test experiments of the crew recovery agent. A monitoring agent class of the crew recovery agent is responsible for monitoring crew events (e.g. non-assignments for some flights) and reporting to the crew finder agent class. The crew finder collects a list of solutions to the problem from the algorithmic agent classes and chooses the cheapest one using the crew payroll information. The authors do not mention what kind of algorithms and heuristics are used in the algorithmic agent classes to find solutions to the recovery problem. Only one test scenario was reported, where 15 crew members with different ranks were set to be absent from their duties at the same base. The results produced by the MAS were compared to the results obtained by a human operator, comparing the solution times and the costs of solutions expressed through the crew payment. The MAS recovery agent came up with a cheaper solution in 25 s compared to the one and a half minutes, which took the operator to find a solution.

2.2.2. Crew recovery with flight cancellations

To our knowledge, the 1994 paper of Johnson et al. [32] is the first published work regarding the airline crew recovery. The problem is formulated as a set covering problem with decision variables allowing flight cancellations, determining the number of deadheading crew on a flight leg and forcing crew to stay at base in the recovery solution. The authors consider the recovery of pilot pairings when a single flight is delayed at a single airport. The approach for identifying crew to be involved in the recovery solution is proposed. Experiments are conducted based on data files supplied by Northwest Airlines. All pairings for the crew recovery problem are generated a priori from a time-line network and the set covering problem is solved using MINTO [46]. Three small test scenarios are described, but the running times are not presented. This research laid the ground for the work by Lettovsky et al. [36], who use the same problem formulation. Preprocessing techniques are used to extract a subset of the schedule for rescheduling. A fast crew pairing generator constructs feasible continuations of partially flown crew trips, and an efficient tree-based data structure is used for storing generated pairings. The crew recovery model is solved with LP relaxation and a branch-and-bound. A three-step branching strategy is used, resolving first cancellation variables, then deadheading variables, and finally performing constraint branching. Test results based on data from a US carrier demonstrate that the applied techniques can be used for managing medium-sized disruptions. The authors conclude that further research is required to handle large-scale disruptions.

Yu et al. [78] report a successful implementation of a crew recovery decision support system CrewSolver in Continental Airlines. The system is interconnected with other systems of the airline. The optimization engine of CrewSolver uses the depth-first search procedure developed by Wei et al. [69], and can generate several solutions to give the operator a flexibility to choose the most suitable recovery solution. Reported test problems with up to 20 affected flights are solved within 1 min, while it takes between 3 and 5 min on average to resolve larger instances.

2.2.3. Crew recovery with departure delays

Stojković and Soumis [58] extend the crew recovery problem of Stojković et al. [60] with a possibility to delay scheduled flights explicitly through the problem formulation. Some flights have fixed departure times, some others have more flexible times in terms of a flight specific time window. The problem is formulated as a multi-commodity network flow with additional constraints, and is solved using column generation with a master problem and a subproblem per pilot. The solution may include the use of reserve pilots, treated as extra artificial commodities in the problem. The model and solution method has been tested on three problems. The largest problem has 59 pilots and 190 flights, of which 52 are originally delayed. All problems are tested with and without reserve pilots, allowing delays of flights and with a fixed flight schedule. The results are encouraging, both in terms of quality and in terms of computing times. Stojković and Soumis [59] builds on the model derived in Stojković and Soumis [58], but extends this to work with multiple crew members. This makes the situation addressed more realistic. The extension is achieved by using a number of copies of each flight corresponding to the number of crew required. A set of constraints ensure that the departure times for all copies of each flight are added to the model. The solution process is similar to that described in Stojković and Soumis [58]. Three different models are tested: one corresponding to that from the previous work with strict flight covering constraints, one in which there is a linear cost for missing crew members, and one with a cost for each flight with missing crew. It is demonstrated that using both the second and the third model, substantial improvements compared to the initial situation can be obtained. However, the solution times experienced for large problems are prohibitive in an on-line situation (more than an hour).

Abdelgahny et al. [1] address the problem of flight crew recovery for an airline with a hub-and-spoke network structure. Several preprocessing steps are applied, including shifting the problem occurrences from the spokes to hubs, adding undisturbed crew to the recovery in order to cover open flights, grouping flights into resource-independent sets, etc. The assignment of crew members to flights is formulated as a mixed integer program, where linear variables for flight departure times allow to minimize the total flight delay in the objective function, while the assignment variables take care of the minimum cost crew assignment to the flights. The recovery horizon is divided into a set of consecutive stages, and the crew recovery problem is solved at each recovery stage in a sequence, using CPLEX Callable Library solver. One disruption scenario from the operations of a major US airline is used as a test case with 18 disrupted crew members and 121 candidate crew members. The number of affected flights is not listed in the paper. The recovery problem was solved within 2 min. The problem formulation of Abdelgahny et al. [1] is transformed into a grey programming model by Zhao et al. [81]. Linear decision variables for departure and arrival times of flights and the linear parameter defining the ready time for crew in the model of Abdelgahny et al. [1] are defined as grey variables in Zhao et al. [81]. A local search heuristic is applied to solve the problem. The basic framework of the implementation is the same as Zhao and Zhu [80], which considers the aircraft recovery. The authors present the same small test case as in Zhao and Zhu [80] without any further details.

2.3. Integrated and passenger recovery

Integrating the recovery of several resources (aircraft, pilots, flight attendants) in the same system is a difficult task, and only a few attempts to integrate resources has been presented in the operations research literature. The 1997 Ph.D. thesis of Lettovsky [35] is the first presentation of a truly integrated approach, although only parts of it are implemented. The thesis presents a linear mixed-integer mathematical problem that maximizes total profit to the airline while capturing availability of the three most important resources: aircraft, crew and passengers. The formulation has three parts corresponding to each of the resources, that is, crew assignment, aircraft routing and passenger flow. In a decomposition scheme these three parts are "controlled" by a master problem denoted the Schedule Recovery Model (SRM). The solution algorithm is derived by applying Benders decomposition. The SRM determines a plan for cancellation, delays and equipment assignment considering landing restrictions. Then for each equipment type f the ARM$_f$ (aircraft recovery model) is solved, and for each crew group c the CRM$_c$ (crew recovery model) is solved returning Benders feasibility or optimality cuts to the SRM. Finally, the PFM (passenger flow model) evaluates the passenger flow. In this way the built-in hierarchy of the framework to a large extent resembles the present manual process at many airlines.

Another work on integrated recovery is reported by Abdelghany et al. [2]. The authors address the situation, where a Ground Delay Program is issued by the US authorities, often due to anticipated adverse weather conditions. A proactive schedule recovery tool DSTAR aims at integrating aircraft, cockpit crew and cabin crew. The recovery process is divided into separate stages in a rolling horizon. Every stage is limited by a number of independent flights that cannot share resources and can therefore be re-assigned to aircraft and crew at the same stage without "competing" for the same resources. At each stage, a simulation model produces the list of disrupted flights for the rest of the horizon, and an optimization solver makes minimum cost resource assignments. The authors present a mixed integer program similar to the formulation of Abdelgahny et al. [1], but where several resources can be rescheduled and flight legs can be cancelled. The authors describe an application scenario with 522 cockpit crew, 1360 pilots, and 2040 cabin crew, where DSTAR saves 8.7% of the total delay. Also, a systematic experimental investigation is reported, which shows that DSTAR offers short computing times and gives savings of approximately 5%. The approach of the paper is very promising when considering larger disruptions, which are foreseeable a number of hours ahead.

The next two papers focus on passenger recovery. Recovering passenger itineraries is an important issue for the airlines, not only due to the operational costs related to passenger delays, but also because continuous flight delays and cancellations can lead to major passenger dissatisfaction and a potential loss of goodwill. When recovering passenger itineraries, it is, however, important to ensure feasibility in the aircraft and crew schedules. Hence, we consider the passenger recovery being an integrated recovery task.

Bratu and Barnhart [13] present two passenger recovery models, which allow to delay or cancel flight departures, and assign reserve crew and aircraft to the flight legs. The models are based on the flight schedule network, where every flight is represented by several arcs, one for each departure time, in order to incorporate the re-timing of flight departures. The same technique is used in e.g. Andersson [4] and Thengvall et al. [66]. While crew regulations for the reserve crew are incorporated into the models, recovery of the disrupted crew is not considered. In the passenger delay model (PDM) delay costs are modelled more exactly by explicitly modelling disruptions, recovery options and delays costs, whereas in the disrupted passenger metric (DPM) model delay costs are only approximate. Based on the single instance for which both methods are tested, the execution time for PDM is roughly a factor 25 higher than for DPM. An operations control center simulator is developed in order to test the models, and data from the domestic operations of a major US airline are provided. The data set contains 302 aircraft divided into four fleets, 74 airports and three hubs. Furthermore, 83,869 passengers on 9925 different passenger itineraries per day are served. Three different scenarios with different levels of disruption are presented. Execution times ranges from 201 to 5042 s. Due to its excessive execution times the PDM is considered unfit for operational use. For all scenarios the DPM generate solutions with noticeable reductions in passenger delays and disruptions.

Another recent work on the passenger recovery problem is reported by Zhang and Hansen [79]. The authors introduce ground transportation modes as an alternative to the passenger recovery by air during disruptions in hub-and-spoke networks. An integer model with a nonlinear objective function allows to substitute flight legs with other form for transportation, respecting the ground transportation times. The objectives of the model are aimed at minimizing passenger costs due to delay, cancellation or substitution, as well as at minimizing the operating cost of the transportation. The problem is solved by first relaxing the integrality constraints and then solving the nonlinear program. After fixing all flight decision variables with the value greater than 0.5 to one and the rest to zero, the original problem is solved in order to find the values for decision variables representing the number of passengers on departure flights. A numerical example includes 40 flights in a 4 h time window. The authors present test results for a disrupted situation, where the capacity of the hub airport drops to half the normal level for 5 h. If the ground transportation substitution is not allowed, 90 passengers are disrupted. With intermodal substitution the number of disrupted passengers decreases to 14. The running time for solving the problem is approximately 1000 s.

3. Disruption management by robustness

An interesting research topic closely related to disruption management is *robust planning* or *schedule robustness*. The goal in robust planning is to make flight and crew schedules and aircraft rotations less sensitive to disruptions. Robustness can be seen as a pro-active way of handling disruptions. The central idea is to incorporate the possibility to either absorb disruptions and remain feasible or facilitate an easy recovery in case of a disruption by enhancing the possibilities of different types of recovery actions. A report from the US Government Accountability Office [27] mentions examples of already established manual methods used by airlines to improve robustness. Among those there are adding buffers in the schedules, having standby reserve crew, partitioning aircraft or crew schedules into sections in order to keep delays occurred in one section from spreading to the remaining flight network.

The first type of robustness is *absorption robustness*. The general goal is to keep the plans feasible in case of smaller disruption events and avoid the knock-on effects. The most obvious way of introducing absorption robustness is to build time buffers into the schedule. However, buffers require a trade-off between robustness and cost: the larger the buffers are, the more robust and costly the operation is in general. There are two important issues when applying the absorption robustness to the schedule. Firstly, how much buffer time is an airline willing to invest in order to increase robustness of the operation, and secondly, exactly where should the buffer times be placed in the schedule? Another way to introduce absorption robustness is to avoid short turn-around times when building the schedules. It should be mentioned that the absorption robustness alone is not able to handle severe disruptions. In case of major disruption good recovery measures are required in order to restore the operation.

Recovery robustness aims at designing rotations and schedules so that the plans fit well to the existing recovery strategies when a disruption occurs. The most common recovery strategies are crew and aircraft swaps, delaying flight departures and cancelling flights covered by the same aircraft rotation cycle. The schedules with incorporated recovery robustness have many possibilities for crew swapping or many short cycles in the aircraft rotations. These plans are more expensive than cost-optimal plans. However, considering the cost of recovery from disruptions, the recovery robust schedules turn out to be cheaper than cost-optimal schedules. Again, there is a trade-off between the cost and the robustness of the schedule.

Robust planning is a difficult task, particularly due to the unpredictability of disruptions. Recently there have been efforts to set up a theoretical framework to evaluate and quantify robustness. The situation, however, resembles that of approximation algorithms: if mathematical proofs are to be given, the results turn out to be weak, and the methods and strategies are far from those known to be most efficient in practice. The need for simulation tools is therefore apparent, and a number of such tools have been built, the most well known and complete being SimAir developed by Rosenberger et al. [49]. More and more publications on robust scheduling appear in the literature. Rosenberger et al. [51], Smith and Johnson [55] consider robust fleet assignment, Ageeva [3], Wu [70], Lan et al. [34] deal with robust aircraft schedules, and Ehrgott and Ryan [24], Schaefer et al. [53], Schaefer and Nemhauser [52], Yen and Birge [75], Shebalov and Klabjan [54], Sohoni et al. [56], Tekiner et al. [62] study robustness in crew schedules, among others. For a comprehensive review of robust planning publications, terminology and concepts, refer to Clausen and Rezanova [21].

4. Discussion and further research

The field of disruption management in the airline industry has been increasingly active over the last decade. In the last years commercial tools for disruption management have also become available. The majority of the publications concentrate on dedicated crew or aircraft recovery, and only a very few researchers integrate recovery of resources during the day of operation. As it is today, the airlines' requirements for recovery decision support systems are still substantially different from the services offered by commercial tools and from most of the prototype tools proposed in the literature.

The optimization problem formulations of recovery models are more or less identical to the formulations of the tactical scheduling problems, like multicommodity network flow problems or set covering/partitioning problems with side constraints. Researchers apply solution methods similar to the state-of-the-art within solution approaches for the tactical planning problems, while reducing the problem space by limiting the recovery time period and the number of crew members or aircraft included into recovery.

The concept of robust planning and methods for achieving robustness in schedules has received an increasing interest over the last years, and promising results have begun to appear. Robustness can be seen as the proactive counterpart of recovery, and we believe that these two concepts will be central in the process of minimizing the effect of disruptions on the daily operation of airline companies.

There is a large number of subjects for further research within the field of disruption management. We mention just a few of these here: quality versus computing time for both dedicated and integrated recovery methods, disruption management versus robustness, disruption management and robustness for other transportation industries, e.g. the railway industry. Therefore we expect that disruption management will be a very active research area over the coming years, both in the context of transportation, and more generally within other areas of logistics, e.g. as a part of supply chain management optimization.

References

[1] Abdelgahny A, Ekollu G, Narisimhan R, Abdelgahny K. A proactive crew recovery decision support tool for commercial airlines during irregular operations. Annals of Operations Research 2004;127:309–31.
[2] Abdelghany KF, Abdelghany AF, Ekollu G. An integrated decision support tool for airlines schedule recovery during irregular operations. European Journal of Operational Research 2008;185:825–48.
[3] Ageeva Y. Approaches to incorporating robustness into airline scheduling. Master's thesis, Massachusetts Institute of Technology; 2000.
[4] Andersson T. The flight perturbation problem—operational aircraft rescheduling. PhD thesis, Linköping University, Sweden, 2001.
[5] Andersson T. Solving the flight perturbation problem with meta heuristics. Journal of Heuristics 2006;12:37–53.
[6] Andersson T, Värbrand P. The flight perturbation problem. Transportation Planning and Technology 2004;27:91–117.
[7] Argüello M. Framework for exact solutions and heuristics for approximate solutions to airlines' irregular operations control aircraft routing problem. PhD thesis, The University of Texas at Austin; 1997.
[8] Argüello M, Bard J, Yu G. A GRASP for aircraft routing in response to groundings and delays. Journal of Combinatorial Optimization 1997;5:211–28.
[9] Argüello M, Bard J, Yu G. Models and methods for managing airline irregular operations. In: Yu G, editor. Operations research in the airline industry. Boston: Kluwer Academic Publishers; 1998.
[10] Ball M, Barnhart C, Nemhauser G, Odoni A. Air transportation: irregular operations and control. In: Barnhart C, Laporte G, editors. Handbook in OR & MS, vol. 14. Amsterdam: Elsevier; 2007.
[11] Bard J, Yu G, Argüello M. Optimizing aircraft routings in response to groundings and delays. IIE Transactions 2001;33:931–47.
[12] Barnhart C, Cohn A, Johnson E, Klapjan D, Nemhauser G, Vance P. Airline crew scheduling. In: Hall RW, editor. Handbook of transportation science. Boston: Kluwer Academic Publishers; 2003.
[13] Bratu S, Barnhart C. Flight operations recovery: new approaches considering passenger recovery. Journal of Scheduling 2006;9:279–98.
[14] Cao J-M, Kanafani A. Real-time decision support for integration of airline flight cancellations and delays, part I: mathematical formulation. Transportation Planning and Technology 1997;20:183–99.
[15] Cao J-M, Kanafani A. Real-time decision support for integration of airline flight cancellations and delays, part II: algorithm and computational experiments. Transportation Planning and Technology 1997;20:201–17.
[16] Castro AJ, Oliveira E. Using specialized agents in a distributed MAS to solve airline operations problems: a case study. In: 2007 IEEE/WIC/ACM international conference on intelligent agent technology (IAT'07), 2007. p. 473–6.
[17] Castro AJ, Oliveira E. A distributed multi-agent system to solve airline operations problems. In: ICEIS 2007. Proceedings of the ninth international conference on enterprise information systems, vol. AIDSS, Funchal, Madeira, Portugal, 2007. p. 22–30.
[18] Clarke M. Development of heuristic procedures for flight rescheduling in the aftermath of irregular airline operations. Working paper, October 1997.
[19] Clarke M. The airline schedule recovery problem. Working paper, October 1997.

[20] Clarke M. Irregular airline operations: a review of the state-of-the-practice in airline operations control center. Journal of Air Transport Management 1998;4:67–76.
[21] Clausen J, Rezanova NJ. Proactive disruption management—developments in robust planning. Working paper, 2009.
[22] Cook A, Tanner G, Williams V, Meise G. Dynamic cost indexing—managing airline delay costs. Journal of Air Transport Management 2009;15:26–35.
[23] Eggenberg N, Bierlaire M, Salani M. A column generation algorithm for disrupted airline schedules. Technical report, Ecole Polytechnique Federale de Lausanne; 2007.
[24] Ehrgott M, Ryan D. Constructing robust crew schedules with bicriteria optimization. Journal of Multi-Criteria Decision Analysis 2002;11:139–50.
[25] Filar J, Manyem P, White K. How airlines and airports recover from schedule perturbations: a survey. Annals of Operations Research 2001;108:315–33.
[26] Filar JA, Manyem P, Panton DM, White K. A model for adaptive rescheduling of flights in emergencies (MARFE). Journal of Industrial and Management Optimization 2007;3:335–56.
[27] GAO-08-1041R. Airline crew scheduling. Published by the United States Government Accountability Office, September 2008.
[28] Gershkoff I. Aircraft shortage evaluator. Presented at ORSA/TIMS Joint National Meeting, St. Louis, MO, October 1987.
[29] Guo Y. A decision support framework for the airline crew schedule disruption management with strategy mapping. In: Operations research proceedings 2004. Berlin, Heidelberg: Springer; 2005.
[30] Guo Y. Decision support systems for airline crew recovery. PhD thesis, University of Paderborn; 2005.
[31] Jarrah A, Yu G, Krishnamurthy N, Rakshit A. A decision support framework for airline flight cancellations and delays. Transportation Science 1993;27:266–80.
[32] Johnson V, Lettovsky L, Nemhauser GL, Pandit R, Querido R. Final report to Northwest Airlines on the crew recovery problem. Technical report, The Logistic Institute, Georgia Institute of Technology, Atlanta, USA; 1994.
[33] Kohl N, Larsen A, Larsen J, Ross A, Tiourine S. Airline disruption management—perspectives, experiences and outlook. Journal of Air Transport Management 2007;13:149–62.
[34] Lan S, Clarke J-P, Barnhart C. Planning for robust airline operations: optimizing aircraft routings and flight departure times to minimize passenger disruptions. Transportation Science 2006;40:15–28.
[35] Lettovsky L. Airline operations recovery: an optimization approach. PhD thesis, Georgia Institute of Technology, Atlanta, USA; 1997.
[36] Lettovsky L, Johnson E, Nemhauser G. Airline crew recovery. Transportation Science 2000;34:337–48.
[37] Liu T-K, Jeng C-R, Liu Y-T, Tzeng J-Y. Applications of multi-objective evolutionary algorithm to airline disruption management. In: 2006 IEEE international conference on systems, man and cybernetics. New York: IEEE; 2006. p. 4130–5.
[38] Liu T-K, Jeng C-R, Chang Y-H. Disruption management of an inequality-based multi-fleet airline schedule by a multi-objective genetic algorithm. Transportation Planning and Technology 2008;31:613–39.
[39] Løve M, Sørensen K. Disruption management in the airline industry. Master's thesis, Informatics and Mathematical Modelling (IMM), Technical University of Denmark (DTU); March 2001.
[40] Løve M, Sørensen K, Larsen J, Clausen J. Using heuristics to solve the dedicated aircraft recovery problem. Central European Journal of Operations Research 2005;13:189–207.
[41] Luo S, Yu G. On the airline schedule perturbation problem caused by the ground delay program. Transportation Science 1997;31:298–311.
[42] Luo S, Yu G. Airline schedule perturbation problem: landing and takeoff with nonsplitable resource for the ground delay program. In: Yu G, editor. Operations research in the airline industry. Boston: Kluwer Academic Publishers; 1998.
[43] Luo S, Yu G. Airline schedule perturbation problem: ground delay program with splitable resources. In: Yu G, editor. Operations research in the airline industry. Boston: Kluwer Academic Publishers; 1998.
[44] Mathaisel D. Decision support for airline system operations control and irregular operations. Computers & Operations Research 1996;23:1083–98.
[45] Medard C, Sawhney N. Airline crew scheduling: from planning to operations. European Journal of Operational Research 2007;183:1013–27.
[46] Nemhauser GL, Savelsbergh MW, Sigismondi GC. MINTO, a mixed INTeger optimizer. Operation Research Letters 1994;15:47–58.
[47] Nissen R, Haase K. Duty-period-based network model for crew rescheduling in European airlines. Journal of Scheduling 2006;9:255–78.
[48] Rakshit A, Krishnamurthy N, Yu G. System operations advisor: a real-time decision support system for managing airline operations at united airlines. Interfaces 1996;26:50–8.
[49] Rosenberger J, Schaefer A, Goldsmans D, Johnson E, Kleywegt A, Nemhauser G. A stochastic model of airline operations. Transportation Science 2002;36: 357–77.
[50] Rosenberger J, Johnson E, Nemhauser G. Rerouting aircraft for airline recovery. Transportation Science 2003;37:408–21.
[51] Rosenberger JM, Johnson EL, Nemhauser GL. A robust fleet-assignment model with hub isolation and short cycles. Transportation Science 2004;38:357–68.
[52] Schaefer A, Nemhauser G. Improving airline operational performance through schedule perturbation. Annals of Operations Research 2006;144:3–16.
[53] Schaefer A, Johnson E, Kleywegt A, Nemhauser G. Airline crew scheduling under uncertainty. Transportation Science 2005;39:340–8.
[54] Shebalov S, Klabjan D. Robust airline crew pairing: move-up crews. Transportation Science 2006;40:300–12.
[55] Smith BC, Johnson EL. Robust airline fleet assignment: imposing station purity using station decomposition. Transportation Science 2006;40:497–516.
[56] Sohoni M, Johnson E, Bailey T. Operational airline reserve crew planning. Journal of Scheduling 2006;9:203–21.
[57] Song M, Wei G, Yu G. A decision support framework for crew management during airline irregular operations. In: Yu G, editor. Operations research in the airline industry. Boston: Kluwer Academic Publishers; 1998.
[58] Stojković M, Soumis F. An optimization model for the simultaneous operational flight and pilot scheduling problem. Management Science 2001;47:1290–305.
[59] Stojković M, Soumis F. The operational flight and multi-crew scheduling problem. Yugoslavian Journal of Operations Research 2005;15:25–48.
[60] Stojković M, Soumis F, Desrosiers J. The operational airline crew scheduling problem. Transportation Science 1998;32:232–45.
[61] Talluri K. Swapping applications in a daily airline fleet assignment. Transportation Science 1996;30:237–48.
[62] Tekiner V, Birbil SI, Bülbül K. Robust crew pairing for managing extra flights. Computers & Operations Research 2009;36(6):2031–48.
[63] Teodorović D, Guberinić S. Optimal dispatching strategy on an airline network after a schedule perturbation. European Journal of Operational Research 1984;15:178–82.
[64] Teodorović D, Stojković G. Model for operational daily airline scheduling. Transportation Planning and Technology 1990;14:273–85.
[65] Teodorović D, Stojković G. Model to reduce airline schedule disturbances. Journal of Transportation Engineering 1995;121:324–31.
[66] Thengvall B, Bard J, Yu G. Balancing user preferences for aircraft schedule recovery during irregular operations. IIE Transactions 2000;32:181–93.
[67] Thengvall B, Yu G, Bard J. Multiple fleet aircraft schedule recovery following hub closures. Transportation Research Part A 2001;35:289–308.
[68] Thengvall B, Bard JF, Yu G. A bundle algorithm approach for the aircraft schedule recovery problem during hub closures. Transportation Science 2003;37:392–407.
[69] Wei G, Yu G, Song M. Optimization model and algorithm for crew management during airline irregular operations. Journal of Combinatorial Optimization 1997;1:305–21.
[70] Wu C-L. Improving airline network robustness and operational reliability by sequential optimisation algorithms. Networks and Spatial Economics 2006;6:235–51.
[71] Yan S, Lin C-G. Airline scheduling for the temporary closure of airports. Transportation Science 1997;31:72–82.
[72] Yan S, Tu Y-P. Multifleet routing and multistop flight scheduling for schedule perturbation. European Journal of Operational Research 1997;103:155–69.
[73] Yan S, Yang D-H. A decision support framework for handling schedule perturbations. Transportation Research Part B 1996;30:405–19.
[74] Yan S, Young H-F. A decision support framework for multi-fleet routing and multi-stop flight scheduling. Transportation Research Part A 1996;30:379–98.
[75] Yen J, Birge J. A stochastic programming approach to the airline crew scheduling problem. Transportation Science 2006;40:3–14.
[76] Yu G, Qi X. Disruption management: framework, models and applications. World Scientific Publishing Company; 2004.
[77] Yu G, Yang J. Optimization applications in the airline industry. in: Handbook of combinatorial optimization Boston: Kluwer Academic Publishers; vol. 2, 1998 p. 635–726.
[78] Yu G, Arguello M, Song G, McCowan SM, White A. A new era for crew recovery at Continental Airlines. Interfaces 2003;33:5–22.
[79] Zhang Y, Hansen M. Real-time intermodal substitution. Transportation Research Records 2008;2052:90–9.
[80] Zhao X, Zhu J. Grey programming for irregular flight scheduling. In: 2007 IEEE international conference on grey systems and intelligent services. New York: IEEE; 2007. p. 1607–11.
[81] Zhao X, Zhu J, Guo M. Application of grey programming in irregular flight scheduling. In: 2007 IEEE international conference on industrial engineering and engineering management. New York: IEEE; 2007. p. 164–8.

24

Planning for Robust Airline Operations: Optimizing Aircraft Routings and Flight Departure Times to Minimize Passenger Disruptions

Shan Lan

John-Paul Clarke

Cynthia Barnhart

Airlines typically construct their schedules assuming that every flight leg will depart and arrive as planned. Because this optimistic scenario rarely occurs, these plans are frequently disrupted and airlines often incur significant costs in addition to those originally planned. Flight delays and schedule disruptions also cause passenger delays and disruptions. A more robust plan can reduce the occurrence and impact of these delays, thereby reducing costs. In this paper, we present two new approaches to minimize passenger disruptions and achieve robust airline schedule plans. The first approach involves routing aircraft, and the second involves retiming flight departure times.

Because each airplane usually flies a sequence of flight legs, delay of one flight leg might propagate along the aircraft route to downstream flight legs and cause further delays and disruptions. We propose a new approach to reduce delay propagation by intelligently routing aircraft. We formulate this problem as a mixed-integer programming problem with stochastically generated inputs. An algorithmic solution approach is presented. Computational results obtained using data from a major U.S. airline show that our approach can reduce delay propagation significantly, thus improving on-time performance and reducing the numbers of passengers disrupted.

Our second area of research considers passengers who miss their flight legs due to insufficient connection time. We develop a new approach to minimize the number of passenger misconnections by retiming the departure times of flight legs within a small time window. We formulate the problem and an algorithmic solution approach is presented. Computational results obtained using data from a major U.S. airline show that this approach can substantially reduce the number of passenger misconnections without significantly increasing operational costs.

Key words: airline operations; aircraft routing; flight scheduling; robust operations

1. Introduction

A common assumption in airline schedule planning (the process of generating the schedule with the greatest revenue potential) is that flight legs will be operated as planned. Because this optimistic scenario rarely occurs, airline schedules are frequently disrupted resulting in significant additional costs to airlines and passengers. It is estimated that the financial impact of irregularities on the daily operations of a single major U.S. domestic carrier may exceed $440 million per annum in lost revenue, crew overtime pay, and passenger hospitality costs (Clarke and Smith 1999). Additionally, the Air Transport Association estimates that when passenger delay costs are considered, delays cost airlines and consumers about $6.5 billion in 2000 (Air Transport Association 2003).

In 2000, approximately 30% of the flight legs operated by one major U.S. airline was delayed, and about 3.5% of these flight legs were cancelled (Bratu and Barnhart 2002). These delays and cancellations lead to disruptions in aircraft routings, crew schedules, and passenger itineraries. A passenger is considered to be *disrupted* if one or more of the flight legs in his/her itinerary is cancelled, or if a flight leg is delayed beyond the point where the passenger can successfully connect to the next flight leg in his or her itinerary. For the same major U.S. airline, it is estimated that approximately 4% of passengers are disrupted (with about half of them being connecting passengers) resulting in (i) very long delays (for example, on a day with adverse weather conditions, disrupted passengers were delayed on average 419 minutes, compared to 14 minutes for nondisrupted passengers), (ii) significant direct revenue loss to airlines and passenger, and (iii) loss of passenger goodwill.

Given the predicted doubling of air traffic in the next 10 to 15 years, the slow growth in aviation system capacity (Mead 2000), and the findings of the MIT Global Airline Industry Program (1999) and Schaefer et al. (2001) that each 1% increase in air traffic will result in a 5% increase in delays, there will likely be more frequent and serious schedule disruptions if nothing is done to change the way airline schedules are developed. Because aviation is such a critical component of the national transportation infrastructure (providing efficiencies in the movement of both people and cargo), there is a clear need for airline schedules that are less susceptible to delays and cancellations.

There is growing consensus among researchers that schedule robustness can be improved by explicitly considering possible delays and cancellations during the creation of schedule plans. However, building robustness into the schedule in this proactive manner presents a number of challenges. First, robustness is difficult to define. A robust plan might be a plan that yields the minimum cost for the worst case, the minimum expected cost, or minimizes costs given a required level of service. Second, it is difficult to capture in a tractable model the complex operations that result when severe weather conditions exist, especially in hub-and-spoke networks. Third, optimization models capturing stochasticity are often computationally intractable when applied to large-scale airline problems. Last, conventional models for airline schedule planning minimize *planned* costs, while airlines' ultimate goal is to minimize *realized* costs, that is, the sum of planned costs and the costs of delays and disruptions. However, it is difficult to estimate a priori the *realized* costs to include them in a planning model.

In this paper, we make two contributions. First, we propose a new approach to generating aircraft routes that minimize delay propagation. We formulate the problem as a mixed-integer program and develop an algorithmic approach to solve it. We investigate the value of our robust plan over the plan generated by conventional approaches using data from a major U.S. airline. The results show that our approach can reduce delay propagation significantly, improve on-time performance, and reduce the number of passengers missing their connections.

Second, we propose a new approach to minimize the expected total number of passenger misconnections. We formulate the problem as mixed-integer program where flight leg departure times are moved within a small time window, analyze the properties of the model, and develop an algorithmic approach. The computational results obtained using data from a major U.S. airline show that this approach, which has desirable computational properties, can significantly reduce the number of disrupted passengers.

The paper is structured as follows. In §2, we survey the literature in the area of robust planning and then provide alternative definitions of robustness and present a modeling framework for robust airline schedule planning. In §3, we present a robust aircraft maintenance routing model and its associated solution approach. By routing aircraft in different ways, we can reduce the delay propagating throughout the network. We also provide proof-of-concept results using data from a major U.S. airline. In §4, we present the idea of rescheduling each flight leg within a small time window to minimize passenger disruptions. We show various ways to model this problem and analyze the properties of the models. We also present and analyze results using data from a major U.S. airline. Finally, in §5, we discuss possible extensions of our robust airline scheduling models.

2. Robust Airline Schedule Planning

There are at least two ways to deal with schedule disruptions. The typical approach is to reoptimize the schedule after a disruption occurs. A more proactive approach is to build robustness into the schedule in the planning stage. To understand how this might be done, it is important to understand the schedule planning process (§2.1), the conventional approach of schedule recovery (§2.2), and previously proposed approaches to robust planning (§2.3).

2.1. The Airline Schedule Planning Process

The airline schedule planning problem has been studied extensively and numerous models and algorithmic approaches have been developed. Barnhart and Talluri (1997) and Cohn and Barnhart (2003) present structural overviews of this planning process and detailed literature reviews. A brief overview is provided here.

Because the airline schedule planning problem is too large to be solved in a single decision model, the problem is traditionally divided into sequential subproblems defined as (i) schedule generation, (ii) fleet assignment, (iii) maintenance routing, and (iv) crew scheduling.

The solution to the schedule generation problem is a schedule defined by markets, frequencies, and the specific departure and arrival times of each flight leg. Because the schedule affects every operational decision, it has the biggest impact on an airline's profitability.

The solution to the fleet assignment problem is the assignment of a specific aircraft type to each flight leg in the schedule, matching as closely as possible the seat capacity of aircraft to the demand, thereby minimizing operating expenses and lost revenue caused by insufficient capacity. Fleet assignment models have been widely applied in practice, and significant savings have been achieved. For example, Subramanian et al. (1994) report $100 million per year in savings at Delta Airlines.

The solution to the maintenance routing problem is a set of routes, one for each aircraft, in which all aircraft are maintained at the right place and right time. The objective of the maintenance routing problem is to find maintenance feasible routes for each aircraft, given a fleeted schedule and the number of available aircraft of each fleet type. This problem is discussed in detail in §3.1.

The solution to the crew scheduling problem is the assignment of cockpit and cabin crews to flight legs that minimize cost and satisfy regulatory agency requirements and collective bargaining agreements.

2.2. Schedule Recovery

When disruptions occur, airlines typically recover from disruptions in stages (Rosenberger, Johnson, and Nemhauser 2001a). In the first stage, new aircraft routings are created by rerouting aircraft and delaying/canceling flight legs. In the second stage, cockpit and cabin crew are reassigned and where necessary reserve cockpit and cabin crew are called. In the third stage, passengers are reaccommodated. Interested readers are referred to Clarke and Smith (2000) and Rosenberger, Johnson, and Nemhauser (2001a) for a detailed review. Related literature includes Teodorovic and Guberinic (1984); Jarrah et al. (1993); Teodorovic and Stojkovic (1995); Yan and Yang (1996); Mathaisel (1996); Cao and Kanafani (1997); Lettovsky (1997); Luo and Yu (1997); Yan and Tu (1997); Thengvall, Bard, and Yu (2000); and Yu et al. (2003).

2.3. Robust Planning

Although robust airline schedule planning is a relatively new concept, "robust planning" has been studied by many researchers and applied in various fields such as robot design, manufacturing, supply chain management and logistics, telecommunications, economics, ecology, water and environmental management, and portfolio management in finance. For detailed reviews, readers are referred to Zimmermann (1991), Watanabe and Ellis (1993), Birge (1995), Kouvelis and Yu (1997), and the Stochastic Programming Community (2003). The methodologies used include stochastic programming (Birge and Louveaux 1997), scenario planning (Mulvey, Vanderbei, and Zenios 1995; Kouvelis and Yu 1997), and fuzzy optimization (Zimmermann 1991; Sakawa 1993).

In part because airlines have incurred billions of dollars in revenue losses due to unplanned disruptions, researchers are beginning to consider possible delays and disruptions in the planning stage. Ageeva and Clarke (2000) present a robust aircraft maintenance routing model to provide opportunities to swap planes. Chebalov and Klabjan (2002) propose a similar idea for crew scheduling. Rosenberger, Johnson, and Nemhauser (2001b) develop a robust fleet assignment and aircraft rotation model with many short cycles. Schaefer et al. (2001) propose a stochastic extension to the deterministic crew scheduling problem. With simulation, they obtain a linear approximation of expected crew costs and then solve the resulting deterministic crew scheduling problem. Yen and Birge (2001) develop a two-stage stochastic integer programming model to minimize total expected crew costs. Kang and Clarke (2002) propose the idea of a degradable airline schedule where a current airline schedule is partitioned into several schedules in independent layers that are prioritized, with higher priority layers recovered first. Independence of layers ensures that disruptions are isolated within a layer, thus preventing disruptions from propagating throughout the network. For a detailed review, readers are referred to Lan (2003).

3. Robust Aircraft Maintenance Routing

3.1. The Aircraft Maintenance Routing Problem

The goal of the aircraft maintenance routing problem is to determine a sequence of flight legs, called *aircraft routings*, to be flown by individual aircraft such that each flight leg is included in exactly one aircraft routing, and all aircraft are properly maintained. In most optimization models for the aircraft maintenance routing problem, the objective is to maximize *through revenue*, the potential revenue obtained by offering passengers the opportunity to stay on the same aircraft when making a connection at an airport. In practice, this additional revenue is very difficult to determine accurately and the financial impact is relatively small (Klabjan et al. 1999, Cordeau et al. 2000). The aircraft maintenance routing problem can thus be cast as a feasibility problem, providing an opportunity to achieve robustness with minimal cost implications.

The FAA mandates four main categories of airline safety checks: A, B, C, and D checks, varying in scope, duration, and frequency (Clarke et al. 1996). Usually, the maintenance routing problem presented in the literature considers only A checks. Among the four safety checks, A checks are the only checks that need to be performed frequently. A checks are required after every 60 hours of flying, although airlines enforce more stringent maintenance requirements and typically perform A checks after every 40 to 45 hours of flying (about three to four calendar days). Because maintenance requires trained professionals and equipment, these checks are only performed at a limited number of airports.

Recent work in the area of maintenance routing includes Feo and Bard (1989), Kabbani and Patty (1992), Desaulniers et al. (1997), Clarke et al. (1996), Barnhart et al. (1998b), Gopalan and Talluri (1998), and Talluri (1998). These models assume that (1) the fleeted schedule will repeat everyday and (2) aircraft that overnight at a maintenance base have the opportunity to undergo maintenance. It is perhaps most important to note (within the context of operational robustness) that none of these models considers the impact of delays and cancellations.

3.2. Delay Propagation

Flight leg delays may be divided into the following two categories.

- *Propagated delay*: Delay that occurs when the aircraft to be used for a flight leg is delayed on its prior flight leg. This delay is a function of an aircraft's routing. For the major U.S. airline for which we have data, propagated delay is approximately 20% to 30% of total delay.

- *Nonpropagated delay*: Delay that occurs for reasons that are not a function of routing. We also call this independent delay (independent of routing).

Figure 1 illustrates the relationships between departures, arrivals, and delays. The solid arrows represent the original schedule for two flight legs i and j. The dotted arrows represent the actual departures and arrivals of these flight legs. PDT refers to planned departure time, and ADT refers to actual departure time. PAT refers to planned arrival time, and AAT refers to actual arrival time. The turn time is the time between the arrival of the aircraft at the gate and the time this aircraft is ready for the next flight. The minimum turn time is the minimum time required to deboard, unload baggage, clean, cater, fuel, load baggage, and board an aircraft. If PTT_{ij} is the planned turn time between flight leg i and flight leg j, and MTT is the minimum turn time, then the slack is the difference between planned turn time and minimum turn time, that is,

$$PTT_{ij} = PDT_j - PAT_i, \quad (1)$$

and

$$Slack_{ij} = PTT_{ij} - MTT. \quad (2)$$

TDD refers to total departure delay, comprised of independent departure delay (IDD) and propagated delay (PD). PD_{ij}, the delay propagated from flight leg i to flight leg j if both flight legs are flown by the same aircraft, can be determined as follows:

$$PD_{ij} = \max(TAD_i - Slack_{ij}, 0). \quad (3)$$

TAD, the total arrival delay, is also comprised of two parts, namely propagated delay (PD) and independent arrival delay (IAD).

3.3. Modeling the Robust Aircraft Maintenance Routing Problem

Because each aircraft routing is a sequence of flight legs flown by a single aircraft, an arrival delay will result in a departure delay if there is not enough slack between two consecutive flight legs in that routing. This "delay propagation" often results in delays for downstream flight legs, and delays and disruptions for crews and passengers. This is especially true at hubs where aircraft, crew, and passenger flows are closely interrelated. Given that flight leg delays are due in part to the propagation of delays along aircraft routings, flight leg delay can be reduced if slack is optimally assigned to aircraft routings (that is, at the airports along aircraft routings where slack is needed most). The underlying premise in our modeling approach is that it is possible to reduce propagated delay and overall flight leg delays by intelligently routing the aircraft, allocating slack optimally to absorb the delay propagation.

Figure 2 illustrates the idea. Assume that flight leg f_1 and flight leg f_3 are in the same route (string) s_1, and flight leg f_2 and flight leg f_4 are in the same route (string) s_2. Suppose, based on historical data, we know that flight leg f_1 is delayed, as shown in the figure, on average to the position of f'_1. This delay is longer than the slack between flight leg f_1 and flight leg f_3, causing delay to propagate from flight leg f_1 to flight leg f_3, and causing flight leg f_3 to be delayed or cancelled if the delay is too long. As a result, passengers connecting from flight leg f_3 to other flight legs will likely be disrupted. Our goal is to consider the historical delay data in selecting aircraft routes, so

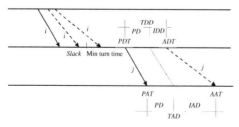

Figure 1 Departures, Arrivals, and Delays

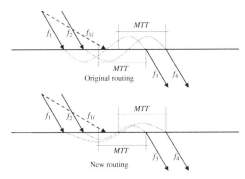

Figure 2   Rerouting and Delay Propagation

that the delay and/or cancellation of flight leg f_3 and the resulting passenger disruptions can be reduced. To illustrate, assume that historical data show that on average flight leg f_2 arrives on time. Then, a better way to construct the aircraft routes is illustrated in the "new routing" shown in Figure 2, that is, to put flight leg f_1 and flight leg f_4 in the same route, and flight leg f_2 and flight leg f_3 in another route. The effect is to add more slack after the often-delayed flight leg f_1 to mitigate the downstream effects of its delay.

This problem can be solved separately for each fleet type. Because delays propagate along the aircraft routes, it is difficult to use leg-based models to track delay propagation. Thus, a routing-based model is more appropriate. Such a model, a string-based formulation for robust aircraft maintenance routing with the objective to minimize total *expected* propagated delay, is presented in this section. A string is a sequence of connected flight legs that begins and ends at maintenance stations (possibly different ones).

3.3.1. Determining Delays for Feasible Routes.

Both propagated delay and total arrival delay are a function of routing. Thus, while historical values for propagated delay and total arrival delay can be computed for each flight leg in existing routings, no such values are available for routings that have not been previously realized. However, because independent arrival delay is not a function of routing, independent arrival delay can be calculated for each flight leg by tracking actual routings of each individual aircraft. The total arrival delays and propagated delays of flight legs in any routing can then be generated, as described below.

ALGORITHM 1: GENERATE DELAY DATA.

1. Determine propagated delays (PD) for each sequence of flight legs i, j in the historical data: $PD_{ij} = \max(TAD_i - Slack_{ij}, 0)$.

2. Determine independent arrival delays (IAD) for each flight leg from historical data: $IAD_j = TAD_j - PD_{ij}$.

3. Determine total arrival delay (TAD) and PD for each flight leg of any routing, given the independent arrival delay (IAD) for each flight leg:
   • For the first flight leg i on each string, $TAD = IAD$; and
   • For subsequent flight legs j in the routing, in sequence: $PD_{ij} = \max(TAD_i - Slack_{ij}, 0)$ and $TAD_j = IAD_j + PD_{ij}$.

3.3.2. Delay Distribution.

We determined the distribution of delay using the Airline Service Quality Performance (ASQP) database. The ASQP database provides flight leg information for all the domestic flight legs of major airlines in the United States (that is, airlines generating revenues of $1 billion or more annually). This database is available to the general public. ASQP provides the following information for each flight leg: planned departure time and arrival time, actual departure time and arrival time (including wheels-off and wheels-on time, taxi-out and taxi-in time, airborne time), and airplane tail number. For cancelled flight legs, reasons for cancellation and airplane tail number are not available.

The arrival delays are usually strongly asymmetric, with some flight legs arriving early (the arrival delays are negative), but most flight legs arriving on time or late. More specifically, most flight legs arrive around the scheduled arrival time, with very few of them arriving very early (more than 20 minutes), and some arriving very late (more than one hour). Therefore, the natural candidates for the arrival delay distributions are the gamma, log-normal, and Weibull distributions.

SAS was used to estimate the parameters and calculate the test statistics. The χ^2 test and/or the Kolmogorov test were used to determine if the total arrival delays follow a specific distribution. We found the log-normal distribution to be the best fit among the distributions listed above. With a significance level of 0.01, the null hypothesis is accepted for 84% of all flight legs, implying that the actual arrival delays for 84% of the flight legs follow a log-normal distribution. For these flight legs, the shape parameters are usually less than one and location parameters are less than zero. The reader is referred to Lan (2003) for details.

3.3.3. Formulation of the Robust Aircraft Maintenance Routing Model.

Let S be the set of feasible strings, F be the set of daily flight legs, F^+ be the set of flight legs originating at a maintenance station, and F^- be the set of flight legs terminating at a maintenance station. We denote the set of ground variables (including the overnight or wraparound arcs to ensure that the flight schedule can repeat daily) as G, the set of strings ending with flight leg i as S_i^-, and the set of strings beginning with flight leg i as S_i^+. We have one binary decision variable x_s for each feasible string s. We have ground variables denoted by y, which are used to count the number of aircraft on the ground at maintenance stations. Let pd_{ij}^s be the delay propagated from flight leg i to flight leg j if flight leg i and flight leg j are in string s. Let a_{is} equal 1 if flight leg i is in string s, and equal 0 otherwise. Ground variables $y_{i,d}^-$ equal the number of aircraft on the ground before flight leg i departs, and ground variables $y_{i,d}^+$ equal the number of aircraft on the ground after flight leg i departs; ground variables $y_{i,a}^-$ equal the number of aircraft on the ground before flight leg i arrives, and ground variables $y_{i,a}^+$ equal the number of aircraft on the ground after flight leg i arrives. r_s is the number of times string s crosses the *count time*, a point in time when aircraft are counted, p_g is the number of times ground arc g crosses the count time, and N is the number of planes available.

The robust aircraft maintenance routing (RAMR) model is written as follows:

$$\min E\left(\sum_{s\in S}\left(\sum_{(i,j)\in s} pd_{ij}^s\right) x_s\right) \quad (4)$$

subject to
$$\sum_{s\in S} a_{is} x_s = 1 \quad \forall i \in F, \quad (5)$$

$$\sum_{s\in S_i^+} x_s - y_{i,d}^- + y_{i,d}^+ = 0 \quad \forall i \in F^+, \quad (6)$$

$$-\sum_{s\in S_i^-} x_s - y_{i,a}^- + y_{i,a}^+ = 0 \quad \forall i \in F^-, \quad (7)$$

$$\sum_{s\in S} r_s x_s + \sum_{g\in G} p_g y_g \le N, \quad (8)$$

$$y_g \ge 0 \quad \forall g \in G, \quad (9)$$

$$x_s \in \{0,1\} \quad \forall s \in S. \quad (10)$$

The objective (4) is to minimize the expected total propagated delay of selected strings. Constraints (5) are cover constraints that ensure each flight leg is in exactly one string. Constraints (6) and (7) are flow balance constraints that ensure the number of aircraft arriving at and departing from a location are equal. Constraint (8) is the count constraint to ensure that the total number of aircraft in use at the count time (and thus at any point in time due to the cyclic, daily nature of the flight schedule) does not exceed the number of aircraft in the fleet. Constraints (9) and (10) force the number of aircraft on the ground to be nonnegative and the number of aircraft assigned to a string to be 0 or 1. Because variable y_g is a sum of binary x variables, the integrality constraints on the y variables can be relaxed, as discussed in Hane et al. (1995).

3.4. Solution Approach

The robust aircraft maintenance routing (RAMR) problem is a stochastic discrete optimization problem. There is extensive literature addressing variants of this problem type. For a detailed literature review, the reader is referred to Kleywegt, Shapiro, and Homem-de-Mello (2001), in which they propose a Monte Carlo simulation-based approach for solving these problems. Their method is particularly applicable when the expected value function in the objective cannot be written in closed form and/or its values cannot be easily calculated. Our model, however, is a stochastic discrete optimization problem without random variables in the constraints, and with an objective function (4) that can be rewritten as:

$$\min E\left[\sum_s x_s \times \left(\sum_{(i,j)\in s} pd_{ij}^s\right)\right]$$

$$= \min \sum_s x_s \times E\left[\sum_{(i,j)\in s} pd_{ij}^s\right]$$

$$= \min \sum_{s\in S}\left(x_s \times \sum_{(i,j)\in s} E[pd_{ij}^s]\right). \quad (11)$$

$E[pd_{ij}^s]$ can be computed offline for each pair of successive flight legs i and j using the approach detailed in Lan (2003). Then, RAMR is a deterministic mixed-integer linear program with a large number of 0-1 variables. For realistic problems, the complete generation of the corresponding instance, let alone its solution, requires prohibitive amounts of time and memory. The problem can be solved, however, using a *branch-and-price* approach. Branch-and-price is branch-and-bound with a linear programming relaxation solved using column generation at each node of the branch-and-bound tree.

3.4.1. Solving the LP Relaxation.
Column generation is used to solve the linear programming (LP) relaxation of the RAMR problem, because it is impractical to enumerate all feasible strings explicitly. The algorithm's steps are summarized as follows.

ALGORITHM 2: SOLVING THE LP RELAXATION OF RAMR.
1. Form the restricted master problem (*RMP*), that is, the *RAMR LP* with only a subset of the variables.
2. Solve the *RMP* to find an optimal primal and dual solution.
3. Using the dual solution of Step 2, solve the pricing problem to identify if one or more variables have negative reduced cost. If so, add them to the *RMP* and go to Step 2; else stop: The *LP* is solved.

3.4.2. The Pricing Problem.
Let $d_s = \sum_{(i,j)\in s} E[pd_{ij}^s]$ represent the total propagated delay along string s,

π_i be the dual variable associated with the cover constraint for flight leg i, δ be the dual variable corresponding to the count constraint, and λ_i be the dual variable corresponding to the flow balance constraint for string s beginning or ending with flight leg i. The reduced cost of a string s beginning with flight leg m and ending with flight leg n is

$$\bar{d}_s = d_s - \sum_i a_{is}\pi_i - r_s\delta - \lambda_m + \lambda_n.$$

Barnhart et al. (1998b) show that the pricing subproblem of their string-based maintenance routing model can be cast as a constrained shortest path problem in a connection network. For our model, however, the pricing problem cannot be cast as a shortest path problem. The reason is that d_s $(=\sum_{(i,j) \in s} E[pd_{ij}^s])$ cannot be assigned to each connection arc (the arc connecting the arrival of one flight leg to the departure of another flight leg at an airport) because the propagated delay for each pair of flight legs depends on the string to which they belong. Thus, we solve the pricing problem approximately without explicitly evaluating the reduced cost for each possible string. We construct a connection network by allocating $-\sum_i a_{is}\pi_i - r_s\delta - \lambda_m + \lambda_n$ to the corresponding flight leg arcs and connection arcs. We then solve shortest path problems for all OD pairs of the network. If the costs for all shortest paths are greater than or equal to zero, then no columns have negative reduced cost, because d_s is greater than or equal to zero, by definition. Thus, no columns will be added and the LP problem has been solved to optimality. For each shortest path with negative cost, we add d_s to its reduced costs and if the resulting total sum is less than zero, then the corresponding column is added to RMP. The augmented RMP is re-solved and the process repeats until a stopping criteria specifying the maximum number of iterations or the minimum objective function improvement is met. Although this method does not guarantee optimality because there might be unidentified paths with negative cost, it is tractable.

3.4.3. IP Solution. An integer solution to the robust aircraft maintenance routing problem can be obtained using a special branching strategy called "branch on follow-ons" (Ryan and Foster 1981, Barnhart et al. 1998b). As proved in Barnhart et al. (1998a), this strategy will generate optimal integer solutions to the problem. This strategy may be summarized as follows.

ALGORITHM 3: BRANCH ON FOLLOW-ONS.

1. If the solution is not fractional, the current maintenance routing problem is solved. If the solution is fractional, identify a fractional string s_1 with $0 < x_{s_1} < 1$. Denote the sequence of flight legs in s_1 as $f_1, f_2, f_3, \ldots, f_{n-1}, f_n$.

Table 1 Characteristics of Four Maintenance Routing Problems

Network	Num of flight legs	Num of strings
N1	20	7,909,144
N2	59	614,240
N3	97	6,354,384
N4	102	51,730,736

2. Identify another string s_2 (one exists) containing flight leg f_i in s_1 but not f_{i+1} in s_1. Define S_L as the set of strings with each string containing flight leg f_i followed by flight leg f_{i+1}.

• On the left branch, force flight leg f_i to be followed by flight leg f_{i+1} with $\sum_{s \in S_L} x_s = 1$. To ensure the pricing subproblem generates strings satisfying this rule, eliminate from the connection network (1) all arcs connecting flight leg f_i to any flight leg other than flight leg f_{i+1}, and (2) all arcs connecting to flight leg f_{i+1} from any flight leg other than flight leg f_i.

• On the right branch, do not allow flight leg f_i to be followed by flight leg f_{i+1}, that is, require that $\sum_{s \notin S_L} x_s = 1$. To ensure the pricing subproblem generates only strings satisfying this rule, eliminate from the network all arcs connecting flight leg f_i to flight leg f_{i+1}.

3.5. Proof of Concept

We used the RAMR model and solution algorithm to create routings for four different fleet types operated by a major U.S. network carrier. Because in practice the model will be built using historical data and then applied to future operations, the routings were created using ASQP (flight leg delay and cancellation) data and passenger booking data for July 2000 and then evaluated using the corresponding data for August 2000. Both flight leg delay and passenger disruption statistics were determined.

3.5.1. Underlying Networks. Table 1 presents the characteristics of the four different maintenance routing problems, each representing a different fleet type. The column "Num of strings" represents all possible strings for each network. Although the number of flight legs in each fleet is relatively small, the number of possible strings is very large.

3.5.2. Computational Results. Our solution algorithm was implemented in C++ and CPLEX 6.5 on a HPC 3000 workstation. The results are presented below.

Flight Leg Delay. Flight leg delay statistics are presented in Table 2. Column "Old PD" indicates the propagated delay in minutes in the historical data; column "New PD" indicates the propagated delay in minutes for our routing solution; column "PD reduced" indicates the reduction in propagated

Table 2 Propagated Delays Based on August 2000 Data

Network	Old PD	New PD	PD reduced	% of PD reduced
N1	6,749	4,923	1,826	27
N2	4,106	2,548	1,558	38
N3	8,919	4,113	4,806	54
N4	14,526	9,921	6,940	48
Total	34,300	21,505	15,130	44

Table 3 Distribution for Propagated Delays

P-delay	(0, 30]	(30, 60]	(60, 90]	(90, 120]	>120	>0
Old (%)	4.8	1.8	1.2	0.5	0.7	9.1
New (%)	2.6	0.9	0.7	0.2	0.6	5.0

Table 4 Distribution for Total Delays and On-Time Performance

	Total delay			On-time rates		
	>15 min	>60 min	>120 min	15 min	60 min	120 min
Old (%)	22.3	7.9	2.9	77.7	92.1	97.1
New (%)	20.7	6.9	2.6	79.3	93.1	97.4

Table 5 On-Time Performance Rank for U.S. Major Airlines

Airlines	Northwest	Continental	Delta	TWA	Southwest
On-time rates (%)	79.2	77.7	77.3	76.7	76.2
Rank	1	2	3	4	5

delay minutes resulting from our new routing solution; and column "% of PD reduced" indicates the percentage reduction in propagated delay. On average, the RAMR model reduces total propagated delay in August by 44% compared to the aircraft routings used by the airline.

The distribution of propagated delays (in August 2000) for both the actual aircraft routings and our routings are summarized in Table 3. The notation "$(a, b]$" indicates that the propagated delay is greater than a minutes and less than or equal to b minutes. The row "Old" represents the percentage of flight legs with propagated delay in the specified ranges for the actual routings, and the row "New" represents the percentage of flight legs with propagated delay in the specified ranges for the new routings. As the table shows, the new routing solution reduces the number of delayed flight legs for each possible range.

The distributions of total delays for both the existing routing and new routings, using August 2000 data for the four networks, are summarized in Table 4. The Department of Transportation (DOT) on-time arrival rate (delay less than 15 minutes) increases 1.6%, while the 60- and 120-minute on-time rates (arrival delay less than 60 and 120 minutes, respectively) are also improved. Note that an increase of 1.6% in the on-time performance of any of the airlines listed in Table 5 (Bureau of Transportation Statistics 2003) would have resulted in at least a one-position improvement for that airline. This is of significance to airlines because the DOT on-time ranking is publicly available and often cited as an important indicator of airline performance.

Passenger Disruptions. We investigated the effect of our routing solution on passenger disruptions by comparing the number of disrupted passengers based on existing routings with those for our new routings.

Figure 3 illustrates some concepts related to passenger disruption. In this section, we consider disrupted passengers to be those passengers who miss their connections because of flight leg delays. As defined in §3.2, PDT refers to planned departure time, and ADT refers to actual departure time. PAT refers to planned arrival time, and AAT refers to actual arrival time. MCT refers to the minimum connecting time needed by a passenger to connect to the next flight leg in his or her itinerary. PCT refers to planned connecting time, and ACT refers to the actual connecting time. Slack is the difference between the planned connecting time and the minimum connecting time. The relationships between these terms are summarized as follows:

$$PCT = PDT - PAT, \quad (12)$$

$$Slack = PCT - MCT, \quad (13)$$

and

$$ACT = ADT - AAT. \quad (14)$$

For any connecting passenger, he/she will be disrupted if

$$ACT < MCT. \quad (15)$$

To determine the number of disrupted passengers, we first compute the departure and arrival times for each flight using Algorithm 1 and then determine the departure and arrival times of each flight leg for our new routings using:

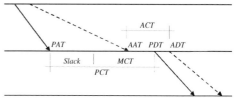

Figure 3   Passenger Disruption

ALGORITHM 4. $ADT_j = PDT_j + TDD_j$, where ADT_j is the actual departure time of flight j expected if our new routing is utilized; and

$AAT_j = PAT_j + TAD_j$, where AAT_j is the actual arrival time of flight j expected if our new routing is implemented.

The next step, calculating the number of disrupted passengers for a given routing solution, is achieved according to the following rules.

1. If a flight leg is cancelled, all passengers on that flight leg are disrupted.

2. If flight leg A is followed by flight leg B and both flight legs are operated, and $ADT_B - AAT_A < T_{\min}$, where $T_{\min}$ is the minimum connecting time for a passenger, then all passengers connecting from flight leg A to flight leg B are disrupted.

3. For those flight legs without ASQP records (that is, flight legs operated by nonjet aircraft), we do not have the data for the actual departure and arrival times. Therefore, we count only the disrupted passengers with connections for which all flight legs have ASQP records.

4. Passengers are counted as disrupted at most once. If a passenger is disrupted on any flight leg of his/her itinerary, that passenger is not counted as disrupted on any other flight leg.

Using the above rules, we estimate the number of disrupted passengers in August 2000 for both the historical routing and our new routing. The results are summarized in Table 6.

Column "Total num of D-pax" represents the total number of disrupted passengers caused by flight leg delays (not by flight leg cancellations) for the historical routing. Because the number of passengers disrupted by flight cancellations in our experiments is independent of the routings, we do not include them in our analysis. In actuality, routings with less propagated delay might result in fewer cancellations, further reducing the number of disrupted passengers. Column "D-pax reduced" represents the reduction in the number of disrupted passengers using our new routing solution, and column "D-pax reduced (%)" represents the percentage reduction in disrupted passengers. On average, our RAMR approach reduces by about 11% the number of passengers disrupted by flight leg delays.

Table 6 Results on Disrupted Passengers

Network	Total num of D-pax	D-pax reduced	D-pax reduced (%)
N1	986	147	14.9
N2	1,070	79	7.4
N3	1,463	161	11.0
N4	3,323	355	10.7
Total	6,842	742	10.8

In summary, our RAMR approach can reduce total propagated delay, improve on-time performance, and reduce the number of disrupted passengers.

4. Flight Schedule Retiming to Reduce Passenger Missed Connections

If connection slack is absorbed by flight leg delay, passengers connecting between two flight legs will be disrupted. Adding more slack can be good for connecting passengers, but can result in reduced productivity of the fleet. The challenge then is to determine where to add this slack so as to maximize the benefit to passengers without requiring additional aircraft to fly the schedule. Moving flight leg departure times provides an opportunity to allocate slack to reduce passenger disruptions and maintain aircraft productivity. In practice, flight leg departure times are adjusted in small time windows beginning several weeks before the flight leg's departure up until the day of departure.

Levin (1971) proposed the idea of adding time windows to fleet routing and scheduling models. Related research can be found in Desaulniers et al. (1997), Klabjan et al. (1999), Rexing et al. (2000), and Stojkovic et al. (2002).

The time window, specifying how much time a given flight leg can be shifted, can be modeled with a simple extension of the basic flight network. By placing copies of a flight arc at specified intervals within that flight's time window and requiring only one of the flight arc copies to be used, we model the choice of flight leg departure time. Because the scheduled time of some flight legs is more flexible than others, the width of each time window is a parameter that can be different for every flight. Moreover, the interval between copies is another parameter, one that can impact the tractability of the model and quality of the solution. To guarantee that flight legs are allowed to depart at any time within the time window, copies should be placed at one-minute intervals. It will be shown, however, in §4.3 that using a narrow interval instead of a broader one causes an explosion in the problem size, but often fails to generate substantially better solutions. We generate *robust schedules* minimizing the number of disrupted passengers by selecting flight leg departure times for specified (relatively short) departure time windows, given the flight schedule, fleet assignment, and aircraft routing decisions.

4.1. Flight Schedule Retiming Models and Their Properties

4.1.1. A Connection-Based Flight Schedule Retiming Model.
Let binary decision variable $f_{i,n}$ for each flight leg i copy n equal one if flight leg i copy

n is selected, and zero otherwise, and let binary variable $x_{i,n}^{j,m}$, representing the connection between flight leg i copy n and flight leg j copy m, equal one if the connection between flight leg i copy n and flight leg j copy m is selected, and zero otherwise. Let $dp_{i,n}^{j,m}$ be the number of disrupted passengers between flight leg i and flight leg j if flight leg i copy n and flight leg j copy m are selected. We denote the set of all flight legs as F, the set of all flight legs to which passengers connect as F^I, and the set of all flight legs from which passengers connect as F^O. Let N_i be the number of copies generated for flight leg i. We denote the set of flight legs with passengers connecting from flight leg i as $C^+(i)$. Similarly, we denote the set of flight legs with passengers connecting to flight leg i as $C^-(i)$. Our objective is to minimize the expected total number of disrupted passengers, subject to the following constraints.

1. For each flight, exactly one copy must be selected.

2. Each selected connection between two flight legs i and j must connect the selected copies of flight legs i and j. For example, if flight leg i copy 2 and flight leg j copy 3 are selected, then the copy of the connection from flight leg i copy 2 to flight leg j copy 3 must be selected, that is, $x_{i,2}^{j,3} = 1$.

3. The current fleeting and routing solutions cannot be altered.

Objective Function. The objective function of our retiming model to minimize the expected number of disrupted passengers can be written as

$$\min E\left[\sum_{i \in F^O} \sum_{n \in N_i} \sum_{j \in C^+(i)} \sum_{m \in N_j} dp_{i,n}^{j,m} x_{i,n}^{j,m}\right]$$

$$= \min \sum_{i \in F^O} \sum_{n \in N_i} \sum_{j \in C^+(i)} \sum_{m \in N_j} x_{i,n}^{j,m} \times E[dp_{i,n}^{j,m}].$$

To compute $E[dp_{i,n}^{j,m}]$, we need to know the distribution of $dp_{i,n}^{j,m}$, that is, the number of disrupted passengers connecting from flight leg i copy n to leg j copy m, for all flight legs i and j and all copies n and m. We assume that if the difference between the actual departure time of flight leg j and the actual arrival time of flight leg i is less than the minimum connecting time MCT, all passengers connecting from flight leg i to flight leg j are disrupted. And, if the difference is at least as great as MCT, connecting passengers are not disrupted. Based on this, the distribution of $dp_{i,n}^{j,m}$ is a binary distribution, namely

$$dp_{i,n}^{j,m} = \begin{cases} c_{ij} & \text{with probability } p \\ 0 & \text{with probability } 1-p, \end{cases} \quad (16)$$

where c_{ij} is the number of passengers connecting from flight leg i to flight leg j. Probability p is determined as follows:

$$p = \text{prob}(ADT_{j,m} - AAT_{i,n} < MCT), \quad (17)$$

where $ADT_{j,m}$ is the actual departure time of flight leg j if copy m is selected, and $AAT_{i,n}$ is the actual arrival time of flight leg i if copy n is selected. As discussed in §3, the distribution of ADT and AAT for each flight leg can be determined for any flight schedule, fleeting, and routing. Then, $E[dp_{i,n}^{j,m}]$ can be determined for each connection between any pair of flight legs.

Model Formulation. The connection-based flight schedule retiming (CFSR) model is written as follows:

$$\text{Min} \sum_{i \in F^O} \sum_{n \in N_i} \sum_{j \in C^+(i)} \sum_{m \in N_j} x_{i,n}^{j,m} \times E[dp_{i,n}^{j,m}] \quad (18)$$

subject to

$$\sum_{n \in N_i} f_{i,n} = 1 \quad \forall i \in F, \quad (19)$$

$$\sum_{m \in N_j} x_{i,n}^{j,m} = f_{i,n} \quad \forall i \in F^O, n \in N_i, j \in C^+(i), \quad (20)$$

$$\sum_{n \in N_i} x_{i,n}^{j,m} = f_{j,m} \quad \forall j \in F^I, m \in N_j, i \in C^-(j), \quad (21)$$

$$f_{i,n} \in \{0,1\} \quad \forall i \in F, n \in N_i, \quad (22)$$

$$x_{i,n}^{j,m} \in \{0,1\} \quad \forall i \in F^O, n \in N_i, j \in C^+(i), m \in N_j. \quad (23)$$

The objective function (18) minimizes the expected total number of disrupted passengers. Constraints (19) are cover constraints that ensure, given the integrality requirements of each variable f (22), exactly one copy will be selected for each flight leg. Constraints (20) and (21), with (22) and (23), jointly ensure that variables f and x are selected consistently. As we explained above, this problem will be solved after solving the fleet assignment and aircraft maintenance routing problems. Therefore, we need to add constraints to maintain the current fleeting and routing solution, as discussed in the next section.

Enabling Current Routings and Itineraries. To maintain the current fleeting, aircraft routings, and passenger itineraries while selecting flight departure times, we must ensure that (1) the planned turn time for each aircraft always exceeds the minimum turn time, and (2) the planned connection time for each passenger always exceeds the minimum connecting time. For example, in Figure 4, suppose flight legs 1 and 2 are in an aircraft route, or in a passenger itinerary. If the time between the arrival of flight leg copy $f_{1,7}$ and the departure of flight leg copy $f_{2,1}$ is less than the minimum turn time, or alternatively the

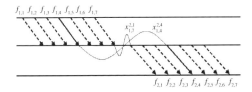

Figure 4 Example: How to Keep Current Routing Solution

minimum connecting time, then flight leg 1 copy 7 and flight leg 2 copy 1 cannot be selected together, implying that $x^{2,1}_{1,7}$ must equal 0. In general, for any pair of flight legs $i-j$ in an aircraft route or passenger itinerary, we can keep the current solution feasible by forcing $x^{j,m}_{i,n} = 0$ if the time between the arrival of flight leg copy $f_{i,n}$ and the departure of flight leg copy $f_{j,m}$ is less than the minimum turn or connecting time. This can be implemented easily by setting to zero the upper and lower bounds for each such x variable, or by not including these variables in the model.

Model Properties. In this section, we analyze the CFSR model properties. Specifically, constraints (23) can be eliminated as shown in the following.

THEOREM 1. *The integrality of the connection variables (constraints (23)) can be relaxed.*

PROOF. Consider flight legs i_1 and j_1 such that flight leg i_1 is followed by flight leg j_1 in an aircraft routing. Constraints (19) and (22) ensure that, for every flight leg, exactly one copy will be selected. Suppose copy n_1 of flight leg i_1 and copy m_1 of flight leg j_1 are selected, then

$$f_{i_1, n_1} = 1; \quad f_{i_1, n} = 0, \quad \forall n \in N_{i_1} \text{ and } n \neq n_1,$$
$$f_{j_1, m_1} = 1; \quad f_{j_1, m} = 0, \quad \forall m \in N_{j_1} \text{ and } m \neq m_1.$$

From constraints (20), we have

$$\forall n \in N_{i_1} \text{ and } n \neq n_1, \quad f_{i_1, n} = 0 = \sum_{m \in N_{j_1}} x^{j_1, m}_{i_1, n}.$$

Because $x \geq 0$, this implies

$$x^{j_1, m}_{i_1, n} = 0, \quad \forall n \in N_{i_1} \text{ and } n \neq n_1, m \in N_{j_1}.$$

Similarly, from constraints (21), we have

$$x^{j_1, m}_{i_1, n} = 0, \quad \forall n \in N_{i_1}, \forall m \in N_{j_1} \text{ and } m \neq m_1,$$

which implies

$$\sum_{m \in N_{j_1}, m \neq m_1} x^{j_1, m}_{i_1, n} = 0, \quad \forall n \in N_{i_1},$$

and

$$\sum_{m \in N_{j_1}, m \neq m_1} x^{j_1, m}_{i_1, n_1} = 0.$$

Thus, together with constraints (20), we have

$$f_{i_1, n_1} = 1 = \sum_{m \in N_{j_1}} x^{j_1, m}_{i_1, n_1}$$
$$= x^{j_1, m_1}_{i_1, n_1} + \sum_{m \in N_{j_1}, m \neq m_1} x^{j_1, m}_{i_1, n_1}$$
$$= x^{j_1, m_1}_{i_1, n_1}.$$

Hence, for any pair of flight legs i_1 and j_1

$$x^{j_1, m_1}_{i_1, n_1} = 1 \quad \text{and} \quad x^{j_1, m}_{i_1, n} = 0,$$
$$\forall n \in N_{i_1}, m \in N_{j_1} \text{ and } n \neq n_1 \text{ or } m \neq m_1. \quad \square$$

The CFSR model can thus be rewritten equivalently by replacing (23) with

$$0 \leq x^{j, m}_{i, n} \leq 1 \quad \forall i \in F^O, n \in N_i, j \in C^+(i), m \in N_j. \quad (24)$$

Alternative, yet equivalent, formulations of the connection-based flight schedule retiming model can be found in Lan (2003). Lan (2003) proves that the LP relaxation of the CFSR model is at least as strong as those of alternative formulations he considers, and can be stronger in some instances.

4.2. Solution Approach

4.2.1. Overview of the Solution Approach. The CFSR formulation is a deterministic mixed-integer program with a large number of variables (recall that in CFSR, we must consider all flight and passenger connections for all fleet types). For practical problems, complete generation of all variables will require prohibitive amounts of time and memory. Thus, we solve these problems using branch-and-price (see §3.4 for a detailed description).

4.2.2. Branching Strategy. After solving an LP relaxation at a node of the branch-and-bound tree, we branch based on the cover constraints:

$$\sum_{n \in N_i} f_{i, n} = 1 \quad \forall i \in F.$$

Building on the results of Hane et al. (1995), we employ special ordered set branching in which we divide the set of variables $f_{i,n}$ for each flight leg i into two sets. We force the sum of the variables in the first set to equal one on one branch, and the sum of the variables in the second set to equal one on the other branch. For fleet assignment problems, Hane et al. (1995) show that this is a more effective branching strategy than branching on individual variables.

4.2.3. Column Generation. At an iteration of the column generation algorithm, let $\pi^j_{i,n}$ be the optimal dual variables associated with constraints (20) and

$\pi_i^{j,m}$ be the optimal dual variables associated with constraints (21). Then, the reduced cost for each connection copy between flight legs i and j is

$$\overline{dp}_{i,n}^{j,m} = E[dp_{i,n}^{j,m}] - \pi_{i,n}^{j} - \pi_i^{j,m}. \quad (25)$$

Because the number of columns is just over one million for a typical airline problem, a large but manageable number, the reduced cost for each copy of each connection can be calculated explicitly and all columns with negative reduced costs are added to the restricted master problem at each iteration.

4.3. Proof of Concept

4.3.1. Underlying Networks. For the computational experiments with our retiming model, we combine the four networks (described in Table 1) to form one network with a total of 278 flight legs and four fleet types. Because there are many passengers connecting in this network, we also consider flight legs in the full airline network that form passenger connections with the flight legs in the 278 flight leg network. For these additional flight legs, we fix the current schedule. The total number of flight legs considered in this expanded network is 1,067.

4.3.2. Data and Validation. We use the same July and August 2000 data used in our computational experiments in §3.5. We solve our robust aircraft maintenance routing model (see §3) using July 2000 data to obtain a routing solution, and then compute the corresponding delays for each flight leg. Given these delays, the expected number of disrupted passengers for each connection copy is estimated. The sample average of the number of disrupted passengers is used as an approximation of the mean. Then, we solve our flight leg schedule retiming models on the July 2000 data to determine flight leg departure times for August 2000. Next, using the departure times selected by our model, we calculate the number of disrupted passengers for August 2000. We also compute the number of disrupted passengers for the actual August 2000 schedule.

4.3.3. Computational Results. The results obtained by applying our flight leg schedule retiming models to the network of a major U.S. airline (described in §4.3.1) are presented below. Problems are solved using CPLEX 6.5 on an HPC 3000 machine with 1 GB RAM.

Size and Bound. Using a 30-minute time window allowing flight legs to depart at most 15 minutes earlier or later than originally scheduled, we generate copies for flight arcs every 5 minutes, for a total of 7 copies in each flight leg's time window. The numbers of constraints, variables, and nonzeros in the CFSR

Table 7 Effects of Retiming on Numbers of Disrupted Passengers (August 2000 Data)

Time window	Old D-pax	New D-pax	D-pax reduced	D-pax reduced (%)
±15 min (7 copies)	18,808	11,348	7,460	39.7
±10 min (5 copies)	18,808	12,732	6,076	32.3
±5 min (3 copies)	18,808	15,042	3,766	20.0

model are 7,506, 27,013, and 59,836, respectively. The LP relaxation of the CFSR model is very tight. For this problem instance, an optimal solution is found at the root node of the branch-and-bound tree, requiring only 13 seconds to find an optimal solution.

Misconnections and Time Window Width. The number of passenger misconnections that can be avoided through retiming is shown in Table 7 for varying time windows. "Time window" indicates the total time (in minutes) flight legs are allowed to shift and the number of copies of flight legs generated in this time window. For example, ±15 min (7 copies) allows each flight leg to depart at most 15 minutes earlier or later than originally scheduled. Because we generate copies for flight arcs every five minutes, there are seven copies in this time window. "Old D-pax" indicates the total number of passenger misconnections in the original schedule, and "New D-pax" indicates the number of passenger misconnections in our new schedule. "D-pax reduced" and "D-pax reduced (%)" indicate the difference in the number (and percentage) of passenger misconnections between the old and new schedules. Note that in our computational experiment, we consider only those passengers whose itineraries have at least 1 flight leg included in the subnetwork with 278 flight legs. The disruption status of all other passengers is unchanged by our retiming solution.

The results obtained by applying our retiming decisions based on July 2000 data to the August 2000 flight network are summarized in Table 7. If flight leg departure times are allowed to shift in a 30-minute time window, about 40% fewer passengers miss their connections, while a 20-minute time window reduces the number of passenger misconnections by over 30%, and a 10-minute time window reduces it by 20%.

Effects of Copy Interval. In Table 8, we provide results of our analysis in which we assumed a minimum connection time of 30 minutes and varied the flight leg copy interval in time windows of various widths. "Increase" indicates the factor increase in the numbers of nonzeros in the model compared to the base case with a five-minute copy interval. In Table 9, "Improve" indicates the percentage reduction in the number of disrupted passengers, again compared to a five-minute copy interval. Generating copies for flight legs every minute results in dramatically increased

Table 8 Comparison of the Problem Sizes (Five-Minute Copy Interval vs. One-Minute Copy Interval)

Time window	Num of constrs	Num of vars	Num of nonzeros	Increase
±15 min (7 copies)	7,506	27,013	59,836	1.0
±15 min (31 copies)	32,514	507,253	1,040,236	17.4
±10 min (5 copies)	5,422	14,085	32,320	1.0
±10 min (21 copies)	22,094	234,213	485,856	15.0
±5 min (3 copies)	3,338	5,325	13,140	1.0
±5 min (11 copies)	11,674	65,373	139,876	10.6

Table 9 Comparison of Numbers of Disrupted Passengers (Five-Minute Copy Interval vs. One-Minute Copy Interval)

Time window	Old D-pax	New D-pax	D-pax reduced	Improve (%)
±15 min (7 copies)	17,459	10,899	6,560 (37.6%)	0.0
±15 min (31 copies)	17,459	10,865	6,594 (37.8%)	0.52
±10 min (5 copies)	17,459	12,070	5,389 (30.9%)	0.0
±10 min (21 copies)	17,459	12,056	5,403 (30.9%)	0.26
±5 min (3 copies)	17,459	14,069	3,390 (19.4%)	0.0
±5 min (11 copies)	17,459	14,058	3,401 (19.5%)	0.28

problem sizes and modest benefit. By placing copies more sparsely, we improve model tractability considerably and obtain solutions that are nearly as good.

Estimating the Impact on Passenger Delays. The passenger delay experienced in August 2000, using historical data, is 419 minutes, with disrupted passengers accounting for 51% of total passenger delay (in minutes). By applying our model (with the minimum connecting time of 30 minutes and flight leg copies generated every 5 minutes within 30-minute time windows), we achieve a reduction of about 40% in the total number of disrupted passengers and a corresponding 20% decrease in total passenger delay. Moving from 30- to 20-minute time windows decreases delay minutes by about 16%, while a 10-minute time window achieves a reduction of roughly 10%.

5. Possible Extensions

5.1. Integrated Robust Aircraft Maintenance Routing and Fleet Assignment

The string-based model proposed by Barnhart et al. (1998b) can solve fleet assignment and maintenance routing problems at the same time. Similarly, one extension for our robust aircraft maintenance routing model is to adopt it to solve integrated fleet assignment and maintenance routing. Adding fleeting decisions results in more feasible strings, potentially leading to improved solutions with reduced delay propagation. When solving integrated fleet assignment and maintenance routing, however, it is inappropriate to minimize delay propagation without considering fleet assignment costs. Applying an idea similar to that proposed by Rosenberger, Johnson, and Nemhauser (2001b), we develop two integrated models for robust aircraft maintenance routing and fleet assignment (see Lan 2003 for details). The first model minimizes total fleet assignment and maintenance routing costs, but constrains total expected propagated delay to a specified threshold value. The second model minimizes total expected propagated delay, and limits fleet assignment and maintenance routing costs to a particular upper bound.

5.2. Robust Aircraft Maintenance Routing with Time Windows

Allowing flight legs to be rescheduled within a small time window and simultaneously determining aircraft routings could lead to a more robust routing solution, one that minimizes delay propagation. To model this problem, the string-based model with copies of each flight leg can be used (see Lan 2003 for details). We can also integrate robust maintenance routing with time windows and fleet assignment to enhance robustness of the plan. Likely, such a model will have tractability issues when solving large-scale problems. Research in this direction should focus on better formulations of the problem and/or new ways to reduce problem size and exploit problem structure.

5.3. Fleet Assignment with Time Window and Passenger Disruption Considerations

Recall in §4, we minimize the number of disrupted passengers by adding a time window for each flight. Integrating this model and the fleet assignment with time windows model allows fleeting decisions to be affected by their impact on passenger disruptions. The difficulty is in determining the costs of passenger disruptions. Passenger disruptions result not only in reaccommodation costs but also in costs associated with loss of goodwill. Thus, similar to what we have done in §5.1, we develop two integrated models for balancing fleet assignment costs with improvements in passenger travel times (see Lan 2003 for details). The first model minimizes the fleet assignment cost but constrains the expected number of disrupted passengers to an upper bound. The second model minimizes the expected number of disrupted passengers and limits fleet assignment costs.

References

Ageeva, Y., J.-P. Clarke. 2000. Approaches to incorporating robustness into airline scheduling. MIT International Center for Air Transportation Report ICAT-2000-6, Cambridge, MA.

Air Transport Association. 2003. http://www.airlines.org/.

AMR Corporation. 2003. http://www.amrcorp.com/.

Barnhart, C., K. Talluri. 1997. Airline operations research, ch.10. *Design and Operation of Civil and Environmental Engineering Systems*. John Wiley and Sons, Inc., New York, 435–469.

Barnhart, C., E. Johnson, G. Nemhauser, M. Savelsbergh, P. Vance. 1998a. Branch-and-price: Column generation for solving huge integer programs. *Oper. Res.* **46**(3) 316–329.

Barnhart, C., N. Boland, L. Clarke, E. Johnson, G. Nemhauser, R. Shenoi. 1998b. Flight string models for aircraft fleeting and routing. *Transportation Sci.* **32** 208–220.

Birge, J. 1995. Current trends in stochastic programming computation and applications. Technical Report 95-15, Department of Industrial and Operations Engineering, University of Michigan, Ann Arbor, MI.

Birge, J., F. Louveaux. 1997. *Introduction to Stochastic Programming.* Springer-Verlag, New York.

Bratu, S., C. Barnhart. 2002. A study of passenger delay for a major hub-and-spoke airline. Working paper, Center for Transportation and Logistics, Massachusetts Institute of Technology, Cambridge, MA.

Bureau of Transportation Statistics. 2003. http://www.bts.gov/oai/.

Cao, J., A. Kanafani. 1997. Real-time decision support for integration of airline flight cancellations and delays. *Transportation Planning Tech.* **20** 183–217.

Chebalov, S., D. Klabjan. 2002. Robust airline crew scheduling: Move-up crews. *Proc. 2002 NSF Design, Service, Manufacturing Grantees Res. Conf.*, San Juan, PR.

Clarke, M., B. Smith. 1999. The development of the airline operations control center. Research paper, Sabre Holdings Corp., Southlake, TX.

Clarke, M., B. Smith. 2000. The impact of operations research on the evolution of the airline industry: A review of the airline planning process. Research paper, Sabre Holdings Corp., Southlake, TX.

Clarke, L., E. Johnson, G. Nemhauser, Z. Zhu. 1996. The aircraft rotation problem. *Ann. Oper. Res.* **69** 33–46.

Cohn, A., C. Barnhart. 2003. Improving crew scheduling by incorporating key maintenance routing decisions. *Oper. Res.* **51**(3) 387–396.

Cordeau, J., G. Stojkovic, F. Soumis, J. Desrosiers. 2000. Benders decomposition for simultaneous aircraft routing and crew scheduling. Technical Report G-2000-37, GERAD, École Polytechnique de Montreal, Montreal, Canada.

Desaulniers, G., J. Desrosiers, M. M. Solomon, F. Soumis. 1997. Daily aircraft routing and scheduling. *Management Sci.* **43** 841–854.

Feo, T. A., J. F. Bard. 1989. Flight scheduling and maintenance base planning. *Management Sci.* **35** 1415–1432.

Gopalan, R., K. Talluri. 1998. The aircraft maintenance routing problem. *Oper. Res.* **46** 260–271.

Hane, C., C. Barnhart, E. Johnson, R. Marsten, G. Nemhauser, G. Sigismondi. 1995. The fleet assignment problem: Solving a large-scale integer program. *Math. Programming* **70** 211–232.

Jarrah, A. I. Z., G. Yu, N. Krishnamurthy, A. Rakshit. 1993. A decision framework for airline flight cancellations and delays. *Transportation Sci.* **27** 266–280.

Kabbani, N. M., B. W. Patty. 1992. Aircraft routing at American Airlines. *Proc. 32nd Annual Sympos. AGIFORS*, Budapest, Hungary.

Kang, L. S., J. P. Clarke. 2002. Degradable airline scheduling. Working paper, Operations Research Center, Massachusetts Institute of Technology, Cambridge, MA.

Klabjan, D., E. Johnson, G. Nemhauser, E. Gelman, S. Ramaswamy. 1999. Airline crew scheduling with time windows and plane count constraints. Technical Report TLI/LEC-99-12, Georgia Institute of Technology, Atlanta, GA.

Kleywegt, A. J., A. Shapiro, T. Homem-de-Mello. 2001. The sample average approximation method for stochastic discrete optimization. *SIAM J. Optim.* **12** 479–502.

Kouvelis, P., G. Yu. 1997. *Robust Discrete Optimization and Its Applications.* Kluwer Academic Publishers, Dordrecht, The Netherlands.

Lan, S. 2003. Planning for robust airline operations: Optimizing aircraft routings and flight departure times to achieve minimum passenger disruptions. Ph.D. dissertation, Massachusetts Institute of Technology, Cambridge, MA.

Lettovsky, L. 1997. Airline operations recovery: An optimization approach. Ph.D. dissertation, Georgia Institute of Technology, Atlanta, GA.

Levin, A. 1971. Scheduling and fleet routing models for transportation systems. *Transportation Sci.* **5** 232–255.

Luo, S., G. Yu. 1997. On the airline schedule perturbation problem caused by the ground delay program. *Transportation Sci.* **31** 298–311.

Mathaisel, D. F. X. 1996. Decision support airline system operations control and irregular operations. *Comput. Oper. Res.* **23** 1083–1098.

Mead, K. 2000. Flight delays and cancellations. Report CC-2000-356, U.S. Department of Transportation, 15.

MIT Global Airline Industry Program. 1999. http://web.mit.edu/airlines/.

Mulvey, J. M., R. J. Vanderbei, S. A. Zenios. 1995. Robust optimization of large-scale systems. *Oper. Res.* **43** 264–281.

Rexing, B., C. Barnhart, T. Kniker, A. Jarrah, N. Krishnamurthy. 2000. Airline fleet assignment with time windows. *Transportation Sci.* **34** 1–20.

Rosenberger, J. M., E. L. Johnson, G. L. Nemhauser. 2001a. Rerouting aircraft for airline recovery. White paper, The Logistics Institute, Georgia Institute of Technology, Atlanta, GA. http://www.tli.gatech.edu/research/papers/files/tli0104.pdf.

Rosenberger, J. M., E. L. Johnson, G. L. Nemhauser. 2001b. A robust assignment model with hub isolation and short cycles. White paper, The Logistics Institute, Georgia Institute of Technology, Atlanta, GA. http://www.tli.gatech.edu/research/papers/files/tli0112.pdf.

Ryan, D. M., B. A. Foster. 1981. An integer programming approach to scheduling. A. Wren, ed. *Computer Scheduling of Public Transport: Urban Passenger Vehicle and Crew Scheduling.* North Holland, Amsterdam, 269–280.

Sakawa, M. 1993. *Fuzzy Sets and Interactive Multiobjective Optimization.* Plenum Publishers, London, U.K.

Schaefer, A. J., E. L. Johnson, A. J. Kleywegt, G. L. Nemhauser. 2001. Airline crew scheduling under uncertainty. White papers and reports, The Logistics Institute, Georgia Institute of Technology, http://www.tli.gatech.edu/research/papers/files/tli0101.pdf.

Stochastic Programming Community. 2003. http://stoprog.org/.

Stojkovic, G., F. Soumis, J. Desrosiers, M. M. Solomon. 2002. An optimization model for real-time flight scheduling problem. *Transportation Res. A* **36** 779–788.

Subramanian, R., R. P. Scheff, J. D. Quillinan, D. S. Wiper, R. E. Marsen. 1994. ColdStart—Fleet assignment at Delta Airlines. *Interfaces* **24**(Jan–Feb) 104–120.

Talluri, K. 1998. The four-day aircraft maintenance routing problem. *Transportation Sci.* **32** 43–53.

Teodorovic, D., S. Guberinic. 1984. Optimal dispatching strategy on an airline network after a schedule perturbation. *Eur. J. Oper. Res.* **15** 178–182.

Teodorovic, D., G. Stojkovic. 1995. Model to reduce airline schedule disturbances. *J. Transportation Engrg.* **121** 324–331.

Thengvall, B. G., J. F. Bard, G. Yu. 2000. Balancing user preferences for aircraft schedule recovery. *IIE Trans.* **32** 181–193.

Watanabe, T., H. Ellis. 1993. Robustness in stochastic programming models. *Appl. Math. Model.* **17** 545–554.

Yan, S., Y. Tu. 1997. Multifleet routing and multistop flight scheduling for schedule perturbation. *Eur. J. Oper. Res.* **103** 155–169.

Yan, S., D. Yang. 1996. A decision support framework for handling schedule perturbation. *Transportation Res. B* **30** 405–419.

Yen, J. W., J. R. Birge. 2001. A stochastic programming approach to the airline crew scheduling problem. *Transportation Sci.* Forthcoming.

Yu, G., M. Arguello, G. Song, S. M. McCowan, A. White. 2003. A new era for crew recovery at Continental Airlines. *Interfaces* **33**(1) 5–22.

Zimmermann, H. J. 1991. *Fuzzy Set Theory and Its Applications.* Kluwer Academic Publishers, Boston, MA.

25

Of plagues, planes and politics: Controlling the global spread of infectious diseases by air

Lucy Budd, Morag Bell, Tim Brown

ABSTRACT

Keywords:
Air travel
Infectious disease
International public health
Disease control

In recent years, the implications of globalisation for the spread of infectious diseases has begun to emerge as an area of concern to political geographers. Unsurprisingly, much of the contemporary literature focuses on the multifarious threats posed by human and, increasingly, non-human mobility. Prompted by current geopolitical concerns surrounding the public health implications of regular international air travel, this paper extends such research by exploring the ways in which the technology of the aeroplane stimulated the production of new international sanitary initiatives aimed at safeguarding global public health in an era of mass aeromobility. By tracing the development of sanitary regulations for aerial navigation, from their origins in the 1920s through the twentieth century in particular, we document the emergence of a series of public health interventions that were designed to limit the public health threat associated with increased international air travel and the concomitant rise in the mobility of infectious diseases. From inoculation certificates to quarantine and the routine 'disinsection' of passenger aircraft with powerful insecticides, modern air travel is replete with a complex set of procedures designed to lessen the risks associated with flying between different climatic and ecological zones. Our detailed examination of the historical context in which these procedures were devised and implemented leads us to consider the importance of time and space, power and efficacy, to the development of a more nuanced understanding of the shifting public health response to an increasingly fluid, mobile, and inter-connected society.

© 2009 Elsevier Ltd. All rights reserved.

Introduction

Since the first heavier-than-air powered flight in 1903, technological developments have enabled aircraft to fly progressively further, faster, longer, and higher, overcoming the tyranny of distance and fundamentally reshaping the patterns and practices of twentieth and early twenty-first century mobilities. Today, nearly two billion passengers a year travel by air and the commercial airline network is routinely depicted as being the metaphorical glue that makes the world go round (Adey, Budd, & Hubbard, 2007; Urry, 2007).

The sheer volume of passenger and freight movements by air combined with, amongst other things, the putative 'mobilities turn' in the social sciences (see Cresswell, 2006; Urry, 2000), has led to a recent surge of academic interest in the multifarious dimensions of aviation. Scholars including Bowen (2002), O'Connor (2003), and Witlox, Vereecken, and Derudder (2004) have shed light on the unfolding networks of air transportation and Adey (2008), Gordon (2008), and others have alerted us to the multiple historical and cultural geographies of the airport terminal. However, while much was made of aviation's importance to the administration and maintenance of 20th century imperial ambitions, including those of Britain (see Cobham, 1926a, 1926b; Hoare, 1927; Salt, 1930; Sykes, 1920), the development of long-haul air routes and the formation of sanitary regulations for aviation is one dimension of the imperial experience that has received scant academic attention to date. This paper addresses this lacuna by tracing what we refer to as the historical 'bio-geopolitics' of passenger aviation.

The 'bio-geopolitics' of aviation

According to Gould (1999), of the near 4000 airports in the world with scheduled international passenger services, no two are more than 36 h flying time apart; leading him to conclude that airports are not just nodes in a global space of air traffic flows but important transit points for the rapid, worldwide spread of disease. The significance of this calculation is, in part, reflected in research which reveals that, in an era of unprecedented global aeromobility when hundreds, if not thousands, of human pathogens are circulating the world's airways (Leibhold, Work, McCollough, & Cavey, 2006; Pavia, 2007), the global airline network plays an important role in the worldwide spread of infectious diseases (Avila, Said, & Ojcius, 2008; Budd, 2008; Cliff and Haggett, 1995; Colizza, Barrat, Barthelemy, & Vespignani, 2006; Mangili & Gendreau, 2005; Tatem & Hay, 2007; Tatem, Hay, & Rogers, 2006). The epidemiological vulnerability of a closely inter-connected and highly aeromobile twenty-first century world was illustrated in 2003, when the SARS (Severe Acute Respiratory Syndrome) virus rapidly spread from East Asia to over 25 countries around the world along the contours of the global airline network (Bowen & Laroe, 2006; Pang & Guindon, 2004), and again in 2009 with the outbreak of H1N1 influenza.

While geographers, including Roger Keil in collaboration with Harris Ali, have explored the implications of globalisation on international biosecurity, especially as it relates to SARS (Ali & Keil, 2006, 2008; Keil & Ali, 2007), much of the contemporary literature focuses on the ways in which national governments and international organisations like the WHO have sought, and are seeking, to strengthen their international borders against what are regarded as the 'wrong' sorts of *human* mobility. Indeed, though the link between public health and international relations – and here we would include all aspects of border control – is not a new one, with many countries responding to the threats from cross-border diseases since at least the fourteenth century, it is only in the last decade or so that it has (re)emerged as a key geopolitical concern (Fidler, 2004a). For Fidler (2004a: 4), as for others (including Garrett, 1995; King, 2002), this is because national governments, especially those of advanced industrial economies, have come to recognise that one of the 'costs' of globalisation is the "growing threat of the microbial world".

This latter point is taken up by Alan Ingram (2005: 532) who, in an essay in which he discusses the 'new' geopolitics of disease, explains that globalisation has come to be associated, at least in the context of global health debate, with the dissolution of "epidemiological space", with the reframing of sovereign power over national borders, and with increasing health insecurity (see also Sparke, in press). One aspect that Ingram flags up for particular attention in his analysis is the suggestion that the forms of global health governance that have emerged to promote health security reflect a shift from Westphalian to post-Westphalian approaches. As Fidler, a key proponent of this argument, suggests, during the period between the emergence of international public health directives in the 1850s and the end of World War Two the question of disease control, in Europe at least, was regarded as the concern of individual sovereign nations who remained free of external intervention in their domestic affairs; that is, it was conducted on 'classic' Westphalian principles (see Fidler 2004a, 2004b, 2004c, 2007).

The shift away from a Westphalian system to a post-Westphalian regime of global health in the post-world war era is centred on the idea that the existing horizontal regime, one "that sought to regulate cross-border microbial traffic" (Fidler, 2004a: 8), was replaced by a vertical, rights-based approach. Here, individual rights to health, as defined in the WHO constitution (WHO, 1946), and national interests were seen to be interdependent and international strategies designed to promote health and prevent disease *within* sovereign nations, such as the WHO's smallpox eradication campaign and its 'Health for All' strategy, were developed. More recent events, including the global response to the HIV/AIDS pandemic and the 2003 SARS epidemic might, according to Fidler, be interpreted as further illustrations of a shift away from a Westphalian rationality, as the desire to contain both epidemics was/is framed by state and non-state interests alike (Fidler, 2004a, 2004b). Although we concur largely with Ingram in his positive appraisal of Fidler's "innovative and sustained analysis" of this shift, the question of whether or not the international response to the many and varied challenges to global health security are seen in Westphalian, post-Westphalian, or indeed other, perhaps imperial, terms, remains.

As Zylberman (2006) notes, our understanding of the relationship between globalisation and the search for international/global health security – of the multiple and varied actors involved, of the technological devices and public health strategies drawn upon to protect and strengthen borders against the agents of disease, and of the geopolitical rationalities that help to shape such international endeavour – should not be reduced to the "rise and fall of Westphalian public health governance". This is, as he quite rightly states, "only part of the full story" (Zylberman, 2006: 35). This point is underlined by the medical historian Alison Bashford (2006a: 1) who notes that, in addition to an understanding of the historical geography of disease, an analysis of global health governance requires an exploration of the geopolitics of disease management. Put differently, she argues that such an analysis should focus on the measures of disease prevention, reduction, and eradication that are implemented and, more importantly here, their spatial implications.

A further point of interest is Bashford's recognition that the interaction between infectious disease management and geopolitics is one that involves borders: "the politics of disease control concerns the governance of *this side* and crucially *that side*, of the border" (Bashford, 2006a: 2. Emphasis in original). In highlighting the centrality of borders to disease management, and to global health governance more broadly, Bashford alludes to the notion that public health intervention occurred outside of the jurisdiction of a sovereign state in the period that Fidler categorises in Westphalian terms. There are many examples of this, and Bashford refers us to, amongst others, European intervention in the former Ottoman Empire and to US public health campaigns in Cuba, Panama, and Puerto Rico. One reason for our raising this here is that Bashford highlights further the limitations of analyses of global health governance that are limited to a Westphalian/post-Westphalian framework. Further, she points researchers in the direction of what we might refer to as a 'bio-geopolitics' of global health governance; a term which reflects the interweaving of bio-political forms of power and geopolitics.

It is with this in mind that we examine the rapid development of long-haul air travel during the twentieth century, the bio-geopolitical challenges posed by this development, and the extent to which the political responses demonstrated a shift away from a Westphalian towards a post-Westphalian regime. We do so because, from its inception, aviation presented a new and challenging set of public health concerns. As we go on to demonstrate, Western nations, in particular, responded with a series of sanitary directives that variously framed certain destinations as being host to an array of 'exotic' or 'tropical' diseases that represented a threat to health and economic development. These directives prescribed a range of interventions, including quarantine and vaccination certificates, which aimed to secure western nations and their citizens from certain microbial threats. At times, however, this desire to provide ontological and material security created geopolitical tensions between those who thought that all possible measures should be taken to safeguard 'global', though perhaps we should read 'national', public health and those who resented the idea that aviation's continued development should be hindered by expensive and time-consuming health checks. As the concern surrounding the H5N1 strain of avian influenza (HPA, 2007; Nerlich & Halliday, 2007) and, more recently, the H1N1 strain, have demonstrated, the trade-offs between screening air passengers at airports and the socio-economic costs associated with implementing such practices remain largely unresolved.

In the analysis that follows, we draw on medical and historical aviation material (the latter sourced from Flight International's digitised online archive and documents deposited in the Transport History Collection at the University of Leicester) to map some of the processes through which the smooth spaces of the air(ways) became increasingly striated as the global airline network developed and highlight the growing anxiety that emerged as public health officials and others began to recognise some of the health-related implications of an increasingly inter-connected aeromobile world. We then explore the gradual, and often contested, development of international sanitary conventions for aviation that emerged in response to this anxiety and offer a bio-geopolitical interpretation of their significance, noting that the international regulatory frameworks that emerged not only sought to manage competing geopolitical interests but also to manage the threat of infection from a range of so-called 'exotic' diseases. The paper concludes with a discussion of the ways in which our analysis informs, and is informed by, recent debate on the broader geopolitical rationality described by Fidler as a shift towards a post-Westphalian global health regime and by others as a, perhaps, more nuanced situation in which western nations sought to secure the health of their populations through a complex array of bio-geopolitical strategies.

Wings around the world: aviation and new global health concerns

As a direct consequence of the metaphorical 'shrinking' of the globe by aircraft during the 1920s and 1930s, nations that had long considered themselves reasonably immune to the diseases of foreign nations, in part due to the security afforded to them by a combination of time and space, found themselves under increased threat. For Australia, the United States, and many of the countries of Western Europe, the time-space compression associated with air travel rendered existing epidemiological surveillance networks almost redundant (Weir & Mykhalovskiy, 2006). The accelerated compression of time and space that aircraft effected meant that, "A man [sic] might fly thousands of miles while incubating a disease, pass medical officials at the destination airport, emerge into a new land, and, a day or two later, go down with an infectious disease that he had picked up on the other side of the world" (Stuart & Baird, 1954: 108–109). Despite this risk, pioneering European air transport companies were encouraged to extend the scope of their passenger operations and to link up territories that were scattered across the globe (Sampson, 1984).

At this time, aviation was considered a powerful tool through which European nations could establish their authority and exert their influence over foreign nations. In the British context, this is reflected in the assumption of responsibility for the Cairo–Baghdad airmail route by Imperial Airways in 1927 and the subsequent, and quite rapid, expansion east; first to Karachi, Jodhpur and Delhi in British India in 1929, then to Calcutta, Rangoon and Singapore in 1933, before finally reaching Hong Kong and Australia in 1934 (Davies, 1964). However, the limited speed, range, and technological capabilities of the early propeller-driven aircraft meant that services could only operate during daylight hours and pilots had to make frequent stops to refuel the aircraft and allow passengers and crew time to rest. By 1934, the 8458-mile Imperial Airways' flight from London to Singapore was achieved in eight days courtesy of intermediate stops at Paris, Brindisi, Athens, Alexandra, Cairo, Gaza, Baghdad, Basra, Kuwait, Bahrain, Sharjah, Gwadar, Karachi, Jodhpur, Delhi, Cawnpore, Allahabad, Calcutta, Akgats, Rangoon, Bangkok, and Alor Star (see Sampson, 1984).

Crucially, however, it was not merely the geographical scope of the early airline networks that was significant, but the reduction in total journey times that aircraft effected. As an editorial in 'Flight' magazine, a publication designed to disseminate news of aeronautical achievement to the British public, cautioned as early as 1920, "Now an aeroplane can cross the Mediterranean from Europe to the African Continent in a night... it would be foolish to ignore the possibility of... pests being introduced into countries hitherto immune by means of the aeroplane... [as]...up to the present time these tropical and Eastern insects and pests had perished before they reached Europe, because the "carriers" had taken days and weeks in a journey" (Flight, 1920a: 454). Though slow by modern standards, the speeds attained by early passenger aircraft revolutionised notions of time and distance: journeys that had once taken weeks or months by surface transport could now be accomplished in a matter of days (Table 1).

As a consequence of this rapid time-space compression (see Janelle, 1969; Simonsen, 2005), many parts of the world could now be reached by air within the incubation period of major infectious diseases (Table 2). The rapid expansion and intensification of global air routes in the early 1930s, and the concomitant rise in passengers and (to a lesser extent) freight volumes worldwide, caused considerable concern among public health authorities (Megonnell & Chapman, 1956). "Nowadays", wrote Air Commodore H. E. Whittingham in 1938, "air-travel is so rapid that an aeroplane departing from the yellow fever zones of West Africa reaches the Sudan in two days, Mozambique in four days, Durban in five days and, by another route, Karachi in five, Calcutta in six... There is, therefore, great danger of yellow fever being spread by air passengers incubating the disease or by infected mosquitoes in the aircraft, unless special precautions are taken" (Whittingham, 1938: 461–462).

As the air routes grew, and new airfields were added to the network, the potential for insects, small reptiles, and mammals to stow away in aircraft and be transported to the next port of call increased. This problem was particularly acute in equatorial Africa, where it was noted that all manner of harmful insects were endemic (Handover, 1936).

Rising appreciation of the increased international mobility of disease and the logistical difficulties associated with maintaining surveillance over rising numbers of passengers resulted in the formation of specific national public health regulations governing aviation. As a direct response to the first flight between England and Australia in 1919, Australia became the first country in the world to apply a quarantine code to aircraft by defining a "vessel" as "any ship, boat, or other description of vessel or vehicle used in navigation by sea or air" (cited in *Canadian Medical Association*

Table 1
'Twice as far in half the time' – by 1935 flying offered significant reductions in journey times, a fact which had serious implications for the spread of disease.

London to -	Time by air (days)	Time by surface transport (days)	Time saved by air (days)
Alexandria	2½	4½	2
Calcutta	6½	16	9½
Rangoon	7	19	12
Singapore	8½	22	13½
Nairobi	5½	19	13½
Johannesburg	8½	18½	10
Cape Town	9	17	8
Brisbane	12½	32	19½

Source: derived from Imperial Airways (1935: 8).

Table 2
The relationship between the incubation period for selected infectious diseases and the journey time between selected endemic zones and the United Kingdom 1938.

Disease	Incubation period (days)	Endemic area	Journey time by air (days)
Cholera	2–5	India	4–5
		Iraq	2–3
Plague	2–6	India	4–5
		Iraq	2–3
		East Africa	4
		West Africa	3–5
		South America	4–5
Smallpox	10–14	India	4–5
		Iraq	2–3
Typhus	5–12	Central Europe	2
		Russia	2
Yellow Fever	3–6	West Africa	3–5
		South America	4–5

Source: Whittingham (1938: 3).

Journal, 1933: 307; see also Bashford, 2004; *Flight*, 1920c, 1920d). A similar definition was adopted by the United States and, in November that year, the US Government decreed that all aircraft entering the country were subject to the same quarantine restrictions as ocean-going ships (*Flight*, 1920e).

Clearly, the development of long-haul commercial air travel had highlighted the threats posed to and by an increasingly 'global' community. As the anxiety surrounding the possibility that aircraft could spread noxious agents around the world became progressively more acute as new destinations were added to the aerial network and passenger numbers increased, international measures were added to these national directives. The *Office International d'hygiène publique* (or the 'Paris Office' as it was also known), one of two European-based international health agencies established in the early 1900s (see Bashford, 2006b; Brown, Cueto, & Fee, 2006; Dorolle, 1968), drafted a precautionary programme of measures that were designed to prevent the spread of yellow fever by air because "while it has been shown that the carrying of adult mosquitoes on [maritime] vessels is not the danger it was once supposed to be, nothing is known of airplane conditions, and there is a rather general belief that a real danger exists" (*American Journal of Public Health*, 1930: 1221).

While the prevalence of insects naturally varied with the geographical site and situation of individual landing grounds, research at Kisumu in Kenya in the early 1930s found that almost half of all aircraft arriving from the north harboured insects despite the eradication measures that were undertaken at intermediate aerodromes to try and prevent their spread (Whittingham, 1938). In response, local health authorities along the route to Durban attempted to restrict the movement of insects by hanging curtains impregnated with paradichlorbenzine, a pungent agent usually used to deter moths, over the doorway of aircraft, placing powerful air blowers by aircraft doors to try and prevent insects from flying in, and physically inspecting aircraft, passengers, and cargo for signs of infestation (Whittingham, 1938: 463). However, no method proved infallible and stowaways were invariably transported (*Flight*, 1920b).

Such interventions created a tension between those who thought all available means should be employed to prevent the spread of infectious disease by air, and those who thought the procedures were too restrictive and unduly hindered the continued development of commercial aviation. One aviation commentator wrote at the time that while "the Colorado Beetle is known to travel by road and rail, the tsetse fly has lived in a sleeping car through Central Africa, and the cockroach first went to the East in a ship, [and] there would seem to be a possibility of the movement of similar "beasties" by air...nothing has eventuated" and observed that the "innocuous" house fly "seems at present to be the only insect that travels unasked on an Imperial Air Route" (Salt, 1930: 220). Nevertheless, despite Salt's apparent lack of concern, the first tentative steps towards the internationalisation of sanitary measures for aviation were taken at the thirteenth International Sanitary Conference in Paris in 1926 (Massey, 1933). Here, it was formally agreed that a period of five days should be universally accepted as the infective period of yellow fever and a compulsory period of observation of six days before embarkation and a further period six days observation upon arrival was imposed in the subsequent Sanitary Convention on all passengers flying from an infected area (*American Journal of Public Health*, 1930: 1221).

The formation of and challenges to international sanitary measures for aviation

It is well established that the geopolitics of disease prevention operates through, and is linked with, the policing of sovereign territory and that the inspection of people, their bodies, identities, and the documents that they carry make "borders more than abstract lines on maps, but a set of practices on the ground." (Bashford, 2006a: 7). Though a system of maritime quarantine had been practised since the fourteenth century and was widely regarded as an essential tool in safeguarding public health (see Fidler, 2001), it was apparent by the mid-nineteenth century that a more extensive 'international' public health framework was required (Harrison, 2006). Within Europe, the desire to internationalise the public health effort was in part linked to the growing realisation that developments in transport and communication systems and the steady growth of transnational flows, especially between European nations and their colonial territories, left the continent vulnerable to the spread of infectious diseases. As many commentators have observed, this vulnerability was especially associated with Europe's eastern borders and the apparent ease with which diseases including cholera and plague were able to cross into the West (see Harrison, 2006; Huber, 2006; Zylberman, 2006).

The beginnings of such a framework emerged through a series of 'international' health conferences, the first of which convened in Paris in 1851 (Harrison, 2006). Though the first of these Sanitary Conferences is often regarded as a failure, in part because only three of the twelve nations that attended actually signed the resulting convention, subsequent conferences nevertheless represented early attempts to promote health and prevent the spread of disease through pre-emptive activity both at, and beyond, the border (Bashford, 2006a). More significantly, in the context of this paper, delegates were required to find a solution to a complex geopolitical problem: namely, how to accommodate the liberalisation of international trade and commerce whilst simultaneously containing threats associated with increased transnational flows of goods and people. As Huber (2006) notes in her detailed analysis of these conferences, for many delegates the solution lay beyond traditional public health practices, such as the imposition of relatively inflexible quarantine or *cordons sanitaires*, as these were considered an "intolerable hindrance to international communications and commerce" (Howard-Jones, 1950: 1034).

Ultimately, the model of international public health that was proposed and partially implemented did not involve direct intervention in the domestic health of other nations. That is, the aim of the various conferences was not to improve the health of those living in countries where diseases such as cholera, plague and yellow fever were endemic. Rather, what was put in place was a series of public health initiatives that sought to distinguish between different types of cross-border enterprise and were sensitive to developments in international communication and transport networks. With regards the former, there was a clear targeting of those 'enterprises' that emanated from the 'East'. Zylberman's analysis of the International Sanitary Conferences and the response of the European delegations to the threat of cholera, particularly after the 1865 epidemic and the opening of the Suez Canal in 1869, are particularly germane here (see also Huber, 2006). As she reveals, political and health-related anxiety, especially surrounding the annual *Hajj* to Mecca, resulted in a 10-day quarantine period being established for the three main pestilential diseases after the 1866 Sanitary Conference in Constantinople. While certain vessels were exempt from such measures, the reality for pilgrims travelling to Mecca along the main sea-routes was that they experienced much longer stays in what Zylberman (2006: 25) describes as a "militarized zone".

Of particular relevance here is the fact that such measures were refined as communication systems became more sophisticated and as transport networks became more advanced. By the time of the 1892 International Sanitary Conference in Venice, delegates were able to agree upon, and subsequently implement, a surveillance system that used telegram communications with ships travelling through the Suez Canal to determine their relative risk. Those ships that carried doctors and appropriate disinfection equipment were allowed to pass unimpeded, those that did not (or contained pilgrims heading for Mecca) were subject to inspection and observation (Huber, 2006). Another, perhaps even more pertinent example came about as a result of the Dresden Sanitary Conference of 1893. Here, delegates recognized that an expanded rail network posed new problems and were forced to consider whether public health inspections, and any resulting isolation measures, should occur at the point of departure or arrival. As Huber (2006: 468) notes, the debate "bore significant parallels to that on passage through the Suez Canal: both were addressing the fact that technology had changed the way in which space was traversed".

The significance of the International Sanitary Conferences, of which 14 were held between 1851 and 1938, is subject to some debate, especially given the failure of some participating nations to ratify many of the conventions that were proposed. As the Editor of *British Medical Journal* (1949: 23) remarked, the conventions "may have been impeccable on the diplomatic level but were often sadly ineffective on the practical level". Though this may be the case, the conferences did represent an early attempt to establish a modern 'international' public health mechanism for dealing with epidemics of infectious diseases in an age of increased trade and mobility, though the conventions designed to tackle threats posed by maritime and rail travel required further consideration before they could deal with the unique challenges presented by commercial aviation (Stock, 1945).

Interestingly, the first multilateral public health agreement to deal expressly with air travel did not come from Europe but from a parallel body, the International Sanitary Bureau, that was established in Washington D.C. in 1902 (García, Estrella, & Navarro, 1999). Following discussion at the (by then renamed) Pan American Sanitary Conference of November 1924, 18 countries in North, Central, and South America signed a Code which called for the "prevention of the international spread of communicable infection of human beings" and, in the event such infections should occur, the adoption of cooperative measures to prevent "the introduction and spread of disease" into other territories that were hitherto unaffected by all means, including the air (cited in García et al., 1999: 28; see also Cheng, 1962).

However, the first truly international, as opposed to regional, public health convention concerned with air travel was the Congress on Sanitary Aviation, which was held in Paris in May 1929 and attended by the representatives of 38 countries (*Flight*, 1930). Six resolutions detailing the extension of sanitary aviation and obligations concerning government assistance were passed (*Flight*, 1930). Four years later, in April 1933, the First International Sanitary Convention for Aerial Navigation was convened in The Hague where the Paris Office and the International Commission for Air Navigation prepared an agreement that provided for the first international sanitary control of aerial navigation (Massey, 1933). The resulting Convention, which became effective in August 1935, contained 67 Articles and dealt with threats posed by Typhus, Smallpox, Plague, Cholera, and Yellow Fever. Medical inspection and control of tropical disease were discussed, and detailed methods of eradicating the vector of Yellow Fever, the *Aëdes aegypti* mosquito, were proposed (Sanitary Convention for Aerial Navigation, 1933). The Convention also established common international sanitary standards for aircraft and landing grounds and provided, amongst other things, for the construction of anti-amaryl aerodromes, the control and/or isolation of air passengers in endemic yellow fever areas, preventative inoculation, and the destruction of insects in aircraft and around aerodromes (Whittingham, 1938).

Significantly, Britain and France, as leading members of the Paris Office, were torn between such hygienic concerns for their populace and the commercial interests of their fledgling airline industries. One of the most contentious issues concerned the treatment of aircraft arriving from endemic disease areas, and opinion polarised between those who favoured stringent regulation and those who did not wish to disrupt air traffic by enforcing time-consuming and expensive disease-control measures (Bell, 1997). This resulted in different interpretations and inconsistent enforcement of the regulations. Some countries demanded that additional disease-control measures, above and beyond those stipulated by the international community, be practised at their frontiers. For example, in the late 1930s, India and the Dutch East Indies prohibited any aircraft from landing that was flying "from areas which can be considered endemic" (Bell, 1997: 169), while the Nigerian health authorities demanded all air passengers provide a week's notice of their proposed departure date and travel itinerary so a decision could be taken on whether to quarantine them prior to departure (Whittingham, 1938). Elsewhere, the Egyptian and Sudanese health authorities required services between Europe and Africa to change aircraft in Alexandria and Khartoum, respectively, to lessen the risk of disease vectors being directly transported into their territory (*Flight*, 1935), while other nations obliged passengers to possess health certificates confirming inoculation against various diseases (Imperial Airways, 1939).

While some of these additional measures can be interpreted as an expression of national autonomy over their borders, some practices, including disinsection (the eradication of insects inside an aircraft using chemical insecticides), had a basis in international aeronautical law and were, theoretically, to be universally applied.

Airlines had first attempted to address the problems of insects, especially the malaria-carrying *anopheles* mosquito, 'hitching rides' in equatorial regions in the late 1920s with hand-held insect sprays, but difficulties regarding the type of insecticide that should be used and the most effective method of delivery took several years to resolve. The legal basis for eradicating insects and other stowaways in aircraft, or 'disinsection' as it was termed, through the application of pesticides and insecticides, was enshrined in Article 5(e) of the 1933 Sanitary Convention. This Article stipulated that all sanitary aerodromes must have the "apparatus necessary for carrying out disinfection, disinsectisation [sic] and deratisation [sic]" of aircraft in order to prevent the spread of disease. However, early experiments with Flit guns, 'Freon bombs', and hand-held aerosols had found them to be largely ineffective as the spray they produced was neither sufficiently fine nor suitably penetrating, while the larger electrical and petrol-driven pressure sprayers that were employed at aerodromes were too heavy and bulky to be used in-flight (Flight, 1947; Whittingham, 1938). Other proposals, including pumping insecticide through special ducts built into the aircraft fuselage were similarly rejected on grounds of weight and cost (Whittingham, 1938) and signatories to the 1933 Convention merely agreed that disinsection should involve the application of "some form of aerial spray containing a rapidly acting insecticide" during flight (Flight, 1947: 95).

Under the direction of their medical adviser, Imperial Airways' Experimental Production section devised a new, more effective, system of disinsection. Constructed from lightweight metal and powered by electricity, the Phantomyst Electrical Disseminator or Phantomyst Vaporiser discharged a fine, dry, near odourless cloud of Pyrethrum-based insecticide into the passenger cabin (Flight, 1938a; Mackie & Crabtree 1938). It was reported that the device leaves:

"no unpleasant odour and [has] no harmful effects on people, clothing or upholstery. Being non-inflammable it may be used in aeroplanes and it is through to be the answer to the yellow fever mosquito and other licentious lice, which attempt to stowaway on aeroplanes in the tropics and spread their doctrines in places hitherto immune" (Flight, 1938b: 327).

During the Second World War, the work of the Paris Office was disrupted and its functions, including those under the 1933 Hague Convention, were temporarily entrusted to the United Nations Relief and Rehabilitation Administration (UNRRA). In anticipation of the rapid post-war growth of civilian aviation, and in light of new epidemiological conditions, scientific innovations, and enhanced medical knowledge, it was decided that the existing 1933 International Sanitary Convention for Aerial Navigation was outdated and required modification. A revised document, which called for "special measures to prevent the spread by air across frontiers of epidemic or other communicable diseases", was opened for signature at Washington in December 1944 and was ratified by 14 countries including the United States and the United Kingdom (United Nations - Treaty Series 106, 1948: 250). The modified Convention introduced new documentation, in the form of aircraft and passenger health declarations, international certificates of inoculation against Cholera, Yellow Fever, Typhus Fever and Smallpox, and certificates of immunity against Yellow Fever. Yet while it was believed that "the spread of disease can be held in check only by a scheme which is internationally sponsored and internationally controlled" (Flight, 1947: 95), the regulations were not uniform in statute or enforcement and the inability to practice global surveillance undermined their effectiveness (Davey, 1948).

As a consequence of the 1944 revisions, the health regulations for air travel became increasingly complex. Not only did the number of required inoculations now depend both on the route that was to be flown, responsibility for complying with the regulations of each country (many of which were contradictory or mutually exclusive) was transferred to individual passengers (Barrett, 1947, 1949). Variations in the validity of immunization certificates, with regards to dates of commencement and cessation (and even the dosage, type, and manufacturer of the serum that could be used), were another source of confusion (Kyle, 1948). For the smallpox vaccine alone, validity varied from a minimum of 12 days to 1 year after vaccination in Thailand to 21 days/2 years in Egypt, even though the international standard was nominally set at 14 days/3 years (Kyle, 1948). One possible explanation for these variations was that the adoption of universal standards would require the partial abrogation of sovereignty on behalf of the individual countries concerned as "the sanitary staff engaged in this work would be responsible not to local directors of medical services, but to the World Health Organisation of the United Nations" (Flight, 1947: 95).

Owing to the different medical requirements demanded by individual states, and the inconsistencies in their policing, many airlines advised passengers to be inoculated against almost every conceivable disease. This situation led to confusion, resentment, and excessive inoculation, with one family who wished to fly from Paris to China "forced to submit to inoculation against smallpox, yellow fever, cholera, plague, typhoid, and paratyphoid" (British Medical Journal, 1949: 23). Moreover, the acquisition of the correct documentation was both time-consuming and expensive. In the UK, only 11 medical institutions were authorised to administer the required vaccines and issue the resulting certificates (Barrett, 1947), and critics of the scheme argued that "the international traveller is increasingly being harassed by demands for certificates of vaccination against a lengthening list of diseases... and the various processes now linked with such documents constitute a distinct obstacle to the free movement of peoples in many parts of the world" (Gear, 1948: 1092).

Questions regarding the suitability of, and reliance upon, personal health certificates as evidence of inoculation were also raised. As Gear (1948: 1092) remarked, "there is considerable difference between recognizing vaccination... as a reliable procedure and acknowledging the obligatory certificate as beyond reproach". Ironically, the authority vested in the very documents that were designed to ensure unfettered access to international aeromobility was increasingly being challenged. Writing on the British experience, 'Flight' magazine remarked that at foreign airports "those who examine the certificates are not always provided with specimens of the various types, or with a list of the medical officers empowered to sign such certificates" and thus "it is not surprising to learn that they have, in the past, been forged, and that it is reported...that on the Continent there is a black market with a recognized tariff for these certificates" (Flight, 1947: 95). It was also alleged that some individuals made false health declarations to avoid being detained at the airport (Stanley-Turner, 1947). A further concern was the suggestion that travellers may be tempted to bribe health officials to bypass health checks. To counter this temptation, passengers were warned, as early as 1924, that they could face a £200 fine for deliberately withholding information from health officials (Imperial Airways Ltd., 1924). Nevertheless, evidence suggests that those with sufficient money and political influence could (and did) buy their way around the regulations (Cobham, 1978: 131).

Despite sustained attempts to create a universal public health response to the disease threats air travel posed, many countries refused to ratify either Sanitary Convention. Only nine nations ratified both Conventions, 16 remained bound by the 1933 convention only and a further nine only ratified the 1944 convention, leaving 36 States not bound by either. As the editor of the British Medical Journal noted with alarm, "since many countries are bound by no particular convention they are free to take the law into their own hands. Some countries refuse to trouble themselves and take few if any precautions, others... have rushed to the other extreme and imposed restrictions which go far in excess of what is required" (British Medical Journal, 1949: 22). Some countries, including the United States, practised highly protectionist policies with respect to foreign quarantine (see American Journal of Public Health, 1952), while others relied on outmoded practices of frontier disease control that were not consistent at all airports (Megonnell & Chapman, 1956).

In recognition that the international regulations concerning quarantine and disease control were in a state of confusion, a global directive aimed at controlling the spread of diseases by air was enshrined in Chapter II, Article 14, of the 1944 Chicago Convention on International Aviation, which stipulated that:

"Each contracting State agrees to take effective measures to prevent the spread by means of air navigation of cholera, typhus (epidemic), smallpox, yellow fever, plague, and other communicable diseases as the contracting States shall from time to time decide to designate, and to that end contracting States will keep in close consultation with the agencies concerned with international regulations relating to sanitary measure applicable to aircraft" (ICAO, 1944).

However, in addition to safeguarding global public health, individual states were also responsible, under Chapter IV, Article 22, to ensure that "the administration of the laws relating to immigration, quarantine, customs, and clearance" does not result in "unnecessary delays to aircraft, crews, passengers, and cargo" (ICAO, 1944). States were thus caught between international obligations to enforce new sanitary regulations and a requirement to avoid unnecessary delays.

Further steps towards the internationalisation of public health measures for aviation occurred on July 22nd 1946, when the constitution of the World Health Organisation was signed in New York. The first assembly of the WHO subsequently convened in Geneva in June 1948 and established an Expert Committee on International Epidemiology and Quarantine with the instruction "to revise the existing International Sanitary Conventions...and combine them into a single body of regulations covering the needs of all travellers". The resulting new regulations were based on a number of principles, including the request that individual member states develop their own internal protection against disease through improvements in sanitation, the control of insect vectors, and national immunization programmes. Significantly, it was also decreed that the public health measures that could be adopted at national frontiers should be the minimum compatible with the existing sanitary situation, as excessive measures would not only interfere with the flow of (air) traffic and have serious economic repercussions, but also, by their very excess, "lead to deliberate evasion of the sanitary control" (Cheng, 1962: 155).

In essence, then, such measures reflect what Fidler views as a shift from Westphalian to post-Westphalian public health: after all, member states were required to take measures that would not only control the spread of infectious diseases between sovereign territory but also prevent the emergence of such diseases in the first place. Yet, as we imply in the opening to our paper, such a reading overlooks the limited power that institutions like the WHO had (and arguably continue to have) in affecting change within nation states and also the tensions that continued to arise between individual sovereign powers in matters of infectious disease management (Davies, 2008). An example of this can be found in the tension that arose, albeit before the new regulations were in place, between Britain and India when it was alleged that practices of infection control had taken on a political as well as a biological dimension. More specifically, in response to Britain's routine disinsection of aircraft arriving from India, the government of India decided in 1946 (one year prior to Indian Independence) that all aircraft arriving in the country from Britain must be similarly treated (Barrett, 1947). Encapsulated in this 'tit for tat' response is what we might regard as the 'bio-geopolitics' associated with the materialization of an international public health framework for aviation. In the final section of this paper, we offer a critical reading of this emergence.

Discussion

"We have reached the stage when we no longer think of countries overseas as being separated by distance, but by time... That is to say that countries where all sorts of unfamiliar diseases flourish are nearer to this country in point of time than the length of their incubation periods" (cited in Stanley-Turner, 1947: 838).

Notions of time and space are crucial to our understanding of the shifting public health response to an increasingly fluid, mobile, and inter-connected society. Referring to Foucauldian-inspired scholarship, Alison Bashford (2004) points, albeit a little sceptically, to the abandonment of crude public health responses to outbreaks of infectious disease in the late-nineteenth and early-twentieth centuries by many Western governments. Here, Foucault's (1977) conceptualisation of a 'plague town', which was defined by the practice of imposing *cordons sanitaires* and concomitant notions of isolation and confinement, was gradually replaced as technological improvements in transport and communications rendered them increasingly ineffective. Developments in shipping, rail travel and, later, aviation, were particularly important in this regard, as they were instrumental in the metaphorical shrinking of space by time.

Clearly, the twentieth century development of air travel had a specific and a profound impact on global public health governance. The technology of the aeroplane, and most notably the speed of travel, has, over the past century, seen 'new' disease threats emerge and 'old' ones appear ever more frightening, in the West at least. As we note in this paper, the realisation that national borders were no longer, if indeed they ever were, 'secure', was highly significant since borders act(ed) both to define the boundaries of a nation and demarcate its lines of quarantine, for it is often at the border where human and non-human bodies and other potentially dangerous 'vessels' are monitored, surveyed, and perhaps excluded. However, as Bashford (2004: 124) rightly observes, "borders aim to regulate and control movement, flow and exchange, not stop it all together". This was a key issue for those trying to establish a public health framework that could respond to the challenges that followed from the emergence of commercial air travel. Of particular concern was how to regulate an increasingly (aero)mobile society while simultaneously accommodating the demand for more liberalised global travel.

Whilst individual countries had instigated their own sanitary procedures by the early 1920s, the first international attempts to bring the public health impacts of aviation under unified control did not occur until the early 1930s. The 1933 Sanitary Convention on Aerial Navigation established the principles and standards on which (inter)national public health measures should be based and, as we reveal above, involved practices that were targeted at both human passengers and at the non-human cargoes that were transported by air. Importantly, the 1933 convention sought to overcome the problem of where such micro-practices of public health should occur. As with other modes of transport, most notably rail travel, the issue was whether public health surveillance should be implemented on departure or arrival; that is at or beyond the sovereign borders of a nation. As we note, one solution was to pass some of the responsibility for implementing public health measures on to the airlines and their passengers. After all, it was the commercial airlines that were required to carry out disinsection, and it was the passengers who were responsible for ensuring that they carried valid documentation detailing the inoculations they had received prior to travel. However, the effectiveness of this system was undermined both by individual passengers and national governments who, frustrated that a supposedly rapid mode of international transport was being hindered by public health bureaucracy, chose to ignore or deliberately circumvent the regulations.

In subsequent decades, the limitations of existing systems of public health regulation became increasingly apparent. The invention of the jet engine, combined with continued innovations in aerodynamics and material sciences, enabled aircraft to fly further, faster, longer, and higher than ever before, revolutionising understandings of travel time and distance and increasing the need for vigilance: "In a world in which carriers of disease can spread with the speed of an aeroplane. A typhus louse or a plague flea, brushed off the rags of a beggar in an Eastern bazaar, can be in Tokyo or Oslo, New York or Moscow, London or Sydney, within a few hours" (Brockington, 1958: 217). In response to such threats, delegates at the Fourth World Health Assembly of May 1951 unanimously adopted a new set of International Sanitary Regulations (Cheng, 1962). According to these regulations, passengers embarking on an international flight to certain destinations had to be in possession of valid immunization certificates as prescribed by the World Health Organisation (not just the receiving country concerned) and rules regarding the mobility of non-human cargoes were also strengthened (*Flight*, 1951; Whittingham, 1953).

Additional sanitary regulations for aviation were adopted at subsequent meetings of the World Health Assembly, and the International Sanitary Regulations of 1951 (which were subsequently renamed the International Health Regulations (IHR) in 1969 and further modified in 1973 and 1981), remained the only global regulations for the control of infectious diseases during the remainder of the twentieth century (Gostin, 2004). The IHR aimed to "ensure the maximum security against the international spread of disease with a minimum interference with world traffic" and, to this end, required countries to notify the WHO of any case of cholera, plague or yellow fever that occurred within their territory and adopt universal hygiene measures at ports, airports and other frontier posts (Gostin, 2004: 2624). While individual countries could request personal health and vaccination certificates from travellers in respect of these three diseases, the health measures the IHR permitted were the maximum measures a State may take for the protection of its territory (Gostin, 2004). However, the narrow scope of the IHR meant the regulations were not only irrelevant for confronting known international public health threats such as HIV/AIDS and hepatitis, but were also non-responsive to the emergence of new infectious diseases such as SARS (Ashraf, 1999). In recognition of the IHR's limitations, a revised draft, which provided for increased surveillance, flexibility, and the global coordination of disease responses, was approved and adopted by member states in May 2005.

Nevertheless, continued difficulties regarding IHR compliance continue to pose significant challenges for global public health governance. Individual countries may choose to ignore international law on grounds of sovereignty, economic self-interest, or because they are incapable of complying due to war, natural disaster, or a lack of resources. As Gostin (2004: 2626) notes, it may even be in a country's interest to overlook WHO regulations in certain situations as compliance "may risk national prestige, travel, trade, and tourism" and thus "reporting a disease outbreak... and offering full cooperation may incur serious economic harm by impeding the flow of people and goods". Clearly, the commercial airline industry continues to present a number of challenges to (inter)national systems of public health and, as we have shown, it is both issues of time and space *and* power and efficacy that lie at the heart of them.

The conceptualisation of a shift in global health governance informs our reading of the emergence of a new international (later global) regulatory regime for commercial aviation in several key ways. On one level, the idea of a shift is useful because we can find some clear evidence of a Westphalian system in practice during the early years of the commercial aviation industry. Indeed, up until the mid-twentieth century, the regulatory ideas concerning the socio-political geographies of aviation, health and governance were emerging within a context in which the European (and here we might add the American and Australian) body/nation was perceived to be threatened by contact with foreign 'Others' (see Anderson, 1996; Bashford, 2004; Farley, 1991; Lyons, 1992). Yet, the creation of the WHO in 1946, and the subsequent establishment of an expert committee on quarantine in 1948, saw an attempt to challenge this Westphalian mentality through the adoption of new international sanitary regulations that aimed to counter the need for restrictive (and time consuming) national border-controls.

It is here, however, that our reading moves away from Fidler's. For although we can see the traces of what might be regarded as a post-Westphalian regulatory system emerging, there is also a clear suggestion that national interests remained at play; many of which were, and perhaps still are (see Aginam, 2003), framed by geopolitical tensions that existed between imperial and post-colonial nations. Thus, despite our analysis largely focusing on the period leading up to the construction of this new regulatory environment in the mid-twentieth century, we argue that it offers important insights into the contemporary situation. As Braun (2007) shows with reference to SARS and other viruses, contemporary global public health security, even in a post-Westphalian system, remains a highly geopolitical entity concerned with the containment of risk and the protection of international borders from diseases whose origins are believed to lie overseas.

Conclusion

A number of key issues are raised by way of conclusion. As regards our methodology, by tracing in detail the 'historical bio-geopolitics' of passenger aviation, including how, when, and why regulations came about, our approach has facilitated a nuanced interpretation of the relations between the rise and expansion of aeromobility as the normal mode of long-distance international travel during the twentieth century and the development of global public health governance. In so doing, we have moved beyond many existing accounts that merely acknowledge that heightened aeromobility was a driver of new international public health regimes.

The paper has also demonstrated how the introduction of various regulatory practices during the opening decades of the twentieth century was an important dimension of the imperial experience and the exercise of power over others (both at the level of the State and the individual). In contrast to many accounts of imperial science and colonial medical practice, however, we have also shown that this regulatory impulse was driven not only by European fears of insects and infectious diseases that were new to western science but, more particularly, by a concern that as a consequence of aeromobility, pathogens in other environments were no longer 'in their place'. Furthermore, our analysis challenges an evolutionary perspective in relation to the expansion of aeromobility and regimes of control. It has illustrated that, during these same early decades of the last century, the impetus to regulate others was accompanied by a broader anxiety that the complexity of commercial air travel posed threats to an increasingly 'global' community, and that national sovereignty must be qualified in an effort to manage the movement of transnational pathogens.

At the heart of this anxiety over the exact place in which border control and surveillance should take place, lies a concern with the enhanced mobility of a range of infectious agents and the vectors that help to transport them. Here our paper engages with current research which explores notions of biopower and biosecurity. Our contribution to this particular discussion has been to identify the emergence of an international regulatory regime for the international commercial airline industry that not only sought to stop the global transfer of non-human disease vectors by the performance of disinsection and other similar methods of insect control but also to enhance the surveillance and regulation of diseased human agents. In this sense, what we highlight are the beginnings of the kind of bio-surveillance regime that Amoore (2006) refers to her recent discussion of the 'biometric border'. For example, the introduction of vaccination certificates might usefully be interpreted as portable devices that enabled increasingly mobile bodies to be surveilled at either side of a border and which acted to govern (but not unduly hinder) the movements of people and (by association) the disease agents they might carry.

In emphasising the significance of time and space, speed and mobility, to the development of this particular aspect of a new regime for global public health governance, the paper also raises important questions about the exercise of power and the efficacy of supranational decision-making. A recurring theme is the geopolitical tensions that emerged between the imperative to safeguard national and global public health and commercial concerns that the continued development of aviation should not be hindered by supposedly expensive and time-consuming health checks. In effect, there were fundamental differences between the demands of an expanding airline industry, for which heightened aeromobility offered opportunities for greater speed and efficiency of movement, and a regulatory regime of surveillance and control that appeared to constrain these opportunities.

It is clear from our evidence that fear can stimulate collective political action and that developments in scientific and medical understanding have failed to eliminate a sense of global risk and, in some cases, may actually enhance it. Equally our findings emphasise the need to distinguish between regulatory standards and practices associated with aeronautical technology and those dealing with individual (aero)mobile human bodies. Whilst certain elements of the global air transport system, such as airport lighting and signage, air traffic control, and safety standards, have been amenable to a degree of consistent setting, interpretation and reinforcing of regulations by supranational organisations such as the International Air Transport Association (IATA) and others, the regulation of humans and their bodies is an altogether more complex, politically sensitive and oft-contested process.

Acknowledgements

We extend our thanks to the three anonymous reviewers for their helpful comments on earlier drafts of this paper.

References

Adey, P. (2008). Architectural geographies of the airport balcony: mobility, sensation and the theatre of flight. *Geografiska Annaler B, 90*(1), 29–47.
Adey, P., Budd, L. C. S., & Hubbard, P. J. (2007). Flying lessons: exploring the social and cultural geographies of global air travel. *Progress in Human Geography, 31*(6), 773–791.
Aginam, O. (2003). The nineteenth century colonial fingerprints on public health diplomacy: a postcolonial view. *Electronic Law Journal*. www.warwick.ac.uk/fac/soc/law/elj/ldg/2003_1/aginam/aginam.rtf. Accessed 22.07.08.
Ali, S. H., & Keil, R. (2006). Global cities and the spread of infectious disease: the case of severe acute respiratory syndrome (SARS) in Toronto, Canada. *Urban Studies, 43*, 491–509.
Ali, H., & Keil, R. (Eds.). (2008). *Networked disease: Emerging infections in the global city*. Blackwell: Oxford.
American Journal of Public Health. (1930). The airplane and yellow fever. (Editorial section). *American Journal of Public Health Nations Health, 20*(11), 1221–1222.
American Journal of Public Health. (February 1952). The new international sanitary regulations. *American Journal of Public Health, 42*, 194–196.
Amoore, L. (2006). Biometric borders: governing mobilities in the war on terror. *Political Geography, 25*, 336–351.
Anderson, W. (1996). Immunities of empire: race, disease, and the new tropical medicine 1900–1920. *Bulletin of the History of Medicine, 70*(1), 94–118.
Ashraf, H. (1999). International health regulations: putting public health on the centre stage. *The Lancet, 354*, 2062.
Avila, M., Said, N., & Ojcius, D. M. (2008). The book reopened on infectious disease. *Microbes and Infection, 10*, 1–6.
Barrett, R. H. (November 1947). Health regulations for air travel. *British Medical Journal, 8*, 741–743.
Barrett, R. H. (1949). Health regulations for air travel (III). *British Medical Journal August, 6*, 329.
Bashford, A. (2004). *Imperial hygiene: A critical history of colonialism, nationalism and public heath*. Basingstoke and New York: Palgrave Macmillan.
Bashford, A. (2006a). 'The age of universal contagion': history, disease and globalization. In A. Bashford (Ed.), *Medicine at the border: Disease, globalization and security, 1850 to the present* (pp. 1–17). Basingstoke and New York: Palgrave Macmillan.
Bashford, A. (2006b). Global biopolitics and the history of world health. *History of the Human Sciences, 19*(1), 67–88.
Bell, H. (1997). *Frontiers of medicine in the Anglo-Egyptian Sudan, 1899–1940*. Oxford: Oxford University Press.
Bowen, J. (2002). Network change, deregulation, and access in the global airline industry. *Economic Geography, 74*(4), 425–440.
Bowen, J. T., & Laroe, C. (2006). Airline networks and the international diffusion of severe acute respiratory syndrome (SARS). *The Geographical Journal, 172*(2), 130–144.
Braun, B. (2007). Biopolitics and the molecularization of life. *Cultural Geographies, 14*, 16–28.
British Medical Journal. (January 1949). International sanitary conventions (Editorial). *British Medical Journal, 1*, 22–23.
Brockington, F. (1958). *World health*. Harmondsworth: Penguin.
Brown, T. M., Cueto, M., & Fee, E. (2006). The World Health Organization and the transition from 'international' to 'global' health. In A. Bashford (Ed.), *Medicine at the border: Disease, globalization and security, 1850 to the present* (pp. 76–94). Basingstoke and New York: Palgrave Macmillan.
Budd, L. C. S. (2008). Pests on a plane. Airports and the fight against infectious disease. *Airports of the World, 18*, 48–53.
Canadian Medical Association Journal. (September 1933). Air traffic and infectious disease. (Editorial comments). *Canadian Medical Association Journal, 29*, 307.
Cheng, B. (1962). *The law of international air transport*. London: Stevens and Sons.
Cliff, A., & Haggett, P. (1995). Disease implications of global change. In R. J. Johnston, P. J. Taylor, & M. J. Watts (Eds.), *Geographies of global change remapping the world in the late twentieth century* (pp. 206–223). Oxford: Blackwell.
Cobham, A. J. (1926a). *My flight to the cape and back*. London: A&C Black.
Cobham, A. J. (1926b). *Australia and back*. London: A&C Black.
Cobham, A. J. (1978). *A time to fly*. London: Shepheard-Walwyn.
Colizza, V., Barrat, A., Barthelemy, M., & Vespignani, A. (2006). The role of the airline transportation network in the prediction and predictability of global epidemics. *Proceedings of the National Academy of Sciences, 103*, 2015–2020.
Cresswell, T. (2006). *On the move: Mobility in the modern western world*. London: Routledge.
Davey, E. L. (1948). Immunization procedures recommended for foreign travel. *Canadian Medical Association Journal, 58*, 77–79.
Davies, R. E. G. (1964). *A history of the world's airlines*. London: Oxford University Press.
Davies, S. (2008). Securitizing infectious disease. *International Affairs, 84*, 295–313.
Dorolle, P. (1968 December 18). Old plagues in the jet age. International aspects of present and future control of communicable disease. *British Medical Journal, 4*, 789–792.
Farley, J. (1991). *Bilharzia: A history of imperial tropical medicine*. Cambridge: University Press.
Fidler, D. P. (2001). The globalization of public health: the first 100 years of international health diplomacy. *Bulletin of the World Health Organization, 79*(9), 842–849.
Fidler, D.P. (2004a). Germs, norms, and power: global health's political revolution. *Law, Social Justice and Development Journal* (An electronic law journal).
Fidler, D. P. (2004b). Caught between paradise and power: public health, pathogenic threats, and the axis of illness. *McGeorge Law Review, 35*(1), 45–104.
Fidler, D. P. (2004c). *SARS, governance, and the globalization of disease*. Houndmills: Palgrave Macmillan.
Fidler, D. P. (2007). Architecture amidst anarchy: global health's quest for governance. *Global Health Governance, 1*(1).
Flight. (1920a). Report on a lecture by Professor Maxwell Lefroy. *Flight, 454*.
Flight. (1920b). Aircraft and insects 1920. *Flight, 643*.
Flight. (1920c). Airisms from the four winds. *Flight, 1067*.
Flight (1920 November 18). Quarantine for aeroplanes. *Flight*.
Flight. (1920e). Airisms from the four winds. *Flight, 1281*.
Flight (1930 September 5). International congress on sanitary aviation. *Flight*.
Flight. (1935 July 25). Oran to Khartoum some incidents during the Duchess of Bedford's recent African flight. *Flight, 110*.
Flight. (1938a). Massacre at Battersea. *Flight, 378*.
Flight (1938 March 31). Commercial aviation. A week at Croydon. *Flight*: 327–328.
Flight (1947 January 23). Spread of disease by air travel an International Organization Suggested. *Flight*: 95–96.
Flight. (1951 May 11). Speaking of bugs. *Flight, 571*.
Foucault, M. (1977). *Discipline and punish: The Birth of the prison*. London: Allen Lane.
Garrett, L. (1995). *The coming plague: Newly emerging diseases in a world out of balance*. New York: Penguin.
García, G. D., Estrella, E., & Navarro, J. (1999). *The pan American sanitary code toward a hemispheric health policy*. Washington, DC: Pan American Health Organization.
Gear, H. S. (1948 June 5). Problems of international travel. *British Medical Journal, 1948*, 1092–1094.
Gordon, A. (2008). *Naked airport a cultural history of the world's most revolutionary structure* (2nd Ed.). Chicago: University of Chicago Press.

Gostin, L. O. (2004 June 2). International infectious disease law revision of the World Health Organization's International Health Regulations. *Journal of the American Medical Association*, 291(21), 2623–2627.

Gould, P. (1999). *Becoming a geographer*. Syracuse, NY: Syracuse University Press.

Handover, D. H. (1936). A new empire link West African colonies linked with empire's air system. *African Affairs*, 35, 413–417.

Harrison, M. (2006). Disease, diplomacy and international commerce: the origins of international sanitary regulation in the nineteenth century. *Journal of Global History*, 1(2), 197–217.

Health Protection Agency (HPA). (2007). *Foreign travel-associated illness England, Wales, and Northern Ireland – 2007 report*. London: Health Protection Agency (HPA).

Hoare, S. (1927). *India by air*. London: Longman's Green and Co.

Howard-Jones, N. (1950 May 6). Origins of international health work. *British Medical Journal*, 1950, 1032–1037.

Huber, V. (2006). The unification of the globe by disease? The International Sanitary Conferences on Cholera, 1851–1894. *The Historical Journal*, 49(2), 453–476.

Imperial Airways. (1935). *Facts*. London: Imperial Airways.

Imperial Airways. (1939). *Information for passengers*. Croydon: Imperial Airways.

Imperial Airways Ltd. (1924). *Pilots handbook and general instructions no. 20*. (Reprinted 1974 London, Ducimus Books). Imperial Airways Ltd.

Ingram, A. (2005). The new geopolitics of disease: between global health and global security. *Geopolitics*, 10, 522–545.

International Civil Aviation Organisation (ICAO). (1944). *Convention on international civil aviation done at Chicago on the 7th day of December 1944*. Chicago: ICAO.

Janelle, D. G. (1969). Spatial reorganization: a model and concept. *Annals of the Association of American Geographers*, 59, 348–364.

Keil, R., & Ali, H. (2007). Governing the sick city: urban governance in the age of emerging infectious disease. *Antipode*, 39, 846–873.

King, N. B. (2002). Security, disease, commerce: ideologies of postcolonial global health. *Social Studies of Science*, 32, 763–789.

Kyle, J. (1948 December 25). Health regulations for air travel (II). *British Medical Journal*, 2, 1115.

Leibhold, A. M., Work, T. T., McCollough, D. G., & Cavey, J. F. (2006). Airline baggage as a pathway for alien insect species invading the United States. *American Entomologist*, 52, 48–54.

Lyons, M. (1992). *The colonial disease a social history of sleeping sickness in northern zaire, 1900–1940*. Cambridge: University Press.

Mackie, F. P., & Crabtree, H. S. (1938). The destruction of mosquitoes in aircraft. *The Lancet*, 235, 447–450.

Mangili, A., & Gendreau, M. A. (2005). Transmission of infectious diseases during commercial air travel. *The Lancet*, 365(12), 989–996.

Massey, A. (1933). *Epidemiology in relation to air travel*. London: H.K. Lewis and Co Ltd.

Megonnell, W. H., & Chapman, H. W. (April 1956). Sanitation of domestic airlines. *Public Health Reports*, 71(4), 360–368.

Nerlich, B., & Halliday, C. (2007). Avian flu: the creation of expectations in the interplay between science and the media. *Sociology of Heath and Illness*, 29(1), 46–65.

O'Connor, K. (2003). Global air travel. Towards concentration or dispersal? *Journal of Transport Geography*, 6(3), 171–186.

Pang, T., & Guindon, E. (2004). Globalisation and risks to health. *European Molecular Biology Organization Reports*, 5, S11–S16, Special Issue-Science and Society.

Pavia, A. T. (2007). Germs on a plane: aircraft, international travel, and the global spread of disease. *The Journal of Infectious Diseases*, 195, 621–622.

Salt, A. E. W. (1930). *Imperial air routes*. London: John Murray.

Sampson, A. (1984). *Empires of the sky the politics, contests and cartels of world airlines*. London: Hodder and Stoughton.

Sanitary Convention for Aerial Navigation (1933). International sanitary convention for aerial navigation Signed 12 April 1933 at *The Hague*.

Simonsen, D. G. (2005). Accelerating modernity: time-space compression in the wake of the aeroplane. *Journal of Transport History*, 26, 98–117.

Sparke, M. Unpacking economism and remapping the space of global health. In Williams, A. & Kay, A. (Eds), *Global health governance: Transformations, challenges and opportunities amidst globalization*. London: Palgrave, in press.

Stanley-Turner, H. M. (1947 November 22). Health regulations for air travel (correspondence). *British Medical Journal*, 1947, 838–839.

Stock, P. G. (1945). The International sanitary convention of 1944. *Proceedings of the Royal Society of Medicine (Section of Epidemiology and State Medicine)*, 38, 309–316, (Sectional: 17–24).

Stuart, F. S., & Biard, H. C. (1954). *Modern air transport*. London: John Long Ltd.

Sykes, F. H. (1920). Imperial air routes. *The Geographical Journal*, 55(4), 241–262.

Tatem, A. J., & Hay, S. I. (2007). Climatic similarity and biological exchange in the worldwide airline transportation network. *Proceedings of the Royal Society B: Biological Sciences*, 274(1617), 1489–1496.

Tatem, A. J., Hay, S. I., & Rogers, D. J. (2006 April 18). Global traffic and disease vector dispersal. *PNAS*, 103(16), 6242–6247.

United Nations – Treaty Series 106. (1948). Sanitary convention for aerial navigation, 1944, modifying the International Sanitary Convention for Aerial Navigation of 12 April 1933. Opened for signature at Washington, on 15 December 1944.

Urry, J. (2000). *Sociology beyond societies. Mobilities for the twenty-first century*. London: Routledge.

Urry, J. (2007). *Mobilities*. Cambridge: Polity Press.

Weir, L., & Mykhalovskiy, E. (2006). The geopolitics of global public health surveillance in the twenty-first century. In A. Bashford (Ed.), *Medicine at the border: Disease, globalization and security, 1850 to the present* (pp. 240–263). Basingstoke and New York: Palgrave Macmillan.

Whittingham, H. E. (1938). Preventive medicine in relation to aviation. *Proceedings of the Royal Society of Medicine*, 32, 455–472.

Whittingham, H. E. (1953 March 7). Medical aspects of air travel 1 – environment and immunization requirements. *British Medical Journal*, 1953, 556–558.

WHO. (1946). *Constitution*. New York: World Health Organization.

Witlox, F., Vereecken, L., & Derudder, B. (2004). Mapping the global network economy on the basis on air passenger transport flows GaWC. *Research Bulletin*, 157. http://www.lboro.ac.uk/gawc/rb/rb157.html. Accessed 17.12.04.

Zylberman, P. (2006). Civilising the state: borders, weak states and international health in modern Europe. In A. Bashford (Ed.), *Medicine at the border: Disease, globalization and security, 1850 to the present* (pp. 21–40). Basingstoke and New York: Palgrave Macmillan.

Index

Aaronson, R. J. 312
Abara, J. 222, 241, 246, 247, 256
Abdelgahny, A. 384, 386, 387
Abdelghany K. F. 387
Abdullah, O. B. 39
Abed, S. Y. 38
Abeyratne, R. I. R. 184, 312
Adey, P. 345–57, 405
Ageeva, Y. 235, 388, 393
Aginam, O. 412
Agin, N. 241
Agre, P. 347, 350
Ahmed, S. 207
Ahuja, R. K. 246, 370
Ali, H. 406
Ali, S. H. 406
Allan, J. R. 312, 313, 316
Alverson, W. S. 312
Amoore, L. 434
Anbil, R. 230, 277, 278
Andersen, K. A. 207
Anderson, W. 412
Andersson, T. 381–4, 387
Andreatta, G. 37
Andreu, P. 351
Andrew, D. 117, 118
Ang, H. -S. A. 290, 293, 294
Argüello, M. F. 375, 379, 381–4
Armacost, A. 222, 230
Armstrong, G. 347
Arnold, G. W. 315
Arnott, D. 62
Ascher, W. 61
Ashford, N. 200
Ashraf, H. 412
Auge, M. 346, 356, 357
Avery, M. L. 316
Avila, M. 406

Bafail, A. O. 38
Bahnisch, M. 348
Baker, J. A. 316

Ballard, J. G. 347
Ball, M. 278, 381
Bandara, S. 202
Barahona, F. 207
Barbot, C. 184
Bard, J. F. 382, 383, 393, 394
Barlas, Y. 43
Barnhart, C. 219–36, 245, 255–75, 277–86, 368, 387, 391–403
Barrat, A. 406
Barrett, R. H. 410, 411
Barros, A. 105
Barthelemy, M. 406
Bashford, A. 406, 408, 411, 412
Basso, L. J. 184
Bass, T. 196
Battersby, A. 347
Batty, M. 354
Bauman, Z. 345, 356
Baumol, W. J. 162
Baxter, A. T. 316, 317
Beasley, J. 278
Becker, G. S. 10, 22
Beckmann, M. 151
Belant, J. L. 316
Bell, A. 101
Bell, H. 409
Bell, M. 405–13
Belobaba, P. P. 41, 240
Benko, G. 356
Bennett, C. J. 348, 324
Benton, T. G. 315
Berge, M. A. 257
Berman, O. 207
Bernhardt, G. E. 316
Best, L. B. 315
Biard, H. C. 407
Birge, J. R. 209, 235, 393
Birkland, T. A. 4, 321–42
Birnbach, R. 300
Bishop, M. 194
Bixby, R. 233, 269

Blaas, E. 80
Black, R. 298
Blackwell, B. F. 311–17
Blake, R. R. 299
Blokpoel, H. 314, 315
Blumstein, A. 130
Blumstein, D. T. 316
Bogard, W. 352
Bollinger, E. K. 316
Bond, D. 339
Bosk, C. 323, 330
Both, C. 317
Bowen, D. E., Jr. 316
Bowen, J. T. 405, 406
Boyfield, K. 183, 184
Braaksma, J. P. 200, 348, 357
Braidotti, R. 347
Bramel, J. 251
Brander, J. A. 167
Brandon, K. E. 316
Bratu, S. 368, 387, 391
Braun, B. 412
Bridgman, C. J. 314
Briggs, D. 62
Brockington, F. 412
Brons, M. 172
Brooks, R. J. 316
Brough, T. E. 314
Brown, K. M. 316
Brown, R. V. 62
Brown, S. 113
Brown, S. S. 11, 29
Brown, T. 405–13
De Brucker, K. 82
Brueckner, J. K. 162, 163, 165, 168, 169, 180, 184
Bruinsma, F. R. 80
Brunetta, L. 37
Bryson, J. M. 58
Buchanan, J. M. 162
Budd, L. C. S. 1–5, 405–13
Busenberg, G. J. 324
Butchers, E. R. 220
Butler, R. E. 307
Butler, S. J. 315
Butterworth, M. 312
Button, K. 184
Byrnes, R. E. 299
Byron, J. 316

Canaday, C. 315
Cao, B. 278
Cao, J. -M. 371, 381, 382, 393
Cappanera, P. 226
Caprara, A. 226
Carlin, A. 3, 151–60, 163
Carrascal, L. M. 316
Carter, A. B. 345, 346
Carter, A. W. 314
Castells, M. 346
Castro, A. J. 386
Caves, R. E. 61, 156
Cavey, J. F. 406
Chace, J. F. 316
Chambers, I. 347
Chang, K. 366
Chang, Z. Y. 200
Chao, C. C. 38
Chapman, H. W. 407, 410
Chavatal, V. 241
Chebalov, S. 235, 393
Chen, C. -H. 2, 37–51
Cheng, B. 411, 412
Chidester, T. R. 301
Cholesky, A. -L. 269, 270
Chou, S. -Y. 2, 37–51
Christou, I. T. 226
Chu, H. 278
Clarke, J. -P. B. 37, 199–215, 391–403
Clarke, L. 224, 226, 228, 394
Clarke, M. D. D. 236, 368, 381–3, 391, 393
Clarke, R. 347, 350
Clausen, J. 364, 368, 377–88
Cleary, E. C. 312, 313
Cliff, A. 406
Clough, P. T. 357
Coase, R. H. 184
Cobb, R. W. 323, 334, 336, 338
Cobham, A. J. 405, 410
Cohn, A. M. 219–36, 277, 281, 392
Cole, J. 291
Colizza, V. 406
Conover, M. R. 315
Cook, A. 384
Cook, T. 220, 221
Cooper, G. E. 297
Cordeau, J. 228, 277, 283, 393
Corrie, S. J. 295
Crabtree, H. S. 410

Crainic, T. 278
Crang, M. 347
Crary, J. 349
Cresswell, T. 346, 347, 357, 405
Crick, H. Q. 317
Cullen, D. 241
Cumming, W. B. 343

Daniel, J. I. 161, 163, 180
Davey, E. L. 410
Davies, R. E. G. 407
Davies, S. 411
Davis, P. K. 63
Davis, S. K. 315
Dawid, H. 226
Day, P. R. 226
Delio, M. 352
Dempsey, P. S. 183, 186
Dempsey, S. 61
De Neufville R. 2, 58, 61
Derudder, B. 405
Desaulniers, G. 226, 233, 239–52, 278, 394, 399
Desrochers, M. 233, 234
Desrosiers, J. 233, 234, 239–52
De Vany, A. S. 2, 9–25
DeVault, T. L. 311–17
Dichter, A. 42
Dill, L. M. 316
Dodson, G. 62
Doganis, R. 27–9, 184
Dolbeer, R. A. 311–17
Donald, P. F. 315
Dorolle, P. 408
Dose, A. 292
Downs, C. T. 316
Dumas, Y. 239

Edmunds, P. 355
Edwards, B. 355
Edwards, E. 297
Eggenberg, N. 382, 383
Ehrgott, M. 388
Elayadath, S. 200
Elle, B. J. 10, 11
Ellis, H. 393
El-Rayes, K. 312
Eppen, G. D. 207
Erdmann, A. 222, 224

Ericson, R. 348
Eschenfelder, P. 312
Estrella, E. 409
Etschmaier, M. M. 241
Evans, A. W. 289

Farkas, A. 240
Farley, J. 412
Feare, C. J. 315
Feo, T. A. 394
Fernandes, E. 38
Fernández-Juricic, E. 311–17
Fidler, D. P. 406–8, 411
Filar, J. A. 381, 384
Flynn, S. E. 346
Forrester, J. W. 38
Forsyth, P. 3, 101–21
Foster, B. A. 234, 397
Fotheringham, A. S. 28, 29, 33
Foucault, M. 347, 349, 411
Foushee, H. C. 298, 299, 301, 302
Fox, A. D. 316
French, S. 357
Frid, A. 316
Fruin, J. J. 200
Fujita, M. 80
Fussell, P. 355

Gallo, G. 226
Galvin, Jr. 39
Gamache, M. 226, 233
Gandy, O. H. 352
García, G. D. 409
Gardner, E. S., Jr. 28
Garges, E. H. 2, 9–25
Garrett, L. 406
Gear, H. S. 410
Gelernter, D. 354
Gelinas, S. 247
Genchi, A. C. 316
Gendreau, M. A. 406
Gershkoff, I. 230, 277, 382
Ghobrial, A. A. 28
Gibson, M. 351
Gilbo, E. 130
Girvin, R. 184
Gopalan, R. 224, 394
Gordon, A. 405
Gormley, W. T., Jr. 346

Gosling, G. D. 61
Gostin, L. O. 412
Gottdeiner, M. 346, 352
Gould, P. 405
Graham, A. 103
Graham, B. 312, 317
Graham, R. L. 312, 317
Graham, S. 351, 352, 356
Graves, G. 277
Gregorich, S. E. 301, 302
Gronau, R. J. 10, 22
Grosche, T. 2, 27–34, 38
Grosse, A. 336, 338
Guberinić, S. 381, 382
Guindon, E. 406
Guiomard, C. 101
Gulding, J. M. 68
Guo, Y. A. 384–6
Gursoy, D. 28
Guyer, C. 312

Haase, K. 384–6
Haggerty, K. 348
Haggett, P. 406
Hamzawi, S. G. 199
Handover, D. H. 407
Hane, C. A. 222, 231, 241, 245, 246, 255–75, 279
Hansen, M. 387
Harrison, M. 408
Hay, S. I. 406
Heinzl, A. 2, 27–34, 38
Helbing, D. 354
Helen, C. 252
Helmerich, R. L. 297–308
Hendriks, N. 117, 118
Higgins, J. 314
Hilgartner, J. 323, 330
Hines, W. E. 301, 302, 304
Hinloopen, E. 87
Hirshleifer, J. 159
Hoare, S. 405
Hoffman, K. L. 230, 278
Hofstede, G. 304
Hogan, O. 103
Holzschneider, M. 105
Homem-de-Mello, T. 396
Hooper, P. 101
Hopperstad, C. A. 257
Horonjeff, R. 349

Houston, C. S. 316
Howard-Jones, N. 408
Howlett, M. 324
Hsu, C. I. 38
Huang, D. S. 30
Huapu, L. 37
Hubbard, P. J. 405
Huber, V. 408, 409
Hudson, R. A. 343
Humberg, L. A. 315
Humphreys, B. 111
Humphreys, I. 312
Hu, P. 37

Ibelings, H. 346
Imrie, R. 349
Ingram, A. 406
Ingram, F. 41
Inzerilli, F. 38
Ioachim, I. 249
Ison, S. 1–5

Jacobs, T. L. 224
James, J. 39
Janardhan, K. S. 200
Janelle, D. G. 407
Janic, M. 289–96
Jarrah, A. I. Z. 235, 381, 382, 384, 393
Jarvis, J. J. 246
Jasimuddin, S. M. 38
Jenkins, D. 346
Jifeng, W. 37
Jim, H. K. 200
Johnson, E. L. 199–215, 255–75, 388, 393, 403
Johnson, V. 384, 386
Johnson, W. C. 317
Johnston, A. C. 290, 293
Jones, I. 183
Jorge-Calderón, J. D. 27–9, 32

Kabbani, N. M. 394
Kanafani, A. 27, 28, 289, 292, 371, 381, 382, 393
Kang, L. S. 393
Karisch, S. E. 226
Kauvar, G. 355
Keil, R. 406
Kelly, T. A. 316
Kelly, T. C. 312, 313
Kershner, E. L. 316

Kessides, C. 42
Khalafalla, A. 312
Kingdon, J. W. 322, 323
King, N. B. 406
Kitowski, I. 316
Kivestu, P. 147
Klabjan, D. 277, 278, 283, 388, 393, 399
Klabjan, J. 228, 235
Kleit, A. 196
Kleywegt, A. J. 396
Knight, R. L. 316
Kobayashi, B. 196
Kohl, N. 226, 246, 363–75, 381, 384
Kokko, H. 316
Kontogiorgis, S. 222
Koopman, B. O. 147
Koppelman, F. S. 221
Kouvelis, P. 393
Krapu, G. L. 315
Kuhlmann, A. 289, 292
Kwakkel, J. H. 3, 55–77
Kyle, J. 410

Langley, P. 42
Lan, S. 388, 391–403
Laroe, C. 406
Larsen, A. 363–75, 377–88
Larsen, J. 363–75, 377–88
Lasdon, L. S. 242
Lauber, J. K. 297
Lavoie, S. 233, 278
Law, R. 349
Lawrence, R. G. 330
Layard, R. 81
Learmount, D. 339
Lee, D. A. 28, 130, 146
Lee, H. 312
Leibhold, A. M. 406
Lemos, P. 355
Lettovsky, L. 368, 384, 386, 387, 393
Levin, A. 241, 399
Levine, D. 278
Levy, F. K. 349
Levy, J. 324
Lima, S. L. 316
Lindblom, C. E. 336
Liner, M. 314
Linnell, M. A. 316
Liu, T. -K. 381, 382, 384
Lloyd, J. 347

Lockyer, K. G. 349
Lohatepanont, M. 221, 230
Longridge, T. 300
Louveaux, F. 393
Løve, M. 371, 382, 384
Lulli, G. 209
Luo, S. 382, 384, 393
Lustig, I. 233
Lyneis, J. 37–9
Lyon, D. 346–9, 352
Lyons, M. 412

McCaughey, N. 101
McCollough, D. G. 406
McCullough, B. F. 200
McGowan, F. 196
McGuire, C. B. 151
McKelvey, F. X. 200, 349
Mackie, F. P. 410
McMaster, D. G. 315
McNally, R. 11
Madsen, J. 316
Madsen, O. B. G. 246
Malone, K. 147
Mangili, A. 406
Marsten, R. E. 233, 234, 255–75
Martin, R. C. 229
Marvin, S. 351, 356
Massey, A. 408, 409
Mathaisel, D. F. X. 241, 381, 382, 393
Matthews, L. 38
May, P. J. 321, 324, 325, 339
Mead, H. 314
Mead, K. 392
Medard, C. 384–6
Megiddo, N. 263
Megonnell, W. H. 407, 410
Mehrotra, A. 234
Merenlender, A. M. 315
Merritt, A. C. 297–308
Metcalf, J. C. 316
Miller, B. 37
Miller, C. K. 316
Miller, S. G. 316
Miser, H. J. 63, 64
Mishan, E. J. 81
Moore, O. E. 29
Morrison, S. 104, 110
Mott, D. F. 315
Mouton, J. S. 298

Mulvey, J. M. 393
Murphy, M. T. 315
Mykhalovskiy, E. 407

Navarro, J. 409
Negroni, C. 332, 343
Nemhauser, G. L. 255–75, 388, 393, 403
Nerlich, B. 407
Newell, G. F. 37, 201
Nice, D. C. 336, 338
Niemeier, H. -M. 117
Nijkamp, P. 3, 79–98
Nissen, R. 384–6
Norris, C. 347

Oates, W. E. 162
O'Connor, K. 405
O'Connor, W. E. 27, 28
Odoni, A. R. 58, 61, 125–49
Ojcius, D. M. 406
O'Kelly, M. E. 29
Older, S. J. 200
Oliveira, E. 386
Orlady, H. W. 299
Osborne, D. R. 316
Oum, T. H. 103, 163, 167
Ouwersloot, H. 85, 96
Owen, D. 291, 292

Pacheco, R. R. 38
Padberg, M. 230, 278
Palomino, D. 316
Pang, T. 406
Park, R. E. 151–60, 163
Pascoe, D. 352, 357
Patrick, F. 252
Patterson, M. P. 315
Patty, B. W. 220, 394
Pavia, A. T. 406
Peer, B. D. 315
Pels, E. 3, 161–81, 184
Pelt, M. J. F. van 82
Perkins, A. J. 315
Perrow, C. 322, 336
Pervan, G. 62
Peterjohn, B. G. 315
Peterson, A. T. 316
Phillips, D. 352
Pinos, A. 312
Poon, P. 62

Poore, J. W. 38
Primo, D. M. 334, 336, 338
Prince, C. 298
Proussaloglou, K. E. 221

Qi, X. 381
Quade, E. S. 63, 64

Rabinbach, A. 349
Rakshit, A. 381, 382
Rao, A. 312
Raven, M. J. 315
Reason, J. 205
Reed, S. E. 315
Reibnitz, U. V. 44
Reijnen, R. 316
Reiss, B. 312
Relph, E. 346
Rengaraju, V. R. 27, 28, 29, 30, 32
Rexing, B. 229–31, 399
Rezanova, N. J. 377–88
Rice, J. 201
Richardson, C. T. 312, 316
Richardson, F. 347
Richardson, G. P. 39
Richardson, W. J. 312, 316
Rietveld, P. 82
Righi, L. 37
Riis, M. 207
Riker, W. H. 183, 184
Riley, N. F. 28, 29
Roberts, A. 278
Roberts, F. L. 200
Robinson, A. P. 317
Rochefort, D. A. 323
Rodgers, J. A., Jr. 316
Rogers, D. J. 406
Rosenberg, B. 292
Rosenberger, J. M. 235, 236, 382, 383, 388, 393, 403
Ross, A. 363–75
Roth, E. 147
Rothlauf, F. 2, 27–34, 38
Rousseau, K. 278
Rouwendal, J. 82
Rowley, J. 355
Rozario, K. 106
Rubin, C. B. 343
Rusch, D. H. 312
Rushmeier, R. 222

Russon, M. G. 28, 29
Ryan, D. M. 226, 232–4, 388, 397

Saaty, T. L. 89
Sabatier, P. A. 324
Sabert, H. 42
Saffarzadeh, M. 200
Sage, A. P. 289, 290
Said, N. 406
St. John, P. 322, 327
Sajjad, M. J. 39
Sakawa, M. 393
Salas, E. 298
Salmon, T. 307
Salt, A. E. W. 405, 408
Salter, M. B. 345, 347, 349, 350
Sampson, A. 407
Sandstrom, U. G. 316
Sarkar, A. K. 200
Sauer, J. R. 317
Savelsbergh, M. W. P. 234
Sawhney, N. 384–6
Sayer, J. 316
Schaefer, A. J. 235, 388, 392, 393
Schafer, L. M. 316, 317
Schiavo, M. 343
Schleusener, M. 28
Schwan, K. 278
Schwikert, S. T. 316
Scott, J. C. 349
Seabright, P. 196
Sealy, K. R. 348
Seamans, T. W. 314, 317
Seetaram, N. 101
Sened, I. 183, 184
Sen, S. 209
Seraj, Y. A. 39
Sergioc, R. 38
Serres, M. 347
Shafer, C. L. 316
Shapiro, A. 396
Shebalov, S. 388
Shen, G. 29
Sherman, P. J. 302, 304
Shiina, T. 209
Sibley, D. 113
Sieg, G. 3, 183–90
Sigismondi, G. 255–75
Simchi-Levi, D. 251
Simonsen, D. G. 407

Sinclair, K. E. 316
Skagen, S. K. 316
Skinner, S. 42
Slack, F. 355
Slowinski, R. 84
Smith, B. C. 220, 226, 388, 391, 393
Smith, H. T. 316
Sodhi, N. 312, 316
Sohoni, M. 388
Solak, S. 199–215
Soliman, A. H. 29
Sol, M. 234
Solman, V. E. F. 312
Solomon, M. M. 239–52
Song, M. 384, 385
Sørensen, K. 382, 384
Soumis, F. 233, 234, 239–52, 384, 386
Sparke, M. 350, 351, 355, 406
Spiller, P. T. 165
Stamatopoulos, M. A. 125–49
Stanley, L. 357
Stanley-Turner, H. M. 410, 411
Starkie, D. 3, 101, 103, 162, 183, 184, 193–8
Sterman, J. 39
Stern, E. 324
Sterner, R. T. 315
Stevens, J. 315
Stewart, S. 291, 292
Stock, P. G. 409
Stojković, G. 235, 368, 381, 382, 393, 399
Stojković, M. 384, 385, 386
Stone, D. 330
Strotz, R. H. 151
Stuart, F. S. 407
Subramanian, R. 241, 393
Sudjic, D. 347, 354
Suryani, E. 2, 37–51
Sutherland, W. J. 316
Svrcek, T. 38
Swaminathan, J. M. 207
Swan, W. M. 38
Swedish, W. J. 139
Sykes, F. H. 405

Tacke, G. 28
Taggart, W. R. 302, 307
Talluri, K. 224, 279, 382, 384, 392, 394
Tanali, I. R. 343
Tanariboon, Y. 200
Tang, H. W. 290, 293, 294

Tatem, A. J. 406
Tekiner, V. 388
Temple, S. A. 316
Teodorović, D. 368, 381, 382, 393
Ter Welle, C. 3
Thalheimer, B. 351, 352
Thamizh Arasan, V. 27, 28, 29, 30, 32
Thengvall, B. G. 236, 382, 383, 387, 393
Thomas, T, C. 154
Thompson, D. 194, 197
Thorpe, J. 312
Thrift, N. 354, 357
Tiourine, S. 363–75
Tomlin, J. A. 246
Toms, M. 117
Torpey, J. 345, 351
Tosic, V. 348, 354
Trick, M. A. 234
Tscharntke, T. 315
Tucker, G. M. 315
Tullo, F. 307
Turban, E. 58
Tu, Y. -P. 382, 383, 393

Ubøe, J. 28
Urry, J. 345, 405

Vance, P. H. 233, 234, 278
Vanderbeck, F. 229
Vanderbei, R. J. 393
van de Riet, O. W. A. T. 63
van der Ploeg, I. 350, 351
van Houtem, H. 356
van Naerssen, T. 356
Vereecken, L. 405
Verhoef, E. T. 161–81, 184
Verleger, P. K. 29
Vespignani, A. 406
Vickery, P.D. 316
Vickrey, W. 151
Virilio, P. 353, 355
Virkler, M. R. 200
Visser, H. G. 58
Vos, D. K. 316
Vreeker, R. 3, 79–98, 312

Wagner, C. 62
Walder, R. 294
Walker, W. E. 3, 55–77
Waller, D. M. 312

Walsh, J. J. 316
Wardrop, J. G. 165, 166, 207
Washburn, B. E. 314
Watanabe, T. 393
Watkins, W. S. 11, 29
Webber, M. J. 28
Wei, G. 384–6
Weikel, D. 312
Weir, L. 407
Welle, C. T. 79–98
Wells, M. P. 316
West, T. 312
White, E. B. 289, 290
White, M. D. 297
Whittingham, H. E. 407–10, 412
Wiener, E. L. 302
Wiest, J. D. 349
Wijnen, R. A. A. 3, 55–77
Wilhelm, J. A. 297–308
Wilson, J. D. 315
Winsten, C. B. 151
Wiper, D. S. 220, 222
Wirasinghe, S. C. 105, 202
Witlox, F. 405
Wolf, G. 351
Work, T. T. 406
Wright, S. E. 312, 316, 317
Wu, C. -L. 388
Wyden, R. 353

Yamaguchi, K. 38
Yang, D. 393
Yang, H. M. 312
Yang, J. 381–3
Yan, S. 381–3, 393
Yates, C. 353, 356
Yen, J. W. 235, 388, 393
Young, H. -F. 382, 383
Young, S. B. 200
Yu, G. 220, 236, 382, 384, 393

Zajac, E. 111
Zenios, S. A. 393
Zhang, A. 101, 167, 184, 185
Zhang, Y. 103, 163, 184, 185, 387
Zhao, X. 382, 384, 386, 387
Zhu, J. 382, 384, 387
Zimmermann, H. J. 393
Zoellick, R. B. 46
Zografos, K. G. 3, 125–49
Zylberman, P. 406, 408, 409